A. B. Amis'

"The Amis, Brewer, Pettey, Langford and Wilson Families of Newton County, Mississippi"

Lucius F. Wright, M.D.

HERITAGE BOOKS
2014

HERITAGE BOOKS

AN IMPRINT OF HERITAGE BOOKS, INC.

Books, CDs, and more—Worldwide

For our listing of thousands of titles see our website
at
www.HeritageBooks.com

Published 2014 by
HERITAGE BOOKS, INC.
Publishing Division
5810 Ruatan Street
Berwyn Heights, Md. 20740

Heritage Books by the author:

*A. B. Amis' "The Amis, Brewer, Pettey, Langford and
Wilson Families of Newton County, Mississippi"*

Southside Virgina Wright Families, 1755–1820

International Standard Book Numbers
Paperbound: 978-0-7884-5566-7
Clothbound: 978-0-7884-9028-6

Preface

In 1936 my great-grandfather, Alphonso Bobbett Amis, wrote a memoir of his family and had seven copies typed—one for each child and one that was placed in the archives at Mississippi State University.[1] Recently, one copy, that of Frances Amis Floyd, has been placed online by the Lauderdale Co., MS, Archives.[2] His work was extended by Alice Amis Hodges, my mother's first cousin.[3] Her work has been widely distributed by online sources, but she did not provide references for her data. I reviewed these works and have confirmed her sources though I disagree with her interpretation of the origins of this Amis family. I have set out an alternative hypothesis linking the Amis families of Granville Co., N. C., to after 1747 (year of death) Joseph Amis of Essex Co., Virginia, (place of death.)[4] This study is presented in Chapter 1.

His son, 1816 William Amis of Granville Co., N. C., did not leave a will, so detailed analysis of Granville Co., N. C., records was necessary to assort the grandchildren to each of his three surviving sons. The descendants of 1825 Lewis Amis of Granville Co., N. C., are considered in Chapter 2. The descendants of 1857 William Amis of Granville Co., N. C., are covered in Chapter 3, along with the information recorded by A. B. Amis for his son, 1849 John Woodson Amis of Scott Co., Mississippi, and his descendants. Finally, the descendants of 1859 John Amis of Marshall Co., Tenn., are considered in Chapter 4.

---

[1] Amis, A. B., Sr. The Amis, Brewer, Pettey, Langford and Wilson Families of Newton Co., Mississippi. (Meridian, MS, mss, 1 August 1936.)

[2] http://www.kithandkinofthesouth.org/a.html. Accessed 24 September 2011.

[3] Hodges, A. A. The Ancestry and Descendants of John Woodson Amis of Granville Co., N. C., and Scott Co., Miss. (Pendleton, S. C., n. p. d., 1978.)

[4] I am indebted to Robert N. Grant for this nomenclature, which is useful where traditional generational numbers cannot be substantiated.

To trace the origins of Wyche Brewer, I conducted a detailed study of the Brewer families of Sumter Co., Ala., from 1837 to 1860. This is presented in Chapter 5. I was also able to establish a probable link to 1808 Malcolm McPherson of Cumberland Co., N. C. This is presented in Chapter 6.

Alice Amis Hodges also published on the ancestry of the Pettey or Petty family,[5] and articulated the traditional view of the Pettey ancestry. New data makes a persuasive argument that this family descends from Hubert Petty of Lancaster Co., Va. This is presented in Chapter 7.

Data on the Langford and Wilson family was accumulated by the late Dan Langford, who generously shared it with me in 2002. The descendants of 1860 Richard Langford of Macon Co., Ala., are presented in Chapter 8. I have been able to link 1810 James Davis of Hancock Co., Ga., to 1706 Robert Davis of Accomack Co., Virginia. This work is presented in Chapter 9.

1820 David Howe of Jones Co., Ga. is presented in Chapter 10. The descendants of 1788 Larkin Wilson of Botetourt Co., Virginia, are presented in Chapter 11.

Finally, I was able to partially determine the ancestry of A. B. Amis' grandmother, Martha Wadkins. This will be presented in Chapter 12.

As part of the research for this work, I found a book published in 1894 that contained the following portrait of the young A. B. Amis.[6]

In selecting a person who is the best educated man that has ever gone from Newton County, it is appropriate that a page should be devoted to his portrait.

---

[5] Hodges, Alice A. Ancestry and Descendants of Dr. John Wright Petty of Madison Co., Ala. (Pendleton, S. C.: n. p. d., 1978.)

[6] Brown, A. J. History of Newton County, Mississippi, from 1834 to 1894. (Jackson, MS: Clarion-Ledger Press, 1894,) pp. 462-466.

A. B. Amis, Esq., now practicing law at Meridian, was born in Scott County, but came with his parents to Newton County when he was quite an infant. Mr. Amis, though himself having some means to assist in educating himself, found the sum inadequate to carry him through, and for a time was thrown upon his own resources in order to make money to complete his education.

He first commenced to go to school in the common schools of the country, and then attended for two terms of nine months each the Connehatta Institute. After that he went to the Chamberlain-Hunt Academy, at Port Gibson, where he attended school for eight months. October 1885 he attended the Tulane University, at New Orleans, but only remained until January of 1886. In October of 1886 he entered the University of Mississippi at Oxford, where he remained successfively until February 1888, when he was compelled to quit and teach in order to obtain means to finish his studies. After teaching the greater part of of the years 1888 and 1889, he returned to the State University and entered the senior class. In June 1890 he completed his course. In July 1890 he was appointed tutor in Medieval and Modern History at the University, which place he held for two years. In the meantime, he took a two year's course in law, and graduated in June 1892 with second honor, with a general average of 98½ percent. During his course at the University, for two years he was a member of the editorial staff of the *University Magazine*, published by the Literary Societies.

In June 1892 he was a member of the faculty of teachers at the Patron's Union Teacher's Normal Institute, held at Lake Camp Ground. In January 1893 he removed to Meridian and entered into the employ of Threefoot Bros. & Co., and Marks, Rothenburg & Co., as their salaried attorney. June 11th, 1893, he was married to Miss Mary S. Langford, of Conehatta. January 1894 he severed his relations as attorney with the above named firms and formed a law partnership with Floyd Y. Lewis, of

Meridian, where they are now practicing their profession.

Mr. Amis is 27 years old; he is a sober, energetic, self-made man, a profound thinker, a fine writer, and a good speaker. He delivered a literary address at Newton at the close of Prof. Mabry's school, June 1893, which did him great credit. Hon. T. C. Catchings, one of the brightest speakers in the State, and Senator A. J. McLaurin, had both favored the schools at Newton with addresses on commencement occasions and Mr. Amis' compared favorably with both of them. His address was not only clothed in elegant language, but it was reasonable and convincing, and delivered in such a way as to show that he was a profound thinker and graceful orator. Taking him in all the phases of his character, and his varied acquirements, this writer feels that no mistake was made in selecting him as the best scholar ever to have gone out from Newton County. Aside from his learning as a literary man and lawyer, his sober habits and attention to business, should recommend him to those needing his services. Newton County feels proud of Mr. Amis.

I have retained the information he recorded throughout this work.[7] It has been more than 75 years since the first edition, and genealogical resources are much more available than they were then, but hopefully I have retained the spirit that motivated his work.

---

[7] I have made minor grammatical corrections as one of the benefits of electronic word processing is the ease with which errors can be fixed without retyping the whole page and the six carbons as my great aunt did with the original. The other change is that I have presented the data in Register format, as it is a widely recognized way of organizing the data, but differs slightly from that used by Judge Amis.

TABLE OF CONTENTS

A. B. AMIS.

Foreword from the Original

For several years past I have had in mind the collection of the necessary data for a biographical sketch of all members of the Amis, Pettey, Langford, and Wilson families; but first one thing and then another has prevented the prosecution of this purpose as seriously as I would have liked. However, I have gathered some data and inasmuch as my time and attention are now devoted to other matters I think it best to make a record of the facts which I have learned from others, as well as those of which I have personal knowledge; so that if someone else shall, at a future date, desire to continue or extend the investigation the work will be, to some extent, facilitated. My data are not complete, and for that reason the sketches are necessarily incomplete; but I believe it is reasonably accurate as far as it goes. Some of the personal sketches are fuller than others for the reason that I knew more about some of them than I did of others.

I have also included a short sketch of the Amis family, in general, and have attempted to trace the genealogy of John Woodson Amis back to the progenitors of the family in America. This attempt is, of course, a mere inference from the data before me, though it seems to be reasonably certain. There may be some errors in names or dates, because I found it a hard matter to keep them straight. Of course, I correct all errors that come to my attention, but there may be some I did not notice. However, I can make the same plea the old fiddler did, who put up a sign in the ballroom: "Don't shoot the fiddler, he's doing his best." And so if any one finds that I have traded off some of his or her children for those of some one else, or have unduly accelerated the birth rate, I hope it will not be thought that it was done intentionally.

Most of the sketches were written and the biographical data was collected and arranged several years ago. The publication was delayed because it

1

seemed that I could not well spare the money to have it done. So I kept waiting until I felt I could spare it, but financial matters do not get any better. So I am making a number of typewritten copies of it for those who may be interested.

I have written these sketches for the information and entertainment of my kindred, as a labor of love for all of them; and I trust they will look with a lenient eye on all imperfections therein contained. But if anyone does not like them, I feel just the same as John Farmer, the hotel keeper at Forest, did about the hound dog. Once when I was there he came out on the front porch and began to ring the bell for dinner, when an old hound, out in the street, threw up his head and began to yowl. John stopped, stared at him for a few seconds and blurted out: "Shut up, sir. You don't have to eat it if you don't want it."

A. B. Amis, Sr.
Meridian, Mississippi
August 1, 1936.

Chapter 1: Origins of the Amis Family

I. Two Branches of the Family
    In my investigations, covering several years, I have found that there are two main branches of the family claiming a common origin and tracing their descent back to old Virginia ancestors. One branch spells the name "Amis" and the other spells it "Amiss."

    The "Amiss" branch does not seem to be quite so numerous nor so widely dispersed as the "Amis" branch. I have located various members of that family in Baton Rouge, Louisiana, Dothan, Alabama, and Luray, Virginia; and the records of the Universities of Virginia and North Carolina show that various members of it have been students in those institutions at various times during the past hundred years. There is a town, or village, in Rappahannock County, Virginia, named "Amissville," but whether any of either branch of the family reside there now I do not know. One member of the family, who lives at Baton Rouge, has accumulated considerable data in reference to the family, and is of the opinion that both families had a common ancestry in Virginia, some two hundred years ago, and that the original spelling of the name was "Amis."

    The "Amis" branch of the family seems to be more numerous and more widely scattered over the country. I have located various members of it in Virginia, North Carolina, South Carolina, Georgia, Alabama, Mississippi, Louisiana, Texas, Arkansas, Oklahoma, Tennessee, Missouri, and New Mexico; and have had a very pleasant correspondence with some of them. Some of the family in various parts of the country have been prominent people, notably Capt. Rufus Amis, of Virginilina, Virginia, Col. James S. Amis, of Oxford, North Carolina, Judge Amis of Arkansas, and his brother, the famous Baptist preacher, who waged such a long and strenuous fight against gambling houses and race track gamblers at Hot Springs, some twenty years ago, or more.

The records of the Universities of Virginia, North Carolina, Arkansas, Alabama, and Mississippi, show that a number of the family have been college students, at various times as far back as 1801, when Thomas Gayle Amis, graduated as a member of the first class of the University of North Carolina. Doubtless the records of many of the other older colleges would show that other members of the family attended as students from time to time; but I have not made any inquiry except as above indicated. Some members of the family have been lawyers, some have been preachers, some doctors, and some merchants; but so far as I have been able to learn, the great majority of them have been, and still are, farmers by occupation. In their religious convictions, most of them are Baptists or Presbyterians, though there are a few Methodists among them, and at least one Methodist preacher, Rev. Lewis Amis, of Columbia, Tennessee.

II. Origins of the family
While it seems to be quite definitely settled that the founder of the American branch of the family settled in America more than two hundred years ago, yet it is not clear to my mind as to what country he came from nor what his original nationality was. Mrs. Margaret Campbell Pilcher (a daughter of Governor Campbell of Tennessee) in her book entitled "Historical Sketeches of the Campbell, Pilcher and Kindred Families," in her sketch of the Amis family says:
There was a settlement of Huguenots on the James River in Virginia, called Manakin Town. It was settled some time in the earlier part of the eighteenth century, and among them was the family Amis. It is supposed that this family left France at the time there was such a great exodus of the best citizens of that country, just after revocation of the Edict of Nantes (1685); but some years previous to this there was a family of Amis in South Carolina. Mrs. William Layman of St. Helena, California, says that her father, Thomas Amis of North Carolina, told her the family were Huguenots, who left France after the

revocation of the Edict of Nantes, going first to the French West Indies, then to Virginia, and that the name was "Amie," not Amis, as it was afterwards spelled in America. Another member of this family says that the family tradition has always been that upon leaving France, just after the Edict of Nantes, the family sailed for Barbados, but remained there only a short time, then went to the Colony of Virginia, and settled in Rappahannock County, establishing themselves in a home and called the settlement Amisville.

On the other hand, Edward McCready, in his book entitled "South Carolina Under Proprietary Government," says that Thomas Amis, or Amys, was a Cacique in the colony of South Carolina in the year 1683 and was a Landgrave in the Colony in 1697.[1] This seems to show that at least one member of the family was in America prior to the revocation of the Edict of Nantes in 1685, and that he was a member of the Colonial nobility, which further indicates that he was a British subject; while the spelling of the name "Amys" corresponds quite closely to the Old English spelling of similar words and names.

Some years ago I met a gentleman, who was a native of Scotland, who told me that the name, Amis, was quite common in his native country. That reminds me that there is quite a large family in northeast Mississippi by the name of McAmis, who claim a Scotch ancestry, and say that the name clearly shows it. Some years ago I met a member of this family at Corinth, Mississippi, and he contended that the Amis family were of Scotch descent too, but that they have been away from the old Highlands so long that they have just lost the Mc. But no matter what country they were from, it seems to be reasonably certain, that the ancestor, or what seems more likely, the ancestors, of the family settled in Virginia, sometime prior to the year 1700, whence they spread south and west, with the general tide of

---

[1] The plan of the government of South Carolina, drawn up by the philosopher, John Locke, provided for Colonial nobility, the lower order being called "Caiques" and the higher order being called "Landgraves."

immigration which subsequently populated this country.

III. Ancestry of John Woodson Amis

The ancestor of the oldest Mississippi branch of the family was John Woodson Amis, who was born in North Carolina, September 22nd, 1795, and died in Scott County, Mississippi, February 4th, 1849. My effort for several years has been to trace his ancestry back to the original progenitor of the family in America. There is no family record to which I have access, which shows definitively who his ancestors were, not even the name or place of residence of his father.

His only child now living, is Mrs. Frances Amis Moore, who resides with her son, C. A. Moore, in Navarro, Texas. She says that her grandfather's name was William; that he lived in Wilmington, North Carolina, and that he married a Miss Woodson. About forty five years ago, Haywood Amis, one of the old Negro slaves of John Woodson Amis, told me that he was born in North Carolina and lived there until he was about fifteen years old; that his "old marster" was named William Amis, who was the father of John Woodson Amis; that his "old marster's wife was a Woodson; and that they lived near Pittsboro, Chatham Co., North Carolina. He further said that shortly after his "old marster" died, John Woodson Amis, who was then living in Wilkinson County, Mississippi, went back to Pittsboro to get his share of his father's estate; that on a division of the estate, he, Haywood, a woman, and two small children, all slaves, were allotted to John Woodson Amis, who loaded them all into a two horse wagon and brought them back with him to his home in Wilkinson County, Mississippi.

It seems reasonably certain therefore, that the father of John Woodson Amis was William Amis, that he married a Miss Woodson, and that he lived and died in North Carolina. I am inclined to think old Haywood was right as to where he lived and died, because he spoke from his own memory. And that was the part of the state in which other members of the family lived, as shown by sundry records which I have investigated.[2]

Mrs. Pilcher, in her sketch of the Amis family....[3] So everything considered, I am persuaded that John Woodson Amis was the son of William Amis and Mirnia Woodson; that William Amis was the son of Thomas Amis and Alice Gayle, and Thomas Amis was the son of John Amis and Mary Dillard, who must have been at least fifty years old at the time of the Declaration of Independence in 1776.

This conclusion is strengthened by the family records in possession of Mr. W. D. Amis, who now lives at Virgilina, Virginia, near the line of North Carolina, and who is now about sixty five years old. His father, Capt. Rufus Amis, was born in 1835, and was a student at the University of North Carolina in 1853 and 1854.[4] The father of Rufus Amis was William Amis, whose father, William, lived in Southampton County, Virginia. William Amis, father of Rufus, moved from Southampton County, Virginia, and settled near Oxford, in Granville County, North Carolina. This was about fifty miles northeast of Chatham County, and about fifty miles west of Halifax County, where Thomas Amis lived when he was elected a delegate to the North Carolina Constitutional Convention in 1775. Mr. W. D. Amis says that his father was the youngest of 13 children,

---

[2] It is important to remember that A. B. Amis was trained as a lawyer and was therefore accustomed to evaluating oral testimony. Note that his conclusions are not quite as specific as the various recollections he cited. Pittsboro, though is southwest of Durham, whereas Oxford, Granville County, is almost equidistant to the northeast of Durham. It also seems likely that the "old marster" was William[2] Amis, rather than William[3] Amis. This suggests that John W. Amis moved to Wilkinson County, Mississippi, rather earlier than his marriage. He was likely 21 when he received his "share" of the estate, which would have been 1816. This suggests that William Amis, Sr., did die within a couple of years of the last recorded deed in 1813.

[3] A. B. Amis summarizes the information contained in Pilcher. Complete reference cited earlier. Interestingly, there are no Y-DNA studies ongoing as of 1 December 2011 to see if the Northampton Co., N. C., and Granville Co., N. C., Amis families are related, and if so, how closely.

[4] Rufus[6] (William[5], Lewis[4], William [3], Joseph[2]) Amis was actually a second cousin of John Woodson Amis.

all of whom were born and reared in Granville County, North Carolina. Now since Rufus Amis was born in 1835, it seems clear that his father William did not move to North Carolina until after the year 1800, or more than twenty-five years after Thomas Amis and William Amis, sons of John Amis and Mary Dillard moved there.

It is undoubtedly true that there were other branches of the family residing in Virginia at the time of the Revolutionary War, in Southampton County, Rappahannock County, and perhaps elsewhere in the State; but none of them except the two sons of John Amis and Mary Dillard, seems to have moved to North Carolina until afterward. I am therefore convinced that the ancestry of John Woodson Amis is as above stated. How many brothers or sisters he may have had, what their names were, or where they lived I have no information, except one sister named Mirnia Woodson Amis. But who she married, or where she lived, I have never heard.[5]

ON EARLY VIRGINIA ORIGINS OF THE AMIS FAMILY

Judge Amis on the basis of the available data concluded they had come from North Carolina and that his great-grandfather was named William. Genealogical research in the past 75 years has not uncovered very many certain items of information about early Amis families, yet the information recorded by Judge Amis seems to be widely cited on the Internet, without any supplemental information.

In 1978 Alice Amis Hodges, his granddaughter, extended his work and showed John Woodson Amis was the son of William Amis of Granville Co., N. C.,

---

[5] Mirnia Woodson Amis is surely Missniah[5] (William[4-3], Joseph[2]) Amis, who never married and died in Maury County, Tennessee, where she had gone to live with some of John Woodson Amis' cousins and sisters.

who died before 10 June 1857.[6] She identified him as a son of William Amis and a grandson of Joseph Amis of Essex Co., Va. She further stated that he moved to Culpeper Co., Virginia, and was father to sons Thomas, Phillip, Gabriel, and William.

The best summary of the available data on early Amis men that I know was published by Laura Collison Ray.[7] She was able to identify that Thomas Amis received a patent on 295 acres of land in Gloucester Co., Va., in 1678. In 1690 John Amis received a patent for 470 acres on the south side of the Rappahannock River at John Meadows' creek, and in 1693 he received a patent for 500 acres on Cockleshell Creek in Middlesex County, Va. She also asserts that Louis Amis was one of the original settlers of Manakintown in 1699/1700.

In addition to the patent records cited above, Thomas Amis was listed as headright of Thomas Symms, Upper Norfolk Co., in 1638.[8] The Quit Rent Rolls of 1704 showed Joseph "Ames" in Accomack Co., Va., James Amis in Petsworth Parish, Gloucester Co., Va., Frances "Amos" and "Nocho Amos" in Parish of St. Peter and St. Paul.[9] Richard Amis witnessed the will of Major Benjamin Berryman in Westmoreland Co., Va., 13 May 1729.[10]

---

[6] Hodges, A. A. The Ancestry and Descendants of John Woodson Amis of Granville Co., N. C., and Scott Co., Miss. (Pendleton, S. C., n. p. d., 1978.) Hodges, Alice A. Ancestry and Descendants of Dr. John Wright Petty of Madison Co., Ala. (Pendleton, S. C.: n. p. d., 1978.) Both of these works appear to have been sold to Family Tree Maker and have been widely copied.

[7] Ray, Laura Collison. The Amiss Family of Amissville, Rappahannock and Culpeper County, Virginia.(Originally published 1952.) Copy located at http://nicbriz.home.mindspring.com/Brisbois/gen_Amiss_Family_by_Ray. html. Accessed 5 October 2011.

[8] Greer, George C. Early Virginia Immigrants, 1623-1666. (repr. Baltimore: Genealogical Publishing Co., 1978; orig. publ. Richmond, Va., 1912,) p. 10.

[9] 1704 Quit Rent Rolls. Located 6 October 2011 at http://files.usgwarchives.net/va/misc/1704va.txt.

[10] Westmoreland Co., Va., Will Book 81:366. [28 August 1729]. http://files.usgwarchives.net/va/westmoreland/wills/b6550001.txt. Accessed 6 October 2001.

As noted, Judge Amis' line can be firmly established as descended from 1857 (year of death) William Amis of Granville Co., N. C., (place of death).[11] An indirect proof is required to show that he was a son of 1816 (year of death) William Amis of Granville Co., N. C., (place of death), since this man left no will and was quite elderly at the time of his death.

William Amis was named as the wife of Hannah in Daniel Daly's will written 17 September 1754 in Essex Co., Va. The parish register of South Farnham Parish is lost so no firm marriage dates for anyone in Essex Co., Va., at this time exist.[12]

William Amis signed an agreement with the Essex Co., Court to take Joseph Evans, orphan of Thomas Evans, as an apprentice to learn the trade of shoemaker 20 August 1751.[13] This deed indicates that he was of age and established in his trade as a shoemaker by this date. From this I infer a birth year that was certainly before 1730, and more likely about 1725. This would also be consistent with having married by 1754 at which time he would be about 30, a common age for me to marry in this era. It would also mean that he was well past 80 at the time of his death.

William Amis appears on a notice presented to the Essex Co., Va., court 18 Jul 1758, of intent to engage in Presbyterian worship on the land of Mr. Thomas Miller in the Parish of South Farnham.[14]

---

[11] My thanks to Robert N. Grant for introducing this nomenclature as a way to sort out persons of similar name where the generational relationship is uncertain.

[12] Personal study of the Pitts family of Essex Co., Va., has given me insight into the records issue. The other problem is that there were problems with the early surveys of Old Rappahannock and early Essex Co., Va., and as a result there are many land deed cases extant. None of these have been researched looking for Amis connections.

[13] Essex Co., Va., Deed Book 25:___; 20 August 1751.

[14] William and Mary Quarterly 26 (ser. 1):65, 1917. The same group certified their presence in a petition to the county court dated 18 July 1758. Hopewell, John S. Presbyterians Certify Their Presence in Essex County, Virginia, 1858. Va. Genealogist 42:146-147, 1998.

William Amis bought a tract of land from Samuel Smith adjoining John Daly for £35 20 September 1756.[15] The land had been purchased from Thomas Pain(e). Both Smith and Daly made a £50 bond that Thomas Pain would be able to remain on the land for the rest of his life, but could not sell the timber. William Amis and his wife, Hannah, sold this 150 acre tract of land, formerly the property of Thomas Pain, dec., to William Brooke 23 July 1768 for £100.[16]

On 2 July 1768 William Cragg[17] and his wife, Christian, of Granville Co., N. C., sold for £37.10 Virginia money to William Amis of Essex County, Virginia, a 100 acre tract of land described as adjacent to Bond and an unnamed branch.[18] The deed was witnessed by Samuel Smith, Mary Smith, and Richard Bush, and was proved by Samuel Smith in the August 1768 Court.

The land can be located more specifically in a deed 20 August 1771 when Edward Bond and his wife, Judy, sold for £125 Virginia money to William Webb of Essex County, Virginia, a 225 acre tract on the east side of Grassy Creek, then east on Smith's land, thence north on William Amis' land, then west to Grassy Creek then south on the meanders of the creek to the beginning.[19] This deed was witnessed by Samuel Smith.

Another early deed of interest dated 4 April 1778 shows that James Hunt sold 200 acres of the tract he bought from William Craig to James Raven "for natural love and affection." The land was adjacent that of William Amis on Grassy Creek, so it is not

---

[15] Essex Co., Va., Deed Book 27:220-223.
[16] Essex Co., Va., Deed Book 30:193.
[17] William Craig sold to James Hunt for £265 Virginia money an 1144 acre tract of land that appears to be located south and east of the tract that he sold to William Amis. [Granville Co., N. C., Deed Book K:167-168, 24 November 1773]
[18] Granville Co., N. C., Deed Book H:451-452.
[19] Granville Co., N. C., Deed Book IJ:385-387. Proved August 1771.

surprising that an Amis girl married John Raven, probably a son of James Raven, and perhaps a grandson of William Craig.

William Amis bought a 640 acre tract of land in Granville County from the State of North Carolina on Beaver Dam Creek adjacent Samuel Smith for 50 shillings in September 1779.[20]

William Amis, Joseph Amis, and Lewis Amis appear among those who took the oath of allegiance to North Carolina in 1778.[21]

On 1 December 1784 he bought from Samuel Smith a 225 acre tract called the Glebe land, previously occupied by the Rev. Patillo, adjacent land of Amis and Smith. The land was bought in their capacity as trustees of the Grassy Creek and Nutbush Presbytery. [22]

On 2 February 1799, William Amis sold to Lewis Amis a 190 acre tract of land on Grassy creek adjacent William Knight's line and James Smith's lines.[23]

William Amis, Sr., of Granville Co., for love and affection transferred title on a Negro boy named Bill to his grandson William Amis, son of John Amis on 13 September 1811.[24] On 8 September 1813, he gave to his son John slaves Ann and "her future increase" and two children Ben and Lilly.[25] The files of his grandson, 1848 William Amis of Granville Co., N. C., son of 1825 Lewis Amis of Granville Co., N. C., who was an attorney, show tax receipts were paid, apparently by him, for his grandfather, William Amis, Sr., in several

---

[20] Granville Co., N. C., Deed Book N:37.

[21] Ardrey, Connie. List of Inhabitants of Granville County who took the oath of allegiance 22 May 1778-2 August 1778. Colonial Records of North Carolina 22:168-179. Located 7 October 2011 online at http://files.usgwarchives.net/nc/granville/court/allegian966w1.txt.

[22] Granville Co., N. C., Deed Book O:361.

[23] Granville Co., N. C., Deed Book Q:229.

[24] Granville Co., N. C., Deed Book V:268.

[25] Granville Co., N. C., Deed Book W:158.

years, the last being 1814 and 1815.[26] This implies that William Amis, Sr., died after 8 September 1813 and certainly before the end of the 1816 tax year. Since he would have been quite elderly, he may very well have used his grandson as his attorney to avoid having to come into the court house to pay the taxes in person. William Amis was taxed on 325 acres of land in the Abraham's Plain district and five slaves in 1788.[27] William Amis is the only man of this surname in Granville Co., N. C., in the 1790 Census.[28] In 1800 William Amis and spouse, both over age 45, are living without any children, but with eight adult slaves.[29] Lewis Amis, aged 26-45 and his wife of similar age, have one boy under 10, two 10-16, and two 16-26, along with three girls under 10. There are also seven adult slaves. The previously cited deed seems to establish Lewis Amis as a son of William Amis. The marriage records of Granville Co., N. C., show many marriages in the appropriate time frame to be children of William Amis and Hannah Daly, although direct proof is lacking. Taken as a whole, it seems clear that William Amis was the father to all the persons of that name living in Granville Co., N. C., in the last part of the eighteenth century.

Review of early Essex County records shows that on 10 March 1702/03 John Amis of Gloucester County purchased 375 acres of land in Essex County for £55 sterling from Henry "Boughan." The tract was described as adjacent Major George Morris, James

[26] Amis-Clark-Puryear Papers, 1760-1849. File #424, box #1, located at Joyner Library Special Collections, East Carolina University, Greeneville, N. C. Accessed 25 February 2012. These papers are further described online at http://digital.lib.ecu.edu/special/ead/findingaids/0474/
[27] Guthrie, Rosie H. 1788 Tax List Granville Co., N. C.
http://files.usgwarchives.net/nc/granville/court/tax1788txt. Accessed 7 October 2011.
[28] 1790 Census Granville Co., N. C., Abraham Plains Twp., p. 9.
[29] 1800 Census Granville Co., N. C., p. 550. (He is recorded two down from Samuel Smith, presumably the son of his cousin Samuel, who died in 1800.

Boughan, Thomas Gaines, and Hoskins' Creek.[30] The same tract of land was sold by Silvester Amis, of Ware Parish, Gloucester Co., Va., to Peter Kemp of Petsworth Parish, Gloucester Co., Va., on 15 December 1732 for £51.13, which appears to have been a slight loss over the intervening 30 years.[31]

John Amis had appeared earlier in Essex Co., Va., records, when the Court ordered him to pay costs to Thomas Short and Abigail Blackburn as the result of him abandoning his suit against them.[32] The basis of the suit was not stated, but Christopher Blackburn had died a short time previously, leaving a wife, Abigail, and children Elias and Mary.[33]

Joseph Amis of Ware Parish, Gloucester Co., Va., bought a tract of land from Gabriel Jones[34] and Mary, his wife, for £96 Virginia money 100 acres from Piscataway Ferry to the Ferry over Hoskins Creek, adjacent Thomas Gaines and Mr. Pettis.[35] Gabriel Jones had previously purchased this tract from Peter Tribble.

This deed seems to establish that Joseph Amis' land is in the same area as that purchased earlier by John Amis, also of Ware Parish, but sold by Silvester Amis of Ware Parish to Peter Kemp of Petsworth Parish about eight years before this deed. This

---

[30] Essex Co., Va., Deeds & Wills 1701-1703:136. Cited by Ruth and Sam Sparacio, (McLean, Va.: Antient Press, 1991,) p. 97.

[31] Essex Co., Va., Deed 19:362-364. (Sparacio.)

[32] Essex Co., Va., Court Orders, 1694-1695:226, 11 February 1694/95. (Sparacio)

[33] Essex Co., Va., Deeds & Wills 1693-1694:277-279. (Sparacio)

[34] Here is another point of confusion. A man named Gabriel Jones moved from Essex Co., Va., and ended up in Frederick Co., Va., where he became a prominent citizen. However, it seems certain that he was born about 1724, so would only be 16 at the time of this deed. While not impossible, it seems unlikely. It is more likely that he is a son/nephew of this Gabriel Jones. It is certainly possible that 1794 Joseph Amis of Culpeper Co., Va., had a close relationship with Gabriel Jones the "valley lawyer." I do not think it proves that 1794 Joseph Amis of Culpeper Co., Va., is the same man as after 1747 Joseph Amis of Essex Co., Virginia.

[35] Essex Co., Va., Deed Book 22:255-259, 6 July 1740/21 July 1741. (Mary released her dower rights on the latter day.)

14

suggests, but does not prove that Joseph was kin to this John Amis of Gloucester Co., Va.

Gloucester Co., Va., records were destroyed by fires in 1820 and 1865, so proving relationships for early settlers of this county is quite difficult, if not impossible. However, we do have the aforementioned Quit Rent Roll of 1704 that showed James Amis in Petsworth Parish, Gloucester County.

The church records for Ware Parish and the Register for Petsworth Parish are not extant, but the Vestry Book for Petsworth Parish has survived and been published.[36] Mr. John Amis and Mr. Thomas Swepson were ordered to procession the 9th Precinct between Chicksak Mill and Richland Swamp 6 April 1709.[37] Mr. James Amis and Mr. William Brookings were ordered to do processioning of the land in the 6th precinct "containing all the land on the left hand side of the road leading to Dragon's Bridge" on 14 September 1715.[38] Mr. James Amis and Mr. Alexander Roane were ordered to procession the 6th Precinct 3 September 1735[39] and again 12 October 1739.[40] Mr. James Amis and William Kenningham (Cunningham?) were ordered to procession the 6th Precinct 5 October 1743[41] and Mr. John Amis and Mr. John Stubbs, Jr., were ordered to procession the 6th precinct 4 September 1751.[42] We cannot be certain that the James Amis of the 1704 Quit Rent Roll is the same James Amis doing the processioning in 1715, but assuming that he is the same man, then it appears

---

[36] Chamberlayne, C. G. The Vestry Book of Petsworth Parish, Gloucester County, Virginia, 1677-1793. (Richmond, Va.: Library Board, 1933.) Cited hereafter as Petsworth Vestry Book.

[37] Petsworth Vestry Book, p. 100. Same data shown again on page 102. Thomas Kemp was listed in the 9th precinct in 1735. (p. 239) It is possible that John Amis moved from Ware to Petsworth Parish between 1702 and 1709, and that this is the same John Amis who purchased land in Essex Co., Va., but this cannot be proved by this record.

[38] Petsworth Vestry Book, p. 130.

[39] Petsworth Vestry Book, p. 239.

[40] Petsworth Vestry Book, p. 259.

[41] Petsworth Vestry Book, p. 269.

[42] Petsworth Vestry Book, p. 290.

15

that he died sometime between 1744 and 1751. For reasons discussed below, this indicates to me that he was an age contemporary of Joseph Amis of Essex Co., Virginia.

Research conducted in the records of Essex Co., Virginia, in 1996 by a grandson of Judge Amis, A. B. Amis, III, proved the following items of information. On 20 October 1747 Joseph Amis and wife Constance sold 100 acres of land for £90 to John Clement, reserving five acres for Constance to live on for life.[43] The land was purchased from Gabriel Jones, who had purchased the land from Peter Tremble.[44] Constant Jones made petition for letters of administration on the estate of her husband, John Jones, deceased on 10 June 1706 and returned the inventory on 10 July 1706 in Essex Co., Va.[45] These data have been interpreted to show that Joseph Amis married Constance Jones, son of John Jones and Constant or Constance, and that she was a brother to Gabriel Jones, and these seem reasonable conclusions.

Daniel Daly wrote his last will and testament in Essex Co., Va., on 17 September 1754 and named his wife Ann, daughters Hannah and Frances, sons John and Isaiah, and his brother-in-law Francis Jones.[46] Hannah was identified as the wife of William Amis and was left first choice of one male slave.

There is minimal information about Lewis Amis, who is said to be associated with the Manakin settlement, but most of this seems based upon the name. I have not been able to find any documentation confirming Lewis Amis as part of the Huguenot

---

[43] John Clement willed "the land I bought of Joseph Amis" to his youngest son, Henry Haggard Clements when he wrote his will 12 November 1766. (Copy located online 9 March 2011 at http://files.usgwarchives.net/va/essex/wills/c4555000.txt.)

[44] Essex Co., Va., Deed Book 24:185; 20 October 1747. This is obviously the same tract of land he purchased as recorded in Deed Book 22:255-259, 6 July 1740/21 July 1741.

[45] Essex Co., Va., Will Book 0:246, 247.

[46] Essex Co., Va., Will Book 10:23.

16

immigration of 1700.[47] It appears that Mrs. Hodges was taking her lead from Mrs. Ray, who asserts that the Culpeper Co. Joseph who died in 1794 is the same as the Essex Co., Joseph.[48] Mrs. Ray also makes the same association with Lewis Amis, "founder of Manakintown." Interestingly, Mrs. Pilcher associates the Culpeper Co., Va., family with Louis Amis, but does not associate them with Joseph Amis.[49]

I have found no evidence the Culpeper Co., Va., Amiss family is the same as the Amis family of Essex Co., Va. The 1783 Personal Property Tax List for Culpeper Co., Va., shows in the list of John Wiginton, Gent., William Amiss, Joseph Amiss (with 10 adult slaves), and Thomas Amiss.[50] However, William Amis, son of Joseph Amis, moved to Granville Co., N. C., in 1768, so he would not be the same man listed in the 1783 personal property tax roll of far distant Culpeper Co., Virginia. The accidental survival of two tithe lists from ca. 1764-1765 shows William Amis with two tithables, himself and a slave named Jenny, with 75 acres of land, which Samuel Smith was taxed for 7

[47] This migration has been studied extensively and reported in the genealogical literature. The Amis family has yet to be proved to be Huguenot. The National Huguenot Society: List of Qualified Ancestors. [http://huguenot.netnation.com/ancestor/AncestorLookup.php] dated 1 September 2011, accessed 20 October 2011.

On the other hand, The Huguenot Society of the Founders of Manakintown in the Colony of Virginia, has accepted six lineages including Louis Amis. Interestingly, none of them seem connected to Joseph Amis of Essex Co., Va. (16 June 2011.)

http://manakin.addr.com/manakin/lineages.php. Accessed 20 October 2011.

[48] Ray, Laura Collison. The Amiss Family of Amissville, Rappahannock and Culpeper County, Virginia. (1952). Accessed 31 March 2009 at http://nickbriz.home.mindspring.com/Brisbois/gen_Amiss_Family_by_Ray.html.

[49] Pilcher, Margaret Campbell. Historical Sketches of the Campbell, Pilcher, and Kindred Families. (Nashville, TN: Marshall & Bruce Co., 1911,) pp. 337ff. Accessed 20 October 2011 at http://www.archive.org/stream/historicalsketch00byupilc#page/n5/mode/2up.

[50] http://files.usgwarchives.net/va/culpeper/census/1783/1783tax01.html. Accessed 10 October 2011.

tithables and 2547 acres of land.[51] A list of Essex County, Va., voters in 1769 shows no one named Amis, and Samuel Smith is also missing. I also think trying to fit the Culpeper and Essex County families together has skewed the chronology. The first useful date is 20 August 1751 when William Amis signed an agreement with the Essex Co., Court to take Joseph Evans, orphan of Thomas Evans, as an apprentice to learn the trade of shoemaker.[52] From this I infer a birth year that was certainly before 1730, and more likely about 1725. This would also be consistent with having married by 1754 at which time he would be about 30, a common age for men to marry in this era. It would also mean that he was 90 or so at the time of his death.[53]

William Amis is the only certain son of Joseph Amis, although I cannot exclude that he had one or more daughters. If we assume Joseph Amis was 25-30 years of age at the time of William's birth, then an estimate for his birth year would be say 1695. This would place him in his early fifties when he disappeared from the Essex County records. Joseph Amis might well be kin to the James Amis of Petsworth Parish who died say 1750 and the John Amis of Ware Parish who died say 1730 and the Thomas Amis who patented land 1678 in Gloucester County.

He is generally assumed to be a brother to the Thomas Amis who appears in the records of Middlesex County, Virginia,[54] and is generally assumed to be a

---

[51] Hopewell, John S. Two Tithable Lists from Essex County, ca. 1764-1765. Va. Genealogist 45:163-177,2001. William Amis is on p. 163 and Samuel Smith is on page 171. There are no other persons named Amis on this list.

[52] Essex Co., Va., Deed Book 25:___; 20 August 1751.

[53] Mrs. Ray documented the remarkable longevity of several of the men clearly related to the 1794 Joseph Amis of Culpeper Co., Virginia.

[54] Parish Register of Christ Church, Middlesex County, Virginia, 1653 to 1812. (Richmond: NSCDA, 1897.) Copy located 8 March 2012 at http://www.archive.org/stream/parishregisterof00chri/parishregisterof00 chri_djvu.txt. The documented facts are that Thomas Amis married Rachel

brother to Ann Amis, who supposedly married Samuel Smith. The last relationship is useful for explaining the observed interactions of the Amis and Smith families in Granville County, North Carolina. The others may be true, but cannot be proved.

Genealogical Summary

1. JOSEPH[2] AMIS was born say 1695 in Ware Parish, Gloucester Co., Virginia, and died after 20 October 1747 in Essex Co., Virginia.[55] He married CONSTANCE JONES say 1725 in Gloucester Co., Virginia.

Joseph Amis was born in Tidewater Virginia in 1710 and married Constance Jones of Essex Co., Va., about 1730. He died in Culpeper Co., Va., in 1794. The names of his parents are not known, but it is believed that he was the brother of Thomas Amis who married Rachel Daniel in 1722 and of Ann Amis who married 1726 Samuel Smith. Descendants of these two couples state that they were the children of Lewis Amis who was born 1670 and died 1750, the son of Thomas Amis who bought land in Gloucester Co., Va. in 1676. The parentage of Constance Jones is also unknown, but a connection with Gabriel Jones who married Margaret Strother seems likely as they were very close friends. I suspect she was a granddaughter of John Jones of Essex Co., Va., whose estate was administered by Constance Jones in 1706. Joseph Amis moved from Essex Co. to Culpeper Co. about 1766. When or where Constance died is unknown. Joseph's estate was administered by his son

---

Daniel on 14 November 1722; John, son of Thomas and Rachel Amis was born 20 August 1724 and baptized 30 August 1724; James Amis married Jane Seager Nichols 17 March 1737/38, and Taylor, son of "Phillis", slave of James Amis was born 28 Mary 1742. While it seems likely that James was a son of Thomas, it is not documented in the parish registry.

[55] I have elected to show Joseph Amis as the second generation as a way of noting that he is not the immigrant ancestor. Perhaps Thomas Amis really was the immigrant, but unless further data are found, this remains speculative, as does the assertion that Thomas was the grandfather, as opposed to the father of Joseph Amis.

Thomas. It is not known whether he had any daughters.[56]

Children of JOSEPH AMIS and CONSTANCE JONES:[57]

3. i. WILLIAM³ AMIS, b. Essex Co., Va.; d. after September 1813 Granville Co., N. C.; m. HANNAH DALY, dau. of DANIEL DALY and ANN ____ before 17 September 1754 Essex Co., Va.

ii. ANN² AMIS died after 17 July 1753 Essex Co., Va. She married SAMUEL SMITH in Essex Co., Va., who died there between 8 October 1734 and 17 May 1737.

Children of ANN AMIS and SAMUEL SMITH are:

1. JOHN³ SMITH.
2. SAMUEL³ SMITH, b.3 December 1729 Essex Co., Va.; d. 6 October 1800 Granville Co., N. C.; m. MARY WEBB May 1761 Essex Co., Va.; b. 1740 Essex Co., Va.; d. 1827 Granville Co., N. C.
3. JANE³ SMITH.[58]
4. MARY³ SMITH.
5. SUSANNAH³ SMITH.

3. WILLIAM³ AMIS, b. about 1725 Gloucester Co., Va., d. after September 1813 Granville Co., N. C. He married HANNAH DALY, daughter of DANIEL DALY and ANN ____ before 17 September 1754 Essex Co., Va.

William Amis, Sr., was probably born in Essex Co., Va., about 1733. His parentage has not been

---

[56] Hodges, A. A. The Ancestry and Descendants of John Woodson Amis of Granville Co., N. C., and Scott Co., Miss. (Pendleton, S. C., n. p. d., 1978,) p. 15.

[57] Many include Thomas Amis, Philip Amis, and Gabriel Amis as sons of Joseph Amis. So far, I have not seen any documentation for this assertion, which seems to depend upon 1794 Joseph Amis of Culpeper Co., Va., being the man appearing in Essex Co., Va., records.

[58] One of the girls married John Young and had three children

proved but the evidence is very strong that he was the son of Joseph Amis and Constance Jones of Essex and Culpepper Cos., Va. This Joseph had a son William who had a son William with him when William Amis, Sr., sold land to his son-in-law Martin Fishback in 1788. William Amis, Sr., married 1754 Hannah Daily, daughter of Daniel Daily of East Farnham, Richmond Co., Va. East Farnham, Richmond Co., Va., is just across the river from South Farnham, Essex Co., Va., where we find William Amis seeking permit to build a Presbyterian Church in 1758.[59] Although he owned land in Culpepper Co., Va., it is not known whether he ever lived there as he referred to himself as of Essex Co., Va., when he purchased land in Granville Co, N. C., in 1768. He and his two eldest sons took the Oath of Allegiance in Granville Co., N. C., 30 May 1778. He first appeared on the "List of Taxables" in Granville Co., in 1778 and last appeared on the tax tables in Culpepper Co. in 1788. The exact date of his move to North Carolina is not known but it was before 1781 when his children were getting married there. The date of his and his wife's death is not known. He was still alive in 1813 when he deeded Negroes to his son John.[60]

I concluded Joseph Amis came from Gloucester Co., Virginia, to Essex Co., Virginia, in 1740, so William would have been born there. I also think he was born earlier than 1733 on the basis of being able to contract with the court in 1751 to take an apprentice. The tax records suggest his death occurred in 1816, so he was about 90 years old. His advanced age may explain his disappearance from the records as well as the lack of a will.

---

[59] William Amis appears on a notice presented to the Essex Co., Va., court 18 Jul 1758, of intent to engage in Presbyterian worship on the land of Mr. Thomas Miller in the Parish of South Farnham. William and Mary Quarterly 26 (ser. 1):65, 1917.

[60] Hodges, A. A. The Ancestry and Descendants of John Woodson Amis of Granville Co., N. C., and Scott Co., Miss. (Pendleton, S. C., n. p. d., 1978,) p. 12.

Children of WILLIAM AMIS and HANNAH DALY are:

i. JOSEPH[4] AMIS, b. before 1756 Essex Co., Va.; d. Guilford Co., N. C., March 1781.

Mrs. Hodges states that Joseph Amis died at the battle of Guilford C. H., North Carolina, and also states he was the eldest son. If William and Hannah used traditional naming patterns this would be a reasonable assumption. Given the range of possible birth years, this would suggest he was born about 1750, which would push his father's birth year closer to 1720, but still consistent with the "about 1725" that I have estimated.

ii. LEWIS[4] AMIS, b. before 1756 Essex Co., Va.; d. before August 1825 Granville Co., N. C.; m. ELIZABETH KNIGHT, dau. of JONATHAN KNIGHT and JUDITH WOODSON 25 December 1781 Granville Co., N. C.

Lewis Amis was old enough to sign the oath of allegiance, and was therefore born before 1756. His marriage in 1781 suggests a birth after about 1750. Their descendants are shown in Chapter 2.

iii. ELIZABETH[4] AMIS, b. 24 March 1755 Essex Co., Va.; d. 15 January 1838 Oglesby, Davidson Co., Tenn.; m. HARRIS OGILVIE 26 October 1781 Granville Co., Tenn., son of WILLIAM OGILVIE and MARY HARRIS; b. 21 March 1758 Granville Co., N. C.; d. 11 November 1823 Oglesby, Davidson Co., Tenn.[61]

iv. WILLIAM[4] AMIS, b. 1765 Essex Co., Va.; d. before 10 June 1857 Granville Co., N. C.; m. JUDITH KNIGHT, dau. of JONATHAN KNIGHT and JUDITH WOODSON 21 January 1789 Granville Co., N. C.

Their descendants are shown in Chapter 3.

v. JOHN[4] AMIS, b. 29 October 1774 Granville Co., N. C., d. 9 September 1852 Culleoka, Maury Co., Tenn.; m. MARY KNIGHT, dau. of JONATHAN

[61] Kristina. Schneider, Jeschke, Linde, Ederer. 13 November 2006. Located at http:// http://wc.rootsweb.ancestry.com, (db. kriss_je)

KNIGHT and JUDITH WOODSON 2 October 1797 Granville Co., N. C.; b. 24 March 1778 Granville Co., N. C.; d. 21 October 1851 Culleoka, Maury Co., Tenn. Their descendants are shown in Chapter 4.

vi. HANNAH⁴ AMIS, b. 1776 Granville Co., N. C.; d. 1830 College Grove, Williamson Co., Tenn.; m. JOHN OGILVIE 20 January 1792 Granville Co., N. C. son of WILLIAM OGILVIE and MARY HARRIS; b. 23 July 1767 Granville Co., N. C.; d. 12 October 1821 College Grove, Williamson Co., Tenn.

"The gravestone for John Ogilvie states: In memory of John Ogilvie who was born July the 23 1767 died Oct the 12 1821 Died a Christian. A stone of identical design and apparent age is next to John's. There is no visible inscription on the stone. According to Ogilvie Kith and Kin, Volume 2 Number 4, it is believed to be the stone of John's wife, Hannah. Hannah lived on John's plantation until the time of her death and it is reasonable to assume that she was buried next to her husband. A complete listing persons known to be buried at the Ogilvie Cemetery (up to 1973) can be found in "Directory of Williamson County, Tennessee, Burials," Volume 1, pages 228-229. Note: the September 1997 issue of Ogilvie Kith and Kin, page 2, gives another possible location for the burial of Hannah. The Word Cemetery in Pleasant Grove, Bedford County, TN, has gravestones for infant children of Frances Ogilvie Robinson and Amy Ogilvie McClure (Hannah's daughters). There is a marker among those children for "H. Ogilvie, Died 1830." It is very possible that Hannah was buried with her grandchildren in Bedford County rather than with her husband in Williamson County.

The last will and testament of John Ogilvie is recorded in the Williamson County, TN, archives in Book C, pages 291-293.

The will states: In the name of God, Amen. I, John Ogilvie, of the County Williamson and State of Tennessee, being in a weak and low (unreadable) of Body but of sound mind and memory do make this my last will and Testament. My soul I commit into the hands of God my creator hoping for mercy thro his Son Jesus Christ my Redeemer and my Body to the Earth in decent Christian Burial at the Burying Ground at Brother Richard Ogilivies and as touching such property as God has been pleased to bless me I give and bequeath in the manner and form following. In the first place my will and desire is that my Family like together in a Family Capacity on the Lands and Plantation whereon I now live and that my negroes remain with them until my daughter Polly arrives at age or marry as the case may be and then my will and Desire is that my wife Hannah Ogilvie have my Negro woman Elisa and her youngest Child at that time and their increase during her life and at her death to be equally divided among my Children and if Circumstances should arise that it would be advisable to make a Division of the Plantation my desire is that my Wife have the dwelling House with half of the improvement adjoining during life and at her death to be buried by my son Lewis Ogilvie. 2nd, I give and bequeath to my son Lewis Ogilvie the other half of my Land when he arives at age and the other half at the death of his mother and the Bay Horse McKinny and a Sorrel Filey now two years old to him and his heirs forever. 3rd, My Will and desire is that the Horse Jack Gin and her colt and the Sorrel Mare with the yoke of oxen remain on the plantation for the use of the Family and that my wife make a choice of twelve head of Cattle, twelve head of Sheep and Hogs sufficient for present support and to raise stock from and the remainder of the Stock of Horses, Cattle, Sheep and Hogs to be sold and the money arisen therefrom after paying my Just Debt to be equally divided among my Children. 4th, I give and bequeath to my daughter Polly when she arrives at age or marries as the case may be a Horse Saddle and Bridle worth ninety five dollars, two beds and Furniture and her choice of a Cow and Calf, one Ewe and Lamb and one Sow and Pigs and Dresser and Kitchen furniture at the discretion of her Mother to be furnished out of the Property on hand in the Family at such time to her and her heirs forever. 5th, My will and desire is that the remainder of Negroes together with their increase when my Daughter Polly arives at age or marry as the case may be should be equally divided among my children to them and their heirs forever. 6th, My Will and desire is that the Crop now on the Plantation together with all the Plantation Tools be disposed of for the benefit of the Family and if it should be necessary that a Division take place in the Plantation, the Plantation Tools, Household and Kitchen Furniture together with the Stock of Horses Cattle Sheep and Hogs to be equally divided between my Wife and son Lewis and at the Death of my Wife her part of this Division then remaining to be equally divided among my Daughters. 7th, and Lastly I constitute and Appoint my trusty friend Doctor Wm S. Webb and my well beloved Wife Hannah Ogilvie Executors in trust of this my Last Will and Testament revoking all others heretofore by me made in Testimony whereof I have hereunto set my Hand and affixed my seal this 5th day of October 1821. (Underlined before signed the words Household and Kitchen Furniture).

An inventory of the estate of John Ogilvie was completed on 12 Feb 1822 by Wm. Webb. The County Commission's Report was dated 19 December 1823. The estate settlement was dated 18 March 1824.

Houston McClure, husband of Amy Ogilvie, petitioned the Williamson County Court on 25 July 1831 to issue subpoenas to Lewis Ogilvie, Wm. Webb, Polly Ogivlie and her husband Thomas Ray, to compel them to provide an accounting of the proceeds of the personal property of John Ogilvie that took place from the time of his death in 1821 until the time of Hannah's death in 1830. The Williamson County Archives has a 103 page record of the case of Houston McClure et al. vs. Lewis Ogilvie et al. McClure admits in his complaint that the personal property and slaves mentioned in the will had been divided equally. His complaint questioned the status of the property that remained with the plantation for its support. He alleged that Lewis Ogilvie had profited from that property (livestock and crops) and had not divided his profits when his mother Hannah died. Lewis countered by saying the property left with the plantation was not sufficient to support the family and everything that he sold was for that purpose and not profit. He said that his mother became insane after the death of John and he had to spend money on her care. He had to purchase additional slaves to maintain the plantation and eventually rented out part of it just to break even. The 103 page case doesn't include a final judgment on who prevailed in the suit."[62]

vii. FRANCES[4] AMIS, m. JOHN RAVEN 7 November 1797 Granville Co., Tenn.

I have found John Raven, Jr., in Abraham Plains District, Granville Co., N. C., in 1790, as well as a John Raven. John Raven and wife, both over 45, are living in Caswell Co., N. C., in 1800.[63] John Raven, 26-45, wife of same age, and one girl 10-16, are living in Greenville Co., S. C. in 1820.[64] I have found John "Ravan" from NC living in Lumpkin Co., Ga., in 1836 and 1850. His estimated birth year is 1799 and his wife, Sarah, was born in the same year in South Carolina, and their daughter Amarillis 25, was born in S. C., suggesting this may be the same family, although their son William was 23 and born in Georgia.[65] Other than these fragments of information, I have

[62] Robinson, Robert. Rob's Family Tree. 19 December 2009. Located at http://wc.rootsweb.ancestry.com, (db. :3366378.)

[63] 1800 Census Caswell Co., N. C., p. 147, [00001-00001]. No other persons named Raven were identified in North Carolina that year.

[64] 1820 Census Greenville Co., S. C., p. 137. [00010-01010].

[65] 1850 Census Lumpkin Co., Ga., Frogtown District, p. 92, #36. There is a James H. Raven, 63, NC living in Sumter Co., Ga., Bottsford Post Office, p. 471, #5/5 and his son, Stewart, p. 472 #10/11. These may be other children of the John Raven who married Frances Amis.

not found solid traces of this couple after their marriage.

On the Knight Family

Given that three sons of William and Hannah (Daly) Amis married daughters of Jonathan and Judith (Woodson) Knight, I have investigated these individuals as well. Like many Virginia families, there seems to be much confusion about the earlier generations of the Knight family. Most of the published studies assert the progenitor of "our" Knight family was Peter Knight, who was a planter in Gloucester Co., Va.[66] He is supposed to be the father of 1702 Peter Knight of Northumberland Co., Va. In turn, Peter is supposed to be the father of 1762 John Knight of Sussex Co., Va., who, in turn, is supposed to be the father of 1772 John Knight of Lunenburg Co., Va. Presently, there is no documentation for this lineage that I have been able to find. However, I have found documentation of 1772 John Knight of Lunenburg Co., Va.

1. JOHN[1] KNIGHT died before 12 March 1772 in Lunenburg Co., Virginia. He married ELIZABETH WOODSON, daughter of ROBERT WOODSON and ELIZABETH WATKINS. She was born after 1710 in Henrico Co., Va., and died after 1784 in Lunenburg Co., Virginia.

John Knight bought 383 acres of land in Brunswick Co., Va., in 1742, likely in the part that was separated into Lunenburg Co., Va., in 1746.[67] John Knight, "of Granville Co., N. C.," obtained patent for 640 acres of land in Granville Co., N. C., in a deed

---

[66] See as an example the posting by Mary Knight, at http://genforum.genealogy.com/knight/messages/693.html. 29 Dec 1998.
[67] Knight, Mary. 19 Dec 2001.
http://genforum.genealogy.com/knight/messages/5423.html.

proved in August 1749. In December 1750, John Knight "of Lunenburg Co., Va.," purchased two parcels of land on both sides of Grassy Creek totaling 1200 acres. It is uncertain if this is two different men named John Knight, or simply the way the deed was recorded.

On 25 February 1762 John Knight of Lunenburg Co., Va., deeded 300 acre tracts of land in Granville, N. C., to Jonathan Knight, William Knight, and Memucan Hunt[68] in indentures recorded in Granville Co., N. C., in May 1762. Jonathan Knight's southern boundary and William Knight's western boundary was shared with Charles Knight, who was presumably granted the remaining 300 acres of land purchased in 1750.

John Knight wrote his last will and testament 7 September 1771, and it was proved in court for Lunenburg Co., Va., 12 March 1772.[69]

In the name of God Amen, I John Knight of Lunenburg County being very sick & weak of Body, but of perfect mind and memory, thanks be given unto God, calling to mind the mortality of my Body and knowing that it is appointed for all men once to die, do make and ordain this my last will and Testament that is to say principally and first of all, I

---

[68] Memucan Hunt (1729–1808) was an early American statesman and the first person to hold the position of North Carolina State Treasurer in its current form. During his term in office, Hunt unwittingly honored fraudulent claims for military service stemming from the Revolutionary War (paying too generously soldiers who had fought in the Revolutionary War, and in some cases, paying soldiers who had not fought at all), which resulted in both litigation and hearings by the General Assembly. While he was not charged with malfeasance, he was defeated for re-election in 1787 by John Haywood. Hunt retired from politics to Granville County, where he became a wealthy planter and served as justice of the peace until 1792. At the time of his death in 1808, at age 79, Hunt owned nearly 16,000 acres (65 km²) of land, 22 slaves, two horses, four mares, 14 head of cattle and 33 hogs. [http://en.wikipedia.org/wiki/Memucan_Hunt. Accessed 28 February 2009.]

[69] Lunenburg Co., Va., Will Book 2:382-387. Transcription posted by Mary Knight 20 December 2001. Located at http://www.genforum.genealogy.com/knight/messages.5429.html.

give and recommend my soul into the hands of Almighty God that give it, and my Body I recommend to the earth to be ____ in decent Christian burial at the discretion of my Executors, nothing doubting but at the general resurrection I shall receive the same again by the might power of God, and as touching my worldly Estate wherewith it has pleased God to bless me in this life I give and devise and dispose of the same in the following manner and form.

Item: Its my will and desire that my whole Estate should be kept together and undivided or separated until all my lawful Debts are paid by means of cropping or otherways to be managed by my Executors hereafter named and after that is fully accomplished it is my further desire that the Estate should be still kept together and managed as aforesaid until the sum of two hundred pounds can be raised and layed out in the purchase of a tract of land for my son Joseph and then to be divided in the form and manner hereafter mentioned.

Item: I lend to my wife Elizabeth during her natural life all that tract of land whereon I now live except one hundred and fifty acres hereafter bequeathed to my son Peter, also five Negroes, viz: Jack, Delcy, Agg, Isaac and Nutty, with all my Household furniture, stock etc and after her decease it is my further will and desire the Negroes should be disposed of as follows.

Item: I bequeath unto my son William after the decease of his mother on Negroe man Jack to him and his heirs forever.

Item: I bequeath unto my son Joseph after the decease of his mother one Negroe man Isaac also a Negroe man Peter to be delivered him at the dividing of the Estate.

Item: I bequeath unto my daughter Rachel after the decease of her mother a Negro girl Nutty also two young Negroes Lewis & Milla.

Item: I bequeath unto my son Peter one moiety of two Negroes Agg and Delcy to be equally divided between him and his Brother John after the decease of their mothers, also one hundred and fifty acres of land more or less joining the tract whereon I now live to be divided by a branch running from near Shelton's Bridge in a straight line to Minors land all the land to the North of that branch is what I bequeath to him and his heirs forever.

Item: I bequeath to my son John one moiety of two Negroes above mentioned after the decease of his mother. \

Item: I bequeath to my son Jonathan one Negroe girl named Fanny to him and his heirs forever.

Item: I bequeath to my son Charles three Negroes Jane, Cesar, and Betta, to him and his heirs forever.

Item: I bequeath to my Daughter Elisabeth a Negroe woman named _____ and her child.

Item: I bequeath to my Daughter Judith Bagley one negroe girl named Beck.

Item: I bequeath to my Daughter Mary Lea two negroe girls Phillies and Tabby during her natural life and if she should die without issue to return to the surviving part of my children to be equally divided between them. It is further my will and desire if she should have an heir or heirs that the Negroes should descend to them as she directs.

Item: I bequeath to my son Woodson two Negroes Tom and Cloe also that tract of land before devised to his mother during her life to him and his heirs forever being the same I now live on with all my stock of every kind and household furniture except three Beds, which I desire may be given to Charles, Joseph and Rachel at the discretion of my beloved wife Elisabeth.

Item: I bequeath to my daughters daughter Lucy Cook one Negro girl named Tamer. It is my will and desire that if any my children should die before dividing the Estate that his or her proportion should be equally divided between the surviving parties. I also desire that every person within mentioned should take in possession their proportion of the Estate as is by this will devised provided it doth not consist in Negroes upwards of ten years of age on that part allotted for the immediate use of my wife Elisabeth.

I do hereby constitute and appoint Joseph Charles and Peter Knight Executors to this my last will and Testament. In witness whereof I have hereunto set my hand and seal seventh day of September one thousand seven hundred and seventy one.

John Knight, Sen. (ls)

Witness
Miller Woodson
Francis (X) Amos
Thomas Jeffress

At a court held for Lunenburg County the 12th day of March 1772 this last will and Testament of John Knight, Sen., was exhibited in court by the Executors therein named and was proved by the oaths of two of the Witnesses thereto subscribed and ordered to be recorded and on the motion of the said Executors who made oath according to law certificate is granted them for obtaining a probate of the said will in due form they giving security whereupon they gave Bond and Security according to law.

Teste: Wm Taylor CLC

Children of JOHN KNIGHT and ELIZABETH WOODSON:[70]

2.   i.   JONATHAN[2] KNIGHT, b. about 1729 Henrico Co., Va.; d. before November 1809 Granville Co., N. C.; m. JUDITH WOODSON 24 February 1757 Goochland Co., Va., dau. of JOSEPH WOODSON and ELIZABETH PARSONS.

     ii. CHARLES[2] KNIGHT, d. after 1819 Nottoway Co., Va.; m. MARY SMITH.

          Charles Knight was head of household in Amelia Co., Va., in 1785. He and his wife, Mary, sold 300 acres of land in to Peter Knight in 1785. Charles Knight was apparently a Tory, and had a

---

[70] Hanke, Douglas. Pierson/Hanke Family Ties. 16 February 2009. Located at http://wc.rootsweb.ancestry.com, (db. dhanke.) The notes are from his posting.

reputation as a receiver of stolen horses and forged tobacco notes.

iii. PETER[2] KNIGHT, d. about 1823 Madison Co., Alabama; m. (1) MASON COLEMAN ANDERSON, d. after 1800 Nottoway Co., Va.; m. (2) PRUDENCE JONES.

Peter Knight and his wife, Mason, sold 150 acres of land to Rice Scott adjacent Woodson Knight 10 March 1786

iv. WILLIAM[2] KNIGHT, m. PALATIA EVANS.

v. JUDITH[2] KNIGHT, m. GEORGE BAGLEY, d. June 1795 Nottoway Co., Va.

George's father sold him 200 acres of land on Woody Creek in Amelia Co., Va., in August 1768. George sold this land to Peter Jones in 1770, when Judith released her dower rights. George Bagley inherited 200 acres of land on the north side of Mallory's Creek, and purchased an additional 403 acres on the same creek from George Foster in January 1770.

George Bagley was first lieutenant of the Amelia Co., militia, contributed 225 pounds of beef to the Revolutionary cause, and was listed in the 1785 "census" of Amelia Co., Va. He died in June 1795 and his will was proved in Nottoway Co., Va., in 1796.[71]

vi. LUCY[2] KNIGHT, m. COOKE.

vii. RACHEL[2] KNIGHT, d. before 2 September 1847 Nottoway Co., Va.; m. WILLIAM DUDLEY 19 August 1784 Lunenburg Co., Va.

viii. ELIZABETH[2] KNIGHT, m. LODOWICK FARMER 11 October 1787; b. 1757; d. 15 September 1816 Lunenburg Co., Va.

Lodowick Farmer married (1) Elizabeth Herring 27 October 1779 Lunenburg Co., Va. Lodowick Farmer and wife Betsy deeded 212 acres of land on Ledbetter Creek Lunenburg Co., Va., to Benjamin Farmer 11 January 1792. He wrote his

---

[71] Nottoway Co., Va., was formed from Amelia Co., Va., in 1789. It consisted of the southern portion of Amelia County and is the northern boundary of Lunenburg Co., Virginia.

will 6 August 1816 in Lunenburg Co., Va., and it was proved 10 October 1816. She received a pension for his Revolutionary War service as 2nd Lieutenant of Capt. Billups company, where she was identified as the daughter of John Knight, a soldier during the Revolution.

ix. JOSEPH[2] KNIGHT, d. before 12 February 1789 Mecklenburg Co., Va.
Joseph Knight was listed as a tithable in his father's household in 1769, which implies a birth year of about 1753. He sold 100 acres of land to James Crook 12 February 1781, so he was certainly born before 1760. He wrote his will in Mecklenburg Co., Va., (WB 3:14), 2 January 1789 and it was proved 12 February 1789. He left the bulk of his estate to his brother, Jonathan.

x. JOHN[2] KNIGHT.[72]

xi. MARY[2] KNIGHT, b. 2 September 1749 Lunenburg Co., Va.; d. after 1810 Chatham Co., N. C.; m. JOSEPH LEA; d. 1805 Chatham Co., N. C.

xii. WOODSON[2] KNIGHT, d. before 9 May 1831 Lunenburg Co., Va.; m. MARTHA WALTON 18 June 1781 Prince Edward Co., Va., dau. of GEORGE WALTON and MARTHA HUGHES; b. 8 June 1762 Prince Edward Co., Va.
Woodson Knight participated in the Battle of Guilford Court House as a militia soldier, and also provided beef and fodder to the Army. His last will and testament was written in Lunenburg Co., Va., 19 March 1831 and proved 9 May 1831.[73]

---

[72] Many online reports indicate he married Rachel Anderson in Cheraw Dist., S. C., 9 January 1774. However, this man "at a young age moved to South Carolina," and appears on the 1777 Will of William MacCormack with Thomas Knight and Zachariah Knight. He served in the 1st Georgia Battalion of Continental Troops from 1 April 1779 to 1 February 1780. He was born 1747 in Virginia and died after December 1822 Wayne Co., Ga. I think it unlikely this is the same man. [Cardell, Richard. Cardell, Roberts, Francis, Elliott. 25 February 2009. Located at http://wc.rootsweb.ancestry.com, (db. gen32207).
[73] Lunenburg Co., Va., Will Book 10:122A,123,123A. Transcription by Jim Dillard. Accessed 28 February 2009 at http://www.vagenweb.org/lunenburg/w0knight_woodson.html.

"I Woodson Knight do hereby constitute this my last will and testament as follows.

First, it is my will that all my just debts be paid out of my personal estate. I direct my land, on which I reside to be divided into two parts by a line commencing at a high rock on the south side of Big Nottoway River where myself and Tarlton W. Knight corners thence pursing the line between said Tarlton W. and myself to the line till it arrives opposite a large forked Red Oak, which is at present a side line to me making a corner on said Oak; thence by a new line running straight through my Plantation till it strikes a large Poplar tree very near my using spring, thence down said spring branch as it meanders, till it intersects the line between me and John H. Knight; the land tying east of these lines and adjoining John H. Knight, I give to my said son John H. Knight and his heirs forever; the land lying west of said lines I give to my son T. W. Knight and his heirs forever. Furthermore, I direct that the graveyard upon the lands I have devised to my son T. W. Knight where many of my kindred has been buried, and where it is my desire that my mortal remains shall be deposited, be laid in a ___ of thirty five yards by twenty and enclosed by my executor, the expense to be paid out of my personal estate; and said graveyard to be held in trust by my son T. W. Knight and his heirs as a burial place for my family; I direct that the residue of my estate that is all my property not herein disposed of, be sold at public auction and the proceeds including all debts due me shall be first as heretofore applied to the payment of my debts, and after such payment, and the payment of the enclosed aforesaid; I give two hundred and forty dollars to my son Tarlton W. Knight in trust for the children of my daughter Betsy W. Williams to be paid to them by an equal division, as they arrive to the age of twenty one years or marry, with interest to commence twelve months after my death. The balance of the money shall be divided into five equal parts; one to be given to my son Robert Knight, one part to my daughter Sally B. Jeffress and the other part to my son T. W. Knight in trust for the children of my daughter Betsy W. Williams to be paid them in equal division as they become twenty one years of age or marry, with interest from the time of said division into five parts. I release my son Thomas Knight the debt he owes me on accounts of the debt paid by me for him to the administrator of John Fowlkes, dec'd. If I am indebted to any of my children who take under this my will, I direct that the request or bequests to such child or children shall extinguish this or debts which he, she or they as the case may be, my claim as due from me, and if any legatee shall elect to claim a debt against my estate instead of a legacy that legacy shall be divided among my other children equally. I hereby appoint my son Tarlton W. Knight executor of this my last will and testament.

Given under my hand & seal this 19th day of March, 1831.

Woodson Knight

Witness: C. D. Smith; John H. Williams; Jordan W. Maxey

In Lunenburg County Court 9th of May 1831; the last will and testament of Woodson Knight, dec'd, was proved by the oaths of the witnesses thereto subscribed and is ordered to be recorded. As on this motion of Tarlton W. Knight the executor named in the said will who having made oath according to the law certificate is granted him for obtaining probate thereof in due form whereupon he entered into and acknowledge bond for that with such conditions as the law required.

2. JONATHAN[2] KNIGHT was born 1729 in Goochland Co., Virginia, and died before November 1809 in Granville Co., North Carolina. He married JUDITH WOODSON 24 February 1757 Goochland Co., Virginia, daughter of JOSEPH WOODSON and ELIZABETH PARSONS. She was born about 1741 in Henrico Co., Virginia, and died about 1820 in Granville Co., N. C.

Jonathan Knight purchased 300 acres of land in Granville Co., N. C., from his father 25 February 1762.[74] He must have moved shortly after this purchase, as he purchased an additional 255 acres of land "adjacent Grassy Creek and Spew Marrow Creek 1 June 1762. On 1 August 1765 Jonathan Knight sold 210 acres of land, and on 3 August 1765, he purchased a 300 acre tract from his father, which appears to be the same plot formerly occupied by his brother, Charles Knight. On 9 August 1771 Jonathan Knight sold 8 acres of this tract, and identified it as the land previously owned by Charles Knight.

Jonathan Knight wrote his will 24 October 1807 in Granville Co., N. C., and it was proved a the November court 1808.[75]

In the name of God Amen, I, Jonathan Knight Senior of the state of N. Carolina & county of Granville, being in a low state of health though of a sound mind and memory doth make and ordain this my last will and Testament in manner and for following to wit:

First: I lend unto my loving wife Judath Knight all the land the East side of the road bound as follows beginning at a white oak on the bank of the Tar River above the bridge running South with the road as it now stands to where the line cross the east to middle Creek thence down the sd creek to the mouth thence up the river to the first beginning, also three Negroes to wit., Jim, Nell & Peter and one mare called Bedford, also all my household & kitchen furniture together with my stock of hoggs, cows & plantation utencils during her natural life, and after the death of my wife, I give unto my daughter Sarah W. Roffe all the Estate lent my wife

[74] Knight, Mary. 19 Dec 2001. Located at
http://genforum.genealogy.com/knight/messages/5423.html.
[75] Granville Co., N. C., Will Book 7:80. Transcription by Mary Knight.
http://www.rootsweb.com/~tnsmith/oldpics/knightjonathanwill2.html.
28 February 2009.

except the negroe boy Peter to her & her heirs and assigns forever.

Item: I give unto my son John Knight all the land lying on the left side of the road where he now lives bounded as follows, to wit, beginning at a white oak on the bank of the Tar River above the bridge, running up the meanders of said river to Nailings corner thence with Nailings line to the main road, thence North with the road as it now stands to the first beginning to him his heirs & assigns forever.

Item: I give unto my grandson Jonathan Knight son of John Knight all the land lying on the East side of middle creek bound by Thos. Person's line & Tarr river & sd. Creek to him his heirs & assigns forever.

Item: I give unto my son Woodson Knight two hundred & fifty nine acres of land whereon my son now lives in Mecklingburg County Virginia and one negroe man Jacob to him his heirs & assigns forever.

Item: I give unto my son William Knight five shillings besides what I have already given him to his heirs and assigns forever.

Item: My will & desire is that after my death that all my estate not given away in this my last will & testament be sold at the descression of my executors hereafter named & the money arising therefrom after paying my just debts be equally divided between Elizabeth Amis, Rachel Dejarnet, Judath Amis, Polly Amis, Jonathan Knight & John Knight to them their heirs & assigns forever.

Item: My will & desire is that after the death of my wife the negroe boy Peter, lent my wife be sold at the descression of my Exrs & the money arising therefrom be equally divided between Elizabeth Amis, Rachel Dejarnet, Judath Amis, Polly Amis, Jonathan Knight & John Knight to them their heirs & assigns forever.

Item: I do hereby appoint Jonathan Knight and William Amis Exrs of this my last will & testament & do revoke all other wills heretofore made by me in witness whereof I have hereunto set my hand and affixed my seal the 24th day of October 1807.

Jona'th Knight (LS)

Wm. Walker
James Richards
Nelson Nailing

State of N. Carolina
Granville County   November Court   1809
The foregoing will & testament of Jonathan Knight Senr was duly proven in open court by the oaths of Wm. Walker & James Richards two of the subscribing witnesses to the same & ordered to be recorded. At the same time William Amis named as Executor of said Will refused to qualify wherefore Jonathan Knight also named as Executor came into court & qualified as such.

Children of JONATHAN KNIGHT and JUDITH WOODSON:

i. WILLIAM[3] KNIGHT, b. about 1758 Granville Co., N. C.; d. 14 November 1839 Bedford Co., Tenn.; m. ELIZABETH MAUPIN.

ii. JOHN[3] KNIGHT, b. about 1760 Granville Co., N. C.; d. 19 October 1843 Smith Co., Tenn.; m. MARTHA MONTAGUE 29 March 1788 Granville Co., N. C.; b. about 1758 Va.; d. 9 September 1838 Smith Co., Tenn.

John Knight was a resident of Jackson Co., Tenn., when he purchased from Ellis B. Beasley 188 acres of land in Smith Co., Tenn., on the north side of the Cumberland River for $600 on 17 November 1815. The land was on Defeated Creek and bounded by Miles West, John Reeves, and Jonathan Beasley.[76] In December 1838 John Knight made a deed to his children of the 188 acre tract and seven slaves. On 1 February 1839 the heirs of John Knight divided the land and the slaves. The heirs were Thomas Latane Knight, William Montague Knight, Henry M. Knight, Ellis E. Knight, Catherine Ramsey, Charlotte Smith,

---

[76] Smith Co., Tenn., Deed Book E:351. (Mary Knight)

wife of Daniel Smith, and Patsy (Martha) West wife of Robert West.[77]

iii. ELIZABETH[3] KNIGHT, b. about 1760 Granville Co., N. C.; d. 1823 Granville Co., N. C.; m. LEWIS AMIS 25 December 1781 Granville Co., N. C. son of WILLIAM AMIS and HANNAH DALY; b. about 1760 Essex Co., Va.; d. 1825 Granville Co., N. C.

iv. WOODSON[3] KNIGHT, b. about 1763 Granville Co., N. C.; d. 1809 Mecklenburg Co., Va.

v. RACHEL[3] KNIGHT, b. about 1765 Granville Co., N. C.; d. 1847 Nottoway Co., Va.; m. BOWLER DEJARNETT.[78]

Bowler DeJarnett was named for his uncle, Bowler Hall. He married (1) Keziah Wooten 11 January 1790 daughter of William Wooten and Lucy Owens. He bought land in Prince Edward Co., Va., in 1790 and sold a portion to Dabney Morris in 1801. Rachel Knight DeJarnett wrote her will 1 July 1847, proved 2 September 1847 Nottoway Co., Va.

vi. JUDITH[3] KNIGHT, b. about 1769 Granville Co., N. C.; d. 1817 Granville Co., N. C.; m. WILLIAM AMIS 21 January 1789 Granville Co., N. C., son of WILLIAM AMIS and HANNAH DALY; b. about 1765 Essex Co., Va.; d. 10 June 1857 Granville Co., N. C.

vii. SARAH WOODSON[3] KNIGHT, b. 1773 Granville Co., N. C.; m. (1) WILLIAM ROFFE, d. about 1816 Granville Co., N. C.; m. (2) WILLIAM AMIS 1817 Granville Co., N. C., widower of her sister Judith.

---

[77] Smith Co., Tenn., Deed Book P:119-121. (Mary Knight)

[78] Hanke, Douglas. Pierson/Hanke Family Ties. 16 February 2009. Located at http://wc.rootsweb.ancestry.com, (db. dhanke.) Hanke has this marriage associated with this Rachel's aunt Rachel, but the will of Jonathan Knight makes it fairly clear that it is his daughter who has married DeJarnett.

viii. JONATHAN[3] KNIGHT, b. about 1775 Granville Co.,
N. C.; d. after July 1821 Granville Co., N. C.;
m. RUTH HIGH.

ix. MARY[3] KNIGHT, b. 24 March 1778 Granville Co.,
N. C.; d. 21 October 1851 Maury Co., Tenn.;
m. JOHN AMIS 7 October 1787 Granville Co., N.
C., son of WILLIAM AMIS and HANNAH DALY; b.
29 October 1774 Granville Co., N. C.; d. 9
September 1852 Maury Co., N. C.

On the Woodson Family

Most of the recorded information about this
family derives from a memorandum written about
1785 by Charles[5] (*Tarleton[4], John[3], Robert[2], John[1]*)
Woodson.[79] The few available data from surviving
public records are consistent with the received
tradition.[80] My review of published data indicate that
Jonathan Knight's wife, Judith Woodson was the
daughter of Joseph[5] (*Joseph[4], Robert[3-2], John[1]*)
Woodson, and his wife Elizabeth Parsons, daughter of
Joseph Parsons and Sarah[4] (*Robert[3-2], John[1]*)
Woodson.

The frequent intermarriage and the repeated
use of the same names has made it difficult to be
certain of much about these persons, and I have not
done significant research in the extant records. It
seems clear, though, that the Amis men were proud of
their connection to the Woodson family, as they used
it in naming their own children.

[79] Woodson, Henry M. Historical Genealogy of the Woodson and Their
Connections. (Memphis: 1915). The copy I found at the Memphis Public
Library had been marred by the theft of some pages, however, a copy has
been located online at books.google.com.

[80] Jester, Annie L., Hiden, Martha W. Adventurers of Purse and
Person: Virginia, 1607-1625. (FFV, 1964), pp. 708-716.

Chapter 2: 1825 Lewis Amis of Granville Co., North Carolina

1. LEWIS[4] (*WILLIAM[3], JOSEPH[2]*) AMIS was born before 1756 in Essex County, Virginia and died before August 1825 in Granville Co., North Carolina. He married ELIZABETH KNIGHT, daughter of JONATHAN KNIGHT and JUDITH WOODSON, 25 December 1781 Granville Co., N. C. She died before 1820 in Granville Co., N. C.

Lewis Amis was listed in the 1810 Census with one son 10-16, one son 16-26, and himself over 45. He had two daughters under 10, and two 10-16. His wife appears to have died before the 1820 Census, as he then had one son 16-26 still living at home and two daughters 16-26, His last will and testament was written in Granville Co., N. C., on 16 July 1825 and was proven at the August 1825 Court.[1]

In the name of God Amen. I Lewis Amis of the County of Granville State of North Carolina being weak in body but of sound mind and perfect memory do make and publish this my last will and testament in manner and form following—

1st It is my wish and desire that my son William Amis should have all the property both real and personal which I have heretofore put him in possession of valued by myself to the sum of Twelve hundred dollars all of which I give to my said son William to him and his heirs forever.

2nd It is my wish and desire that my son Thomas Amis should have all the property both real and personal which I have heretofore put him in possession of valued by myself to the sum of Eighteen hundred dollars all of which I give to my said son Thomas to him and his heirs forever.

---

[1] Granville Co., N. C., Will Book 10:56-57. My transcription from microfilm copy at the Richard Thornton Library, Oxford, N. C.

3rd It is my wish and desire that my son Lewis Amis should have all the property both real and personal which I have heretofore put him in possession of valued by myself to the sum of Eighteen hundred dollars all of which I give to my said son Lewis to him and his heirs forever.

4th It is my wish and desire that my son Joseph Amis should have all the property both real and personal which I have heretofore put him in possession of and valued by myself to the sum of Two thousand dollars all of which I give to my said son Joseph to him and his heirs forever.

5th It is my wish and desire that my daughter Elizabeth Graves should have all the property which I have heretofore put her in possession of valued by myself to the sum of Fifteen hundred dollars to my said daughter Elizabeth to her and her heirs forever.

6th It is my wish and desire that my daughter Nancy Graves should have all the property which I have heretofore put her in possession of valued by myself to the sum of fifteen hundred dollars all of which I give to my said daughter Nancy to her and her heirs forever.

7th It is my wish and desire that my said son John Amis should have all the property which I have heretofore put him in possession of both real and personal, valued by myself to the sum of Two thousand dollars all of which I give to my said son John to him and his heirs forever.

8th It is my wish and desire that my daughter Hannah Sanford should have all the property which I have heretofore put her in possession of valued by myself to the sum of Twelve hundred dollars to my said daughter Hannah her and her heirs forever.

9th It is my wish and desire that my daughter Frankey Puryear should have all the property both real and personal which I have heretofore put her in possession of and valued by myself to the sum on Nineteen hundred dollars to her and her heirs forever.

(obscured microfilm copy of will)...two hundred dollars each out of the property not heretofore distributed then if any balance should remain in the hands of my Executor after paying all of my just debts, it is my desire that it should be equally divided between all my children and each child is to share and share alike.

It is also my wish and desire that my Executor should choose 2 or 3 reputable men of the neighborhood for the purpose of valuing the remaining Negroes not heretofore disposed of for the purpose of enabling my Executor to make each child equal portion up to the value of $2000 by giving property to each at valuation—and it is my wish that each of my grown Negroes which have not heretofore been disposed of should have the privilege of choosing which of my children they wish for their master, and it is my wish that each child should have them provided such child will give or allow the price the Negro or Negroes may be valued by the persons heretofore chosen by my Executor.

Lastly I do hereby constitute and appoint all my sons William Amis, Thomas Amis, Lewis Amis, Joseph Amis, and John Amis Exccutors to this my last will and testament.

Signed, sealed and acknowledged this 16th day of July Eighteen hundred and twenty five in the presence of   LEWIS AMIS (LS)
Alxr Smith
John L. Patillo

State of No. Carolina) August Court A. D. 1825
Granville County   )
The execution of the foregoing last will and testament of Lewis Amis, deceased, was duly proven in oath and in open court by Alexander Smith and John L. Patillo the subscribing witnesses thereto and was ordered to be recorded. At the same time came forward William Amis, Joseph Amis, and John Amis named as three of the executors in said will and duly qualified as such. (signed by clerk of court)

On 27 February 1828 in Giles Co., Tenn., William C. Graves and Sterling Graves gave Thomas Neal of Giles Co., a power of attorney to represent them on behalf of their wives, Elizabeth Graves and Nancy Graves, children of Lewis Amis, deceased, and to obtain their share of his estate from the executors William Amis, Joseph Amis, and John Amis.[2] Some inferences can be drawn from the fact that John[3] Amis had moved with his family to Tennessee by 1820 and William[3] Amis appears to have had only two sons: Jonathan and John Woodson Amis, who was the grandfather of A. B. Amis. Jonathan does not appear in the record, so it seems probable that all of the other men named Amis up through the 1850's are sons and grandsons of Lewis Amis and Elizabeth Knight. Thomas and William Amis are certainly brothers, as attested by correspondence saved by William Amis that included a letter written 11 October 1826 that mentions, among other things, settlement of the estate, presumably of their father, Lewis Amis.[3]

The court documents establish that both Thomas and Lewis Amis were not in Granville County in 1825. From the letter we can confirm that Thomas was in Oglethorpe County, and Lewis Amis was in Person Co., N. C., based upon his marriage certificate.[4]

Children of LEWIS AMIS and ELIZABETH KNIGHT are:

---

[2] Giles Co., Tenn., Deed Book G:418, 21 April 1828. Accessed online 20 November 2011 at http://files.usgwarchives.net/tn/giles/deeds/deed-1.txt.

[3] Letter from Thomas Amis to William Amis with the salutation "Dear Brother" and dated in a postscript 11 October 1826. Amis-Clark-Puryear Papers (#474), Special Collections Department, J. Y. Joyner Library, East Carolina University, Greenville, North Carolina, USA. Accessed at http://digital.lib.ecu.edu/special/ead/findingaids/0474/ 27 November 2011.

[4] He is not listed in the 1820 Census for Person Co., N. C., but the records are incomplete and many counties have been lost. I have not reviewed the county tax records.

2. i. WILLIAM[5] AMIS; b. 11 December 1782 Granville
Co., Ga.; d. 28 December 1848 Granville Co.,
N. C.; m. ELIZABETH PURYEAR 3 December 1804
Granville Co., N. C.; b. 11 February 1788
Granville Co., N. C.; d. 26 April 1859 Granville
Co., N. C.

ii. THOMAS[5] AMIS, b. 1785 Granville Co. N. C.; d.
1858 Oglethorpe Co., Ga.; m. SARAH WYNNE
about 1806 Wilkes Co., Ga.[5]

Thomas Amis was the son of Thomas Amis Sr.
and was born in the western part of the county on
Big Creek....He was one of twelve children, all of
whom lived to the age of maturity and were
married. His father came from North Carolina to
Georgia about the time of the great influx of
population....after the war of the Revolution. His
father and grand-father who lived in N.C. were
machinists. They all had a genius for machinery
and were successful millmen,.... were all men of
great energy, ... producers, all alike being
successful farmers.[6]

In 1850, Thomas and Sarah, both 65, b. N. C.,
have Lewis, 24 and Mary, 20, and their two sons,
John, 3, and Lewis, 2, living with them in
Oglethorpe Co., Ga.[7] In 1860, Sarah is living with
daughter, Mary Brooks, 50, and her children and
grandchildren.[8]

Thomas Amis' will was written 29 March 1851
and proved 11 October 1858.[9] He noted that he
had already advanced $1,000 by his estimation, to
each of his children: Elizabeth Trammell, Mary
Brooks, Nancy Aycock, William Amis, Amanda

---

[5] Craig, W. B. Old Georgia: Amis, Belcher, Hogan & Affiliates. 12
June 2011. Located at http://wc.rootsweb.ancestry.com, (db. oldgeorgia.)
His documentation seems much more careful than some of the other
posters on this family.

[6] From Thomas Amis, Jr.'s obituary January 1900, Lexington,
Oglethorpe Co., Ga. Cited by W. B. Craig.

[7] 1850 Census Oglethorpe Co., Ga., Div. 66, p. 8B, #105.

[8] 1860 Census Oglethorpe Co., Ga., Mil. Dist. 227, p. 606, #26.

[9] Oglethorpe Co., Ga., Will Book D:384. Abstracted by McRee, Fred W.
Oglethorpe County, Georgia, Abstracts of Wills, 1794-1903. (Lexington,
GA: Historic Oglethorpe, 2002,) p. 188.

Martin, Joseph Amis, John L. Amis, Lucy Smith, Thomas Amis, Sarah Smith, Frances Walters, and Lewis Amis. The arrangement of names suggests they are in birth order, as confirmed by available dates. He specified that his wife, Sarah, was to receive $1,000 from his estate plus sharing equally with the other children, who were to receive an additional $1,000. Richard Aycock had executed a bond 16 September 1846 for $1002.41, which was to be rounded to $1,000 for the accounting. The share bequeathed to Mary Brooks, wife of Thomas P. Brooks, was placed in the hands of Thomas Amis, trustee, with the specification that Thomas Brooks was to have no share of the money. The sons were all named as executors, and the will was witnessed by John F. Biggers, William McLane, and William L. Meese.

The marriages for Elizabeth, Mary, Nancy, Amanda, Lucy, and Sarah Amis were found online.[10]

Children of THOMAS AMIS and SARAH WYNNE are:

1. ELIZABETH[6] AMIS, b. 16 May 1808 Oglethorpe Co., Ga.; d. 23 January 1892 Jefferson Co., Ala.;[11] m. ROBERT TRAMMELL 17 May 1826 Oglethorpe Co., Ga.[12]

2. MARY[6] AMIS, b. 5 January 1810 Oglethorpe Co., Ga.; d. 4 October 1888 Oglethorpe Co., Ga.;[13] m. THOMAS PRICE BROOKS 24 January 1826 Oglethorpe Co., Ga.; b. 12

---

[10] Oglethorpe County Marriages, 1825 to 1865. Accessed 23 March 2014 at http://genealogytrails.com/geo/oglethorpe/marriages-1.htm. The same information is in McRee, Fred W. Oglethorpe County, Georgia, Marriage Records, 1794-1852. (Lexington, Ga.: Historic Oglethorpe, 2005.)

[11] Harmony Baptist Church Cemetery, Empire, Ala. The stone is inscribed "Mother of Robert Trammell." http://www.findagrave.com., #65962103. They were in Clarke Co., Ga., in 1850, and Paulding Co., Ga., in 1860. He served as Captain, Troop D, 1st Ga. Cavalry, and, along with many of his men, bought land in then Jefferson Co., Ala., from the L & N Railroad Co.

[12] He reportedly died in 1830 and she remained a widow the rest of her life, raising their four children.

[13] W. W. Brooks Family Cemetery, Oglethorpe Co., Ga. http://www.findagrave.com., #31885715.

March 1803 Buckingham Co., Va.; d. 13
November 1876 Panola Co., Texas.[14]

3. ANN W.[6] AMIS, b. 3 March 1811 Oglethorpe
Co., Ga.; d. 1888 Dade Co., Ga.; m.
RICHARD M. AYCOCK 24 January 1828
Oglethorpe Co., Ga.

4. WILLIAM[6] AMIS, b. 24 June 1812 Oglethorpe
Co., Ga.; d. 24 August 1888 Carroll Co.,
Ga.;[15] m. JANE ELIZA PINSON 10 December
1833 Clarke Co., Ga.; b. 22 January 1817
Clarke Co., Ga.; d. 10 February 1884 Carroll
Co., Ga.[16]

5. AMANDA FITZLAND[6] AMIS, b. 8 May 1814
Oglethorpe Co., Ga.; d. 8 January 1864
Coweta Co., Ga.;[17] m. ELIJAH MARTIN 1
April 1832 Oglethorpe Co., Ga.; b. 3 June
1807 Oglethorpe Co., Ga.; d. 30 September
1878 Coweta Co., Ga.;[18] he m. (2)
ELIZABETH HOGAN about 1866 Troup Co.,
Ga.

6. JOSEPH[6] AMIS, b. 1816 Oglethorpe Co., Ga.;
d. 15 January 1891 Griffin, Ga.; m.
ELIZABETH PRICE 13 October 1836
Oglethorpe Co., Ga.; b. 1819 Clarke Co.,

---

[14] Thomas P. Brooks was apparently estranged from his wife when
John Amis wrote his will in 1851. By 1860 he lived in Texas with their
sons William T., and John R. Brooks. Mary is buried in Temple Methodist
Church Cemetery, Oglethorpe Co., Ga., on Brooks land deeded to the
church in 1890 by her eldest son W. W. Brooks. He is buried in Sugar Hill
Cemetery, Panola Co., Texas. Thomas Brooks was named as the son of
Wilson Brooks in the latter's will dated 12 August 1846 and proved 9
November 1846. [Oglethorpe Co., Ga., Will Book D:192. McRee, p. 150.]

[15] He is buried in Oak Hill Cemetery, Newnan, Coweta Co., Ga.
http://www.findagrave.com., #117784747. "He prospered as a planter,
and in 1855 bought a mill site on Snake Creek at Banning, Carroll County.
With the War's onset, he moved to Banning and began making yarn for the
C.S.A. cause. After the war, William built 'a fine merchant mill with new
machinery' there, processed cotton and wool into cloth, & diversified into
grain, lumber, and leather processing. In 1878, at age 66, Mr. Amis sold
off his factory." Cited by W. B. Craig, although it appears to be from a
nineteenth century county history.

[16] Oak Hill Cemetery, Newnan, Ga. http://www.findagrave.com.,
#117784787.

[17] Martin Cemetery at Brookhaven, Sharpsburg, Ga.
http://www.findagrave.com., #59525746.

[18] Martin Family Cemetery, Coweta Co., Ga.
http://www.findagrave.com., #59526152.

Ga.; d. about 1897 Newnan, Coweta Co., Ga.[19]

7. JOHN L.[6] AMIS, b. 1818 Oglethorpe Co., Ga.; d. about 1868 Copiah Co., Miss.; m. LUCY SMITH 24 November 1845 Oglethorpe Co., Ga.; b. February 1822 Clarke Co., Ga.; d. about 1905 Forest Hill, Copiah Co., Miss.

8. LUCY[6] AMIS, b. 1820 Oglethorpe Co., Ga.; d. before 1899 Coweta Co., Ga.; m. WILLIAM E. SMITH 14 September 1836 Oglethorpe Co., Ga.; b. 7 August 1811 Oglethorpe Co., Ga.; d. 7 April 1854 Coweta Co., Ga.[20]

9. THOMAS[6] AMIS, JR., b. 22 September 1822 Oglethorpe Co., Ga.; d. 31 December 1899 Oglethorpe Co., Ga.;[21] m. EVALINE A. MOORE 20 November 1850; b. 27 January 1820 Sampson Co., N. C.; d. 26 May 1895 Oglethorpe Co., Ga.[22]

10. SARAH[6] AMIS, b. 22 September 1822 Oglethorpe Co., Ga.; d. about 1865 Coweta Co., Ga.; m. HARDAWAY SMITH 2 November 1843 Oglethorpe Co., Ga.; b. 29 September 1816 Oglethorpe Co., Ga.; d. about 1895 Coweta Co., Ga.[23]

11. FRANCES[6] AMIS, b. 18 September 1824 Oglethorpe Co., Ga.; d. 31 March 1913 Haynesville, Claiborne Parish, La.; m. BURWELL AYCOCK WATTERS about 1845; b.

---

[19] Both are buried in Whitesburg, Carroll Co., Ga.

[20] He is buried in the Smith Family Cemetery; she does not have a marker stone.

[21] From his obituary in the Lexington, Ga., paper. He was engaged in farming and milling on Big Creek until the fall of 1867, when he moved to the Gresham place on Long Creek, where he successfully engaged more extensively in farming and milling. People came from far and near to the "Amis mill"....The mills were running night and day for months at a time. Sometimes he was misunderstood. His pushing energetic way gave him the appearance of a cold man of the world, yet he was tender hearted..... It was a matter of pride with him in his old age that no one ever went from his home hungry.... His love for his father and mother was beautiful. In his old age he often spoke of them with childlike affection..... Cited by W. B. Craig.

[22] Buried in the family plot on Long Creek.

[23] Both plots are unmarked, but are presumed to be in the Smith Family Cemetery, Coweta Co., Ga.

1 March 1822 Oglethorpe Co., Ga.; d. 24 January 1890 Haynesville, Claiborne Parish, La.[24]

12. LEWIS[6] AMIS, b. 16 August 1826 Oglethorpe Co., Ga.; d. 3 February 1883 Ozark, Franklin Co., Ark.; m. MARY JANE DEAN 5 February 1846 Clarke Co., Ga.; b. 18 September 1829 Clarke Co., Ga.; d. May 1888 Franklin Co., Ark.[25]

iii. LEWIS[5] AMIS, b. 1788 Granville Co., N. C.; d. 22 January 1858 Fayette Co., Tenn.; m. CHARLOTTE PULLIAM 4 September 1811 Person Co., N. C.; b. 27 August 1787 Person Co., N. C.; d. 10 October 1856 Fayette Co., Tenn.

Lewis Amis. 62, and Charlotte, 63, are listed in 1850 with her sister, Jane Pulliam, 56, Elizabeth Amis 33, and Mary A. Amis, 19.[26] John and Lewis Amis, Jr., 29, and Catherine 32, are nearby,[27] and Joseph Amis, 35, and Annis, 36, are in the 1st Civil District.[28] William Amis, 30, and Ellen, 30, are in the 6th Civil District.[29]

Children of LEWIS AMIS and CHARLOTTE PULLIAM:

1. JOSEPH[6] AMIS, b. 1813 Granville Co., N. C.; d. 18 February 1876; m. ANNIS SATTERFIELD 9 December 1833 Person Co., N. C., dau. of WILLIAM SATTERFIELD and NAOMI LEE; b. 1814 Caswell Co., N. C.; d. 7 November 1879.[30]

---

[24] Both are buried in Friendship Cemetery.

[25] Both are buried in Mountain View Cemetery, Franklin Co., Ark.

[26] 1850 Census Fayette Co., Tenn., 8th Civil District, p. 291B, #821/821.

[27] 1850 Census Fayette Co., Tenn., 8th Civil District, p. 298B, #911/911. John Amis, 24, is working at the next door neighbors, #910/910.

[28] 1850 Census Fayette Co., Tenn., 1st Civil District, p. 234A, #41/41.

[29] 1850 Census Fayette Co., Tenn., 6th Civil District, p. 278B, #645/645. He is working as an overseer, as he was in the 1860 Census.

[30] Information obtained from the Bible of their son, Edwin H. Amis. http://www.tngenweb.org/records/henderson/misc/gm/gm4-17.html. 26 November 2011. The marriage date if from Fox, John. Fox and Graham Family. 16 December 2010. Located at http://wc.rootsweb.ancestry.com, (db. johnfox38.) I have communicated with Mr. Fox about the Mecklenburg Co., Va., Fox family related to my Wright family. Edwin H. Amis (1845-

2. WILLIAM L.[6] AMIS, b. 16 October 1832; d. 21 January 1918 Henderson Co., Tenn.[31]
3. JOHN[6] AMIS.
Additional work on marriages will need to be done, but there is a tombstone in Hood Cemetery, Fayette Co., Tenn., for Katie E. Amis, b. 8 March 1870; d. 12 August 1871, daughter of J. S. and E. J. Amis.[32]
4. JAMES[6] AMIS,
6. ELIZABETH[6] AMIS, m. _____ LOVELADY.
7. SAMUEL SATTERFIELD[6] AMIS, b. 10 December 1840; d. 2 February 1897; m. A. A. AMIS 5 January 1875.[33]
8. MARY E.[6] AMIS., b. 31 January 1852, d. 1874

iv. JOSEPH[5] AMIS, b. 1790 Granville Co., N. C.; d. before August 1840 Granville Co., N. C.; m. ELIZABETH DOWNEY 3 March 1818 Granville Co., N. C., dau. of JAMES DOWNEY; d. 1848 Granville Co., N. C.[34]

Joseph Amis died testate, but did not list his minor children. As it happens, his executor and executrix both died before completion of his probate, with the result that there is a suit on file in the Archives where William Amis and Ann S.

1874) and Adrin A. Amis, (1849-1922) are both listed in Nebo Cemetery, Henderson Co., Tenn., along with others who are likely related to this branch of the family. (Donahue, David. Located 16 December 2011 at http://files.usgwarchives.net/tn/henderson/cemeteries/Nebo.txt.

[31] His death record recorded his parents as Joseph Amis and Annis Satterfield. Accessed 26 November 2011 at
https://familysearch.org/pal:/MM9.1.1/NSM9-84Y. (He was recorded as "Billie." He was 84 years old and single. He is buried in Nebo Cemetery, Henderson Co., Tenn., without dates on the marker.
http://files.usgwarchives.net/tn/henderson/cemeteries/nebo.txt.
Accessed 16 December 2011.

[32] Hensley, Cindy. Hood Cemetery, Warren, Fayette Co., Tennessee. http://files.usgwarchives.net/tn/fayette/cemeteries/Hood.txt. Accessed 16 December 2011.

[33] This may well be Adrienne A. Amis, daughter of Joseph Amis and Annis Satterfield, b. 10 June 1849 Fayette Co., Tenn. (Bible of Edwin H. Amis.)

[34] Joseph Amis served as a militia colonel in the War of 1812, and was a Presbyterian, according to a biography of his son, Lewis Amis, of Princeton, Arkansas. [Biographical and Historical Memoirs of Southern Arkansas, 1890: Chapter 27:209, Dallas County.] This Lewis Amis' first wife was Martha Amis, daughter of William[4] Amis.

Amis, guardians for Susanna S. E., Amis, Rosaltha A. Amis, and William J. Amis, minor children of Joseph Amis and Elizabeth Amis petitioned for the sale of slaves that they held as tenants in common with their siblings. The document states that the will appointed Elizabeth Amis, widow of Joseph Amis as executrix, and his son Lewis Amis, and son-in-law Lewis Amis, as executors. His son had not originally qualified, but both Lewis Amis the son-in-law, and Elizabeth Amis were dead by 1846 (when the suit was filed). Named as defendants were Lewis Amis (son) as executor, Joseph N. Barnett and wife Mary, Lewis B. Norwood and his wife Jane, James A. Amis, and Judy F. Amis the latter two also minor children of Joseph Amis, deceased.[35]

Children of JOSEPH AMIS and ELIZABETH DOWNEY:

1. ELIZABETH[6] AMIS, b. 1819 Granville Co., N. C.; d. 1843 Granville Co., N. C.; m. LEWIS AMIS 1836 Granville Co., N. C., son of WILLIAM AMIS and ELIZABETH PURYEAR; b. 1809 Granville Co., N. C.; d. 1843 Granville Co., N. C.

2. JANE D.[6] AMIS, m. LEWIS B. NORWOOD 1846 Granville Co., N. C.

3. LEWIS[6] AMIS, b. 22 December 1822 Granville Co., N. C.; d. 19 July 1894 Dallas Co., Arkansas; m. (1) MARTHA AMIS October 1848 Granville Co., N. C., dau. of WILLIAM AMIS and ELIZABETH PURYEAR; b. 1825 Granville Co., N. C.; d. May 1850 Granville Co., N. C.;[36] m. (2) MARTHA DANIEL 1 June 1852 Granville Co., N. C.; b. 16 August

---

[35] Estate File of Joseph Amis. Microfilm copy reviewed at Thornton Library, Oxford, N. C., 27 February 2012 Information on children obtained from biographical sketches of their sons, Lewis and James A. contained in Biographical and Historical Memoirs of Southern Arkansas, 1890, Chap. 27:709, Dallas County. Copy located at http://books.google.com, accessed 18 November 2011. Joseph Amis' will was recorded in Will Book 14:567 and listed "Betsy" Lewis, James, and Joseph. Lewis was identified as the third child in his biographical sketch..

[36] Her death from "dropsy" at age 25 is recorded in the 1850 Mortality Schedule Granville Co., N. C. I suspect this was pre-eclampsia.

1835 Granville Co., N. C.; d. 10 August 1889 Dallas Co., Ark.[37]

4. MARY[6] AMIS, m. JOSEPH N. BARNETT.

5. JAMES A.[6] AMIS, b. 8 May 1829 Granville Co., N. C.; d. 24 March 1904 Dallas Co., Ark.;[38] m. ELIZABETH (TAYLOR) PHELPS 2 January 1868 Union Co., Ark.; b. 11 September 1843 Wetumpka, Coosa Co., Ala.; d. 17 July 1930 Fordyce, Dallas Co., Ark.; m. (1) FRANKLIN PHELPS 5 September 1859 Union Co., Ark.[39]

6. JUDITH F.[6] AMIS, b. 1833 Granville Co., N. C.

7. ANN S.[6] AMIS, b. 1834 Granville Co., N. C.[40]

8. SUSANNAH[6] AMIS, b. 1838 Granville Co., N. C.[41]

9. ROSALTHA[6] AMIS, b. 1839 Granville Co., N. C.[42]

---

[37] Louis Amis, 27, Judith, 17, Joseph 3, and Martha "1 month" are living in the County Line District of Granville Co., N. C., in 1850. This Judith is almost surely his sister. Although Martha is said to be 1 month old, her mother had died in May, so the date is probably off slightly. At any rate, this establishes the children he had by Martha Amis.

Louis Amis patented land in Dallas County, Arkansas, in section 29, twp. 108, range 12W in October 1860.Fisher, Joy. BLM records for Dallas Co., Arkansas. Located at

http://files.usgwarchives.net/ark/dallas/land/dallas.txt. 16 December 2011.

[38] Buried Oakland Cemetery, Fordyce, Ark. (W. B. Craig.) He also lists Mary W. Amis, Ann L. Amis, and Judith Frances Amis (m. John Henry Webb 5 June 1855 Granville Co., N. C.) as daughters, presumably based upon their mother's estate records. He had no other information about these persons. Gwynn's abstract of Joseph's estate included another Joseph.

[39] Buried in Oakland Cemetery, Fordyce, Arkansas. Data from Medley, Linda. Warner Brown Family—Virginia to Arkansas. 2 June 2011. Located at http://wc.rootsweb.ancestry.com, (db. laaymedley.)

[40] I believe she is the Ann E. Amis living with John T. and Mary A. A. Blackwell in the Nutbush District in 1850. [1850 Census Granville Co., N. C., Nutbush District, p. 210, #50/50.

[41] Living with her uncle, John Amis, along with Rosaltha and William (J.). 1850 Census Granville Co., N. C., Abraham Plains District, p. 202B, #41/41. She may be the Susan Amis who married Mason Gates Granville Co., N. C., 23 March 1868, but there is also a Susan Amis who married Daniel Cooper Granville Co., N. C., 6 August 1870.

[42] Rosa A. Amis married Lewis E. Amis Granville Co., N. C., 29 October 1859. Since they were living in the household together, this seems possible. On the other hand, L. E. Amis m. Bettie R. Scott Granville Co., N. C., 12 February 1867. While it is possible Rosaltha Amis died, the possibility of a divorce is raised, since Rosa Amis married Addison Cannady Granville Co., N. C., 26 December 1873 and Rosetta Amis

10. WILLIAM J.[6] AMIS, b. 1840 Granville Co., N. C.

v. ELIZABETH[5] AMIS, b. 11 October 1794 Granville Co., N. C.; d. 31 August 1864 Howard Co., Ark.;[43] m. WILLIAM C. GRAVES 10 September 1811 Granville Co., N. C.; b. 25 December 1791; d. 8 November 1874 Howard Co., Ark.

vi. JOHN[5] AMIS, b. 1800 Granville Co., N. C.; d. about 1866 Granville Co., N. C.; m. MARY HUNT 21 July 1824 Granville Co., N. C.[44] John Amis was apparently a millwright. He built a mill that still stands on Grassy Creek in Granville Co., N. C.[45] His house was also

---

married John Satterwhite Granville Co., N. C., 23 November 1870. These relationships have not been pursued to establish a firm connection.

[43] Tombstone for both Elizabeth and William C. Graves, Sr., are in Graves Cemetery, Howard Co., Ark. Accessed 27 November 2011 at http://www.genealogyshoppe.com/arhoward/gravecem.htm.

[44] John Amis, 50, and Mary Amis, 42, are living with their family in Abraham Plains in 1850 along with Lucy Hunt 66, presumably her mother. 1850 Census Granville Co., N. C., Abraham's Plains, p. 202B, #41/41.

[45] An architectural history of the county shows a photograph of the mill with the following legend. "Rising three-and-a-half stories, the Amis-Dalton Mill is the county's most imposing non-residential structure. Thought to have been built, during the second quarter of the nineteenth century, by John Amis (b. 1800), the grist mill is one of the oldest and largest in the eastern Piedmont. A prominent northern Granville County resident, Amis owned approximately 400 acres of property in addition to his extensive milling operation. He donated, in 1855, the land upon which the eponymous Amis Chapel Baptist Church was raised. In 1900 Amis' nephew, James S. Amis (1826-1903), sold the mill to Arthur S. Carrington and his son, Luther, for $1650. Luther and Mary Carrington sold it thirteen years later, for $2800, to John T. and Mary Dalton, in whose family it remains.

The mortised, tenoned, and pegged structure was originally raised on stone piers and sheathed in weatherboards. Though the stones have been supplemented with adjacent concrete piers, and many of the weatherboards have peeled away, the mill and its site probably look much as they did when built...

Numerous millstones are scattered throughout the structure's milling floors, as well as the steep slope to its rear. A variety of chutes, bins, gears, and grinders, and other milling equipment are still in place. Also in place is the mill race, which runs to the east, terminating in a rock and concrete dam that once regulated the flow of the water driven mill's power source, Grassy Creek."

substantially made, and it too has been photographed.[46]

John Amis and his family are living in the Abraham's Plains District in 1850. He has his brother Joseph's three youngest children living with him.

Children of JOHN AMIS and MARY HUNT are:

1. JAMES S.[6] AMIS, b. 1825 Granville Co., N. C.; d. 5 November 1903 Granville Co., N. C.; m. MARY NASH SCOTT about 1849 Granville Co., N. C.; b. 1827; d. February 1908 Granville Co., N. C.[47]

Children of JAMES AMIS and MARY SCOTT:

a. MARY[7] AMIS, b. 19 January 1852 Granville Co., N. C.; d. 11 April 1938

---

[46] "If only in whispers, the remaining finish of this substantial timber frame house still proclaims the presence of a once fine dwelling. John Amis, (b. 1800), who built the house, probably before the close of the first third of the nineteenth century, was also the builder and owner of the Amis-Dalton Mill to the north. The exceptional size of his mill and the finish of his house, along with his substantial land holdings, indicate that he was one of the wealthier members of the community he served. After Amis, the house's next owner is said to have been Samuel Cash, (1856-1936), whose family it left, only to be reacquired in 1971 by a grandson, also named Samuel Cash.

The unusual number of bays that cross the house's front façade, as well as their placement—four in number, they are asymmetrically aligned—suggest it may originally have a hall parlor, or even a side hall plan. Now divided by a center hallway, the stairs of which climb up to the second floor and down to a brick walled cellar, the house retains some of its Federal style interior finish, including heavily articulated, flush sheathed wainscoting and a reeded mantle. Federal style surrounds also inframe the front block's seven panel entry door and rectangular transom and its 9/9 windows, many of which retain remnants of early or original louvered shutters.

A collapsing one story ell at the house's rear, probably original, is surprisingly well finished. Lit by 9/9 windows set in three part surrounds, it retains part of the paneled underside of a boxed stair and broken stretches of plaster cling to its exposed lath walls."

[47] James Amis and Mary Amis, along with daughter Mary, age 8, and John B. Lancaster, age 10, are living in County Line District in 1860, [1860 Census Granville Co., N. C., County Line District, p. 40.] By 1870, James S. Amis and Mary N. Amis are living with Ernest B., age 9, J. H. Minor, a 60 year old woman who was teaching; J. E. Lancaster, a 22 year old woman with no occupation, and Mary Amis, 30, teaching school. [1870 Census Granville Co., N. C., Oxford Twp., p. 40, #83/87.]

Waynesboro, Virginia; m. JAMES ALBERT FISHBURN 29 August 1882 Granville Co., N. C.[48]

b. ERNEST R.[7] AMIS, b. 1867 Granville Co., N. C.; m. GERTRUDE R. VAUGHN 8 November 1894 Winston Twp., Forsyth Co., N. C.

2. LEWIS E.[6] AMIS, b. 1827 Granville Co., N. C.; m. (1) ROSA E. AMIS 29 October 1859 Granville Co., N. C.; b. 1839 N. C.; d. before 1867;[49] m. (2) BETTIE R. SCOTT 12 February 1867 Granville Co., N. C.[50]

vii. NANCY[5] AMIS, b. say 1797 Granville Co., N. C.; m. STERLING GRAVES 26 December 1817 Granville Co., N. C. ; b. 23 April 1793 Granville Co., N. C.; d. 1836 in Tenn.

viii. HANNAH[5] AMIS, b. 1802 Granville Co., N. C.; d. before 1880 Holloway Twp., Person Co., N. C.; m. JAMES LANKFORD[51] 22 April 1822 Granville Co., N. C.

ix. FRANCES[5] AMIS, b. 1804 Granville Co., N. C., d. before 1880 Granville Co., N. C.; m. PEYTON PURYEAR 5 November 1822 Granville Co., N. C.

2. WILLIAM[5] (*LEWIS[4], WILLIAM[3], JOSEPH[2]*) AMIS was born 11 December 1782 in Granville Co., N. C., and died 28 December 1842 in Granville Co., N. C. He married

[48] Information from files collected by Francis B. Hays from newspaper clippings and now stored at the Robert Thornton Library, Oxford, N. C. Accessed 27 February 2012.

[49] This is probably Rosaltha Amis, minor child of Joseph[5] (Lewis[4], William[3], Joseph[2]) Amis and Elizabeth Downey.

[50] Lewis Amis is living with Judith Amis, age 17, Joseph 3, and Martha, b. October 1850. He is in County Line District near his brother, James. [1850 Census Granville Co., N. C., p. 178, #7/7.] He is living with his parents in 1860, along with William, 18, and Rose 21. [1860 Census Granville Co., N. C., Abram's Plains District, p. 32, #236/232.] In 1870 he is head of household and has Mary A. or Mary H., 62, probably his mother, Bettie B. S., 35, and Bettie S., 5, in his household. [1870 Census Granville Co., N. C., Sassafras Fork, p. 24, #149/234. (also called p. 331B.|]

[51] Name has also been read as Sandford, but cannot find anyone of that surname in the appropriate census lists.

ELIZABETH PURYEAR 3 December 1804 in Granville Co., N. C. She was born 11 February 1788 in Granville Co., N. C., and died 26 April 1859 in Granville Co., N. C.

William Amis was an attorney in Granville Co., N. C., and he left extensive records which have been placed in the archives at East Carolina University, where I reviewed them in February 2012.[52]

"Correspondence of Amis family members consists largely of notes and letters requesting loans and making arrangements to sell brandy and corn. Items of interest include a letter (Oct. 1, 1826) which briefly mentions a decline in cotton and corn prices and deaths resulting from an epidemic of colds, and a letter (Dec. 9, 1835) requesting settlement of the Archibald Clark estate.

Among legal and estate papers are receipts for the payment of public, county, and poor taxes (1800-48) and various promissory notes. Of interest are receipts (Oct. 11, 1822; Dec. 15, 1829) for payments on tracts of land, bills (Sept., 1830) for William Amis's law services, and a receipt (Nov. 29, 1833) for the cost of an equity suit between William Amis and John Puryear.

Financial papers reflect the social and economic life of the Amis family. Business-related financial materials includes receipts for a donation for building the Grassy Creek Baptist Meeting House (Dec. 23, 1832), charges for lodging a traveler and his horse (Oct. 13, 1836), expenses at the Washington Hotel (1838), and the expenses of maintaining a Negro woman and her two children (July 24, 1846). An item of particular interest is a document (undated) recording the age and valuation of slaves received by Elizabeth Amis when she

[52] Amis-Clark-Puryear Papers (#474), Special Collections Department, J. Y. Joyner Library, East Carolina University, Greenville, North Carolina, USA. Accessed 27 November 2011 at http://digital.lib.ecu.edu/special/ead/findingaids/0474/.

married. In general, business receipts record purchases and sales of such items as horses, lumber, tobacco, iron, and corn.

Among the domestic financial papers are receipts (July 14, 1814; July 28, 1832) for medical services, including prices and prescriptions for the Amis family and its slaves. Tuition receipts (Dec. 10, 1824; Feb. 2, 1831; Jan. 28, 1832; Mar. 6, 1833; May 12, 1834) and receipts for subscriptions to the Raleigh Register and North Carolina Gazette (Mar. 8, 1829), the Oxford Examiner (Aug. 21, 1830), and the Oxford Mercury (Nov. 8, 1843) are found in the domestic financial material. Overall, this group of papers contains accounts and receipts documenting purchases of items such as foodstuffs, clothing, and household goods."

The letter mentioned was sent to Lewis Amis from his brother, Thomas Amis of Oglethorpe Co., Ga.,[53] In addition to discussing the drought, Thomas asks how settlement of the estate is going. Although he does not say "our father's estate" or any other such identification, the letter is dated 1 October 1826, and almost surely the reference is to the death of Lewis Amis.

William Amis, Esq., paid his own taxes as early as 1805, where he is identified as "the younger" to distinguish him from his grandfather, and he also entered into a bond with Lewis Amis, Sr., on 19 March 1810 for £41, 19.3 to John Downey. All of this indicates that William was not enumerated in the 1810 Census with his father, Lewis, and thus that the older son at home was likely Thomas, who can now be proved to be in Oglethorpe Co., Ga., by 1826, and probably somewhat before that.

The papers also make it clear that William Amis, Esq., was the administrator for the estate of John Puryear. He filed suit with his wife "and others"

---

[53] The letter is addressed "Dear Brother".

against John Puryear for which he paid court costs of $18.40 on 29 November 1833. However, on 1 March 1834, D. T. Wilkerson, George W. Tucker, John Y. Wilkerson, and John Puryear entered into a bond for William Amis in the amount of $399.37 against the estate of John Puryear, deceased. All of this is additional evidence for the marriage of William Amis and Elizabeth Puryear.

Rufus Amis, youngest son of William Amis and Elizabeth Puryear was also an attorney and left an extensive correspondence as well as Bible records which are on file at the University of North Carolina, Chapel Hill. Copies of the Bible records were reviewed at the Richard Thornton Library in Oxford, N. C., in February 2012. They establish the dates of birth and death for William Amis and Elizabeth Puryear.

William Amis left a very extensive estate settlement file, but no will. A microfilm copy was reviewed and showed several items of interest. First, Elizabeth Amis sued John Amis & others in a petition for her dower rights. Since Thomas Amis, William Amis, and Alexander Amis were non-residents, notice was published in the Raleigh Times of an intent to grant the petition at the August Court for Granville Co., N. C.[54]

Elizabeth Amis received her dower land in a survey by a commission on 3 October 1849.

State of N Carolina)
Granville County)   We the undersigned subscribers being lawfully summoned and empowered according to law as Jurors to allot & lay off the dower of Elizabeth Amis, widow of William Amis, decd., we have this day met on the premises and have viewed the said lands and have laid off the same and have given the boundary as follows to wit: beginning at J...Amises corner pine on Aaron's Creek thence East 291 poles to pointers,

---

[54] Notice was dated 16 June 1849.

thence North 152 poles to a pine in Bohannon's line, thence West 16 poles to pointers, thence South 25 poles to a corner a litewood stake then West on Zaney's line 162 to his corner pointers, thence North 246 poles to a Redd Oak in the Virginia line then west by the Virginia line to Aaron's Creek, thence up the creek as it meanders to the mouth of the first branch which falls into the said creek on the west side of said creek below where the old road crosses the said creek as it meanders to Winfrees line, thence south by Winfrees to Robert Waids corner on the bank of Aaron Creek and then up the said creek as it meanders to the beginning, containing 540 acres more or less and we have put her in possession of the same given under our hands and seals this 3rd of October AD 1849.[55]

Attached to this document was the sheriff notice where Elizabeth Amis had petitioned for her dower rights against her children, John Amis, James Amis, Lewis Amis and Martha P. Amis, his wife, Mary Amis, Rufus Amis, Susannah E. Amis, Rosaltha A. Amis, William J. Amis, Thomas Amis, William Amis, and Alexander Amis as defendants.

The file also included powers of attorney which help to locate the children of William Amis.

Know all men by these presents that I James Amis of Ouachita County & State of Arkansas for divers good causes and considerations me hereunto receiving do have nominated and appointed and by these presents do nominate and appoint John Amis, Junr., of the County of Granville & State of North Carolina my true and lawful attorney for me and in my name and for my own purposes use & benefit to ask, demand, sue for recovery, & receive from and of

---

[55] The jurors are signed in their own hand, and I cannot make out most of the names with certainty. Those that are clearly legible in the microfilm are E. Royster, who signed by mark, Robert Sandford, W. G. Thomas, L. Williamson, Thos. Chandler. The Sheriff listed all the jurors in his attachment to the deed.

the Clerk and Master of the Court of Equity of the said county of Granville and from any & all other persons such sums or sum of money as I am or may be entitled to as one of the children and heirs at law of the said William Amis, decd., ...whereof I have hereunto set my hand & seal this 10th day of May 1851. signed James Amis; witnessed by James Winfree; Joel Chandler.

Know all men by these presents that I William Amis of the County of Henry and State of Georgia for divers good causes and considerations hereunto moving have nominated and appointed and by these presents do nominate and appoint John Amis, Junr., of the County of Granville and State of North Carolina my true and lawful attorney for me and in my name and for my own purposes use and benefits ask, demand, sue for, recover, and receive of and from James Amis, Administrator of William Amis, decd.,....as one of the children and distributees of the said decd....I have hereunto set my hand and seal this 21st day of December 1849. signed William Amis; witnessed by Joel Sh..ny; Gabriel Jones.

Lewis E. Amis in right of his wife, Rosa, and William J. Amis petitioned the court as tenants in common to divide the slaves of William Amis, decd., at the November term of court 1859. A total of 24 names were listed. The court ordered a panel to separate these 24 slaves into two lots as equal as possible, and to let the petitioners choose their lot.

The file also includes a plat for a tract of 126 acres sold by Peyton Puryear to William Amis, described as part of the Harris tract lying along the west side of the Oxford Road and on the east Spring Green Meeting House is identified about half way along the north-south boundary line. Newman's Store is identified at the narrow southern end of the plat. There is a tract of land described as belonging to William Amis' heirs, surveyed 10 October 1849 and containing 201 acres lying on Aaron's Creek. There is another plat for a 100 acre tract adjacent William Chandler. He also had a tract of 436½ acres, described as the Wade tract, touching on Aaron's Creek. Finally there is a 159½ acre tract lying just south of the Virginia line and to the west of Aaron's Creek where it crosses that boundary. It is unclear to me if these properties were excluded from calculation of the widow's dower of 540 acres, but they total to 997 acres, which would give the widow somewhat more than 1/3 of the land accounted for by these various plats. I have not tried to research William Amis' land purchases and sales in the deed books.

Children of WILLIAM AMIS and ELIZABETH PURYEAR:

  i. THOMAS[6] AMIS, b. 1805 Granville Co., N. C.; d. after 1860 Ouachita Co., Ark.; m. MARTHA ANN BOYD 22 April 1830 Halifax Co., Va.

  ii. LEWIS[6] AMIS, b. 1809 Granville Co., N. C.; d. 1843 Granville Co., N. C.; m. ELIZABETH AMIS 1836 Granville Co., N. C., dau. of JOSEPH AMIS and ELIZABETH DOWNEY.[56]

  iii. WILLIAM[6] AMIS, JR., b. 18 August 1811 Granville Co., N. C.; d. 16 October 1881 Henry Co.,, Ga.; m. ANN WHITE about 1833 Granville Co., N. C.; b. 18 August 1811 in Virginia; d. 28 June 1869 Henry Co., Ga.[57]

  iv. JOHN[6] AMIS, b. 1814 Granville Co., N. C.; d. 1898 Granville Co., N. C.[58]; m. CATHERINE S. _____ about 1839 Granville Co., N. C.[59]

---

[56] Obviously this represents a first cousin marriage, but it is not the only one I have found in this generation.

[57] Buried McDonough City Cemetery.

[58] Buried in Amis Chapel Baptist Church Cemetery. Located online 11 March 2012 at http://cemeterycensus.com/nc/gran/cem242.htm.

[59] John Amis, 36, is living in Goshen District with Catherine S., 24. James Amis, 27, and Marsha A. Amis, 21, are also living in Goshen District. 1850 Census Granville Co., N. C., Goshen District, p. 185B,#86/86. James is #88/88. John Amis, 35, is living with Catherine, 27, m. about 1839 in County Line District, as is Lewis Amis, 27. Based upon the family clusters, I have decided this John Amis is the man living in Goshen District.

A respected citizen and well known lawyer of Granville was born in this county, educated at Caldwell Institute in Greensboro, afterwards at Chapel Hill from which he graduation in 1846. He was engaged as a teacher a year at the first mentioned institution, later studied law under Judge Battle and was admitted to the bar in 1848 and to the Supreme Court in 1849. He practiced till 1856 and then retired to his farm and came again to the courts after the war. In 1852-3-4 he was representative to the State Legislature and in 1854 was the Whig candidate for the Speakership of the House. During the war he was Colonel of the militia stationed in this county. In 1862 and again in 1864 he was elected to the House of Representatives. In 1866 he was elected County Solicitor serving till reconstruction in 1868. From 1872 to 1878 he was chairman of the county Democratic Executive Committee, of which he is still a member, from 1877 to 1878 he was on the Board of Directors of the State Insane Asylum. In all the various positions Colonel Amis has acted unselfishly and energetically and has shown himself fully worthy of the trusts submitted to him. Since the war he has had his law office in Oxford, now in the bank building and being a well read lawyer enjoys a good practice in this and Vance counties. He is a member of the Presbyterian body. He married a Hillsboro lady and has two of a family.[60]

Children of JOHN AMIS and CATHERINE S. ____:

1. JOANNA[7] AMIS, b. 1840 Granville Co., N. C.
2. NANCY[7] AMIS, b. 1842 Granville Co., N. C.; m. JAMES A. JONES 14 December 1866 Granville Co., N. C.
3. ELMIRA C.[7] AMIS, b. 1844 Granville Co., N. C.; m. S. L. PURYEAR 6 December 1868 Granville Co., N. C.
4. SOPHRONIA[7] AMIS, b. 1847 Granville Co. N. C.

[60] A Historical and Descriptive Review of the State of North Carolina 1885. (Charleston, S. C.: Empire Publishing Co.,1885) p. 116

v. ALEXANDER[6] AMIS, b. 6 April 1816 Granville Co.,
    N. C.; d. 28 July 1858 Dallas Co., Ark.; m.
    HENRIETTA LEWIS 17 February 1840 Granville
    Co., N. C.[61]
        Alexander Amis obtained a patent for 80
    acres of land in section 32, twp. 98, range 13 west
    in Dallas County, Arkansas on 1 December
    1857.[62]

    Children of ALEXANDER AMIS and HENRIETTA:[63]
        1. ELIZABETH[7] AMIS, b. 1841 Granville Co., N. C.
        2. WARREN[7] AMIS, b. 1843 Granville Co., N. C.
        3. WILLIAM[7] AMIS, b. 1844 Granville Co., N. C.
        4. JOSEPH[7] AMIS, b. 1847 Tennessee
        5. male, b. April 1850, Dallas Co., Ark.

vi. WARREN[6] AMIS, b. 1818 Granville Co., N. C.; d.
     July 1844 Granville Co., N. C., (unm.)

vii. JAMES S.[6] AMIS, b. about 1823 Granville Co., N.
     C.; d. before 9 November 1853 Ouachita Co.,
     Arkansas; m. MARSHA A. JUNIEL 1847 Halifax
     Co., Va.[64]
        James Amis, 27, and Marsha A. Amis, 21, are
     living in Goshen District in 1850, two houses
     down from John and Catherine S. Amis.[65]

viii. MARTHA P.[6] AMIS, b. about 1825 Granville Co., N.
      C.; d. about 1850 Granville Co., N. C.; m.
      LEWIS AMIS 1844 Granville Co., N. C., son of
      JOSEPH AMIS and ELIZABETH DOWNEY; b. 22
      December 1822 Granville Co., N. C.; d. 19
      July 1894 Dallas Co., Ark.; m. (2) MARTHA J.
      DANIEL 1 June 1852 Granville Co., N. C.[66]

---

    [61] Buried Juniel Cemetery, Dallas Co., Ark.
    [62] BLM records compiled by Joy Fisher. Located online 16 December
2011 at
http://files.usgwarchives.net/ar/dallas/land/dallas.txt. This land is not
in the townships being settled by John N. and Louis Amis.
    [63] 1850 Census Dallas Co., Ark., Princeton Twp., p. 81A, #540/540.
    [64] 1850 Census Granville Co., N. C., Goshen District, p. 196B,
#88/88. They have no children listed.
    [65] 1850 Census Granville Co., N. C.,
    [66] Data from Biographical and Historical Memoirs of Southern
Arkansas, 1890, Chapter 27:709, Dallas County. Copy located on line at

viii. MARY[6] AMIS, b. 1833 Granville Co., N. C.[67]

3. ix. RUFUS[6] AMIS, b. 24 January 1835 Granville Co., N. C.; d. 29 October 1903 Granville Co., N. C.; m. (1) ELIZABETH ANN RAGLAND 14 November 1855 Halifax Co., Va.; b. 1836 Virginia; d. 1900 Granville Co., N. C.;[68] m. (2) CARRIE (____) HUDGINS 19 December 1900 Baltimore, Baltimore Co., Maryland.[69]

3. RUFUS[6] (*WILLIAM[5], LEWIS[4], WILLIAM[3], JOSEPH[2]*) AMIS was born 24 January 1825 Granville Co., North Carolina, and died 29 October 1903 Granville Co., N. C. He married (1) ELIZABETH A. RAGLAND 14 November 1855 Halifax Co., Virginia. She was born 18 April 1834 and died 20 April 1900. She is the mother of all his children. He married (2) CARRIE (____) HUDGINS 19 December 1900 Baltimore, Baltimore Co., Maryland.

Children of RUFUS AMIS and ELIZABETH RAGLAND:[70]

i. WILLIAM DABNEY[7] AMIS, b. 25 January 1862 Granville Co., N. C.; d. 5 December 1927

---

http://books.google.com. Louis Amis obtained patents in sections 29 and 30 of township 108, range 12W in 1859 and 1860. Cited by Fisher, Joy, *op cit.*

[67] Living with Rufus Amis and wife Elizabeth in the 1860 Census Granville Co., N. C., Buchanan P. O, p. 467, #184/180. Next door is John Amis, 46, wife Catherine, 37, Joanna, 20, Nancy, 17, Eltamira, 14, and Frances 13, all daughters. Two more houses down is Peyton Puryear, so it appears they are living on the tract along the Oxford Road.

[68] Rufus Amis Papers #3158-z, Southern Historical Collection, The Wilson Library, University of North Carolina at Chapel Hill. Accessed 7 October 2011 at http://www.lib.unc.edu/mss/inv/a/Amis.Rufus.html. The records apparently include genealogical materials which I have not yet consulted.

[69] The marriage was proved by a copy of the license and also the Bible records accessed in Oxford, N. C. There was also a newspaper clipping about the marriage.

[70] Data are from his Bible, which was kept in the Chandler Family. Copy located at the Robert Thornton Library, Oxford, N. C., 27 Feb 2012.

Granville Co., N. C.; m. PEARL LUCK 1 January 1895 Granville Co., N. C.; b. 1873; d. 1948 Granville Co., N. C.[71]

Children of W. D. AMIS and PEARL LUCK are:

1. ELIZABETH LOUISE[8] AMIS, b. 25 April 1896;
2. WILHELMINA[8] AMIS, b. 7 April 1898;
3. ROBERT THOMAS[8] AMIS, b. 23 January 1900;
4. CORNELIA ROSE[8] AMIS, b. 17 June 1901 Granville Co., N. C.; d. 28 January 1902 Granville Co., N. C.[72]
5. WILLIAM DOWNEY[8] AMIS, b. 13 September 1903;

ii. HARRIET ELIZABETH[7] AMIS, b. 21 May 1864 Granville Co., N. C.; d. 24 August 1946 Granville Co., N. C.; m. JAMES P. CHANDLER 3 November 1886 Granville Co., N. C.; b. 22 July 1844; d. 25 July 1926 Granville Co., N. C.[73]

Children of HARRIET AMIS and JAMES CHANDLER:

1. MARY ELIZABETH[8] CHANDLER, b. 26 February 1889; d. 12 August 1983.
2. JULIA AMIS[8] CHANDLER, b. 4 September 1891; d. 26 March 1974.
3. RUFUS EDWARD[8] CHANDLER, b. 18 January 1894; d. March 1991.
4. SALLIE ANN[8] CHANDLER, b. 25 March 1897; d. 15 February 1990.
5. ROBIE THOMAS[8] CHANDLER, b. 11 April 1900; d. 29 March 1991.
6. JAMES LEE[8] CHANDLER, b. 31 December 1902; d. June 1957.

iii. ROBERT THOMAS[7] AMIS, [74] b. 4 September 1866 Granville Co., N. C.; d. 27 February 1900

---

[71] Both are buried in Amis Chapel Cemetery. Located online 11 March 2012 at
http://cemeterycensus.com/nc/gran/cem242.htm.

[72] Buried in Amis Chapel Cemetery.

[73] Buried in Amis Chapel Cemetery.

[74] Even though his name was spelled out as Robert Thomas Amis, he appears everywhere else in the Bible as Robert L. Amis. I have no explanation for the discrepancy.

Granville Co., N. C.; m. ANNIE H. CHANDLER 28
November 1888 Granville Co., N. C.; b. 2
October 1867; d. 7 August 1924, Granville
Co., N. C.[75]

Children of R. L. AMIS and ANNIE CHANDLER:

1. RUFUS THOMAS[8] AMIS, b. 19 August 1889;
2. LILLIE MAE[8] AMIS, b. 14 May 1891;
3. JANIE LEE[8] AMIS, b. 18 July 1892; m.
   EUGENE WARREN WHITAKER 9 November
   1912.
4. CHARLES JAMES[8] AMIS, b. 18 November 1895;
5. EVELYN MARIAN[8] AMIS, b. 15 September 189_.

iv. RUFUS EDWARD[7] AMIS, b. 15 August 1878
Granville Co., N. C.; d. 22 February 1975
Granville Co., N. C.; m. LILLIAN CHANDLER 30
April 1901 Granville Co., N. C.; b. 16 October
1879 Granville Co., N. C.; d. 2 June 1920
Granville Co.,. N. C.[76]

Children of R. E. AMIS and LILLIAN CHANDLER:

1. RUBY ELIZABETH[8] AMIS, b. 11 January 1902,
   d. 23 November 1953.
2. MARY LYLE CHANDLER[8] AMIS, b. 25 July
   1903, d. 19 May 1941.[77]

---

[75] Buried in Amis Chapel Cemetery.
[76] Buried in Amis Chapel Cemetery.
[77] Buried in Amis Chapel Cemetery.

Chapter 3: 1857 William Amis of Granville Co., North Carolina

1. WILLIAM[4] (*WILLIAM[3], JOSEPH[2]*) AMIS was born 1765 in Essex Co., Virginia and died before 10 June 1857 in Granville Co., N. C. He married (1) JUDITH KNIGHT, daughter of JONATHAN KNIGHT and JUDITH WOODSON, 21 January 1789 in Granville Co., N. C. He married (2) SARAH (KNIGHT) ROFFE.

> William Amis, Jr., was born in 1765 in Virginia. He married first Judith Knight on 21 Jan 1789, in Granville Co., N. C. William Amis, Jr. died 10 June 1857 leaving a will dated 15 June 1842 in which he names his wife as Sarah. As one of the descendants of his daughter, Lucy, who married Thomas Reavis has stated that his wife was a Miss Roffe of Virginia, I believe that he married secondly Sarah Knight Roffe, the widowed sister of his first wife. Both Sarah Roffe and Judith Amis are named as daughters in the will of Jonathan Knight which was filed November 1809 in Granville Co., N. C.[1] I have not located any record of his second marriage.[2]

William Amis obtained his tract of land from his father-in-law, Jonathan Knight, and appears to have stayed there his entire life. He appears to have played

---

[1] Granville Co., N. C., Will Book 7:80-81. Cited in Gwynn, Zae Hargett. Abstracts of the Wills and Estate Records of Granville County, North Carolina, 1808-1833. (Rocky Mount, NC: Joseph W. Watson, 1976.) p. 12. Jonathan Knight, Sr., willed to his wife Judith all land on the east side of the road, three Negroes, and household furniture. Son John received the land to the left side of the road whereon he was then living, and grandson John, son of John, received land on the east side of Middle Creek. Son Woodson Knight received 250 acres in Mecklenburg Co., Va., and son William received 5 shillings plus what he had already received. The residue of the estate was left to Elizabeth Amis, "Rachal" DeJarnat, "Judath" Amis, Polly Amis, Jonathan and John Knight.

[2] Hodges, A. A. The Ancestry and Descendants of John Woodson Amis of Granville Co., N. C., and Scott Co., Miss. (Pendleton, S. C., n. p. d., 1978,) p. 10.

a much less prominent role in local affairs than his nephew, William Amis, son of Lewis.

William Amis, 82, was living with Lewis and Rachel Parham in 1850.[3]

William Amis last will and testament was proved at the November 1857 Court of Granville County.[4]

I William Amis of the County of Granville and State of North Carolina do make and ordain this my last will and testament in manner and form following.

Item: I give and bequeath to my beloved wife Sarah the following slaves, to wit, Calann, Granville, and Clarey, the tract of land where I know reside with the exception of the land given to Alfred Knight and sold to John D. Bryant, Jr., during the term of her natural life, and after her death, to return to my estate. I also give to my wife Sarah the sum of six hundred dollars--$600—to her and her heirs forever. I leave to my wife all my household & kitchen furniture and at her death to return to my estate. It is also my will that my executors allot to my wife, Sarah, ( ) years plentiful support for herself and family from the time of my death.

Item: I give and bequeath to my daughter, Missinia, the following Negro slaves to wit, Anderson and Rachel, to her and her heirs forever, two cows and calves, one bureau and good feather bed and furniture, one saddle & bridle, to her and her heirs forever. My object is to make an equal distribution of my estate amongst all my children and having made advancements to them of various amounts whatever each one may be hereinafter charged with must account for the advance before they can claim any portion of my estate. I have advanced to my son Johnathan Amis the sum of eleven hundred dollars--$1100—which he is to account for at my death,

---

[3] 1850 Census Granville Co., N. C., Tabs Creek District, pp. 83A-B, #71/71.

[4] Granville Co., N. C., Will Book 20:340-343. My transcription from the microfilm copy.

without interest until my death. I have advanced to Judith W. Parham, wife of Williamson Parham, the sum of six hundred dollars--$600—in Negro girl Sophia, one horse and saddle, and cash (illegible) my son John W. Amis ( ) in Negroes William and Haywood. I have advanced to Sarah Bryant, wife of John W. Bryant, the sum of one thousand dollars...I have advanced to Rachel Parham, wife of Lewis Parham, the sum of five hundred dollars--$500—in Negro girl Mariah and horse and saddle. I have advanced to Mary Montague, wife of Samuel Montague, the sum of five hundred dollars--$500—in Negro girl Mary and horse and saddle. I have advanced to Elizabeth Bryant, wife of Edward Bryant, the sum of five hundred dollars in Negro boy Randall horse and saddle, etc. I have advanced to Susan Bryant, wife of Patterson Bryant, the sum of five hundred dollars in Negro girl Emily horse & saddle, etc. I have advanced to Martha Cheatham, wife of Thomas Cheatham, the sum of five hundred dollars--$500—in Negro boy Aaron, horse, saddle, etc. I have this day executed to Alfred Knight a deed to a certain tract or parcel of land as an advancement to Frances Knight, wife of said Alfred Knight, for which the said Alfred Knight is to account for the sum of five hundred dollars--$500. I have advanced to Lucy Reavis, wife of Thomas Reavis, the sum of seven hundred dollars--$700—in Negro woman Lacey and child, horse & saddle, etc.

I have sold to John W. Bryant, Junr., the tract of land on which he lives for the sum of one thousand dollars, which I consider as an advancement to the children of Harriet Bryant, who was the wife of said John W. Bryant, to wit, Wesley S. Bryant, Sara Bryant, Judith Bryant, William Bryant, Pamina Bryant. And it is further my will that my executors collect the said thousand dollars from said John F. Bryant, when due and as the said children of the said Harriet Bryant, deceased, shall arrive at the age of twenty one years, to give each and all of them their portion of the said amount share & share alike.

It is my will and desire that after each of my children shall have accounted for the amounts I have charged as advancements that the residue of my estate be equally divided between my twelve children, to wit, Johnathan, Judith, John, Sarah, Rachel, Elizabeth, Mary, Ann, Martha and the children of Harriet Bryant, deceased, Frances, Lucy to them and their heirs and assigns forever.

I will and bequeath to my wife Sarah one good horse and saddle, two feather beds and furniture, two tables, two ( ), one trunk, one ( ), to her and her heirs forever. Finally I nominate and appoint my two sons-in-law Alfred Knight and Thomas Reavis my executors to carry out this my last will and testament, thereby making this my last will and testament by me made witness my hand and seal the 15th June 1842.   signed William Amis
Witness: D. A. Paschall; Sea. Parham

State of North Carolina)
Granville County)   I William Amis of the above county & state do hereby make and ordain and declare this Codicil a part of my last will and testament in the following words, to wit, I have omitted to charge my daughter Elizabeth Bryant in my will above written dated 15th June 1842 with the sum of seventy five dollars for a wagon and gear furnished her and in the settlement of my estate she must account for said sum of seventy five dollars. I also give to my daughter Missniah one Negro boy named Armistead instead of and to make up for one Negro boy named Anderson given to her in my will and who has since died. In witness of which I have hereunto set my hand and affixed my seal this 24th day of July 1848.   signed William Amis
Witness: Richard Obritton; D. A. Paschall

Several of the daughters of William Amis and Judith Knight married men named Bryant, and they all appear to have gone to Maury Co., Tennessee, about the same time William's brother, John Amis moved there.

70

Children of WILLIAM AMIS and JUDITH KNIGHT are:

i. JONATHAN D.[5] AMIS, m. ELIZA HILL 3 September 1820 Granville Co., N. C.

ii. JUDITH[5] AMIS, b. 1791 Granville Co., N. C.; d. April 1870 Granville Co., N. C.; m. WILLIAMSON PARHAM 12 December 1807 Granville Co., N. C.; b. 1788 Granville Co., N. C.

They are living with Asenath, 35, Asa, 27, and Louisa, 20, in Granville Co., N. C., in 1850.[5] In 1860, they have all three children and have been joined by Emily S. Jackson, 50, and "Neah" Amis, 48.[6] Living next door is Joseph Parham, 37, and wife "Mursouria", and three children, with Ann Kelly, 34, David Owen, 11, John Owen, 9, Sally Kelly, 2, and Mary 6/12.[7] The relationship to Joseph is established not only by proximity but by a deed from Williamson Parham to Joseph D. Parham in 1849 for two slaves.[8]

Children of JUDITH AMIS and W. PARHAM:

1. EMILY[6] PARHAM, b. about 1810 Granville Co., N. C.; m. SAMUEL J. JACKSON 31 December 1838 Granville Co., N. C.;[9] b. about 1817 Virginia.[10]

    Emily, 69, is living with her nephew, John H. Owens, Ann Kelly, 54, Louisa Parham 50, and Asenath Parham, 70, in 1880.[11]

2. JOSEPH[6] PARHAM, b. about 1813 Granville Co., N. C.

---

[5] 1850 Census Granville Co., N. C., Raglands, p. 96A, #59.

[6] 1860 Census Granville Co., N. C., Ragland, p. 311, #47. A number of Internet sources list his date of death as 9 September 1857, but he is still living in 1860 as judged by the census.

[7] 1860 Census Granville Co., N. C., Ragland, p. 311, #48.

[8] Granville Co., N. C., Deed Book 15:182-183. Cited by Kimberly. My Comprehensive Genealogy File. 27 August 2007.
http://wc.rootsweb.ancestry.com, (db. onebigfamily100.)

[9] Holcomb, Brent. Marriages of Granville Co., North Carolina, 1753-1858, (2003.) p. 180. Accessed 1 March 2014 at Ancestry.com.

[10] 1850 Census Granville Co., N. C., Napp, p. 171A, #17. He is living in a household headed by Judith Jackson, 96, and Emily is listed as being 40. No children.

[11] 1880 Census Granville Co., N. C., Henderson, ED 98, p. 289A, #305.

3. ASENATH[6] PARHAM, b. about 1815 Granville Co., N. C.

4. ASA COLLIN[6] PARHAM, b. 23 June 1821 Granville Co., N. C.; d. 17 April 1902 Granville Co., N. C.;[12] m. SALLIE A. PASCHALL 16 February 1864 Granville Co., N. C.;[13] b. about 1838 North Carolina.

    Asa C. Parham and wife Sally, 32, are head of household that includes Asenath Parham, 50, Louisa Parham, 35, Emily Jackson, 48, Ann A. Kelly, 36, and her two daughters in 1870.[14] It does not appear they had any children of their own.

5. ANN[6] PARHAM, b. about 1826 Granville Co., N. C.; m. (1) JOHN H. OWEN 3 November 1842 Granville Co., N. C.;[15] m. (2) GEORGE J. KELLY 23 September 1857 Granville Co., N. C.[16]

6. LOUISA[6] PARHAM, b. about 1830 Granville Co., N. C.

iii SARAH WOODSON[5] AMIS, b. 1 April 1794 Granville Co., N. C.; 14 April 1870 Marshall Co., Tenn.;[17] m. JOHN FARRINGTON BRYANT 3 November 1812 Granville Co., N. C.;[18] b. 14 May 1790 Granville Co., N. C.; d. 6 December 1857 Mooresville, Marshall Co., Tenn.[19]

---

[12] Elmwood Cemetery, Oxford, N. C. http://www.findagrave.com, #28316235.

[13] Holcomb, p. 252. Accessed 1 March 2014 at Ancestry.com.

[14] 1870 Census Granville Co., N. C., Henderson, p. 232A, #509

[15] Holcomb, p. 251. Accessed 1 March 2014 at Ancestry.com.

[16] Holcomb, p. 193. Accessed 1 March 2014 at Ancestry.com.

[17] Bryant Cemetery, Lewisburg, Marshall Co., Tenn. http://www.findagrave.com, #85613165.

[18] Andrew D. Bryant, from whom the station takes its name was born in Franklin Co., N. C., 14 March 1825, son of John F. and Sarah W. Amis Bryant who located near Mooresville 1837. http://books.google.com/books?id=9dQBAAAAMAAJ&pg=PA4&dq=maury +tennessee+records&hl=en&ei=diDDTqTjO4a4twfCxry3DQ&sa=X&oi=book _result&ct=result&resnum=2&ved=0CEYQ6AEwAQ#v=onepage&q=Amis&f =false. Accessed 20 November 2011.

[19] Bryant Cemetery, Lewisburg, Marshall Co., Tenn. http://www.findagrave.com, #85612834. An extended genealogy of the relevant Bryant family was posted by Clements, Virginia. 7 March 2011. http://genforum.genealogy.com/bryant/messages/10708.html.

John F. Bryant, 60, Sarah W., 56, and children, Henrietta, 28, John A., 21, Rollin F., 19, Sarah J., 16, and William A., 11, are living in Marshall Co., Tenn., in 1850.[20] All of the children except William were born in North Carolina.

In 1860, Sarah, 62, has Henrietta, 38, John A., 30, Sarah 25, and two girls, whose names appear to be Eudora, 15,[21] and Lura, 16, both born in Tennessee.[22]

The Bible record of John Farrington Bryant has been published,[23] but I have no found a will.

Children of SARAH AMIS and JOHN BRYANT:

1. JAMES JACKSON[6] BRYANT, b. 2 June 1815 Granville Co., N. C.; d. 20 January 1892 Bosque Co., Texas;[24] m. (1) REBECCA JANE REAVIS 14 November 1838 Granville Co., N. C.;[25] b. 12 October 1813 Vance Co., N. C.; d. 19 September 1845 Maury Co., Tenn.; m. (2) MARTHA ANN MALONE 20 June 1846 Maury Co., Tenn.;[26] b. 8 December 1828 N. C.; d. 15 November 1898 Bosque Co., Texas.[27]

"J. J." Bryant, 34, and Martha, 21, are living with Sarah, 8; Hannah, 6, and Mary, 2; in Maury Co., Tenn.[28]

"J. J." Bryant, 65, and M. A. Bryant, 52, with some of their children and grandchildren are living in Maury Co., Tenn., in 1880.[29]

---

[20] 1850 Census Marshall Co., Tenn., CD 13, p. 125A, #398. William A., appears to be the eldest son of James J. Bryant. He may have moved in with his grandparents after the death of his mother.

[21] Dora Bryant, b. 1844; d. 1900, is buried in Bryant Cemetery, Lewisburg, Marshall Co., Tenn. http://www.findagrave.com, #86806717.

[22] 1860 Census Marshall Co., Tenn., CD 13, p. 115, #98/73.

[23] Accessed 1 March 2014 at
http://trees.ancestry.com/tree/5890313/person/-1378562157/storyx/23c8e1ce-43dc-4183-b68e-8901ce03d8e7?src=search

[24] Cedron Cemetery, Bosque Co., Texas. http://www.findagrave.com, #16247489.

[25] North Carolina Marriage Collection, 1741-2004. Accessed 1 March 2014 at Ancestry.com.

[26] Tennessee State Marriages, 1780-2002. Accessed 1 March 2014 at Ancestry.com.

[27] Cedron Cemetery, Bosque Co., Texas. http://www.findagrave.com, #16247459.

[28] 1850 Census Maury Co., Tenn., CD 11, p. 350B, #1526.

2. ROBERTSON[6] BRYANT, b. 4 January 1817 Granville Co., N. C.; d. 1 February 1880 Dallas Co., Ark.;[30] m. MARY JANE H. EDWARDS 10 February 1845 Franklin Co., N. C.;[31] b. 11 May 1823 Granville Co., N. C.; d. 2 August 1899 Dallas Co., Ark.[32]

> "Robison" Bryant, 33, and Mary, 25, with John, 5, and Louis, 2, are living with John W. Ricard in Marshall Co., Tenn., in 1850.[33] In 1860 Rob, 43, and Mary, 38, are with children John, 14; Louis, 11; Alexander, 8; George, 6; and Vincent, 4; along with Elizabeth Edwards, 21.[34]

3. ALEXANDER[6] BRYANT, b. 14 December 1818 Granville Co., N. C.;[35] m. MARIA G. WILKES 5 September 1842 Marshall Co., Tenn.[36]

> Alexander Bryant, of Marshall County, Tenn., is a son of John F. and Sarah (Amis) Bryant, and was born in Granville County, N.C., December 14, 1818. His parents were also born in North Carolina, and were married in that State, and became the parents of ten children. The father was a well-to-do farmer, and lived in his native State until 1837, and then moved to Tennessee, and located in Marshall County, and there died in 1857. He was a Democrat and for several years held the position of magistrate. The mother died in 1870. Alexander's early school advantages were very limited, never having attended school more than twelve months. After attaining manhood he began farming and has followed that calling through life. In 1842 he

---

[29] 1880 Census Maury Co., Tenn., CD 4, ED 157, p. 145A, #3.

[30] Bryant Cemetery, Dallas Co., Ark. http://www.findagrave.com, #104349506.

[31] Date of bond. NC Marriage Bond #46950. NC Marriage Bonds, 1741-1868. Accessed 1 March 2014 at Ancestry.com.

[32] Bryant Cemetery, Dallas Co., Ark. http://www.findagrave.com, #104348855.

[33] 1850 Census Marshall Co., Tenn., CD 15, p. 108A, #189

[34] 1860 Census Dallas Co., Ark., Jackson, p. 1067, #764. Lewis Amis and wife Frances are on the same page at #759.

[35] An online source says he died in Marshall Co., Tenn., 29 February 1904, and that she was the daughter of John Wilkes and Martha P. Fortune, b. 30 July 1820 Marshall Co., Tenn., and d. there 28 October 1888.

[36] Tennessee State Marriages, 1780-2002. Accessed 1 March 2014 at Ancestry.com.

wedded Maria Wilkes, by whom he had eleven children. Both he and Mrs. Wilkes are members of the Cumberland Presbyterian Church. Mr. Bryant is a Democrat and as a farmer has met with well deserved success. He has been a resident of Marshall County for twenty-seven years, and has the confidence and respect of all who know him.

4. HENRIETTA[6] BRYANT, b. 8 December 1820 Granville Co., N. C.; d. 31 October 1915 Marshall Co., Tenn.;[37] m. THOMAS B. TAYLOR 29 August 1860 Marshall Co., Tenn.;[38] b. 9 March 1819 Wilson Co., Tenn.; d. 13 April 1879 Wilson Co., Tenn.[39]

5. WILLIAM THROWER[6] BRYANT, b. 12 July 1822 Granville Co., N. C.; d. 25 May 1861 Marshall Co., Tenn.;[40] m. MARY ELIZABETH HILL 5 January 1846 Maury Co., Tenn.; b. 10 February 1824; d. 19 May 1905 Marshall Co., Tenn.[41]

    William T. Bryant, 27, NC, Mary Bryant, 25, and John R. Bryant, 4, are living with Burrell Wilkes and wife Elizabeth and family in Marshall Co., Tenn., in 1850.[42]

6. ANDREW DANIEL DAILY[6] BRYANT, b. 14 March 1825 Granville Co., N. C.; 21 May 1910 Marshall Co., Tenn.;[43] m. SARAH WILLIAMS HILL 4 January 1852 Maury Co., Tenn., dau. of ISAAC HILL and MARGARET STEELE;

---

[37] Bryant Cemetery, Lewisburg, Marshall Co., Tenn. http://www.findagrave.com, #85607765. Her death record specifically lists her parents as John F. Bryant and Sarah Amis and gives the same dates. [Tennessee Deaths and Burials Index, 1874-1955. Accessed 1 March 2014 at Ancestry.com.]

[38] Tennessee State Marriages, 1780-2002. Accessed 1 March 2014 at Ancestry.com.

[39] Leesville Cemetery, Wilson Co., Tenn. http://www.findagrave.com, #29146348.

[40] Bryant Cemetery, Lewisburg, Marshall Co., Tenn. http://www.findagrave.com, #101864957.

[41] Bryant Cemetery, Lewisburg, Marshall Co., Tenn. http://www.findagrave.com, #101864913.

[42] 1850 Census Marshall Co., Tenn., CD 13, p. 128B, #447.

[43] Bryant Cemetery, Lewisburg, Marshall Co., Tenn. http://www.findagrave.com, #85608280.

b. 20 August 1827; d. 22 September 1889 Marshall Co., Tenn.[44]

Andrew D. Bryant, one of Maury County's most enterprising citizens, was born in Franklin County, North Carolina, March 14, 1825, and is the son of John F. and Sarah W. (Amis) Bryant, who were born in 1790 and 1794 respectively.[45] The father, John F., was the son of Roland and Mary (Hunt) Bryant, and Roland was the son of William Bryant, who was born in Ireland. John F. was a successful farmer, was married in 1814, and was the father of 10 children. He died December 6, 1857, and his wife followed him to the grave in 1870. Our subject was reared on a farm and obtained a limited education in the country schools, and followed farming for eight years in Dallas County, Arkansas. He then moved to Maury County, Tenn., where he now resides, engaged in farming and stock raising, in which he has been quite successful. He was married, January 4, 1852, to Sarah Hill, a native of Tennessee, born in June 1828, and the daughter of Isaac and Margaret (Steele) Hill. Isaac Hill was born in North Carolina, in 1800, and died in Marshall County, Tenn., in 1840. To our subject and wife were born eight children...Mr. Bryant has given his children a good education and has reason to be proud of them. In 1874 he was engaged in building two miles of railroad and also built switch and station houses. In 1877 he engaged in the saw and grist mill business. He took an active part in the Confederate service during the late war, enlisting in Co. H., 53rd Regt. [TN Inf.] and served two years. He was first lieutenant, and his captain being wounded at Fort Donelson, Mr. Bryant took his place as captain. Our subject was captured and taken to Indianapolis, Johnson's Island, Camp Chase, and at Vicksburg, where he was exchanged...

7. PATRICK HENRY[6] BRYANT, b. 14 March 1827 Granville Co., N. C.; d. 4 June 1862 Dallas

---

[44] Bryant Cemetery, Lewisburg, Marshall Co., Tenn. http://www.findagrave.com, #85607906.

[45] Goodspeed's History of Maury Co., Tenn., located 1 March 2014 at http://trees.ancestry.com/tree/5890313/person/-1378562193/mediax/2?pgnum=1&pg=0&pgpl=pid|pgNum

Co., Ark.;[46] m. REBECCA FRANCES EDWARDS 8 January 1852 Dallas Co., Ark.;[47] b. 18 January 1835; d. 12 August 1912 Dallas Co., Ark.[48]

Patrick Bryant, 23, is living with his cousin, "Aley" Amis and wife Henrietta, 28, in Dallas Co., Ark., in 1850.[49]

8. JOHN AMIS[6] BRYANT, b. 28 June 1828 Granville Co., N. C.; d. 21 November 1889 Marshall Co., Tenn.;[50] m. SARAH C. FRY 8 December 1860 Marshall Co., Tenn.;[51] b. 9 May 1835; d. 1904 Marshall Co., Tenn.[52]

John A. Bryant, farmer, is a son of John F. and Sarah W. (Amis) Bryant, both natives of North Carolina, the father born in 1790 and the mother in 1794.[53] After marriage, in 1837, they removed from their native State and came to Marshall County, where the spent the remainder of their days. This family consisted of ten children, six of whom are living. The father was an industrious tiller of the soil, owning nearly 800 acres of land. He was a Democrat and a man of fair education and good business qualities. His death occurred in 1857. After his death the mother lived a widow on the old homestead until 1870, when she, too, was called away. Our subject was born in North Carolina June 28, 1828, and his ancestors on both sides were of Irish extraction. He was reared on the farm, and owing to the demand for his services at home, received a very limited education. He worked for his father till twenty-one years of age, and then

---

[46] Bryant Cemetery, Dallas Co., Ark. http://www.findagrave.com, #40805334.

[47] Arkansas, County Marriages Index, 1837-1957. Accessed 1 March 2014 at Ancestry.com.

[48] Bryant Cemetery, Dallas Co., Ark. http://www.findagrave.com, #40805381.

[49] 1850 Census Dallas Co., Ark., Princeton, p. 40B, #540.

[50] The date given is from his biography. The date on his tombstone says he was born 21 June 1829. Bryant Cemetery, Lewisburg, Marshall Co., Tenn. http://www.findagrave.com, #85608546.

[51] Tennessee State Marriages, 1780-2002. Accessed 1 March 2014 at Ancestry.com. Her name is given as Sarah A. Fry.

[52] Bryant Cemetery, Lewisburg, Marshall Co., Tenn. http://www.findagrave.com, #86806828.

[53] Goodspeed's History Marshall Co., Tenn.

began his career as an independent farmer. In 1860 he wedded Sallie C. Fry, a native of Marshall County, born May 9, 1835, and to them were born four children. In 1862, Mr. Bryant enlisted in Company E. Eleventh Tennessee Confederate Cavalry and after twelve months' service was appointed brigade forage master, and a year later held a position in the ordnance department. During three years of faithful service he was never wounded nor taken prisoner. After peace had been declared he returned to the more peaceful pursuits of farming. He is a member of the Presbyterian Church, and for eight years held the position of magistrate. He is a Democrat in politics. He owns over 500 acres of land, and for forty-nine years has been a resident of Marshall County.

    9. ROWLAND FARRINGTON[6] BRYANT, b. 26 January 1837 Granville Co., N. C.; d. 10 October 1861.[54]

    10. SARAH JUDITH[6] BRYANT, b. 27 December 1834 Granville Co., N. C.; m. JOHN N. TAYLOR 11 March 1862 Marshall Co., Tenn.[55]

iv. RACHEL[5] AMIS, b. 1794 Granville Co., N. C.; d. before 1860 Granville Co., N. C.; m. LEWIS PARHAM 5 October 1816 Granville Co., N. C.; b. 1790 Granville Co. N. C.;[56] d. before 1870 Granville Co., N. C.

    Lewis Parham and family are in Tabs Creek District in 1860.[57] Rachel Amis is dead by the time of this census. Lewis is dead by the time of the 1870 Census.[58]

---

[54] He was on active duty with the CSA. Memorial located in Bryant Cemetery, Lewisburg, Marshall Co., Tenn. http://www.findagrave.com, #85607712.

[55] Tennessee State Marriages, 1780-2002. Accessed 1 March 2014 at Ancestry.com.

[56] 1850 Census Granville Co., N. C., Tabs Creek, p. 83A, #71/71 William Amis, 82, is living with them.

[57] 1860 Census Granville Co., N. C., Tabs Creek District, p. 145, #910.

[58] Irene. Morris, Ellsworth, Butler and Adams Lineage. 15 June 2010. Located at http://wc.rootsweb.ancestry.com, (db. morris-butler) reports that Lewis R. Parham sold Lewis Parham his interest in a 21 year old male slave named Anderson, (Granville Co., N. C., DB 11:410); Lewis Parham and Asa Parham sold a slave to James Floyd, (DB 7:260); Lewis

2. v. JOHN WOODSON[5] AMIS, b. 22 September 1795 Granville Co., N. C.; d. 4 February 1849 Scott Co., Miss.; m. MARTHA WADKINS 10 February 1824 Copiah Co., Miss; b. 10 June 1805 Montgomery Co., Tenn.; d. 10 September 1887 Scott Co., Miss.

vi. ELIZABETH[5] AMIS, b. 22 September 1797 Granville Co., N. C.; d. 9 October 1876 Maury Co., Tenn.;[59] m. EDWARD T. BRYANT 17 February 1818 Granville Co., N. C.; b. 7 October 1778 Granville Co., N. C.; d. 23 September 1845 Maury Co., Tenn.; m. (1) NANCY PARHAM.

"Elizabeth Amis was 20 in 1818 when she became the second wife of Edward Bryant who was twice her age. They had eleven children: William Rowland, Albert (or Abner), Harriett D., Lewis Amis, Lucy H., Ellen G., Martha, Elizabeth, James D., Lucius Rhodes, and Thomas H. In 1841, her son William R. Bryant married Sarah Anthony. Her daughter Harriett married Archelause M. White. Four years later, her husband Edward and four other children died during an epidemic, probably cholera. Ellen, 19 years old, died first, on August 8. Lewis, 23, died the next month on September 19, and his father four days later. Albert, 25, died on October 3. Lucy, 20, died on November 16. The documents relating to the settlement of her husband's estate show that it took many years before it was completed. Elizabeth was not alone in this task— the epidemic raged almost ten years and often killed whole families. Her uncle John Amis, his wife Polly Knight, and their son Josiah died of the same cause a few years later. In the 1860 census, Elizabeth was recorded as being 62 years old and living with two sons, Lucius (22) and Thomas (20).

Parham sold Albert Parham an eight year old slave girl named Ida for the use of his grandchildren, Lucy and Sarah. (DB 20:214.)

[59] Tombstones for both are found in Friendship Baptist Church, Culleoka. http://www.findagrave.com, #32238822 and #32238844.

She lived as a widow for more than 30 years, dying October 9, 1876 at the age of 79."[60]

Edward T. Bryant wrote his will 20 July 1836 at it was proved between 1 and 21 October 1845 in Maury Co., Tenn.[61]

Children of ELIZABETH and EDWARD BRYANT:

1. WILLIAM ROWLAND[6] BRYANT, b. 1819 Granville Co., N. C.; d. about 1870 Weakley Co., Tenn.; m. (1) SARAH D. ANTHONY 7 October 1841 Maury Co., Tenn.; b. 1825 Tenn.; d. about 1859 Madison Co., Tenn.; m. FLORENCE SNODGRASS 5 August 1861 Madison Co., Tenn.;[62] b. about 1841 Miss.; d. before 1880 Weakley Co., Tenn.

   William R. Bryant, 31, and Sarah, 25, are living with children Josephus, 7; Lewis, 5; and Emily, 3, in Maury Co., Tenn., in 1850.[63] In 1860 William Bryant, 41, is living with James, 17; Louis, 14; Emily, 12; Mary, 10; Ellen, 7; Hiram, 4; and Frances, 8/12, in Madison Co., Tenn.[64] W. R. Bryant is on the Weakley Co., Tenn., tax list for 1869.[65]

   In 1870 William R. "Briant" is listed with Frances, 39, b. Miss.; Mary, 20; Ellen, 16; Hiram 14;[66] Fanny 9; Sally, 7; Virginia 5; William, 3;

---

[60] Green, Virginia Pearson. As I Have Been Told. Updated April 1998. http://homepages.rootsweb.ancestry.com/~aihbt/profiles/amis.html. 29 November 2011.

[61] Maury Co., Tenn., Will Book A2:292. There was no certificate of probate; the date range is from the items above and below it on the page. He left all of his property to his wife, Elizabeth Bryant, except for 4 shillings to son John F. Bryant and daughter Mary Fuller, wife of Samuel Fuller. The remainder of his children, not named, were apparently underage. John is not included in the Bible record, and Mary could be a daughter from his first marriage.

[62] The name comes from J. B. Hitt. http://wc.rootsweb.ancestry.com, (db. jbh.)

[63] 1850 Census Maury Co., Tenn., CD 4, p. 320B, #1088.

[64] 1860 Census Madison Co., Tenn., CD 11, p. 154, #1447/1478.

[65] http://www.rootsweb.ancestry.com/~tnweakle/1869taxlistB.htm, Accessed 2 March 2014. Further research shows he was in District 8, http://www.rootsweb.ancestry.com/~tnweakle/1869taxlist_8.htm, which includes the town of Sharon.

[66] In 1880, Hiram is by himself in Palestine, Obion Co,. Tenn., ED 111, p. 144D, #94/97. He is working on the farm of Eugene A. Lawson and wife Mary E. In 1900 he is back in Weakley County, CD 8, ED 121, p. 14B,

and Lucas, 7/12 (January); along with Joseph "Briant," 27, TN, and Florence, 3.[67]

In 1880 Josephus S. Bryant, 36, wife Mary C., 35, and children Nannie L, 5; William V., 3; and Lucius F., 6/12; also having living with them his step brothers and sisters Sarah B. Bryant, 17, William S. Bryant, 12, and Lucius J. Bryant, 10.[68]

2. ALBERT[6] BRYANT, b. 22 October 1820 Granville Co., N. C.; d. 3 October 1845 Maury Co., Tenn.[69]

3. HARRIET D.[6] BRYANT, b. 25 July 1823 Granville Co., N. C.; d. 5 December 1902 Jackson, Madison Co., Tenn.;[70] m. ARCHELOUS M. WHITE 12 August 1841 Maury Co., Tenn.;[71] b. 2 January 1815 Virginia; d. 13 May 1879 Madison Co., Tenn.[72]

4. LEWIS AMIS[6] BRYANT, b. 27 March 1822; d. 19 September 1845 Maury Co., Tenn.[73]

5. LUCY H.[6] BRYANT, b. 26 February 1825; d. 16 November 1845 Maury Co., Tenn.[74]

#301, with his wife of 8 years, Roxey A., 28, and three children. He was b. June 1857, she was b. Dec. 1871. In 1910, they are in Justice Precinct 2, Red River Co., Texas, ED 120, p. 8A, #66. In 1920, Hiram, 62, is with wife Della R., 48, and son Hiram L., b. 1911 Texas, are in Bentley, Atoka Co., Okla., ED 1, p. 2A, #28/29. Hiram Lucius Bryant's birth certificate (#37623, accessed on Ancestry.com 2 March 2014) in Cuthand, Red River Co., Texas, shows he was born 7 October 1910 to Hiram Bryant and Roxie Adella Wilson. However, this was based on an affidavit filed 10 October 1975 by his sister, Georgia B. Whitten.

[67] 1870 Census Weakley Co,. Tenn., CD 8, p. 139, #135. http://www.rootsweb.ancestry.com/~tnweakle/1870_page139.htm. This district is NOT included in the census on Ancestry.com.

[68] 1880 Census Weakley Co., Tenn., Sharon Station, ED 171, p. 253B, #337.

[69] Friendship Baptist Church Cemetery, Culleoka, Tenn. http://www.findagrave.com, #32238818.

[70] Hollywood Cemetery, Jackson, Tenn. http://www.findagrave.com, #92219554.

[71] Tennessee State Marriages, 1780-2002. Accessed 2 March 2014 at Ancestry.com.

[72] Hollywood Cemetery, Jackson, Tenn. http://www.findagrave.com, #92219362.

[73] Friendship Baptist Church Cemetery, Culleoka, Tenn. http://www.findagrave.com, #32238931.

[74] Friendship Baptist Church Cemetery, Culleoka, Tenn. http://www.findagrave.com, #32238947.

6. ELLEN G.[6] BRYANT, b. 1 November 1826; d. 8 August 1845 Maury Co., Tenn.[75]

7. MARTHA[6] BRYANT, b. 14 October 1828; d. 16 September 1863 Maury Co., Tenn.;[76] m. SAMUEL JEFFERSON FITZPATRICK 10 February 1849 Maury Co., Tenn., son of JOHN FITZPATRICK and LUCY FREEMAN; 1818 Maury Co., Tenn.; d. 22 July 1893 Maury Co., Tenn.;[77] m. (2) SARAH VIRGINIA AKIN 1 June 1873 Giles Co., Tenn.; b. 31 December 1844 Virginia; d. 17 July 1930 Giles Co., Tenn.[78]

8. ELIZABETH[6] BRYANT, m. JOSEPH A. GREEN 11 December 1850 Maury Co., Tenn.

9. JAMES D.[6] BRYANT, b. about 1835 Maury Co., Tenn.

10. LUCIUS RHODES[6] BRYANT, b. August 1837 Maury Co., Tenn.; d. 12 July 1908 Hopkins Co., Texas; m. (1) MARTHA E. BRANCH 16 November 1865 Maury Co., Tenn.; d. before 1880 Maury Co., Tenn.; m. (2) FRANCES CORDELIA (GARRETT) RENFRO 9 February 1881 Marshall Co., Tenn.;[79] dau. of THOMAS GARRETT and MARY BRANCH; b. 16 August 1852 Maury Co., Tenn.; d. 5 November 1931 Culleoka, Maury Co., Tenn.[80]

Lucius R. Bryant enlisted as a private in Company F, 48th Tenn. Inf.[81] On 10 March 1923, Mrs. Frances Cordelia Bryant made application

---

[75] Friendship Baptist Church Cemetery, Culleoka, Tenn. http://www.findagrave.com, #32238862.

[76] Friendship Baptist Church Cemetery, Culleoka, Tenn. http://www.findagrave.com, #32284458.

[77] http://www.findagrave.com., #114049741. He was probably not buried in this cemetery, although his second wife was.

[78] Arlington Cemetery, Mt. Pleasant, Maury Co., Tenn. http://www.findagrave.com, #71066184.

[79] Tennessee State Marriages, 1780-2002, shows L. R. Bryant married Mrs. F. C. Renfro 9 February 1881 in Marshall Co., Tenn. In the 1900 census they claimed to have been married in 1881.

[80] Mother's surname and dates of birth and death are from Tennessee Deaths and Burials Index, 1874-1955. Accessed 2 March 2014 at Ancestry.com. She is buried at Friendship Baptist Church Cemetery, Culleoka, Tenn. http://www.findagrave.com, #32238888.

[81] National Park Service, U. S. Civil War Soldiers, 1861-1865. Accessed 2 March 2014 at Ancestry.com.

for a pension based on her husband's service in Hopkins Co., Texas. She stated that she married Lucius Rhodes Bryant 15 February 1882 in Maury Co., Tenn., and that they moved to Sulphur Springs 23 years ago, or in 1900, where he died 12 July 1908.[82]

In 1880 he is a widower living with children Lillie M., 12; William, 9; Lucius, 8; and Ezra, 5.[83] He was listed in Maury Co., Tenn., in 1900.[84]

Delia Garrett was listed with her parents in 1870,[85] and with her first husband, James H. Renfro in 1880.[86]

11. THOMAS H.[6] BRYANT, b. August 1839 Maury Co., Tenn.;[87] d. 1926 Maury Co., Tenn.;[88] m. EMILY J. HOWARD 30 January 1866 Maury Co., Tenn.;[89] b. February 1847 Tenn.

vii. MARY[5] AMIS, b. 1800 Granville Co., N. C.; d. 15 September 1875 Granville Co., N. C.;[90] m. SAMUEL MONTAGUE 25 April 1818 Granville Co., N. C.; b. 27 February 1791 Granville Co., N. C.; d. 8 July 1873 Granville Co., N. C.[91]

---

[82] Texas State Library and Archives Commission; Austin, Texas; Confederate Pension Applications, 1899-1975. Accessed 2 March 2014 at Ancestry.com.

[83] 1880 Census Maury Co., Tenn., Dist. 6, ED 159, p. 174D, #172/177. He was born in Tenn., and both parents were b. NC. His son, Lucius, may be the man who married Miss. Sallie F. Howlett 15 December 1904 Maury Co., Tenn.

[84] 1900 Census Maury Co., Tenn., CD 6, ED 70, p. 5A, #89. Both of his parents were said to have been born in Virginia. Children include Malam, b. August 1882; Lizzie M., b. January 1885; and Naomi H., b. May 1896. He is living next door to Thomas H. Bryant.

[85] 1870 Census Marshall Co., Tenn., CD 13, p. 161B, #39/41.

[86] 1880 Census Marshall Co., Tenn., CD 13, ED 144, p. 446A, #43/55. They are living with her parents.

[87] 1900 Census Maury Co., Tenn., CD 6, ED 70, p. 5B, #90. They have children, Frank S., b. June 1876; Bessie, b. February 1885.

[88] Friendship Baptist Church Cemetery, Culleoka, Tenn. http://www.findagrave.com, #32238967.

[89] She may be Emma Bryant, b. 1847, d. 1901 Maury Co., Tenn. Friendship Baptist Church Cemetery, Culleoka, Tenn. http://www.findagrave.com, #32238877.

[90] Perry Burial Ground, Creedmoor, Granville Co., N. C. http://www.findagrave.com, #90239981.

[91] Perry Burial Ground, Creedmoor, Granville Co., N. C. http://www.findagrave.com, #90239865.

Samuel Montague and Mary (Amis) Montague are in Granville Co., N. C., in 1850.[92]

Children of MARY AMIS and SAMUEL MONTAGUE:

1. ALFRED KNIGHT[6] MONTAGUE, b. 1826 Granville Co., N. C.; d. 1887 Granville Co., N. C.;[93] m. SARAH ANDREWS 10 May 1855 Granville Co., N. C.;[94] b. 4 December 1837; d. 8 January 1913 Granville Co., N. C.[95]
2. MARY[6] MONTAGUE, b. 1830.
3. ARCHIBALD PITTARD[6] MONTAGUE, b. 1 February 1831 Granville Co., N. C.; d. 28 April 1881 Ohio Co., Ky.;[96] m. NANCY ELLEN LEACH dau. of JOSEPH LEACH and ALTHA S. MILLER; b. 7 December 1832 Ohio Co., Ky.; d. 15 February 1896 Caldwell Co., Ky.[97]
4. EDWIN[6] MONTAGUE, b. 1834.
5. THOMAS[6] MONTAGUE, b. 1836.
6. ELLEN[6] MONTAGUE, b. 24 March 1840 Granville Co., N. C.;[98] d. 29 January 1903 Granville Co., N. C.; m. JOSEPH FREEMAN USRY 23 January 1866 Granville Co., N. C.;[99] b. 22 December 1838; d. 3 December 1918 Granville Co., N. C.[100]

---

[92] 1850 Census Granville Co., N. C., Ledge of Rock District, p. 313, [157A] #118/118
[93] Montague Family Cemetery, Oxford, N. C. http://www.findagrave.com, #90645179.
[94] North Carolina Marriage Collection, 1741-2004. Located 2 March 2014 at Ancestry.com.
[95] Montague Family Cemetery, Oxford, N. C. http://www.findagrave.com, #90645570.
[96] East Providence Cemetery, Prentiss, Ky. http://www.findagrave.com, #67824167.
[97] East Providence Cemetery, Prentiss, Ky. http://www.findagrave.com, #67824377.
[98] Corinth Baptist Church Cemetery, Oxford, N. C. http://www.findagrave.com, #21275330.
[99] North Carolina Marriage Collection, 1741-2004. Located 2 March 2014 at Ancestry.com.
[100] Corinth Baptist Church Cemetery, Oxford, N. C. http://www.findagrave.com, #21274663.

7. ADOLPHUS[6] MONTAGUE, b. August 1842 Granville Co., N. C.;[101]; d. after 1910 Granville Co., N. C.; m. EMILY USRY 30 January 1868 Granville Co., N. C., dau. of WILLIAM USRY and JANE FOWLES; b. 13 September 1848 Granville Co., N. C.; d. 29 November 1927 Granville Co., N. C.[102]

8. PROTHEUS GRAVES[6] MONTAGUE, b. 13 October 1843 Granville Co., N. C.; d. 8 April 1935 Raleigh, Wake Co., N. C.; [103] m. (1) SARAH F.; b. 16 March 1848; d. 6 April 1880 Person Co., N. C.;[104] m. (2) ELIZABETH F. LINK; b. 21 June 1848; d. 17 March 1935 Person Co., N. C.[105]

9. SARAH JUDITH[6] MONTAGUE, b. 22 June 1848 Granville Co., N. C.; d. 11 December 1927 Portsmouth, Va.;[106] m. JEPHTHA FULLER LEIGHTON 19 November 1874 Norfolk, Virginia;[107] b. 1854; d. 17 July 1926 Portsmouth, Va.[108]

viii. NANCY[5] AMIS, b. 11 September 1801 Granville Co. N. C.; d. 6 September 1868 Maury Co., Tenn.; m. ROBERTSON BRYANT 19 February 1818 Granville Co., N. C.; b. 11 February 1795

[101] 1900 Census Granville Co., N. C., Fishing Creek, ED 56, p. 12B, #213/221. She was buried at home. Accessed 2 March 2014 at Ancestry.com.

[102] N. C. Death Certificate 395492, Granville Co., N. C., Fishing Creek,

[103] N. C. Death Certificate District 92, 230. Accessed 2 March 2014 at Ancestry.com. He was living in a VA home, but was from Granville Co., N. C. The names given for his parents do not match, but it does not appear that the informant was a close relative. Buried Mill Creek Baptist Church Cemetery, Person Co., N. C. http://www.findagrave.com, #97727567.

[104] Mill Creek Baptist Church Cemetery, Person Co., N. C. http://www.findagrave.com, #97727893.

[105] Mill Creek Baptist Church Cemetery, Person Co., N. C. http://www.findagrave.com, #52317172.

[106] Oak Grove Cemetery, Portsmouth, Va. http://www.findagrave.com, #74966398.

[107] Ancestry.com. No reference is given and I have not found the marriage listed in Virginia, Select Marriages, 1785-1940.

[108] Oak Grove Cemetery, Portsmouth, Va. http://www.findagrave.com, #74966376.

Granville Co., N. C.; d. 2 February 1872 Maury Co., Tenn.[109]

Robertson Bryant died testate.[110]

I Robertson Bryant of the County of Maury and State of Tennessee do make and publish this my last will and testament, hereby revoking and making void all other wills by me at any time made.

Item 1st: I direct that my funeral expenses and all my just debts be paid as soon after my death as possible, out of any moneys that I may die seized and possessed of or may first come into the hands of my executors.

Item 2: I will that after my death my daughter, Francis D. Bryant, and my daughter, Missniah E. Bryant and Rowland E. Bryant, my son, shall each have one well furnished featherbed and clacking and bedstead.

Item 3: I next will that after my death my executor shall sell at public sale on 12 months credit all my perishable and personal property, stock, and crop and farming utensils, household and kitchen furnishings, all sums under five dollars to be cash, the purchaser giving bond and good security the proceeds of which is to be equally divided between my daughter, Francis D. Bryant and my son Wm H. Bryant and Isaiah B. Bryant, Louisiana Bee Kelley and Livinia L. Moore, Rowland E. Bryant and Misiniah E. Bryant, and my Grandson, Robertson B. Nolen.

Item 4: I have given to my son Robert D. Bryant a liberal education and the use of a negro boy Rowland which I value to him at five hundred dollars of my estate already received by him and also I have given to my son Archibald S. Bryant

[109] Nancy is not a legatee of William Amis, but he is the only person likely to have a daughter of this age. Data are from Robertson Bryant's Bible, located online 23 November 2011 at http://www.tngenweb.org/maury/bible/rbryant.html. Robertson Bryant is buried in the Bryant Family Cemetery, Maury Co., Tenn. http://www.findagrave.com, #33160542.

[110] Maury Co., Tenn., Will Book F:419, 6 February 1872]. Transcription by Lucy Bryant Duanaway Zeier. Located 10 November 2011 at http://tngenweb.org/maury/wills/rbryant.html.

the advantages of a good education and the use of a negro boy Albert, which I value to him at four hundred dollars already received by him as a part of my estate, and I have given to my daughter, Martha E. Jackson, the advantages of a good education and the use of a negro girl Mariah which I value to her at three hundred and fifty dollars as a part of my estate already received by her; there is no interest to be claimed off the three legatees last named for the amt they have already received until the final settlement of my estates.

Item 5: I will that when my youngest child, Misniah E. Bryant, shall arrive at the age of twenty-one yrs that all my land shall be equally divided between all my children. But if said land cannot be satisfactorily divided I will that my executor shall sell it to the highest bidder after giving thirty days notice in the public news paper of the County and at other places in the neighborhood and I authorize my Executor to divide the land into lots if it is considered by him to be to the advantage of the legatees and the items of the sale be determined by my Executor and I hereby authorize and empower him to make the title to the land if sold by him and the proceeds to be so divided among all my children viz: Robert D. and Archibald S. Bryant's children Raph and Archibald one share Francis D. Bryant and Mary J. Nolen's son, Robertson B. Nolen, one share Wm H. Bryant, and Martha E. Jackson, Isaiah B. Bryant and Louisiana B. _eelley, Lavinia Lemon Moore and Rowland E. Bryant and Misniah E. Bryant that they be made equal in the final distribution of my estate, taking into consideration the advancements I have already made.

Item 6: I will the Stock I own in the Nashville and Decatur Railroad is equally divided among all my children as above named and Grand children as above named, viz: Archibald S. Bryant's two sons to receive one share and Robinson B. Nolen to receive one share.

Item 7: I will that if any dissatisfaction should arise among my legatees about my will and the distributions I have made of my estate that my Executor shall call in 3 disinterested parties and lay the difficulty before them and there decision shall be a final settlement of the matter. But if any legatees should carry it to court of law or equity, I hereby disinherit them and will that they shall receive no part of my estate.

Item 8: I hereby nominate and appoint Henry Harris Executor of this my last will and testament, this in witness where of and whereby set my pen this 19th day of February 1867.

S/   Robertson Bryant, Esq.

Witnesses: W.A. Henderson
Williamson Denton

Children of NANCY AMIS and ROB. BRYANT:[111]

1. ROBERT D.[6] BRYANT, b. 28 January 1819 Granville Co., N. C.; d. 28 April 1871 Bells, Haywood Co., Tenn.; m. MARTHA C. JACKSON 20 December 1849 Maury Co., Tenn.

2. MARY JUDITH[6] BRYANT, b. 10 October 1820 Granville Co., N. C.; d. 29 April 1844 Williamson Co., Tenn.; m. MILTON BERRY NOLEN 27 August 1843 Maury Co., Tenn.; m. (2) LOUISE WHITE 21 November 1855 Davidson Co., Tenn.[112]

3. FRANCES DAILY[6] BRYANT, b. 10 August 1822 Granville Co., N. C.; d. 27 April 1906 Bedford Co., Tenn.[113]

4. ARCHIBALD S.[6] BRYANT, b. 20 February 1824 Granville Co., N. C.; d. 8 October 1862

---

[111] Robertson Bryant's Bible Record was annotated by Lucy Bryant Dunaway Zeier and posted at http://www.findagrave.com., #33160542.

[112] Tennessee State Marriages 1780-2002. Located 1 March 2014 at Ancestry.com.

[113] Pleasant Mount C. P. Church Cemetery, Maury Co., Tenn. http://www.findagrave.com, #9012408.

Perryville, Ky.; m. JANE WATTS GRESHAM 11 January 1855 Marshall Co., Tenn.[114]

5. ANN ROBERTSON[6] BRYANT, b. 9 February 1826 Granville Co., N. C.; d. 26 September 1860 Maury Co., Tenn.[115]

6. MARTHA ELIZABETH[6] BRYANT, b. 13 April 1828 Maury Co., Tenn.; d. 31 March 1925 Austin, Travis Co., Texas; m. JOSEPH THOMAS JACKSON 10 February 1847 Maury Co., Tenn.

7. WILLIAM H.[6] BRYANT, b. 20 May 1830 Maury Co., Tenn.; d. March 1880; m. ASENATH MORRISON MCCONNELL 12 November 1857 Marshall Co., Tenn.,[116] dau. of JEREMIAH MCCONNELL and ANNABELL MARTIN; b. 28 September 1836 Marshall Co., Tenn.; d. 11 January 1908 Maury Co., Tenn.[117]

8. MINERVA EMALINE[6] BRYANT, b. 3 July 1832 Maury Co., Tenn.; d. 20 March 1833 Maury Co., Tenn.

9. ISAIAH BURNEY[6] BRYANT, b. 5 March 1834 Maury Co., Tenn.; d. 10 July 1917 Maury Co., Tenn.;[118] m. EMILY LEWIS FREY 20 September 1866 Maury Co., Tenn.; b. 27 February 1840; d. 26 May 1928 Maury Co., Tenn.[119]

10. LOUISIANA BEE[6] BRYANT, b. 10 July 1836 Maury Co., Tenn.; d. 21 May 1919 Maury Co., Tenn.;[120] m. WILLIAM SAMUEL LEE NEELLEY 15 November 1860 Maury Co.,

---

[114] Tennessee State Marriages 1780-2002. Located 1 March 2014 at Ancestry.com.

[115] Bryant Family Cemetery, Maury Co., Tenn. http://www.findagrave.com, #33160558.

[116] Tennessee State Marriages 1780-2002. Located 1 March 2014 at Ancestry.com.

[117] Pleasant Mount C. P. Church Cemetery, Maury Co., Tenn. http://www.findagrave.com, #9012414.

[118] McCains Cemetery, Maury Co., Tenn. http://www.findagrave.com, #11150596.

[119] McCains Cemetery, Maury Co., Tenn. http://www.findagrave.com, #52733581.

[120] McCains Cemetery, Maury Co., Tenn. http://www.findagrave.com, #14893821. Her death record confirms her parentage. [Tennessee, Deaths and Burials Index, 1874-1955. Located 1 March 2014 at Ancestry.com.]

Tenn.,[121] son of WILLIAM LEE NEELEY and NETTIE SMITH; b. 21 November 1836; d. 15 June 1903 Maury Co., Tenn.[122]

11. JAMES ALONZO[6] BRYANT, b. 21 September 1839 Maury Co., Tenn.; d. 13 September 1840 Maury Co., Tenn.

12. LAVINIA LEMON[6] BRYANT, b. 25 February 1842 Maury Co., Tenn.; d. 16 August 1931 Maury Co., Tenn.;[123] m. ROBERT HAWKINS MOORE 17 April 1866 Maury Co., Tenn.;[124] b. 3 January 1844; d. 3 March 1918 Maury Co., Tenn.[125]

13. THEOPHILUS COMPTON[6] BRYANT, b. 26 November 1844 Maury Co., Tenn.; d. 26 July 1864 Fort Delaware, Delaware.

14. ROWLAND EDWARD[6] BRYANT, b. 12 July 1847 Maury Co., Tenn.; d. 20 August 1894 White Co., Ark.; m. FRANCINA ALMETA SMITH 25 February 1873 Maury Co., Tenn.

15. MISSNIAH EUGENIA[6] BRYANT, b. 24 July 1850 Maury Co., Tenn.; d. 3 July 1919 Maury Co., Tenn.; m. WILLIAM SPARK CASKEY 22 December 1870 Maury Co., Tenn.,[126] son of ROBERT CASKEY and JANE HILL; b. 19 July 1833 Maury Co., Tenn.; d. 10 July 1897 Maury Co., Tenn.[127]

ix. HARRIET[5] AMIS, d. before 1837 Granville Co., N. C.;[128] m. JOHN FARRINGTON BRYANT 23 December 1824 Granville Co., N. C; m. (2)

---

[121] Tennessee State Marriages 1780-2002. Located 1 March 2014 at Ancestry.com.

[122] McCains Cemetery, Maury Co., Tenn. http://www.findagrave.com, #14893798.

[123] Pleasant Mount C. P. Church Cemetery, Maury Co., Tenn. http://www.findagrave.com, #13409418.

[124] Tennessee State Marriages 1780-2002. Located 1 March 2014 at Ancestry.com.

[125] Pleasant Mount C. P. Church Cemetery, Maury Co., Tenn. http://www.findagrave.com, #8973033.

[126] Tennessee State Marriages 1780-2002. Located 1 March 2014 at Ancestry.com.

[127] Pleasant Mount C. P. Church Cemetery, Maury Co., Tenn. http://www.findagrave.com, #23741107.

[128] Deceased when her father wrote his will, but named her children.

MARTHA KITTRELL 1 January 1837 Granville
Co., N. C.;[129] b. about 1817 N. C.

John F. Bryant 44, born NC, is also in Maury
Co., Tenn., in 1850. Listed second is Martha, 24,
but I think she should have been listed as 34.[130]

Martha J. Bryant, 43, b. NC, is head of
household with James, 20; Alexander H., 19,
Louis R., 19, Sarah F., 17, Martha G., 16,
Elizabeth, 12, Cordelia Z., 9, and Alfred R., 8.[131]
By dates, these are all her children.

The inventory of John F. Bryant was recorded
28 September 1852 in Maury Co., Tenn., and
totaled $396.70.[132]

Children of HARRIETT AMIS and JOHN BRYANT:[133]

1. WILEY T.[6] BRYANT, b. 1827 Granville Co., N.
   C.; m. ELIZABETH S. WALLACE 31 July 1851
   Maury Co., Tenn.; b. 1837 Maury Co., Tenn.
       He is living in Dallas Co., Mo., next door
   to "James A." Bryant in 1860, with wife Sarah,
   18, b. Tenn., and children William H., 4, and
   Virginia H., 1, both b. Mo.[134] I have not located
   them after this census.

2. WILLIAM D.[6] BRYANT, b. 1830 Granville Co.,
   N. C.; d. 15 May 1864 Resaca, Ga.;[135] m.
   HANNAH M. SCOTT 6 July 1853 Maury Co.,
   Tenn.; b. about 1838 Tennessee; d. 23 June
   1895.[136]
       In the 1860 Census William D. Bryant,
   28, Hannah, 22, have Harriet J., 6, Laura E., 4,
   Luella E., 3, and Juda J., 6/12, living with them

---

[129] Holcomb, p.42. Accessed 3 March 2014 at Ancestry.com.

[130] 1850 Census Maury Co., Tenn., CD 24, p. 283B, #562.

[131] 1860 Census Maury Co., Tenn., CD 24, p. 513, #820.

[132] Maury Co., Tenn., Will Book 4:599.

[133] Children probably born to Martha, b. NC, are James, 12;
Alexander, 9; Louis 7; Sarah, 6; born Tenn., Martha, 5; Elizabeth, 3, and
Cordelia, 1.

[134] 1860 Census Dallas Co., Mo., Jackson, p. 223, #332/71.

[135] NPS. U. S. Civil War Soldiers, 1861-1865. Note attached by J.
Sager. Accessed 3 March 2014 at Ancestry.com.

[136] Rock Springs Cemetery, Maury Co., Tenn.
http://www.findagrave.com, #72438244.

in Maury Co., Tenn.[137] They are living next to Martha J. Bryant.

3. JUDITH W.[6] BRYANT, b. 1833 Granville Co., N. C.; d. before 1900 Arkansas; m. (1) ROBERT S. WALLIS 7 August 1851 Maury Co., Tenn.; divorced about 1870 Dallas Co., Ark.; b. 8 May 1834 Maury Co., Tenn.; d. 6 January 1903 Rockdale, Milam Co., Texas.;[138] m. (2) SIMON J. RUSSELL 12 October 1870 Dallas Co., Ark.; b. September 1838 Tenn.; d. 28 July 1928 Little Rock, Pulaski Co., Ark.[139]

This is probably "Judia" Wallace, b. 1835 NC, living with R. S. Wallace, 26, TN, in Webster Co., Mo., in 1860.[140] He is listed as a physician.

Judith Wallace, 37, NC, is living with Frances Knight, 60 NC,[141] and probably her children, Bettie F., 18, and son "Lulen W.," 13, both born NC, in Dallas Co., Ark., in 1870.[142] Robert Wallis m. Bettie W. Wilcox 2 June 1870 in Dallas Co., Ark.[143] He was listed as a physician-minister. Judith Wallace married Simon J. Russell 12 October 1870 in Dallas Co., Ark. She was 38, he was 33.

In 1880, Lyman Russell 40, and Juda Russell, 46, b. NC, are in Owen, Dallas Co., living near her cousin, Mary (Bryant) Williams.[144] She has two sons from this second marriage: William S. 8, and Thomas A., 6.

---

[137] 1860 Census Maury Co., Tenn., CD 24, p. 513, #821.

[138] Odd Fellows Cemetery, Rockdale, Texas. http://www.findagrave.com, #49611992. His second wife, Elizabeth Wilcox Wallis, was born 31 August 1845 in Dallas Co., Ark., dau. of Robert J. Wilcox and Jane Davis. (She was living in the household of R. S. and Judith (Bryant) Wallace in the 1860 Census.) She died 10 April 1927 in Rockdale, Texas, and is buried next to her husband. (#52036621.)

[139] Little Rock National Cemetery, Ark. http://www.findagrave.com, #3142793.

[140] 1860 Census Webster Co., Mo., Marshfiled, p. 806, #718/714. They have James C., 5; Jane E., 3; and Robert D., 1/12, all b. Mo.

[141] I think this is Frances Amis Knight, husband of Alfred Knight, and so Judith's maternal aunt.

[142] 1870 Census Dallas Co., Ark., p. 431B, #21.

[143] Arkansas, County Marriages Index, 1837-1957. Accessed 3 March 2014 at Ancestry.com.

[144] 1880 Census Dallas Co., Ark., Owen, ED 70, p. 212D, #28

In the 1900 Census he was a widower.[145] Clearly Judith and Robert S. Wallis divorced about 1870 in Dallas Co., Ark.

4. JUNIUS A.[6] BRYANT, b. July 1834 Granville Co., N. C.; d. 10 December 1911 Greene Co., Mo.;[146] m. SARAH J. HARKNESS 1858, dau. of JOHN W. HARKNESS and PENELOPE CHAPMAN; b. 23 February 1842 Maury Co., Tenn.; d. 11 December 1911 Greene Co., Mo.[147]

He is listed as "James A.", 25, living in Jackson, Dallas Co., Mo., in 1860 with son Columbus.[148] Junius A. Bryant, 36, living with wife, Sarah J., and children in Greene Co., Missouri, in 1870.[149] The eldest child, Columbus, was born in Mo., in 1860. They are still there in 1880,[150] and in 1900, when he said they had been married 42 years.[151] I have not found a record of the marriage, but it was probably in Maury Co., Tenn.

x. FRANCES[5] AMIS, b. about 1811 Granville Co., N. C.; m. ALFRED KNIGHT 16 December 1829 Granville Co., N. C.; b. about 1807 Granville Co., N. C.; d. August 1870 Dallas Co., Ark.[152]

Alfred Knight, 43, and Frances, 39, are living in Granville Co., N. C., in 1850.[153] I have not found them in the 1860 Census, but she is in

---

[145] 1900 Census Clark Co., Ark., Manchester, ED 11, p. 1A, #6.

[146] Bass Chapel Cemetery, Greene Co., Mo. http://www.findagrave.com, #84465633. The date of birth is listed as 23 February 1842, and he was said to have served as a Sergeant in Co. I, 8th Wisconsin Inf., which does not seem to match for this man, and does not match the census data showing he was born in NC as were his parents.

[147] Bass Chapel Cemetery, Greene Co., Mo. http://www.findagrave.com, #84465639. Data quote from her death certificate.

[148] 1860 Census Dallas Co., Mo., Jackson, p. 223, #331/70

[149] 1870 Census Greene Co., Mo., Jackson, p. 189B, #53/54. Sarah was b. Tenn.

[150] 1880 Census Greene Co., Mo., Robberson, ED 33, p. 40D, #142.

[151] 1900 Census Greene Co., Mo., Jackson, ED 52, p. 1B, #22.

[152] 1870 Federal Census Mortality Index. Accessed 3 March 2014 at Ancestry.com.

[153] 1850 Census Granville Co., N. C., Tabs Creek, p. 80A, #30. Susanna A. Hester, 21, is living in the household.

Dallas Co., Ark., in 1870 living near her children.[154]

Children of FRANCES AMIS and ALFRED KNIGHT:

1. SUSAN[6] KNIGHT, b. 27 February 1831 Granville Co., N. C.; d. 12 March 1886 Dallas Co., Ark.;[155] m. GEORGE A. HARRISON 23 February 1857 Granville Co., N. C.;[156] b. 7 March 1833 Granville Co., N. C.; d. 30 July 1889 Dallas Co., Ark.[157]

> George Harrison, 27, and Susan B. Harrison, 29, are head of household in Dallas Co., Ark., in 1860 and have her brother and his wife and children living with them.[158] By 1870, they have had four daughters: Mary F., 7, Lucy W., 5, Susan C., 3, and Bettie G., 2.[159] They are living next door to Frances Knight.

2. LEWIS[6] KNIGHT, b. 1835 Granville Co., N. C.; m. SALLIE M. DUKE 7 February 1855 Granville Co., N. C.;[160]

> Louis B. Knight, 26, Sallie M. Knight, 21, "Lewellin" 4, and Francis, 2, are living with his sister in Dallas Co., Ark., in 1860.[161] Llewellyn may be the Lulen Knight living with his grandmother in 1870, and the Bettie F., 18, may be Frances. I have not found either Lewis or Sallie in 1870 or 1880, which is consistent with this notion that their children are living with his mother.

3. WOODSON[6] KNIGHT, b. 1837; d. before 1870 Dallas Co., Ark.; m. MARY M. WILLIAMS 16

---

[154] 1870 Census Dallas Co., Ark., p. 431B, #21.

[155] Sardis Cemetery, Pine Grove, Ark. http://www.findagrave.com, #6678756.

[156] Holcomb, p. 148. Ceremony performed by L. K. Willie, M. G. Accessed 3 March 2014 at Ancestry.com.

[157] Sardis Cemetery, Pine Grove, Ark. http://www.findagrave.com, #6678745. His father may be Kenelm Harrison (1806-1875) #6662939.

[158] 1860 Census Dallas Co., Ark., Owen, p. 996, #320.

[159] 1870 Census Dallas Co., Ark., Owen, p. 431A, #20.

[160] Holcomb, p. 198. Ceremony performed by L. K. Willie, M. G. Accessed 3 March 2014 at Ancestry.com.

[161] 1860 Census Dallas Co., Ark., Owens, p. 996, #320. All were listed as born in N. C., suggesting a move about 1858.

August 1865 Dallas Co., Ark.;[162] b. 1840
Alabama.

Mary Knight, 28, b. Alabama, with her
son, Woodson, 3, Ark., is living with her mother
Mary B. Williams in a row with her extended
family in 1870.[163]

4. JUDITH C.[6] KNIGHT, b. 1842 Granville Co., N.
C.; m. PATRICK H. WILLIAMS 24 July 1869
Dallas Co., Ark.;[164] b. 1827 Tenn.

Patrick and Judith Williams are living
next to his mother in Dallas Co., Ark., in 1870.[165]
In 1880 they are still in Dallas County, but not
living in a row with his family.[166] In 1900 the
younger children are all living together in Dallas
County, and I cannot find either Judith or
Patrick suggesting they died before that date.[167]

5. MARY[6] H. KNIGHT, b. September 1843
Granville Co., N. C.; d. 1926 Dallas Co.,
Ark.;[168] m. CHRISTOPHER C. WILLIAMS 16
October 1861 Dallas Co., Ark.;[169] b. about
1837 Tenn.;[170] d. 17 April 1898 Dallas Co.,
Ark.[171]

They are in Owen, Dallas Co., Ark., in
1870,[172] 1880,[173] and she is living there as a
widow in 1900,[174] 1910[175] and 1920.[176]

---

[162] Arkansas, County Marriages Index, 1838-1957. Accessed 3 March
2014 at Ancestry.com.

[163] 1870 Census Dallas Co., Ark., Owen, p. 431A, #19.

[164] Arkansas, County Marriages Index, 1838-1957. Accessed 3 March
2014 at Ancestry.com. He was listed as "P. H." In the 1880 Census he is
Patrick Williams. [Dallas Co., Ark., Owen, ED 70, p. 211A, #6.

[165] 1870 Census Dallas Co., Ark., Owen, p. 431A, #18.

[166] 1880 Census Dallas Co., Ark., Owen, ED 70, p. 211A, #6

[167] 1900 Census Dallas Co., Ark., ED 19, p. 12A, #203/206

[168] Williams Cemetery, Dallas Co., Ark. http://www.findagrave.com,
#104343977.

[169] Arkansas, County Marriages Index, 1838-1957. Accessed 3 March
2014 at Ancestry.com.

[170] 1850 Census Carroll Co., Tenn., CD 15, p. 132A, #1751. His
parents are James R. Williams, and Susan Williams.

[171] Arkansas, Confederate Veterans Pension Records, 1891-1935.
Accessed 3 March 2014 at Ancestry.com. She applied for his pension in
1901. Also Williams Cemetery, Dallas Co., Ark.
http://www.findagrave.com, #104343920.

[172] 1870 Census Dallas Co., Ark., Owen, p. 433A, #43/42. This time
he was said to have been born in Alabama.

[173] 1880 Census Dallas Co., Ark., Owen, ED 70, p. 212D, #32.

[174] 1900 Census Dallas Co., Ark., Nix, ED 18, p. 3A, #38/39.

xi. MARTHA[5] AMIS, b. about 1808 Granville Co., N. C.; m. THOMAS CHEATHAM 29 October 1830 Granville Co., N. C.; b. about 1809 Granville Co., N. C.

Thomas and Martha Cheatham are living in Maury Co., Tenn., in 1840,[177] 1850,[178] 1860,[179] 1870,[180] and 1880.[181]

Children of MARTHA and THOMAS CHEATHAM:

1. FLETCHER H.[6] CHEATHAM, b. 31 August 1833 Maury Co., Tenn.; d. 9 July 1909 Culleoka, Maury Co., Tenn.;[182] m. (1) MARTHA ANN MARTIN 1 May 1856 Maury Co., Tenn.; b. about 1834 Maury Co., Tenn.; d. about 1874 Maury Co., Tenn.; m. (2) LOUIZA C. HICKS 15 April 1875 Giles Co., Tenn.; b. 26 September 1842 Giles Co., Tenn.; d. 22 July 1920 Giles Co., Tenn.[183]

2. MARY E.[6] CHEATHAM , b. 2 September 1835[184] Maury Co., Tenn.; d. 18 May 1910 Waco, McLennan Co., Texas;[185] m. LEWIS ROBERTSON CHEATHAM 12 November 1850 Maury Co., Tenn.; b. 1828 Maury Co.,

---

[175] 1910 Census Dallas Co., Ark., Nix., ED 27, p. 3A, #40.

[176] 1920 Census Dallas Co., Ark., Nix, ED 32, p. 20A, #393/394.

[177] 1840 Census Maury Co., Tenn., p. 300. He has three sons: one 15-19; one 5-9; one under five, and three daughters under five. The list from 1850 apparently does not include several older children.

[178] 1850 Census Maury Co., Tenn., CD 6, p. 323A, #1124.

[179] 1860 Census Maury Co., Tenn., CD 6, p. 342, #603. Judith is gone and William has a wife, Nancy P., 20.

[180] 1870 Census Maury Co., Tenn., CD 6, p. 287A, #303. Only Martha H., and James are still at home.

[181] 1880 Census Maury Co., Tenn., CD 6, ED 159, p. 167A, #48/50.

[182] Miller Cemetery, Giles Co., Tenn. http://www.findagrave.com. #19109532.

[183] Miller Cemetery, Giles Co., Tenn. http://www.findagrave.com. #30663509.

[184] So stated in her application for a pension 6 April 1907 based on his service for three years in Co. E, 48th Tenn. Infantry. Texas Confederate Pension Application #12996. Accessed 3 March 2014 at Ancestry.com.

[185] Oakwood Cemetery, Waco, Texas. http://www.findagrave.com. #100247693.

Tenn.;[186] d. 15 March 1907 Waco, McLennan Co., Texas.[187]

3. WILLIAM[6] CHEATHAM, b. 1838 Maury Co., Tenn.

4. JUDITH C.[6] CHEATHAM, b. 25 November 1838 Maury Co., Tenn.; d. 23 September 1882 Limestone Co., Texas;[188] m. JAMES E. BRYANT 15 October 1856 Maury Co., Tenn.; b. 28 September 1834 Maury Co., Tenn.; d. 10 May 1885 Limestone Co., Texas.[189]

5. NANCY P.[6] CHEATHAM, b. 1842 Maury Co., Tenn.; m. J. F. EXUM 16 June 1863 Maury Co., Tenn.

6. AMANDA[6] CHEATHAM, b. 1843 Maury Co., Tenn.

7. SARAH A.[6] CHEATHAM, b. 1844 Maury Co., Tenn.

8. MARTHA H.[6] CHEATHAM., b. 1 August 1845 Maury Co., Tenn.; d. 12 June 1889 Hill Co., Texas;[190] m. THOMAS P. SMITH 28 September 1875 Maury Co., Tenn.;[191] b. 3 July 1835 Tenn.; d. 23 January 1914 Hill Co., Texas.[192]

    They are in Giles Co., Tenn., in 1870,[193] and Hill Co., Texas, in 1880.[194]

9. JAMES[6] CHEATHAM, b. 1848 Maury Co., Tenn.

---

[186] Boone White said he was the son of John Cheatham and Elizabeth Amis, so was probably born in Williamson Co., Tenn. I have not seen any proof of that statement, though.

[187] Oakwood Cemetery, Waco, Texas. http://www.findagrave.com. #8254545.

[188] Mt. Antioch Cemetery, Prairie Hill, Texas. http://www.findagrave.com, #41961168.

[189] Mt. Antioch Cemetery, Prairie Hill, Texas. http://www.findagrave.com, #41961155.

[190] Fairview Cemetery, Hubbard, Hill Co., Texas. http://www.findagrave.com. #11276592.

[191] Tennessee State Marriages 1780-2002. Accessed 3 March 2014 at Ancestry.com.

[192] Fairview Cemetery, Hubbard, Hill Co., Texas. http://www.findagrave.com. #11276582.

[193] 1870 Census Giles Co., Tenn., CD 11, p. 224B, #88.

[194] 1880 Census Hill Co., Texas, Precinct 5, ED 75, p. 385A, #205.

x. MISSNIAH[5] AMIS, b. 11 July 1811 Granville Co., N. C.; d. 22 September 1882 Maury Co., Tenn.[195]

xiii. LUCY[5] AMIS, b. 4 April 1814 Granville Co., N. C.; d. 20 June 1889 Vance Co., N. C.; m. THOMAS HILL REAVIS 20 October 1838 Granville Co., N. C.; b. 31 March 1808 Granville Co., N. C.; d. 20 September 1869 Granville Co., N. C.[196]

Mrs. Lucy D. Reavis, relict of Thomas Reavis deceased, died at her home near Henderson, N.C., June 20th 1889, aged 75 years, 2 months and 10 days. The deceased was born in Granville county, N.C.; and was a daughter of William and Judith Amis. She embraced religion in her girlhood and at once joined the M.E. Church, in which she lived a pious, useful member until her earthly pilgrimage ended. She was a devoted Christian, and loved the church of her choice very much, but did not fail to love all Christians. We have often seen her cup of Christian joy full and overflowing, and heard shout the praises of God. Her home was the Christian's home, and there many ministers of the gospel of Christ found a welcome reception and hospitable entertainment. In extolling her many virtues much could be said, but let it suffice to say that her life was but a living epistle of good works, to be read and admired by all who knew her. Her death was as calm as her life was pure. At a ripe old age her lamp of life went out; or, rather she fell asleep....[197]

Children of LUCY AMIS and THOMAS REAVIS:

---

[195] She is buried in Friendship Baptist Church Cemetery, also known as Culleoka Cemetery. She is specifically identified as a daughter of William and Judith Amis. Hawkins, Fred L., Jr. Maury County, Tennessee, Cemeteries, (Columbia, TN, 1989,) p. 480. She appears to have been living with her sister, Elizabeth Amis Bryant.

[196] 1850 Census Granville Co., N. C., Henderson, p. 64B, #71/71. http://familytreemaker.genealogy.com/users/r/e/a/David-C-Reavis/GENE36-0008.html#CHILD37. 29 November 2011.

[197] Obituary by her daughter Roberta Reavis Renn. Cited by David Reavis.

1. WILLIAM AMIS[6] REAVIS, b. 31 January 1842 Granville Co., N. C.; d. 6 February 1926 Franklin Co., N. C.;[198] m. CYNTHIA ELIZABETH CHEATHAM 19 December 1866 Granville Co., N. C.;[199]

2. MARTHA E.[6] REAVIS, b. 5 November 1843 Granville Co., N. C.; d. 3 January 1922 Marshall Co., Tenn.;[200] m. (1) GRANDISON FAIN 23 February 1867 Granville Co., N. C.;[201] m. (2) ANDREW BRYANT 1894 Maury Co., Tenn.;[202] b. 12 March 1825; d. 21 May 1910 Marshall Co., Tenn.[203]

3. ANN ELIZA[6] REAVIS, b. 10 August 1845 Granville Co., N. C.; d. 12 April 1920 Oxford, Granville Co., N. C.;[204] m. DAVID T. CHEATHAM 19 December 1866 Granville Co., N. C.,[205] son of JAMES CHEATHAM and REBECCA CREWS; b. 2 February 1838 Granville Co., N. C.; d. 9 December 1915 Oxford, Granville Co., N. C.[206]

4. MARY GREEN[6] REAVIS, b. 1847 Granville Co., N. C.; m. JOHN W. VAUGHN 25 July 1867 Granville Co., N. C.

5. JOHN T.[6] REAVIS, b. 1 June 1849 Granville Co., N. C.; d. 10 March 1918 Henderson,

---

[198] Trinity Methodist Church Cemetery, Franklin, N. C. http://www.findagrave.com., #6811220.

[199] Holcomb, p. 278. Accessed 4 March 2014 at Ancestry.com.

[200] Bryant Cemetery, Lewisburg, Tenn. http://www.findagrave.com, #85608331.

[201] North Carolina, Marriage Collection, 1741-2004. Accessed 4 March 2014 at Ancestry.com.

[202] Amis, Bryant, Burnett, Dunaway, Frey, Reavis, and More. Accessed 4 March 2014 at http://trees.ancestry.com/tree/12698139/person/-201166046?ssrc=

[203] Bryant Cemetery, Lewisburg, Tenn. http://www.findagrave.com, #85608280. His first wife was Sarah Williams (1827-1889.)

[204] Elmwood Cemetery, Oxford, N. C. http://www.findagrave.com, #28502428.

[205] Holcomb, p. 60. Accessed 4 March 2014 at Ancestry.com.

[206] Elmwood Cemetery, Oxford, N. C. http://www.findagrave.com, #28502688.

Vance Co., N. C.;[207] m. LENORA ____ 1879 N. C.; b. May 1857 N. C.[208]

6. LEWIS[6] REAVIS, b. November 1854 Granville Co., N. C.[209]

7. ROBERTA[6] REAVIS, b. 1855 Granville Co., N. C.; d. before 1900 Granville Co., N. C.; m. JOSEPH J. RENN 24 November 1884;[210] b. 8 November 1860 N. C.; d. 7 April 1915 Granville Co., N. C.[211]

8. JOSEPH WOODSON[6] REAVIS b. 10 May 1857 Granville Co., N. C.; d. 11 December 1942 Maury Co., Tenn.;[212] m. CORNELIA BRYANT, dau. of I. B. BRYANT and EMMA FRY; b. 20 October 1869 Tenn.; d. 9 January 1953 Marshall Co., Tenn.[213]

9. SAMUEL JONES[6] REAVIS, b. November 1859 Granville Co., N. C.; m. IDA BRYANT 17 November 1885 Maury Co., Tenn.;[214] b. November 1861 Tenn.

Samuel and Ida Reavis were in Maury Co., Tenn., in 1900,[215] 1920,[216] and 1930.[217]

---

[207] N. C. Death Certificate #381. Accessed 4 March 2014 at Ancestry.com.

[208] 1900 Census Vance Co., N. C., Middleburg, ED 86, p. 17A, #285/299; living on Hawkins Avenue.

[209] Unmarried and living with John T. in Warren Co., N. C., in 1900. [Hawtree, ED 94, p. 13B, #222/223.

[210] Amis, Bryant, Burnett, Dunaway, Frey, Reavis, and More. Accessed 4 March 2014 at
http://trees.ancestry.com/tree/12698139/person/-201166046?ssrc=

[211] Elmwood Cemetery, Oxford, N. C. http://www.findagrave.com., #29237826. He married Meta Kimball, and she was his wife in the 1900 census.

[212] Tennessee Death Certificate, Dist. 611, #292, #25607. Accessed 4 March 2014 at Ancestry.com.

[213] Tennessee Death Certificate 53-01286. Accessed 4 March 2014 at Ancestry.com.

[214] Tennessee, State Marriages, 1780-2002. Accessed 4 March 2014 at Ancestry.com.

[215] 1900 Census Maury Co., Tenn., CD 4, ED 68, p. 7B, #143.

[216] 1920 Census Maury Co., Tenn., CD 4, ED 115, p. 1A, #5; living on Columbia Road.

[217] 1930 Census Maury Co., Tenn., CD 4, ED 10, p. 1A, #2; living on Highway 80.

2.   JOHN WOODSON[5] (*WILLIAM[4-3]*, *JOSEPH[2]*) AMIS was
born 22 September 1795 in Granville Co., North
Carolina and died 4 February 1849 in Scott Co.,
Mississippi. He married MARTHA WADKINS 10 February
1824 in Copiah Co., Mississippi, daughter of JAMES
WATKINS and LUCRETIA CURL. She was born 28 June
1805 in Montgomery Co., Tennessee, and died 10
September 1887 in Scott Co., Mississippi.

*My information about John Woodson Amis was
derived in large measure from my Mother, who heard
her father, Albert G. Petty, speak of him; from
Haywood Amis, the old Negro slave, above
mentioned, and Calvin H. Doolittle, son-in-law of
Ascension Amis Blalock, with whom I had quite a
long conversation on the day of her funeral in 1905.
My maternal grandfather, Albert G. Petty, and old
Haywood knew him personally, and Calvin H.
Doolittle got his information from his mother-in-law,
Ascension Amis Blalock, who was the oldest child of
John Woodson Amis, and I am convinced that my
information is reasonably accurate.*

*As above stated, he was born September 22nd,
1795, in North Carolina, and grew to manhood there.
After reaching his majority, sometime about the year
1820, he went west across the Cumberland
Mountains, to some point on the Cumberland River,
but just where is not known. There he took passage
on a flat boat, the only kind then in use, down the
Cumberland, Ohio, and Mississippi Rivers and
landed at Natchez, Mississippi. By occupation he was
a millwright, that is, a builder of grist mills, flour
mills, and cotton gins, to be operated either by water
power or animal power. After landing at Natchez he
followed his trade of millwright in Adams, Copiah,
Wilkinson and adjoining counties. And while engaged
on a job of that sort, he met Martha Wadkins, who
with her sister, was living with her uncle, Seth*

Corley, in Copiah County.[218] Subsequently on February 10th, 1824, he and Martha Wadkins were married. After his marriage he settled near Woodville, in Wilkinson County, where he continued to reside until about 1838 or 1839. He became a landowner and a slave holder, as most other men of means were, and seems to have been highly esteemed by the people of his community. About 1838 or 1839 he moved to Newton County and settled on a tract of land about halfway between Newton and Decatur, just north of a large plantation then owned by Millanton Blalock, now owned by Tom Doolittle and others. About 1845 or 1846, he moved to Scott County and settled on the old stage road running from Jackson, Mississippi, to Livingston, Alabama, at the eastern end of the old turnpike across Tuscalameta Swamp, where he died February 4th, 1849. He was buried on his own farm, in the old Amis graveyard, about five or six miles northwest of Conehatta. For many years this grave yard was the neighborhood burial ground although no one has been buried there for ten or fifteen years past. A tombstone was erected at his grave many years ago, but it is now fallen down and broken in pieces.

Physically he was of spare build and a little below medium height, and at some time during his life he had lost one eye. Those who knew him after he moved to Newton County say that he was a one-eyed man. How or when he lost his eye I never heard. He was a vigorous, active man and had considerable influence in his community. In temperament he was somewhat taciturn and sometimes a little obstinate, not being inclined to argue matters much. He was rather sensitive concerning the honor of himself and his family and was not quick to forgive an injury to either. In politics he was a Whig and always voted the straight ticket. In religion he was a Baptist, being a member of old Sulphur Springs Baptist Church at the time of his death. He was a royal arch mason,

---

[218] Seth Corley was actually Temperance Wadkins' husband, and thus Martha Wadkins' brother-in-law, as is developed in the section of information on her family.

being a member of the Hillsboro lodge at the time of his death. I have in my possession the original copy of the resolution of respect and condolence passed by Hillsboro Lodge, after his death, March 25th, 1849, a copy of which is shown in the appendix to these sketches. His neighbors, widely scattered, in those days of sparse population, were the ancestors of the Graham, Brewer, Pettey, Eastland, Blalock, Keith, Carleton, Doolittle, Wilson, Smith, and Johnson families of Newton and Scott Counties. All of them were of the old pioneer stock, whose memory has almost faded. Their like will never be seen again.

Martha Wadkins Amis, familiarly and affectionately known as "Old Mother," was born at, or near, Macon, Georgia, June 28th, 1805.[219] Her mother was a Curle, but I do not know anything of her father or mother. She had one sister named Tempe, but if she ever had a brother I do not know it. Their father and mother died when they were quite young, and they were reared by their uncle, Seth Corley. Whether this uncle lived in Georgia or Mississippi, I do not know; but at any rate they were both living with, or visiting one of their uncles in Mississippi in 1824, and both of them married from his home. Which was the older and which married first, I have never heard, but Tempe married and settled in Copiah County and her descendants are there yet, but I do not now anything about them.

On February 10th, 1824, when she was not quite nineteen years old, Martha was married to John W. Amis, with whom she lived until his death in 1849, and to whom she bore four sons and five daughters. In 1849, at the age of forty four, she was left a widow, but never married again. She took charge of the plantation and the slaves and reared her family to manhood and womanhood. Her youngest daughter

[219] Actually, she was born in Montgomery Co., Tennessee, and moved with her family to Jones County, Georgia, which is just northeast of Macon, Ga., about 1809. The parents had died by 1815 when court records establish that Temperance Wadkins avoided an appointed guardian by marrying Seth Corley, and Martha Wadkins became the ward of her uncle, Kinchen Curl. She said she was born in Tennessee in the 1850 Census.

Frances married in 1869 and a short time afterward, I do not know just when, she sold the old home to her son-in-law J. D. Graham, and "broke up housekeeping." She then began to live around among her children, though for many years she kept her clothing and had her headquarters at the old home with Uncle Dock and Aunt Wootie. Finally, however, a few years before her death she went to live with her youngest daughter, Frances, at the old Ed Moore place, where she lived until she died September 10th, 1887. She was buried beside her husband in the old Amis graveyard, and a tombstone marks her grave.

My recollection of her is very vivid, as is that of all who knew her; because she was a vigorous woman of strong personality and great courage. As an instance of her courage, it is related that shortly after her husband's death, one of her Negro slaves, a man, rebelled against her authority and refused to obey her; but instead of being frightened or of calling some neighbor man to chastise him, as was the custom of widows in such cases, she proceeded without assistance to administer the punishment suitable to his offence. After that she never had any trouble with the Negroes.

It is also related that Sherman's army marched right by her place at one time during the Civil War, and she knew that the soldiers would steal everything that they could lay their hands on. All her sons were gone to the war and there was no one home except herself, her daughters, and the Negro slaves. So when she heard the army approaching, she had her few valuables, and all her bacon, lard, and other foodstuffs, brought in and piled in the middle of her room, which was the main living room of the family. She then got her daughters in and sat herself down in a chair in the open doorway and waited. Shortly the soldiers came and spread all over the place, into the smokehouse, the corn-crib, the dairy, and everywhere else, and some even tried to get past her into her room; but she calmly sat there and kept them back. In a little while she saw an officer approaching, whereupon she called to him, identified herself as a master mason's widow, and asked for a detail of soldiers to guard her residence, which was immediately given her. Knowing her as I did, I can well understand why any skulking thief, soldier or not, would stop when he tried to pass her sitting in that open doorway.

And yet, everybody loved her, and all the children in the whole countryside, and many of the grown folks, called her "Old Mother." And when she would pass a house going from one child's house to another, the children would come running to meet her and she would always stop and talk to them or to anyone else she met, even a Negro, and seemed to be greatly interested in their welfare.

An amusing story used to be told about Jeffie Wilson, daughter of Uncle Henry Wilson, who lived in the neighborhood. All the children, except Jeffie, were accustomed to calling her "Old Mother." Jeffie, however, always called her "Mrs. Amis." As Old Mother would pass along the road by Uncle Henry's place, the children would always run out to meet her shouting "Howdy, Old Mother." So, when they ran out to meet her, Jeffie in the lead, she shouted "Howdy, Old Mrs. Amis." The children teased her about it for years afterward.

In going from one child's house to another, she nearly always walked, and usually had one or two children along to carry her bundles. But very often she would go alone. When she got tired she would stop at the first house and rest awhile; and if it was near mealtime, she would always stay and eat with the family. She was always welcome everywhere and the children were glad to see her. She always had an apple, a marble, or some little thing for them, and what was better, a smile and a hug. She used to make trips that way for twenty miles or more. It would take her two or three days, but she never got in a hurry and always arrived safely.

She would ride in an ox wagon or a mule wagon, if the mules were old and slow; but she did not like to ride in a buggy or hack with spirited horses. They went too fast for her. I remember, once, my mother induced her to have me carry her from our house to Uncle Dock's, about five miles, in a buggy; but from the way she looked and held on, I am sure it was a journey in which she took no pleasure. She went to Texas once, about 1880, but when she got back, she said never again, it was all too fast for her. I wonder what she would have thought of the swift moving automobiles of these speed-mad days, and whether she would have ridden in one of them.

She was a member of the Baptist Church and a devout believer in the over-ruling providences of God, yet she had a great fund of common sense and homely philosophy, and firmly believed that "God helps only those who help themselves." Once, when my father was a candidate for office, she told him that if he set himself up as a target he might expect to be shot at; and the last time I ever saw her alive, she told me that if I ever got a handle to my name, folks would take hold of it and shake it. She had a little money, which she kept loaned out, and was always very particular to collect her "intrust" as she called it. And I remember one day, when one of the borrowers paid her the "intrust," she said to him , with a chuckle, "That's what you pay me for trusting you with my money." And while that does not coincide with the definition given by the lexicographers or the law writers, yet every lender knows that she was right, because the custom is, that the greater the risk of losing the principal the higher is the rate of interest charged.

She had great faith in the virtues of castor oil in generous doses as a remedy for childish ailments and seldom suggested anything else. She also believed that a jug of good whisky—with some rock candy and various kinds of barks in it, was mighty good to cure a cold if you have one and to keep it off if you didn't. And I think she was right. In fact, I wish I had a little of that same kind of medicine (with the barks left out), because I am liable to catch a cold most any time.

Old Mother was of Scotch-Irish ancestry. When I can first remember her, she was nearly seventy years old, but was still vigorous. She was a little below medium height and was somewhat corpulent. Her complexion, even at seventy, was ruddy. After each meal she smoked a pipe of tobacco, but not often at other times. She had an old clay pipe and a cane stem that she carried around in her bag—I think it was called a reticule in those days—and she would get it out and fill it, and many a time I have dipped it in hot ashes for her or handed her a live coal to light it. And then she would sit and puff, the perfect picture of peace and contentment. And yet they say, in these days of equal rights for women, that ladies should not smoke! O tempora! O Mores! Dear Old Mother, I loved her well, as did all who knew her. May she rest in peace.

Children of JOHN W. AMIS and MARTHA WADKINS:

i. ASCENSION LUCRECY[6] AMIS, b. 28 December 1824 Wilkinson Co., Miss.; d. 3 May 1905 Newton Co., Miss.; m. SAMUEL BLALOCK son of MILLANTON BLALOCK 12 March 1840 Newton Co., Miss.; d. 11 March 1852 Newton Co., Miss.

Ascension L. Amis, oldest daughter of John W. Amis and Martha Wadkins, was born in Wilkinson County, December 28th, 1824 and grew to womanhood there. About 1838 or 1839 her father moved to Newton County and settled on a tract of land just north of the plantation of Millenton Blalock, now known as the Doolittle place. There she met Samuel Blalock, son of Millenton Blalock, and they were married March 12th, 1840. They lived together until his death, March 11th, 1852, and had three children: John M., Harriet P., and Louisa L. Blalock. She never remarried, but remained a widow until her death, May 2nd, 1905.

From the time of her marriage until her death she lived at Newton, first with and among the family of her husband, and later with her children and grandchildren. I never knew her very intimately, but would visit her occasionally after I reached manhood. She was a quiet, soft-voiced, delicate old lady, with a slow, sweet smile, and features that showed she was quiet a beauty in her younger days. Evidently she developed into womanhood early, because she married when she was but a few months above the age of fifteen years.

On the day of her funeral, in 1905, her son-in-law, Cal Doolittle, showed me some of her keepsakes, and among them was a formal, printed invitation to Miss Ascension Amis, to attend a grand ball in the town of Woodville, in Wilkinson County, which, as I remember bore the date of 1836, but it may have been 1838. Well, well, folks, talk about how precocious the modern flapper is, and how they have "dates" when they ought to be playing dolls; but how about the old days when a twelve or fourteen year old Miss was formally invited to attend a grand ball, where the belles and beaux of the Southland danced away the fleeting hours, in the moonlight's mellow glow, in the old time town of Woodville, nearly a hundred years ago!

O time and change what has thou wrought
Of all that scene of yesteryear!
The forms are faded that the moonbeams sought,
And the hearts are still that were then so dear;
But life ever laughs your havoc to nought,
And youth is the same from year to year.

And so it was that good old "Aunt Tent" sipped life's nectar in the early morning of youth, when her dreams were sweet; but when she met her mate her soul was satisfied. And though he was taken from her when she was only twenty eight years old, she never sought another, but for more than half a century trod her lonely way, content with her memories, and the love and care of her children and grandchildren, in the full faith that somewhere, sometime, all would be well. Such constancy! What was it that held her so true through all those years?

What was it? Alas, who knows!
What sage or seer hath ever told;
Or whence it comes, or wither goes,
Or how to win, or how to hold.

It blushes like a summer's dawn,
Then like the noontide sun it glows;
Or like a brook it babbles on,
Then like the mighty river flows.

It whispers low in soundless sigh
A story that no tongue can tell—
That lifts us up above the sky
Or drags us downward into hell.

It makes or mars each human life
Nor counts the cost in pain or tears;
But leads us on to joy or strife
In endless cycles through the years.

A passion born of nature's urge,
Repressed, refined through long control;
But when its fires begin to surge
'Tis master of the human soul.

And when its fires consume the dross
And fill our souls with perfect trust,
Then each will bear the other's cross
Till dust returnest unto dust.

And though one fall beside the way
Their spirits nought will e'er dissever,
For the lonely one will wait the day
They meet to part no more forever.

Children of ASCENSION and SAMUEL BLALOCK:

1. JOHN MILLANTON[7] BLALOCK, b. 6 July 1842;
   d. 24 July 1856 Newton Co., Miss.
2. HARRIET PARISADE[7] BLALOCK, b. 18 June
   1844 Newton Co., Miss.; d. 16 January
   1890 Newton Co., Miss.; m. CALVIN H.

DOOLITTLE 18 June 1863 Newton Co., Miss.; d. 13 March 1906 Newton Co., Miss.

3. LOUISA LAVINIA[7] BLALOCK, b. 25 February 1847 Newton Co., Miss.; d. 4 November 1892 Newton Co., Miss.; m. WAD H. THOMPSON about 1866 Newton Co., Miss.; d. 12 September 1882 Newton Co., Miss.

These were two daughters of Samuel Blalock and Ascension Amis, and were born, reared and lived out their lives at or near Newton.

They were my cousins, but as they were both older than my mother, I was never familiar with either of them. In fact, because of the distance they lived from the rest of the kindred, I never knew either one of them very well and know but little of their lives or characteristics. My information is, that when Millenton Blalock, their grandfather, died shortly prior to the Civil War, they inherited considerable property from his estate. But the administration dragged along in the courts for many years, and then the War came on and freed the slaves and destroyed the value of the land. And the result of it all was that their inheritance was never of much benefit to them.

Lou married Wad Thompson, and while I used to hear my father speak of him, I never knew him. He died when I was about fifteen years old and up to that time I had scarcely ventured so far from home as Newton was then. It was a whole lot further then than it is now in these days of the Ford car and good roads.

Harriet married Cal Doolittle, whom I knew well, but not until after she was dead. Cal was the oldest son of Roger Doolittle, one of the pioneer settlers of Newton County. He was a man of intelligence and judgment and was popular in his community. For a long time he was Justice of the Peace at Newton, and was a good one too, as I can testify, having tried many cases in his Court. He had an accurate and retentive memory and a wealth of information about local people and conditions, extending back several years before the Civil War, and I always enjoyed hearing him tell of early times and conditions.

My information is that Harriet and Lou, as well as their husbands, are buried in the old Doolittle burial ground, just north of Newton.

Robert W. Thompson, son of Wad Thompson and Louisa Blalock, familiarly known as Bob, was born October 7th, 1872. He was a locomotive engineer of the Gulf and Ship Island Railroad, and was killed in the performance of his duties on the 9th day of July 1916. He married Maud Doolittle, daughter of Thomas I. Doolittle, of Newton, Mississippi, about the year 1899. He left surviving him his widow, Maud Thompson, who is now matron of Gulfpark College at Gulfport, and two children, Robert and Loucidel. Bob was genial and accommodating and well liked by all who knew him. Children were especially fond of him, and that, it my opinion, is the supreme test of a man's goodness of heart. His death was accidental, caused by a washout on the main line of the railroad, his engine turning over and the steam scalding him. After his death, the officials of the railroad were very considerate of his widow and children and made a liberal settlement with them without any suit in the courts.

ii. TEMPERANCE PARISADE[6] AMIS, b. 18 September 1826 Wilkinson Co., Miss.; d. 10 May 1908 Conehatta, Newton Co., Miss.; m. (1) B. O. SWINNEY 21 March 1844 Newton Co., Miss.; m. (2) CHARLES W. DAY 3 March 1853 Scott Co., Miss.

Temperance Parisade Amis, (Aunt Pod), daughter of John W. Amis and Martha Wadkins, was born in Wilkinson County, September 18th, 1826. On March 21st, 1844, she was married to B. O. Swinney. She lived with him only a short time, but just how long I do not know. He was cruel to her and she left him and returned to her father's home. Swinney promised to reform and tried to get him to return to her, but she would not consent, and her father, on pain of death, forbade him coming to see her. My maternal grandfather, Albert G. Petty, was a friend to both of them and tried to effect a reconciliation without success. I do not know whether Swinney died or they were divorced, but at any rate on March 3rd, 1853, she was married to Charles W. Day, with whom she lived until she died May 10th, 1908. She never had any children by Swinney that I ever heard of. By her

111

second husband, Uncle Charley Day, she had two children: Emma and Loula.

Uncle Charley and Aunt Pod, as they were familiarly and affectionately known, lived all their lives within five miles of the present village of Conehatta, in Newton County, and for a larger part of the time in the village itself. And for me it is impossible to think of or write about them separately, for while they were unlike in appearance, yet they were truly one in spirit.

Aunt Pod was a great cook of the old southern style, and Uncle Charley gloried in her excellence. The form of his blessing at mealtime was the shortest I ever heard. It was: "Dear Lord, bless us and dinner," or supper, or breakfast as the case might be; and when Aunt Pod had prepared something which specially suited his taste, he would add: "and the old woman for cooking it." And that reminds me of the story of Uncle Charley and his false teeth. When he began to get along in years, he had all his teeth pulled, and a full set of artificial teeth, but upper and lower plates, made. In due time the dentist delivered and fitted them, and Uncle Charley was quite proud of them, though I know he felt like he had a couple of wheelbarrows in his mouth. That day for dinner, Aunt Pod baked some sweet potatoes, of which he was specially fond. And so when dinner was ready, he sat down and said his usual grace, with a special blessing for the cook, and taking one of the potatoes he pulled off the skin and took a huge bite. Now that potato was soft, sticky, and quite hot, as he discovered when he bit into it, but it stuck in his teeth and he could neither swallow it nor spit it out; and the more he tried to swallow it the more it stuck, the more it got under his plates and the more it burned him. He struggled and sputtered for awhile, and finally took the whole mess out with his fingers, laid it on his plate and said: "Now, damn you. Lie there and blaze." After that, those teeth were a matter of ornament, not of use; for he laid them up on the mantel, cussed 'em, and swore he would "gum it" for the rest of his days. And so he did.

Like many oldtimers, Uncle Charley had no liking for paper money, "Greenbacks," as it used to be called. In his opinion, gold was the only real safe money. And so when he would hear of anyone having gold, he would go and trade for it, even if he had to pay a premium, which he often did. He was a frugal man, and in this way accumulated quite a sum in gold, for the proverbial rainy day. How much he had or where he kept it, I never knew, but I know he had it, and it was a source of great comfort to them in their old age when the "rainy day" came.

Uncle Charley was a very large man, and as so often happens in matrimonial affairs, Aunt Pod was a small woman, though in her old age she became quite corpulent. They were quiet, peaceful old people, and were liked by all who knew them. They seemed to be wholly satisfied by their surroundings and with each other; and I feel sure that for more than forty years before they died, neither of them ever went as much as ten miles from home. Nothing ever seemed to disturb the even tenor of their lives, but secure in the esteem and affection of their friends and kindred, they lived out their days in peace, if not in plenty. They were buried side by side in the old Amis graveyard, but no tombstone marks their graves.

And there they sleep the years away
Patiently awaiting the judgment day,
For under the sod, as well as the stone,
God will claim and keep his own.

Children of PARISADE AMIS and CHARLES DAY:

1. EMMA[7] DAY, b. 8 June 1863 Newton Co., Miss.; d. 8 October 1945 Athens, Henderson Co., Texas; m. NATHAN CLARKE MURRELL 6 October 1887 Newton Co., Miss.; b. 14 August 1860 Newton Co., Miss.; d. 17

August 1933 Athens, Henderson Co., Texas.[220]

2. LOULA[7] DAY, b. 12 September 1867 Newton Co., Miss.; d. 26 September 1927 Chattanooga, Hamilton Co., Tennessee; m. THOMAS P. WILLIAMS about 1889 Newton Co., Miss; b. 8 August 1861; d. 4 March 1950 Newton Co., Miss.[221]

Loula Day, daughter of Charles W. Day and Parisade Amis, was born September 12, 1867, in Newton County and grew to womanhood there. During most of her life she resided in the village of Conehatta. She attended the High School there and as I remember graduated about 1889, and in the fall of that year was married to Thomas P. Williams. Her sister Emma had previously married Clarke Murrell and they had moved to Texas. So after her marriage, Loula and her husband lived with her father and mother in the village until about 1901 or 1902 when they moved to the old Thornton homestead about half a mile north of the village where they lived for several years, after which they returned to the village and lived in the old Giles Brunson homestead. About 1927 or 1928 they moved to Chattanooga, Tennessee, to live with their daughter, where she died about the year 1930.

As a girl she was tall and rather slender with black hair and eyes. Her complexion, while it had a tinge of red in the cheeks, was not so ruddy as was that of her mother and sister Emma. She did not have that quickness of motion or characteristic of the Amis strain, but like her father, was deliberate in all she said or did. She was a lovely winsome girl, and I thought very beautiful.

We were nearly the same age and took great delight in each other's society and companionship. When Emma, who was several years older than we were, had a beau to church, or an entertainment in the village, we played the part of chaperone and tagged along behind; and just for

[220] Tombstones are in Athens Cemetery, Athens, Henderson Co., Texas. Located 4 December 2011 at http://www.findagrave.com.

[221] Both markers are in the Conehatta Methodist Church Cemetery, Newton Co., Miss., although hers notes she is buried in Chattanooga. (Smith, Bonnie A., Smith, Jackson E., Smith, Robert E. Newton County, Mississippi: A Cemetery Census, 1782-1995. (Decatur, MS: EBRS Publishing, 1997,) p. 95.

fun, we often tried to hear the love making going on ahead of us. And one time we crept up rather close and heard John Bishop trying to tell her how pretty she was and how much he loved her. But he stammered so much and got so badly stalled in the effort, that we laughed out loud and put an end to the romantic scene. Another time we were tagging along, one beautiful moonlight night, behind our mutual cousin Ella Graham and her beau. Ella grew sentimental and looking up at the moon she said, "The moon, the moon, the pale yellow moon." Her beau did not know any poetry, but not to be outdone, he said, "The sun, the sun, the red hot sun." Again, we laughed and ruined the love making.

She bore and reared ten children and gave her life, with patient cheerfulness to their service and that of her husband. Her father and mother lived in the same house with her all her life, and when they became old and decrepit she cared for them and nursed them in that sweet spirit of kindness and gentleness so characteristic of her. Like her mother, she stayed home and seldom went visiting or traveling. Until she and her husband went to Chattanooga to live with their daughter, I do not think she had been out of the county since her marriage.

Her life was one of service and self denial for those she loved. And the Master said "Greater love hath no man than this, that he giveth his life for his friends." Measured by that standard, she had no superior. Like deep waters, her life flowed on to the ocean of eternity without a ripple, without a murmur of complaint or note of discontent. To the great world of men she was unknown, unhonored, and unsung. But in her own sweet gentle way her life was a benediction, a hymn of love, and a prayer of service. Many a flower blooms by the wayside, and dies unseen by the hurrying throng. But its beauty and fragrance is just as great as if the multitude had stopped to enjoy it. And I am sure that as the sun of life was setting, she saw the stars shine through the gathering gloom, and heard a voice whisper to her fading consciousness, "Well done, thou good and faithful servant." For again the Master said, "He that is greatest among you shall be your servant."

iii. WILLIAM ALEXANDER[6] AMIS, b. 24 July 1829
Wilkinson Co., Miss.; d. 7 November 1862
Scott Co., Miss.; m. MARGARET BURLESON 3
February 1858 Scott Co., Miss.; d. 27
December 1862 Scott Co., Miss.

*William Alexander Amis, son of John W. Amis
and Martha Wadkins, was born in Wilkinson
County, July 24th, 1829. He was about eight or
nine years old when his father moved to Newton
County. He remained a bachelor until he was
nearly thirty years old, and on February 3rd, 1858,
he married Margaret Burleson. They had two
children, George W., and Rankin H., Jr.,[222]
otherwise known as "Little Tank."*

*Uncle William, as I was taught to call him, was
a very small man physically, and so were both his
sons, neither of them being more than five feet four
inches high. Before his marriage he was rather
wild, and was of no help to his mother in rearing
the younger members of the family. He kept the toll
gate on the turnpike across Tusculameta Swamp
and the grocery, as they then called it, connected
therewith, for Col. Boyd, the owner; and like many
other men of that day, drank more whisky than
was good for him. When the war came on he
enlisted as a private soldier in the Confederate
Army, and while in camp at Vicksburg, he
contracted what was then known as camp fever,
which subsequently came to be known as typhoid
fever. His mother sent for him and brought him
home, where his wife tenderly nursed him until he
died November 7th, 1862. While nursing him, his
wife contracted the disease, and she too died,
December 27th, 1862.*

*His mother took his two sons, George and
Tank, and kept them until she broke up
housekeeping about 1873 or 1874, when George
went to live with Uncle Charley and Aunt Pod, and*

---

[222] In today's nomenclature, we would call him Rankin Haywood Amis,
II, to note that he was not the son of Rankin Haywood Amis, the elder, who
was his uncle.

Tank came to live with my father, Albert G. Amis, where they continued to live until they were grown.

In the year of 1879 Tank and Walter Willis, a young man about the same age, went to Texas. From there they both drifted up into Oklahoma—then Indian Territory—and married. I have not heard from Tank directly in more than forty years. About a year ago, Nettie Parks Hankey, of San Saba, Texas, wrote me that Tank died in the summer of 1925 and that his family lived in Tulsa, Oklahoma.[223] I wrote his widow a letter, but never had any reply. About 1881 or 1882, George also went to Texas. For a time he lived in or near San Saba, with his uncle James Parks, but later drifted northward and married. I have not heard from him directly for more than thirty years. About a year ago, Nettie Parks Harkey wrote me that he was living in Mangum, Oklahoma. I wrote him at once, but never had any reply.

Both William Amis and his wife are buried in the old Amis graveyard, but no one now living can locate their graves.

Children of WILLIAM AMIS and MARGARET:

1. GEORGE WASHINGTON[7] AMIS, b. 1 December 1858 Scott Co., Miss.; d. 5 January 1941 Hughes Co., Oklahoma.[224]

    George Amis, 61, was widowed, and living as "father-in-law" in the household of "Willie" Morgan, b. 1892, and Hubert Morgan, 45, in 1920. They also have Maxine Amis, 18, living with them.[225] In 1930, George, now 71, is living with the Morgans in Wetumka, Hughes Co., Oklahoma. His daughter is Willa U. Morgan, 38.[226] Maxine is not living with them any more. From the data, we can conclude that George Amis' wife died between 1902 and 1920, and that he

---

[223] He apparently changed his name to John Rankin Amis. He was buried in Rose Hill Memorial Park, Tulsa, Oklahoma, 5 June 1925. http://www.findagrave.com, accessed 3 December 2011.

[224] Buried in Wetumka Cemetery, Hughes Co., Okla. http://www.findagrave.com, accessed 3 December 2011.

[225] 1920 Census Muscogee, Oklahoma,

[226] 1930 Census, Wetumka, Hughes Co., Oklahoma,

had at least two children, Maxine, born 1902, and
Willa U. (Amis) Morgan.[227]

2. RANKIN HAYWOOD[7] (JOHN RANKIN) AMIS, b.
28 March 1861 Scott Co., Miss.; d. 4 June
1925 Tulsa, Tulsa Co., Oklahoma; m.
AMANDA AVIS MULKEY 11 December 1884
San Saba, San Saba Co., Texas, dau.
WILLIAM ROSS MULKEY and MARGARET
REBECCA HUDSON; b. 4 April 1866 San
Saba Co., Texas; d. 20 December 1933
Tulsa, Tulsa Co., Okla.[228]

Children of JOHN AMIS and AMANDA MULKEY:

a. WILLIAM ALVIN[8] AMIS, b. 1886 Cherokee
Nation, Oklahoma, Indian Terr.; d.
before 25 June 1969;[229] m. KATHRYN
_____; d. before 17 December 1971.

b. JAMES EARL[8] AMIS, b. 1889 Cherokee
Nation, Oklahoma, Indian Terr.; d.
before 6 July 1935; m. MARGARET _____;
d. before 4 May 1940.[230]

c. EDWIN R.[8] AMIS, b. 1892 Cherokee
Nation, Oklahoma, Indian Terr.; d.
before 3 October 1949;[231] m. AMANDA
OTIS; d. before 22 December 1933.

---

[227] Willie Morgan was born 22 January 1892 and died 31 August
1960. She is buried in Wetumka Cemetery.

[228] Council, Jess. Sanders-Nelson Family Tree. 19 October 2009.
Located at
http://wc.rootsweb.ancestry.com, (db. jsan-nel.) The family is present in
the Cherokee Nation in the 1900 census, and in Washington, Oklahoma, in
1920. Both are buried in Rose Hill Cemetery, Tulsa, Oklahoma.
(http://www.findagrave.com, accessed 3 December 2011.) According to the
Dawes Record (family #5077) cited by Mr. Council, Mrs. Amis was part
Cherokee, so she may have thought her husband's Mississippi kinfolks
would not be interested in knowing her, and so not responded to the letter
A. B. Amis sent to her.

[229] Buried that day in Rose Hill Memorial Park, Tulsa, Oklahoma.
(http://www.findagrave.com,) accessed 3 December 2011. I have imputed
the marriages based upon location in the cemetery.

[230] Of course, I can't be sure this is not the sister.

[231] Edwin R. Amis is on the list of Oddfellows who completed military
service in World War I. He was a member of Romona Lodge, #338, in
Washington Co., Oklahoma. Located online at
http://files.usgwarchives.net/ok/ioof/military/wwihonorroll.txt. Accessed
4 December 2011.

        d.   MARGARET E.[8] AMIS, b. 1892 Cherokee Nation, Oklahoma, Indian Territory.

   iv. JAMES C.[6] AMIS, b. 20 January 1832; d. 26 January 1832, Wilkinson Co., Miss.

    v. RANKIN HAYWOOD[6] AMIS, b. 25 May 1834 Wilkinson Co., Miss.;[232] d. 4 April 1910 Newton Co., Miss.; m. (1) ELIZABETH KIMBALL 21 December 1854 Newton Co., Miss.; m. (2) ELIZABETH WINDHAM 3 April 1897 Newton Co., Miss.

Rankin Haywood Amis, generally known as Tank Amis, was a son of John W. Amis and Martha Wadkins. He was born May 25th 1834 in Wilkinson County, and died in Newton County, April 4th, 1910, and was buried in the old Amis graveyard.

He married Elizabeth Kimball, December 21st, 1854, who bore him one son and five daughters, namely, Frances, John, Mattie, Eliza, Mollie, and Emma. Soon after their marriage they settled on a farm about half a mile from White Plains Church and resided there until sometime after the Civil War. They then moved to a farm they purchased from Uncle Charley Day, near the junction of the old Jackson road with the Lake and Carthage road, where they resided the balance of their lives. About 1896 his first wife died and on April 3rd, 1897, he married Elizabeth Windham, who survived him and is still living on the old homestead. He had no children by his last wife.

He enlisted as a private soldier in the Confederate Army and served throughout the war. He was a master mason, being a member of White Plains Lodge at Sebastopol, at the time of his death. He was a consistent and devout Christian and a member of Sulphur Springs Baptist Church; and yet he believed in enjoying all the good things in life in a sane, sensible sort of way. To him life

[232] Newton Co., Miss., Chancery Court Petition #1308, Will Book 1:367-3. Will was signed 14 December 1900 by Rankin H. Amis and witnessed by A. B. Amis and J. W. Gill. Accessed 24 March 2014 at https://familysearch.org/pal:/MM9.3.1/TH-1961-31023-25697-15?cc=2036959&wc=M7MJ-4P8:344548501,344602501

was neither a joke nor a funeral; but like a summer day, was full of sunshine as well as shadows. Like other people, he devoutly believed in a future life, but he was sure of this one, and enjoyed it fully. When there was sorrow among his neighbors and friends, he was there to aid and comfort them, and when there was joy and gladness, he was there to share it with them.

Uncle Tank was one of the finest and most loveable men I ever knew. He was jolly, even tempered and kind to everyone. He never borrowed trouble, but said and believed that everything would always work out for the best in the end, if he would just do his part. He was frugal and industrious, but believed fully in the proverb that haste makes waste; and so, no matter what the task was, he never got in a hurry, but went at it steadily and deliberately until it was finished. His idea was that if a man worked reasonably in the daytime, he was entitled to rest and sleep at night; and so he never tried to turn night into day to complete any task. No matter how pressing the farm work was, nor how fast the grass was growing in his crop, he never went to work until after the sun was up, nor even then until he had sat down after breakfast and smoked a pipe or two of tobacco.

He had an original idea about paying debts. No matter when a debt was due by its terms, he thought it was all right if he paid up by Christmas each year, so he was able to start the new year with a clean slate on the first day of January. And with him the rule worked both ways. He was always perfectly satisfied if anyone owing him paid up by Christmas. And when one thinks of it, as customs were then, there was a good reason for his idea. At that time cotton was the sole money crop of the farmer; and it took him till the end of the year to cultivate, gather and market it, and he was fortunate if he could pay in full year by year. So why not everybody be satisfied if there was full payment by Christmas?

Another original notion of his was that everyone was entitled to feel rich once a year; and so, when he went down to Newton and settled up his debts just before Christmas, he would get him a jug of whisky, and as long as it lasted, he kept pretty mellow and felt mighty rich, much to the scandal and disgust of Aunt Betty, his good old wife. But when it was gone, that was the end of his spree until about the same time next year.

He was of medium height with a ruddy complexion and black hair and beard. He had a quick ready smile, a short chuckling laugh, and sly wit that was often very amusing. For example, while he believed in education he did not think it ought to make a fool of anybody; and so if any of the young folks got a little too precise in conversation, "too proper," as he called it, he would suddenly lapse into a regular Negro dialect, which seldom failed to take the starch out in a very short time.

In his later years, he became almost blind, but that did not change his disposition or his outlook on life in the least. He still had the same cheery smile and mirth-provoking chuckle that made one know he had a clean mind and a pure heart. And it seemed to be really true, as he told me on my last visit to him, that his last days were his best days. And God was good to him, because he passed on without pain. He just went to sleep and never waked up.

Uncle Tank and Aunt Betty, how everyone loved them and enjoyed visiting them; and home much at home they made everyone feel. And they loved to have their friends and neighbors with them, for as he often said: "When Betty has company, I get treated like company, too." They are both gone the way of all flesh, and lie side by side in the old Amis graveyard. Their like we will not see again soon. May the sod lie lightly above them until the Master calls.

Children of RANKIN AMIS and ELIZABETH KIMBALL:

1. FRANCES VIRGINIA[7] AMIS; b. 5 October 1855
   Newton Co., Miss.;[233] m. (1) E. W. T.
   HORTON 16 December 1875 Newton Co.,
   Miss.; d. 15 July 1900; m. (2) M. W.
   BRIDGES 24 November 1904.

2. JOHN DAVIS[7] AMIS, b. 3 May 1858 Newton
   Co., Miss.; d. 16 March 1934 Newton Co.,
   Miss.; m. (1) SUSIE DOWDLE 12 January
   1882 Newton Co., Miss.; b. 8 March 1863
   Newton Co., Miss.; d. 12 August 1900
   Newton Co., Miss.[234]; m. (2) ELIZA ANDREWS
   23 January 1901 Newton Co., Miss.;[235] b. 1
   December 1878 Scott Co., Miss.; d. 29
   January 1938 Newton Co., Miss.

   *John Davis Amis, son of Rankin H. Amis
   and Elizabeth Kimball, was born May 3, 1858, in
   Newton County and lived there all his life. By the
   time he was old enough to go to school, the Civil
   War had been fought to a conclusion and the South
   was prostrate. The people were too poor to support
   private schools and the public schools were taught
   by ignorant Yankee teachers only a few months in
   the year. The result was that he never had the
   opportunity to attend any other sort of school. And
   while he learned the three Rs, readin', 'ritin, and
   'rithmetic, he had no other "book learning." But like
   all the Amis's he was a good farmer. He knew good
   land when he saw it and how to make it produce
   good crops. So as soon as he reached his majority
   he bought a tract of valley land on Bougephalia
   Creek adjoining his father's farm, and went to
   work. There he lived all his life and there he died in
   March 1925. On January 12, 1882, he married
   Susie Dowdle, daughter of that fine old Irishman,
   Uncle Jim Dowdle. She died in 1900, but bore him
   seven children. Afterwards, on January 23, 1901,
   he married Eliza Andrews who survived him and
   still resides on the old homestead. She bore him
   seven children, some of whom are now dead.*
   *Though he was unlearned in books yet he
   was a man of quick perception and vigorous*

---

[233] Living in Stamps, Lafayette Co., Arkansas, in 1936. No record of
burial there so they may have moved afterward.
[234] Buried in Erin Cemetery, Newton Co., Miss. Data from Boone
White.
[235] Newton Co., Miss., MB A:576. (Boone White.)

intelligence. His motions and speech were quick and decisive. And I used to wonder how he and his first wife, Susie, ever carried on a conversation; because she spoke so slowly and deliberately while his words came like the chatter of a machine gun. He was genial and jolly and always full of fun, playing pranks and telling amusing stories on his sisters and other kindred. When Will Horton, his oldest sister's first husband died, she married a man named Windom Bridges, and John in speaking of him to his sister, always called him Windy Britches. He nearly worried the life out of his sister Mattie about having to prompt her husband, Alex, when he forgot part of his sermon. I have heard him tell, with great glee, about how Alex got "in a weaving way" in one of his sermons and the congregation was enthralled with his eloquence, when Mattie blurted out "You've skipped a page, Alex."

He was an inveterate talker and he laughed almost as much as he talked. Like his father he enjoyed life in his own way among his friends and neighbors. And they were all his friends. While he lived the frugal life of a well to do farmer, he never accumulated or hoarded money. I do not think he cared for it further than to pay his just debts and provide the comforts of himself and family. His sense of right and wrong was as keen and clear as any man I ever knew. And for that reason his judgment was respected by all who knew him. When his older children grew up and married, some of them went to Texas, some to New Mexico, and one to California. He visited them one or more times and they tried to induce him to "go West and grow up with the country" as they had. But he said no, he had grown up already. To him the scenes and friends of his youth and earlier manhood were too sacred for him to abandon. And so he lived his life out within a mile of the place where he was born, and now lies buried in the churchyard at Sulphur Springs, scarcely two miles away.

Children of JOHN AMIS and SUSIE DOWDLE:

a. JAMES RANKIN[8] AMIS, b. 3 December 1882 Newton Co., Miss.; d. 3 November 1883 Newton Co., Miss.[236]

b. ALMA[8] AMIS, b. 8 January 1884 Newton Co., Miss; d. 20 January 1913 Newton Co., Miss.; m. JOSEPH BENJAMIN VANCE 23 November 1902 Newton Co., Miss.; b. 11 June 1882 Newton Co., Miss.; d. 12 April 1960 Newton Co., Miss.[237]

c. WILLIAM ANDREW[8] AMIS, b. 18 July 1886 Newton Co., Miss.; d. 30 December 1892 Newton Co., Miss.[238]

d. GEORGE GROVER[8] AMIS, b. 24 March 1889 Newton Co., Miss.; m. MITTIE ELOISE RUSSELL 23 September 1915 Newton Co., Miss.

e. NETTIE MOORE[8] AMIS, b. 19 September 1891 Newton Co., Miss.; m. CLAUDE BARBER 1 September 1911 Newton Co., Miss.

f. JOHN LEON[8] AMIS, b. 9 August 1894 Newton Co., Miss.; m. JULIA STANLEY 6 June 1925.[239]

g. MORRIS PARKER[8] AMIS, b. 17 October 1897 Newton Co., Miss.; d. 11 December 1967 Newton Co., Miss.; m. SARAH ANN EZELL 30 April 1919 Newton Co., Miss.; b. 28 May 1900 Newton Co., Miss.; 5 January 1987 Newton Co., Miss.[240]

Children of JOHN AMIS and ELIZA ANDREWS:

h. LENA RIVERS[8] AMIS, b. 17 October 1901; d. before 1936.

i. WILLIAM RANKIN[8] AMIS, b. 1 October 1903 Newton Co., Miss.; d. 14 March 1982 Newton Co., Miss.; m. MINNIE

---

[236] Buried in Amis Cemetery, Scott Co., Miss.
[237] Buried in Erin Cemetery, Newton Co., Miss.
[238] Buried in Amis Cemetery, Scott Co., Miss.
[239] Boone White says the marriage was in Lancaster, California.
[240] Buried in Erin Cemetery, Newton Co., Miss. Boone White also lists a Johnnie Amis, b. 11 July 1900, d. 30 September 1900, buried in Amis Cemetery.

EUNICE VANCE 9 August 1934 Newton Co., Miss.; b. 26 July 1902 Newton Co., Miss.; d. 26 August 1999 Meridian, Lauderdale Co., Miss.[241]

j. CHARLES H.[8] AMIS, b. 23 October 1905 Newton Co., Miss.; d. 29 January 1972 Dona Ana Co., N. M.; m. LILLIAN GYLES 11 December 1926; b. 17 November 1906; d. 10 April 1976 Dona Ana Co., N. M.[242]

k. EDGAR H.[8] AMIS, b. 23 December 1907 Newton Co., Miss.; d. 16 February 1994 El Paso, El Paso Co., Texas;[243] m. ELVA ELOISE MULLOY; b. 23 November 1921; d. 1998 Dona Ana Co., N. M.

l. MURRAY[8] AMIS, b. 30 March 1911 Newton Co., Miss.

m. JOHN D. AMIS, JR., b. 15 February 1913 Newton Co., Miss.; d. 19 June 1915 Newton Co., Miss.

n. HERBERT BAILEY[8] AMIS, b. 21 December 1916 Newton Co., Miss.

3. MARTHA SUSAN[7] AMIS, b. 24 September 1863 Newton Co., Miss.; d. 22 March 1922, Farrar, Limestone Co., Texas; m. ALEX T. BRUNSON 27 February 1879 Newton Co., Miss.

Mattie was the daughter of Rankin H. Amis and Elizabeth Kimball and was born and reared in Newton County, Mississippi. In 1879 she married Alex Brunson, and continued to reside there until 1884 when the family moved to Texas. After moving to Texas, Alex was actively engaged in the ministry and in the pursuit of his calling, moved from place to place in the state until the family finally located at Farrar, Texas, where she died March 22, 1922, and was buried there. Although

---

[241] Buried at Sulphur Springs Baptist Church. Marriage date from Boone White.

[242] Both of their stones are in the Masonic Cemetery, Las Cruces, Dona Ana Co., N. M. along with a son, Charles H. Amis, Jr., (1935-1978). Located at http://findagrave.com. Accessed 4 December 2011.

[243] Buried Anthony Cemetery, Anthony, Dona Ana Co., N. M. (near Las Cruces.) Her end date is not on the stone. Located at http://findagrave.com. Accessed 4 December 2011.

they were a few years older than I, yet I remember them both as young people before as well as after their marriage.

As I remember Mattie, she was rather more of her mother's type than that of her father's people. She was a great singer, and had all the songs, words as well as notes, in the old Sacred Harp "on the tip of her tongue." And so did Alex, her husband. And after they married and moved off to themselves, the neighbors used to say that the last thing they heard before they went to bed and the first thing they heard when they waked in the morning, was Alex and Mattie singing. But they were young and light-hearted and didn't care what their neighbors said about it, but just kept on singing whenever they felt like it. A short time after their marriage, Alex felt he had a call to preach and began preparing to enter the ministry. And John, Mattie's brother, used to nearly tease the life out of her about how Alex would first try his sermons out on her, to see how they worked, before he tried them on his congregation. And with great glee used to tell me many amusing stories about them. I never knew how much truth there was in them and always thought they were mostly pure fabrication; but I also suspect that Alex, like most other husbands, appreciated his wife's kindly sympathy and criticism, especially in the earlier days of his Ministry. But, like her mother, Mattie was always a good sport, a happy go lucky sort of woman, who took a joke well, and never suspected anyone of intentionally mistreating her. And this, as well as her many other admirable traits, made her a great favorite of all who knew her.

She was a member of the Baptist Church and when I knew her was a zealous worker in the vineyard, and always took a keen interest in the Ministerial work of her husband. She lived to see all of her children married and settled in homes of their own, and to live over again the days of her young motherhood, in the caresses and prattle of her grandchildren; than which there is no greater comfort or joy to the aged.

4. ELIZA[7] AMIS, b. about 1866 Newton Co., Miss.; d. about 1892; m. J. T. WESTERFIELD about 1888 Newton Co., Miss.

5. MALLIE[7] AMIS, b. 15 April 1869 Newton Co., Miss.; d. 1930 Scott Co., Miss.; m. G. A. MCILHENNY December 1888 Newton Co., Miss.

Mallie Amis, daughter of Rankin H. Amis and Elizabeth Kendall was born April 15th, 1869, in Newton County and was reared there. She attended the High School at Conehatta, but I do not think she graduated. During the Christmas holidays in December 1888 she married Dr. G. A. McIhenny, a dentist who then lived near Hillsboro, in Scott County. He was well liked by everyone, and the only person to object to the marriage was old Steve Graham, a Negro neighbor of Uncle Tank, who insisted that no man could make a living for a woman "jest pullin' a toof here and a toof dar." After their marriage, they lived for some years on a farm about two miles east of Hillsboro. Subsequently they moved to Forest, where they continued to live until she died and was buried there in 1930. They had three children, Oliver, Elizabeth, and George, all of whom survived her and are now married and have families of their own. She was a fair, slender girl, of her mother's type of face and figure. Her personality was winsome, and her manner charming to all who knew her. She was greatly attached to her husband and children, and they in turn almost worshipped her. When slightly teased, her little giggling laugh was the most delightful I ever heard. As a consequence, I used to tease her, just to hear that laugh. And I think Uncle Dock did too. She and her sister Emma, and Lula Day, were near my own age. Naturally they were my favorite cousins and I loved them very much. After Mollie and and Dock moved to Forest I went to see her every time I was there and always enjoyed the visit. Her last illness was long and painful, and though she knew the disease was incurable, she bore the suffering with a patience and fortitude which none could excel. Dock spared neither pains nor expense to provide the best medical care and skill and care for her, but without avail. The grim reaper came and naught could stay his hand.

O spirit fair, where art thou now,
In all the expanse of earth and sky?
Dost linger here to soothe the brow
Of loved ones, when pain and anguish are nigh?

When the stars are shining throughout the night
Dost flit above them as they sleep?
Or mid heaven's bright celestial light
Sittest thou thy watch and ward to keep?
Dost pluck aside death's dismal veil
To share their griefs and quell their fears—
To give them strength lest courage fail?
Or hast thou fled this veil of tears?
In all the realms of boundless space
Where art thou now, O spirit sweet?
Dost gaze upon thy Maker's face,
Or dost thou sit at Jesus' feet?
Beyond the bounds of space and time
And faintest gleam of sun or star
Mid angel throngs and scenes sublime
Dost hold the gates of heaven ajar?
Who knows? We may not lift the veil
That hides what lies beyond the grave—
We can but hope, within life's pale,
To live   so that His grace will save.

6. EMMA[7] AMIS, b. 15 November 1871 Newton
Co., Miss.; d. 1932 Newton Co., Miss.; m.
JOHN M. WILLIS about 1894 Newton Co.,
Miss.; b. 18 March 1866 Newton Co., Miss.;
d. about 1909.[244]

John M. Willis, (Reb) a son of James M.
Willis, of Newton County, was born March 18th,
1866, and was reared on a farm near Decatur.
About 1894 he married Emma Amis, a daughter of
Rankin H. Amis and Elizabeth Kimball. After their
marriage, they resided at his father's old farm,
which he purchased, until his death, about the
year 1909. He was murdered by a Negro, one of
the tenants on his farm, who was afterward duly
tried, convicted, and executed for the crime. His
widow never remarried, and continued to reside at
the old homestead, and for a number of years was
a teacher in the public schools of the county. She
died in 1932 or 1933.

Emma Amis, daughter of Rankin H. Amis
and Elizabeth Kimball, was born November 14,
1871, in Newton County and lived there all her life.
In her young womanhood she attended the High
School at Conehatta, but I do not think she

---

[244] Both are buried at New Hope Church near Stratton, Newton Co.,
Mississippi.

graduated. About the year 1894 she married John M. (Reb) Willis. For several years they lived just north of Cross Roads Church on the Newton and New Ireland road. When Reb's father, James M. Willis, died, they purchased they purchased his place and moved on it. In 1909 her husband was murdered by one of his Negro tenants and she was left with a family of five small children to rear and educate; and what was equally perplexing to her, a considerable sum of debts due by her deceased husband. But like her father, whom she resembled very much, she set herself to the task with grim determination, and slowly, but surely paid the debts and reared her family to manhood and womanhood in a creditable manner.

To do this she managed the farm, kept the home, and taught the neighboring school for a number of years. She died on Sunday with all her children about her. She had requested them to visit her on the previous day when she divided all her property among them. The next day she went to Church came back home and died that afternoon. I do not remember the date of her death, but I think it was in the summer of 1932. She was buried beside her husband at New Hope Church near Stratton.

She was the youngest of six children and was as much like her father as it was possible for a woman to be. She had the same ruddy complexion, the same quick step, the same chuckling laughter and ready wit, the same patience and perseverance under difficulties, and the same genial disposition that made both of them well liked by all who knew them. When she was young, she was more handsome than beautiful. There was something about her that was masculine. Her voice had none of the feminine treble in it, but was somewhat husky, as though it was about the halfway mark between the masculine and the feminine.

While rearing her children she took part in their pleasures for she was a good sport and loved a joke or a laugh as well as they did. Occasionally she visited me and I always stopped with her when I was in that part of the country. I well remember the last time I spent the night at her home. We laughed and talked about old times and the old timers until after midnight. And it rained

that night and the car got stuck on the way back to
Decatur next morning.

I knew her husband Reb quite well and
liked him; but I have often wondered who was the
better businessman, he or his wife. He was
inclined to be a plunger in financial matters, but his
wife was more careful and frugal. She never made
a debt until she knew how she could pay it, a trait
he did not have. And I am not sure that she did not
succeed, financially, as well or better than if he
had lived. All of which reminds me of Uncle Tank's
maxim that everything works out for the best in the
end if we only do our best. And the energetic,
courageous soul that she was did her best. No one
could do more.

vi. MARTHA JANE[6] AMIS, b. 11 March 1838 Newton
Co., Miss.; d. 12 November 1909 San Saba
Co., Texas; m. (1) E. A. GRAHAM 4 March 1858;
m. (2) JAMES M. PARKS 10 February 1867.

"Martha Jane Amis, daughter of John W. Amis
and Martha Wadkins, was born March 11, 1838, I
believe in Newton County, Mississippi, and died
November 12th, 1909, in San Saba County, Texas.
She married E. A. Graham, March 4th, 1858, but
had no children by that marriage.

What became of E. A. Graham; whether he was
killed during the war or died after the war, or
whether they were divorced, I do not know; but the
old family record shows this marriage. It also
shows that she was married to James M. Parks,
February 10th, 1867, who at that time was a
widower with two daughters living. He built, and
was the owner of the Wanita Woolen Mills, at
Wanita, in Clarke County, about eight miles from
Enterprise. About the year 1875 he sold the woolen
mills and with his wife and three daughters, moved
to San Saba County, Texas, where they lived the
balance of their lives.

Aunt Martha never had but one child, Nettie,
who was born a year or so after her second
marriage. Sometime prior to 1889 Nettie married a
Mr. Harkey and both of them live in San Saba,
Texas.

I never knew very much of Aunt Martha and my recollection of her is not very vivid. She married Uncle Jim about the time I was born and went to live at Wanita, about thirty or forty miles away from where the balance of the kindred lived. In fact, I do not remember ever having seen her but once, when she came to visit us. As I remember her, she was a rather tall, handsome woman, and, as I thought, very finely dressed. In fact, for some unknown reason, I was a bit afraid of her. But somehow, although Uncle Jim was a bluff, hearty, loud voiced man, I was not afraid of him at all; but would sit and listen to him talk by the hour. I remember he was slightly deaf, and so was Old Mother, but neither of them appreciated just how deaf the other was. Somehow, each one thought the other was very deaf, and when they got together and began to talk, they made the shingles rattle on the roof. It was a source of great amusement to my father, and I halfway suspect he was the cause of the impression each one had of the other."

3. vii. ALBERT GALLATIN[6] AMIS, b. 15 January 1841 Newton Co., Miss.; d. 31 July 1878 Conehatta, Newton Co., Miss.; m. MARY AUGUSTA PETTY, 16 December 1865 Newton Co., Miss.; b. 8 April 1849 Scott Co., Miss.; d. 9 July 1922 Meridian, Lauderdale Co., Miss.; m. (2) WILLIAM BUYCK THORNTON.

vii. MIRNIA WOODSON[6] AMIS, b. 27 February 1844 Newton Co., Miss.; d. 29 December 1897 Newton Co., Miss.; m. J. D. GRAHAM 14 January 1864 Newton Co., Miss.; d. 21 June 1896 Newton Co., Miss.

"Mirnia Woodson Amis, Aunt Wootie, daughter of John W. Amis and Martha Wakdins, was born February 27th, 1844, in Newton Co., Mississippi. She married J. D. Graham, Uncle Dock, January 14th, 1864. He died June 21st, 1896, and soon thereafter, on December 29th, 1897, she followed him. They had nine children: Harvey, Ella, Walter, Ida, Mattie, Jimmie, William, John, and Ruby, all of

131

whom, except Mattie, lived to be grown and married.

Aunt Wootie was rather taller than any of her sisters, unless it was her sister, Martha. She and Aunt Martha were never as stout as the others; and as I remember them, their complexion was not as ruddy as was that of all the others. She was a very kind, motherly sort of woman, but she never fussed or worried about the children. Her son Harvey was just a little older than I was, and I remember that I always enjoyed visiting him very much, because she would let us do almost anything we wanted to, except tear the house down or set something afire. We would go fishing, hunting, make blow-guns, play "injun," or yoke up the yearlings and haul with the wood wheel wagon and never heard a word of protest from her. And Uncle Dock was the same way. They seemed to think the Lord took care of boys and there was no use to worry about us. And they were right about it, for I guess we would have done it anyway, even if we had to sneak off.

Uncle Dock was a happy-go-lucky sort of man, full of fun and a great practical joker. He and his neighbors, Ferd Petty, Pate Finlayson, and Jim Wilson were always playing pranks on each other, like grown up boys, much to their own amusement and that of everyone else in the neighborhood. Nor were Uncle Dock's pranks confined to them, but often included others as well.

He knew that Uncle Charley Day liked his "dram" as well as anybody, if not a little better, especially in cold weather. In going to Newton to market, he had to pass through the village of Conehatta. On one occasion, just before Christmas, he carried a load of cotton to Newton. While there he bought a jug of whisky and a jug of cottonseed oil and placed them both in the back end of his wagon among the various other articles he had purchased. Of course, he took a few "nips" out of the whisky jug himself on his way home, but just before he got to Conehatta, he drove the stopper down tight in the whisky jug and left the one in the oil jug loose so it could be pulled out easily.

When he reached the village, he stopped his wagon right in front of Uncle Charley's house and began to talk loud to a crowd of on one of the store galleries. Pretty soon Uncle Charley came over and after he got a whiff of Uncle Dock's breath, he asked him if he had any left. In a maudlin, half drunk manner Uncle Dock said: "Yes, plenty in the back end of the wagon, help yourself." Without waiting for a second invitation, Uncle Charley went and pulled out the loose stopper and there, before the whole crowd, proceeded to take a good long swig of cotton-seed oil, before he discovered his mistake. Although he got plenty of the contents of the other jug to take the taste out, I do not think Uncle Charley ever fully forgave him.

And shortly before Dr. McIlhenny married Uncle Tank's daughter, Mollie, Uncle Dock told him, in the greatest confidence, that there was a great secret about the Amis family that he ought to know, but which he could not tell. Doctor was greatly worried, but of course could not ask Mollie to tell him. So he got very confidential with her and told her all manner of yarns about his folks, mostly in the hope that she would tell him the great family secret. But this availed him nothing and he was still mystified the day of the wedding when Uncle Dock, leading a mangy, bob-tailed cur, waylaid him on his way to the wedding and after presenting him with the dog, told him that the secret was that every Amis son-in-law must own a bob-tailed dog.

It would take a volume to record all the pranks he played on his neighbors and kindred, and yet he was a good neighbor and friend. His pranks served to drive away the tedium of life and the dull carking care that sits, too often, on the brow of those who dwell on the farm and toil with their hands alone in the fields.

"The evil men do lives after them, the good is oft interred with their bones," wrote the great bard of Avon, but I prefer to remember the good rather than the evil; and to record that which makes life a little better and a little brighter. Like an old preacher friend of mine, now passed to his reward, I would *rather make men laugh than to make them cry, and if I were permitted to amend the "Beatitudes" I would add: "Blessed are the mirth makers, for theirs is the kingdom of gladness."*

Laugh and the world laughs with you,
Weep, and you weep alone.
For the sad old earth must borrow its mirth,
It has troubles enough of its own."

Children of MIRNIA AMIS and J. D. GRAHAM:

1. HARVEY JORDAN[7] GRAHAM, b. 1866 Scott Co., Miss.; d. 1925 Lubbock, Texas; m. ELIZABETH HARDING.[245]

    Harvey J. Graham, son of J. D. Graham and Mirnia Woodson Amis, was born about 1866 in Scott County, Mississippi, and grew to manhood there. In his early boyhood, he, along with Jesse Willis, Thomas Wilson, and myself, attended a school, at Old White Plains, in the winter of 1873 and 1874 taught by an old Yankee school teacher named Rhodes. All four of us were in the same class in spelling, which, by the way, we all studied, or pretended to study. We "said three lessons" every day, or in modern phraseology, recited, three times every day. And that old scoundrel whipped each one of us nearly every time we "said a lesson," or rather tried to say it, for we were so scared of him we couldn't "say" what little we did know. And then to add insult to injury, he often kept us, six and seven year old boys, in after school until sundown, and we had to walk home, two or three miles, after dark. I believe he just hated every white skin in the South and tried to take it out on us children. And because of his cruelty, his patrons finally ran him off.

    Later, Harvey attended High School at Conehatta, where we both at last, began to learn a little. After he grew to manhood, he went to Texas and for some years worked for his uncle, James M. Park, at San Saba, Texas. Later he

---

[245] In 1920 Harvey J. Graham 54, MS, and his wife, Betty, 53, were living with Robby, 19, Jeffie 17, and Murrie (f.) 12 in Dawson Co., Texas. [1920 Census, Dawson Co., Texas, Commissioner's Precinct 3, ED 250, p8A, #172/172.] The county seat is Lamesa, and it is closer to San Antonio than anywhere else.

married Elizabeth Harding, and, as I understand, accumulated considerable property. At the time of his death, in 1925, he lived in or near Lubbock, Texas, but I cannot get any information as to his family, although I have tried repeatedly. In our boyhood, Harvey and I were great friends and playmates, and we spent many happy hours together in boyish sports. And, by the way, even old Rhodes didn't get ahead of us much by keeping us in after school; because we took a lot of splinters and our dog with us to school, and would sometimes catch possums on the way home at night. So then, as now, every bitter had its sweet.

2. ELLA[7] GRAHAM, b. 15 April 1868 Scott Co., Miss.; m. WILLIAM H. LACK 6 September 1886 Scott Co., Miss.; b. 12 January 1858 Newton Co., Miss.; d. 25 July 1925 Norton, Miss.

   William H. Lack, familiarly known as Bill, was the son of Dr. Lack of Hillsboro, Mississippi, where Bill was born January 12th, 1858, and was reared there. On September 6th, 1886, he married Ella Graham, daughter of J. D. Graham and Mirnia Woodson Amis. After their marriage they lived for several years at Conehatta, Mississippi, where he engaged in farming and for several years was a Deputy Sheriff of the County. Subsequently the family moved to Bay Springs, Miss., where they resided for a number of years, and finally moved to Norton, where he died, July 25th, 1924. His widow still resides at Norton.[246]

3. WALTER WOODSON[7] GRAHAM, b. 11 June 1869 Scott Co., Miss.; d. 6 November 1954 Newton Co., Miss.;[247] m. MARTHA PETTEY 15 October 1879 Scott Co., Miss.; b. 13 October 1879; d. 23 August 1957 Newton Co., Miss.

4. IDA V.[7] GRAHAM, b. 10 May 1872 Scott Co., Miss.; d. 14 June 1911 Jackson, Hines Co., Miss.; m. OLLIE L. LACK 17 December 1891 Scott Co., Miss.

---

[246] I have been unable to locate Norton, although there is a Bay Springs in both Jasper and Smith County. The former seems more likely.

[247] Buried Sulphur Springs Baptist Church Cemetery.

Ida Graham, daughter of J. D. Graham and Mirnia Woodson Amis was born in Scott County, Mississippi, May 10th 1872. While she was a young girl, her father's family moved to Conehatta, where for a time she was a student at the High School there. On December 17th, 1891, she married Ollie L. Lack, a son of Dr. Lack, of Hillsboro, Mississippi. After their marriage, they continued to reside for some time in and near Conehatta, but finally moved to Jackson, Miss., where she died June 14th, 1911.

5. JIMMIE[7] GRAHAM, b. 12 July 1876 Scott Co., Miss; m. J. D. COLEY 6 December 1900 Scott Co., Miss.

6. JOHN D.[7] GRAHAM, b. 12 March 1881 Scott Co., Miss.; d. 30 June 1950 Hillsboro, Scott Co., Miss.; m. CARRIE E. HOLLINGSWORTH 12 December 1913 Scott Co., Miss; b. 12 November 1893 Scott Co., Miss.; d. 16 September 1983 Scott Co., Miss.

7. WILLIAM ALBERT[7] GRAHAM, b. 11 December 1881 Scott Co., Miss.; d. 5 November 1951 Scott Co., Miss.; m. MARY LOIS LEACH; b. 22 July 1903 Scott Co., Miss.; d. 19 October 1987 Newton Co., Miss.

8. RUBY[7] GRAHAM, b. 8 September 1885 Scott Co., Miss.; d. 24 November 1962; m. RUFUS F. UNDERWOOD 12 November 1905 Scott Co., Miss.; b. 17 December 1879; d. 25 February 1969 Newton Co., Miss.

ix.   FRANCES[6] AMIS, b. 28 January 1848 Scott Co., Miss.; m. WILLIAM H. MOORE 18 February 1869 Newton Co., Miss.; d. 1 January 1908.

"Frances Amis, daughter of John W. Amis and Martha Wadkins, was born January 28th, 1848, a little more than a year before her father died. She married William H. Moore, February 18th, 1869. He died January 1st, 1908, but she is still living and, like Old Mother, lives with and among her children, sometimes with her daughter, Nettie Moore Harper, at Wolfe City, Texas, and sometimes with her son, Almon Moore, at Navarro, Texas.

I remember her back as far as fifty years ago and I always thought she was more like her mother than any of her sisters. She always had the same little motions and mannerisms that distinguished Old Mother from all other people I ever knew. And while I have not seen her for many years, I am told by those who have that she grows more and more like her as she grows older. She was the baby child of the family, and I always thought, my father's favorite sister.

When I can first remember, she and Uncle Bill lived within a mile or so of my father's home, and the families visited each other often. And one of the most vivid recollections I have is how he used to tease her, or else one of her children until he got one or both of them crying. And when she began to scold him, he and Uncle Bill would pick up their hats and go off laughing, with me trudging along at their heels. She always called him Albert, but when she got angry and began to scold him, she said is so quick it sounded like "Abbott" instead of Albert. And yet, with all his teasing and her scolding, they were very fond of each other. And when Old Mother was too feeble to travel around among her children, she chose her baby as the one with whom she would spend her last days. And her trust was not misplaced, for she was lovingly and tenderly cared for until the end.

Aunt Frances for nearly twenty years has been a widow, and yet she lives on. She has lived out her allotted of three score and ten years and, by reason of strength, has almost reached four score. But the years come on apace and the shadows are lengthening around her. The pathway is darkening and just over the hill lies the Valley of the Shadow. Conscious of a life well spent, she patiently awaits the Master's summons, in the blessed assurance that all will be well when her "ship puts out to sea." May her last days be glad days, and when the end comes, may she be—

Sustained and soothed by an unfaltering trust
Like one who wraps the drapery of his couch
About him, and lies down to pleasant dreams.

Uncle Bill was a bluff, hearty man, with a deep, bass voice, and a slow, rumbling laughter that seemed to come from the depths of his being. He was fond of children, especially boys, and made companions of his sons. He was a man's man, and took great pleasure in their company and conversation. He seldom borrowed trouble or took things too seriously. He seemed to believe in the proverb: "Don't trouble trouble, till trouble troubles you," and as a result he escaped many of the needless worries and anxieties of life.

He like to hunt and fish, and especially to trap partridges. He used to have a net and a pony trained for the business; and when he went out on a damp, drizzly day along in the fall, he seldom failed to bag a covey. Some of the gun club members might say that he was not sportsman-like. But he wouldn't have cared if they had. He was out after the birds and he got them just like a modern hunter with three or four dogs and a pump gun does. What's the difference, the birds get killed either way. The only difference is that when Uncle Bill bagged more than he needed for his own table, he divided with his neighbors; while the latter-day pump-gun hunter puts all his kills in cold-storage and keeps them for his own use. As between the two, I vote for Uncle Bill.

Uncle Bill is gone, and so are most of the birds and nearly all the fish and squirrels. Canals have been dug along the streams and the fishing is ruined. The forests have been cut down and destroyed and there is no place for the game to hide and nothing for them to feed on. The only hiding places left are the sedge fields and the briar patches, and about the only game that thrives there are the cotton-tail rabbits, which the small boy and his hound pup still chase over hill and dale, to the great amusement of all concerned."

Children of FRANCES AMIS and WILLIAM MOORE:

1. WILLIS WATKINS[7] MOORE, b. 15 August 1870; m. (1) ANNIE M. ESTES 1 February 1906; m. (2) CLARABEL FREEKET December 1924.
2. CLARENCE ALMOND[7] MOORE, b. 12 April 1873; d. 26 May 1941 Navarro, Navarro Co.,

Texas; m. KATIE ISABELLE THOMAS 18 August 1901 Texas; b. 14 August 1880 Corsicana, Navarro Co., Texas; d. 22 May 1952 Navarro, Navarro Co., Texas.

3. NETTIE B.[7] MOORE, b. 19 April 1874; m. T. B. HARPER 14 November 1899 Wolfe City, Hunt Co., Texas.

4. EFFIE D.[7] MOORE, b. 2 January 1876 Newton Co., Miss.; d. 22 March 1909 Lake, Scott Co., Miss.; m. CLAUDE G. MCCLANAHAN 28 December 1902 Newton Co., Miss.

> *"Effie Moore, daughter of W. H. Moore and Frances Amis, was born January 2nd, 1876, in Newton County, and was reared there. When she was a young girl her parents moved to Conehatta and for a time she was a student at the High School there. Afterward her parents moved to Harpersville, and she was a student in the High School there for a time. On December 28th, 1902, she married Claude G. McClanahan, of Hillsboro, where they resided for some years after their marriage. Later, they moved to Lake, where she died, March 22nd, 1909. She left three children, all boys, surviving her. She was a shy sweet girl, as modest and shrinking as a violet that blooms by the wayside, and gladdens the eye with its beauty and loveliness. In memory, I can still see her sweet face and timid winsome smile, that won the hearts of all who knew her. The dread white plague, tuberculosis, laid its hand upon her, and at the touch of its blighting breath, she faded away."*

3. ALBERT GALLATIN[6] (*JOHN W.[5], WILLIAM[4-3], JOSEPH[2]*) AMIS was born 15 January 1841 in Scott Co., Mississippi and died 31 July 1878 in Conehatta, Newton Co., Miss. He married MARY AUGUSTA PETTY 16 December 1865 Newton Co., Miss., dau. of ALBERT G. PETTY and LUVENIA BREWER. She was born 8 April 1849 in Scott Co., Miss., and died 9 July 1922 in Meridian, Lauderdale Co., Miss. She married (2) WILLIAM BUYCK THORNTON September 1879 Newton Co., Miss. He died February 1897 in Gulfport, Miss.

Albert Gallatin Amis, son of John W. Amis and Martha Wadkins, was my father. He was born January 15th, 1841, and died July 31st, 1878. He served as a soldier in the Confederate Army, first as a private for fourteen months in the 6th Mississippi Infantry Regiment, and then for thirty four months as 2nd Lieutenant of Company K, 34th Mississippi Cavalry Regiment. He was wounded at the battle of Shiloh, and subsequently took part in the Georgia campaign, when General Johnston's Army retreated from Chattanooga across Georgia to the sea and thence north into the Carolinas.

On the evacuation of Richmond in 1865, the specie, (gold and silver) in the Richmond banks was loaded into army wagons and started south under military escort. When this money train, as it was called, reached the Carolinas in the military area under the command of General Johnston, a squadron of cavalry under the command of Col. William Preston Johnson, was assigned to guard it in its movement to the southwest; and Co. K, 34th Mississippi Cavalry was one of the units assigned to that duty. When that command reached Forsyth, Georgia, they learned that General Johnston had surrendered his entire army and thereupon the officer in command distributed twenty dollars in silver to each soldier and placed the balance of the specie in a brick storehouse and waited for the Federal troops. On their arrival, the Confederates surrendered. They were paroled and permitted to keep their horses and the officers to retain their side-arms.

My father brought home two "Navy six" cap and ball pistols and his sword. He gave the sword to China Grove Lodge of Masons at Conehatta, Mississippi, and it was used by them as the tyler's sword, the last I knew of it. He sold one of the pistols when I was a boy, but he kept the other until his death, and he was an expert in the use of it. He said it saved his life once in the army and he would not part with it.

After having surrendered, he, in company with Lt. Robert Burton of Lawrence, Steve Daniels of Union, and Clay McMullan, now living at Decatur, rode home across the country, where they arrived on the third Sunday in June 1865. On arriving home, he found the family had gone to church, at old Sulphur Springs, a couple of miles away and so he rode over there. When he arrived the pastor was in the midst of his sermon; but some members of the congregation seeing him ride up on his old cavalry horse, clad in his worn and faded uniform, forgot the solemnities of the occasion, and blurted out: Yonder comes Ab Amis." With that, his mother and sisters, and the whole congregation, preacher and all, rushed out of the church to greet and welcome one whom they had already begun to mourn as dead. And they all say there was no more preaching that day.

On December 6th, 1865, he married Augusta Petty, daughter of Albert G. and Luvenia Brewer Petty, and soon thereafter, bought and settled a tract of land about a mile and a half northwest of Prospect Church, in Newton County, where he continued to reside until January 1878, when he moved to Conehatta, where he died in July following.

He was an excellent farmer and a good businessman. He was a member of the Baptist Church, a Royal Arch Mason, an enthusiastic Granger, and was, at various times, master of his Lodge and his Grange. He was active in politics and was one of the political leaders of the county. In 1876 he was a candidate for Representative from Newton County, but was defeated by a margin of four votes in the single primary election of those days, in which there were five candidates.

He was a handsome man, about five feet eleven inches high, broad shouldered and erect. His complexion was ruddy, his eyes were gray, his beard was luxuriant and his black hair was worn rather long, in the style of the old south. At home he dressed as other farmers; but when he "went abroad" as the saying was, dressed in his broadcloth suit, polished, high heel calfskin boots, and broad-brimmed black hat, he was a striking figure in any crowd. He was a great talker in private, but could never make a public speech. He was an inveterate tease, and kept his sisters and sisters-in-law in constant dread of him, and yet they all loved him.

As a businessman, he was prompt in the performance of his obligations, and insisted that others do likewise. He bought his first tract of land on credit, but he paid for it when it was due, and after that, he never bought anything on credit of more than thirty days. He realized the power of cash in driving business deals, and always took advantage of it. And as far back as I can remember he always kept a cash reserve of five hundred dollars in gold, in an old leather trunk in his bedroom. At it was there when he died.

Although he was just a farmer, he kept an old single entry ledger on the old high boy in the "big room" and every night he would enter into it a record of the day's transactions, whether with his tenants, wage-hands, or others with whom he had business. When his cotton was ready for market, he would always send his wagons on ahead and then he would bathe, shave, and dress, mount his saddle-horse and get there before they did. He would the sell his cotton, purchase his supplies, load them on the wagons, and then beat them back home. I think he had the idea, now generally recognized, that a man's personal appearance counts in business of any sort.

Of course, he was my ideal man. When I was a boy he would often take me with him when he went hunting, and I remember that I would try to tread in his tracks as I trudged along behind him. And though he has been dead more than fifty years, I have tried through the years, though often unsuccessfully, to tread in his tracks. And to me, though dead, he yet liveth.

He left surviving him my mother and four children; myself, two sisters, Elvy and Bertha, and my brother Alvin; all of whom, except my mother and my sister Elvy, are still living.

My mother, Augusta Pettey, was born April 8th, 1849, and was only twenty nine years old when my father died. And in September 1879 she married William Buyck Thornton, of Conehatta, Mississippi, by whom she had one child, Ruby, born in 1881. After the marriage of my mother the family resided at Conehatta until 1896, when they moved to Gulfport, Mississippi, where my step-father died in February 1897. My mother continued to reside at Gulfport until 1905 when she moved to Meridian and lived in her own home, beside mine, until she died July 9th, 1922, and was buried in Magnolia Cemetery, at Meridian.

No children ever had a more faithful, kind, tender and loving mother that was ours. Year in and year out, she loved us, toiled for us and cared for us. She often denied herself the comforts of life that we might have the best. True to our father's ambition as well as her own, she struggled and toiled to earn the money to send us all to college.

It would be ungrateful in me not to record here a tribute to our step-father, because he, too, helped to care for us, educate us; and without his help, I do not believe our mother would have succeeded half as well as she did. And the fact that he was a college man himself contributed to give us a broader vision and encouraged us to take a collegiate education. His financial career was a varied and stormy one, for he was sometimes prosperous and sometimes poor.

But whatever he had, he shared with us, and when he lay dying, with full knowledge that the end was near, he prayed "for his children, all five of them," that God would keep and guard them. "After life's fitful fever he sleeps well" in the Methodist Church Yard at Conehatta. His only child, Ruby, now Mrs. J. H. Matthews, resides with her husband and three children at Gulfport, Mississippi.

Children of ALBERT G. AMIS and AUGUSTA PETTY are:

4.   i.   ALPHONSO BOBBETT[7] AMIS, b. 7 February 1867 Scott Co., Miss.; d. 6 July 1949 Meridian, Lauderdale Co., Miss.; m. MARY SALOME LANGFORD 11 June 1893 Newton Co., Miss.; b.

1 February 1868 Newton Co., Miss.; d. 7 December 1942 Meridian, Lauderdale Co., Mississippi.

ii. ELVY ZERAH[7] AMIS, b. 13 December 1868 Newton Co., Miss.; d. 26 June 1900; m. EUGENE E. KELLEY 12 February 1895 Newton Co., Miss.

Elvy Amis, daughter of Albert G. Amis and Augusta Pettey, was born December 13th, 1868, in Newton County and was reared there. In her girlhood, she attended, along with me, the old time Yankee teacher schools, and later the High School at Conehatta. When she was nearly grown, she attended the East Mississippi Female College at Meridian for two or three years. On February 12th, 1895, she married Eugene Kelly, of Conehatta, and they continued to reside in our old home until her death June 26th, 1900. She was buried in the Methodist Churchyard at Conehatta. She was about five feet high and weighed about a hundred pounds. She had a ruddy complexion, black eyes, and hair that reached almost to her knees. She was always neat in appearance, sprightly in disposition, and kind in word and deed. She died of an internal hemorrhage and was conscious until almost the end. When the eternal shadows began to fall about her she thought it was only the night coming on; and with a tired sigh, murmuring, "I'll be better in the morning," she fell asleep to wake no more.

> *The moving finger writes and having writ*
> *Moves on; nor all our piety nor wit*
> *Shall lure it back to cancel half a line*
> *Nor all our tears wash out a word of it."*

And while we cannot understand the inscrutable decrees of Providence, nor plumb the depths of His wisdom, yet we are comforted by the reflection that somewhere "Behind the dim unknown, standeth God within the shadow, keeping watch above His own. Like a flower in the springtime, she lived only to bloom and die, but-

> *A lily of a day is fairest in May*
> *Although it fall and die that night—*

It was a plant and flower of light.

Children of EUGENE KELLEY and ELVY AMIS:

1. FRANK EDWARD[8] KELLEY, b. 28 January 1896; m. (1) BERNICE RUSS 28 July 1918, divorced; m. (2) RUTH WOOSTER June 1926.
2. AMIS WILLIAM[8] KELLEY, b. 28 October 1898; m. JENNIE MEYER 18 October 1918.

iii. BERTHA[7] AMIS, b. 11 February 1873 Newton Co., Miss.; d. 11 June 1951 Moss Point, Jackson Co., Miss.;[248] m. JACOB NATHANIEL RAPE 11 November 1897 Newton Co., Miss.; b. 18 February 1859 Harpersville, Scott Co., Miss.; d. 4 February 1935 Moss Point, Miss.[249]

Jacob Nathaniel Rape was born about 1858 in Scott County, Mississippi, and was reared on a small farm a few miles north of Lake near Old Salem Church. I never knew his father, but I think his name was Cyrus Rape. My information is that he died in early manhood leaving his widow and two children, both boys, Jacob and John. All the property they inherited from their father was a small farm and the necessary plow animals and farming implements. And so from the time of his death the boys had to work the farm in order that they and their mother might have a living. The result was that they had very little schooling and when Jacob reached his majority he was scarcely able to read and write. Realizing the advantages of an education he went to work to acquire it. He first attended the common schools of the neighborhood and then the High School at Conehatta where I first knew him. At that time he was a grown man with a heavy moustache, the envy of the rest of us, who could only sport a few hairs on the upper lip, about eight on one side of the nose and nine on the other.

He was a hard working, industrious student and his progress was steady, though not rapid.

---

[248] Griffin Cemetery, Moss Point, Miss. http://www.findagrave.com., #53146667.

[249] Griffin Cemetery, Moss Point, Miss. http://www.findagrave.com., #53271533.

After graduating at Conehatta High School he studied medicine, but I have forgotten which college he attended. I think it was Tulane University in New Orleans, but it may have been Mobile Medical College. After graduating in medicine he located near Chula, in Holmes County, where he stayed some years on a large plantation as plantation physician. On November 11, 1897, he married Bertha Amis, daughter of Albert G. Amis and Augusta Pettey. On their wedding trip they spent a month or six weeks in New York City where he took a special course at Bellevue Hospital. On their return, they located in the town of Chula until the fall of 1900 when they moved to Moss Point, Miss., where they resided as long as he lived. He died in February 1935 and was buried at Moss Point.

In appearance he was rather tall and slender and always had a moustache, though in later years he kept it cut short. He was one of the neatest men I ever knew; and while he never wore fine clothes yet they always fit him well and it seemed that he never got them soiled. Some men are that way and he was one of them. I never could understand how they do it. His manners were polite, kind, and courteous; and that was true at home as well as abroad. He was patient and even tempered. In fact I do not think I ever saw him angry or out of humor in my life, though I knew him for nearly fifty years. He was a devout Christian and was sober and temperate in all things. He was an excellent physician and enjoyed a good practice from which he accumulated considerable money. But unfortunate investments and bank failures caused him to lose rather heavily. However, at his widow sufficient for her comfortable maintenance. His widow and four sons survived him. She is now and has been for several years a teacher in the Moss Point public schools. Two of the sons reside with her in the old family homestead and two of them live in Gulfport.

His obituary was posted on the findagrave website.

"Dr. Jacob N. Rape, physician and prominent citizen of Moss Point, died at his home in Moss Point on Monday, February fourth, after an illness of one month.

The funeral was held on Wednesday, from late home of the deceased, Rev. W. O. Sudler and Rev. W. H. Lewis, officiating, assisted by Revs. J. F. Brock, B. A. Meeks of Moss Point, and Rev. W. P. Baggett of Kreole.

Interment was in the family plot in the Griffin Cemetery, the following being pall bearers: Dr. J. F. Colley, A. L. Monroe, C. M. Fairley, K. W. Burnham, W. M. Alexander, and B. D. Spann. The honorary pallbearers were the members of the Jackson County Medical Society.

Dr. Rape was 75 years, 11 months, and 17 days old, being born in Forest, Miss., and came to Moss Point in 1900, where he has lived ever since. He is survived by his widow, four sons, and one grandchild.

He was a member of the Methodist Church and the Moss Point Masonic Lodge, a competent and popular physician, a good citizen, and a most loveable man. His loss will be keenly felt by the entire community as well as those who knew him intimately and all will join this paper in expressions of sympathy for the bereaved family."

Children of JACOB RAPE and BERTHA AMIS are:

1. CYRUS AMIS[8] RAPE, b. 14 January 1900; d. 13 May 1962 Gulfport, Harrison Co., Miss.;[250] m. ADELE YELVERTON 20 September 1928 Harrison Co., Miss.; b. 20 May 1902; d. 1 October 1996 Gulfport.[251]
2. JOHN WOODSON[8] RAPE, b. 28 August 1902 Moss Point, Miss.; d. 23 December 1970 Moss Point, Miss.;[252] m. BEULAH SHAMPINE,

[250] Floral Hills Memorial Gardens, Gulfport, Miss. http://www.findagrave.com., #106351674.
[251] Floral Hills Memorial Gardens, Gulfport, Miss. http://www.findagrave.com., #106351410.
[252] Griffin Cemetery, Moss Point, Miss. http://www.findagrave.com., #40244665.

b. 22 March 1912; d. 23 October 1984 Moss Point, Miss.[253]

3. JACOB NATHANIEL[8] RAPE, JR., b. 12 August 1904 Moss Point, Miss.; d. 1963 Gulfport, Harrison Co., Miss.;[254] m. RUTH ALDERMAN; b. 30 October 1903; d. 22 March 1991 Gulfport;[255] m. (2) JOHN ALEXANDER FUREY 17 March 1966 Harrison Co., Miss.

4. ALFONSO GALLATIN[8] RAPE, b. 12 June 1906; d. 13 June 1907.[256]

5. KATHERINE[8] RAPE, b. 21 March 1908; d. 4 July 1909.[257]

6. WILLIAM PETTEY[8] RAPE, b. 1 January 1910; d. 31 July 1911.[258]

7. GRAHAM PETTEY[8] RAPE, b. 1 September 1911 Moss Point, Miss.; d. 22 December 1999 Pascagoula, Miss.;[259] m. LUCILLE M. FAGGARD; b. 18 July 1905; d. 31 January 1984 Jackson Co., Miss.[260]

iv. ALVIN WOODSON[7] AMIS, b. 6 January 1875 Newton Co., Miss.; d. January 1944;[261] m. PATTI MAUD BROOKS 2 October 1904; b. 14 February 1877 Noxubee Co., Miss.; d. 1964.[262]

Born January 6, 1875, student University of Mississippi at various times from 1891 to 1898;

[253] Griffin Cemetery, Moss Point, Miss. http://www.findagrave.com., #40244688.

[254] Floral Hills Memorial Gardens, Gulfport, Miss. http://www.findagrave.com., #106242572.

[255] Floral Hills Memorial Gardens, Gulfport, Miss. http://www.findagrave.com., #106242807.

[256] Griffin Cemetery, Moss Point, Miss. http://www.findagrave.com., #40244740.

[257] Griffin Cemetery, Moss Point, Miss. http://www.findagrave.com., #28945543.

[258] Griffin Cemetery, Moss Point, Miss. http://www.findagrave.com., #28945520.

[259] Griffin Cemetery, Moss Point, Miss. http://www.findagrave.com., #53275369.

[260] Griffin Cemetery, Moss Point, Miss. http://www.findagrave.com., #53271559. He was her third husband.

[261] Floral Hills Memorial Gardens, Gulfport, Miss. http://www.findagrave.com., #101683424. Stone says "1943."

[262] Floral Hills Memorial Gardens, Gulfport, Miss. http://www.findagrave.com., #86388860.

graduated at the University of Mississippi 1898; employee of G&SI RR from 1900 to 1925; auditor of G&SI RR from 1915 to 1925; real estate and insurance business since 1925; secretary and treasurer, Gulfport Baptist Church; Secretary Building & Loan Assn., Gulfport; Superintendent of Baptist Sunday School. Married Patty Brooks October 3, 1904.

Children of ALVIN AMIS and PATTI BROOKS:

1. ALVIN WOODSON[8] AMIS, JR., b. 15 October 1905 Moss Point, Miss.; d. 1980 Gulfport, Harrison Co., Miss.;[263] m. MILDRED KELLER 10 September 1927; b. 1906; d. 1988 Gulfport.[264]

2. WAYNE BROOKS[8] AMIS, b. 28 August 1910 Moss Point, Miss.; d. 1996 Gulfport, Harrison Co., Miss.;[265] m. MYRTICE (BATSON) SMITH, dau. of JAMES C. BATSON and IDA LOTT; b. 1911 Lumberton, Miss.; d. 19 June 2000, Gulfport.[266]

4. ALPHONSO BOBBETT[7] (*ALBERT G.[6], JOHN W.[5], WILLIAM[4-3], JOSEPH[2]*) AMIS was born 7 February 1867 in Scott County, Mississippi, and died 6 July 1949 in Meridian, Lauderdale County, Mississippi. He married MARY SALOME LANGFORD 11 June 1893 in Newton Co., Miss., daughter of THOMAS DAVIS LANGFORD and LUCY FRANCES WILSON. She was born 1 February 1868 in Newton Co., Miss., and died 7 December 1942 in Meridian, Lauderdale Co., Mississippi.

---

[263] Floral Hills Memorial Gardens, Gulfport, Miss. http://www.findagrave.com., #86389097.

[264] Floral Hills Memorial Gardens, Gulfport, Miss. http://www.findagrave.com., #101683434.

[265] Evergreen Cemetery, Gulfport, Miss. http://www.findagrave.com., #101683440.

[266] Floral Hills Memorial Gardens, Gulfport, Miss. http://www.findagrave.com., #71510500. Date from her obituary. She was the widow of Esco Smith when she married Wayne B. Amis. She had one daughter, Ida Sue Harrell, wife of Dr. Tommy Harrell of Houma, La.

A. B. Amis: A Meridianite who achieved prominence in legal circles in the course of a long career, A. B. Amis attended Tulane University in 1885 and the University of Mississippi from 1886 to 1892, before beginning his Meridian law practice in 1893. Amis served as city attorney from 1912 to 1931. In 1930, he became Chancellor of the Second District, earning distinction for his judicial decisions. Among his many accomplishments are his contributions to domestic relations law in Mississippi. His "Amis on Divorce and Separation" laid the foundation for equity court statues in the state and remains in use today.[267]

Judge Amis moved to Meridian in 1893 to establish his law practice, and acquired the blocks between 12th and 14th Streets and 38th and 40th Avenues. He built the main house at 1201 38th Avenue, which was occupied by my grandparents when I was a child. Behind the main house, on the 12th Street side were the houses occupied by Merle and Aud, who were the Judge's cousins, and then the house occupied by Junie Cleveland, his first cousin. Junie's brother was Dr. Grover Cleveland, who was still in practice when I was a child. I also got to know Junie's brother Mimms Cleveland. When I first went to Birmingham to start medical school, Mom had told me to look them up. I did so, and they invited me out to visit. They also had an old oscillating fan that they gave me, since the apartment where I was living did not have air conditioning. I still have that fan. Mimms and Emily fed me and my roommate many Sunday dinners those first couple of years. I was always struck by the ease with which the claims of kinship could be made, as I had never met these folks before. All I had to do when I called was to identify myself as Augusta's grandson..

---

[267] From *Paths to the Past-An Overview History of Lauderdale County, Mississippi*, by Fairley and Davison, quoted by Dan Langford. This seems to be taken from Brown, quoted fully in the foreword.

My mother, Mary Mina Whitener, wrote a recollection of her grandparents in 2000. "Since I have become an ancestor, I have been thinking about my ancestors. What do I remember about them?

I suppose that I was closest to my maternal grandmother, whom we called "Mammy." We lived right next door to her and Grandpaw . And, I spent most of my growing up time at Mammy's house. I remember that the rest of the family called me Mammy's shadow.

Though I spent a good deal of time with her, I never knew she had false teeth. That is until one time we were on the screen porch in the swing when she sneezed! Lo and behold her teeth flew out of her mouth over the railing and into the flower bed. Needless to say I was very agitated. I thought something was wrong. I guess I was about 5 years old at that time. It took some explaining from my mother to quiet me down.

Mammy loved to fish and she and Miss Madge, Grandpaw's secretary, would go every time they could get away. And, I was allowed to tag along. Mostly we fished with live earth worms but once in a while Mammy would decide she wanted to use Catalpa worms. They were big green worms that I could never get on my hook. They bled green. I think Mammy was very disappointed that I was never able to bait my hook with one of them.

She also loved to garden. She had a plot down the hill on 12th street where the Negro Junior College is now located. Of course, Willie did the plowing and all the hard work, but Mammy did the harvesting and some hoeing. I used to go down there and "help" her pick beans and peas. I was not allowed to pull the corn, though, as I had a tendency to break the stalk as I pulled. Just didn't have the knack to break the ear from the stalk. She usually was already down there by the time I was awake and looking for her.

That didn't stop me from going on down the hill to find her.

After she returned from the garden with her harvest to the back steps was the most fun. Mamma, Frannie and Mary would come over to decide what they would have for dinner (which was always at noon.) They would shell peas, shuck the corn and just visit. Most of us grandchildren would help shell the peas or just sit and listen to the grown ups.

Usually after all the vegetables were ready to be cooked we would adjourn to the side yard and eat watermelon. From the 4th of July until well into the fall, Mammy had a watermelon every day. Toward the end of the summer, she would buy a whole truck load of melons from one of the Negroes who came by everyday and store them in the cellar. It was dark and damp down there but it kept the melons fresh for her one a day habit.

Holidays were one big get together with the whole family. B and Polly, Sonny and Paul would come up from Newton and spend the day. And, of course, Mamma and Daddy, Jim and Frannie, Mary and Donovan, and all the sundry kids were on hand. Some times Mammy and Grandpaw had one of Edna's kids living with them and they were there, too. In fact there were so many of us that we had a second table where the kids ate. I really wanted to make the big table, but never did while Mammy was alive. When Mamma moved into the big house, I finally made it one time before the house was sold.

Getting ready for dinner was a big deal. Black Mammy (Jean, the cook) always was in charge of the turkey which was always at least a 25 pound Tom Turkey. A couple of days ahead we made a pound cake and the ambrosia. I was allowed to sit in the pantry and cream the butter, real butter, which I did in a big wooden bowl with my hands. There were no mixers at that time. While I "played" with the butter, Mammy measured a pound of sugar, a pound of flour, separated one dozen eggs and then added it to my butter. I can smell it all now. In getting the ambrosia ready somebody always scraped their fingers grating the coconut and bled into the mix. Added flavor, I suppose.

Grandpaw always carved the turkey at the table. And, we all had to wait til he finished before we could eat. I remember that he ate with his knife and I could never figure out why he didn't cut himself and how in the world he could pick up peas. But he did.

I was very fortunate to know all four of my grandparents. However, I knew my maternal ones best because they lived next door to us until we moved to Louisiana. I have already talked about Mammy. Grandpaw Amis was not a lovable personality; admirable, yes, but I don't ever remember having a conversation with him. I most remember his whittling. He always had a piece of cedar in his hand. He didn't make anything but was always surrounded by shavings. He always smelled like cedar.

I remember he walked a lot, up and down the sidewalk in front of the house. George and Bill would follow him around. Perhaps they had conversations with him.

Grandpaw at one time must have played a fiddle. I remember one summer he gave his old fiddle to Margaret and showed her how to get noise out of it. I was somewhat jealous because he didn't give it to me, tho, I have not a musical bone in my body. That is the only time I saw or heard of the fiddle.

When Luke was born, we took him to see his great grandpaw because not too many people had great grandparents. Luke must have been all of three months old, but he saw his great grandpaw! Grandpaw didn't ooh and aah over him but did pronounce that he would be plenty smart because he had a lot of head between his ears and the top of his head!

I suppose that is enough reminiscing. I had a wonderful carefree childhood. Not only did my aunts live next door but Junie and Merle lived on the block, too. And, I had the roam of the whole block. I was always visiting some one. And, I was allowed to walk to the store three blocks away to buy candy when I had a penny or two. Neighborhoods were safe then.

My descendants can't live that kind of life. But, I could wish for them the joy of knowing their family. And, the love that surrounds them."

A. B. Amis, III, mother's first cousin, also wrote his recollections of his grandfather for this work 6 December 2000. "Dr. Luke Wright has asked me to write up a personal sketch about my Grandfather, and his Great-grandfather, A.B. Amis, Sr. I undertake the task cheerfully: I enjoy writing, as Grandpa did also, and I would hope to afford succeeding generations a bit of insight into this brilliant and strongly-motivated man, whose smart and self confident Amis genes they still carry.

Certainly there are other of my cousins still living who would have been better able to write from their own personal recollections of Grandpa—cousins who spent most of their youth on "Grandpa's block" in Meridian and grew up seeing him daily and calling him "Mawka." He was never "Mawka" to me, so I'll be writing primarily about things I've heard and read about Grandpa. But because I'm his namesake, perhaps I've been a more careful collector and saver of things written about Grandpa.

At one time during the 1930s Grandpa had populated a full city block running from 12th to 13th Streets and from 38th to 39th Avenues atop one of Meridian's higher hills, only a few blocks from Highlands Park. I don't know exactly when Grandpa bought this property or started building on it, but I expect it was soon after he came to Meridian in early 1893 as a newly graduated and newly married 25-year-old lawyer just starting his practice. I've always had the impression that my Father and most of his brothers and sisters were born and raised in the large two-story house that still stands on that lot now, more than a hundred years later. Grandpa presumably had that house built, and probably expanded later to accommodate a growing family, as permitted by a successful law practice. Upstairs rooms later became "apartments" which were way stations where my Father and many of his siblings spent the early months or years of their marriages. Grandpa probably made the offer, and people generally didn't argue with Grandpa. Then later he presumably offered lots on his block to his three daughters, and they all dutifully built homes adjacent to his. The other two building lots on his block were occupied by homes owned by two of Grandpa's cousins—one of whom became a caretaker and housekeeper for him in his last years.

I grew up seeing Grandpa somewhere between weekly and monthly, when Daddy would drive us the 30 miles from Newton to Meridian for Sunday afternoon visits—a practice that continued until Grandpa died in 1949. Up until the time of Mammy's death in 1942, the whole Amis clan was expected to gather around her large dining table on special occasions like Thanksgiving or Christmas; then Grandpa would offer the simple "Amis blessing" (the one I still use and have passed on down to my children), make a ceremony of carving the turkey, and finally inquire about the "sweet by and by" (dessert) after the main courses were all completed. While others might opt for the ambrosia or ice cream, Grandpa usually seemed satisfied to just spread a generous layer of butter on a large slab of the delicious yellow pound cake Mammy always included in her dessert offerings. Apart from these ceremonial gatherings and Sunday visits, I've been told the story that I spent several days in quarantine with Grandpa once when both of us must have had something contagious like mumps or measles. Whatever it was, we needed to be kept away from bright light, so we stayed in Grandpa's dark bedroom, where I taught him to play a child's card game—the only card game he ever learned, because he wasn't one to waste time in play.

Brilliant, yes; energetic, yes; motivated, yes; witty, enough; playful, no. My Father used to opine that Grandpa's one shortcoming was that he'd never learned to play. I expect Grandpa disdained adult play as a waste of time— somewhat in the same category as politicking and much of purely social interaction. Even at the ceremonial family gatherings, the men would retire to the sitting room or porch, to be joined later by the ladies after the dishes had been cleared and the children attended to, and Grandpa would lead the conversation around to important issues of the day rather than personal talk about the children or family happenings. When my mother first came into the family, she said she felt very much intimidated by all the smart people and bright conversation, and confided this concern to one of the sisters, who advised her "Just don't say anything and they'll think you're smart too." Grandpa's preoccupation with productive, rather than time wasting, activities no doubt set him apart from most people and likely came across as aloofness and a lack of warmth. In a 1938 newspaper editorial endorsing Grandpa's successful candidacy for a third four-year term as Chancellor, the editor had this to say:

God blessed this man with rare intelligence and a full understanding of the Law, and had the Maker of men given him the ability to acquire friends easily and a more full use of the tongue, he might have been one of the nation's contemporary greats.

It was this man who fashioned the first commission form of government for municipalities in Mississippi. It was this man who dreamed once of a great and beautiful city administration building, and we know it now as the most attractive structure of

156

its kind in the commonwealth. It was this man who made our present Mattee Hersee hospital a possibility. As he designed our city hall, so is his influence seen in the architectural plans of this medical institution.

In a paid advertisement in that same newspaper issue, Grandpa, himself, had this to say:

> I was reared in Newton County. Forty-five years ago I moved to Lauderdale County where I have lived ever since. During all those years I have been a part of the community life of the County. As a man, a lawyer and a judge I have walked among you and dealt with you. I have tried, as best I could, to live the life of an honest, sober, and industrious man and useful citizen. How well I have succeeded I leave to your judgment.
>
> I know nothing of the arts or guile of the politician. All I know in that regard, is hard work and honest, faithful service. I am deeply grateful for the honor of serving you in the past and in return I have given to your service all the mental, moral and physical powers I possess. I desire the honor of serving you another term, and to that end respectfully solicit your votes.

In those 45 years referred to by Grandpa, he had raised a family (and meddled, benevolently by his reckoning, in their affairs), established a successful law practice, served as Meridian City Attorney for 19 years and Chancellor for 8 years, and participated in various civic organizations and causes where he felt he might contribute productively. Grandpa was supremely confident—when he saw something that he thought needed doing, he undertook to get it done. When he saw something that he thought needed fixing, he undertook to fix it, with never a doubt that he could, indeed, fix it: he would simply read everything he could about it, think hard about it, and then write down instructions for others how it should be fixed.

As Chancellor, Grandpa heard civil cases involving all manner of disputes relating to property, debts, damages, etc., but certainly his greatest expertise and contributions were in matters of divorce, probate, and guardianship. One of his early acts after taking the bench as Chancellor in 1930 was to write, publish, and distribute at his own expense three thousand copies of a pamphlet on the "Duties of Executors, Administrators, and Guardians." Quoting from a letter written some years later by an associate who had practiced law in his Court:[268]

> When he took office, he found the probate business of his district in a sad and derelict condition...Chancellor Amis went diligently to work to straighten out his probate dockets, to restore the estates to solvency where possible and to pursue the wasters and looters wherever practicable throughout the district.
>
> His bar had so long neglected efficiency in this branch of their work that to aid them and himself in his efforts, he wrote and had printed at his own expense a paper bound booklet on probate practice which he distributed to the lawyers of his district.
>
> I doubt that Chancellor Amis had any statute of another state which he followed. He didn't need any to show him the way or how to proceed. He was a statesman judge, with a creative and searching mind...and he had the patriotic willingness to labor to correct such evils as these statutes and others he drew were designed to eradicate.

Grandpa then turned his attention to bank failures, which had become commonplace during the great Depression of the 1930s. Perceiving that there was nothing to guide lawyers in liquidating the failed

---

[268] The letter was written to Hon. Phil Stone, Oxford, Miss., 23 May 1952, but the signature is not legible on the copy I have.

banks and administering the assets, he again made a study of the banking system, thought hard about it, and then wrote and distributed to the lawyers of his district an outline of procedures to be followed.

In 1935 Grandpa published what he described as "A Brief on the Law of Divorce and Separation in Mississippi." This 500 page "brief" served as the preeminent reference on divorce in Mississippi for lawyers and professors for decades following its issue. In his Foreword to this book, he says:

GENTLEMEN OF THE BAR: This book is a brief in fact as well as in form. The only excuse for its preparation and publication, if any be required, is that I felt that something of the sort was needed; and since no abler man, of whom there are many, would undertake the task, I assumed to do it. .

The brief was prepared in a sort of desultory manner, at times when I was not engaged in the discharge of my official duties. For that reason, as will be observed, there is more or less repetition in it, a fact of which I am fully conscious. But if that be considered a literary sin, my defense is, that law like religion cannot be learned in a moment, but must be conned by littles, precept upon precept, rule upon rule, line upon line, here a little and there a little, over and over, until it becomes an integral part of the mental and moral nature. And besides that the various subjects are often so blended that it is difficult to trace the line of demarcation between them. However well or ill the task may have been performed, it has been a pleasant and profitable one to me, in that it has greatly increased my own knowledge of a subject matter, concerning which my ideas had previously been very hazy and uncertain.

During this same productive period, the mid-1930s, Grandpa also researched and recorded quite a lot of material on his own and Mammy's ancestries.

I believe I've read that Grandpa had sandy brown or reddish hair as a young man, but by the

159

time I have any recollection of him he was already in his mid-sixties or beyond, and projected a very distinguished appearance in his customary attire of a suit, with a black string bow tie and black high top shoes setting off his silver hair. Before stepping outside the house he'd take a hat from a hat rack and select a walking stick from a china urn, both just inside the front door. A medium size man in height and weight, he usually smelled of cedar, for it was his habit to carry a small knife with a keen blade and a stick of red cedar, and while taking testimony in court or even just conversing, he'd whittle small curly shavings from the stick. He explained that this helped him focus on what was being said rather than being distracted by other things going on around him. Grandpa never learned to drive as far as I know, and relied on trains or else getting a ride with his long time court reporter for travel to the various county seats in his district for terms of court.

Grandpa was 75 when he voluntarily stepped down from the bench in 1942 after three terms as Chancellor, and he received many public accolades for his distinguished service. While still sound of mind and body, age had nevertheless begun to take a toll on Grandpa, particularly a facial skin cancer condition for which he finally resorted to surgery in the late 1930s or early 1940s. My Father accompanied Grandpa to St. Louis for the surgery, and then Grandpa remained there at the Biltmore Hotel for several weeks afterwards, recuperating. In a letter to Mammy he wrote:

As you know I dreaded the trip and its possible results more than anything in recent years. Yet it has not been unpleasant. Everyone has been uniformly kind to me and I have made a number of pleasing acquaintances. And the numerous letters I have received show me that I have many friends who love me with genuine affection. That has been a source of much joy. I am keeping them for you to read. But the greatest thing is the burden of apprehension that the doctor has removed by his assurances that I need not have any further fear of cancer. The spectre that I would have my face eaten off by a slow cancer and thus become an object of pity and disgust to all with whom I might come in contact was almost more than I could stand. The doctor assures me that will not happen. He also says my eye will close naturally. But even if it does not I am content to escape what I feared so much - a cancer. I have been fighting it 20 years and I pray God that it does not recur. If it does not, I feel that I will live and work at least 10 years more. For I feel fine every other way and life seems good and sweet, among those whom I love and who love me - of whom you, my dear, are the most beloved.

Grandpa probably figured right about living for another 10 years, but after stepping down from the bench and then Mammy slipping away in her sleep just months later, the two things that had made life most worthwhile for him were now ended. A place was made for Grandpa in a son-in-law's law firm, and he practiced a little law and agitated a little in the local city courts about issues that attracted his interest like lax and unequal enforcement of prohibition statutes, but in truth he was now redundant and he realized it. He continued to go to the office every day and became a figure recognized by the townspeople as he charged across the busiest intersections in the heart of Meridian, against traffic, with his cane raised in the air commanding everyone to make way for him to cross.

Grandpa knew his Bible and could quote Scriptures in support of any lesson he was trying to illustrate relating to how men should conduct themselves. But he wasn't a Bible thumper. Much of his faith was in himself, I think, and he probably had less need of Biblical interpretations of God than most.

He revered "the Word," but wasn't beyond making light of some of its institutions sometimes out of fear of being instantly struck down by a thunderbolt. In writing of a despised "old Yankee school teacher named Rhodes" who had mistreated him badly in his first years of school right after the end of the Civil War, he said:

> And that old scoundrel whipped each one of us nearly every time we 'said a lesson', or rather tried to say it, for we were so scared of him we couldn't 'say' what little we did know. And then to add insult to injury, he often kept us, six and seven year old boys, in after school until sundown, and we had to walk home, two or three miles, after dark. I believe he just hated every white skin in the south and tried to take it out on us children. When I get up before the bar of Judgment, if old Saint Peter asks me whether I have any hatred in my heart, I am going to inquire where old Rhodes is, and if I find out he is where I think he ought to be, then I will forgive him; but if he is inside the pearly gates, dressed up in a halo and a pair of wings, playing 'Yankee Doodle' on a jews-harp, I don't believe I would enjoy going to Heaven.

As noted, the 1930's were a productive time for A. B. Amis as an author. He also wrote a small pamphlet titled "Recollections of Social Customs in Newton and Scot Counties, Mississippi, Fifty Years Ago."[269] Among the papers collected by his grandchildren was a story, undated, titled "My First Law Suit." Although his grandchildren did not think he had a sense of humor, this story suggests otherwise.

> When I first opened a law office in the small town of Mendenhall, very wise, ambitious, and feeling

---

[269] Privately published in 1934. A. B. Amis, III, made an OCR copy and posted it online. It was found 27 March 2014 at http://www.scottlee.com/recollections.html.

secure in my ability to cope with all things, my library sisting of the code of 1892 and three sheet redacts of the legislature, a second-hand typewriter, stationery emblazoning my name at large, a 75 cent sign at the foot of the stairy telling all that I was a good lawyer awaiting them upstairs, I sat down for about two weeks without having my door darkenend. My pangs of disappointment grew more acute as the footsteps of those seeing other occupants of the building would turn into other doorways.

Finally a denizen of Sullivan's Hollow, whom I now know to have been in very great need of a green lawyer, one of that shade of sincere inexperience who could readily see the law as confirming to the vehement facts related to him by his prospective client who was preparing to "have the law on his offending neighbor," came in, looked around and asked if I were a lawyer. Upon my informing him that I was and in that manner benefiting the occasion, that I was a good one, too, he blurted out, "I may want to hire you. What's the law on truspass?"

After quizzing him I found that the cause of his ire was that a man in the community who "had it in for him" and who "was agin' him," had "tore down his fence," maliciously, malevolently, with malice aforethought, and with venom and hatred in his heart, had cared to "trespass" and injure the property of my client.

I, of course, assured him that the law was against this sort of "truspass" and that when its might and power were properly invoked by a mighty wielder of the law, the proper vengeance would be wreaked upon the offender, the cruel wrong would be righted by fine and imprisonment, and the imprisonment would be especially inflicted. This line of talk seemed to get over and he want to know, "What'll you ax me to go down to Sarytogy Satidy and put it to him? The court will be held two miles out from Sarytogy at the Shiloh school house." I explained to him that because of the importance of his case and the expense of railroad fare being $1.60, that I would have to charge him $10.00 cash. We traded by splitting the fee in two payments—half cash and half at the court.

My train got to Saratoga at 7 o'clock in the morning, and I proceeded to walk out to Shiloh and sit around for an hour or so before anybody came up. After awhile the natives began to straggle in. There came up from one of the dim pathways a tall, barefooted, angular, and most voluble man carrying a long, single barreled shot gun. His repertoire was complete with all the jokes with which Solomon regaled his court, and the witty and funny things which wer no old no doubt in the days of Noah. His guffaw was loud and long at all his witty sayings and stale repartee. His toes spread apart and each toe had an individual motor. If, by chance, one of those large red ants got on his toe, without moving his foot or flicking a muscle, that toe would go into action like a mule's tail switching a horse fly, carrening the said ant so far that he could hardly crawl back that day.

Court was duly opened, the case proceeded to tril. My client put on his evidence, which almost made out a case, and if the opinion of my client and strong, unimpeachable, and hearsay evidence competently made out a prima facie case, which I maintained that it did, then we had enough to go to the consideration of the court. The defense was, as related by the defendant, that it was merely an accident. He told how he had come around a little dim road to the back of my clients field after a load of light wood and at one joint where the dim road came too near the rail fence that his wagon accidentally jerked a couple of panels of his fence down.

Among defendant's witnesses was the tall individual already referred to. He took his seat on the witness stand, crossed his legs and spit off about six or eight feet in a long, thin squirt—every drop of it went through a crack in the floor of the school house. (I verily believe he could have spit a fly off a door knob ten feet away and not hit the door.) He related how he had "overtuk" the defendant in the case while out hunting; how he was walking along, talking with him when the accident occurred; that it was purely accidental, with no taint of maliciousness in what he did. When he wound up, I sailed into him and the following examination took place.

Lawyer: "Why didn't this defendant drive his wagon further awy from this fence so that it would not be struck by the hub of the wagon?"

Witness: "Wal, sir, because it wuz a non-possibility."

Lawyer: "Why was it a non-possibility?"

Witness: "Because thur wuz a mud hole that coulda bogged 'im down."

Lawyer: "Why didn't he go around the mud hole?"

Witness: "Wal, sir, that wuz a non-possibility."

Lawyer: "Why was that a non-possibility?"

Witness: "Because there wuz a big stump agin the mud hole on the other side."

Lawyer: "Why didn't he straddle the stump?"

Witness: "Because that wuz a non-possibility."

Lawyer: "Why was that a non-possibility?"

Witness: "Because the stump wuz too high and it woulda caught on the axle."

Lawyer: "Why didn't he go around the stump?'

Witness: "Wal, sir, that wuz a non-possibility."

Lawyer: "Whey was that a non-possibility?"

Witness: "Because a big gulch made off from agin the stump and went on down to the crick bottom."

The lawyer by this time was somewhat bewildered and he hurled this question: "What do you mean by a non-possibility."

Witness: "Wal sir, I'd say it's a non-possibility fer you to stretch your mouth any wider cep'n you get your years a little fudder back."

Moral: Don't ask a witness one question too many.

Children of A. B. AMIS and MARY LANGFORD are:

i. MARSHALL WILSON[8] AMIS, b. 13 September 1894 Newton Co., Miss.; d. 11 July 1986 Fort Worth, Tarrant Co., Texas; m. ALICE MARY SMITH 21 July 1917 Memphis, Shelby Co., Tenn.; b. 25 March 1896; d. 7 February 1985.

Marshall Wilson Amis received his BS and LLB degrees from the University of Miss. in 1917. He served in World War I as Captain, Battery A, 334th Field Artillery from 15 Aug 1917 until 7 Mar 1919. From 1919 until late 1933 he practiced law in Meridian, Miss. In Dec. 1933 he joined the Legal Division of the Public Works Administration where he served until March 1938 when he joined the staff of the United States Housing Authority. In 1939 he became the Director of the Fort Worth Regional Office FPHA. In 1948 he was recalled to Washington to serve as General Counsel for the USHA. In 1953 he returned to Fort Worth as Regional Director. He retired September 1964. [270]

I met Marshall, or Buddy as he was called in the family, only twice. The first occasion was the marriage of my uncle, George Whitener in 1958. Of that meeting I have no distinct recollection of him. However, he visited with my parents and grandmother in Memphis in the summer of 1984 at which time he had turned 90. He had just returned from visiting a grandson who was serving in the Navy and was deployed with the Fleet. He was a very small man, much as his father was described, and of light frame. He was still mentally alert, despite his advanced age, but was becoming physically infirm.

Children of MARSHALL AMIS and ALICE SMITH:

1. ALICE MARY[9] AMIS, b. 20 August 1920 Meridian, Lauderdale Co., Miss.; d. April 1993 Anderson Co., S. C.; m. HODGES, VERNON SEYMOUR HODGES 9 April 1955; b.

---

[270] Hodges, Alice A. Ancestry and Descendants of Dr. John Wright Petty of Madison Co., Ala. (Pendleton, S. C.: n. p. d., 1978,) p. 12. (this was her father.)

16 August 1912; d. 11 February 1980 Pendleton, Anderson Co., S. C.[271]

2. MARGARET BROOKS[9] AMIS, b. 18 December 1922 Meridian, Lauderdale Co., Miss.; m. JAMES ALBERT DICKIE 14 February 1950 Alexandria, Va.

3. MARSHALL WILSON[9] AMIS, JR., b. 31 December 1927 Meridian, Lauderdale Co., Miss.; m. ELIZABETH HOYE.[272]

ii. MAURICE BREWER[8] AMIS, b. 11 March 1896 Newton Co., Miss.; d. 11 November 1980 Midland, Midland Co., Texas; m. VIOLET BOLTON 3 May 1920; b. 1899; d. 1981 Midland, Midland Co., Texas.[273]

Maurice Brewer Amis attended the University of Mississippi 1912-1913 and graduated from the University of Alabama in 1918. During World War I he served as a sergeant in the 605th Engineers, U. S. Army A. E. F. He was discharged June 1919. His hearing was damaged during this conflict. Until he retirement he was Chief Chemist, Standard Oil Refinery, Baton Rouge, La. [274]

Child of MAURICE AMIS and VIOLET BOLTON:

1. VIOLET[9] AMIS; m. (1) LELAND ELLIS 16 October 1942, divorced; m. (2) WILLIAM CAMERON BANKS 1959.

iii. ALPHONSO BOBBET[8] AMIS, JR., b. 20 August 1899 Newton Co., Miss.; d. 28 February 1972 Newton, Newton Co., Miss.; m. PAULINE HARDIN 25 April 1923 Hattiesburg, Miss.; b. 27 February 1901 Light, Miss.; d. 18 November 1982 Newton, Newton Co., Miss.

---

[271] Both death dates and his birth date are from the SSDI.

[272] She was the granddaughter of Clarence V. Hoye who was A. B. Amis, Sr.'s, roommate at the University of Mississippi according to handwritten notes by Frances Amis Floyd.

[273] Resthaven Memorial Park, Midland, Midland Co., Texas. Located on http://www.findagrave.com.

[274] Hodges, Alice A. Ancestry and Descendants of Dr. John Wright Petty of Madison Co., Ala. (Pendleton, S. C.: n. p. d., 1978,) p. 15.

A. B. Amis, Jr., attended Miss. A & M College and the University of Mississippi, where he received his law degree in 1922. He practiced law in Lauderdale and Newton Cos., Miss. He was a member of the Mississippi State Legislature from Lauderdale County from 1924-1928. [275]

A. B. was the uncle about whom the most stories were told that I recall hearing as a child. One that my grandmother swore to was that he had flunked ninth grade three times, when his father told him that he had been enrolled at the University of Mississippi as a freshman. He was told that if he flunked out, that he would be on his own. As noted, he became an attorney and practiced for awhile in Lauderdale County before moving back to Newton.

One famous story told in the family concerned a time when he was arguing a case in front of his father. The judge was prone to whittle while sitting on the bench, and did not appear to be paying all that much attention. At one point, the opposing counsel was making a point, and A. B. stood and made an objection. The judge overruled him. This prompted A. B. to suggest that "perhaps the court is in doubt about the ruling." The judge responded, "Sir, I may be in error, but I am never in doubt." Of course this was told to illustrate what a terror the judge was supposed to be, at least in the minds of his daughters.

A. B. was the uncle I got to know best as a child, as he lived nearby when we lived in Meridian in 1954-1956. He like to fish more than he liked to practice law, and had a sign on the wall of his boathouse that I recall said "The world is six sevenths water, so evidently God intended man to spend six days out of seven fishing."

A. B. was considerably more fleshy than the pictures of his father, or as I recall his eldest brother, Marshall. His wife, Pauline, or Polly as she was called, was a very slow talker, and had a

[275] Hodges, Alice A. Ancestry and Descendants of Dr. John Wright Petty of Madison Co., Ala. (Pendleton, S. C.: n. p. d., 1978,) p. 15.

very gravelly, raspy voice that was certainly lower than my boyish treble. I recall her having a dry wit, though, to go with it, and she clearly ruled the house. I remember eating Thanksgiving dinner at her house, probably in either 1954 or 1955, and being introduced to things like mincemeat and pumpkin pie. I may have been exposed to them earlier, but that is the first occasion I recall specifically. A. B. died of lung cancer in 1972, and Polly died 10 years later.

Children of A. B. AMIS and PAULINE HARDIN:

1. A. B.[9] AMIS, III, b. ; m. FRANCES HOLLADAY September 1949; b. 2 February 1926 Newton Co., Miss.; d. 31 August 2009 Grant, Fla.

> Sonny, as my mother always called him, was her favorite cousin. He was a couple of years younger than she, but was around a good deal in the early years and shared similar interests. As a result, he was the only cousin of the Amis surname that I really ever got to know. His wife, Frances, died a couple of years ago, and he sent me a copy of her obituary, which I have inserted here.

> Frances Amis passed away on Monday, August 31st, 2009 at her home. Born in Newton, MS, on 2/2/1926, to the late William Byron Holladay and Lydia Bounds Holladay, Frances's depression era upbringing as the second eldest of six siblings (oldest girl) instilled traits of responsibility, hard work, and love of family that stayed with her throughout her life. Completing public schools in Newton in 1944, Frances was valedictorian of her graduating class. After graduation, she worked for one year at the Mississippi Employment Service in Jackson before returning home to Newton to attend Clarke Memorial College and later work as a bank secretary up to the time of her marriage to A.B. Amis, III in 1949. She continued secretarial work at banks in Atlanta, GA, and Evansville, IN, while A.B. attended college and worked at his first job, before moving to Melbourne in 1953.

She is survived by her husband, A.B.; their two sons, William Paul and Richard Mark, by Mark's wife, Sandra, and grandchildren Simon and Hannah. Other survivors from Frances's immediate family are brother Wilbur Holladay, Macon, GA; sister's Mildred Valentine and Jennie Brady, Meridian, MS; Bobbie Miller and her husband Robert Miller, Lake Placid, FL; sister-in-law Agnes Holladay of Fairview, NC; one aunt, Sarah Massey, from Meridian, MS; special niece Julie Holladay Strahle, of Melbourne, who has been like a daughter; and numerous other nieces and nephews.

A member of the First Baptist Church of Melbourne since moving to Melbourne in 1953, Frances was a Florida Master Gardener for 20 years and also loved golf, gourds, RV travel, and bluegrass music.

Memorial services will be held at Brownlie-Maxwell Funeral Home in Melbourne on Friday, September 4th at 3:30 p.m. In lieu of flowers, donations may be made to Vitas Hospice or to the Alzheimer's Association.

2. PAUL HARDIN[9] AMIS.

iv. AUGUSTA[8] AMIS, b. 22 July 1902 Meridian, Lauderdale Co., Miss.; d. 30 November 1998 Memphis, Shelby Co., Tenn.;[276] m. GEORGE ALVIN WHITENER 18 July 1924 Meridian, Lauderdale Co., Miss., son of JOHN A. WHITENER and MINA ELIZABETH VINCENT; b. 30 August 1899 Cleveland, Bradley Co., Tenn.; d. 27 February 1962 Jackson, Rankin Co., Miss.

Children of ALVIN WHITENER and AUGUSTA AMIS:

1. MARY MINA[9] WHITENER, b. 8 September 1925 Meridian, Lauderdale Co, Miss.; m. LUCIUS FEATHERSTONE WRIGHT, JR., 27 January 1947 Alexandria, Rapides Parish, Louisiana, son of LUCIUS F. WRIGHT, SR., and KATHRYN PEARL DENNY.

---

[276] She is buried in Magnolia Cemetery, Meridian, Miss.

Children of MARY MINA and LUCIUS WRIGHT:

a. LUCIUS FEATHERSTONE[10] WRIGHT, III, b. 10 April 1948 Fort Sill, Comanche Co., Okla.; m. CYNTHIA MANN 23 June 1973 Memphis, Shelby Co., Tenn. *Children:* Kathryn (William Webb) Myers; David (Vickie Ellis) Wright; Frances (Duncan Kirk) Breland; Marian Wright; *Grandchildren:* Mary Olive and Charles Allen Myers; Eli Augustus and David Lawrence Breland.

b. JUDITH[10] WRIGHT, b. 17 December 1950 Fort Sill, Comanche Co., Okla.; m. WALTER EDWIN PIERCE 14 August 1976 Memphis, Shelby Co., Tenn. *Children:* Melissa Leigh (Emmett Joseph) Webb; Michael Edwin (Belee Jones) Pierce; *Grandchildren:* Caroline Leigh, Ella Marie, and Emmett Joseph Webb, Jr.

c. GEORGE DENNY[10] WRIGHT, b. 26 November 1966 Washington, D. C.; m. SUSAN DAWN MILLER 3 June 1989 Memphis, Shelby Co., Tenn. Children: Rebecca Suzanne; Amy Elizabeth; Stephen Daniel.

2. GEORGE AMIS[9] WHITENER, b. 9 August 1934 Meridian, Lauderdale Co., Miss.; m. JOAN ANDERSON 9 August 1958 Woodville, Wilkinson Co., Miss.

George received in bachelor's degree from Millsaps College in 1956. He went into the Army for two years, serving as a company clerk, prior to marring Joan. George then obtained his master's degree from George Peabody College, now part of Vanderbilt University in 1959. He then took a job teaching high school history and coaching the golf team at Herndon High School in Fairfax County, Virginia, where he stayed until retirement. Joan also graduated from Millsaps College, and taught elementary school in Herndon. Following her retirement, they moved to Leesburg, Loudon County, Virgnia, where they live now.

Children of GEORGE WHITENER and JOAN:

    a. GEORGE AUSTIN[10] WHITENER, b. 11 October 1962 Leesburg, Loudon Co., Va.; m. DIANE LEROUX 27 June 1992.

    b. LESLIE CAROL[10] WHITENER, b. 24 November 1965; m. ROBERT BROYLES TURNER 17 July 1993; children: Jessica Lauren, b. 31 December 1994; Kelly Morgan, b. 22 August 1996; Caroline Elizabeth, b. 3 May 1999.

    c. SUSAN MARIE[10] WHITENER, b. 9 February 1967.

    d. JOHN ANDERSON[10] WHITENER, b. 11 July 1969; m. (1) KARIN CUMMINS 24 October 1996; m. (2) ALLISON DIMSKI 15 May 1999; children: Elizabeth Augusta, b. 22 July 2000; Amy Anderson, b. 16 December 2003.

v. FRANCES[8] AMIS, b. 30 May 1904 Meridian, Lauderdale Co., Miss.; d. 26 May 1994 Meridian, Lauderdale Co., Miss.; m. JAMES COMBS FLOYD 26 September 1927 Meridian, Lauderdale Co., Miss.; b. ; d. 12 December 1968 Meridian, Lauderdale Co., Miss. (d. s. p.)

vi. MARY[8] AMIS, b. 16 October 1908 Meridian, Lauderdale Co., Miss.; d. May 1984 New Orleans, La.; m. JOHN DONOVAN READY 4 January 1929 Meridian, Lauderdale Co., Miss.; d. 11 April 1960 Meridian, Lauderdale Co., Miss.

Children of DONOVAN READY and MARY AMIS:

1. JOHN DONOVAN[9] READY, JR.; b. 9 January 1930 Meridian, Lauderdale Co., Miss.; d. 3 October 1993 Austin, Travis Co., Texas;[277] m. LESSIE CLYDE BOLER 26 December 1953.

2. WILLIAM EMMETT[9] READY, m. JULIA BANKS 26 June 1954 DeSoto Co., Miss.

3. MARY FRANCES[9] READY.

---

[277] SSDI listing.

Chapter 4: 1852 John Amis of Maury Co., Tenn.

1. JOHN[4] (*WILLIAM[3], JOSEPH[2]*) AMIS was born 29 October 1774 in Granville Co., N. C., and died 9 September 1852 in Culleoka, Maury Co., Tennessee. He married MARY KNIGHT 2 October 1797 Granville Co., N. C., daughter of JONATHAN KNIGHT and JUDITH WOODSON. She was born 24 March 1778 in Granville Co., N. C., and died 21 October 1851 in Culleoka, Maury Co., Tennessee

    John Amis appeared with his brother William Amis in the 1810 Census for Granville Co., N. C., age 26-45 with a wife, five sons and one daughter.[1] John Amis appears to have been the youngest son of William Amis, who was disposing of his slaves in 1813 just prior to his death.

    John Amis and his family moved to Williamson Co., Tenn., along with his sisters Mary and Hannah and the Ogilvies, where he appears in the 1820 Census.[2] Elizabeth Amis married John Cheatham 4 March 1820 and William Amis married Polly Anderson 26 March 1822 in Williamson County, Tennessee.[3]

    John Amis was in Maury County, Tennessee, by October 1828, when

> ...John Farney, John Amis, Stephen W. Smith, Peter Acres, Joseph Bellefant, Joseph Brown, & Nathaniel Steele were ordered to make a new road of the 3rd class begging near Michael Baldridge's to intersect the other Pulaski road at or near Howland's horse mill.[4]

---

[1] 1810 Census Granville Co., N. C., p. 274 (p.909) His family structure is 22110-10010.

[2] 1820 Census Williamson Co., Tenn., p. 121. His family structure is now 211401-11010. He was reportedly the father of 12 children, so at least 2 are missing from this list.

[3] Bejach, Wilena R., and Gardiner, Lillian J. Williamson County, Tennessee, Marriages, 1800-1850. (1957), p. 7. Cited hereafter as Bejach.

[4] Loose Maury County Road Minutes. Historic Maury 7(3):87, 1971.

The 1840 Census for Maury Co., Tenn., shows John Amis, age 60-70 with one male 30-40 and one male 20-30 and no women in the household living in the 6th Civil District.5 Also living in the 6th Civil District are Lewis Amis, 30-40,6 and Thomas Amis, 30-40.7 Jonathan Amis is in the 7th Civil District,8 and William Amis is in the 25th Civil District.9

In 1850 John Amis, 75, and Mary, 72, both born in North Carolina are still in the 6th Civil District.10 He and Mary are buried in Amis Cemetery on Valley Creek Road, Culleoka, Maury Co., Tenn., along with their youngest son, Josiah D. Amis, b. 10 April 1819; d. 4 April 1852.11 John Amis' inventory was filed 8 February 1853 by J. E. Thomas, administrator.12 He left moveable property valued at $3885.55, had outstanding loans totaling almost another $1000, and had 16 slaves plus property, establishing that he was quite wealthy. The estate sale shows purchases by Jonathan, William, Lewis, Thomas, and John Amis, Jr., as well as John and James A. Cheatham.

The 1850 Census also shows Lewis Amis, 41, and Louiza, 39,13 are living next door to John and Mary Amis with their family, and Thomas Amis, 49,

---

5 1840 Census Maury Co., Tenn., 6th Civil District, p. 303. [000011001-0].

6 1840 Census Maury Co., Tenn., 6th Civil District, p. 303. [10000001-21001].

7 1840 Census Maury Co., Tenn., 6th Civil District, p. 302. [010001-121001].

8 1840 Census Maury Co., Tenn., 7th Civil District, p. 306. [1001001-121001].

9 1840 Census Maury Co., Tenn., 15th Civil District, p. 392. [0200001-1120001].

10 1850 Census Maury Co., Tenn., 6th Civil District, p. 331A, #1243/1243.

11 Gray, R. and Gray A. Amis Cemetery. Accessed 22 October 2011. at http://freepages.rootsweb.ancestry.com/~maury/cemetery/Amis.txt.

12 Maury Co., Tenn., Will Book 4:615-624.

13 1850 Census Maury Co., Tenn., 6th Civil District, p. 331A, #1244/1244.

and Hannah, 50, are three families away.[14] Jonathan Amis, 50, and Elizabeth, 52, are in the 5th Civil District with their family, and William Amis, 52, and Nancy 50, with their family are in the 21st Civil District.[15]

The 1860 Census shows Thomas Amis, 55, and Hannah, 58, in the 6th Civil District (Culleoka),[16] Lewis Amis, 50, and Louiza 48, in the 7th Civil District (Bigbyville),[17] with Jonathan Amis, 60, and Elizabeth 61 nearby,[18] and William Amis, 61, and Nancy F., 60, in District 24 (Columbia.)[19]

Marriage records of Maury Co., Tenn.,[20] show that William Amis married Nancy F. Wilson 28 September 1843, which seems likely to be a second marriage for him. Thomas Amis married Hannah Kennedy 12 October 1827, and Lewis Amis married Louisa Y. Johnson 12 July 1830. I have attempted to sort the daughters based on marriage records and the census records, although some remain uncertain.

Alice Hodges cited a Bible record to establish the birth dates for most of the children.[21] Cemetery records for Maury Co., Tennessee, confirm the dates and establish some of the family relationships listed.[22]

Children of JOHN AMIS and MARY KNIGHT are:

   i. WILLIAM WOODSON[5] AMIS, b. 4 December 1798 Granville Co., N. C.; d. 19 July 1865 Maury Co., Tenn.; m. (1) MARY J. ANDERSON 26 March

---

[14] 1850 Census Maury Co., Tenn., 5th Civil District, p. 306A, #875/875.

[15] 1850 Census Maury Co., Tenn., 21st Civil District, p. 263B, #277/277. Dorothy Amis, 15, is at school in the 9th District, (p. 270B, #376).

[16] 1860 Census Maury Co., Tenn., 6th Civil District, p. 337, #529.

[17] 1860 Census Maury Co., Tenn., 7th Civil District, p. 345, #15.

[18] 1860 Census Maury Co., Tenn., 7th Civil District, p. 346, #24.

[19] 1860 Census Maury Co., Tenn., 24th Civil District, p. 516, #856.

[20] Sistler, Byron and Sistler, Barbara. Early Middle Tennessee Marriages. (Nashville, 1998). Grooms Vol. 1:11; brides 2:12.

[21] Hodges, A. A., pp. 13-14.

[22] Hawkins, Fred. Maury County, Tennessee, Cemeteries. (Columbia, TN; 1989,) cited as Hawkins.

1822 Williamson Co., Tenn., dau. of JOEL ANDERSON and SARAH J.[23]; b. 3 January 1805 Virginia; d. 9 January 1832 Williamson Co., Tenn.;[24] m. (2) NANCY F. WILSON 28 September 1843 Maury Co., Tenn.

William Amis served as bondsman for the marriages of James Walker to Polly Thompson 8 March 1821,[25] Abner Lambert to "Ibby" Scott 27 April 1825,[26] and Elias Burke to Hannah Kincaid 30 October 1827.[27]

Children of WILLIAM AMIS and MARY ANDERSON:[28]

1. MARTHA JASPER[6] AMIS, b. 1 January 1828 Williamson Co., Tenn.; d. 5 January 1877 Maury Co., Tenn.; m. JESSE E. EVANS 19 December 1845 Maury Co., Tenn.; b. 24 March 1805 Williamson Co., Tenn.; d. 20 September 1862 Maury Co., Tenn.; m. (2) SQUIRE HAMILTON TIMMONS 12 April 1864 Maury Co., Tenn.; b. 4 April 1813 Williamson Co., Tenn.; d. 24 April 1884 Maury Co., Tenn.

2. NANCY[6] AMIS, b. 29 January 1829 Maury Co., Tenn.[29]

---

[23] Joel Anderson died intestate, leaving his widow, Susan J. Anderson as administrator. His children petitioned for division of the estate, including Thomas Amis, John Amis, and Henrietta Amis, children of deceased daughter, Polly. Williamson Co., Tenn., Record Book 7:86, November 1853 and RB 7:116, March 1854. Lynch, Louise G. County Court of Williamson County, Tennessee, 1821-1872, Books 2-8. (1974,) pp. 118, 122. Cited hereafter as Lynch.

[24] She is buried in Joel Anderson Cemetery, Williamson Co., Tenn. Lynde, Louise G. Directory Williamson County, Tennessee, Burials, Vol. 1. (Williamson Co., Hist. Soc., 1972), p. 5.

[25] Whitley, Edythe R. Marriages of Williamson County, Tennessee, 1804-1850. (Baltimore: Genealogical Publ. Co., 1982), p. 193.

[26] Whitley, p. 109.

[27] Whitley, p. 24.

[28] White, Boone. Boone White Family. 18 January 2011. Located at http://www.wc.rootsweb.ancestry.com, (db.1553blw.) Cited hereafter as Boone White. I have been in contact with him occasionally over the years. Nancy, John, Thomas and Henrieta are still at home in the 1850 Census for Maury Co., Tenn. 21st Civil District, p. 263B, #277. Boone White also lists Benjamin Franklin Amis and Francis Nemaris Amis as the two eldest children, but I have not seen a source for this, and their birth years are estimates only.

3. SARAH D.⁶ AMIS, b. 12 February 1832 Williamson Co., Tenn.; d. 12 March 1909; m. JAMES W. NICHOLSON 12 January 1848 Maury Co., Tenn.; b. 30 June 1809 Franklin Co., Ala.; d. 7 April 1862 Maury Co., Tenn.

4. JOHN D.⁶ AMIS, b. about 1833 Maury Co., Tenn.; m. (1) MARGARET H. DANIEL 8 June 1852 Maury Co., Tenn.; b. 29 October 1831; d. 29 April 1853 Maury Co., Tenn.;[30] m. (2) MARGARET D. HARDISON 19 October 1854 Maury Co., Tenn.

5. THOMAS J.⁶ AMIS, b. about 1834 Maury Co., Tenn.; d. 31 May 1862 Shiloh Chapel, Hardin Co., Tenn.; m. ELIZABETH ANN JACKSON 16 January 1860 Mt. Moriah, Benton Co., Tenn.[31]

6. MARY HENRIETTA⁶ AMIS, b. 17 October 1836 Maury Co., Tenn.[32]

ii. JONATHAN KNIGHT⁵ AMIS, b. 23 April 1800 Granville Co., N. C.; d. 6 November 1869 Maury Co., Tenn.;[33] m. (1) NANCY BOYD 21 December 1825 Williamson Co., Tenn.,[34] dau.

---

[29] Nancy A. Amis married Pleasant H. Wilson 8 October 1849. Since Nancy was still at home in the 1850 census, I am assigning this marriage elsewhere. Boone White did make the assignment, but I found a grave for Nancy Nelson, b. 29 January 1820; d. 17 April 1891 in McCain's Cemetery, Maury Co., Tenn., which is the death date Boone White gave to this Nancy, even though she was born 10 years later.

[30] Hawkins, p. 93. He adds that she was the daughter of Simm and Eliza (Hardison) Daniel. She was identified on her tombstone as the consort of John D. Amis. This is the only John of the appropriate age to be this man.

[31] Boone White says he was shot at the Battle of Shiloh 7 April 1862 and died of his wounds on the date indicated.

[32] Boone White says she married Squire Hamilton Timmons as his third wife about 1878 after the death of her older sister, Martha Jasper Amis.

[33] Reece's Chapel Cemetery, Hawkins, p. 599. Hodges listed birth as 25 April 1800.

[34] Jonathan "Amos" married Nancy Boyd 21 December 1825 in Williamson Co., Tenn. [Bejach.] Jonathan Amis and Nancy Amis sold land to James G. Swisher in Williamson County, Tenn., in 1829. (Court Minute Book 10/208). [cited in Johnson, Albert L. Minute Book Genealogy of Williamson County, TN, 1799-1865, p. 65.]

of JAMES BOYD and NANCY;[35] m. (2) ELIZABETH POLK HENDERSON; b. 16 August 1798; d. 21 June 1860 Maury Co., Tenn.[36]; m. (3) CATHERINE FARLEY 28 November 1863 Maury Co., Tenn.[37]

In 1840 Jonathan Knight Amis has one son 15-19, one son under 5, and four girls, one under 5, two 5-10, and one 10-15. In 1850 he has Dorinda 16, and Felix 14, living with him. These are clearly the two youngest children. Since I do not have a death date for Nancy Boyd Amis, I am not sure who the mother was.

Children of JONATHAN KNIGHT AMIS are:

1. male, b. abt 1827
2. female b. about 1830
3. female b. about 1832
4. female b. about 1834
5. DORINDA A.[6] AMIS, b. about 1835 Maury Co., Tenn.; m. DAVID S. MAXWELL 9 September 1852 Maury Co., Tenn.
6. FELIX G.[6] AMIS, b. about 1836 Maury Co., Tenn.; d. 8 February 1861 Maury Co., Tenn.[38]

iii. JOHN[5] AMIS, b. 25 March 1802 Granville Co., N. C.; d. 15 April 1859 Giles Co., Tenn.; m. MARTHA ANN WILKINSON, dau. of THOMAS WILKINSON and MARY ROBERTSON 14 August

---

[35] James Boyd d. testate 24 May 1821 naming his widow, Nancy, as executor. Jonathan Amis and Nancy, his wife, daughter of James Boyd, received 110 acres of land from that will. Williamson Co., Tenn., RB 4:292, October 1828. Lynch, p. 49.

[36] Her dates are from her tombstone adjacent to his in Reece's Chapel Cemetery.

[37] Boone White identifies her maiden name as Wright. (http://wc.rootsweb.ancestry.com, db. 1553blw.) I was in contact with him about 10 years ago, and he was a cousin collector.

[38] His obituary was published The Maury Press, Vol. 2, #5, 14 February 1861. Accessed 20 November 2011 at http://files.usgwarchives.net/tn/maury/newspapers/newsmisc.txt. He died from a fall off a horse at "about age 25."

1823 Williamson Co., Tenn.;[39] b. 27 January 1805 Va.; d. 7 March 1881 Giles Co., Tenn.[40]

John "Ames" is in the 7th Civil District Tax List of Giles Co., Tenn., in 1836, with 30 acres of land, two town lots in Pulaski, and one slave and one white poll.[41]

John "Amus" is listed in the 6th Civil District of Giles Co., Tenn., in 1850 as a machinist, b. in North Carolina. Martha Ann is 44 and born in Virginia.[42] Martha "Amos" is head of household in the 1860 Census.[43] Martha is in Pulaski in the 1870 Census with "Jeff" 36, farmer, Lewis, 35, a dry goods merchant and five young black children who are listed as cotton factory hands.[44] Dates for the males were identified from Giles County cemetery records.[45]

Probate files show a will for John Amis written in 1859 naming his wife, Martha, who was to have the home tract plus six named adult slaves and their unnamed children.[46] Lewis Amis was named trustee for Mary Ann Smith, wife of "B." Smith, and her children, James F. Amis and Eliza Jane Amis, and named James F. and Lewis Amis executors. The will was witnessed by Thomas Davenport and Miller Doggett.

Martha Amis wrote her will in 1879 and it was proved in 1881.[47] She named her son Frank,

---

[39] Data obtained from a Goodspeed's biography of their son, Lewis Amis contained in the Giles County chapter. Accessed 20 November 2011 at http://www.tngenweb.org/records/giles/history/goodspeed/bios.html.

[40] Smith, Jonathan K. T. Death Notices From The Christian Advocate, Nashville, Tenn., 1880-1882. 14 May 1881.
[http://www.tngenweb.org/records/tn_wide/obits/nca/nca7-04.html. Accessed 20 November 2011.]

[41] McDonald, Joyce. Accessed 24 November 2011 at http://tngenweb.org/giles/tax/1836/1836-07.html.

[42] 1850 Census Giles Co., Tenn., 6th Civil District, p. 401, #5/#5.

[43] 1860 Census Giles Co., Tenn., Vale Mills, p. 113, #178/154. James F., Lewis, and Eliza J. Amis are still at home.

[44] 1870 Census Giles Co., Tenn., Pulaski, p. 103, #188/188.

[45] http://www.findagrave.com/ Accessed 24 November 2011. The burials were all in Maplewood Cemetery.

[46] Parker, Clara M. Giles County, Tennessee, Will Abstracts, 1815-1900. (1988), p. 4, loose will. Cited hereafter as Parker.

[47] Parker, p. 4.

daughter-in-law Rebecca Amis, Martha Smith, and Johnny ___. Executors were J. F. and Lewis Amis, witnesses Mary E. Rainey and Gertrude A. Anderson.

Children of JOHN AMIS and MARTHA WILKINSON:[48]

1. MARY ANN[6] AMIS, b. about 1824 Giles Co., Tenn.; m. BUCKNER SMITH,[49] b. about 1820 Tennessee;[50] d. after 1893 Giles Co., Tenn.[51]
2. NANCY[6] AMIS, d. young.
3. MARTHA JANE[5] AMIS, b. 30 November 1827 Giles Co., Tenn.; d. 7 October 1828 Giles Co., Tenn.[52]
4. JOHN W.[6] AMIS, b. 25 May 1834 Giles Co., Tenn.; d. 15 December 1859 Giles Co.,

---

[48] Lewis Amis, of the firm of L. Amis & Bro., dealers in groceries and general merchandise, at Vale Mills, Giles Co., Tenn., was born December 5, 1836, in Pulaski, Tenn. He is a son of John and Martha A. Amis, both natives of North Carolina. John Amis was the son of John and Pollie Amis, natives of Granville County, N. C., and Martha Amis was the daughter of Thomas and Pollie (Robertson) Wilkinson, natives of North Carolina. The parents of our subject were married August 14, 1823, in Williamson County, and to them were born eight children, named Mary A., Nancy, Martha J., John W., James F., Field R., Lewis and Nancy E. J. Our subject was educated in the district schools, and his occupation has been merchandising and farming from early boyhood. In 1866 he was married to Rebecca E. Summerhill, daughter of Horace and Parmelia Summerhill, of Lauderdale County, Ala. To our subject and wife was born one son, John L. The Amis Bros. are Democrats in politics, and our subject is a member of the F. AZ A. M. and also the A. L. of H. The Amis family are members of the Methodist Episcopal Church South, and in high standing. They have been successful men in all their undertakings, and are regarded as prosperous and industrious business men. The older members of the family came here at an early date and have been known in this State for nearly a century. They are of Scotch-Irish descent. [Goodspeed's History accessed online 20 November 2011 at
http://www.tngenweb.org/records/giles/history/goodspeed/bios.html.]

[49] His name was established by the will of J. F. Amis, written 1893 and proved 1913 where he left his sister, Mary, wife of Buckner Smith, $500 to her and to her heirs if she pre-deceased him, but not to her husband. If she contested the will, then the $500 was to be given to friend John T. Allen if the will was challenged. Clearly, Buckner Smith did not have the good opinion of his in-laws. Parker, p. 151.

[50] 1850 Census Giles Co., Tenn., Civil Dist. 7, p. 337A, #128. Martha Smith is their eldest daughter, b. 1847.

[51] 1880 Census Giles Co., Tenn., Pulaski, ED 105, p. 125C, #200/237. He is listed as a butcher.

[52] Maplewood Cemetery, Pulaski, Tenn. http://www.findagrave.com., #15575126.

Tenn.;[53] m. REBECCA EMILY SUMMERHILL 1 December 1858 Giles Co., Tenn., dau. of HORACE SUMMERHILL and PERMELIA _____; b. 26 August 1839; d. 6 December 1908 Giles Co., Tenn.[54]

5. JAMES FRANKLIN[6] AMIS, b. 7 January 1833 Giles Co., Tenn.; d. 15 October 1913 Giles Co., Tenn.[55]

6. FIELD R.[6] AMIS.,[56] d. young.

7. LEWIS[6] AMIS, b. 5 December 1836 Giles Co., Tenn.; d. 6 May 1887 Giles Co., Tenn.;[57] m. REBECCA EMILY SUMMERHILL, dau. of HORACE SUMMERHILL and PERMELIA _____.; b. 26 August 1839; d. 6 December 1908 Giles Co., Tenn.[58]

8. NANCY E. J.[6] AMIS, b. 1841 Giles Co., Tenn.

iv. THOMAS[5] AMIS, b. 3 October 1803 Granville Co., N. C.;[59] d. 19 January 1867 Maury Co., Tenn.; m. HANNAH KENNEDY 12 October 1827 Maury Co., Tenn.; b. 25 November 1800; d. 2 March 1878 Maury Co., Tenn.

Hannah (Kennedy) Amis' obituary was published in *The Christian Advocate*, (Nashville, TN) for 6 April 1878.[60]

Hannah Amis, nee Kennedy, wife of Thomas Amis, born Maury Co., Tenn., Nov. 25, 1800, married October 1827; mother of

---

[53] Maplewood Cemetery, Pulaski, Tenn. http://www.findagrave.com., #44268933.

[54] Maplewood Cemetery, Pulaski, Tenn. http://www.findagrave.com., #15575353. "At rest between her two loving husbands."

[55] Maplewood Cemetery, Pulaski, Tenn. http://www.findagrave.com., #44268936.

[56] His name was given in the biography of Lewis Amis, but he is not in the 1850 or 1860 Census with his parents.

[57] Maplewood Cemetery, Pulaski, Tenn. http://www.findagrave.com., #15575388.

[58] Rebecca E. Summerhill first married John W. Amis 1 December 1858 in Giles Co., Tenn.

[59] Mrs. Hodges gives his date of birth as 11 October 1803. Dates are from his tombstone in Wilkes (Old Campground) Cemetery, Maury Co., Tenn., Hawkins, p. 499. Most of this family is buried in the cemetery allowing for fairly good dating.

[60] Located at http://www.tngenweb.org/records/tn_wide/obits/nca6-04.html. Accessed 27 November 2011.

7 children all of whom "died years ago"; had six surviving grandchildren (four children of Rev. W. H. Wilkes and two children of Erastus Amis); died March 2, 1878.[61]

Children of THOMAS AMIS and HANNAH KENNEDY:

1. MARY KENNEDY[6] AMIS, b. 18 October 1828 Maury Co., Tenn.;[62] d. 2 March 1856 Maury Co., Tenn.; m. WILLIAM HARRIS WILKES 6 January 1848 Maury Co., Tenn.; b. 7 May 1821 Maury Co., Tenn.; d. 16 October 1895 Maury Co., Tenn.; m. (2) ZERALDA AMIS.

2. ZERALDA[6] AMIS, b. 17 November 1830 Maury Co., Tenn.; d. 28 February 1860 Maury Co., Tenn.; m. WILLIAM H. WILKES 30 December 1856 Maury Co., Tenn.

3. JOHN ERASTUS[6] AMIS, b. 26 September 1831 Maury Co., Tenn.; d. 12 March 1862 St. Louis, Mo.; m. REBECCA J. THOMAS 12 October 1857 Maury Co., Tenn., dau. of JAMES E. THOMAS and MARTHA C. ADKISSON; b. 1 November 1838 Maury Co., Tenn.; d. 5 March 1903 Maury Co., Tenn.[63]

---

[61] I have only been able to find six children. Perhaps the other was an infant death. However, she certainly outlived the six children I have been able to find.

[62] Boone White listed her as the eldest daughter. The remainder are listed in the 1850 Census.

[63] Wilkes Cemetery, Maury Co., Tenn. http://www.findagrave.com., #15182036. "Mrs. Rebecca T. Amis, a native of Maury County, Tenn., was born in 1839 and is a daughter of Col. Jonas and Martha (Adkisson) Thomas, who were both born in the "Old Dominion." The father came to Tennessee at an early day, and became an eminent lawyer and politician. He represented Maury County in both branches of the State Legislature, and was speaker of the State Senate one term, and as parliamentarian had no superior. He was once nominated for Congress, but owing to ill health was compelled to withdraw from the race. His demise occurred August 3, 1856. The mother died January 14, 1870. Mrs. Amis, our subject, was married October 13, 1857 to John E. Amis, and two children blessed their union, Bruce E. and Jonas T. Mr. Amis took an active part in the late was and was a member of the gallant Forty-eighth Tennessee Infantry. He was captured at the fall of Fort Donelson and died in prison in St. Louis, Mo., in 1863. Mrs. Amis is a finely educated woman, and has won quite a reputation as an instructress, having taught at the Atheneum at Columbia, and in the Tennessee College at Franklin, and alos in public schools at

4. TALITHA C.[6] AMIS, b. 18 November 1832 Maury Co., Tenn.; d. 12 March 1854 Maury Co., Tenn.; m. CARTER WITT 6 January 1853 Maury Co., Tenn.

5. EMILY[6] AMIS, b. 15 July 1838 Maury Co., Tenn.; d. 23 November 1855 Maury Co., Tenn.

6. MCCOY CAMPBELL[6] AMIS, b. 27 February 1841 Maury Co. Tenn.; d. 5 February 1863 Maury Co., Tenn.[64]

v. ELIZABETH[5] AMIS, b. 15 January 1806 Granville Co., N. C.; d. 11 May 1845 Giles Co., Tenn.[65]; m. JOHN CHEATHAM 4 March 1820 Williamson Co., Tenn.; b. 16 January 1798 Granville Co., N. C.; d. 24 July 1873 Culleoka, Maury Co., Tenn.[66]

vi. LEWIS[5] AMIS, b. 15 March 1809 Granville Co., N. C.; d. 19 June 1873 Maury Co., Tenn.;[67] m. LOUISA YEOMANS JOHNSON 12 July 1830 Maury Co., Tenn., daughter of ALEXANDER JOHNSON and MARY _____; b. 11 October 1811.[68]

The dreadful story of infant mortality is detailed in the tombstone inscriptions surround Lewis Amis and Louisa Johnson in the Johnson-Amis Cemetery in Maury Co., Tenn.[69]

---

that place. She is a member of the Presbyterian Church." From Goodspeed's History. Accessed online 20 November 2011 at http://freepages.genealogy.rootsweb.ancestry.com/~maury/biog.htm.

[64] He served in Co. E.; 3rd Tenn. Infantry, CSA.

[65] Evans Cemetery, Giles Co., Tenn. http://www.findagrave.com. #30191911.

[66] Wilkes Cemetery, Maury Co., Tenn. http://www.findagrave.com. #17864313. (This is the same cemetery where Thomas and Hannah Amis are buried.)

[67] In addition to his tombstone, there was an obituary notice in *The Mail* (Columbia, Tenn.,) vol. 1:22, 26 June 1873. Accessed 15 November 2011 http://files.usgwarchives.net/tn/maury/newspapers/newsmisc.txt.

[68] These dates are from a family Bible owned by a descendant of this Lewis Amis. She is buried along with Lewis Amis in the Johnson-Amis Cemetery, Maury Co., Tenn., but there are no dates given on the stone. Hawkins, p. 496.

[69] Hawkins, p. 446.

Children of LEWIS AMIS and LOUISA JOHNSON:[70]

1. MARY F.[6] AMIS; b. 1832 Maury Co., Tenn.; m. JAMES W. NANCE 13 December 1860 Maury Co., Tenn.

2. ELIZA ANN[6] AMIS; b. 30 November 1833 Maury Co., Tenn.; d. July 1834 Maury Co., Tenn.

3. AMANDA MALVENA[6] AMIS, b. 23 July 1835 Maury Co., Tenn.; d. 31 August 1840 Maury Co., Tenn.

4. SARAH[6] AMIS, b. 11 August 1837 Maury Co., Tenn.; d. 14 December 1914 Pulaski, Giles Co., Tenn.;[71] m. DAVID C. SCOTT 6 September 1858; b. 11 April 1826; d. 23 November 1907 Pulaski; Giles Co., Tenn.

5. JOHN ALEN[6] AMIS; b. 20 June 1839 Maury Co., Tenn.; d. 24 July 1840

6. OP[6] AMIS; b. 6 May 1842 Maury Co., Tenn.; d. 26 June 1843 Maury Co., Tenn

7. RUTH ADELIA[6] AMIS, b. 1843 Maury Co., Tenn.[72]

8. ALEXANDER JOHNSON[6] AMIS, 20 September 1845 Maury Co., Tenn.; d. 20 January 1847 Maury Co., Tenn.

9. WILLIAM[6] AMIS, b. 1847 Maury Co., Tenn.

10. JOSEPH D.[6] AMIS, b. 11 August 1849 Maury Co., Tenn.; d. 15 August 1865 Maury Co., Tenn.

11. WALTER WOODSON[6] AMIS, b. 3 June 1851 Maury Co., Tenn.;[73] d. 31 January 1927 Springfield, Greene Co., Missouri;[74] m. BELLE CHURCHILL LYNES 22 December 1885 Calloway Co., Mo.; b. 22 July 1855 in

---

[70] List from the tombstone, census, and Boone White.

[71] Tombstones i Maplewood Cemetery, Pulaski, Giles Co., Tenn. She is actually listed as Sarah H. Amis on the double stone.

[72] Sarah Ruth is living with William Amis is Columbia, age 22, in the 1860 Census for Maury Co., Tenn. (Civil District 24, p. 516, #856/856.) His wife is now Nancy F. Amis, b 1810 in North Carolina.

[73] Boone White indicates he lived in Cape Girardeau, Mo., and also indicates that Ruth married a man in Missouri. Will look for them in the census.

[74] Tombstone in Hazlewood Cemetery, Springfield, Greene Co., Mo. Accessed 26 November 2011 at http://www.findagrave.com.

184

Missouri; d. 28 February 1937 Springfield, Greene Co., Mo.

Walter W. Amis and Belle Lynes have not been identified in the 1880 Census, but are living in Cape Girardeau, Missouri, in 1900, along with Mary, b. January 1888 and Everett b. May 1890.[75] In 1910, the family is living in St. Louis, where Walter was working as a salesman.[76] In 1920, Belle and Walter Amis appear to be separated. Belle is living with her older sister, "Statie" Fisher and her mother, Mary E. Lynes, age 98.[77] Walter is living with his daughter Mary A. Luster and her husband Lewis, 45, attorney.[78]

Children of WALTER AMIS and BELLE LYNES:

a.   MARY L.[7] AMIS, b. 13 January 1888 Union City, Obion Co., Tenn.; m. LEWIS LUSTER about 1920.

b.   EVERETT LYNES[7] AMIS, b. 18 May 1890 Calloway Co., Mo.; m. MARY ORME 7 June 1916 Hugo, Choctaw Co., Oklahoma; b. 11 Jan 1890 Hardeman Co., Tenn.[79]

---

[75] 1900 Census Cape Girardeau, Mo., 4th Ward Cape Girardeau, p. 132B, SD12, ED26, sheet 19B. Walter, b. June 1851; Belle, b. July 1855 Missouri. The marriage date is from an IGI file that has provable errors, so I will need to confirm it, but I think it probable. Mary was born in Tennessee, and Everett in Missouri, and there is evidence they were in Obion Co., Tenn.

[76] 1910 Census St. Louis Co., Mo., 28th Ward, St. Louis, p. 108, #5727/110/331. Mary L. Amis was also counted that year in the 2nd Ward Lebanon, LaClede Co., Mo., p.229, #254/263. I suspect she was actually living there and was simply listed at her "permanent" address by her parents as well.

[77] 1920 Census Greene Co., Mo., 4th Ward Springfield, p. 35A, #50/51.

[78] 1920 Census Greene Co., Mo., Campbell Twp., p. 4. The Lusters have one daughter, Nancy L., b. June 1919.

[79] Robert W. Amis, 85, died in Minneapolis, MN, on October 17, 2008. Preceded in death by father Everett L. Amis, mother Mary O. Amis, brother Everett, sisters Polly Spaar, and Mary Elizabeth Knorr. Survived by wife, Lucille Hamer of Brownsville, TN; sons Robert (Gretchen) and Allan (Ginna); grandchildren Lucille, Brian, Susan, Julia, Alison, and Mary; and sister Jeanne (Robert) Jernigan. Bob grew up in Dyersburg, TN, graduated from Rhodes College, and lived in Memphis with his wife, Lucille, until they moved to Minneapolis in 1966. Bob's life was full of hard work, devotion to his wife and family, and random whimsical acts. His courage, dignity, and sense of humor during his prolonged battle with heart and lung disease were a powerful testament to the character and spirit of this noble man.

12. LOUISA J.[6] AMIS, b. 1852 Maury Co., Tenn.[80]

13. LEWIS RANDOLPH[6] AMIS, b. 7 December 1856 Maury Co., Tenn.; d. 16 December 1904 Nashville, Davidson Co., Tenn.; m. AGNES FULTON 26 June 1884 Maury Co., Tenn.[81]

vii. MARY[5] AMIS, b. 18 October 1811 Granville Co., N. C.; d. 21 June 1894 Mooresville, Marshall Co., Tenn.;[82] m. JAMES FRY about 1838 Maury Co., Tenn.[83]

viii. JAMES[5] AMIS, b. 8 May 1814 Granville Co., N. C.; m. MARY ANN _____ about 1835 Giles Co.,

---

Memorials preferred to Rhodes College, 2000 North Parkway, Memphis, 38112. The Commercial Appeal (Memphis, TN) 16 November 2008. Located at http://www.commercialappeal.com/obituary-archives/ Accessed 23 December 2011.

[80] Boone White indicated she married Mr. Vaught.

[81] Louis Randolph Amis was born December 7, 1856 in Maury County, Tennessee, the son of Lewis Amis and Louisa Johnson Amis, and the grandson of John Amis and Mary (Polly) Knight Amis. He married Agnes Fulton in 1884. They had five children. Louis Amis received his education at the Webb Brothers Training School and at Vanderbilt University. He taught in the Webb Brothers Training School in 1883/1884. He was a Methodist minister. He died December 16, 1904, in Nashville. [Excerpt from Goodspeed's History accessed online 20 November 2011 at http://freepages.genealogy.rootsweb.ancestry.com/~maury/biog.htm.] Lewis Randolph Amis was born 7 Dec 1856 in Maury County, Tennessee, the youngest child of Lewis Amis and Louisa Yeomans Amis. He united with the Methodist Church in Sept 1867. He entered the Tennessee Methodist Conference as preacher in Oct 1878. From 1880-1895, he served as assistant secretary of conference. He began serving as secretary of the conference in 1895, a position he held until his death. On 26 Jun 1884 in Maury County, he united in Holy Matrimony with Agnes Jane Fulton, daughter of Josiah Fulton and Martha White. This union was blessed with the birth of five children: Fulton (died as an infant), Louise (lived to age one), Agnes (never married), Ruth (wife of Frank Burke Wilkes), and Lewis Randolph Amis Jr. (husband of Anne Cole Townsend). Lewis died at Nashville, Tennessee on 16 Dec 1904. He is buried at Zion Presbyterian Church Cemetery in Maury County, Tennessee. [http://www.findagrave.com, accessed 26 November 2011.]

[82] Tombstone in Old Bear Creek Cemetery, Marshall Co., Tenn.

[83] There is a marker in Old Bear Creek Cemetery, Marshall Co., Tenn., for Joseph Fry, b. 19 September 1800; d. 31 October 1858. James and Joseph seem likely to be the same person. Located at http://www.findagrave.com. Accessed 26 November 2011.

Tenn.; b. 20 March 1818 Tennessee; d. 11 January 1886 Madison Co., Tenn.[84]

James "Amus" and Mary Ann are in Giles County, Tennessee, in the 5th Civil District along with seven children.[85] James Amis and Mary Ann are living in Hardin Co., Tenn., in 1860.[86] The list of children is from that census. I have not yet found him in 1870, but in 1880 he and Mary Ann are living in the 10th Civil District of Madison Co., Tenn.[87]

Children of JAMES AMIS and MARY ANN:

1. JOHN A.[6] AMIS, b. 25 November 1836; d. 6 November 1852 Hardin Co., Tenn.[88]
2. JAMES M.[6] AMIS, b. 1841 Giles Co., Tenn.
3. WILLIAM[6] AMIS, b. 1843 Giles Co., Tenn.[89]
4. JOSEPH T.[6] AMIS, b. 29 June 1844 Giles Co., Tenn.; d. 22 October 1922 Madison Co., Tenn.;[90] m. SUSAN TAMYRA NOEL about 1870;[91] b. 22 September 1845 Tenn.; d. 17 January 1917 Madison Co., Tenn.
5. CORNELIA[6] AMIS, b. 1846 Giles Co., Tenn.

---

[84] The burial was apparently originally in Pleasant Hill-Gilmore Cemetery, Madison Co., Tenn. Her burial was not recorded in the Hollywood Cemetery database.

[85] 1850 Census Giles Co., Tenn., 5th Civil District, p. 373, #79/79. He is living between Samuel Harwell and Frederick Harwell, both of whom are about his age, suggesting his wife may be a Harwell.

[86] 1860 Census Hardin Co., Tenn., 12th Civil District, Coffee Landing, p. 379B, #1354/1402.

[87] 1880 Census Madison Co., Tenn., 10th Civil District, SD 5, ED 5, p. 51, #408/409. Laura J. Amis, 20, is still living at home.

[88] Amis Cemetery, Milledgeville, "son of J. and M. A. Amis."

[89] 1880 Census Madison Co., Tenn., Jackson, SD 5, ED 101, p. 9, #59/68. He is listed as a railroad gate keeper, and is a boarder in the home of John D. Parham, who was a fire insurance agent. There does not appear to be a direct link between this Parham and the family of the same name associated with the Amis family in Granville Co., N. C.

[90] Dates and her name are from their tombstones in Riverside Cemetery, Jackson, Tenn. His will was written 27 January 1917 and proved 4 January 1923 Madison Co., Tenn., Will Book C:343. On page C:474 his date of death is given as 29 October 1922.

[91] 1880 Census Madison Co., Tenn., 10th Civil District, SD 5, ED 5, p. 51, #406/407.

6. TOLBERT F.[6] AMIS, b. 23 August 1847 Giles
     Co., Tenn.; d. 29 January 1927 Madison
     Co., Tenn.;[92] m. TENNIE _____ about 1870.[93]
7. LAURA J.[6] AMIS, b. 1859 Hardin Co., Tenn.

ix. ALEXANDER[5] AMIS, b. 27 April 1817.

x. JOSIAH D.[5] AMIS, b. 11 April 1819 Williamson
     Co., Tenn.; d. 4 April 1852 Maury Co., Tenn.[94]

xi. JUDITH[5] AMIS, b. 12 October 1821 Williamson
     Co., Tenn.; m. JOHN H. WALKER 16 December
     1836 Maury Co., Tenn.; b. about 1812
     Tennessee.

     John H. Walker, 38, TN, and Judith are living
in Maury Co., Tenn., in 1850 along with five
children: John, 12, Benjamin, 10, Mary, 8, Nancy,
5, and Elizabeth, 2.[95] I have not been able to
locate him with certainty thereafter, although
there is a John F. Walker, b. 17 January 1821, in
Giles County, Tenn., about the same time.[96]

---

[92] Maple Springs Cemetery, Madison Co., Tenn.

[93] 1880 Census Madison Co., Tenn., 10th Civil District, SD 5, ED 95, p. 29, #221/222. A Mary Ann Amis is also buried in Maple Springs Cemetery with dates 17 August 1846-25 June 1825. Presently I am not sure if this is another wife or the same woman.

[94] Buried with his parents and apparently did not marry.

[95] 1850 Census Maury Co., Tenn., Civil Dist. 6, p. 324B, #1143.

[96] Stella Cemetery, Giles Co., Tenn. http://www.findagrave.com., #44988363.

Chapter 5: Brewer Families of Sumter Co., Alabama to 1860

My interest in the Brewer families of Sumter County, Alabama prior to the Civil War stems from tracing the ancestry of 1877 (year of death) Wyche Brewer of Scott Co., Miss. (place of death). Wyche Brewer's great-grandson, A. B. Amis, wrote of his grandmother and great-grandfather: "

> *Wytche Brewer was a Tennessee Mountaineer, but I do not know when or where he was born. About 1822 he married Flora McPherson and for a time lived in Sumter County near Livingston. About 1835 he moved to Scott County, Mississippi, and settled on a farm about a mile northwest of where Sulphur Springs Baptist Church is now located, where he died in 1877 at the age of eighty five years. He was buried in the old Amis Graveyard. He had ten children, all of whom are long since dead.*

1877 Wyche Brewer of Scott Co., Mississippi

The birth and death dates and the fact of their marriage for Wyche Brewer and Flora McPherson were obtained from the tombstones in the Amis Cemetery, 5mi north of Conehatta, Miss.[1] Judge Amis thought that the Brewers had come to Scott Co., Miss., from Sumter Co., Alabama. In the 1850 Census for Scott Co., "Wicht" Brewer's family is located between the Amis and the Petty families. He is shown as 52 years old, born in Georgia. His wife, Flora, is shown as 48, born in Mississippi. There are eight children, seven girls, still living at home. Luvenia is shown as married to Albert Petty. Christianna, the wife of John W. Petty,

---

[1] Transcription by Elvy Hammond. Located on the Scott Co., Miss., page www.usgenweb.org.

living next door, is 24 and born in Alabama. She is shown as another daughter in Petty family data.[2]

Wyche Brewer first appears in the 1830 Census of Butler County, Alabama,[3] with one male 30-40, three females under five, one female 5-10, and one female 20-30, which matches the later data. He is only one person removed from Malcolm McPherson, who has one male under 5, one male 5-10, one male 10-16, and one male 30-40, two females under five, one 5-10, and one female 30-40. Butler County was organized in 1819, and a census was done, but it has not survived. However, it was formed in part from Conecuh County, and the 1820 Census for this county does survive. This census shows William Brewer and William McPherson living next door to each other.

Wyche Brewer purchased 40 acres of land on May 15, 1837, in St. Stephen's Twp., Sumter Co., Alabama.[4] He is in the 1840 Census for Sumter Co., Ala., between 40 and 50 with a wife between 30 and 40, and one son under five. He has two girls under five, three between 10 and 15, and one between 15 and 20.[5]

The following deed is of interest:

The State of Alabama Sumter County Know and see by these present that I William Brewer and Mary Brewer in consideration of the sum of three hundred and fifty six dollars in hand paid and bargained granted sold released and conveyed and by these presents do bargain grant and release and convey to Wiche Brewer all the described tract or parcel of

---

[2] 1850 Census, Scott Co., Miss., p. 258.

[3] 1830 Census, Butler Co., Ala., p. 298.

[4] Bureau of Land Management Document #9631, Alabama, Serial #AL3420-186. This was a cash entry sale for 40.03 acres located in Township 19N, Range 2W, Section 13. The file is accessible through links on the Alabama home page for www.usgenweb.org.

[5] 1840 Census, Sumter Co., Ala., p. 137.

190

land located in the county of Sumter and state aforesaid to whit the North end of the East half of the South East quarter of section fourteen township nineteen Range two and to the amount of fifty acres - containing 50 acres all lying in the district of lands sold at the land office at Demopolis. To have and to hold all and singular the aforesaid. s/William Brewer Mary Brewer.[6]

Wyche Brewer purchased for $300 a tract of land in Scott Co., Miss., 26 March 1845 from Jeremiah Putnam and his wife Elizabeth.[7] The tract was described as the east half of the southeast quarter of section 23 in township 8, range 9E, containing 80.17 acres more or less. He purchased from Carolinus and Mathilda Boyd for $25 the northeast quarter of section 24, township 8, range 9E on 1 July 1848.[8] On 18 September 1859 he purchased from J. E. Dunlap and wife Elizabeth for $485.56 the west half of the southwest quarter of section 24, township 8, Range 9E containing 64 acres more or less.[9] Charles W. Gascoigne and R. E. Cunningham, executors of Charles Gascoigne late of Mobile, Ala., sold to Wyche Brewer the northwest corner of section 24, township 8, Range 9E containing 130 acres on 1 October 1859.[10] He purchased on 23 November 1860 from Anderson B. Smith for $144 the south half of the northeast quarter Section 28, township 8, Range 9E.[11]

The 1880 Census in Mississippi for Lake County[12] showed William Owens 48, m, Ala., NC, TN; Harriet, wife, 42, f, Ala., Ga., NC; James, son, 10, m, Miss., Ala., Ala.; Oscar, son, 6, m, Miss., Ala., Ala.;

[6] Sumter Co., Ala., Deed Book G:722, [23 December 1842.]
[7] Scott Co., Miss., Deed Book C:466-67, 2 May 1845.
[8] Scott Co., Miss., Deed Book E:4, 1 July 1848.
[9] Scott Co., Miss., Deed Book I:513, 26 July 1860.
[10] Scott Co., Miss., Deed Book I:254, 5 October 1859.
[11] Scott Co., Miss., Deed Book J:84, 23 November 1860.
[12] 1880 Census Lake Co., Miss., Beat 5, District 52, p. 230, #253.

Lawrence, son, 6, m, Miss., Wyche, son, 4, m, Miss., and Martha Brewer, 55, f, Ala., Ga., NC, sister-in-law.[13] These dates match the estimated birth years from the 1850 census fairly well for two of Wyche and Flora Brewer's daughters.

Genealogical Summary

1. WYCHE[1] BREWER, b. 6 July 1798 in Georgia, d. 17 March 1877 Scott Co, Miss. He married FLORA MC PHERSON about 1821 Conecuh Co., Ala., daughter of WILLIAM MC PHERSON and CHRISTIAN MC DONALD. She was born 1 December 1803 in North Carolina and died 6 February 1866 Scott Co., Miss.

Children of WYCHE BREWER and FLORA MCPHERSON:

    i. MARTHA[2] BREWER, b. 14 October 1823 Butler Co., Ala.; d. 15 January 1911 Leake Co., Miss.[14]

        She is living with her sister Henrietta in Leake Co., Miss., in 1880.[15]

    ii. LUVENIA[2] BREWER, b. 11 February 1825 Butler Co., Ala.; d. 18 February 1897 Newton Co., Miss.; m. ALBERT GALLATIN PETTY about 1845 Scott Co., Miss., son of JOHN WRIGHT PETTY and ANNA HARRIS; b. 29 May 1820 Lincoln Co., Tenn.; d. 2 June 1879 Scott Co., Miss.

        Luvenia Brewer was born 11 Feb. 1825 in Sumter Co., Ala. She moved with her father to Scott Co., Miss., about 1836. In 1881, after the death of

---

[13] Lentz, Wanda Eakin. 3 Jul 2002. http://genforum.genealogy.com/brewer/messages/6110.html.

[14] Mount Zion Cemetery, Leake Co., Miss. http://www.findagrave.com, #36709489. Judge Amis stated that she never married.

[15] 1880 Census Leake Co., Miss., Walnut Grove, ED 37, p. 14A, #221.

her husband, she moved to Union, Newton Co., Miss., where she died 18 Feb. 1897. [16]

iii. CHRISTIANA[2] BREWER, b. 14 March 1827 Butler Co., Ala.;[17] d. 14 Jun 1909 Scott Co., Miss.;[18] m. JOHN WRIGHT PETTY, about 1846, Scott Co., Miss., son of JOHN WRIGHT PETTY and ANNA HARRIS; b. 12 November 1826 Madison Co., Ala.; d. 27 March 1858 Scott Co., Miss.

Children of CHRISTIANA and JOHN PETTY:

1. VIRGINIA[3] PETTY, b. 20 June 1849 Scott Co., Miss; d. 17 December 1925 Cameron Co., Texas;[19] m. DICK CLOUD.[20]
2. WRIGHT[3] PETTY, m. MARY MILLSAPS.[21]
3. WILLIAMS[3] PETTY, m. EMMA WALL.[22]
4. ANN[3] PETTY, unm.

iv. LENORA[2] BREWER, b. 13 October 1828 Butler Co., Ala., d. 13 August 1915 Bosque Co., Tex.; m. WILLIAM MATTHEW THOMAS about 1850 Scott

---

[16] Hodges, Alice A. Ancestry and Descendants of Dr. John Wright Petty of Madison Co., Ala. (Pendleton, S. C: n. p. d., 1978,) p.7. In fact she was born in Conecuh or Butler Co., Ala. Mrs. Hodges got her data from Judge Amis, who spelled the county "Sumpter."

[17] Pollard Clements Family. Accessed 13 February 2014 at http://trees.ancestry.com/tree/56615385/person/40011004778.

[18] Sulphur Springs Baptist Church. Remember Me. Directories of Cemeteries in Scott Co., MS. Printout obtained from library in Forest, Miss., March 2012.

[19] LaFeria Cemetery, Cameron Co., Texas. http://www.findagrave.com, # 20409828.

[20] They had seven children (Cloud): May; Dell m. Robert McDill; Fate, m. Emma Enderson; Leona; Johanna, m. Singleton Hunt; William. (A. B. Amis.)

[21] They never had any children. She is dead and he has remarried and lives at Harpersville, Miss. (A. B. Amis)

[22] Three children: Nina, Lilla, and Fannie. Address: Conehatta, Miss. (A. B. Amis.)

Co., Miss.;[23] b. 19 June 1828 South Carolina; d. 18 April 1904 Bosque Co., Texas.[24]

William M. Thomas and Lenora, 31, are living in Scott Co., Miss., in 1860.[25] Judge Amis said "They moved to Texas about 1870 and I have no information as to the family."

Children of LENORA and WILLIAM THOMAS:

1. MADISON[3] THOMAS, b. 1852 Scott Co., Miss; d. young
2. EMANUEL WAYMIRE[3] THOMAS, b. 13 Jan 1854, Scott Co., Miss.; d. 19 November 1949 Johnson Co., Tex;[26] m. MARY ELIZABETH PORTER, dau. of JOHN F. PORTER and CAROLYN SELF; b. 23 October 1855; d. 8 August 1948.[27]
3. JEFFERSON DAVIS[3] THOMAS, b. 9 March 1856, Scott Co., Miss.; d. 31 January Fort Worth, Tarrant Co., Texas, unm.[28]
4. JOHN WRIGHT[3] THOMAS, b. 5 April 1858 Scott Co., Miss.; d. 17 May 1930 Cisco, Eastland Co, Texas;[29] m. OPHELIA TRAMMELL 21 December 1880 Bosque Co., Texas; b. 12

---

[23] McCollough, ElaRuth. Personal communication 12 July 2002. Her connection was through Lenora. She also is the source of the dates, which matches the census estimate, and come from her tombstone in Kopperl Cemetery, Bosque Co., Texas. Also posted 18 December 2006 at http://www.findagrave.com, #17065778.

[24] Kopperl Cemetery, Bosque Co., Texas. http://www.findagrave.com, #26939640.

[25] 1860 Census Scott Co., Miss., Dist. 5, p. 4, #23. At #24 are John Thomas, 57 SC, and Mary Thomas, 50 SC, who are probably his parents.

[26] Grandview Cemetery, Grandview, Johnson Co., Tex. http://www.findagrave.com, #32057037.

[27] Grandview Cemetery, Grandview, Johnson Co., Tex. http://www.findagrave.com, #32057038.

[28] Texas Death Certificate 4842. Burial was in Kopperl. Pollard Clements Family. Accessed 13 February 2014 at http://trees.ancestry.com/tree/56615385/person/40011004778.

[29] Texas Death Certificate 23314. He was a minister and died of uremia. Pollard Clements Family. Accessed 13 February 2014 at http://trees.ancestry.com/tree/56615385/person/40011004778.

March 1861 Montgomery, Ala.; d. 10 January 1944 Cisco, Eastland Co., Texas.[30]

5. BABS[3] THOMAS, b. 1860 Scott Co., Miss; d. young.

6. WESLEY BARNES[3] THOMAS, b. 20 May 1862 Scott Co., Miss.; d. 6 June 1950 Stamford, Jones Co., Texas;[31] m. LAURA A. BRADSHAW; b. 28 September 1863 Ga.; d. 22 February 1960, Stamford, Jones Co., Texas.[32]

7. CLINTON H.[3] THOMAS, b. 20 February 1866 Scott Co., Miss.; d. 5 August 1941 Colorado City, Mitchell Co., Texas;[33] m. EDNA C. BODINE, dau. of WILLIAM H. BODINE and MARTHA JOANNE PUTNAM; b. 6 May 1883 Ala.; d. 18 November 1959 Colorado City, Mitchell Co., Tex.

8. ALBERT WYCHE[3] THOMAS, b. 14 June 1867 Scott Co., Miss.; d. 13 July 1949 Bosque Co., Tex.;[34] m. JESSIE MCKISSICK; b. 20 September 1874; d. 18 September 1936.

9. MELISSA TENNESSEE[3] THOMAS, b. 21 June 1873 Bosque Co., Texas; d. 1930 Bosque Co., Tex.;[35] m. SAM BAYLOS POWELL, b. 1870; d. 1942.[36]

v. MARY[2] BREWER, b. about 1830 Butler Co., Ala; d. before 1880 Scott Co., Miss.; m. ROMULUS DAY

---

[30] Texas Death Certificate 1888. Pollard Clements Family. Accessed 13 February 2014 at http://trees.ancestry.com/tree/56615385/person/40011004778.

[31] Highland Cemetery, Stamford, Haskell Co., Tex. http://www.findagrave.com, #34495346.

[32] Highland Cemetery, Stamford, Haskell Co., Tex. http://www.findagrave.com, #34495725.

[33] Loraine Cemetery, Mitchell Co., Tex. http://www.findagrave.com, #59346082.

[34] Morgan Cemetery, Bosque Co., Tex. http://www.findagrave.com, #17465414.

[35] Kopperl Cemetery, Bosque Co., Texas. http://www.findagrave.com, #16368804.

[36] Kopperl Cemetery, Bosque Co., Texas. http://www.findagrave.com, #16368794.

about 1851 Scott Co., Miss; b. about 1832 Mississippi.[37]

He was a widower in the 1880 Census.[38]

Children of MARY BREWER and ROMULUS DAY:

1. MALVINA[3] DAY, m. FINIS BAILEY.[39]
2. FLETA IRENE[3] DAY, b. 18 July 1856; d. 5 January 1925 Neshoba Co., Miss.;[40] m. JAMES M. SMITH,[41] b. 29 September 1842; d. 1 December 1923 Neshoba Co., Miss.[42]
3. HELENA[3] DAY, m. GEORGE UNDERWOOD.
4. MARY[3] DAY, m. ABSALOM LOPER, d. s. p.

vi. ELIZA[2] BREWER, b. 8 September 1832 Sumter Co., Ala.;[43] d. 26 February 1903 Kaufman Co., Texas;[44] m. LUNSFORD B. JONES about 1852 Scott Co., Miss.; b. about 1828 Tenn.; d. before 1870.[45]

Children of ELIZA BREWER and LUNSFORD JONES:

1. MILDRED[3] JONES, m. WORTH BAILEY,[46] b. June 1848; d. 10 September 1899 Leake Co., Miss.[47]
2. LAFAYETTE[3] JONES.[48]

---

[37] 1860 Census Scott Co., Miss., Dist. 5, p.17, #104/104.

[38] 1880 Census Scott Co., Miss., Beat 5, ED 83, p. 101A, #74/79. He is living near the Pettys.

[39] Six children: Charley, Minnie, Effie, Edith, Betty, and Finis, Jr. (A. B. Amis.)

[40] Neshoba Cemetery, Neshoba Co., Miss. Located at http://www.findagrave.com, #108995569.

[41] Seven children: Irvin, Romulus, Monroe, Eugene, Jewell, Flora, and Amos. (A. B. Amis.)

[42] Neshoba Cemetery, Neshoba Co., Miss. Located at http://www.findagrave.com, #108994848.

[43] Smith, Donna. Personal communication 10 Jul 2002 gives a birth date of 7 April 1834. She does not give the source, but it is probably an IGI file. Her connection was through Lenora.

[44] Hillcrest Cemetery, Forney, Kaufman Co., Texas. http://www.findagrave.com, #105692674.

[45] She is a widow in 1870 Census. May be the Lafayette B. Jones

[46] Three children: Laura, Jones, and Fletcher. (A. B. Amis.)

[47] Salem Cemetery, Leake Co., Miss. http://www.findagrave.com, #37118370

3. JAMES[3] JONES.[49]

4. TENNESSEE[3] JONES, b. 14 August 1862 Scott Co., Miss.; d. 2 March 1943 Ray, Pinal Co., Arizona;[50] m. ALBERT FINLEY,[51] b. 27 August 1859 Scott Co., Miss.; d. 17 October 1923 Roswell, Chaves Co., N. M.[52]

"Tennessee was born in Scott Co., Mississippi, near where her future husband's family lived. She later married Albert Brown Finley; they moved to Haskell, Texas, and later homesteaded in Roswell, N. M., where they are both buried next to their son, Austin Arthur Finley, my husband's father."[53]

vii. NANCY[2] BREWER, b. about 1834 in Alabama;. m. (1) JOHN ARNOLD; b. about 1832 Miss., son of WILLIAM ARNOLD and EMILY;[54] d. before 1870 Newton Co., Miss.; m. (2) _____ HATTAWAY about 1855 Newton Co., Miss.; d. before 1870 Newton Co., Miss.

Nancy Hattaway, b. about 1837 in Alabama, is head of household in Newton Co., Miss., in 1870 with Edward E., 13, John W., 11, and Albert, 5.[55]

Nancy Arnold is head of household in Neshoba Co., Miss., in 1880 with Christopher C. Arnold, 24, and Albert A. Hattaway, 15.[56]

Children of NANCY BREWER and JOHN ARNOLD:

---

[48] Married and went to Texas about forty years ago. No information as to his family. (A. B. Amis.)

[49] Married and went to Texas about forty years ago. No information as to his family. (A. B. Amis.)

[50] South Park Cemetery, Roswell, Chaves Co., N. M. Located at http://www.findagrave.com, #99322763.

[51] Married and went to Texas about forty years ago. No information as to his family. (A. B. Amis.)

[52] South Park Cemetery, Roswell, N. M. http://www.findagrave.com, #99322670

[53] Kendra. Located at http://www.findagrave.com, #99322763.

[54] 1850 Census Leake Co., Miss., Beat 3, p. 46A, #666.

[55] 1870 Census Newton Co., Miss., twp. 8, range 10, p. 496A, #120. She is two houses removed from Rankin Amis and three away from Allen Langford.

[56] 1880 Census Neshoba Co., Miss., Dixon, ED 59, p. 507B, #127/130.

1. CHRISTOPHER COLUMBUS[3] ARNOLD, b. 24
   April 1856; d. 28 May 1917 Neshoba Co.,
   Miss.;[57] m. ____ RISHER.[58]
2. JOHN[3] ARNOLD, JR., m. (1) MARY JACKSON;
   m. (2) AMANDA CLEVELAND.[59]

viii. HENRIETTA[2] BREWER, b. 8 July 1836 Sumter Co.,
Ala.; d. 2 October 1930 Leake Co., Miss.;[60] m.
(1) BENNETT BISHOP; m. (2) WILLIAM OWENS
before 1868; b. 12 December 1831; d. 9 May
1915 Leake Co., Miss.[61]

Child of HENRIETTA and BENNETT BISHOP:

1. LITA[3] BISHOP; m. WILLIAM COX.

Children of HENRIETTA and WILLIAM OWENS:

2. IRVIN[3] OWENS, b. 25 May 1870 Miss.;[62] d. 15
   March 1965 Hennepin Co., Minn.;[63] m.
   ADALINE MCADAMS about 1905, dau. of and
   JAMES MCADAMS and ALICE CURRIE; b. 22
   March 1882 Tarrant Co., Texas; d. 3
   January 1969 Hennepin Co., Minn.[64]
3. WILLIAM OSCAR[3] OWENS, b. 20 June 1873
   Miss.; d. 20 June 1913 Leake Co., Miss.[65]

---

[57] High Hill Baptist Church Cemetery, Dixon, Neshoba Co., Miss.
http://www.findagrave.com, #98169189.

[58] Lived in Leake Co., Miss., (A. B. Amis.)

[59] Three children: Georgia, m. Joe Collins; Pearl, m. Mr. Russell; and
Jenner. (A. B. Amis.)

[60] Mount Zion Cemetery, Leake Co., Miss. http://www.findagrave.com,
#36709402.

[61] Mount Zion Cemetery, Leake Co., Miss. http://www.findagrave.com,
#36709412.

[62] 1880 Census Leake Co., Miss., Walnut Grove, ED 37, p. 14A, #221.

[63] Certificate #5919, record #1597560. Minnesota Death Index, 1908-
2002. Located at Ancestry.com, 14 February 2014. His mother's maiden
name was stated as Brewer. He was apparently a veterinarian.

[64] Certificate #569, record #1729007. Minnesota Death Index, 1908-
2002. Located at Ancestry.com, 14 February 2014. Her mother's maiden
name was stated as Curry. Her maiden name is derived from the listing of
her parents in their household in 1910. [Tarrant Co., Texas, Fort Worth
Ward 8, ED 133, p. 6B, #132.]

[65] Mount Zion Cemetery, Leake Co., Miss. http://www.findagrave.com,
#36709420.

4. JOHN LAWRENCE[3] OWENS, b. 20 June 1873 Miss.[66]; d. after 1930 Leake Co., Miss.[67]

5. BENJAMIN WYCHE[3] OWENS, b. 3 January 1876 Miss.; d. 15 April 1963 Leake Co., Miss.[68]

ix. MELISSA[2] BREWER, b. 15 June 1840 Sumter Co., Ala.; d. 8 January 1912 Leake Co., Miss.;[69] m. IRVIN MILLER 4 Dec 1856 Scott Co., Miss.;[70] b. 11 November 1836 Ky.; d. 20 May 1906 Leake Co., Miss.[71]

Irvin and Melissa Miller are in Scott Co., Miss., in 1860,[72] and in Leake County in 1880,[73] and 1900.[74]

Children of MELISSA BREWER and IRVIN MILLER:

1. JOHN[3] MILLER, b. 1857 Scott Co., Miss.

2. ADDIE[3] MILLER, b. April 1863 Miss.; m. W. W. GRAHAM 25 December 1886 Leake Co., Miss.; d. before 1900 Leake Co., Miss.[75]

---

[66] 1880 Census Leake Co., Miss., Walnut Grove, ED 37, p. 14A, #221.

[67] 1930 Census Leake Co., Miss., Beat 5, ED 12, p. 5B, #99/101. He said he married at age 42, but has no wife listed with him in 1930 at age 56. Henrietta, 93, is living with him at that time.

[68] Mount Zion Cemetery, Leake Co., Miss. http://www.findagrave.com, #36709395.

[69] Golden-Johnson-Rock Hill Cemetery, Leake Co., Miss. http://www.findagrave.com, #61570476.

[70] Biographical and Historical Memoirs of Mississippi. (Chicago: Goodspeed Publ. Co., 1891,) p. 438.

[71] Golden-Johnson-Rock Hill Cemetery, Leake Co., Miss. http://www.findagrave.com, #61570883. "They had several children, among whom was John, Addie, Jennie, Gussie, Irvin, and Edith, but I have no information about their families." (A. B. Amis.)

[72] 1860 Census Scott Co., Miss., District 5, p. 12, #72. He is described as a merchant and has William Andrews, 20, Ga., clerk, and son John, 3. He seems likely to be the 14 year old boy in 1850 living with David and Elizabeth Phillips in District 1, Marion Co., Ky., [p. 343A, #214.]

[73] 1880 Census Leake Co., Miss., Walnut Grove, ED 52, p. 459B, #519/582.

[74] 1900 Census Leake Co., Miss., Walnut Grove, ED 37, p. 11A, #187.

[75] 1900 Census Leake Co., Miss., Walnut Grove, ED 37, p. 11A, #188. Her son, Miller Graham, registered for the WWI draft listing his date of birth as 21 September 1887 in Walnut Grove, Miss., and said he was supporting his mother and one brother. [WWI Draft Registration Hancock Co., Miss. Accessed 14 February 2014 at Ancestry.com.]

3. JENNIE[3] MILLER, b. 23 March 1867 Miss.; d. 22 December 1942 Leake Co., Miss.;[76] m. WILLIAM A. KELLY 24 December 1887 Leake Co., Miss.;[77] b. 26 July 1860; d. 27 October 1919 Leake Co., Miss.[78]

4. GUSSIE[3] MILLER, b. November 1869 Miss.;[79] m. LUTHER STARLING 5 May 1890 Leake Co., Miss.[80]

5. IRVIN KAVANAUGH[3] MILLER, b. 18 August 1878[81] Leake Co., Miss.; d. 1958 Allen Par., La.;[82] m. MARY V. BROWN about 1902,[83] dau. of JOHN F. BROWN;[84] b. 1883; d. 1978 Allen Par., La.[85]

6. EDITH[3] MILLER, b. about 1882 Leake Co., Miss.

x. WILLIAM[2] BREWER, b. about 1840 Sumter Co., Ala.; d. Civil War; m. MELISSA GUNN, dau. of ANDREW C. GUNN and SARAH LOUISE TUCKER b. 21 July 1845; d. 18 July 1883 Hempstead Co., Ark.; m. (2) BENJAMIN FRANCIS LANG 21 December 1866 Leake Co., Miss.; b. 5 June 1844 Leake Co., Miss.; d. 1920 Pulaski Co., Ark.[86]

---

[76] She is buried as Virginia M. Kelly. Old Walnut Grove Cemetery, Leake Co., Miss. http://www.findagrave.com, #11753345.

[77] Mississippi Marriages 1776-1935. Accessed 14 February 2014 at Ancestry.com.

[78] Old Walnut Grove Cemetery, Leake Co., Mississippi. http://www.findagrave.com, #11753282.

[79] 1900 Census Leake Co., Miss., Walnut Grove, ED 37, p. 11A, #189.

[80] Mississippi Marriages 1776-1935. Accessed 14 February 2014 at Ancestry.com. Gussie and Luther Starling were living in Leake Co., in 1935, but moved to Jackson, Hinds Co., Miss., by 1940. [2116 Capital Way, ED 25-24A, p. 15A.

[81] WW1 Draft Registration Card, Allen Par., La. Accessed 14 February 2014 at Ancestry.com.

[82] Resthaven Cemetery & Mausoleum, Oakdale, Allen Par., La. http://www.findagrave.com, #72128993.

[83] 1910 Census Grant Par., La., Police Jury Ward 5, ED

[84] 1940 Census Allen Par., La., ED2-14, p. 8B, 1022 Main Street. John F., Brown, 87, father-in-law is living with them.

[85] Resthaven Cemetery & Mausoleum, Oakdale, Allen Par., La. http://www.findagrave.com, #72129017.

[86] Pollard Clements Family. Accessed 13 February 2014 at

"He died during the Civil War and his widow re-married and went to Texas, about 1870. I have no information as to their families."[87]

Pvt. William Brewer, Co. F., 43rd Mississippi Infantry, died 25 May 1863.[88] Company F was originally raised in Lowndes Co., Miss., and the regiment mustered initially at Gainesville, Ala.[89]

Clearly, Wyche Brewer was associated with William Brewer, but which William Brewer?

About three miles from town, on this road, was where William Brewer settled about 1830. He lived here near Holihta Creek and was known in this time as "Holeeta Bill" to distinguish him from another William Brewer who lived on Cedar Creek, who was called "Cedar Creek Bill."

The wife of Holihta Bill Brewer was a Miss Bates, related, so it said, to Thomas Jefferson. The Brewers had a number of children amongst them Robert Brewer, Mrs. William Lockard, and Mrs. Thomas Lockard, Jr.

Robert Brewer married a Miss Hadden, who was related to the noted Presbyterian preacher of that day, Isaac Hadden. Among the children of Robert and his wife were Lewis and Willis Brewer. Lewis served as a Confederate and Willis, in after years, served in Congress and wrote a history of Alabama.[90]

---

http://trees.ancestry.com/tree/56615385/person/40011004778.

[87] Judge Amis stated that he had two daughters and that his wife and children moved to Texas about 1870. Clearly there is no possibility of y-DNA testing to link Wyche Brewer to the family of George Brewer in Brunswick Co., Virginia. It may still be possible to link through a descendant of William Brewer, who is clearly a male relative, although not the father of Wyche Brewer.

[88] Cedar Hill Cemetery, Vicksburg, Warren Co., Miss.

[89] http://en.wikipedia.org/wiki/43rd_Mississippi_Infantry. Accessed 15 December 2013.

[90] Spratt, Robert D. The History of the Town of Livingston, Alabama. (1928, repr. 1974, Sumter Co., Hist. Society), p. 44,

Mrs. Miriam Brewer Richardson of Montgomery, a daughter of the late Willis Brewer, informs me that "Holihta Bill" and "Cedar Creek Bill" were distantly related, and that Brewersville was named for "Holihta Bill's brother Matthew Brewer, who lived there in 1832.[91]

William (Cedar Creek Bill) Brewer of Sumter Co., Alabama

William Brewer of Cedar Creek, Sumter Co., Alabama, was born 14 September 1770 in North Carolina and died 26 March 1852 Sumter Co., Alabama. He is buried, along with his wife, Mary, and son William P. Brewer in the New Prospect Baptist Church Cemetery, near Bluffport, Sumter Co., Alabama.[92] Mary Brewer was born in Virginia 12 February 1774 and died in Sumter Co., Alabama 11 January 1859.[93]

Based upon the data for their children, (see below) William Brewer and Mary married in Georgia before 1803, but probably no earlier than 1799. They probably lived in Georgia at least through 1808 based upon the census data for their children, although Jackson Brewer, who appears to be the eldest child, was reportedly born in Alabama in 1803 according to his entry in the 1850 Census for Harrison Co., Texas.

William Brewer appears in Conecuh Co., Alabama after 1816[94] and before 1818.[95] William Brewer was in Conecuh Co., Alabama in 1820.[96] He

---

[91] Spratt, Robert D. The History of the Town of Livingston, Alabama. (1928, repr. 1974, Sumter Co., Hist. Society), p. 146,

[92] Cemetery reading kindly provided by LeSabre Hoit.

[93] The 1850 Census Sumter Co., Ala., p. 330, #1150, shows William Brewer, 76, NC, Mary Brewer, 72, VA,

[94] Davis, Joyce. Alabama Early Settlers, 1816. (Hanceville, AL: Briarwood Press, 1983.)

[95] Names of Persons Owning or Holding any Taxable Property, Conecuh County, 1818. (Typescript transcription in the Conecuh County Library, Evergreen, Alabama. (n. p. d.)

[96] 1820 Census Conecuh Co., AL, p. 28, (2-5-1-3).

was still there in 1830 when had four sons, two of whom were born 1820-1830, and three daughters, one of whom was born 1820-1830. This means one of the sons has been "lost" and presumably married prior to 1830. Thus, in 1820 he has one adult male and two of the five minor males who cannot be his sons. I am reasonably confident that Wyche Brewer, b. 1798, is the other adult male. Could the extra three males be from a previous marriage? The probate records provide absolutely no indication that any of the nine children were by any mother other than Mary Brewer, widow and relict of William Brewer.

In 1820 he has three girls. He added one more daughter 1825-1830. Assuming all of the girls in his household in 1820 were daughters, we can account for four of the six known. Presumably, the two missing girls have married prior to 1820.

The 1820 Census for Conecuh Co., Alabama also shows two other adult males named Brewer: James Brewer[97] and George Brewer.[98] George Brewer is on the same page as William Brewer. The 1830 Census of Alabama shows a James Brewer in Pike Co., who may or may not be the same man, and Wyche Brewer in Butler Co. (q.v.) At least one of the minor children appears likely to be living with Henry Brewer in 1830.

From the land records in Sumter Co., Ala., the third male appears to be John M. Brewer.[99] When the land patents were registered William Brewer took out tracts in township 19, range 2W (St. Stephen's Meridian)[100], along with Wyche Brewer[101], Seaborn

---

[97] 1820 Census Conecuh Co., Ala., p. 26, (1-1-0-1).

[98] 1820 Census Conecuh Co., Ala., p. 30, (1-1-1-1).

[99] The land records also make it likely there is a second William Brewer, who is associated with Matthew Brewer, patenting land in Sumter Co., Ala., at the same time. As will be shown in his section, this man probably lived in Choctaw Co., and was Matthew's brother.

[100] BLM documents 2620, 80 acres in section 8 (W ½ SE); 3112, 80 acres in section 26 (E ½ NE) along with Samuel H. Coffman, who also

Brewer, and Jackson Brewer. He also took out a patent on 80 acres in section 31, township 20N, range 2W,[102] at the same time as John M. Brewer.[103]

The early records of Conecuh Co., Ala. have been lost, but a memorial regarding Leroy Brewer was published in the 1930's asserting that he was born in Conecuh Co., Alabama in 1818 and moved with his family to Sumter Co., Ala., in 1832. (q.v.) This is the only direct statement I have found showing that William Brewer of the 1830 Census in Conecuh Co., Ala., is the same man as William Brewer of the 1840 Census in Sumter Co., Ala[104]., but there are also no other possibilities to be found from examination of the 1830 Alabama Census.

The data suggest, then, that William and Mary Brewer married in Georgia about 1800 and that he became the guardian for his nephews, George, James, Wyche, John M., and one whose name is yet to be discovered. Since Wyche Brewer is known to have been born 6 July 1798 in Georgia,[105] it seems reasonable to conclude that his father died in Georgia after about 1805 and before 1814.[106]

---

patented land with Jackson Brewer; 3114, 80 acres in section 11, twp. 19N, range 4W.

[101] BLM document 9632, 40 acres in section 13 (SWNW aliquot), dated 15 May 1837.

[102] BLM document 2621, 15 Mar 1837 (W ½ NW aliquot.)

[103] BLM document 2622, 15 Mar 1837 (E ½ SE aliquot.)

[104] 1840 Census Sumter Co., Ala., (00110001-01001001) Who the female b. 1835 to 1840 is remains unknown. It is possible she died before William Brewer and so was not mentioned in his probate papers. Otherwise the data are consistent with William P. Brewer as the youngest son, with Leroy Brewer and Elizabeth Brewer still living at home.

[105] Amis Family Cemetery, Conehatta, Scott Co., Miss. Transcription by Elvy Hammond. Located on the Scott Co., Miss., page www.usgenweb.org.

[106] Wyche Brewer would not have needed a guardian after age 16, and would likely not have been living in association with William Brewer most of his adult life.

Last Will and Testament of William Brewer, Sumter Co., Alabama[107]

The State of Alabama, Sumter. I William Brewer...If my beloved wife Mary should survive me, it is my will and desire that she shall have all my property, both real and personal so long as she shall live, and at her death to be legally divided amongst my legal distributees just in the same manner as is presented out by the statute of distributions of the State of Alabama...I hereby appoint my son William T. (P) to be my executor. As witness my hand and affixed my seal this 21st day of December 1850. Wit: Matthew C. Houston, Edwin Gibbs, David Hitt.

Codicil: As a codicil to the foregoing will, I will and bequeath to Martha E. Monett wife of James Monett as a separate estate to be free from the debts, contracts and liabilities of her said husband or any future husband, the sum of six hundred dollars...this the 15th day of January A. D. 1851. Signed, sealed, published and declared before Benjamin J. H. Gaines, William S. Tuneman. {Will recorded October 11, 1852} Ben. J. H. Gaines, Judge P. C.]

Fortunately, the loose probate records survive, and include the following document which spells out those entitled to receive a distribution from his estate.

To the Honorable the Judge of Probate of the County of Sumter & State of Alabama[108]

The undersigned administrator with the will annexed of all & singular the goods & chattels, rights & condits which were of William Brewer deceased represents to your Honorable Court that the sale of the perishable property ordered by your

---

[107] Sumter Co., Ala., Will Book 2:20 (p. 35 when renumbered). Cited in Hester, G. Sumter County, Alabama Wills:1828-1872. (Dallas: Southern Roots, 1998,) p. 144.

[108] Loose estate papers, Sumter Co., Alabama, Estate of William Brewer, item 1146-1148

Honorable Court to be sold and the proceeds of the crop now gathered and being gathered will be sufficient to play the debts of decedent & to discharge the special legacy made by decedent, that the salves of the estate should therefore be distributed. The heirs & distributees are as follow.

1.   Mary Brewer of Sumter County widow of decedent, who has dissented from the will.

2. Serena Jones, a female of age of Sumter County, daughter of decedent.

3.   Sarah Summerlin daughter of decedent of age, wife of William D. Summerlin of Sumter County, she marred before the year 1848.

4.   Elizabeth S. M. Beazley, daughter of decedent and wife of petitioner, of age & of Sumter County. She married before 1848.

5.   William P. Brewer of age and of Sumter County, son of decedent.

6.   Leroy Brewer, son of decedent, of age, of the County of Mobile, State of Alabama

7.   Henry Brewer, son of decedent, of age, of the County of Covington, State of Alabama

8.   Serena Summerlin, of age, wife of Fesenton Summerlin, William E. Briggs of age, both of Yellowbusha (sic) County, Mississippi, Henry Briggs, aged about eighteen years, Leroy Briggs, aged about 12 years, Mary Briggs, aged about eleven years, all of Sumter County, Alabama. These are all children of Nancy Briggs, who died before petitioner's decedent.   Said Mary was the daughter of petitioner's decedent.

9. Margaret E. Monett of age, wife of James Monett of said County of Sumter, Mary L. Brewer, aged about fourteen years, John H. Brewer aged about twelve years, Thomas P. Brewer aged about ten years, Sarah Brewer aged about years, all of Harrison County, Texas. These are children of Jackson Brewer, deceased, said Jackson was the son of petitioner's decedent & died before petitioner's decedent.

Your petitioner also shows that about seventeen years since Seaborn Brewer, a son of decedent, went to Kentucky on business, expecting shortly to return. He has not been heard of since he reached Louisville & it is supposed he died long since.

Your petitioner begs your honor to cause the slaves of decedent to be distributed according to law & the will of decedent, and your petitioner as on duty bound will ever pray, etc.

Sworn to, subscribed before me

B. J. Gaines, J. P. C.   s/ Wm. H. Beazley

Confirmed

    James P. May

    Robert H. Houston

    Josiah Moore

    Wm. V. Bevill

    James H. Soutston (?)

Although William Brewer's will provided his wife with a life estate, the decision was made to proceed with a sale of his multiple properties, which are itemized in the following two documents, again from his loose probate records.

The State of Alabama[109]

Sumter County

To the Honorable B. J. H. Gaines, Judge of Probate for said county

Your petitioner William H. Beezley respectfully shows to your Honor that he is administrator, with the will annexed, of William Brewer, dec'd, late of said county; that by the terms of the will the widow was entitled to a life estate in the property of the deceased, and that after her death the residue was directed to be distributed according to the Laws of Alabama; that the said widow has dissented from

---

[109] Loose estate papers, Sumter Co., Alabama, Estate of William Brewer, item 1100-1101

the will and had her dower assigned her in the land hereafter mentioned. Your petitioner is advised and believes that the lands above referred to remain as if no will had been made.

Your petitioner further shows the deceased died seized and possessed of the following land in said county--

SW 1/4 of	section	13	in Township
19, R. 2W			
W 1/2 of SE 1/4	"	13	"
NW 1/4 "	24		"
W 1/2 of NE1/4	"	24	"
W 1/2 of SE 1/4	"	14	"
S. end of E 1/2 of SE 1/4"		14	"
NW 1/4	"	23	"
NE 1/4	"	23	"
N. side of SW 1/4"	23		"

The sixth mentioned tract being 30 acres and the last 40 acres.

The said lands are so situated in reference to the number of heirs that the same cannot be equitably divided among them without a sale. The following are the names of the heirs. (Henry Brewer scratched out) Serena Jones, Elizabeth H. Beazley, wife of your petitioner, Sarah Summerlin, wife of Wm. D. Summerlin, William P. Brewer all of age and in this county; Leroy Brewer of Mobile; Henry Brewer of Covington Co., Ala., who are of age; William E. Briggs, Serena Summerlin, wife of Fessenden Summerlin, both of whom are of age and live in Mississippi; and the following minors who live in Sumter Co.; Ann Briggs (over 14), Leroy Briggs & Mary E. Briggs, (both under 14); Emeline Monett, wife of James Monette of this county, Mary L. Brewer (over 14), John H. Brewer, Thomas J. Brewer, and Sarah E. Brewer, under 14, all of the State of Texas.

Wherefore your petitioner asks that the said lands may be sold for equitable division, as the Statute directs, and that the ___citations ___, and, a guardian ad litem may be appointed for the said minors; and that such other order may be made as may be necessary to give your honor jurisdiction, and to provide a trial of the facts stated in this petition; and that your honor may make such further order as the merits of the case may justify. Baldwin and Wetinon (?) for the petitioner.

The State of Alabama
Sumter County
c/o the Hon. B. J. H. Gaines, Judge of Probate for said county:[110]

The undersigned administrators with the will attached of the estate of William Brewer deceased reports to your honor that, in pursuance of a ____ of your honor, and after advertising more than thirty days in the Sumter County Whig, we did, on the 7th day of November 1853, at the usual hour, expose to sale, before the Court house door in said County, the following land of said estate.

Lot No. 1   W 1/2 of SE1/4 of sec 14; W 1/2 of NE 1/4 sec 23; 40 acres on the south of SW1/4 of sec. 23, all in township 19 of Range 2W containing 360 acres.

Lot No. 2 E1/2 of NE1/4 of sec 23, 30 acres on the south end of the E1/2 of SE1/4 of sec. 14 all in the same township & range containing 110 acres.

Lot No. 3 SW 1/4 of sec 13, less 10 acres on the NW corner, W1/2 of SE1/4 of sec 13, NW1/4 of sec 14; W1/2 of NE1/4 of Sec 24, all in the same township and range, containing 470 acres.

All sold on twelve months credit.

W. Waldo Shermer being the highest bidder, bought the first lot at Six 50/100 dollars per acre, and ____, and therefore his note for two thousand three hundred & forty dollars, with Marcus Parker & Socrates Parker securities, which note was accepted by the undersigned.

---

[110] Loose estate papers, Sumter Co., Alabama, Estate of William Brewer, pp. 1080-1081.

Geo. B. Saunders, being the highest bidder, bought the second Lot at six 62 1/2/100 dollars per acre, and executed therefore his note for seven hundred & twenty eight 75/100 dollars, with Wm. B. Suanders, & Reuben Thorne his securities, which note was accepted by me.

Mary Brown being the highest bidder, bought the last named parcel her designated as Lot No. 3, at one 60/100 dollars per acre, and executed therefore her note for seven hundred & fifty one dollars, with Wm. P. Brown, Wm. D. Summerlin & Syrena Jones, sureties, which note was accepted by the undersigned.

The undersigned asks that the said sales be confirmed, and reports that he has fully complied with the order of the Probate Court.

The undersigned also reports the following claims due the estate, in addition to those previous returned; and if any of the same have been previously returned, he merely reports them now, with the caution that he be not charged twice of the same debts,

1. Note on Leroy Brown, due Apl 10 1852, given for money obtained of decedent $50.00
2. Note on Wm. P. Brown for rent due Jany 1 1854
$5.25
3. Note on Syrena Jones for ginning cotton due July 1 1853 $15.00
4. Note on J. A. Abraham and Robt Arrington for rent due Jany 2 1854 $31.25
5. a/c on Wm. D. Summerlin for ginning & ____ due Jany 13 1853 $19.56
6. a/c on undersigned for rent due July 1 1853 $18.75

Dec. 1, 1853   s/ Wm. H. Beazley

Genealogical Summary

2. WILLIAM[2] BREWER was born 14 September 1770 in North Carolina and died 26 March 1852 Sumter Co., Alabama.   He married MARY ____ about 1800 in

Georgia. She was born 12 February 1774 in Virginia and died 11 January 1859 Sumter Co., Ala.

Children of William Brewer and Mary are:

i. JACKSON[3] BREWER, b. 1803 Alabama; d. about 1851 Harrison Co., Texas; m. HARRIET (SAVAGE) GORDON.

Jackson Brewer patented 160 acres of land in twp. 19N, range 2W along with his father and brother on 15 March 1837.[111] George W. Harper was listed as a secondary patentee.[112]

Jackson Brewer's children are described as being in Harrison Co., Texas, in 1854. The 1850 Census for Harrison Co., Texas shows "J" Brewer, 47, b. "Alabama," with his wife "H", b. Georgia, also 47 along with children William Brewer, 22, Alabama, M., (f.12), J. H., (m 9), T. P., (m 8) and S. A. G., (f 6) all born in Texas.[113] It is not clear that William Brewer, 22, is a son—he may be William P. Brewer of Sumter Co., Ala., who managed to get counted twice in this census.

Blanche Hancock Turlington, a descendant of Jackson Brewer reported that his wife's name was Harriet (Savage) Gordon, and that she moved to Ashley Co., Ark., after Jackson Brewer's death. Mrs. Turlington was descended from their youngest daughter, Sarah Brewer.[114]

---

[111] BLM document 3605 Section 25, NW aliquot.

[112] I have looked for a possible connection with the Harper family in Greene Co., Ga. There are two possible clues. The first is George Weldon Harper, b. 25 Sep 1807 in Ky., married Malinda F. Moore 1827 Sumter Co., Ala. Moved to Scott Co., Miss, Gonzales Co., Texas, and Medina Co., Texas. He married (2) Ann L. King in Hondo, Texas. [Lee, Bebe. 14 Jul 2003. http://genforum.genealogy.com/harper/messages/6374.html.] The second is Wyatt Harper, b. 1799 in Ga., m. Sophia (Coats) Bates 21 Dec 1825 Greene Co., Ala., and moved to Sumter Co., Ala., shortly thereafter. Children include John E., James W., Robert S., Wyatt Judson, George G., Louis Pink, and Zachary C. Harper. [Holt, Olivia. 11 Sep 1999. http://genforum.genealogy.com/harper/messages/1677.html.]

[113] 1850 Census Harrison Co., Texas, p. 74, #360.

[114] Personal communication, T. Daniel Knight, 15 Feb. 2005.

Harriett Brewer married Charles Herman 13 October 1852 in Ashley Co., Arkansas.[115] Online sources state, without documentation that she died 18 April 1859.

The 1860 Census shows the children spread out. Thomas Brewer, 19, is living with J. H. Peddy and Elizabeth.[116] Henry Brewer, 13, is living with M. H. Christian.[117] The dates don't match the other census data that well. There are an "E" and an "Elizah [Elijah]" Brewer living with members of the Noble family, but I have not found Harriett there.

On 26 June 1858 James W. M. Kirkpatrick of Ashley Co., Ark., appointed William P. Brewer as his attorney to settle with the guardian of Thomas P. Brewer and Sarah A. E. Brewer.[118] This is consistent with the notion that Mary L. Brewer had married "Kirkpatrick" after the death of her grandfather. Presumably, they were also keeping her two younger siblings, Thomas P., and Sarah A. Elizabeth."

The *Voice of Sumter* for 17 May 1836 reported the deaths of James Gordon, aged 10 years, from scarlet fever on 12 May, and of George W. Gordon, aged 5 years, on May 15th, both sons of Mrs. Jackson Brewer.[119] This item indicates that Jackson Brewer married the widow Gordon between 1831 and 1836.

The Governor for use of Simmons v. Hancock and Harris. Writ of error to County Court of Sumter Co.[120]

---

[115] Arkansas Marriages 1779-1992. Accessed 14 February 2014 at Ancestry.com.

[116] 1860 Census Ashley Co., Ark., Carter, p. 208, #757/773. Mr. Peddy is a hotel keeper, so he appears to be living there in a boarding house.

[117] 1860 Census Ashley Co., Ark., Carter, p. 210, #767/778. This is also a boarding house.

[118] Sumter Co., Ala., Deed Book P:244-245. Transcribed by Linda Essary.

[119] Gandrud, Pauline. Alabama Records, Vol. 164, p. 4.

[120] Minors Court Book 10:296, [August 1841], cited in Gandrud, Pauline. Alabama Records, Vol. 70, p. 78.

Action of debt on a sheriff's bond against the defendants, who signed the same as sureties for William Johnson, Sheriff. Attachment was issued at suit of Mrs. Anne Simmons against the estate of Jackson Brewer to secure a debt of $1400. Brewer had removed all his property from this county.

Jackson Brewer received a conditional patent for land in the Republic of Texas on 7 Jul 1838, in the so-called 2nd class, for 1280 acres of land in San Augustine Co., in which he said he arrived in Texas in January 1837.[121] The grants were conditional upon three years residence in the Republic, an attempt to prevent fraud and land speculation. The patent was confirmed in Harrison Co., Texas on 2 December 1844.

Harriet Brewer had her son-in-law, J. W. Monette, acting as guardian for her minor children on 4 April 1853.

"The Children of Jackson Brewer are as follows:[122]

1. Martha A. Monett & her husband J. W.
2. Mary L. Brewer, now the wife of Kirkpatrick (but was not married April 4, 53)
3. John Henry Brewer, a minor
4. Thomas Pinkney, a minor
5. Sarah Elizabeth, a minor

J. W. Monett was appointed guardian of all said four & was so acting the 4th of April 1853.

In witness before

B. J. H. Gaines, J. P. s/ Wm. H. Beazley"

---

[121] White, Gifford. 1840 Citizens of Texas, Vol. 1, Land Grants. (Nacogdoches, Texas: Ericson Books, 1983,) p. 28.

[122] Sumter Co., Ala., William Brewer's Loose estate papers, item number not copied.

Children of JACKSON BREWER are:

1. MARGARET EMMELIN[4] BREWER, b. about 1832 Alabama; d. after 1920 Wilcox Co., Ala.;[123] m. JAMES W. MONETTE 2 November 1850 Sumter Co., Ala.;[124] b. about 1828 Alabama; d. after 1880 Mobile Co., Ala.

    Margaret Brewer and James Monette are said to be living in Sumter Co., Alabama in 1854. They are present there in 1860,[125] and 1870.[126] They moved to Mobile by 1874, and were there in 1880.[127]

    The Livingston Journal for 24 November 1876 reported the death of George Monette, son of Richard and Mary E. Felder on November 4th, and the death of Mollie E., wife of Richard Felder, and daughter of Capt. J. W. and Emma Monette and niece of L. Brewer on 19 November 1876.[128]

2. MARY L.[4] BREWER, b. about 1839 Harrison Co., Texas; d. before 1860 Ashley Co., Ark.; m. JAMES W. M. KIRKPATRICK 24 November 1852 Ashley Co., Ark.;[129] b. about 1832 Georgia;[130] d. after 1880;[131] m. (2) S. C.; m. (3) JOSEPHINE E. MCCOMBS 13 February 1868 Ashley Co., Ark.;[132] d. before 1880 Ashley Co., Ark.

---

[123] 1920 Census Wilcox Co., Ala., Clifton, ED 165, p. 6A, #107. This was a boarding house.

[124] Alabama Select Marriages 1816-1957. Accessed 14 February 2014 at Ancestry.com.

[125] 1860 Census Sumter Co., Ala., Southern Division, p. 538, #556.

[126] 1870 Census Sumter Co., Ala., Twp. 19, range 1, 2, 3, and 4. (Livingston, which is actually range 2), p. 220A, #48/39. He was listed as a "cotton weigher."

[127] 1880 Census Mobile, Mobile Co., Ala., ED 130, p. 218A, #325/429. He is again listed as a cotton weigher.

[128] Gandrud, Pauline. Alabama Records. Vol. 70, p. 60.

[129] Arkansas Marriages 1779-1992. Accessed 14 February 2014 at Ancestry.com.

[130] 1860 Census Ashley Co., Ark., White, p. 170, #480/484. J. W. M. is living in the household of his father, "E." Kirkpatrick, 52, retired merchant, b. Georgia, with S. C., 26, b. Ga., and M. L., 5F, b. Ark.

[131] 1880 Census Ashley Co., Ark., Portland, ED 10, p. 151A, #212/218.

[132] Arkansas Marriages 1779-1992. Accessed 14 February 2014 at Ancestry.com.

3. JOHN HENRY[4] BREWER, b. about 1841 Texas
4. THOMAS PINCKNEY[4] BREWER, b. 9 April 1843 Marshall, Harrison Co., Texas;[133] d. 9 June 1914 Mobile, Mobile Co., Ala.;[134] m. EMMA C. MCKEAN 1873 Mobile, dau. of WILLIAM P. MCKEAN and MARTHA W. MCCLESKY; b. 21 September 1845 Mobile; d. 11 January 1933 Chicago, Cook Co., Illinois.[135]

Thomas P. Brewer enlisted as a private in Co. K., 3rd Arkansas Infantry and was mustered out at Appomattox C. H. 9 April 1865 as a Captain.[136]

Thomas P. Brewer was City Treasurer of Mobile. His father was identified as Jackson Brewer and his mother was identified as Harriett Savage.[137]

5. SARAH ELIZABETH[4] BREWER, b. 4 February 1844 Marshall, Harrison Co., Texas; d. 22 April 1919 Ashley Co., Ark.;[138] m. (2) WILLIAM MARCUS NOBLE 4 October 1866 Ashley Co., Ark.;[139] b. 21 December 1848 Jefferson Co., Ark.; d. 16 June 1919 Ashley Co., Ark.[140]

ii. HENRY[3] BREWER, b. 1805 Georgia; m. MARY ____ about 1829 Covington Co., Ala.(?); b. 1816 South Carolina.

---

[133] Alabama Census of Confederate Soldiers, 1907-1908. Accessed 14 February 2014 at Ancestry.com.

[134] Magnolia Cemetery, Mobile, Mobile Co., Ala. http://www.findagrave.com, #116132301.

[135] Illinois Deaths and Stillbirths Index, 1916-1947. Accessed 14 February 2014 at Ancestry.com.

[136] US Civil War Soldier Records and Profiles, 1861-1865. Accessed 14 February 2014 at Ancestry.com.

[137] Alabama Deaths and Burials Index, 1881-1874. Accessed 14 February 2014 at Ancestry.com.

[138] Bethel Cemetery, Crossett, Ashley Co., Ark. http://www.findagrave.com, #11067808.

[139] Arkansas Marriages 1779-1992. Accessed 14 February 2014 at Ancestry.com. She is identified as Sallie A. Hendrick.

[140] Bethel Cemetery, Crossett, Ashley Co., Ark. http://www.findagrave.com, #11067805.

Henry Brewer is in Covington Co., Ala., in the 1830 Census.[141] He has a teenaged male with him, who may be one of the "extra" males in the household of William Brewer in the 1820 Conecuh Co., Ala., census. He is listed there in 1840, again with the extra adult male, and with four daughters.[142] In the 1850 Census he has four daughters and three sons, but the ages are such that he is missing three older daughters, who have either died or married. Henry Brewer was living in Covington Co., Alabama in 1854 according to the estate records of his father.

A history of Covington Co., Ala. reports that Henry Brewer was among the men known to have served as a county prosecutor prior to the Civil War.[143]

On 30 September 1831 Henry Brewer, Reuben L. Jones, and Jacob Briggs, among others, supported the appointment of Eli N. Briggs for sheriff in a petition sent to the Governor.[144] (The previous sheriff had resigned.) Reuben L. Jones married Syrena Brewer, as discussed below. The name of Nancy Brewer's husband was known to be Briggs, but his first name has yet to be discovered by me. However, it seems probable that he is related to these men named Briggs.

Henry Brewer apparently lived near Montezuma originally and then moved to Andalusia after the first town was abandoned as too unhealthy.

"A few new residents had moved to Montezuma in the late 1820's and early 1830's, the most notable of these being John G. Barrow, David Dunn and Henry Brewer."[145]

---

[141] 1830 Census Covington Co., Ala., p. 235, line 7, (00011-0001).

[142] 1840 Census Covington Co., Ala., p. 327, line 18 (000011-21101).

[143] Ward, Wyley D. Early History of Covington County, Alabama, 1821-1871. (Spartanburg, SC: The Reprint Co., 1991,) p. 51. Cited hereafter as Ward.

[144] Ward, p. 54,

[145] Ward, p. 148.

He was appointed provost marshal of the 60th Regt., 11th Brig., 5th Div., Alabama militia on 26 February 1841.[146]

"By 1850 the town of Andalusia was beginning to take shape, John Nicholas and Isaac Smith had established stores in the town, David Dunn was operating a blacksmith shop nearby, and Josiah Jones had opened a law office in the town. In addition to these the families of Henry Brewer, Seth and John B. Dixon, William T. Acree, and Charles A. Stanley were living in the village." [147]

Henry Brewer represented the Andalusia Baptist Church at the Bethlehem Association meetings in 1852 and 1858,[148] and on 27 August 1864, Henry Brewer, 59, was listed on the muster roll for Co. A., Covington County Reserves.[149]

In 1880 M. E. Brewer, 65, b. S. C., widow, is identifiable as the mother of "G. A." Holley, in Green Bay, Covington Co., Ala.[150]

Children of HENRY BREWER and MARY are:

1. SARAH[4] BREWER, b. 1839 Covington Co., Ala.
2. GATSIE[4] A. BREWER, b. 5 February 1842 Covington Co. Ala.; d. 6 April 1919 Okaloosa Co., Fla.; m. 1) JEREMIAH HOLLOWAY about 1860; m. 2) WILLIAM F. HOLLEY about 1868; b. 6 September 1848 Coffee Co., Ala.; d. 4 Mar 1926 Tallahassee, Fla.[151]
3. NANCY[4] BREWER, b. 1844 Covington Co., Ala.
4. WILLIAM[4] BREWER, b. 1846 Covington Co., Ala.

---

[146] Ward, p. 309.
[147] Ward, p. 151.
[148] Ward, p. 136.
[149] Ward, p. 316.
[150] 1880 Census Covington Co., Ala., Green Bay, ED 54, p. 339D, #37.
[151] Bryan, Bob. Bryans of NW Florida/South AL/SC and Related Families. 9 July 2004. Located on http://worldconnect.rootsweb.com, (db bbryan84).

5. JACKSON[4] BREWER, b. 1848 Covington Co., Ala.; m. AMANDA CAROLINE HOLLEY; b. about 1853 Coffee Co., Ala.[152]

6. SYRENA[4] BREWER, b. 1850 Covington Co., Ala.

7. three daughters yet to be identified from marriage records before 1850.[153]

iii. SYRENA[3] BREWER, b. 1808 Georgia; d. before 5 Jan 1863 Sumter Co., Ala.; m. REUBEN L. JONES Conecuh Co., Ala.(?); b. 1800-1810; d. before 1850 Sumter Co., Ala.

Reuben L. Jones along with Henry Brewer signed a petition asking the governor to name Eli N. Briggs sheriff of Covington Co., Ala., on 30 September 1831.[154] There are two mentions of Reuben Jones, "L" not specified, that may be his father. Reuben Jones signed a petition supporting the appointment of William Hewitt as sheriff on 11 December 1823.[155] Reuben Jones was appointed lieutenant of the 46th Regt., 11th Brig., 4th Div., Alabama militia on 20 January 1829.[156]

Reuben L. Jones is living between William Brewer and Wyche Brewer in the 1840 Census Sumter Co., Ala.[157] Syrena Jones, 42, Ga., along with William Jones, 19, Ala., is living five houses away from William Brewer in 1850.[158]

On 13 September 1849 Syrena Jones gave consent for the marriage of her daughter, Mary E. Jones, to marry Wesley A. Mundy.[159] Sadly, the Sumter Democrat of 12 June 1852 noted that " Died at the residence of her Mother, Mrs. Jones in this county, on 3rd inst., Mrs. Mary, consort of

---

[152] Ibid.

[153] In the 1860 Census, Eliza M. Brewer, 30, is living with Henry, 55, and Mary E., 45, and Sarah S., 20.

[154] Ward, p. 53.

[155] Ward, p. 27.

[156] Ward, p. 308.

[157] 1840 Census Sumter Co., Ala., p. 137, line 6. (010001-010001)

[158] 1850 Census Sumter Co., Ala., p. 330B, #1155.

[159] Sumter Co., Ala., Marriage Book 2:69. Cited in Gandrud, Pauline. Alabama Records, Vol. 176, p. 85.

Wesley A. Mundy, aged about 20 years." In the 1850 Census Mary A. E. Mundy is 18 and living nine houses away from her mother.[160] These ages match the data for Reuben L. Jones in the 1840 Census reasonably well.

Syrena Jones died testate in Sumter Co., Alabama, naming her "beloved brother, William P. Brewer" as executor.[161] She left four slaves to her grandson, Pinckney L. Mundy, son of Wesley A. Mundy, and bequeathed her share of her mother's estate to William Jones, Jerome Jones, and Joseph Jones, sons of her son William H. Jones. She also mentioned her daughter-in-law Elizabeth Jones. It is this will which establishes the death of Mary Brewer, wife of William[3] Brewer

Children of SYRENA BREWER and REUBEN JONES:

1. WILLIAM H.[4] JONES, b. 1831 Covington Co., Ala.; d. before 8 December 1866 Sumter Co., Ala.; m. ELIZABETH W. GRAHAM 17 February 1857 Sumter Co., Ala.[162]

    William H. Jones is living with his mother in 1850,[163] and her will in 1862 lists three sons for him. The Livingston Journal for 6 Dec 1866 shows William P. Brewer acting as administrator for both Syrena Jones and William H. Jones.[164]

    W. H. Jones, 38, NC, is living by himself in 1860.[165]

    Children of WILLIAM JONES and ELIZABETH:

    a. WILLIAM[5] JONES.
    b. JEROME[5] JONES.
    c. JOSEPH[5] JONES.

2. MARY E.[4] JONES, b. 1832 Covington or Sumter Co., Ala., d. 3 June 1852 Sumter

---

[160] 1850 Census Sumter Co., Ala., #1146.

[161] Sumter Co., Ala., Will Book 2:264(552); 11 Nov 1862/5 Jan 1863.

[162] Alabama Marriage Collection, 1800-1969. Accessed 16 February 2014 at Ancestry.com.

[163] 1850 Census, Sumter Co., Ala., p. 331A, #1155

[164] Gandrud, Pauline. Alabama Records, Vol. 44, p. 18.

[165] 1860 Census Sumter Co., Ala., Southern Div., p. 549, #641.

Co., Ala.; m. WESLEY A. MUNDY 13 September 1849 Sumter Co., Ala.

Child of MARY JONES and WESLEY MUNDY:

a. PINCKNEY L.[5] MUNDY, b. 2 July 1850 Sumter Co., Ala.; d. 2 June 1929 Sumter Co., Ala.;[166] m. EMMA E. TATE 24 January 1872 Sumter Co., Ala.;[167] b. 11 April 1855 Sumter Co., Ala.; d. 8 May 1893 Sumter Co., Ala.[168]

iv. NANCY[3] BREWER, b. about 1811; d. about 1842 Sumter Co., Ala.; m. ELI NELSON BRIGGS about 1830 Covington Co., Ala., son of ELKAHAH BRIGGS; m. (2) MARY ELIZABETH LONG 10 January 1843 Sumter Co., Ala.; m. (3) ELIZABETH CARR 21 January 1859 Clarke Co., Miss.

As noted under the discussion for Henry Brewer, it seemed likely that Nancy Brewer was married to one of the several Briggs men resident in Covington Co., Ala.[169]

The area along the eastern side of Pigeon Creek near the present Loango Community in the western part of Covington County was one of the first places in the county to be settled. A wagon road leading from the early settlements in Conecuh County to the Falls of the Conecuh River was

---

[166] Alabama Deaths and Burials Index, 1881-1974. Accessed 16 February 2014 at Ancestry.com.

[167] Alabama Marriages, 1808-1920. Accessed 16 February 2014 at Ancestry.com.

[168] Coke's Chapel Cemetery, Ward, Sumter Co., Ala. http://www.findagrave.com, #5812575. She was identified as the wife of "P. L." and has a son, William (11 July 1874-11 September 1879) buried there as well. (#5812585.)

[169] 1830 Census Covington Co., Ala., p. 232 Eli N. Briggs (00001-00001) and p. 236 Simeon Briggs (000001-0001). In 1840, p. 231 Simeon Briggs (2001001-010001), is the only one present, and in 1850 p. 295, #277 Simeon Briggs, 50 GA, Sarah, 48 SC, James, 13, John, 10, Michael, 5, and also William, Eliza, and Sarah Maxy. At a guess, Sarah's maiden name was Maxy or Maxey.

possibly cut through this area as early as 1816, and by 1819 the first whites had probably settled near the point where this road crossed the Sepulga River about one mile below the junction of Pigeon Creek.

The land in the Loango area was thought to be some of the best in the county and when it was first placed on sale on December 9, 1823, members of the wealthy Bradley family.....1824 Elkanah Briggs and Simeon Briggs purchased land nearby. In addition...Eli N. Briggs...had settled in the Loango area during the 1820's.[170]

In 2012, Susan Holman posted a response to an earlier version of this report outlining the reasons why Nancy Brewer married Eli Nelson Briggs, son of Elkanah Briggs of Covington Co., Ala.[171] She shows that Eli N. Briggs was on a poll list in Livingston, Ala., in 1841, and stood security with William Brewer for William D. Summerlin as guardian of Calvin F. and Pheasanton Summerlin 1 April 1841 in Sumter Co., Ala.[172]

The children of Nancy Brewer, William E. Briggs, 20, Henry, 16, Ann, 14, Leroy 11, and Mary A., 10, are living with their grandfather, William Brewer, in 1850.[173]

Children of NANCY BREWER and ELI BRIGGS:

1. SYRENA[4] BRIGGS, b. 1832 Alabama; m. PHEASANTON K. SUMMERLIN 2 March 1848

---

[170] Ward, Wyley D. Early History of Covington County, Alabama, 1821-1871. (Spartanburg, SC: The Reprint Co., 1991,) pp. 159-160.
[171] Holman, Susan. Re: Brewers of Sumter Co., Ala., before 1860—Wyche, William, Matthew. 18 March 2012.
http://genforum.genealogy.com/brewer/messages/8817.html.
[172] Jenkins, Nelle M., Stegall, Elizabeth B. Sumter County, Alabama, Records, 1833-1845, p. 263; from Orphans Book 1. Holman.
[173] 1850 Census Sumter Co., Ala., Scatterling, p. 300B, #1150.

Sumter Co., Ala.,[174] son of WYLIE SUMMERLIN; b. about 1826 N. C.

"P. Summerlin" is living in the northern district of Yalobusha Co., Miss., age 24, NC, along with Sarah 18, Ala., and Henry, 2, Miss.[175]

Child of SYRENA BRIGGS and P. SUMMERLIN:

a. HENRY[5] SUMMERLIN, b. 1848 Yalobusha Co., Miss.

2. WILLIAM E.[4] BRIGGS, b. February 1831 Covington Co., Ala.; d. after 1900 Limestone Co., Tex.;[176] m. ELIZA JANE BURNS 26 July 1855 Yalobusha Co., Miss.[177]; b. 3 May 1837 Ala.; d. 29 September 1892 Limestone Co., Texas.[178]

William E. Briggs is also said to be resident of Yalobusha Co., Miss., in 1854. In 1860 he was in Limestone Co., Texas, where he apparently lived the rest of his life.[179] William Briggs was a sergeant in Co. K., 27th Texas Cavalry.[180]

3. HENRY[4] BRIGGS, b. about 1836

4. LEROY MARSHALL[4] BRIGGS, b. 14 May 1839 Sumter Co., Alabama;[181] d. 4 February 1916

---

[174] Sumter Co., Ala., Marriage Book 2:19. Cited in Gandrud, Pauline. Alabama Records, Vol. 176 (Sumter Co.), p. 60.

[175] 1850 Census Yalobusha Co., Miss., p. 409, #470/470. I have not been able to find him afterward.

[176] In the 1900 Census Limestone Co., Texas, Justice Prct. 5, ED 60, p. 11A, his wife is listed as Emma, 45, and they have been married 10 years. The February 1831 date of birth for him is from this census.

[177] Mississippi Marriages, 1776-1935. Accessed 16 February 2014 at Ancestry.com. He is listed as "William S." in the index.

[178] Eutaw Cemetery, Kosse, Limestone Co., Texas. http://www.findagrave.com, #14518413.

[179] 1860 Census Limestone Co., Texas, Pct. 2, p. 319-320, #86/82. He was said to be 27; wife is listed as "E. J.", 22, b. Ala.

[180] http://www.findagrave.com, #14518407. There is no tombstone listed for Eutaw Cemetery, accessed 15 February at http://files.usgwarchives.net/tx/limestone/cemeteries/eutaw.txt. There is a death record in Kosse, Limestone County, for "M. E. Briggs" 76, on 23 January 1908, which seems likely to be William E. Briggs. Accessed 16 February at http://files.usgwarchives.net/tx/limestone/obits/groesbek.txt

[181] Briggs/York/Anderson Family Tree. Accessed 16 February 2014 at http://trees.ancestry.com/tree/9277284.

Falls Co., Tex.;[182] m. MARY ANN (_____) HAILEY 26 September 1869 Falls Co., Texas;[183] b. 15 November 1847 Houston Co., Texas; d. 8 July 1945 Falls Co., Texas.[184]

5. MARY[4] BRIGGS, b. August 1842 Sumter Co., Alabama.;[185] d. 1929 Pontotoc Co., Okla.;[186] m. JOHN W. HAMMOND about 1872 Limestone Co., Tex.;[187] b. 1852 Mississippi;[188] d. 1933 Pontotoc Co., Okla.[189]

v. ELIZABETH S. MARSHALL[3] BREWER, b. 1813 Alabama; d. before 1870; m. WILLIAM H. BEASLEY 10 May 1844;[190] b. about 1813 South Carolina; d. after 1870.

---

[182] Calvary Cemetery, Marlin, Falls Co., Texas. http://www.findagrave.com, #29905730. He was a private in Co. K., 15th Texas Infantry. Interestingly, his birth year was estimated at 1843 through the 1880 Census Limestone Co., Texas, Kosse, ED 93, p. 315D, #30/36. He was living two houses up from W. E. and E. J. Briggs.

[183] Texas State Library and Archives Commission: Confederate Pension Applications, 1899-1975. Located 16 February 2014 at Ancestry.com. Application #32561. Mary Ann Briggs applied for a widow's pension, 7 March 1916. She stated her husband's full name was Leroy Marshall Briggs, that she was 68 and born in Houston Co., Texas, and that he had applied as pension #27531, and that she had been living in Marlin, Texas, for 8 years. The marriage of L. M. Briggs to Mrs. M. A. Hailey occurred 26 September 1869 in Falls Co., Texas. Accessed 16 February 2014 at http://files.usgwarchives.net/tx/falls/vitals/marriages/1869/1869marr.txt

[184] Calvary Cemetery, Marlin, Falls Co., Texas. http://www.findagrave.com, #29905748.

[185] 1900 Census Indian Territory, Chickasaw Nation, Twp. 2, ED 133, line 100. (The numbers have been overwritten.)

[186] East Hill Cemetery, Roff, Pontotoc Co., Okla. http://www.findagrave.com, #52693268.

[187] Allen, Nadene. Mary E. Briggs, b. 1843 AL. http://genforum.genealogy.com/briggs/messages/38.html.

[188] 1880 Census Limestone Co., Texas, Kosse, ED 93, p. 333D, #345/358. His wife, "M. E." is 37, Ala., Ala., Ala., and "G. A." Briggs, niece, 17, are living with him.

[189] East Hill Cemetery, Roff, Pontotoc Co., Okla. http://www.findagrave.com, #52693107.

[190] Sumter Co., Ala., MB 1:288. Cited in Gandrud, Pauline. Alabama Records, Vol. 132, p. 76.

William H. Beasley, 39, SC, and his wife "Marshall E.," 37, Ala., are living in "Scattering," Sumter Co., Ala., in 1850 with no children.[191]

William Beasley was acting as administrator of the estate at the time the probate record was made which lists the children and heirs of William Brewer. He is listed in the 1870 Census with "Emma" age 25.[192] Elizabeth is not listed, and is presumed dead.[193]

vi. SEABORN[3] BREWER, b. before 1817; d. about 1838 Louisville, Ky.

Seaborn Brewer patented land in twp. 19N, range 2W, Sumter Co., Ala., on 15 Mar 1837 along with his father and brother.[194] Both of his tracts listed Samuel H. Coffman as a patentee, as did a tract by William Brewer.[195] By implication, he was at least 21 years old on that date.

The last will and testament of Samuel H. Coffman was written 4 Oct 1839 and probated 9 November 1839 in Sumter Co., Ala. He mentions his mother, Mary Coffman of Shenandoah Co., Va., his wife, Susan B. Coffman, now pregnant, his daughter Virginia Elizabeth Coffman, and his three brothers, Samuel, Erasmus, and DeWitt Coffman.[196] His connection with the Brewer family is not evident from these data.

Susan Holman has provided data showing that Emeline Briggs, daughter of Elkanah Briggs of Butler Co., Ala., married a man named Brewer. Elkanah Briggs died testate before 23 Jan 1855,

---

[191] 1850 Census Sumter Co., Ala., p. 295, #592/601.

[192] 1870 Census Sumter Co., Ala., Beat 12, Sumterville, p. 40, #346.

[193] There is also a William Beasley living in Crenshaw Co., Ala., in 1870, age 54, SC, living in twp. 11. (p. 147, #349.) He has Eliza, 22, Margaret 18, Julia 14, Victoria, 11, and Alexander 4. These children do not match the 1850 report, where there were no children.

[194] BLM documents 3603 Section 24 (E ½ SE) and 3604 Section 23 (W ½ SW), both 80 acres. These tracts would abut each other, leading to a total tract of 160 acres.

[195] BLM document 3112 Section 26 (N ½ E).

[196] Sumter Co., Ala., Will Book 1:60. Cited in Gandrud, Pauline. Alabama Records, Vol. 91, p. 20.

[197] and a legal notice published in "The South Alabamian" of Greenville, Alabama, reported a citation to the sheriff to summon Simeon Briggs of Covington Co., Ala., Emeline Brewer of Sumter Co., Michael Briggs of Pickens Co., Thomas H. Briggs of Butler Co., and Jacob Briggs of Pike Co., to appear in regard to settling his estate. Emeline Briggs may have been the wife of Seaborn Brewer, as there are no other males who seem to be likely candidates.

vii. LEROY[3] BREWER, b. 19 February 1818 Conecuh Co., Ala.; d. 1893 Mobile, Ala.; m. EMMA O. PHARES 1884 Sumter Co., Ala.

Leroy Brewer, aged 28, b. Alabama, is living alone in Kemper Co., Miss., in 1850.[198] Leroy Brewer was living in Mobile Co., Alabama in 1854 according to his father's estate papers.

In an article in *The Birmingham News* 19 February 1934 the following information about Leroy Brewer was published.[199]

> Leroy Brewer born in Conecuh Co., Ala., Feb. 19, 1818 and died in Mobile 1893. The family moved to Livingston, Sumter Co., Ala., in 1832. In 1884, he married Emma O. (Phares) Hopper of Sumter Co., Ala., and they had one son and one daughter.

viii. SARAH[3] BREWER b. 1820 Conecuh Co., Ala.; m. WILLIAM D. SUMMERLIN 8 September 1838 Sumter Co., Ala.;[200] b. about 1815 North Carolina.

---

[197] Butler Co., Ala., Will Book 1:56. His son Thomas H. Briggs was named, but no other children. Holman, Susan. 18 June 2006. Located at http://boards.ancestry.com/mbexec?htx=messages&r=surnames.brewer&m=3232.1

[198] 1850 Census Kemper Co., Miss., p. 186, #684.

[199] Gandrud, Pauline. Alabama Records, Vol. 52, p. 93.

[200] Sumter Co., Ala., Marriage Book 1:83. Cited in Gandrud, Pauline. Alabama Records, Vol. 128 (Sumter Co.), p. 1. She married with the consent of her father, William Brewer.

In the 1850 Census Sarah Summerlin listed her age as 28, born in Alabama.[201]

Children of SARAH and WILLIAM SUMMERLIN:

1. CORNELIA A.[4] SUMMERLIN, b. 1839 Sumter Co.; Ala.
2. LAVINIA A.[4] SUMMERLIN, b. 1841 Sumter Co., Ala.
3. CALVIN L.[4] SUMMERLIN, b. 1845 Sumter Co., Ala.
4. MARGARET A.[4] SUMMERLIN, b. 1848 Sumter Co., Ala.

ix. WILLIAM PINCKNEY[3] BREWER, b. 5 May 1822 Conecuh Co., Ala.; d. 23 November 1907 Sumter Co., Ala.; [202] m. ELIZA JANE TALBOT 21 January 1854 Sumter Co., Ala., dau. of WILLIAM HARVEY TALBOT and CAROLINE TALBOT; b. 16 Jan 1832 Greene Co., Ala.; d. 29 September 1904 Sumter Co., Ala.[203]

The Sumter Democrat for 28 January 1854 reported the marriage of William P. Brewer to Eliza Jane Talbot, daughter of William Talbot, Esq., on January 21st.[204]

The 1855 Census for Sumter Co., Alabama shows William P. Brewer with one white male under 21, one white male over 21, and 17 slaves.[205]

William P. Brewer and Eliza J. T. Brewer are living in Bluff Port, Sumter Co., Ala., in 1880.[206]

---

[201] 1850 Census Sumter Co., Ala., p. 262, #84/85. In the 1870 Census a William Summerlin is living at Fuller's Cross Roads, Crenshaw Co., Ala., but his wife's name is Elizabeth. The youngest child living at home was Needham, b. 1855, and the names do not match.

[202] New Prospect Cemetery, Livingston, Sumter Co., Ala. http://wwww.findagrave.com, #73035775.

[203] New Prospect Cemetery, Livingston, Sumter Co., Ala. http://wwww.findagrave.com, #73035628.

[204] Gandrud, Pauline. Alabama Records, Vol. 128, p. 45.

[205] Hester, Gwendolyn L. 1855 Census Sumter County, Alabama. (Dallas: Southern Roots, 1988.)

[206] 1880 Census Sumter Co., Ala., p. 484A. He is residence 60, family 62, on p. 9 of the Bluff Port census.

He is said to be 58, born in Alabama with parents born in Ga., and Va. She is said to be 48, born in Alabama with parents born in Georgia and Tennessee. However, they clearly spent time in Louisiana after the Civil War based upon the birthplaces of Mary G. Brewer. This was confirmed by this notice published in *The Livingston Journal* for 25 December 1874.[207] "Mr. W. P. Brewer who moved to Louisiana soon after the surrender, this week returned to Sumter Co., to stay."

Children of WILLIAM BREWER and ELIZA: [208]

1. RHODA AMELIA[4] BREWER, b. 1858 Sumter Co., Ala., unmarried 1896.
2. DELLA LEE[4] BREWER, b. 1864 Sumter Co., Ala.; m. FRANK L. CLEMENT.
3. JULIA WEBB[4] BREWER, b. 1866 Sumter Co., Ala.; m. JOHN F. BATES.
4. MARY GERTRUDE[4] BREWER, b. 1871 in Louisiana, unmarried 1896.
5. WILLIAM A.[4] BREWER, died young.
6. CAROLINE TALBOT[4] BREWER, died young.
7. WILLIE EDITH[4] BREWER, died young.
8. JAMES HARVEY[4] BREWER, b. 1857 Sumter Co., Ala., unmarried 1896.

William (Holihta Bill) Brewer of Sumter Co., Alabama

William Brewer appears in the 1840 Census of Sumter Co., Ala., as aged 60-70, with one male 20-30, two females 5-10, 1 female 15-20, and one female 40-50.[209] Holihta Bill Brewer also patented land in 1837, but the sequence numbers of the grants establishes

---

[207] Gandrud, Pauline. Alabama Records, Vol. 52, p. 78.
[208] Additional data provided by LeSabre Hoit, who quotes from the Talbot family history.
[209] 1840 Census Sumter Co., Ala., p. 146, #1. (00010001-021001).

that he was associated with the family of Matthew H. Brewer.

The family relationships among these men is established by a letter written by Willis Brewer in 1911.[210]

> William Brewer, our direct ancestor, lived on one side of the Savannah River in the early part of the last century. With a rifle on his shoulder he walked alone through Georgia and Alabama, then occupied mostly by Indians, to Washington County. He left there to return home and was never heard from after. He had three sons, Matthew, Willis, and William. Willis, your grandfather, who fought at the Battle Autussee, as I suppose you already know. He left two sons, William George and Sam. Matthew Brewer had three sons, the name of one I have forgotten, but he went westward and I do not know what became of him. Thos. J. Brewer died in Sumter leaving children. The third son, George W. Brewer, lived in Brewersville, merchandized there and the place is named for him...
>
> My grandfather, W. Brewer, the third son, had two surviving sons, Robert W. Brewer (my father) and Capt T.C. Brewer. He had sisters, one of whom married the famous Sam Hale of Sumter, brother of John P. Hale of New Hampshire and the Abolition candidate for President in 1852.[211]

As described previously, Robert Spratt identified Holihta Bill Brewer's wife as a Miss Bates,

---

[210] Phyllis. 24 Dec 2002. Located at
http://boards.ancestry.com/mbexec?htx=message&r=rw&p=surnames.brewer&m= 2671.1.1.2. (two line URL.) Below is the contents of a 1911 letter written by Mr. Willis Brewer. I obtained this copy through the Alabama Department of Archives & History. The late Mr. Brewer is the author of several Alabama books. I have no proof that his information is accurate.

[211] Although Willis Brewer does not say so, it appears that all of the Washington Co., Ala., Brewer family are descended from George Brewer. Unfortunately, he does not say if George was William's brother, cousin, or nephew.

and elsewhere identified her as "Ann." There is a marriage record in Elbert Co., Ga., for William Brewer and Ann Bates 12 October 1810.[212]

Willis Brewer's biography says that William Brewer moved to Perry Co., Alabama from Wilkes Co., Ga., in 1818.[213] The 1820 Census for Alabama shows four men named William Brewer: the one in Conecuh Co., that I have identified as 1852 William Brewer of Sumter Co., Ala., one in Washington Co. who is too young,[214] and two in Fayette Co., Ala. The first, who is listed by himself, is also too young,[215] but the second, who appears in association with Thomas Brewer, John Brewer, and Ransom Brewer, is about the right age.[216] However, "old" William is still present in Fayette Co., Ala., in 1840, along with Thomas and John.[217]

William Brewer witnessed the sale of an 80 acre tract of land in Perry Co., Ala., from Asa Folly to William J. Harper on 15 January 1831.[218]

Of significance as to the origin of the Brewer family is the following deed:[219]

---

[212] Elbert Co., Ga., Will Book (1809-1812):136. Reference courtesy of Linda B. Essary.

[213] Owen, Thomas. History of Alabama and Dictionary of Alabama Biography. (Chicago: S. J. Clarke, 1921,) pp. 211-214. Cited by Blackman, L. and Blackman E. Blackman-Farmer Roots. 8 Feb 2005. Located on http://worldconnect.Rootsweb.com, (db blackman-farmer.)

[214] 1820 Census Washington Co., Ala., p. 251 (000001-3001).

[215] 1830 Census Fayette Co., Ala., p. 202, #10 (101001-110011).

[216] 1830 Census Fayette Co., Ala., p. 202, #23 (00010001-0001); #21 Ransom Brewer (20001-0101); #22 Thomas Brewer (10001-10001), #24 John Brewer (00001-1001).

[217] 1840 Census Fayette Co., Ala., p. 199, #17, 18, and 19.

[218] Perry Co., Ala., Deed Book B:136, [1 Aug 1831.] Morgan, Cathy. (http://boards.ancestry.com/mbexec?htx=message&r=rw&p=localities.nort ham.usa.states.alabama.counties.perry&m=459). , 12 May 2000. Any connection with George W. Harper, who patented land with Jackson Brewer in Sumter Co., Ala., is unknown to me.

[219] Perry Co., Ala., Deed Book B:90-91, [23 Nov 1830.] Morgan, Cathy, (http://boards.ancestry.com/mbexec?htx=message&r=rw&p=localities.nort ham.usa.states.alabama.counties.perry&m=411) Accessed 27 April 2000.

The State of Alabama: Know all men by these presents that we Burrel Taylor, James Scarborough,[220] Burrel Brewer, Uriah Taylor, Thomas Welch and William Taylor all of Perry County in the State aforesaid except Burrel Brewer of Chesterfield District in the State of South Carolina in consideration of Five hundred and twenty (seventy?) Dollars to us paid by Brisband Taylor of Perry County in the State aforesaid have granted bargained sold and released and by these presents do grant bargain sell and release unto the said Brisband Taylor all the Fractional North West Quarter of Section Twenty five in Township nineteen of Range Eight in District of Cahaba containing eighty acres originally granted to Anna Taylor The seventeenth day of July one thousand eight hundred and twenty nine and by consent of the Legatees has been sold to the aforesaid Brisbond Taylor together with all and singular the rights members heriditament and appurtenances to the said premises belonging or in any wise incident or appertaining to have and to hold all and singular the premises before mentioned unto the same Brisbond Taylor his heirs and assigns forever And we do hereby bind ourselves our heirs executors and administrators to warrant and forever defend all and singular the said premises unto the said Brisbond Taylor his heirs and assigns against ourselves and our heirs and against every person whomsoever lawfully claiming or to claim the same or any part thereof. Witness our hands and seals this 18th day of November 1830 in the year of our Lord one Thousand Eight hundred and thirty and in the fifty fifth year of Independence of the United States of America. Burrel Taylor, Hughria Taylor, Burris

---

[220] Just to confuse the issue, William P. Brewer, son of 1851 William Brewer witnessed the will of Abner R. Scarborough 27 August 1887, Sumter Co., Ala. Abner had a son named James T. Scarborough. Sumter Co., Ala., Will Book 3:189 [8 May 1889.] Copy provided by Mary Anne Habbe on the Sumter Co., Ala. GENWEB site in 2002.

Brewer, Thomas Welch, William Taylor ,Jas. L. Scarborough. Executed in the presence of Pinckney Holley, Robert Brown.

The 1850 Census for Macon Co., Ala., lists William Brewer, 65, born in Georgia, landlord, and Anna C. Brewer, 55, born in South Carolina, living in the household of David Clopton.[221] Also living there are Harriet M., 18, and Augusta A. F. Brewer, 16, both born in Alabama. Living two doors down is Thaddeus C. Brewer, 28, born in Alabama, with his wife, Anna F. Brewer, 19.[222]

William Brewer died testate in Macon Co., Alabama, 28 August 1858, and his probate establishes conclusively that this is the man known as "Holihta Bill."[223]

The State of Alabama
Macon County   To   the   Honorable   Lewis Alexander, Judge of Probate for said county—
The petition of Thomas N. McMullen administrator of the said Anna Brewer, respectfully shows that William Brewer lately an intestate (? Inhabitant) of this county departed this life in said County on the 28th day of August, 1858, leaving a last will and testament which is herewith filed and offered for probate.

Your petitioners that your petition and Thadus C. Brewer, are named in said Will as Executor. They further state that Anne C. Brewer one of the petitioners is widow of deceased and that the heirs at Law of deceased are Thadeus C. Brewer, Son of deceased of full age and resides as petitioner believes in Tusculoosa in this state, Robert Brewer a son of deceased of full age and resides in Sumter

---

[221] 1850 Census Macon Co., Ala., 71st Dist., p. 192, #12/12.
[222] 1850 Census Macon Co., Ala., 71st Dist., p. 192, #14/14
[223] Macon Co., Ala., Record Book 7:640-643, [13 December 1858]. Transcription courtesy of Linda B. Essary.

County Alabama—Hulda Lockard Wife of William Lockhard, daughter of deceased of full age and resides in Sumter County Alabama. Augustus Key a daughter, of deceased of full age and wife of Henry Key who resides in Macon County Alabama. Harriet McMullen wife of Thomas N. McMullen one of petitioners of age and who resides in said County.

Your petitioners pray to your Honor to make all neadfull orders in etc promises to appear notices to the parties entitled to notices and to open subpoenas for the witnesses to said will and on a day Set for a hearing may it please your honor, to admit and order the said Will and codicel, to probate, and may it please your Honor to grant Letters testamentary to your petitioner, both of whom are of full age, and citizens of the state and petitioners will pray &c.
Thomas N. McMullen
Anne C. Brewer

In the Name of God amen, I William Brewer, of the County of Macon and state of Alabama, being of sound and disposing Mind and Memory do Make and ordain this my last will and testament,
Item 1st. It is my will and desire that my Executors shall so soon as practicable, after my decease, collect such debts as may be due me and with the proceeds and such moneys, as may be on hand, at the happening of that event, pay my just debts.
Item 2nd. I give and bequeath unto my Grand daughter, Lenor Lockhard, to her sole and separate use, & free from the Controle or Contracts or desposition of any husband that she may hereafter have, a Negro girl child, named Seby.
Item 3rd. I devise give and bequeath unto my beloved wife Ann C. Brewer, an estate for life and to determine at her decase [sic]—in the following property to wit, lots of Land adjoining and situate in the town of Tuskegee & said county known as lots no. one (1), two (2), three (3), ten (10), eleven (11),

twelve (12), thirteen (13), and fourteen (14), and one hundred feet, of the back part of lot no 7, eight (8) and (9) and fifty five feet, of the Back part of lot no. (4) and (5) all being Block no. (12) and, city Hotel which I now Keep, and the improvements &c. connected there with and, by her held, and enjoyed to her sole and separate use during her life.

Item 4th. It is my will and desire that should either my daughters or my said children should depart this life before the death of the said Ann C. Brewer, then in that event such issue shall take and receive in the proceeds of said last mentioned item 5, that its parent would have taken and received under this will if in life.

Item 6th. I hereby appoint my beloved wife, Ann C. Brewer, and my son Thadeus C. Brewer, and my son in law, Thomas N. McMullin Executrix and Executors of this my will

In testimony whereof I hereunto set my hand and seal this the 6th day of January A. D. 1852.

William Brewer

Test:
J. W. Willis
W. G. Brewer
R. M. Willis

The State of Alabama
Probate Court
In the Matter of the application to Probate the will of William Brewer, deceased—before me Lewis Alexander Judge of Probate for said County— Personally appeared William G. Brewer, who being by me duly sworn, and Examined doth depose and say on oath that he is a subscribing witness thereto attended (appended) and which perports to be the will of said William Brewer, late inhabitant, of said County of Macon. That said William Brewer signed and Executed Said instrument and declared the same to be his last will and testament in his

presence and in presence of J. W. Willis and R. M. Willis the other subscribing witnesses to said instrument, and that they the said other subscribing witnesses Signed their names and in the presence of the said William Brewer. And at the time of signing the same the said William Brewer was in the opinion of deponant of sound mind and full capable of Making his Will.

Wm. G. Brewer

Sworn and subscribed Before me this AD December 1858
Lewis Alexander Judge of Probate.

I William Brewer desiring to alter some of the provisions of my will do hereby declare the following Instead of vesting in the lots land of Tavern and Hotel property mentioned and described in 3rd item of my will, in my wife Ann C. Brewer in for life I hereby direct that my Executors so soon after my death as practicable sell the said Lots and Hotel to the best advantage and I direct that they invest the proceeds of such sale, in such manner as for the principal to be safe and so that the same shall yield eight per cent interest which interest I desire and direct shall be collected and paid over to my beloved Wife Ann C. Brewer, and that she have the same, absolutely for and during her life, and after the said principal being the proceeds of ithe sale, of the Hotel property be disposed of by my executors in the manner and subject to the restrictions, specified in item 4 and 5 of my will directing the manner of disposing of the proceeds of the sale of the said Hotel property after the death of my wife.

In testimony of which I, the said William Brewer, have hereunto set my hand and seal, this 24th day of July, 1854.

In presence of, attest: Per W. G. Brewer
W. G. Brewer
E. M. Moore
Seaborn Williams

The State of Alabama
Macon County, Probate Court
In the Matter of the Probate of the Will of William
Brewer deceased
Before me Lewis Alexander Judge of Probate for said
County personally appeared in open court William
G. Brewer and Seaborn Williams who, being by me
Sworn depose and say that they are each
subscribing witnesses to the instrument hereto
attached and which perports to be the codicil to the
will of William Brewer, deceased, late an inhabitant
of said County—that the said William Brewer, now
deceased requested his name signed and Executed
said instrument, as codicil to the will previously
made by him and W. G. Brewer signed the name of
said William Brewer in the presence of deponent and
E. M. Moore and that they the said deponents signed
said instrument together with E. M. Moore the other
subscribing witness thereto in the presence of the
said William Brewer, on the day that said
instrument bears date. And at the time of Executing
said codecil the said was of sound Mind and fully
Capable of Making his will.
Seaborn Williams
W. G. Brewer
Sworn & subscribed Before me this 13th day of
December 1858,
Lewis Alexander, Judge of Probate.

A certified copy of the Brewer Family Bible of
Ann Bates Brewer, wife of William Brewer, is on file in
the records of the National Society Daughters of the
American Revolution records.[224] This document states
that William Brewer and Anna Clarke Bates married
22 November 1810, and further states that William
Brewer, son of William Brewer and Elizabeth Holman,
was born 21 February 1785, and that Anna Clark

---

[224] Transcription furnished courtesy of Linda B. Essary.

Bates, daughter of Fleming Bates and Margaret McCarter, was born 25 January 1795.[225] The information from the Bible record is incorporated in the genealogical summary.

The statement that 1858 William Brewer of Macon Co., Ala., is the son of William Brewer and Elizabeth Holman helps establish the parentage of both William and 1853 Matthew Brewer of Choctaw Co., Ala. DAR Application #569650 of Helen Walpole Brewer says that William Brewer, Sr., was born about 1758 and married Elizabeth Holman "about 1780." He died after 1818 in Oglethorpe Co., Ga., and Elizabeth died in 1800. [226] After study of the issues, Mrs. Essary believes the DAR file is correct, and that William Brewer, father of 1858 William Brewer of Macon Co., Ala., can be equated to 1818 William Brewer of Oglethorpe Co., Ga. William Brewer and Elizabeth Brewer served as executors of the estate of Burwell Brewer and returned his inventory on 6 March 1799 in Oglethorpe Co., Ga.[227] William Brewer is listed as a son of Burwell Brewer in a family history written in 1871 by George W. Paschal.[228] Burwell Brewer, in turn, is thought to be an unnamed younger son of 1744 George Brewer of Brunswick Co., Va., although documentation of this point is lacking. One of his other sons was 1760 George Brewer of Brunswick Co., Va., who married Abigail Wyche. This suggests that "Cedar Creek Bill" is a descendant of the younger

---

[225] Mrs. Essary also reported that the will of Fleming Bates is recorded in Abbeville, S. C., Will Book 1:296 [2 July 1804] and the file is in Box 105, pkg. 2655, which proves the parentage of Anna Clarke Bates.

[226] No source was given for these statements. Matthew H. Brewer was born 1774-1776 in South Carolina, so the marriage was probably earlier than this. The information in this file was given to me courtesy of Linda B. Essary.

[227] Oglethorpe Co., Ga., Probate Case #89. (FHL USCAN #1893076). Courtesy of Linda B. Essary.

[228] Paschal, George W. Ninety-Four Years, Agnes Paschal.. (Washington D. C.: M'Gill & Witherow, 1871,) repr. Spartanburg, SC: Reprint Co., 1974. [FHL US/CAN 962822, item 3.]

George, which would perhaps make Burwell Brewer his great uncle.

1853 Matthew Brewer of Choctaw Co., Alabama

The earliest probable reference to Matthew Brewer is the 1810 Census for the Abbeville District, South Carolina.[229] This may be the same man who appeared in the 1816 Tax List in Clarke Co., Ala. However, I have not been able to find him in either 1820 in South Carolina, Georgia, or Alabama, but the 1820 Census in Alabama is incomplete. The only Brewer I can find in Clarke Co., Alabama in 1830 is James L. Brewer,[230] who is too old to be a son of Matthew H. Brewer.

"Mathew" H. Brewer, age 50-60 is in Perry Co., Ala., in 1830, along with one son, 15-20 and one daughter, and his wife.[231]

Matthew H. Brewer patented 80 acres of land in section 21, twp. 18N, range 1W in Sumter Co., Alabama, on 15 May 1837.[232] George W. Brewer took out a patent on an adjacent aliquot the same day.[233] George Brewer also obtained a patent on a 160 acre tract with Thomas I. Brewer as a secondary patentee,[234] and an 80 acre tract in section 8, twp. 18N, range 1W, with Joseph Lake as a patentee.[235]

From the document sequence numbers, it appears that William Brewer patented 80 acres of land

---

[229] 1810 Census Abbeville Dist., S. C., p. 13, #4. Matthew Brewer (2001-2001). If Matthew was b. 1774 as indicated by his 1850 Census report, he would have been 46, whereas the census shows one male 26-45. However, there are no other probable names on the list, and the same source indicates we should look for him in South Carolina.

[230] 1830 Census Clarke Co., Ala., p. 24. (2120011-10021.)

[231] 1830 Census Perry Co., Ala., p. 50, line 1.

[232] BLM document 2309, (W ½ SW aliquot.)

[233] BLM document 2308, 80 acres (E ½ SW aliquot.)

[234] BLM document 2448, 15 March 1837, section 21, NW aliquot.

[235] BLM document 2307, 15 May 1837, (E ½ SE aliquot.)

at the same time as Matthew H. Brewer and George W. Brewer in section 18, twp. 20N, range 2W with Lewis S. Brown as a secondary patentee.[236] William Brewer also patented an 80 acre tract in section 13, twp. 13N, range 2W, Choctaw Co., Alabama, with Benjamin Needham as a secondary patentee.[237] Census data suggest he lived in Choctaw Co., Alabama.

Matthew H. Brewer deeded one acre of land in SW quarter of section 21, twp. 18N, range 1W on 27 May 1838 to Christian Valley Primitive Baptist Church.[238] Matthew H. Brewer patented land in section 19N, range 2W on 15 May 1837,[239] and on 16 April 1839.[240] This meant he was living in proximity to 1851 William Brewer.

M. H. Brewer is living in Sumter Co., Alabama in 1840, aged 60-70, along with one woman, aged 60-70 and one woman aged 20-30.[241]

Matthew H. Brewer is living in the household of Thomas J. Brewer in the 1850 Census.[242] Thomas J. Brewer, 36, was born in Georgia, and had a son named Seaborn.

The Sumter Democrat for 2 April 1853 reported the death of Matthew Brewer.[243]

Died at James Bluff, Choctaw County on 6th (Mrs. J. copied it 19th) Mr. Mathew H. Brewer aged about 80 years, native of South Carolina but one of the first settlers of this section of Alabama. Had been a citizen of this county until recently, for the last

---

[236] BLM document 2313, 15 March 1837, (E ½ SW aliquot.)

[237] BLM document 2311, 15 March 1837, (N ½ NW aliquot.) William Brewer also patented 40 acres (NENE aliquot) in section 14, twp. 13N, range 3W on 1 Aug 1837 (BLM document 10951), and 40 acres (NESW aliquot) in the same section on 2 Nov 1837 (BLM document 11967.)

[238] Sumter Co., Ala., Deed Book E:30 [22 Sep 1838.]

[239] BLM document 2310, 40 acres in section 33, (NESE).

[240] BLM document 12430, 40 acres in section 33, (SESE)

[241] 1840 Census Sumter Co., Ala., p. 129, #4.

[242] 1850 Census Sumter Co., Ala., p. 265.

[243] Cited in Gandrud, Pauline. Alabama Records, Vol. 176, p. 21.

twenty years, where he has left many relatives and friends to mourn his loss.

Genealogical Summary

3. WILLIAM[3] (*BURWELL[2], GEORGE[1]*) BREWER, b. about 1756; d. about 1818 Oglethorpe Co., Ga.;[244] m. ELIZABETH HOLMAN before 1774, daughter of SAMUEL HOLMAN; d. before 10 October 1805 Clarke Co., Ga.

Georgia)[245]
Clarke Co.)
    Know all men by these presents that I William Brewer Senr. of the State and County aforesaid for diverse good causes and considerations me there unto moving do nominate constitute and appoint by these presents have nominated constituted and appointed my Son Matthew Brewer my full and lawful power of attorney to do and transact all money and things relative to me and in my name and more especially to Sue for and collect all debts and legacies that I the said William Brewer am or may be entitled to by law as the last Will and testament of Samuel Holding, Senr., dec'd., of the County of Wake and the state of North Carolina. I the said William Brewer, Sr., claiming as heir and representatives of my dec'd wife Elizabeth Brewer daughter of the aforementioned Samuel Holding, Sen., of the county and state aforesaid and I the said William Brewer, Senr., do by these presents as fully authorize and empower my said Son Matthew Brewer to take a proper and lawful measure to sue for and collect all and every part of the aforesaid Samuel Holdin, Senr., dec'd., estate that I the sd. William Brewer could do though I was there in my own proper person and when collected or received to

---

[244] Again, Willis Brewer does not say if his ancestor lived north or south of the Savannah River. Since Matthew was b. SC according to his obituary, it seems likely that it was north.
[245] Clarke Co., Ga., Deed Book B:356. Transcription by Linda Essary.

grant receipts when so granted to said son Matthew Brewer for any money or other property that he may receive in law thereof shall be obligatory on me as witness my hand an seal this tenth day of Oct. 1805.

s. William Brewer

Wm. Depon, JP
Spencer Frazer, Clerk

Children of WILLIAM BREWER and ELIZABETH HOLMAN:

    i. MATTHEW[4] BREWER, b. about 1774 South Carolina; d. 6 March 1853 Choctaw Co., Alabama; m. ELIZABETH HAMPTON.[246]

Children of MATTHEW BREWER and ELIZABETH:

    1. THOMAS J.[5] BREWER, b. about 1814 Georgia; d. about 1852 Sumter Co., Ala.

Thomas J. Brewer is in Sumter Co., Ala., in 1850.[247] Matthew is living in his household that year. His wife apparently died sometime between 1840 and 1850.

Brewer vs. Brewer & Logan
Error to Chancery Court of Sumter[248]

Thomas J. Brewer filed his bill against George W. Brewer and Benjamin F. Logan in Chancery Court at Livingston. Bill alleges that in 1834 the complainant was in possession of a certain quarter section of land to which he had a pre-emption right; that being unable to pay the entrance money, his brother, George W. Brewer agreed to pay it and let him redeem it when able. In the year 1839, before George W. Brewer had parted with the legal claim, he stated to James Curry that there was a bargain between him and his brother that he, George, was to pay the pre-emption money.

---

[246] King, Syble Brewer. 4 Oct 2001.
http://genforum.genealogy.com/brewer/messages/5226.html.
[247] 1850 Census Sumter Co., Ala., p. 265.
[248] Orphans Court Book 19, part 1, p. 204, June term 1851. Cited in Gandrud, Pauline. Alabama Records, Vol. 91, p. 69.

Thomas J. Brewer was then lying sick and George W. Brewer was leaving home with view to be married.

Thomas J. Brewer was poor and had a family dependent upon his labor for support.

Children of THOMAS J. BREWER are:

a.   JOHN H.[6] BREWER, b. June 1830 Alabama; d. 16 December 1917 Winn Parish, La.;[249] m. HARRIET C. JOHNS; b. 29 November 1837 Miss.; d. 12 May 1900 Winn Parish, La.[250]

b.   SEBORN FRANKLIN[6] BREWER, b. 1832 Alabama; m. MARTHA J. NABBER 24 December 1854 Sumter Co., Ala.; b. about 1835 Alabama.[251]

c.   ELIZABETH A.[6] BREWER, b. March 1837 Alabama; d. 16 May 1920 Marengo Co., Ala;[252] m. JAMES M. MATTHEWS 23 November 1856 Sumter Co., Ala.;[253] b. November 1826 S. C.; d. after 1900 Sumter Co., Ala.[254]

---

[249]   Zion Hill Cemetery, Tannehill, Winn Parish, La. http://www.findagrave.com, #47657688. The stone notes that he served in Co. I, 4th Louisiana Infantry.

[250]   Zion Hill Cemetery, Tannehill, Winn Parish, La. http://www.findagrave.com, #47657764.

[251] Alabama Marriages, 1808-1920. Accessed 28 February 2014 at Ancestry.com; also 1860 Census Sumter Co., Ala., Southern Half, p. 538, #496. They have a daughter, "M," age 2.

[252] 1920 Census Marengo Co., Ala., Demopolis, ED 48, p. 12B, #364, 333 Washington St. She is living with her daughter Annie M. Janes. Date of death is from Alabama, Deaths and Burials Index, 1881-1974. Accessed 28 February 2014 at Ancestry.com. Her death record lists her father as Thomas J., and her mother's maiden name as Curry, with husband J. M. Matthews.

[253] Alabama Marriages, 1808-1920. Accessed 28 February 2014 at Ancestry.com. James M. Matthews, 23, SC, is living in Bluff Port, Sumter Co. Ala., in 1850, [p. 266B, #181] with his wife, Mary J. Matthews, 23, and two daughters, Rosane E, 3, and Laura F., 1. Evidently this was the second marriage for him. Rose Anne apparently did not marry.

[254] 1900 Census Sumter Co., Ala., Belmont, ED 96, p. 13A, #335/336. He was listed as a wheelwright, b. SC, father b. England, mother b. South Carolina. They were listed as married 56 years. I suspect his first marriage

d.   THOMAS G.[6] BREWER, b. 1838 Alabama

e.   PHILEMON H.[6] BREWER, b. 1841 Sumter Co., Ala.

f.   SARAH A.[6] BREWER, b. 1844 Sumter Co., Ala.; m. WILLIAM MAIDEN 18 December 1866 Sumter Co., Ala.; [255] b. 1840 Alabama.[256]

2. GEORGE W.[5] BREWER, m. SARAH ANN MAXWELL 24 March 1839 Dallas Co., Ala.[257]

George W. Brewer has also turned out to be hard to find. Despite Willis Brewer's confident assertion he was to be found in Brewersville, "which he founded" I cannot find him in the Census for Sumter Co., Ala., in either 1840 or 1850. He may be in Marengo Co., Ala., based upon analysis of the land patents described above.

ii. WILLIAM[4] BREWER, b. 21 February 1785 in Oglethorpe Co., Ga.; d. 28 August 1858 Tuskegee, Marion Co., Ala.; m. ANN BATES 22 October 1810 Elbert Co., Ga., daughter of FLEMING BATES and MARGARET MCCARTER; b. 25 January 1795 Abbeville Dist., S. C.; d. 28 May 1872 Macon Co., Ala.

Children of WILLIAM BREWER and ANN BATES:[258]

1.   BENJAMIN B.[5] BREWER, b. 11 Oct 1811, Ga.; d. Jan 1840 Sumter Co., Ala.

2.   MARGARET HULDA[5] BREWER, b. 24 June 1813 Ga.; d. 10 Mar 1886; m. WILLIAM

---

was in 1844, but their marriage is of record. Rose Anna, 52, is living with them.

[255] Alabama Marriages, 1808-1920. Accessed 28 February 2014 at Ancestry.com.

[256] 1870 Census Sumter Co., Ala., Belmont, p. 263A, #913/865. I have not been able to locate them afterward. In 1870 he was living with "Ed." Maiden, 37, and his family, who appear in Limestone Co., Texas, in 1880.

[257] Dallas Co., Ala., Marriage Book 1:130. (Courtesy of Linda B. Essary.)

[258] Brewer Family Bible located in NSDAR records, cited above. The places have been entered based upon the migration from Georgia to Perry Co., Alabama in 1818, to Sumter Co., Ala., in 1832, and to Macon Co., Ala., in 1846 or so.

LOCKARD 10 Sep 1831 Sumter Co., Ala., son of THOMAS LOCKARD, SR., and MARY HALSELL; d. 22 May 1872 Sumter Co., Ala.[259]

William Lockard obtained a patent for 159.52 acres in Sumter Co., Ala., on 15 March 1837, being the NE aliquot of section 17, twp. 19N, 2W. He is present in the 1840 census with himself, his wife, three daughters, and 12 slaves.[260] In 1850 he is shown as 45, born in SC, with wife Margaret, 36, b. SC, and their children.[261]

3. AMANDA FLEMING[5] BREWER, b. 28 June 1815 Ga.; d. 1 Jul 1882, Livingston, Sumter Co., Ala.; m. THOMAS LOCKARD 2 December 1835 Sumter Co., Ala.,[262] son of THOMAS LOCKARD, SR., and MARY HALSELL; b. 31 March 1813 SC; d. 28 Nov 1854 Chickasaw Co., Miss.

Dr. Spratt reported that Amanda T. Brewer Lockard went with her husband to Aberdeen, Miss., where he died. She then returned to Sumter Co., Ala., about 1855 with all of her children except her eldest daughter.

4. JOHN M.[5] BREWER, b. 6 Dec 1817 Ga.; d. 4 Dec 1840 Sumter Co., Ala.

5. ROBERT WILLIS[5] BREWER, b. 1819 Perry Co., Ala.; d. 6 May 1876; m. JANE HADDON 13 February 1841 Sumter Co., Ala.[263]

Robert W. Brewer is in the 1850 Census for Sumter Co., along with his two sons.[264] Interestingly, the census makes it clear that Willis is actually named Constantine Willis

---

[259] Gandrud, Pauline. Sumter Co. Records, p. 110.

[260] 1840 Census Sumter Co., Ala., p. 137, line 15.

[261] 1850 Census Sumter Co., Ala., p. , #63.

[262] Information about this family is in the Bible Record of Mrs. Amanda Fleming Brewer Lockard, copied by Mrs. Miriam Brewer Richardson on 15 Oct. 1929, and placed on file in the NSDAR. Information courtesy of Linda B. Essary, who is a descendant of Amanda Fleming Brewer.

[263] Sumter Co., Ala., Marriage Book 1:163. Cited in Gandrud, Pauline. Alabama Records, Vol. 128, page 1.

[264] 1850 Census, Sumter Co., Ala., p. 268.

Brewer, which is not seen in any of his biographical reports.

Children of ROBERT BREWER and JANE:

    a.   LEWIS W.[6] BREWER, b. 1842 Sumter Co., Ala.

    b.   CONSTANTINE WILLIS[6] BREWER, b. 14 March 1844 Sumter Co., Ala.; d. before 2 December 1913 Montgomery Co., Ala.; m. MARY E. BAINE.[265]

6. THADDEUS CONSTANTINE[5] BREWER[266] b. 25 December 1821, Perry Co., Ala.; d. 4 Feb 1873; m. ANNA F. COTTRELL 12 December 1848 Macon Co., Ala.; b. 27 Mar 1833 Abbeville Co., S. C.; d. 19 Aug 1866 Claiborne, Monroe Co., Ala.[267]

7. WILLIAM F.[5] BREWER, b. 23 September 1825, Perry Co., Ala.; d. 29 September 1829 Perry Co., Ala.

8. ELIZABETH EVELINA[5] BREWER, b. 7 May 1828, Perry Co., Ala.; d. 28 June 1848 Greene Co., Ala.; m. LEONIDAS LUCKIE 5 February 1846 Sumter Co., Ala.[268]

9. HARRIETTE M.[5] BREWER, b. 20 Dec 1830, Perry Co., Ala.; d. 26 Jan 1893; m. THOMAS N. MCMULLEN 31 October 1850 Macon Co., Ala.

10.AUGUSTA A. F.[5] BREWER, b. 13 Aug 1833, Sumter Co., Ala.; d. 28 Feb 1896; m. HENRY KEY 21 Nov 1855 Macon Co., Ala.

        Linda Essary found a tombstone recording the dates for Augusta (Brewer) Key. Henry Key was present in the 1860, but not 1870

---

[265] Montgomery Co., Ala., Will Book 8:294, LWT of Willis Brewer written 11 Apr. 1912.

[266] Willis Brewer called him "Capt. T. C. Brewer" but a biographical dictionary lists Willis' full name as Thaddeus Constantine Willis Brewer. I suspect he was named for his uncles.

[267] Gandrud, Pauline. Alabama Records, v. 125, p. 3. Courtesy of Linda B. Essary. She was living in Wilcox Co., and is buried in Camden Cemetery, Wilcox Co., Ala.

[268] Green Co., Ala. Marriages (1836-1846):393. Courtesy of Linda B. Essary.

244

Census and is presumed to have died during that decade.

iii. ___ BREWER, m. SAMUEL HALE.

iv. WILLIS[4] BREWER, b. 20 Feb 1790 Milledgeville, Baldwin Co., Georgia; d. 25 February 1869 Aberdeen, Monroe Co., Miss.; m. WALPOLE, MARY SPENCE 8 November 1819 Madison Co., Ala.;[269] b. 16 Sep 1802 Edgefield Co., S. C.,; d. 1 Jun 1873 Aberdeen, Monroe Co., Miss.[270]

The only Willis Brewer in the Census identified so far is Willis H. Brewer, b. 1790 Ga., living 1850 in Monroe Co., Miss., with his wife Mary S. 48, b. SC, and his children, Richard M., 27, Daniel A., 19, Samuel B., 19, Julia 15, and Mary E., 11, all born in Mississippi.[271] This may be the same Willis H. Brewer who married Mary Walford   or Walpole on 8 November 1819 Madison Co., Alabama.[272] This does not match, of course, with the information provided by Willis Brewer in his 1911 letter

Another family researcher has stated that Willis Hamlin Brewer did marry Mary Spence Walpole of Madison Co., Ala., on 8 November 1819, and that he had a son who married in Monroe Co., Miss. In 1846.[273]

"Willis Brewer fought at the battle of Autosse, having enlisted with a Georgia Company in 1812, and accompanied General Floyd into that region to quell Indian disturbances.   Riding over the country after the battle, his curling blue-black hair straying beneath the picturesque helmet of 1812, he flicked silky eyelashes over the alluring

---

[269] Alabama Select Marriages 1816-1957. Accessed 16 February 2014 at Ancestry.com.

[270] Dates from DAR Application #569650, Cyble Brewer King. Information provided by Linda B. Essary.

[271] 1850 Census Monroe Co., Miss., p.22, #299/311.

[272] Alabama Marriages to 1825. Located on the Alabama GENWEB site.

[273] Parry, Jack. 30 May 2001.
http://genforum.genealogy.com/brewer/messages/4657.html.

landscape and declared that the country should be the home of his descendants, and for a hundred and seventeen years they have occupied it. One of his sons, William George Brewer, was one of the earliest attorneys of Tuskegee, dying at an advanced age in 1896."[274]

Children of WILLIS BREWER and MARY:[275]

    1. WILLIAM GEORGE[5] BREWER.
    2. SAMUEL[5] BREWER.

---

[274] Brewer, Miriam Richardson. Obituary for Judge Samuel L. Brewer. *Montgomery Advertiser*, 1932, copy furnished by Linda B. Essary.

[275] The 1850 Census for Sumter Co., Ala., shows Andrew J. Brewer, b. about 1824 in Georgia. His household included his wife Mary, a daughter Louisa, b. 1848, and a son James, b. 1849. 1850 Census Sumter Co., Ala., p. 329.

Chapter 6: Ancestry of 1866 Flora (McPherson) Brewer of Scott Co., Mississippi

William McPherson is not in the 1818 tax list for Conecuh County, but is listed in the 1820 census,[1] with two adult males, five under age males, two adult women and two under 21. He follows William Brewer in the list. Assuming one of the adult women is his wife, Christian, then there are three women who could be his daughters, and six possible sons. There are no civil records from Conecuh County extant from this early date, and a McPherson family history found at the Conecuh County Library lists seven sons, but only one daughter. However, I have concluded that Flora McPherson, who married Wyche Brewer, is the second daughter of William and Christian (McDonald) McPherson.

1. MALCOLM[1] McPHERSON was born 1734 in Argyle, Scotland, and died before 25 January 1808 in Cumberland Co., North Carolina. He married (1) CHRISTIAN DOWNEY about 1760 in Argyle. She was born 1744 in Argyle and died 1780 in Cumberland Co., N. C. He married (2) MARY ____. She died after 1808.

> Malcolm McPherson, Sr., was born in 1734 in Glen Orchy, Argyllshire, in the western highlands of Scotland. Glen Orchy is located about 22 miles east of Oban.[2] The Orchy River flows from Loch Tulla, under the Bridge of Orchy to Loch We. This area is about 50 miles west of Newtonmore, site of the McPherson Castle and the traditional home of the McPherson Clan...

---

[1] Owen, Marie Bankhead. *Alabama Census Returns, 1820.* (Baltimore: Genealogical Publishing Co., 1967,) p. 38.

[2] McPherson, Daniel G. *McPherson Family Genealogy.* (Long Lake, MN: 2000). Copy located at the Butler County Historical and Genealogical Society Library, Greenville, Alabama, 24 June 2003.

In 1774 Malcolm McPherson, age 40 and his wife
Christine Downie, age 30 and their children Janet,
10, and William, 9...On 22 August 1774, Malcolm
and his family boarded the ship *Ulysses* at the Port
of Greenoch with 84 others bound for the Port of
Wilmington, North Carolina. The reason given for
their emigrating, as with most of the other
passengers, was "Rents and Oppression."[3]

It was, and still is, customary for immigrants
when moving to a new country to try to settle near
people of their own kind. Better yet to setle near
friends, or even family if possible. In 1739, a
contingent of 51 Scots emigrated from Argyllshire,
Scotland on the bark *Thistle* landing in
Brunswicktown on the Cape Fear River in the area
of what is now Williamstown, North Carolina. One of
these was John McPherson who settled near what is
now Fayetteville, N. C. He had two sons, Alexander
and Daniel and one daughter, Catherine who
married a Monroe. He was 14 years older than
Malcolm, so could not have been Malcolm's father,
however, it is very likely that John was either a
brother, nephew, or a cousin of Malcolm. The first
parcel of land that Malcolm purchased he bought
from Alexander McPherson, and this land abutted
Alexander's property as is mentioned in Malcolm's
will in 1800. (John died in 1789.)

Malcolm acquired a number of parcels in
addition to the 100 acres he bought from Alexander
McPherson on the east side of Beaver Creek in 1780.
By 1800 his total holdings grew to 1450 acres, all
located in what is now the southwest part of
Fayetteville, N. C. Malcolm Sr. died some time
between 1800 and 1808. He willed all of this land to
his sons, William, John, Daniel, and Malcolm, jr.
Malcolm, jr., born in 1792, was too young to qualify
for his inheritance, so in 1808 when he reached age
16, his brothers deeded parcels of land to him that
were his rightful inheritance. This document was

---

[3] The file included a copy of the passenger list compiled by R. E.
Philips and dated 8 May 1775, the ship *Ulysses*, James Wilson, master,
and the ship *Christy*, Hugh Rellie, Master.

signed by Malcolm, Sr's, widow Mary McPherson. Since Christian Downie McPherson, Malcolm's first wife would have been 58 at the time of Malcolm Jr.'s, birth it is obvious that she had died and Malcolm, Sr., remarried Mary some time after they arrived in N. C. Janet and William are Christian's children, Malcolm, Jr., is Mary's son, but it is unclear who was the mother of Daniel and John...Note: The original copies of these deeds may be found in Columbus County, N. C., Public Library; N. C. Archives in Raleigh, N. C.; and Cumberland County Courthouse, Fayetteville, N. C. My sister, Louise McPherson Selleck, was a legal secretary at one point in her career, and her husband Everett's father had been an abstractor so both of them were familiar with the format and terminology of deeds and wills. They agreed to study these documents and transcribe them. Copies of their transcriptions are attached.

Will of John McPherson[4]
In The Name of God, Amen. I, John McPherson, Senr of the County of Robeson and State of North Carolina, being weak in body but of perfect mind and memory, do make this my Last Will & Testament in manner and form following, viz.
1. I give and bequeath to my grandson Neil McPherson and to Danl McPherson, my two Negroes, James & Peter.
2. I given & bequeath to my grandson Arch. McPherson son of Danl McPherson, three of my Negroes, viz. Dick, Ben, & Cramson, to be theirs and their heirs forever, but if either Neil of Arch die without issue I desire that the living may heir the heirs right of & to Negroes.
3. I likewise give & bequeath to my grandson Neil McPherson one Hundred & sixty acres of land at the juniper & one Hundred acres of land lying at the upper end of the Bear Pond, joining McBride's land,

---

[4] Robeson Co., N. C., Will Book A:363, May Ct. 1838.

it being part of a survey of 200 acres, to be his and his heirs forever.

4. I likewise give & bequeath to my grandson Arch. McPherson, one hundred acres, to with, the Plantation I now live upon, together with one Hundred acres below me in two surveys, & likewise one Hundred acres above me, being the other half of the above 200 acres, likewise fifty acres lying between the Bear Pond & the Big Pond and another Fifty lying between the Bear Pond & the Raft Swamp, to be his and his heirs forever.

I give and bequeath to my son, Alexander McPherson, one Crown Sterling, of my estate after my dissolution.

I likewise give and bequeath to my son Daniel McPherson one Crown Sterling to be paid to him out of my estate after my dissolution.

I likewise give & bequeath to my son in law Lewis Monroe one Crown Sterling to be paid him out of my estate after my dissolution.

I likewise give & bequeath to my Beloved wife my two Negroes Charley & Bettey, & all the cattle & moveables that I am now possessed with & I desire that the cattle be divided among my grand daughter & my daughter Catherine Campbell after our dissolution. In Witness Whereof I hereunto set my hand and seal this 26th day of Oct. in the year of our Lord 1789.

/s/   John McPherson

Signed & Sealed in the Presence of us
Test: Neil Smith and Daniel Patterson

Malcolm McPherson bought 100 acres on the east side of Beaver Creek from Alexander McPherson of 5 March 1778; recorded in Cumberland County, N. C., January 1784. He bought and additional 100 acre tract and a 200 acre tract on Beaver Creek, and 100 acres between Beaver Creek & Buckhead on the headwaters of Little Rockfish, Cumberland County,

N. C., from the state 18 May 1789.[5] He bought 50 acres near Duncan McPherson's line from the state on 18 December 1800.[6] On 25 June 1800 the state granted 900 acres in Cumberland County to William, John, Daniel, & Malcolm McPherson, which appears adjacent to the previously patented land.[7]

William McPherson of Richmond Co., N. C., presumably acting as eldest son and executor of his father, distributed the share due to his brother, Malcolm, Jr., in 1808.[8]

William McPherson &
Donald McPherson
To
Malcolm McPherson

Be it known that we William McPherson of the County of Richmond and State of North Carolina and Donald McPherson of the County of Cumberland and state aforesaid doth ___ and give up to Malcolm McPherson of the County of Cumberland and state aforesaid his heirs and assigns forever certain pieces or parcels of land part of it being the property of Malcolm McPherson beginning at a (?) & two maples on the east side of Beaver Creek and (?) in the West side of Alexander McPherson's line...We hereby warrant and forever acquit and give up from ourselves our assigns the above described lands and premises to Malcolm McPherson his heirs and assigns. In Witness whereof we have hereunto set our hands and seals this 25th day of January eighteen hundred and eight.

/s/ Donald McPherson
/s/ William McPherson

Teste: Malcolm MacPherson, Jnr.

---

[5] Grant #675; #414; #441. Cited in the McPherson genealogy.

[6] Grant #2252. Cited in the McPherson genealogy.

[7] Grant #1950. Cited in the McPherson genealogy. He notes that Donald and Daniel in Scottish naming were essentially the same.

[8] McPherson argues that Malcolm, Jr., was 16 in 1808, but it seems more likely he was 21. This would give him a birth year of about 1786. The distinction is important, because William named his eldest son Malcolm, and he was estimated to have been born in 1792.

Mary McPherson (X her mark)
State of North Carolina
Cumberland County June term 1827
   Then was the execution of this Deed from Mary
McPherson so ordered to be registered.

   Daniel McPherson thought his line came
through the children of Malcolm McPherson the
younger, although he offered no evidence to that
effect. The will of Malcolm McPherson was written in
Chesterfield District, S. C., 16 September 1850. The
1850 Census shows him as 68, born in North
Carolina.[9] He has no family, which is consistent with
the bequests in the will to nieces and nephews. The
will also shows he had sisters not recorded by
McPherson, whom I think likely to be children of the
second wife.

   Children of MALCOLM and CHRISTIAN DOWNIE:

   i. JANET[2] MCPHERSON, b. 1764 Argyle;
2. ii. WILLIAM[2] MCPHERSON, b. 1765 Argyle; d.
      December 1825 Conecuh Co., Ala.; m.
      CHRISTIAN MCDONALD 1788 Cumberland Co.,
      N. C.; b. 1766 Argyle; d. after 1850 Conecuh
      Co., Ala.
 iii. DANIEL[2] MCPHERSON,
 iv. JOHN[2] MCPHERSON,

   Children of MALCOLM MCPHERSON and MARY are:

  v. MALCOLM[2] MCPHERSON, b. 1782 Cumberland
      Co., N. C.; d. after 16 September 1850
      Chesterfield District, S. C., unm.
        The State of South Carolina Chesterfield
      District[10]
        I, Malcolm McPherson Senr, of the District and
      State afroesaid being reminded by bodily

---

[9] 1850 Census Chesterfield Co., S. C., p. 115B, #268.
[10] Accessed 9 December 2013 at
http://trees.ancestry.com/tree/13671730/person/740185717/storyx/ala
0e550-79b7-4c19-9a0e-713e65b61e6c?src=search

infirmities that an end shall come to the life which I now live in the flesh, but still, being of sound and disposing mind and memory, and desiring now to direct what disposition shall be made after my decease, of alt my wordly goods do make. ordain and publish my last Will and Testament as follows: that is to say:

First: It is my will and desire, and my Executor hereinafter named shall at such early time after my decease, as to him shall seem proper, sell for cash, or good interest bearing securities, all my personal estate of what kind soever it may be, except such portions and particulars thereof as are hereinafter specifically bequeathed — and from and out of the proceeds thereof, and out of any money and the proceeds of any chooses in action which shall be in my possession, or in the possession of any other for me, or which shall be due and owing unto me, my said Executor shall first pay and discharge in full, all my just debts, and the Expenses of my last Illness and decent interment. — and then the pecuniary legacies hereinafter mentioned and given:

Item: I give and devise unto my nephew, Malcolm McNair, all that Tract of Land. lying on Big Black Creek, in the District of Chesterfield aforesaid, containing Eight Hundred and fifty acres more or less, which was purchased by me. on the sixth day of March A.D. 1848, at a Sale, made by order of the Court of Ordinary for said District, of the real estate of Jane McLaughlin deceased and conveyed to me by William L. Robeson, Sheriff of said District, by deed bearing date on the Eighth day of March aforesaid and recorded in the Register's Office for said District in Book P. pages 411 & 412 - to the said Malcolm McNair. his heirs and assigns forever.

Item: I give and bequeath unto my niece, Catharine Powers, my negro woman slave, named Nancy, to the said Catharine and her assigns forever:

Item: I give and bequeath unto Malcolm Hugh Campbell, son of my nephew Daniel Campbell, my negro woman Lucy and her four children, Margianna, Sarah, John and Ned, with the future increase of the females to the said Malcolm Hugh Campbell and his assigns forever – subject however to a charge of the sum of Five Hundred Dollars to be by or on behalf of the said Malcolm Hugh Campbell, within two years _____ [a blank, drawn line in document] after my decease unto John M. Campbell, Ann Campbell, Catharine Campbell and Gracey Downey Campbell, the children of my nephew John P. Campbell by his second marriage, the said sum of Five Hundred Dollars to be equally divided between and among the said children - and for the payment of which said sum, the said negroes shall be held security.

Item: I give and bequeath unto Nancy, the daughter of Malcolm McNair, one cow and calf to be selected out of my Stock by my Executor.[this item crossed through lightly in document]

Item: I give and bequeath unto my sister, Mary McCall, now in Florida, the sum of One Hundred Dollars - but if my said sister shall not be living at my decease, the said sum of One Hundred Dollars shall be given to and equally divided between my nephews Malcolm McPherson and William McPherson who are now in the State of Alabama.

Item: I give and bequeath unto my niece, Sarah Porter, wife of Henry Porter, the sum of Five Hundred Dollars, [this item completely crossed through in document]Item-1' give and bequeath unto my Grand Nephew William Campbell, son of John P Campbell, the sum of One Hundred Dollars, [this is completely crossed through in the document)

Item: I give and bequeath unto my sister Nancy McNair, the sum of Three Hundred Dollars($300.)

Item-1 give and bequeath unto each one of my nieces, Gracey Alford. Nancy Brown and Flora Brown, the sum of Fifty Dollars, [this item completely crossed through in document]

Item- All the rest residue and remainder of my estate, real and personal in possession, remainder reversion or in action, and of the proceeds thereof, I give, devise and bequeath unto my nephew Daniel Campbell. and to the aforesaid Nancy McNair, Sarah Porter [crossedthrough] and Catharine Powers to be equally divided among them. Share and share alike.

Lastly: I nominate, constitute and appoint, my nephew Daniel Campbell. to be sole executor of this my Will. hereby revoking all former wills.

In witness whereof I have hereunto set my hand and seal this 16th day of September in the year of our Lord One Thousand eight hundred and fifty.

Mal.m McPherson

Done by the said Malcolm McPherson in our presence, who at his request, in his presence and in the presence of each other, signed as witnesses

John C. Pervis

Lauchlin McKinnon

Geo. W. Bell

vi. NANCY[2] McPHERSON, b. say 1778 Cumberland Co., N. C.; m. McNAIR.

The nephew, Malcolm P. McNair, is living in Chesterfield Co., S. C., in 1850, age 46, with wife "Effa", 40, and children.[11] Both are buried in Douglass Cemetery, Chesterfield. He was born 5 February 1804 and died 4 August 1879.[12] She was born 17 December 1809 and died 27 March 1881.[13] If he is the first born son of Nancy McPherson and Malcolm McNair, then they married about 1802, which suggests a birth year for her of say 1784.

Malcolm P. McNair was living in Rutherford Co., N. C., in 1840.[14]

Living with them in 1850 was Nancy McLaurin, 68, who seems likely to be Effie's mother.

---

[11] 1850 Census Chesterfield Co., S. C., Chesterfield, p. 107A, #135.

[12] http://www.findagrave.com, #41151207.

[13] http://www.findagrave.com, #41151163.

[14] 1840 Census Rutherford Co., N. C., Rockingham Dist., p. 249, (he was 30-39, one son under 5; she was also 30-39, one daughter under 5.)

The only likely Nancy McNair I have found in the census was living in Barbour Co., Alabama, in 1850.[15] She was 72, so born about 1778, in North Carolina. She was living in a household headed by John P. McNair, 40, NC, and next door to Randall McNair, 36, NC, who are surely her sons.

If this is the correct, person, she was probably a daughter of Christian Downey, not Mary ____.

vii. MARY[2] MCPHERSON, m. MCCALL.

Although Malcolm McPherson said Mary McCall lived in Florida in 1850, I was not able to locate a likely candidate. However, Mary McCall, 56 NC, head of household with six adult children is living in Lowndes Co., Ala.[16] This person died there 17 June 1881 at age 87, (b. 1794.)[17]

viii. Daughter, d. before 1850; m. CAMPBELL about 1800; b. about 1774 Scotland; d. after 1850 Chesterfield Co., S. C.

The will also names nephews named Campbell, which implies the existence of another sister, who was deceased in 1850. Daniel Campbell, the nephew named is probably the man present that year in Chesterfield Co., S. C., 49, b. S. C.[18] He and his wife are buried in St. Mary's Presbyterian Church Cemetery. Daniel was born 9 May 1802 and died 13 December 1857.[19] Effie (McArn) McPherson was born 15 March 1806 and died 25 November 1866.[20] Their children are buried in Patrick Cemetery.

The census suggests two possible men as father of Daniel Campbell. The first is Malcolm Campbell, 84, born in Scotland,[21] who is living next door to Malcolm McPherson, who separates

---

[15] 1850 Census Barbour Co., Ala., Div. 23, p. 228B, #1870.

[16] 1850 Census Lowndes Co., Ala., p. 164A, #952. Children b. Alabama; Eli, 29, lawyer; William T., 27, physician; Franklin, 24, clerk; Robert 21, mechanic; Ellen, 17; Charles, 26, overseer.

[17] Alabama Deaths & Burials Index, 1881-1974. Accessed 9 December 2013 at ancestry.com.

[18] 1850 Census Chesterfield, Chesterfield Co., S. C., p. 115B, #267.

[19] http://www.findagrave.com, #47830358.

[20] http://www.findagrave.com, #47837196.

[21] 1850 Census Chesterfield, Chesterfield Co., S. C., p. 115B, #269.

him from Daniel. This seems most likely. There is a 90 year old Alexander Campbell with wife Isabella, 85,[22] and Daniel Campbell, 76, born in Scotland,[23] who are other, but in my view, less likely candidates.

2. WILLIAM[2] MCPHERSON was born 1765 in Argyle, Scotland, and died December 1825 in Conecuh Co., Alabama. He married CHRISTIAN MCDONALD 1788 in Cumberland Co., N. C. She was born 1766 in Argyle and died after 1850 Conecuh Co., Ala.

Copies of family group sheets for Malcolm McPherson and William McPherson were found at the Conecuh County Library, Evergreen, Alabama.[24] The data for William McPherson are transcribed below. From the records listed under Malcolm McPherson it appears that William was born in Glen Orchy, Argyllshire, Scotland, lived in Montgomery and Richmond Counties, N. C., and as will be shown here, probably in Marion Co., S. C., prior to his move to Conecuh County, Alabama.

There are two men named William McPherson in Richmond Co., N. C., in 1790 with the same family structure.[25] In 1800 there is one William McPherson,[26] who has four sons under ten, and one daughter 11-16. This structure is consistent with either of the two listed in 1790. In 1810, William McPherson has two sons under 10, three 11-16, one 16-26, and two daughters, one under 10 and one 16-26.[27]

---

[22] 1850 Census Chesterfield, Chesterfield Co., S. C., p. 129A, #472.

[23] 1850 Census Chesterfield, Chesterfield Co., S. C., p. 147B, #757.

[24] Donald Robert McPherson, Star Rte. 2 Box 277 A-435, Canyon Lake, Texas, 78133; Oct. 1988. He listed his phone number then as (512) 935-4506.

[25] 1790 Census Richmond Co., N. C., p. 172, (1-1-2-0); and p. 179, (1-1-2-0).

[26] 1800 Census Richmond Co., N. C., p. 252, (40010-01010-1).

[27] 1810 Census Richmond Co., N. C., p. 191.

William McPherson is not in the 1818 tax list for Conecuh County, but is listed in the 1820 census, with two adult males, five under age males, two adult women and two under 21.[28] He follows William Brewer in the list. Assuming one of the adult women is his wife, Christian, then there are three women who could be his daughters, and six possible sons. The McPherson family history found at the Conecuh County Library lists seven sons and only one daughter, which suggests Flora McPherson, who married Wyche Brewer, is the second daughter of William and Christian (McDonald) McPherson.

The 1830 census for Conecuh County, Alabama, shows John McPherson (30-40) and his wife, 20-30, with no children (p. 95) living near William Brewer (also p. 95) while Eliza McPherson, (20-30) is living with one male 5-10; two females under five; one 5-10; and two 10-15.[29] James McPherson, (20-30); is living with his wife, also 20-30, and one son under five.[30]

The 1850 Census[31] for Conecuh County shows Eliza McPherson, 47, b. SC, with Flora, 11, born in Alabama, and William C. McPherson, 26 M, born Alabama, overseer William McPherson, 37 M, farmer, NC is living with Mary, 38F, S. C., and Mary J., 13; Christian, 9F; Grace 7; Frances 4F; and John 1, all born in Alabama. (No. 3). Also shown in Mrs. C. McPherson, 84 F, born Scotland, living alone. (No. 92).

The 1830 Census for Butler County shows Wyche Brewer, age 30-40, Flora, age 20-30, no sons, three daughters under five, and one daughter 5-10, followed by William Skeins, then Malcolm McPherson, (30-40) with his wife, 20-30; one son 5-10; one male

28 Owen, Marie Bankhead. Alabama Census Returns, 1820. (Baltimore: Genealogical Publishing Co., 1967,) p. 38.
29 1830 Census Conecuh Co., Ala., p. 107.
30 1830 Census Conecuh Co., Ala., p. 113.
31 1850 Census Conecuh Co., Ala., p. 769, #796.

10-15; one male 15-20; two daughters under five, and one 5-10. Malcolm McPherson is still present in Butler County, Alabama in 1840, age 40-50, with his wife, 30-40, two sons under five, one 10-15, one 15-20, one 20-30; and one daughter under five, one 5-10; and one 10-15. Also living in Butler County in 1840 is John McPherson, 30-40, with two women 30-40, and one son 5-10. The only Brewer is Tabitha Brewer with one woman 60-70, one 30-40, and one girl under five, one 5-10, and two 10-15, along with one son 5-10. Although the census does not indicate this, it is likely that Tabitha is the woman who is the mother of the children, and thus the one 30-40. The older woman is presumably her mother. These data are consistent with the report that John McPherson moved to Butler County from Conecuh County in 1832.[32] He presumably moved to the area where John F. McPherson lived, which was described as "five miles up the creek from where Garland now is."[33]

Murdock McPherson acquired land near Sparta, Conecuh County, Alabama, described as in township 4, range 10, on 17 February 1824.[34] "John McLeod opened the first school. [in Sparta, Conecuh Co., Alabama.] He was followed by Murdock McPherson, who is said to be the first Mason buried with full Masonic honors, in Conecuh County."[35]

Unfortunately, the court house in Conecuh County was burned in 1858, and the court house in Butler County burned in 1853, so there is no direct proof that Flora McPherson was the daughter of William McPherson and Christian McDonald. However, her birth date, fits into a gap in the recorded

[32] Little, John Buckner. History of Butler County, Alabama, 1815-1885. (Cincinnati: Elm St. Printing, 1885, repr. 1971,) p. 216.

[33] Ibid., p. 154. John F. McPherson was listed as one of the contributors of data to the work by the author in his foreward.

[34] Hahn, Marilyn Davis. Old Sparta and Elba Land Office Records and Military Warrants, 1822-1860. (Easley SC: Southern Hist. Press, 1983,) p. 4.

[35] Brantley, Mary E. From Cabins to Mansions: Gleanings From Southwest Alabama. (Huntsville, AL: Strode Publ., 1981,) p. 79.

birth dates and is consistent with the 1800 and 1810 census data from Richmond Co., N. C. The will of 1850 Malcolm McPherson of Chesterfield Co., S. C., also suggests that William McPherson had a daughter named Flora.

John McPherson, brother of Malcolm and uncle of John F. McPherson moved from South Carolina and settled in Lowndes County, Alabama, near Letohatchee. Wife's name was Polly, (Family name unknown.) He was a slave owner and prosperous planter. When slaves were freed, they all left the plantation and went to Montgomery expecting to be given provisions by the Carpet Bag Government. Upon learning that his ex slaves were starving, John McPherson went to Montgomery and carried them all home to their own cabins, gave them work, and at the time of this death, they were still there.

John F. McPherson's uncle William went to Texas. No further record.

John and William also had a sister (assumed to be Janet) who married a Mr. Brown. She was the mother of Liza and Jenny Brown who died in Andalusia, Alabama and of Dr. Dan Brown and Tom Brown (who) for many years associated with Brown-Broughton Drug Co. in Andalusia. (now deceased). Bill Brown lived and died at Owassa, [Conecuh Co.] Alabama.

I think it was William McPherson, son of William and Christian (McDonald) McPherson, who "went to Texas," since Christian was still living in Conecuh County, Alabama, in 1850. John F. McPherson's tombstone lists his date of birth as 4 March 1817 and his date of death as 30 August 1887.[36] I think "uncle John" was Flora's brother, born 1797, which matches the available census data.

------

[36] Hahn, Marilyn Davis. Butler County in the Nineteenth Century. (1978, n. p.d.) He is buried in Sellers Cemetery, 3 miles south of Georgiana, Butler County, and in the area where he owned land.

Children of WILLIAM and CHRISTIAN MCDONALD are:

i. MALCOLM[3] MCPHERSON, b. about 1792 North Carolina.

> Malcolm McPherson, 58, is in Butler Co., Alabama, in 1850.[37] It appears his wife was dead by that date.

ii. JOHN[3] MCPHERSON, b. 4 May 1797 Robeson Co., N. C.; d. 19 May 1885 Ft. Deposit, Lowndes Co., Ala.;[38] m. MARY BETHUNE 1825 Marion Dist., S. C.; b. about 1802 South Carolina; d. 9 August 1875 Ft. Deposit.[39]

> John and Mary McPherson are in Butler Co., Ala., in 1850, along with Isabella McPherson, 48, SC, and William Thompson, 16.[40]

iii. JAMES[3] MCPHERSON, b. 1801; d. 1869 Sumter Co., Ala.; m. ELIZA TAYLOR; b. 1809 Georgia.

> James and Eliza McPherson are in Butler Co., Ala., in 1850.[41] They have seven children living with them and a boarder, Hansford B. Williams, a teacher.

iv. FLORA[3] MCPHERSON, b. 1 December 1803 N. C., d. 6 February 1866 Scott Co., Miss.; m. WYCHE BREWER about 1821 Conecuh Co., Ala.; b. 6 July 1798 probably Hancock Co., Ga.; d. 17 March 1877 Scott Co., Miss.

v. GRACIE[3] MCPHERSON, b. 12 March 1806; d. 23 October 1886[42] Marion Co., S. C.; m. NEILL LITTLE ALFORD, son of WARREN ALFORD and

---

[37] 1850 Census Butler Co., Ala., Twp. 11, p.252A, #134. He was b. NC, and had in his household Christian, 21F,; Duncan, 14, Mary, 11, and Malcolm, 9, all born Alabama. Daniel McPherson, 23M, Ala., clerk, is #130 in household of James Wall. This is likely his eldest son.

[38] Little Sandy Ridge Cemetery, Fort Deposit, Ala. http://www.findagrave.com., #88563771.

[39] Little Sandy Ridge Cemetery, Fort Deposit, Ala. http://www.findagrave.com., #88563609.

[40] 1850 Census Butler Co., Ala., Beat 4, p. 210A, #472.

[41] 1850 Census Sumter Co., Ala., Bellmont, p. 303B, #735.

[42] Alford Cemetery, Minturn, Dillon Co., S. C. http://www.findagrave.com, #62930092.

BARBARA LITTLE; b. 5 March 1799; d. 1 July 1866 Minturn, S. C.[43]

vi. WILLIAM[3] MCPHERSON, b. 15 September 1813; d. 13 February 1882 Falls Co., Texas; m. MARY BROGDON 24 February 1840 Conecuh Co., Ala.; b. about 1812 South Carolina; d. before 1880 Falls Co., Texas.

William and Mary McPherson are in Conecuh Co., Ala., in 1850 with six children.[44] They are still there in 1860, with two more children.[45] They moved with at least five of their children to Falls Co., Texas, by 1870.[46]

William McPherson was a charter member of the Presbyterian Church of Marlin, Falls Co., Texas, 2 May 1874.[47]

William McPherson is widowed, head of household including his widowed daughter, Christian Tomlinson and her children, and daughter Frances, in 1880.[48]

vii. MURDOCH[3] MCPHERSON, d. 7 November 1829 Conecuh Co., Ala.; m. ELIZA CATER about 1823 Conecuh Co., Ala.

viii. DUNCAN[3] MCPHERSON, d. 20 June 1835 Conecuh Co., Ala.

ix. DANIEL[3] MCPHERSON, d. 15 January 1838 Conecuh Co., Ala.

---

[43] Alford Cemetery, Minturn, Dillon Co., S. C. http://www.findagrave.com, #62928881.

[44] 1850 Census Conecuh Co., Ala., p. 332A, #3.

[45] 1860 Census Conecuh Co., Ala., p. 1089, #954/917.

[46] 1870 Census Falls Co., Texas, Precinct 5, p. 117B, #317/314.

[47] Renfrow, Joan. Falls County Historical Markers. Accessed 11 December 2013 at http://files.usgwarchives.net/tx/falls/history/histmrk.txt

[48] 1880 Census Falls Co., Texas, ED 41, p. 252C, #180.

Chapter 7: Descendants of 1750 Thomas Petty of Orange Co., Virginia

Albert G. Pettey, a son of Dr. John Wright Pettey, was born May 20, 1820, in Madison County, Alabama, and was reared there. About 1843 he came to Scott County, Miss., and for a time taught various schools in the neighborhood. About the year 1845 he married Luvenia Brewer, daughter of Wytche Brewer and Flora McPherson, and settled on a farm about a mile northeast of Sulphur Springs [Baptist] Church, where he died June 2, 1879. They had eight children, three sons and five daughters whose names and descendants are shown later in these sketches. He was a man of medium height, and weighed about one hundred and forty pounds, and when I knew him, his hair and beard were white. He was intelligent and well educated for those times and was a man of influence in the community. He was a Master Mason, a Granger, a member of Sulphur Springs Baptist Church, and for many years before his death, was the church clerk. He was buried in the old Amis graveyard.

The traditional view of the Petty family was presented by Alice Amis Hodges in her study of the Petty family of Madison County, Alabama.[1] She argued that Thomas Petty, wife of Catherine Garton, was the son and grandson of men named Thomas Petty or Pettus. This analysis was apparently popularized in the 1940's, but Mrs. Hodges did not cite her references.

However, James Petty has presented evidence that seems to indicate that Thomas Petty was, in fact, the son of a man named Hubert[2], whose last name

---

[1] Hodges, Alice Amis. Ancestry and Descendants of Dr. John Wright Petty of Madison Co., Ala. (Pendleton, S. C., 1978.)

[2] Petty, James W. 10 Sep 1998.
http://genforum.genealogy.com/petty/messages/253.html.

was usually rendered Patey or Patty. His evidence, which I have not confirmed, but find convincing, is as follows:

1.   On 6 March 1700/01 Thomas and Katherine Petty appeared with Martha Garton, Katherine's mother, to settle the estate of John Garton. [Richmond Co., Va., Court Orders 3:85, 168.]
2.   On 13 October 1701 Thomas Petty and his wife, Katherine, sold land in Lancaster Co., Va., on Morratico Creek, which land was bequeathed to him in the will of his father Hubert Petty. [Lancaster Co., Va., DB 7:36.]
3.   On 2 November 1699 Thomas Petty sued Dennis and Jane Cameron, "the executors of Walter Welch, dec'd., who was executor of Hubert Patty" for Thomas' inheritance, which he had not received. On 3 April 1700, Thomas Petty and his wife, "Kat." Won their case and received "four cows, and their increase since he came of age." [Richmond Co., Va., Court Order Book 3:24.]
4.   In the Spring term 1687, Hubert Petty/Patey of Lancaster Co., Va., died leaving a will naming his wife Faith, and his minor son, Thomas.   Hubert bequeathed all of his land and property to Thomas and named his executor, Walter Welch, as Thomas' guardian. [reference not given.]

Further information on Hubert Patey has also been developed and republished online.[3] Although the records spell his name several ways, I will simplify them and call him Hubert Patey. He came to Maryland in 1650 in the household of William Turner. He is listed as a plaintiff in suit against John Wakefield in 1654.[4] It is unclear if he was still indentured at that

[3] McGee, Barbara. Located online 3 April 2010 at http://www.pettygenealogy.com/HMTL%20files/pafc05.htm#209C14. Referred to hereafter as McGee.
[4] Browne, William Hand, ed. *Judicial and Testamentary Business of the Provincial Court* 10: (1649/50-1657):368-369, 6 April 1654.

point, but he appears in Norfolk Co., Virginia, in 1660 when he was an administrator appointed to an estate.

Hubert Patey purchased 150 acres of land on Morratico Creek in Lancaster Co., Virginia, 20 November 1665 from Abraham Bush. Two years later he and his wife, Rebecca, sold half of this tract. He made application for a land patent in 1672, which is apparently the only time his name appears in the records as Petty. He wrote his will in 1687 naming his wife Faith and minor son, Thomas.[5] Walter Welch was named as guardian for son Thomas. There is some indirect evidence to suggest that Walter Welch may have been Hubert Patey's uncle, although the scanty data are subject to interpretation. Some believe that Walter Welch may have been a brother to Rebecca, first wife of Hubert. Although there are no data, the fact that Thomas appears to have been an only child suggests that Rebecca died in childbirth or while Thomas was quite young, and then Hubert died shortly after his marriage to Faith.

The traditional view links Thomas Petty to the Pettus family, members of the minor nobility.

The tradition has developed among researchers of the Petty family over the years that Thomas Petty was the son of Thomas Pettit/Petty and Rachel Wilson of Essex County, Virginia, and the grandson of Col. Thomas Petty and Catherine Morris of Rappahannock Co., Virginia. This line is further traced back to Thomas Pettus, who resided in Norwich, England in 1492. Thomas Pettit, the supposed father of the subject of this article, died in 1720, and named a son Thomas in his will. This has been the sole source of proof tying the lines together.[6]

---

[5] Lancaster Co., Va., Will Book 5:113, 2 June 1687.
[6] McGee.

As a result, many still accept this interpretation rather than the more humble origins of Hubert, who appears to have been a carpenter, based upon his will, and who certainly was a commoner. Personally, I find the links outlined above reasonably convincing. However, I have chosen to start the summary with Thomas[2] Petty,[7] about whom more documentation is established.

Genealogical Summary

1. THOMAS[2] PETTY was born 1673 in Lancaster Co., Virginia, and died before 24 May 1750 in Orange County, Virginia. He married CATHERINE GARTON about 1699 in Richmond Co., Virginia, daughter of JOHN GARTON and MARTHA _____. She was born about 1675 in Rappahannock Co., Virginia, and died 3 January 1748/49 in Orange Co., Virginia.

Thomas Petty's year of birth is estimated from a Northumberland Co., Va., court record dated 6 November 1689 involving the probate of his guardian, Walter Welch. At that time, Thomas bound himself out to John Davis to teach him the trade of carpentry. His term was for five years, which implies he was 16, since he was able to make his own decision, and also implying he would be 21 by November 1694. Both of these considerations seem to establish his birth year in 1673, although it is going a bit far to say that he was born in November of that year.

Thomas Patty sued Dennis Cameron and wife Jane Cameron, as executors of Walter Welch, who was the executor of Hubert Patey, for the portion of the inheritance he had not received on 2 November 1699 in Richmond Co., Virginia. He received four cows and their calves.[8]

---

[7] The Scott County family spelled the name Pettey, but it appears both ways in the records. For consistency I have chosen to spell the name Petty.

[8] Richmond Co., Va., Court Order Book 3:24, 3 April 1700.

Thomas Petty, Katherine Petty, and Martha Garton were awarded 300 pounds of tobacco as settlement of a suit against Robert and Anna Post concerning the estate of John Garton.[9] Thomas and Katherine Patty and Ruth Boyd sued Hannah Port for a portion of the estate of John Garton that they had not received in the initial settlement.[10]

Thomas and Katherine Petty and Ruth Garton Boyd applied for letters of administration for the estate of John Garton, the younger, 6 April 1721. David Boyd filed a complaint against Thomas Petty 2 August 1721, but it was dropped.[11] Ruth Boyd and Thomas Patty gave security as executors of the will of David Boyd 2 October 1728. Thomas asked for release from his duties 2 March 1731/32 and was replaced by his son-in-law, Thomas Sims.

All of these chancery actions establish the connections between Thomas Petty and Catherine Garton and her family, which included her parents, John and Martha, her sister Ruth Boyd, wife of David Boyd, and John Garton the younger, who apparently died without leaving a wife or children.

Land deeds show that Thomas and Catherine Garton sold 65 acres of land on Morratico Creek, adjoining the lands of Abraham Bush, 13 October 1702 in Lancaster Co., Virginia.[12] As noted earlier, this land appears consistent with that purchased by Hubert Patey from Abraham Bush. Since I have not read the original deed, I do not know if he specifically established his ownership by inheritance, or if he simply assert his title, as was done more commonly.

Thomas Patty purchased 150 acres of land on Bare Branch of Rappahannock Creek from Thomas Barker in Richmond County 6 October 1703.[13]

[9] Richmond Co., Va., Court Order Book 3:85, 6 March 1700/01; and 3:186, 7 May 1702.
[10] Richmond Co., Va., Court Order Book 9:48, 5 April 1722.
[11] Richmond Co., Va., Court Order Book 9:14, 2 August 1721.
[12] Lancaster Co., Va., Deed Book 7:36, 13 October 1702.
[13] Richmond Co., Va., Deed Book 3:118, 6 October 1703.

Thomas Patty sold 50 acres of this tract to his son John 2 January 1727/28.[14] Thomas and Catherine Petty and John and Rebecca Petty sold their tracts of land to William Jordan 4 November 1732.[15] Both families leased land in then Spotsylvania Co., Virginia, 23 October 1734, which became Orange County 1 January 1734/35.[16]

Thomas Patty was sued for debt 17 March 1735/36 by William Jordan and was awarded 570 pounds of tobacco. Thomas Patty was also ordered to perform road work service apparently in lieu of court costs, but asked to be excused on the basis of being 75 years old.[17] Although the evidence suggests he was closer to 65 years old, this would still have been considered quite elderly for the time and place.

Thomas Petty wrote his will 31 January 1748/49 and it was proved in Orange County, Virginia, 24 May 1750.[18]

In the name of God Amen, Jan. 31 1748 I Thomas Petty of Orange Co. St. Thomas Parish being sick and weak of body but of sound and perfect mind and memory praise be to God for the same do make and ordain this my last will and testament in writing and hereby do also make void all former wills or testaments by me heretofore, made. Imprimis, I give and bequeath my soul to God that gave it in hopes of full assurance to receive the same again at the Resurrection at the last day by the merit of my Lord Saviour Jesus Christ and my body I bequeath to the Earth from Whence it came to be buried in decent manner according to the discretion of my executors and executrix hereafter mentioned.

Item. I give and bequeath to my son John Petty one Shilling.

[14] Richmond Co., Va., Deed Book 8:249, 2 January 1727/28.
[15] Richmond Co., Va., Deed Book 8:622-624, 4 November 1732.
[16] McGee.
[17] Orange Co., Va., Court Order Book 1:146.
[18] Orange Co., Va., Will Book 2:144-145.

Item. I give and bequeath to my son William one Shilling.

Item. I give and bequeath to my son Thomas Petty one Shilling.

Item. I give and bequeath to my son James Petty one Shilling.

Item. I give and bequeath to my daughter Rebecca Sims one Shilling.

Item. I give and bequeath to my daughter Mary Wright one Shilling.

Item. I give and bequeath to my son George Petty and my daughter Martha Petty all my estate both real and personal after my debts being paid and the legacies aforesaid to be equally divided between my well beloved children George Petty and Martha Petty to them and their heirs forever. Lastly, I nominate my son George Petty executor and my daughter Martha Petty executrix of this my last will and testament as witness my hand and seal this day and year above mentioned.

Thomas (X) Petty

Signed, sealed and delivered
in the presence of us
Solomon Ryan, Wm. Sims
Thomas Petty younger

May 24, 1750 at a court held for Orange Co. Thursday 24 May 1750 will was presented by Geo. and Martha Petty exrs. and ordered recorded.

Children of THOMAS PETTY and CATHERINE GARTON are:

i. REBECCA[3] PETTY, b. about 1701 Richmond Co., Va.; d. before April 1784 Culpeper Co., Va.; m. THOMAS SIMS 30 November 1725 Richmond Co., Va.; d. before 18 July 1785 Culpeper Co., Va.

Thomas Sims wrote his will 21 April 1784 and it was proved 18 July 1785 in Culpeper Co., Virginia.[19] Rebecca was dead when he wrote his will.

---

[19] Culpeper Co., Va., Will Book E:342.

ii. JOHN[3] PETTY, b. about 1703 Richmond Co., Va., d. before 27 September 1770 Orange Co., Va.; m. REBECCA SIMS.

John Petty wrote his will 26 July 1768 Orange Co., Virginia, and it was proved 27 September 1770.[20]

In the name of God, Amen; I John Petty, being of the County of Orange, Parish of St. Thomas, being in perfect sense and memory, do make and ordain this my last will and testament Imprimis: I lend my beloved wife, Rebecca, the land and plantation whereon we now live, containing 122 acres during her natural life or widowhood, also my negro fellow Punch and negro woman Maoll, together with all my other estate, during her natural life or widowhood, and after her decease my will and desire is that my estate be divided amongst my children in manner and form to wit;

Item; I leave to my eldest son Thomas Petty 5 shillings current money to be paid to him by my executors when demanded and it is my will and desire that my said son have no other part of my estate.

Item; I give and bequeath to my daughters Sarah Corley and Tabitha Edwards and to my son Luke who are now in Carolina, the sum of 5 shillings each.

Item; I give and bequeath to my granddaughter Ann Ford the feather bed that she lies on with the furniture belonging to it.

Item; I give and bequeath to my son-in-law William Ransdall my large church Bible.

Item; I give and bequeath to my son Francis Petty one horse to the value of £8.

Item; I give and bequeath to my son Abner Petty my negro man named Punch, but in case Abner should die before he arrives to the age of 21 yrs or has heirs of his body lawfully begotten, then it is my will and desire that my said negro Punch be sold and the money divided amongst my other children who I have not cut off with 5 shillings.

---

[20] Orange Co., Va., Will Book 2:422.

Item; I give and bequeath to my son George Petty after his mother's decease, the land and plantation whereon I now live and one negro woman named Moll. With her future increase to him and his heirs forever but in case that George should have died before he arrives to the age of 21 yrs or has heirs of his body lawfully begotten then it is my will and desire that the land and plantation go to my son John Petty and his heirs forever and the negro woman named Moll be sold to the highest bidder and the money to be equally divided betwixt all my children who have not been cut off 5 shillings.

It is my will and desire that in case my wife Rebecca Petty should marry after my decease that then she should have no more of estate than the law here after mentioned, vis.; Alizia Ford, John Petty, Zachariah Petty, Ann Ransdall, Rebecca Boston, Susannah Hawkins, Jemima Boston, Francis Petty, and Abner Petty, and I do appoint my beloved wife Rebecca Petty Extrx., and my son Zachariah Petty and William Ransdall executors of this my Esate will and testament this 26th day of July 1768.

John Petty signed, sealed and delivered in the presence of us: Alexander Waugh Jr., Absalom Wood, William Wood.

Since the signing of the above will, I have been informed of the death of my eldest son, Thomas Petty, therefore to prevent his children from having any part of my estate, I give to my grandson Reuben Petty, son of Thomas Petty, one shilling sterling in witness thereof, I have hereunto set my hand and seal this 20th day of Feb 1770.

John Petty Signed, sealed, and delivered in the presence of Catty Petty and Alexander Waugh Jr.

2. iii. THOMAS[3] PETTY, b. 1706 Richmond Co., Va.; d. after 1756 Lunenburg Co., Va.; m. ELIZABETH MOORE 24 August 1727 North Farnham Parish, Richmond Co., Va.

iv. CHRISTOPHER[3] PETTY, b. about 1708; d. before
1765 Culpeper Co., Va.; m. MARTHA _____.
v. WILLIAM[3] PETTY, b. about 1710; m. ELIZABETH
_____.

William Petty purchased a lease in Orange Co.,
Virginia, in 1741 in which he named his sons
Theophilus and William Petty. The family left
Orange County in May 1748 and appear in
Brunswick Co., Va., where on 27 September 1750
William Petty and his wife Elizabeth sold a tract of
land to John Marshall of Charles City Co.,
Virginia. No record has been found of their
acquisition of the land, so it is possible that it was
through an inheritance from her family. Her
surname has not been established from the
records.

William Petty and family moved to nearby
Lunenburg Co., Virginia, where he appears in the
1751 Tithe List. Theophilus is also listed,
indicating he was born before 1734. William Petty
appears in court records with children of Thomas
Petty, Jr., until July 1756, a suit between Richard
Taylor and William Petty was dismissed because
William had moved away from Lunenburg Co., Va.

William Petty received land grants in Orange
Co., N. C., that he later divided amongst his
children. He appears for the last time in court
records from 1769. His son, William Petty, Jr.,
used the "Jr." in August 1770, and did not in
November 1770, suggesting his father had died in
the interim.

The only proven children of William and
Elizabeth Petty are Theophilus and William. He is
supposed to have had two other sons, Hubbard
and John, although proof is lacking.[21]

vi. MARY[3] PETTY, b. about 1714; m. THOMAS KNIGHT.

---

[21] Information was reported by McGee, but appears to be a verbatim
quote from Hodges, p. 22. Just to confuse the issue, Mrs. Hodges probably
has Thomas and William confused in her records. Since she does not cite
her sources, I cannot back track to figure out how to correct the
information. It seems clear that Thomas Petty was the father of the William
Petty, grandfather of John Wright Petty.

vii. MARTHA[3] PETTY, b. about 1717; m. R____
    BOSTON.
viii. JAMES[3] PETTY, b. about 1720; d. before 3
    November 1806 Union Co., S. C.; m. MARTHA
    ____.

James Petty and his family appear to have moved to Bute Co., N. C., before 1768, and then to Chatham Co., N. C., and then to Union Co., S. C., about 1785. He wrote his will there 14 March 1806 and it was proved 3 November 1806.[22]

In the name of God, Amen, I James Petty of the State of South Carolina, Union District, farmer, being of sound body mind and memory and understanding, praised be God for the same, do make this my last Will and Testament in manner and form following: first I commit my soul to God who gave it and my body to be buried in a Christian manner at the discretion of my Executors and as for my worldly goods I dispose of in the following manner:

First: it is my will that all lawful debts be paid together with funeral expenses, probate of will and etc. Then I it is my will that my beloved wife Martha enjoy as her right all my estate and real and personal during her life or widowhood (excepting for...of five shillings to each of my children : Viz: Ambrose, James, Absalom, Joshua, Thomas, and George, and also the same moiety of five shillings to each of my daughters namely: Rachel, Sarah, Martha, Catharine, and Polly to be paid to each of them by my executors at the Death or Marriage of my beloved wife.) At her Death or Marriage I give my plantation and land containing 325 Acres, more or less, to my son Gabriel Petty in fee simple and also two thirds of my personal estate; and the other third part I give to my beloved wife to dispose of at her discretion—and lastly I constitute ordain and appoint my trusty

---

[22] Union Co., S. C., Will Book A:232. Transcript located online 8 April 2012 at
    http://www.archivesindex.sc.gov/onlinearchives/Thumbnails.aspx?recordId=299028.

and well beloved wife Executrix and my son
Gabriel and my trusty friend, Nicholas Corry,
Executors of this my last Will and Testament,
hereby revoking and making void all and every
other will and wills at any time heretofore by me
made and declare this to be my last will and
testament In witness whereof I have hereunto set
my hand and seal this 14th of March in the year
of our Lord 1806.

Signed and declared published by the above
named J.P. the testator as and for his last will and
testament in the presence of us who at his request
and in his presence have subscribed our names as
witnesses.

Signed: James Petty

Witnesses: Charles Petty, Jeptha Harrington &
John Petty

ix. GEORGE[3] PETTY, b. about 1723; d. 1752 Orange
Co., Va.; m. JEMIMA _____.
George Petty's will was written 3 January 1751
and proved 28 May 1752 in Orange Co., Va.[23]

2. THOMAS[3] (*THOMAS[2], HUBERT[1]*) PETTY was born about
1708 in Richmond Co., Virginia, and died about 1770
in Orange Co., Virginia. He married ELIZABETH MOORE
24 August 1727 North Farnham Parish, Richmond
Co., Virginia, daughter of FRANCIS MOORE and ANN
_____.

Very little firm information has been collected
on this man other than the information recorded in
the Registry of North Farnham Parish.

Children of THOMAS PETTY and ELIZABETH MOORE
are:

---

[23] Orange Co., Va., Will Book 2:165.

i. FRANCIS MOORE[4] PETTY, b. 27 June 1728
Richmond Co., Va.; d. before 26 February
1816 Halifax Co., Va.; m. MARY _____.

Francis Moore Petty was witness for a deed of
Thomas Petty and Francis Moore in Lunenburg
Co., Va., 16 February 1757. He wrote his will 9
September 1802 and proved 26 February 1816.[24]

In the name of God amen, I Francis Moore
Petty of Halifax County in the state of Virginia,
being weak of body but sound of mind and
memory, Thanks be to God Almighty for the same,
do make this my last will and testament in the
manner and form following.

First I consign my body to the dust and my
soul to God that gave it.

Secondly my will and desire is that all my
debts be paid by my executor hereafter to be
mentioned.

Item - I lend to my beloved wife Mary during
her natural life or pleasure, all of my estate both
real and personal now in my possession.

Item - I give and bequeath to my son Joseph
one negro woman named Ann, now in his
possession with all of her increase for the year
One Thousand Seven Hundred and Seventy Five
to him and his heirs forever.

Item - I give and bequeath to my daughter
Mary Bosticke one negro woman named Dorcas
now in her possession with all of her increase for
the year One Thousand Seven Hundred and
Eighty Eight to her and her heirs forever.

I give and bequeath to my son Garton One
Hundred Fifty pounds to be paid on application,
in lieu of land I intended to give him.

Item - I give and bequeath to my son Davis all
the tract of land on Whitewater Saw, where
Andrew now lives, containing his Hundred and
Fifty Three acres be the same more or less, to him
and his heirs forever.

Item - I give and bequeath to Coleman
Hawkins, son of Milly Hawkins Twenty Five

---

[24] Halifax Co., Va., Will Book 10:424.

pounds to be paid by my executor on his coming of age twenty one years old.

After the death of my wife, or if she should wish to divide my estate it is my will and desire that all of my estate such as land, slaves, stock and all kinds of furniture so lent to my wife be sold by my executor and the money arriving from such sale together with all the money I may have or had as due me by bond or likewise be equally divided among my children, except my son Joseph who is to secure One Hundred pounds over and above what I have before given him, to them and their heirs forever. My will and desire further is that no part of my estate be appraised, and lastly I mandate, constitute and appoint my son Joseph and my son Garton Petty executors of this my last will and testament, hereby revoking all others.

In testimony whereof I have set my hand this 9th Day of September One Thousand Eight Hundred and Two.

Francis Moore Petty

Signed, Sealed and Acknowledged in presence of us,

Peter Barksdale, John ? and Richard ?

   ii. ANN[4] PETTY.

3. iii. WILLIAM[4] PETTY, b. about 1730 Richmond Co., Va.; d. before 27 May 1805 Clark Co., Kentucky; m. LETITIA _____.

   iv. LAVINIA[4] PETTY.

   v. ELIZABETH[4] PETTY.

   vi. JOSEPH[4] PETTY, b. 1738 Orange Co., Va.

3. WILLIAM[4] (THOMAS[3-2], HUBERT[1]) PETTY was born about 1730 in Richmond Co., Virginia, and died before 27 May 1805 Clark Co., Kentucky. He married LETITIA _____.

The history of the Reverend William Petty, Sr., Baptist minister of early Surry County, North

Carolina, has been the subject of many genealogical researchers.[25] Though not all of their conclusions are fully proven, we must remember that we are dealing with the Colonial Period and that surviving records are scanty. Some of the material which follows is not documented but is presented as hypotheses in the hopes of guiding further research.

The Reverend William Petty is reputed to have been the second son of Thomas Petty IV, who married Elizabeth Moore in Richmond County, Virginia, on August 24, 1727. Their oldest son, Francis Moore Petty, was born June 27, 1728, as shown by a baptismal record in North Farnham Parish where they married. William's name first appears in a 99 year lease recorded in 1735 in Orange County, Virginia; so his birth date has been estimated as being about 1730. The absence of a church record for him in North Farnham probably indicates that his parents had moved to Spotsylvania County, Virginia, prior to his birth.[26] The use of the youngest son's name in a land lease was customary when leasing land for a longer period than the probable life span of the parent.

The Petty family settled in an area near the meeting of the Rappahannock and Rapidan Rivers. In 1734 this land became a part of Orange County. (The 1735 land lease mentioned previously also mentions Thomas Petty IV's younger brother, another William (b. 1710) and William's son Theophilus. According to a 1775 land record of Chatham County, North Carolina, this William, brother to Thomas, also had another son, William, Jr., born about 1740. The presence of this other William Petty (b. 1710) and his son William Petty, Jr.

[25] Pettey, Harry, Medlin, Doris, and Parks, Vivian. The Pettey's of East Texas. Cited by Mike. 1658-1758 Charles Co., MD, Families, "The First 100 Years." 8 April 2012. Located online at http://wc.rootsweb.ancestry.com, (db. mrmarsha.)

[26] My interpretation is that he had become Baptist by the time his second son was born and therefore had no intention of having him baptized in the Anglican church. Further, even good Anglicans do not appear to have thought it that important to have each child christened in the church.

(b. 1740), has complicated the interpretation of existing records. Comments on this William, Jr., will be limited to the hypothesis that he was the Revolutionary soldier who married Mildred Phelps about 1774 and died in Halifax County, Virginia, in 1827 (Rev. Pension Record W-18747).

1756 land records indicate that Thomas Petty IV and his brother William (b. 1710) had moved their families to Lunenburg County, Virginia, possibly as early as 1751. Halifax County was formed from Lunenburg in 1752, Charlotte from Lunenburg in 1765, and Pittsylvania from Haliax in 1767.An understanding of the sequence of county formation in Colonial Virginia is important to an interpretation of Petty family history through land records.

Our subject William Petty (b. ca 1730) married about 1754 in Culpeper County, Virginia to one Lettice _____. Some researchers say he was married twice but there is no evidence to support the theory that his first wife was the Elizabeth Petty listed as a daughter in the 1794 will of Thomas Marshall of Culpeper County, Virginia; but there is ample evidence that it was William's cousin, Zachariah Petty, who married this Elizabeth Marshall about 1762. The colonial records for a William and Elizabeth Petty in the Lunenburg County area are probably for William Petty (b. 1710) our subject's uncle, who is reported to have married an Elizabeth in Orange County about 1734. Assuming, as it now seems proper to do, that our subject William Petty (1730), son of Thomas Petty IV, was not the William Petty on record in Lunenburg with wife Elizabeth, where was he? Did he remain in Northern Virginia and marry there when his father went South to Lunenburg County along with other Petty relatives? If so, no records have been found to indicate it save perhaps the sworn statement of his son William in his pension application that he was born in Fauquier or Stafford County, Virginia on March 13, 1764. Wherever he and his family may have been from 1764 and earlier, our subject William Petty (1730) purchased 200 acres of land on

Wallace Creek in Charlotte County, Virginia on August 1, 1770, from William and Joseph Crews (Charlotte County Deed Book 3, p. 330). Whether our William Petty ever lived in Charlotte County is not certain from information at hand; but he was a resident of neighboring Pittsylvania County by 1773 when "William Petty of Pittsylvania County" sold land he purchased from William and Joseph Crews (Charlotte County Deed Book 3, p. 360).

His wife Lettice (Lettie, Letty, Lettitia) relinquished her dower right, and in so doing forged one of the strongest links between the William Petty of Pittsylvania County, Virginia, in 1773 and the William Petty whose will was probated in Clark County, Kentucky, on May 27, 1805, naming among others his widow Lettis and his daughter, Elizabeth Dodson. Even before selling his land in Charlotte County, William Petty had on January 1, 1772, purchased 150 acres of land on both sides of Double Creek in Pittsylvania County (Pittsylvania County Deed Book 2, p. 437) which he sold in two separate tracts on August 17, 1778, while still listed as a resident of Pittsylvania County (Pittsylvania County Deed Book 5, pp. 23 and 25).

In my view, this appears to be the most balanced attempt to "sort out" the various men named William Petty who lived in the southern counties of Virginia before the Revolution.[27] From the information that appears validated, William Petty moved many times in the course of his life, presumably founding churches. For instance, his son, William, asserted he was born in 1764 in either Fauquier or Stafford Co., Virginia, but enlisted in the Revolutionary cause in Surry Co., N. C., in 1780. (see his entry below.)

---

[27] A somewhat more traditional, but apparently undocumented, interpretation says that 1805 (year of death) William Petty of Clark Co., Ky., (place of death), was married twice. By his supposed first wife, Elizabeth Ransdell, he had either 8 or 10 children. He married secondly to Letitia Thornton, by whom he had an additional 4 or 5 children.

As noted in the quotation above, there is good reason to think that in 1771 William Petty had purchased 200 acres of land on Wallace Creek in Charlotte Co., Virginia from William and Joseph Crews,[28] and was living in Pittsylvania County when he and Lettice sold the tract in 1773.[29] He had previously purchased 150 acres of land on both sides of Double Creek in Pittsylvania County on 1 January 1772,[30] and sold the tract in two parcels in August 1778.[31]

William Petty obtained a land grand from the state of North Carolina for a 300 acre tract of land on the waters of Deep Creek adjacent Henry Hambrick, Millington (Millanton?) Blalock, and Richard Blalock 9 August 1787.[32] William Petty, Sr., sold a 300 acre tract of land on Deep Creek adjacent Henry Hambrick and William Blalock to Christian Fender for £32 North Carolina money in 1792.[33]

The 1790 tax list for Surry Co., N. C., shows Ransdale Petty with 300 acres of land and 1 poll, William Petty with 400 acres of land and no polls, Zachariah Petty with 140 acres and 1 poll.[34]

The 1790 Census for Surry Co., N. C., shows Ransdall Petty with himself, his wife, and one son.[35] William Petty was shown with three males under 16, two over 16, three women, and one slave.[36] Zachariah Petty is shown with himself, one son under 16, and five women.[37] In 1800 William Petty, Sr., was listed in

---

[28] Charlotte Co., Va., Deed Book 3:330, 1 August 1770.

[29] Charlotte Co., Va., Deed Book 3:360.

[30] Pittsylvania Co., Va., Deed Book 2:437, 1 January 1772.

[31] Pittsylvania Co., Va., Deed Book 5:23, 25, 17 August 1778.

[32] Surry Co., N. C., Deed Book D:41, 9 August 1787. Located 19 April 2012 at http://genforum.genealogy.com/hamrick/messages/961.html.

[33] Surry Co., N. C., Deed Book E:228, 14 January 1792. Located 19 April 2012 at http://www.moonzstuff.com/fender/nimrod1766.html.

[34] Captain Hudspeth's District. Located online 19 April 2012 at http://newrivernotes.com/nc/surry/1790tl.html.

[35] 1790 Census Surry Co., N. C., p. 519. (This list is roughly alphabetized, but the names are not adjacent to each other.)

[36] 1790 Census Surry Co., N. C., p. 519.

[37] 1790 Census Surry Co., N. C., p. 519.

Morgan, Wilkes Co., N. C., over 45, with one male 16-25, and one 10-15, his wife, over 45, 1 woman 16-25, and one 10-15, and one slave.[38] William Petty, probably his son, is 26-45, as is his wife, and they have 3 boys under 10, and two 10-15, and also two girls under 10, and one girl 10-15 years old.[39]

William Petty founded a Baptist Meeting House on Deep Creek in 1788. The church is now known as the Flat Rock Baptist Church and is in present day Yadkin Co., N. C.

In the year 1786, eleven churches, which had been previously gathered about the head of the Yadkin and its waters, began to hold yearly conferences, as a branch of the Strawberry Association in Virginia. The proceedings of this conference were annually submitted to the Association to which it had attached itself, for their inspection, and were borne thither by delegates appointed for the purpose. But in 1790, the churches, composing this conference, were, upon their request, dismissed, and formed a distinct Association. The ministers belonging to this body at its commencement, were George M'Neal, John Cleaveland, William Petty, William Hammond, Cleaveland Caffee, Andrew Baker, and John Stone. This Association, like Sandy-Creek, transacted its business, or at least, held its sessions, for a number of years, without a moderator. Some of their scrupulous brethren, it seems, were opposed to order, or formality, as they esteemed it, in their religious proceedings, and pleaded that it was an infringement of Christian liberty, and too much like worldly assemblies, to have a moderator at their head, whom they must address when they spoke, and whose liberty they must request, etc. In 1793, Mr. John Gano, who then lived in Kentucky, visited this Association, and found many difficulties among them on account of these things. But he knew very

---

[38] 1800 Census Wilkes Co., N. C., Morgan, p. 57.
[39] Same page, although he is listed two lines above his father.

well how to manage prejudices so whimsical and absurd, and prevailed on them to choose a moderator and establish rules, by which their business was afterwards conducted with much decorum.[40]

William Petty and his wife moved to Winchester, Clark Co., Kentucky, between 1800 and 1804, when he wrote his will there.[41] He named his wife, Lettis, his youngest son Thomas, then his sons Francis, Zachariah, William, Randell, John, and James, and daughters Rhoda Cast, Elizabeth Dodson, Rachel Russell, Hannah Ward, and Sarah Stevens. Wife Lettis and son Thomas were named as executors. Witnesses were Charles and Sarah Tracy.[42]

Children of WILLIAM PETTY and LETTICE _____ are:[43]

- i. FRANCIS MARION[5] PETTY, d. March 1857 Tipton, Willow Fork Twp., Moniteau Co., Mo.; m. SARAH RAGLAND 2 December 1802 Clark Co., Ky.
- ii. ZACHARIAH[5] PETTY d. 1835 Surry Co., N. C.; m. NANCY ANNE DODSON.
- 4. iii. WILLIAM[5] PETTY b. 3 March 1764 Fauquier or Stafford Co., Va.; d. 26 September 1834 New Market, Madison Co., Alabama; m. LUCRETIA WRIGHT 25 January 1783 Wilkes Co., N. C., daughter of JOHN WRIGHT and ANN WILLIAMS; b. 7 July 1765 Fauquier Co., Va.; d. 16 August 1842 Madison Co., Alabama.

---

[40] Benedict, David. A General History of the Baptist Denomination in America and Other Parts of the World. (London: Lincoln & Edmonds, 1813.) Quotation cited was located online 19 April 2012 at http://www.fbinstitute.com/baptist-in-america/benedict29.html.

[41] Clark Co., Kentucky, Will Book 2:41, 1 May 1804/27 May 1805.

[42] Ellsberry, Elizabeth Prather, comp. *Will Records of Clark County, Kentucky.* (Chillicothe, MO: Elizabeth Prather Ellsberry, circa 1965.) Located online 20 April 2012 at Ancestry.com. *Clark County, Kentucky Wills 1792-1826, Vol. 1-2* [database on-line]. Provo, UT, USA: Ancestry.com Operations Inc, 2001.

[43] Additional data are from McGee.

iv. RANSDELL[5] PETTY, m. P. ELSEY DODSON.

v. JOHN[5] PETTY m. MARY SANDERS 5 January 1791 Wilkes Co., N. C.

vi. JAMES[5] PETTY b. 13 September 1771 Culpeper Co., Va.; d. 14 July 1847 Franklin, Williamson Co., Tenn.;[44] m. KIZIAH JANE SANDERS.

vii. THOMAS[5] PETTY, b. 1780 Wilkes Co., N. C.; d. 1838 Montgomery Co., Ky.; m. REBECCA _____ about 1808 Clark Co., Ky.

viii. RHODA[5] PETTY d. 1823 Warren Co., Ohio; m. ELISHA CAST 10 March 1804 Clark Co., Ky.; b. say 1780 Iredell Co., N. C.; d. 1822 Warren Co., Ohio.

ix. ELIZABETH[5] PETTY, m. CALEB DODSON; b. 1752 Fauquier Co., Va.; d. 1836 Halifax Co., Va.

Caleb Dodson is in Meadsville, Halifax Co., Va., in 1820.[45] In 1830, he and his wife, both 70-79, were still in Halifax Co., Va.[46] Caleb Dodson made application for a Revolutionary War pension 23 September 1832 in Halifax Co., Va.[47] He stated he was 81 years old and born in Fauquier Co., Va., and moved to Halifax Co., Va., when about 12 years old.

x. RACHEL[5] PETTY, m. BUCKNER RUSSELL 1790 Wilkes Co., N. C.; b. 1751 Va.; d. after 15 January 1836 Weakley Co., Tenn.

Buckner Russell's Revolutionary War pension application 15 January 1834 in Weakley Co., Tenn., is of record.[48] He stated he was 83 years of age, entered service in Wilkes Co., N. C., in 1780, and served two enlistments. He was at home and was taken prisoner 10 March 1781 by soldiers under command of General Cornwallis. He

---

[44] Buried in Rowe Cemetery. Not located on findagrave.com.

[45] 1820 Census Halifax Co., Va., Meadsville, p. 70. He was over 45, and had 1 son 10-15, one daughter 16-25, and his wife, over 45.

[46] 1830 Census Halifax Co., Va., p. 387.

[47] Revolutionary War Pension Application, R 2996. Accessed 2 May 2014 at Ancestry.com.

[48] Revolutionary War Pension Application, S4166. Accessed 2 May 2014 at Ancestry.com.

escaped and served a third term. He signed his name to the application. The claim was not allowed.

Buckner Russell was recorded in Wright's District of Surry Co., N. C., in 1786.[49] He obtained land grants on Big Barren River, Green Co., Kentucky 4 April 1799 and 19 October 1804.[50] He is probably the Buckner Russell, Sr., in Monroe Co., Ky., in 1820.[51] I have not identified him in the 1830 Census.

xi.   HANNAH[5] PETTY, d. 1845 Hendricks Co., Ind.; m. JOHN R. WARD 1778 Wilkes Co., N. C.

xii. SARAH[5] PETTY, m. RICHARD STEVENS.

4.   WILLIAM ELI[5] (*WILLIAM[4]*, *THOMAS[3-2]*, *HUBERT[1]*) PETTY was born 3 March 1764 in either Fauquier or Stafford Co., Virginia, and died 26 September 1834 in New Market, Madison Co., Alabama. He married LUCRETIA WRIGHT 25 January 1783 Wilkes Co., N.C., daughter of JOHN WRIGHT and ANN WILLIAMS. She was born 7 July 1765 in Fauquier Co., Virginia, and died 16 August 1842 in New Market, Madison Co., Alabama.

William Eli Petty is one of the better documented ancestors from this period I have investigated, as his application for a Revolutionary War pension is extant as are family Bible records. He was born in Virginia, but in his pension application cannot say if it was in Fauquier or Stafford County. As noted above, his father was a pioneering Baptist minister, who moved fairly regularly, founding new meeting houses as he went. William Eli Petty was also a Baptist minister, but he spent most of his life in

---

[49] North Carolina Compiled Census and Census Substitutes Index, 1790-1890. Accessed 2 May 2014 at Ancestry.com.

[50] The Kentucky Land Grants, Vol. 1, part 1. Accessed 2 May 2014 at Ancestry.com.

[51] 1820 Census Monroe Co., Ky., p. 195, [01001-01001].

North Carolina before moving to Madison County, Alabama, about 1815.[52]

State of Alabama)[53]
Madison County)

On this 29th day of October 1832 personally appeared in open court before the judge of the circuit court now sitting William Petty a resident of the county of Madison and State of Alabama aged sixty eight years who being first duly sworn according to law, doth, on his oath, make the following dictation in order to obtain the benefit of the Act of Congress passed June 7th, 1832.

That he entered the service of the United States under General Rutherford, Colonel Armstrong, and Capt. Absalom Bostwick who was his immediate commander—he marched from Surry County, North Carolina, as a drafted militiaman through Salisbury, from there to Cheraw Hills, and somewhere in the neighborhood of Rugby Mills he joined Gen'l. Gates army, with which he remained until a few days before the engagement in which Gates was defeated. He was detached with about 300 men under to command of Major Elisha Isaacs to inform Gen'l. Sumpter whom he joined in the neighborhood of Candis and remained until his defeat, in this campaign he was in service about three months— after the close of which he was engaged in scouting parties until he again entered the service as a substitute for a man whose name he has entirely forgotten—he however recollects that he was commanded by Major Francis Hargrove and Pendleton Isbell after the close of this last campaign he was engaged in guarding the legislature of North Carolina he was almost continually engaged in scouting parties which at that time was considered

[52] Campbell, Vera M. Pettey, Howard, Carleton and Golden Families. In The Heritage of Madison County, Alabama. (Clanton, Ala.; Heritage Publishing Consultants, 1998.)
[53] Revolutionary War Pension Application of William Petty, S-17016. Copy located on Heritage Quest 21 April 2012.

very ___ service. He served more than six months, but how long he does not know—during the first campaign he thinks Major Micajah Lewis and Major John Armstrong were in the same town and in the regular service. He further states that he was frequently sent on express. He has no documentary evidence of his service.

He hereby relinquishes any claim whatever to a pension or annuity except the present and declares that his name is not on the pension rolls of the agency of any State.

Sworn to and subscribed the date and year aforesaid in open court.

(signed) William (P) Petty, his mark.

Interrogation propounded to William Petty an applicant for a pension in the War of the Revolution.

1st Where and in what year were you born? Ans. I was born in the county of Fauquier or Stafford, State of Virginia—I do not know which—on the 13th day of March 1764.

2nd Have you any record of your age and if so where is it? Ans. I have a ___ in my family Bible which I made myself from what my parents have told me.

3rd Where were you living when called into service; where have you lived since the Revolutionary War, and where do you live now? Ans. I lived in Surry County, North Carolina, when I entered the service, and continued to live there until the close of the Revolutionary War. I then moved to Wilkes Co., N. C., and lived there until the year 1817 when I moved to Madison County, Alabama Territory, now state of Alabama, and have lived there since and still do.

4th How were you called into service; were you drafted, did you volunteer, or were you a substitute, and if a substitute for whom? Ans. I was once drafted and once was a substitute—but I have entirely forgotten for whom—he was a stranger to me when I engaged as his substitute—I knew him afterward, but cannot recollect his name—I was at that time 16 years of age.

5th State the names of some of the regular officers who were with the troops where you served; such regimental and militia regiments as you can recollect, and the general circumstances of your service. Ans. I cannot state now particularly than I have done in my declaration to which I refer in answer to this interrogatory.

6th Did you receive a discharge from the service; and if so, by whom was it given, and what has become of it? Ans. I never did receive any discharge—it was at that time considered of no value.

7th State the names of persons to whom you are known in your present neighborhood and who can testify as to your character for veracity, and their belief of your service as a soldier of the Revolution. Ans. Drury Allen and Samuel Chapman are present, any others to whom I am known I believe would do the same.

(signed) Wm Petty

On 30 May 1835 Lucy Petty appointed Theophilus Lacy her attorney to receive the pension due to William Petty from the 4th day of September 1833 to the 26th day of September 1834, due to her in consequence of the death of William Petty.

William Petty died testate in Madison Co., Alabama.[54] Two Bible records of descendants list the dates of birth for their children. William Petty and Lucy Wright Petty's dates are from their tombstones.

As a small child growing up in west Huntsville, I can remember my mother, Mary Lou Driver Harbin, and my grandmother, Mildred "Meldie" Vodrine Petty Driver, talking about the Petty's of New Market and

---

[54] Madison Co., Alabama, Probate Record 7:61, 26 April 1834/17 March 1835. He named his wife Lucretia Petty, daughters Nancy Hickerson, Amelia Carlton, and Eliza Eastland, and sons Eli, Lazarus, John Wright, Zachariah, William Thornton, James William, Thomas Merce, Benjamin Franklin, and Thomas Harrison. One deceased daughter was not named.

Hazel Green. My mother was very leery of whom we dated, even from Huntsville. It seems that the Pettys and the Wrights married into all the Madison County families.[55]

Children of WILLIAM PETTY and LUCRETIA WRIGHT:

i. NANCY[6] PETTY, b. 28 February 1785 Surry Co., N. C.; d. 7 September 1854 Coffee Co., Tenn.;[56] m. JOHN HICKERSON, son of DAVID HICKERSON and SARAH TALLIAFERRO; b. 19 April 1792 Wilkes Co., N. C.; d. 19 August 1845 Coffee Co., Tenn.[57]

I John Hickerson do make and publish this as my last will and testament hereby revoking all former wills by me at any time made.[58]

Item 1st—I wish my executors hereafter named to pay all my said debts as soon after my death as possible.

Item 2—I wish my wife to have my Hazel Patch Lands which includes all the lands that adjoins the old Hazel Patch Place during her life and at her death my will is that they be equally divided between my two youngest sons John W. and Little Hickerson which I release to them at four thousand dollars in the distribution of my estate.

Item 3—My further will and wish is that all my Negroes and other property remain with my wife during her life ____ to her control and that the labor of my Negroes over and above what may be necessary to the support of my wife go to the payment of what debts I may owe at my death. If however what debts I have coming to me & the proceeds of the proceeds of the labor of my

[55] Harbin, William Wayne. Wright/Wrta/Wryta Families. In The Heritage of Madison County, Alabama. (Clanton, Ala.; Heritage Publishing Consultants, 1998.)

[56] Hickerson Cemetery, Rutledge Falls, Coffee Co., Tenn. http://www.findagrave.com., #21846004.

[57] Hickerson Cemetery, Rutledge Falls, Coffee Co., Tenn. http://www.findagrave.com., #21845965.

[58] Coffee Co., Tenn., Will Book O:53. Accessed 12 May 2014 at http://trees.ancestry.com/tree/11997654/person/-355017264/storyx/00149d87-c89e-4625-bb92-acf009adab5c?src=search

Negroes is not sufficient to pay my debts by the time my executors are complied to meet them then they are directed to sell such of the Negroes or of the property as may be necessary for such purpose and my executors are directed to take all said steps and do all such things as maybe necessary to promote the comfort of my said wife and enhance the interest of the estate.

Item 4—My will is that after the death of my wife (or during her life she & my executors ____theretofore) the balance of whatever property _____personal that I may ____ seized and possessed of be equally divided between the following. (Each are for accounting for whatever advancements they may have accured heretofore and my two younger sons first accounting for the sum of two thousand dollars each the value of the land divided to them in this will) to wit: Effa Powers, Delpha Powers, Synthia Bowden, William P. Hickerson, Charles Hickerson, John W. Hickerson, D. Litle Hickerson, Lucy Timmins wife of Ambrose Timmins her portion I give to her for her own seperate use free from the contracts of her said husband and for her support of herself and children also the portion of Eliza Aldridge to be for her support and to her own seperate use free from the influence and control of her husband John Aldridge (the two last mentioned devises are also first to account for any advancements heretofore made to them or their husbands.

Item 5—I do hereby nominate and appoint Thomas Powers & W. P. Hickerson executors of this my last will and testament signed and sealed this 16 day of July 1845.

John Hickerson

Signed and sealed by the Testator in presence of us & subscribed by us in presence of the Testator and in presence of each other this 17 day of July 1845

A.M. Holt

D.V. Davidson

ii. ELI WILLIAMS[6] PETTY, b. 26 December 1786 Surry Co., N. C.; d. 1 July 1854 Franklin Co., Tenn..;

m. DIANE HARRISON MARTIN 3 March 1810
Wilkes Co., N. C.; d. before 1850 Franklin Co.,
Tenn.; m. (2) SARAH ELIZABETH STEPHENS, b.
1824 Wilkes Co., N. C.[59]
He is a widower in the 1850 Census.[60] He had
married Sarah, 36, by 1860.[61]

iii. LAZARUS D.[6] PETTY., b. 7 June 1789 Surry Co.,
N. C.; d. 7 October 1843 Madison Co.,
Alabama; m. SARAH.

5. iv. JOHN WRIGHT[6] PETTY, b. 28 February 1791
Wilkes Co., N. C.; d. 23 September 1876
Madison Co., Alabama; m. ANNA HARRIS 18
March 1817 Wilkes Co., N. C.; b. 18 January
1798 Montgomery Co., N. C.; d. 13 June 1869
Madison Co., Alabama.

v. ZACHARIAH[6] PETTY, b. 28 May 1793 Wilkes Co.,
N. C.; d. 8 July 1854 Madison Co., Alabama;[62]
m. REBECCA SHACKELFORD 2 January 1823
Madison Co., Alabama, dau. of RICHARD
SHACKELFORD and MARY ANN;[63] b. 26
December 1790 S. C.; d. 26 May 1875
Madison Co., Alabama.[64]

vi. AMELIA[6] PETTY, b. 20 July 1795 Wilkes Co., N.
C.; 17 November 1867 Sherman, Grayson Co.,
Texas; m. DAVID CARLTON 26 September 1814
Wilkes Co., North Carolina.

---

[59] SAR Application of Palmer R. Petty, #93831, citing the 1860
Census. Online database accessed 12 May 2014 at Ancestry.com.
[60] 1850 Census Franklin Co., Tenn., Dist. 8, p. 64B, #856. He has
Elizabeth Stephens, 34, NC, living in his household, and they are next door
(#857) to Collin Stephens, 58, NC. At #855 is Robert Petty, 36, NC,
probably a son.
[61] 1860 Census Franklin Co., Tenn., Dist. 8, p. 146, #1307/1286.
[62] Petty Cemetery, New Market, Madison Co., Ala.
http://www.findagrave.com., #84235013.
[63] Will of Richard Shackelford, 29 December 1823, Madison Co., Ala.,
Probate Record Book 3:70, File 647. Accessed 12 May 2014 at
http://trees.ancestry.com/tree/23421804/person/13572595908/storyx/
2c79cc80-ca02-49db-9674-69ee51615a62?src=search
[64] Petty Cemetery, New Market, Madison Co., Ala.
http://www.findagrave.com., #84235013.

vii. WILLIAM THORNTON[6] PETTY, b. 29 September 1797 Wilkes Co., N. C.; d. after 26 April 1834 and before 1840 Lincoln Co., Tenn.; m. ABIGAIL BAYLESS 3 December 1821 Madison Co., Alabama; b. 20 January 1802 Washington Co., Tenn.; d. 20 December 1883 Lamar Co., Texas.

William T. Petty was living in Lincoln Co., Tenn., in 1830.[65] Abigail Petty was listed as head of household in Madison Co., Tenn., in 1840.[66] Abigail Petty is head of household in Lamar Co., Texas, in 1850,[67] 1860,[68] and 1870.[69]

viii. SALLY[6] PETTY, b. 11 August 1799 Wilkes Co., N. C.; d. 11 February 1801 Wilkes Co., N. C.

ix. JAMES WILLIAM[6] PETTY, b. 12 October 1801 Wilkes Co., N. C.; d. 29 September 1843 Limestone Co., Ala.; m. ELIZABETH FISHBACK MORGAN 4 August 1825 Limestone Co., Ala.

He is probably the "Wm. Pitty" living in Limestone Co., Ala.[70]

6. x. THOMAS MERCE[6] PETTY, b. 5 October 1803 Wilkes Co., N. C.; d. 1887 Hillsboro, Scott Co., Miss.; m. LOUISA WHYTE ROBERTS 4 August 1825 Madison Co., Ala.; b. 19 December 1808 Tennessee; d. 1 January 1889 Ruston, Lincoln Par., La.

xi. BENJAMIN FRANKLIN[6] PETTY, b. 4 November 1805 Wilkes Co., N. C.; d. 6 March 1875 Wilkes Co., N. C.; m. (1) CYNTHIA BRYAN 29 January 1829 Wilkes Co., N. C.; b. 1800 North Carolina; d. 7

---

[65] 1830 Census Lincoln Co., Tenn., p. 264. He had five daughters and no sons listed, who were clearly in addition to the children listed in 1850.

[66] 1840 Census Madison Co., Ala., p. 134. She has one son, four daughters still at home, and seven slaves.

[67] 1850 Census Lamar Co., Tex., Precinct 9, p. 302B, #473. She has children Nancy E., 19, Sarah E., 18, and William H., 17. Nancy was b. Alabama, the others born Tennessee.

[68] 1860 Census Lamar Co., Tex., Precinct 9, p. 128, #127.

[69] 1870 Census Lamar Co., Texas, Beat 1, p. 201A, #289.

[70] 1840 Census Limestone Co., Ala., p. 161.

March 1851 Wilkes Co., N. C.; m. (2) JANE AMANDA NESBITT about 1852 Wilkes Co., N. C.

xii. ELIZA WRIGHT[6] PETTY, b. 28 August 1808 Wilkes Co. N. C.; d. 1839 Scott Co., Miss.;[71] m. ALFRED EASTLAND 2 June 1825 Madison Co., Ala.; b. 10 February 1806 Newberry Dist., S. C.; d. 24 April 1870 Waco, McLennan Co., Tex.[72]

Alfred Eastland was in Lincoln Co., Tenn., in 1830.[73] He was in Scott Co., Miss., in 1850 with what appears to be a blended household,[74] and in 1860 is living in his son-in-law's household.[75]

xiii. DANIEL HARRISON[6] PETTY, b. 28 February 1812 Wilkes Co., N. C.; d. 7 June 1895 Madison Co., Ala.;[76] m. SUSAN ANN STONE 5 November 1833 Madison Co., Ala.; b. 25 May 1816 Madison Co., Ala.; d. 9 January 1859 Madison Co. Ala.[77]

5. JOHN WRIGHT[6] PETTY was born 28 February 1791 in Wilkes Co., North Carolina, and died 23 September 1876 in Madison Co., Alabama. He married ANNA HARRIS 18 March 1817 in Wilkes Co., N. C. She was born 18 January 1798 in Montgomery Co., North Carolina, and died 13 June 1869 in Madison Co., Alabama.

[71] http://trees.ancestry.com/tree/20702711/person/1016255550
[72] First Street Cemetery, Waco, Tex. http://www.findagrave.com., #7055475.
[73] 1830 Census Lincoln Co., Tenn., p. 199, three sons under five, himself 30-39, and his wife, 20-29.
[74] 1850 Census Scott Co., Miss., Hillsboro, p. 260A, #92.
[75] 1860 Census Scott Co., Miss., Hillsboro, p. 32, #207. Next door are Dr. J. W. Lack and Mary Lack, noted elsewhere.
[76] Locust Grove Cemetery, Madison Co., Ala. http://www.findagrave.com., #73942398.
[77] Stone Cemetery, Madison Co., Ala. http://www.findagrave.com., #6256042.

Dr. John Wright Petty[78] was born in North Carolina, but moved to Lincoln Co., Tenn., following his marriage to Anna Harris. He then moved to the adjacent Madison Co., Alabama. There is on record in Madison Co., Ala., a deed of gift dated Feb. 17, 1823, from Sarah Harris of Montgomery Co., N. C., to her beloved daughter Ann Harris and John Wright Petty, her husband, of two slaves. This deed was filed 17 Feb 1823. John Wright Petty and his wife lived for a while in Lincoln Co., Tenn., before moving to Madison Co., Ala. These two counties are adjacent to one another. He died 23 September 1876 and she died 13 June 1869. Both are buried in Madison Co., Ala. John Wright Petty was a physician.

It appears that John Wright Petty and his children were the ones who decided to add an "e" to the spelling of the surname, which is the way the family in Scott Co., Mississippi, spelled the name. For simplicity, I have retained the previous spelling.

Children of JOHN WRIGHT PETTY and ANNA HARRIS:

    i. CLINTON ROWLAND[7] PETTY, b. 25 December 1817 Wilkes Co., N. C.; d. 8 January 1897 Lincoln Co,, Tenn.;[79] m. ELIZA ANN PALMER 9 September 1850 Madison Co., Ala.; b. 1831; d. 1899 Blanche, Lincoln Co., Tenn.[80]

        Hearts have been made sad in our community since we wrote you last. On Friday morning, the 8th inst., at about 2 o'clock, Mr. Clinton Pettey died of old age and the grippe. He was one of our best citizens, a quiet Christian man and beloved by all who knew him. He leaves a wife and a large family of grown children to mourn his death. For a number of years he was a member of the M. E.

---

[78] Hodges, Alice Amis. Ancestry and Descendants of Dr. John Wright Petty of Madison Co., Ala. (Pendleton, S. C., 1978,) p. 7.

[79] Buried in Blanche Cemetery, Blanche, Lincoln Co., Tenn. Located 28 April 2012 at http://findagrave.com.

[80] Buried in Blanche Cemetery, Blanche, Lincoln Co., Tenn. Located 28 April 2012 at http://findagrave.com.

Church, but for months past he was too feeble to often get to the house of God. On Saturday, after funeral service by Rev. Wood Bouldin, he was laid to rest in the cemetery at Blanche to await the resurrection morn.[81]

  ii. WILLIAM W.[7] PETTY, b. 15 May 1819 Wilkes Co., N. C.; d. 30 March 1904 Fresno, California.[82]

7. iii. ALBERT GALLATIN[7] PETTY, 29 May 1820 Lincoln Co., Tenn.; d. 2 June 1879 Scott Co., Mississippi; m. LUVENIA BREWER about 1845 Scott Co., Miss., dau. of WYCHE BREWER and FLORA MCPHERSON; b. 11 February 1825 Butler Co., Alabama; d. 18 February 1897 Newton Co., Miss.

  iv. SARAH ANN[7] PETTY, b. 7 January 1822 Madison Co., Ala.; d. 6 March 1854; m. ELI MITCHELL 8 September 1841 Madison Co., Ala.

  v. WILLIAM HOWARD[7] PETTY, b. 20 February 1823 Madison Co., Ala.; d. 28 August 1860 Nacogdoches, Texas;[83] m. SARAH POWER 19 September 1845 Madison Co., Ala.[84]; b. 20 April 1828; d. 24 December 1885 Nacogdoches Co., Texas.[85]

  vi. NANCY[7] PETTY, b. 26 January 1826 Madison Co., Ala.; d. 6 December 1846 Madison Co., Ala.

8. vii. JOHN WRIGHT[7] PETTY, b. 12 November 1826 Madison Co., Ala.; d. 27 March 1858 Scott Co., Miss.; m. CHRISTIANA BREWER about 1846 Scott Co., Miss., dau. of WYCHE BREWER and

---

[81] *The Fayetteville (TN) Observer* 21 January 1897. (Attached to the photo of his tombstone at location above.)

[82] There are a number of Pettys buried in Odd Fellows Cemetery, Fresno Co., California, who are likely his children, but I have not found a record of his burial.

[83] Buried in Redland Cemetery, Douglass, Nacogdoches Co., Texas. Located 28 April 2012 at http://findagrave.com.

[84] There is also a marriage of William H. Petty and Ann Roberta Ricks 10 March 1848 in Lincoln Co., Tenn. (Tennessee State Marriages 1780-2002. Online database at Ancestry.com, accessed 28 April 2012.)

[85] Buried in Redland Cemetery, Douglass, Nacogdoches Co., Texas. Located 28 April 2012 at http://findagrave.com.

FLORA MCPHERSON; b. about 1827 Butler Co., Ala.

viii. ANN ELIZA[7] PETTY, b. 30 August 1827 Madison Co., Ala.; d. 7 April 1909 Ala.; m. WILLIAM HOWARD 24 November 1852 Madison Co., Ala.; b. 16 April 1826; d. 12 June 1913 Madison Co., Ala.[86]

ix. RICHARD P. [7] PETTY, b. 8 January 1829 Madison Co., Ala.; d. 31 October 1890 Fayetteville, Lincoln Co., Tenn.; m. MARGARET NORRIS.

x. CORNELIA[7] PETTY, b. August 1833 Madison Co., Ala.; d. 17 January 1882. unm.

xi. LUCY[7] PETTY, b. 2 January 1835 Madison Co., Ala.; d. 19 December 1915 Fayetteville, Lincoln Co., Tenn.; m. THOMAS LOVE 26 September 1856 Madison Co., Ala.

xii. NEWTON ELI[7] PETTY, b. 16 April 1838 Madison Co., Ala.; d. August 1924 Madison Co., Alabama.; unm.

xiii. DANIEL BOONE[7] PETTY, b. 25 November 1839 Madison Co., Ala.; d. 2 May 1869 Madison Co., Ala.; unm.

6. THOMAS MERCE[6] PETTY was born 5 October 1803 in Wilkes Co., North Carolina, and died 4 August 1885 in Hillsboro, Scott Co., Mississippi. He married LOUISA WHYTE ROBERTS 4 August 1825 in Madison Co., Alabama. She was born 19 December 1809 in Tennessee and died 1 January 1889 in Ruston, Lincoln Par., Louisiana.

Children of THOMAS PETTY and LOUISA ROBERTS are:

i. ROBERT L.[7] PETTY, b. about 1826 Bedford Co., Tenn.; d. 7 June 1899 Scott Co., Miss.; m.

---

[86] Both are buried in Foster Cemetery, Madison Co., Alabama. Located 28 April 2012 at http://www.findagrave.com.

MARY ANN BUTLER about 1850 Scott Co., Miss.; b. 2 May 1831 Rankin Co., Miss.; d. 27 March 1892 Scott Co., Miss.

ii. HIRAM F.[7] PETTY, b. 1830 Lincoln Co., Tenn.; m. ALMEDA _____.

Hiram F. Petty enlisted as a private in Co. I, 28th (Gray's) Louisiana Infantry on 11 May 1862.[87] H. F. Pettey and Almeda are living in Ward 6, Athens, Claiborne Par., Louisiana, in 1870.[88] Children listed are Imogene, 10, Thomas L., 8, Lathenia (f) 3, and John R., 11/12. All of the children were born in Louisiana. Almeda was born in Georgia.

iii. NANCY[7] PETTY, b. 17 July 1833 Scott Co., Miss.; d. 4 March 1926 Palestine, Anderson Co., Texas; m. SAMUEL CURTIS 1850 Scott Co., Miss.; b. about 1817 Tenn.[89];

iv. BENTON[7] PETTY, b. about 1835 Scott Co., Miss.

Benton Petty appears only on the 1850 Census. I have not been able to locate him in any subsequent records. I have also found no record of his gravestone.

v. W. FERDINAND[7] PETTY, b. about 1837 Scott Co., Miss.; m. ELIZABETH _____.[90]

Ferdinand and Elizabeth are living in Scott Co., Miss., in 1880. She is 35, b. MS, and the children are William 16, May 14, Oliver 10, Floy (f) 8, and Percy 5. Martha Amis is living with her daughter Frances Moore at #84/89, and James Graham and his wife Woodson are living between them.

vi. AMERICA[7] PETTY, b. about 1839 Scott Co., Miss.

---

[87] Confederate Research Sources, 3:125. Online database located on ancestry.com 29 April 2012.

[88] 1870 Census Claiborne Parish, La., p.174B, #151.

[89] 1850 Census Scott Co., Miss., p. 258A, #64/64. Samuel Curtis, M. D., 33, and wife Nancy, 17, are living with her parents next door to Albert G. Petty and John W. Petty. An ancestry file says he was born in Stewart Co., Tenn., and that they married 2 April 1846, which would have made her not quite 13. I think this is unlikely to be the correct date. His date of death is given as 17 August 1874.

[90] 1880 Census Scott Co., Miss., Beat 5, p. 102C, ED 83, #87/92.

vii. AMELIA TENNESSEE[7] PETTY, b. 7 June 1843 Scott Co., Miss.; m. JOSEPH (CUDGE) MCGOWAN about 1860 Scott Co., Miss.[91]

> Tennessee McGowan and her husband "Cudge" are living in Scott Co., Mississippi in 1880.[92] Contrary to his son's statement, he was born in Georgia, not Ireland, and his parents were born in Georgia and South Carolina. They are listed on the same page as Martha Amis, Frances (Amis) Moore, James and Mirnia Woodson (Amis) Graham and Ferdinand Petty.

viii. ANDREW J.[7] PETTY, b. about 1845 Scott Co., Miss.

ix. EMMA[7] PETTY, b. 15 September 1847 Scott Co., Miss.; d. 27 May 1903 Claiborne Parish, La.; m. JOHN FRANKLIN EVERS about 1866 Scott Co., Miss.; b. 30 March 1840 Monroe Co., Ga.; d. 28 August 1897 Claiborne Parish, La.

x. JULIETTA JOSEPHINE[7] PETTY, b. 11 October 1849 Scott Co., Miss.; d. 13 December 1932 Louisiana; m. JAMES RICHARD CARVER 27 May 1869 Scott Co., Miss.; b. 19 February 1846 Autauga Co., Ala.; d. 24 April 1911 Louisiana.[93]

7. ALBERT GALLATIN[7] PETTY was born 29 May 1820 in Lincoln County, Tennessee, and died 2 June 1879 in Scott Co., Mississippi. He married LUVENIA BREWER about 1845 Scott Co., Miss., daughter of WYCHE BREWER and FLORA MCPHERSON. She was born 11

---

[91] Their son, Joseph Manisco McGowan died 23 May 1956 in Cleburne, Johnson Co., Texas, and the death record listed his birth in Scott Co., Miss., 16 June 1885. He stated that his father was born in Ireland. [Texas Deaths 1890-1976. Online database accessed 29 April 2012 at familysearch.org.]

[92] 1880 Census Scott Co., Miss., p. 102C, ED 83, #89/96.

[93] Bluemel, Daniel. Bluemel Family History. 25 October 2011. Located at http://wc.rootsweb.ancestry.com, (db. danielbluemel.) Some of his locations are wrong, but the dates are quite specific.

February 1825 in Butler Co., Alabama, and died 18 February 1897 in Newton Co., Mississippi.

> *Albert G. Petty moved to Madison Co., Ala., when he was an infant. About 1843 he moved to Scott Co., Miss., where he taught at various schools. He married Luvenia Brewer, daughter of Wyche Brewer and Flora McPherson. They settled on a farm about a mile northeast of Sulphur Springs Baptist Church in Scott County. He was a man of medium height and weighed about 140 pounds. He was intelligent and well educated for a man of those times and was a man of influence in his community. He was a Master Mason, a Granger, and a member of the Sulphur Springs Baptist Church where he served for many years as the church clerk. He is buried in the Amis graveyard near Conehatta, Miss.*

Children of ALBERT PETTY and LUVENIA BREWER are:

i. ANNA MISSOURI[8] PETTY, b. 12 March 1847 Scott Co., Miss; m. WARNER BLEDSOE about 1864 Scott Co., Miss.

> *After their marriage, they resided for several years near Sulphur Springs Church, but about 1881 they moved to Union, in Newton County, where they resided for some years. About the year 1889 they moved to Texas and later to McAllister, Oklahoma, where they lived the balance of their lives. They both have been dead several years.*

Children of ANNA PETTY and WARNER BLEDSOE:

1. ANNA CELESTIA[9] BLEDSOE, b. 1866; d. 1950;[94] m. STEPHEN N. ROSS[95] 1899,[96] son of BENJAMIN A. ROSS and ELIZABETH;[97] b.

---

[94] Leonard Cemetery, Fannin Co., Texas. http://www.findagrave.com, #8236922.
[95] Resided in Whitesight, Texas. (A. B. Amis.)
[96] 1900 Census Fannin Co., Texas, Leonard, ED 66, p. 3A, #53.
[97] 1850 Census Edgefield Dist., S. C., p. 32A, #488.

1845 Edgefield Dist. S. C.; d. 1926 Fannin Co., Texas.[98]

In 1940 Anna C. Ross, 74, widowed, is living with Frances Pittman in McAlester, Okla. She was listed as a sister.[99] With her full name, she can be found in 1910[100] and 1920.[101]

2. HIRAM FLOYD[9] BLEDSOE, b. 18 July 1869 Newton Co., Miss.; d. 29 October 1958 Dennison, Grayson Co., Texas;[102] m. SARAH ELIZABETH PAYNE,[103] b. 11 October 1872; d. 19 August 1960 Dennison.[104]

3. FRANCES DELIA[9] BLEDSOE, b. 1876; d. 1941 McAlester, Pittsburg Co., Okla.;[105] m. FORTUNATUS D. PITTMAN,[106] b. 1874, d. 1937 McAlester, Pittsburg Co., Okla.[107]

ii. MARY AUGUSTA[8] PETTY, b. 8 April 1849 Scott Co., Miss., d. 9 July 1922 Meridian, Lauderdale Co., Miss; m. (1) ALBERT GALLATIN AMIS 16 December 1865 Newton Co., Miss., son of JOHN WOODSON AMIS and MARTHA WADKINS. He was b. 15 Jan 1841 Scott Co., Miss., d. 31 July 1878 Newton Co., Miss.; m. (2) WILLIAM BUYCK THORNTON September 1879 Scott Co., Miss., son of JAMES J. THORNTON and SARAH J.

---

[98] Leonard Cemetery, Fannin Co., Texas. http://www.findagrave.com, #8736922

[99] 1940 Census Pittsburg Co., Okla., McAlester, ED 61-36, p. 2A, 305 E. Jackson St.

[100] 1910 Census, Fannin Co., Texas, Leonard, ED 39, p. 5B, #102.

[101] 1920 Census, Fannin Co., Texas, Leonard, ED 46, #141/148. She listed her parents as being b. Georgia/Mississippi, where she had said both in Mississippi previously.

[102] Fairview Cemetery, Dennison, Grayson Co., Texas. http://www.findagrave.com, #92286731.

[103] They have one child, Elizabeth; reside in Denison, Texas. (A. B. Amis.) She was b. 4 September 1907; d. 25 September 2001 Dennison. Fairview Cemetery, http://www.findagrave.com, #92286711. Apparently never married.

[104] Fairview Cemetery, Dennison, Grayson Co., Texas. http://www.findagrave.com, #92286771

[105] Oak Hill Memorial Park, McAlester, Pittsburg Co., Okla., http://www.findagrave.com, #21512761.

[106] Resided in McAlester, Okla., no children. (A. B. Amis.)

[107] Oak Hill Memorial Park, McAlester, Pittsburg Co., Okla. http://www.findagrave.com, #21517252.

BUYCK;[108] b. 3 April 1856 Alabama; d. 1 Feb 1897 Gulfport, Harrison Co., Miss.

Mary Augusta Pettey, daughter of Albert G. Pettey and Luvenia Brewer was born April 8, 1849. She married Albert G. Amis December 16, 1865. After their marriage they lived on a farm in the northwestern part of Newton County until January 1878 when they moved to Conehatta, where her husband died July 31, 1878. They had four children: Bobbet, Elvy, Bertha, and Alvin. In September 1879 she married William Buyck Thornton by whom she had one child, Ruby. After their marriage they lived at Conehatta until 1896 when they moved to Gulfport, where her second husband died in February 1897. She continued to reside at Gulfport until 1905 when she moved to Meridian and lived there until she died July 9, 1922. She was buried in Magnolia Cemetery, at Meridian. The record of all her Amis children is shown in the sketch of that family. She had one child by her second husband, Ruby, who was born July 21, 1881, was educated at E. M. F. College at Meridian and married John H. Matthews, November 21, 1906. They reside at Gulfport, Miss.

Child of MARY PETTY and WILLIAM THORNTON is:

1. RUBY[9] THORNTON, b. 21 July 1881 Newton Co., Miss.; d. 10 November 1967 Gulfport, Harrison Co., Miss.; m. JOHN H. MATTHEWS 21 November 1906 Gulfport, Harrison Co., Miss.; b. 1874 Mobile, Ala.; d. 7 June 1937 Gulfport, Harrison Co., Miss.[109]

Children of RUBY and JOHN MATTHEWS:

a. RUBY ABERNATHA[10] MATTHEWS, b. 23 September 1907 Gulfport.[110]
b. SARAH HARRIS[10] MATTHEWS, b. 23 July 1915 Gulfport.

---

[108] 1870 Census Newton Co., Miss., Twp. 7, range 10, p. 462B, #24.
[109] Buried Evergreen Cemetery.
http://trees.ancestry.com/tree/56016355/
[110] Graduated from Gulfport High School; now student in Greenville Woman's College, Greenville, S. C. (A. B. Amis.)

300

c. JOHN WILLIAM[10] MATTHEWS, b. 4 March 1917 Gulfport.

iii. FRANCES MADORA[8] PETTY, b. 15 Sep 1851 Scott Co., Miss., d. 16 June 1929 Meridian, Lauderdale Co., Miss.; m. J. M. CLEVELAND 2 June 1882 Scott Co., Miss.

Frances Madora Pettey was born September 15, 1851 and married Dr. J. M. Cleveland of Union, Miss., June 3, 1882. After their marriage they lived at Union, where he died in 1895. In December 1903 she and her family moved to Meridian, where she still resides at 3818 Twelfth Street. They had three children.

Children of FRANCES PETTY and J. CLEVELAND:

1. JUNIE[9] CLEVELAND, b. 6 September 1889 Newton Co., Miss.; d. September 1979 Meridian, Lauderdale Co.,. Miss.

    Junie lived two houses behind the big house, at the corner of 12th Street and 39th Avenue. She was interested in family, and lived long enough for me to know as a teen.

2. THOMAS GROVER[9] CLEVELAND, b. 9 October 1885 Newton Co.,. Miss.; d. June 1966 Meridian, Lauderdale Co., Miss.; m. LILLIAN YARBROUGH.

    Dr. Cleveland was often used as the family doctor. When I was a boy, I received allergy shots regularly. Once, when on vacation in Meridian, I needed one of my shots, so Mom took me in to see him. He got an old fashioned glass syringe and needle out and loaded the serum, but then decided the needle looked dull. He said as much, then reached in his desk drawer, pulled out a file, sharpened the bevel, and then gave me the shot. Mom was aghast at his lack of sterile technique.

3. MIMMS I.[9] CLEVELAND, b. 6 September 1889 Newton Co., Miss.; d. 4 July 1973 Birmingham, Jefferson Co., Ala.; m. EMILY MALONE 1922, dau. of JANETTE;[111] b. 13

---

[111] 1920 Census Birmingham, Jefferson Co., Ala., ED 108, p. 7B, #132, address 930 Adams Street. She was a chemist in a steel mill.

March 1894 Ala.; d. 17 August 1996 Houston, Harris Co., Texas.

When I went to Birmingham to start medical school in 1970, my grandmother told me I should call cousin "Mimms and Emily" and gave me their phone number. I did, and they asked me how I was faring. It was hot that September, and I did not have a fan. They invited me to dinner the next night and gave me an old oscillating fan they no longer needed, which I still have.

They fed me and my roommate several meals that first year, before Mimms got sick and I lost touch with them. I recall one evening, probably in the spring of 1971, when they reminisced about life in Birmingham in the 1920's. Mimms commented that he wore celluloid collars with his white shirts and the air around the steel mills in West Birmingham was so bad he had to change them out at noon to keep them looking respectable. After telling several funny stories, Emily commented: "We had good times back then. We had our troubles, too, but I prefer to remember the good times." I have always thought that was a good attitude—realistic, but cheerful.

iv. CORINE FLORENCE[8] PETTY, b. 16 Oct 1853 Scott Co., Miss; d. 15 May 1942 Mills Co., Texas;[112] m. BENJAMIN FRANKLIN BLEDSOE about 1872 Scott Co., Miss., son of BAILEY BLEDSOE and MARY DANIEL JEAN; b. 15 April 1847 Carroll Co., Ga.; d. 3 March 1925 Mills Co., Texas.[113]

After their marriage they resided in the northwestern part of Newton County until about 1889, when they moved to Texas and settled in Mills County, about eight miles from Goldthwaite. Her husband died in 1925. She still resides in the old home. They had twelve children.

Children of CORINE PETTY and FRANK BLEDSOE:

---

[112] Tombstone records her date of birth as 15 November 1852. Goldthwaite Cemetery, Mills Co., Texas. http://www.findagrave.com, #110290830.

[113] Goldthwaite Cemetery, Mills Co., Texas. http://www.findagrave.com, #110290815.

1. MARY ALVIA[9] BLEDSOE, b. 14 September 1872 Newton Co., Miss.; d. 11 April 1947 Mitchell Co., Texas;[114] m. JOHN R. OGLESBY 17 December 1893, son of ROBERT D. OGLESBY and CAROLINE A. ROBERTS; b. 23 February 1870 Mississippi; d. 12 August 1958 Mitchell Co., Texas.[115]

2. ARTHUR FRANKLIN[9] BLEDSOE, b. 5 July 1874 Meridian, Lauderdale Co., Miss.; d. 31 January 1957 Colorado City, Mitchell Co., Texas;[116] m. MATTIE J. WEAVER 9 March 1897 Mills Co., Texas, dau. of BRADFORD K. WEAVER and MARY WEST; b. 20 January 1876 McLennan Co., Texas; d. 6 November 1971 Brookshire, Waller Co., Texas.[117]

Arthur Franklin Bledsoe, 82, died Thursday afternoon at his home after a long illness.

Mr. Bledsoe was born July 5, 1874, in Meridian, Mississippi, but had lived in Mitchell County since 1918. He was a retired farmer, a member of the Baptist Church and Masonic Lodge. He married Miss Mattie Weaver, March 9, 1897, in Goldthwaite...He is survived by his wife, two sons, Marion C. Bledsoe, Dallas, and Hollis D. Bledsoe, Albany, Calif.; four daughters, Mrs. J. D. Kennedy, Stephenville, Mrs. E. W. Montgomery, Odessa, Mrs. Bill Hague, Lamesa, and Mrs. Charles Walters, Brookshire; one brother, C. D. Bledsoe, Stephenville; six sisters, Mrs. George Mauldin, Texas City, Mrs. Earl Bailey, Wichita Falls, Mrs. Daisey Sellers, Goldthwaite, Mrs. Mark Dawson, Loraine, Mrs. A.

---

[114] Westbrook Cemetery, Mitchell Co., Texas. http://www.findagrave.com, #38070289. "Lives at Westbrook, Texas, and have six children, several of whom are married." (A. B. Amis.)

[115] Westbrook Cemetery, Mitchell Co., Texas. http://www.findagrave.com, #38070138.

[116] Colorado City Cemetery, Mitchell Co., Texas. http://www.findagrave.com, #79609581. "...who married and lives at Westbrook, Texas. He has five children, several married." (A. B. Amis.)

[117] Colorado City Cemetery, Mitchell Co., Texas. http://www.findagrave.com, #79615028.

F. King, Colorado City, and Miss Gussie Bledsoe, McLean...[118]

3. ALBERT PERCY[9] BLEDSOE, b. 25 March 1877 Newton Co., Miss.; d. 5 March 1950 Coleman Co., Texas.[119]

4. ALONZO BAILEY[9] BLEDSOE, b. 15 August 1878 Newton Co., Miss.;[120] d. before 1 February 1957.[121]

5. PEARL[9] BLEDSOE, m. EARL BAKER.[122]

6. GUSSIE[9] BLEDSOE, b. 4 August 1885 Scott Co., Miss.; d. 2 May 1979 Clovis, Curry Co., N. M.[123]

Funeral services for Miss Gussie Bledsoe, 93, who died Wednesday at a local nursing home, will be conducted at 2:30 PM Friday from the First Church of the Nazarene...Miss Bledsoe was born August 4, 1885, at Sebastopol, Miss., and had been a resident of Clovis for the past 10 years. She was a school teacher in McLean, Texas, and retired at the age of 72 after a career of teaching for 47 years...[124]

7. FANNIE[9] BLEDSOE, m. MARK DAWSON.[125]

8. CARL DAVIS[9] BLEDSOE, b. 10 June 1888 Newton Co., Miss.; d. 27 October 1974 Stephenville, Erath Co., Texas;[126] m. FANNIE

---

[118] *Big Spring Daily Herald*, 1 February 1957. Dennis Deel, posted at http://www.findagrave.com, #79609581.

[119] Goldthwaite Cemetery, Mills Co., Texas. http://www.findagrave.com, #110290881. "Unmarried, address Goldthwaite, Texas." A. B. Amis.

[120] Goldthwaite Cemetery, Mills Co., Texas. http://www.findagrave.com, #110290905. The entry lists his date of death wrong.

[121] He pre-deceased his brother according to the obituary, which matches the other data I have found. "Unmarried." (A. B. Amis.)

[122] "...married a man named Baker. Address unknown." (A. B. Amis.)

[123] Lawn Haven Memorial Gardens, Clovis, Curry Co., N. M., http://www.findagrave.com, #102449790. "...who is unmarried. Lives in New Mexico." (A. B. Amis.)

[124] Clovis (N. M.) News Journal, 3 May 1979. Brett L. Rowland, Lawn Haven Memorial Gardens, Clovis, Curry Co., N. M., http://www.findagrave.com, #102449790.

[125] "...married Mark Dawson and lives at Roscoe, Texas. They have four children." (A. B. Amis.)

[126] Goldthwaite Cemetery, Mills Co., Texas. http://www.findagrave.com, #110290851. "...who married Fannie Forehand and lives at Goldthwaite, Texas. They have five children. He is Sheriff of Mills County." (A. B. Amis.)

AURA FOREHAND, b. 12 May 1890 Mills Co., Texas; d. 25 July 1984 Mills Co., Texas.[127]

9. CLARENCE WARNER[9] BLEDSOE, b. 20 November 1890 Meridian, Lauderdale Co., Miss.; d. 17 September 1937 Berino, Dona Ana Co., N. M.; m. INA L. SCHREEFER 25 January 1924 El Paso, Texas.[128]

10. DAISY MAE[9] BLEDSOE, b. 4 May 1894 Texas; d. 29 July 1973 Houston, Harris Co., Texas;[129] m. LEMUEL M. SELLERS, b. 1891; d. 1936.[130]

11. JEWELL[9] BLEDSOE, b. 3 January 1892; d. 30 September 1961 Colorado City, Mitchell Co., Texas;[131] m. AUGUST F. KING, b. 16 August 1890 Milam Co., Tex.; d. 26 June 1959 Colorado City, Mitchell Co., Texas.[132]

12. RUBY[9] BLEDSOE, d. after 1957 Galveston Co., Texas; m. GEORGE MAULDIN.[133]

v. THOMAS WRIGHT[8] PETTY, b. 12 August 1855 Scott Co., Miss; d. 1 October 1913 Scott Co., Miss.; m. SARAH AGNES MAJURE 18 December 1878 Leake Co., Miss.;[134] d. 1919 Meridian, Lauderdale Co., Miss.

He married Sallie Majure about 1878. After their marriage they bought the old Wyche Brewer place, near Sulphur Springs Church and they lived there several years. About 1888 they moved to

---

[127] Goldthwaite Cemetery, Mills Co., Texas.
http://www.findagrave.com, #110290867.

[128] Goldthwaite Cemetery, Mills Co., Texas.
http://www.findagrave.com, #9097339. "..who married and lives at El Paso, Texas.. He has one child." (A. B. Amis.)

[129] Goldthwaite Cemetery, Mills Co., Texas.
http://www.findagrave.com, #110291398. "...who married Lem Sellers and has two children. Address Goldthwaite, Texas."

[130] Goldthwaite Cemetery, Mills Co., Texas.
http://www.findagrave.com, #110291420.

[131] Colorado City Cemetery, Mitchell Co., Texas.
http://www.findagrave.com, #46528346. "...who married August King. They have no children. Address, Westbrook, Texas."

[132] Colorado City Cemetery, Mitchell Co., Texas.
http://www.findagrave.com, #46528363.

[133] "...they have two children. Address, Breckenridge, Texas."

[134] Mississippi Marriages, 1776-1935. Accessed 2 February 2014 at Ancestry.com.

Conehatta, and lived there until about 1892 when they returned to their old home, where they continued to live until he died in 1913. After he died, his widow went to live with her daughter Merle McCord, until she died in 1919. They were both buried in the churchyard at Sulphur Springs.

Children of THOMAS PETTY and SARAH MAJURE:

1. MATTIE[9] PETTY, b. 13 October 1879 Scott Co., Miss.; d. 23 August 1957 Newton Co., Miss.;[135] m. WALTER GRAHAM 15 October 1897; b. 11 July 1869 Scott Co., Miss.; d. 6 November 1954 Newton Co., Miss.[136]

2. ALBERT LAFAYETTE[9] PETTY, b 12 July 1881 Scott Co., Miss.;[137] m. EULA MAE HORTON 25 September 1910; b. 20 May 1891; d. 10 December 1981 Scott Co., Miss.[138]

3. AUDIE[9] PETTY, b. 5 August 1883; d. 27 November 1955 Meridian, Lauderdale Co., Miss.;[139] m. GROVER C. HAMILTON about 1912; b. 1 July 1884; d. 28 January 1941.[140]

     Merle and Aud lived behind the "big house" on 12th Street when I was a child. I remember the house as being dark and them being old, although they were contemporaries of my grandfather Wright. In retrospect, Aud may have been sick. I was probably influence by knowing they were my great-grandfather's first cousins.

4. MERLE[9] PETTY, b. February 1886; m. GEORGE C. MCCORD 5 May 1910.

---

[135] Sulphur Springs Baptist Church Cemetery, Conehatta, Newton Co., Miss. http://www.findagrave.com, #88970978.

[136] Sulphur Springs Baptist Church Cemetery, Conehatta, Newton Co., Miss. http://www.findagrave.com, #88970937.

[137] WWI Draft Registration Card. 4 February 2014 at Ancestry.com.

[138] Sulphur Springs Baptist Church Cemetery, Conehatta, Newton Co., Miss. http://www.findagrave.com, #88964367.

[139] Sulphur Springs Baptist Church Cemetery, Conehatta, Newton Co., Miss. http://www.findagrave.com, #88961297.

[140] Sulphur Springs Baptist Church Cemetery, Conehatta, Newton Co., Miss. http://www.findagrave.com, #88961263. Also located there is an interment for Sgt. George T. Hamilton, Battery C., 149th AA Battalion; b. 8 November 1914; d. 26 September 1945. http://www.findagrave.com, #88961337.

After Merle died, my grandmother took me over to the house, where she gave me one of her father's old rocking chairs. It seems he had bought a dozen, half in oak and the other half in maple. I put it in the back of the car and took it back to Birmingham with me. My wife refinished it many years later and now my oldest daughter has it—the fifth generation.

vi. SARAH ELIZABETH[8] PETTY, b. 20 Sept. 1857 Scott Co., Miss., d. 6 March 1901 Louisville, Winston Co., Miss.;[141] m. JOHN BASSETT PARKES 7 December 1875 Scott Co., Miss.,[142] son of WILLIAM T. PARKES and HARRIET I.,[143] b. 10 December 1855 Ga.; d. 31 January 1928 Louisville;[144] m. (2) MARGARET J. GREER; b. 18 June 1868; d. 5 May 1951 Louisville, Winston Co., Miss.[145]

After their marriage they resided for a few years on a farm on the old Jackson road adjoining his father's farm. About 1880 they sold the farm and moved to Philadelphia, in Neshoba County, where they lived for several years. Later they moved to Attalla County and settled on a farm where she died in the fall of 1898 or 1899. Subsequently her husband remarried and now lives at Louisville, Mississippi.

In 1920, he was living in Louisville with Margaret J., 57, and had Harry Parkes 14, and Kendall Parkes, 7, living with him.

Children of SARAH PETTY and JOHN PARKES:

1. LUTHER TILDEN[9] PARKES, b. 15 September 1876; d. 26 November 1965 Fearns Springs,

---

[141] Masonic Cemetery, Louisville, Winston Co., Miss. http://www.findagrave.com. #104315283.

[142] Mississippi Marriages, 1776-1935. Located at Ancestry.com 2 February 2014.

[143] 1900 Census Leake Co., Miss., Edinburg, ED 29, p. 9B, #156. His parents are both living in his household and are identified as such.

[144] Masonic Cemetery, Louisville, Winston Co., Miss. http://www.findagrave.com. #104252786.

[145] Masonic Cemetery, Louisville, Winston Co., Miss. http://www.findagrave.com. #104252822.

Winston Co., Miss.;[146] m. ANNIE ANDERSON; b. 6 February 1881; d. 9 December 1962 Fearns Springs.[147]

> Their children are listed in the 1920 Census as Mary, 16, Tilden, 14, and Mildred, 11.[148] In 1930, they still have Tilden, Jr., at home, but are also caring for Virginia's sons, John P. Kirby, 15, and Albert Kirby, 11.[149]

2. TOMPIE[9] PARKES, b. August 1878; d. about 1918.

3. HARRIET LOU[9] PARKES, b. April 1882 Neshoba Co., Miss.; d. before 1908; m. FRANCIS BOWEN KIRBY about 1908, son of EDWARD KIRBY and ELIZABETH MCCARVER; b. 13 January 1870 Mason, Bolivar Co., Miss.; d. 11 December 1951 Kerrville, Kerr Co., Texas.[150]

4. SARAH FLO[9] PARKES, b. 24 November 1883 Neshoba Co., Miss.; d. 2 April 1931 Pontotoc, Pontotoc Co., Miss.;[151] m. JAMES THOMAS PENNY; b. 9 August 1877; d. 15 December 1958 Pontotoc.[152]

> In the 1900 Census her birth year was given as September 1884.

5. ALBERT[9] PARKES, b. about 1885; d. before 1930, unm.

6. VIRGINIA MAE[9] PARKES, b. April 1887; d. 1927; m. FRANCIS BOWEN KIRBY about 1908, son of EDWARD KIRBY and ELIZABETH MCCARVER; b. 13 January 1870 Mason,

---

[146] Good Hope Cemetery, Fearns Springs, Winston Co., Miss. http://www.findagrave.com. #28819300.

[147] Good Hope Cemetery, Fearns Springs, Winston Co., Miss. http://www.findagrave.com. #28819299.

[148] 1920 Census Winston Co., Miss., Beat 2, ED 131, p. 16A, #280.

[149] 1930 Census Winston Co., Miss., Southeast, ED 4, p. 9A, #182/183. In all the census data he is recorded as a general practitioner.

[150] Kerrville National Cemetery, Kerrville, Kerr Co., Texas. http://www.findagrave.com. #3060053.

[151] Pontotoc Cemetery, Pontotoc Co., Miss. http://www.findagrave.com. #120639085.

[152] Pontotoc Cemetery, Pontotoc Co., Miss. http://www.findagrave.com. #120639174.

Bolivar Co., Miss.; d. 11 December 1951 Kerrville, Kerr Co., Texas.[153]

Virginia Kirby, 22, with F. B. Kirby 39, Albert Parkes 20, Lamar Parkes, 15, and a daughter, Virginia Kirby, 1 4/12 years, are living in Quanah, Hardeman Co., Texas, in 1910.[154] In 1920 they are living in Somervell Co., Texas, and have five children.[155]

His obituary described him as Judge Frank B. Kirby, 81, San Antonio Spanish-American War veteran, born January 13, 1870, in Mason, Mississippi. He was survived by a daughter, Mrs. H. Thomas of San Antonio. His death certificate says he was a resident of 138 Funston Place, San Antonio, and that he died of advanced tuberculosis.[156]

7. LAMAR B.[9] PARKES, b. 6 July 1894 Neshoba Co., Miss.; d. 31 December 1963 Douglas, Cochise Co., Ariz.[157]

vii. JOHN DAVIS[8] PETTY, b. 24 Oct 1861 Scott Co., Miss.; d. 1952 Neshoba Co., Miss.;[158] m. (1) MOLLIE NICHOLSON; m. (2) VIRGINIA S. GULLEY about 1895 Newton Co., Miss.; b. 11 October 1868 Miss.; d. January 1967 Neshoba Co., Miss.[159]

For some years he lived at Union, then later at Neshoba, and for four years at Philadelphia while he was Clerk of the Chancery Court. He now resides at Neshoba, Mississippi.

---

[153] Kerrville National Cemetery, Kerrville, Kerr Co., Texas. http://www.findagrave.com. #3060053.

[154] 1910 Census Hardeman Co., Texas, Quanah, ED 129, p. 2B, #44/49. He was listed as a real estate agent.

[155] 1920 Census Somervell Co., Texas, Justice Pct. 1, ED 80, p. 2A, #29. He was listed as a land title abstractor.

[156] Texas Death Certificates 1903-1982, accessed 2 February 2014 at Ancestry.com.

[157] Julia Page Memorial Park, Douglas, Cochise Co., Ariz. http://www.findagrave.com. #39798925. A. B. Amis said he was not married.

[158] Cedar Lawn Cemetery, Philadelphia, Neshoba Co., Miss. http://www.findagrave.com. #30778344.

[159] Cedar Lawn Cemetery, Philadelphia, Neshoba Co., Miss. http://www.findagrave.com. #30778417.

John D. Petty, 38, and Virginia S., 30, are living in Newton Co., Miss., in 1900.[160] In 1910, Miller is identified as William M., and "Litti Gennie" is 4.[161]

Child of JOHN PETTY and MOLLIE NICHOLSON:

1. MILLER MCELROY[9] PETTY, b. 25 January 1890 Newton Co., Miss.; d. 25 July 1938 Neshoba Co., Miss.;[162] m. CORIN W.; b. 1890; d. 1954 Neshoba Co., Miss.[163]

Children of JOHN PETTY and JENNIE GULLEY:

2. MARKS R.[9] PETTY, b. 4 June 1895 Newton Co., Miss.; d. 16 January 1961 Neshoba Co., Miss.[164]

3. JOHN DEWEY[9] PETTY, b. 16 June 1898 Newton Co., Miss.; d. 6 August 1976 Neshoba Co., Miss.;[165] m. (1) NANNIE GERTRUDE HUNTER 4 February 1920 Neshoba Co., Miss.;[166] m. (2) MITTIE THEO SKINNER; b. 18 September 1911; d. 30 April 2002.[167]

4. GLADYS[9] PETTY, b. 9 April 1901 Neshoba Co., Miss.; d. 9 February 1993 Neshoba Co., Miss.;[168] m. ROBERT HICKS VERNON; b. 13 September 1906; d. 31 January 1991 Neshoba Co., Miss.[169]

---

[160] 1900 Census Newton Co., Miss., Beat 2, ED 50, p. 10A, #168.

[161] 1910 Census Neshoba Co., Miss., Beat 4, ED 81, p. 9A, #103/104.

[162] Cedar Lawn Cemetery, Philadelphia, Neshoba Co., Miss. http://www.findagrave.com. #30779033.

[163] Cedar Lawn Cemetery, Philadelphia, Neshoba Co., Miss. http://www.findagrave.com. #30779103.

[164] Cedar Lawn Cemetery, Philadelphia, Neshoba Co., Miss. http://www.findagrave.com. #30778459.

[165] Golden Grove Cemetery, Neshoba Co., Miss. http://www.findagrave.com. #27802462.

[166] Mississippi Marriages, 1776-1935. Accessed 2 February 2014 at Ancestry.com.

[167] Golden Grove Cemetery, Neshoba Co., Miss. http://www.findagrave.com. #27802509.

[168] Cedar Lawn Cemetery, Philadelphia, Neshoba Co., Miss. http://www.findagrave.com. #30778589.

[169] Cedar Lawn Cemetery, Philadelphia, Neshoba Co., Miss. http://www.findagrave.com. #30778682.

5. RUTH[9] PETTY, b. 3 February 1903 Neshoba Co., Miss.; d. 24 January 1991 Union, Neshoba Co., Miss.;[170] m. ROBERT LUTHER ASHMORE; b. 26 June 1900; d. 30 March 1950 Neshoba Co., Miss.[171]

Funeral services for Ruth Pettey Ashmore were held Tuesday, January 26th from the chapel of Stevens Funeral Home in Union.[172] Rev. Johnny Collins officiated with burial in the Cedar Lawn Cemetery in Philadelphia.

Mrs. Ashmore, 95, died January 24th at Magnolia Regional Personal Care Home in Union. She was retired owner and operator of Union Florist.

Survivors include one son, Jim Ashmore of Union, sister Jackie Pettey of Union; one grandson; three great-grandchildren.

6. JENNY JACQUELINE (JENCINE)[9] PETTY, b. 1904 Neshoba Co., Miss.; d. 25 July 2007 Oxford, Lafayette Co., Miss.[173]

Graveside services for Jennie Jacqueline Pettey were held Thursday, July 26, 2007, at 10 a. m. from Cedar Lawn Cemetery under the direction of McClain-Hayes Funeral Service, Inc. Tom Pettey officiated.

Miss Pettey, 102, died Wednesday, July 25, 2007, in Hermitage Gardens of Oxford in Oxford.

She was born a reared in Neshoba County and was a graduate of Philadelphia High School. She made her home in Memphis, Tenn., most of her life, where she retired as a secretary from Baptist Hospital. She made her home in Union for a number of years and had made her home in Oxford for the past five years.

Miss Pettey was a member of Prescott Baptist Church in Memphis, Tenn. Survivors include eight nieces and nephews.

---

[170] Cedar Lawn Cemetery, Philadelphia, Neshoba Co., Miss. http://www.findagrave.com. #30778790.

[171] Cedar Lawn Cemetery, Philadelphia, Neshoba Co., Miss. http://www.findagrave.com. #30778849.

[172] Union Appeal, Union, Miss., Wednesday, 3 February 1999. Dottie Gilder. http://www.findagrave.com. #30778790.

[173] Cedar Lawn Cemetery, Philadelphia, Neshoba Co., Miss. http://www.findagrave.com. #21677436. The obituary was from this site.

7. LEROY[9] PETTY, b. 14 April 1911 Neshoba Co., Miss.; d. 30 July 1982 Neshoba Co., Miss.;[174] m. PEARL BURT; b. 26 July 1922; d. 19 August 1993 Neshoba Co., Miss.[175]

viii. ALBERT GALLATIN[8] PETTY, b. 29 July 1865 Scott Co., Miss; d. 1 March 1930 Newton Co., Miss.; m. (1) EMILY CARSON about 1903 Scott Co., Miss.; b. 7 May 1885; d. 25 January 1925 Scott Co., Miss.; m. (2) PEARL NESTER December 1926 Lake Co., Miss.; b. 14 July 1890; d. 27 April 1947 Newton Co., Miss.[176]

After they married they lived at Conehatta, Miss., until about 1924, when they moved to Lake, where she died in March 1925. About December 1926 he married Pearl Nester. He was a practicing physician and resided at Lake, where he died in 1929.

Albert G. Pettey and family are listed in the 1920 Census for Beat 3, Newton County.[177] The family is headed by "A. G.," female, 39, in 1930, evidently Pearl.[178] She had her nephew, Lelus Cooper, 18 months, living with her. Next door was J. C. Cooper, 44 year old Methodist Episcopal Church minister, likely a brother or brother-in-law.

Children of ALBERT PETTY and EMILY CARSON:

1. THOMAS C.[9] PETTY, b. 1909 Newton Co., Miss.
2. CHRISTINE[9] PETTY, b. 1911 Newton Co., Miss.
3. MARY FRANCES[9] PETTY, b. 7 August 1912 Newton Co., Miss.; d. 30 January 1933 Newton Co., Miss.;[179] m. H. C. SMITH.

---

[174] North Bend Methodist Church Cemetery, Neshoba Co., Miss. http://www.findagrave.com. #29117034.

[175] North Bend Methodist Church Cemetery, Neshoba Co., Miss. http://www.findagrave.com. #29117043.

[176] All three are buried in Conehatta Methodist Cemetery, Newton Co., Miss. (Located at http://www.findagrave.com. Accessed 29 April 2012.

[177] 1920 Census Newton Co., Miss., Beat 3, ED 95, p. 12B, #203/205.

[178] 1930 Census Scott Co., Miss., Lake, ED 4, p. 2B, #39/46. They lived on Loper Street.

[179] Conehatta Methodist Church Cemetery, Newton Co., Miss. http://wwwfindagrave.com, #88392580.

4. SAMUEL[9] PETTY, b. February 1916 Newton Co., Miss.
5. LUVENIA[9] B. PETTY, b. July 1919 Newton Co., Miss.
6. CLARENCE[9] PETTY, b. about 1920 Newton Co., Miss.
7. KATIE RUTH[9] PETTY, b. about 1922 Newton Co., Miss.

8. JOHN WRIGHT[7] PETTY was born 12 November 1826 in Madison Co., Alabama, and died 27 March 1858 in Scott Co., Mississippi. He married CHRISTIANA BREWER about 1846 in Scott Co., Miss., daughter of WYCHE BREWER and FLORA MCPHERSON. She was born about 1827 in Butler Co., Alabama.

Children of JOHN W. PETTY and CHRISTIANA BREWER:

i. VIRGINIA[8] PETTY, m. MARCUS LAFAYETTE CLOUD 30 April 1874 Scott Co., Miss.; b. 22 December 1842; d. 14 August 1903 Scott Co., Miss.
ii. WRIGHT[8] PETTY, m. MARY MILLSAPS.
iii. JOHN WILLIAMS[8] PETTY, b. 16 November 1854 Scott Co., Miss.; d. 22 December 1936 Scott Co., Miss.; m. EMILY S. WALL 22 November 1893 Scott Co., Miss.; b. 28 May 1866 Newton Co., Miss.; d. 6 May 1902 Scott Co., Miss.
iv. FLORA ANN[8] PETTY, b. 30 September 1852 Scott Co., Miss.; d. 26 September 1935 Scott Co., Miss.[180]

[180] Sanders, Delores Pickering. Remember Me: Scott County [MS] Cemetery Census, 2nd Ed., 1999, Sulphur Springs Baptist Church, p. 2266.

Chapter 8: Descendants of 1860 Richard Langford of Macon County, Alabama

The father of Dr. T. D. Langford was born in the earlier part of the last century and lived and died near Auburn, Alabama. He had two daughters, Scrap, who married William Langford, and Emma, who married a man named Jeffreys. He had four sons: Thomas Davis, Henry, Joel, and Philip. Philip married and settled in Montgomery and was a merchant there. Henry married and settled in Leake County, Miss., where he reared a large family, but I never knew any of them. Joel married and settled in Newton County, Miss. He had two daughters, Mollie, who married Dempsey Pace, and Sallie, who married Fred Weaver. Both are now dead. He had five sons, Bill, John, Eck, Henry, and Charley, who went to Texas more than forty years ago and all trace of them is lost.[1]

Genealogical Summary

1. RICHARD[1] LANGFORD was born 9 October 1772 in Hanover Co., Virginia, and died 12 May 1860 in Macon Co., Alabama. He married (1) AMELIA SOPER 22 May 1801 in Montgomery Co., Maryland, daughter of ZADOK SOPER and ANN _____. She was born in Prince Georges Co., Maryland, and died about 1823 in Hancock Co., Georgia. He married (2) NANCY HEATH 2 December 1824 in Putnam Co., Georgia. She was born 1800 in Georgia and died 1872 in Lee Co., Alabama.

The information presented was first collected by Dan Langford,[2] whose father was a first cousin of Mary Salome (Langford) Amis. He told me by e-mail in 2001 that his father had always been grateful to

---

[1] A. B. Amis goes on to state the biography of Dr. T. D. Langford, which is quoted under his entry.

[2] Dan Langford was living in Spring, Texas, in 2001, and died in 2006.

Judge Amis, who took him under his wing when his parents died, and paid for his education. He had originally been in contact with Frances (Amis) Floyd, and copies of that correspondence were available. He also published an earlier version of his findings in a local genealogy journal.[3]

According to Dan's notes, Richard Langford was born in Hanover Co., Virginia, but moved to the Eastern Shore of Maryland as a child. Efforts to use this clue to locate the parents of Richard Langford have not, as yet, borne fruit.[4]

Richard Langford has not been identified in the 1800 or 1810 census, but is recorded the Register of St. George's Parish, then Montgomery Co., Maryland, now District of Columbia. The Register records his marriage to Amelia Soper 22 May 1801, and the birth of his first child, Henry Norman Langford, b. 13 March 1802, baptized 25 April 1802. The Register also records the births of Ann Turner Langford and Langford, Carmila.

According to his obituary, Richard Langford was a "mechanic" who was involved in the building of the United States Capitol. Richard Langford bought

[3] Langford, Dan A. The life of Richard Langford as Gleaned from Public Records. Tap Roots 1993;30(3):101-104.

[4] Peden, Henry C. Revolutionary Patriots of Worcester & Somerset Counties, Maryland, 1775-1783. (Westminster Md.: Willow Bend Books, 2000,) pp. 174-175 shows the following data about people named "Lankford." Benjamin Lankford (1758-   ) Son of Lazarus & Rachel Lankford, b. in Coventry Parish Sept. 12, 1758. Elijah Lankford (1752-   ), applied for a pension in Somerset Co. on April 16, 1818, at age 66. Wife may have been named Hannah. Ephraim, Ezekiel, Jacob, and Jesse, John, Joseph, Joshua, Killum, Levi, & Thomas Lankford were privates in Somerset militia, 1780. Jesse is probably Jesse Maddux Langford (1760-   ) son of Lazarus and Rachel Lankford, b. in Coventry Parish Oct. 4 or 5, 1760. William Lankford, (1761-   ) Son of William and Rachel Lankford, born in Coventry Parish Jan. 9, 1761.

Since Richard Langford was in Prince Georges Co., Maryland, when he first appeared in public records, it is possible there is a connection to a different family, in this case Robert Langford, carpenter, of Prince Georges Co., Maryland, who bought a tract of land there 27 Feb 1743, and sold it 5 October 1745. (See my note: Robert Langford, Anne Arundel and Prince Georges Co., Maryland, 1745.

http://genforum.genealogy.com/langford/messages/1688.html.

115 acres of land in Montgomery Co., Md., from John Turner, executor for the estate of Shadrack Turner on 5 September 1812 for $500. On 24 June 1813 Richard Turner mortgaged the property for $200 to Thomas Cramphin, which he apparently repaid, as he sold the tract to George Moore on 2 May 1815 for $741.44. All told, he appears to have recouped the initial purchase price, covered the $200 mortgage, and made $41.44 from the transaction.

Richard Langford had service during the War of 1812. He served as a draftee in an Extra Battery of Maryland militia attached to the 4th Brigade from 26 July to 2 September 1813. A detachment of this unit under Captain Riley marched to Annapolis on 12 & 13 August 1813, with Richard Langford among the men in this detachment.

Richard Langford does not appear in either the 1800 or 1810 census, perhaps because he was living in the District of Columbia. He moved from the District to Hancock Co., Georgia between 2 May 1815, when he sold his land, and 1817, when he appears on a list of purchasers in Hancock Co., Georgia. He appears on the 1820 Census in Hancock Co., Ga.[5] In the 1821 Land Lottery, Richard Langford of Hancock Co., Ga. He was on the tax rolls there as late as 1824.[6] He married Nancy Heath in neighboring Putnam Co., Ga., 2 December 1824.

Before his marriage, Richard Langford made a deed 1 December 1824 Putnam Co., Ga., conveying

---

[5] 1820 Census Hancock Co., Ga., p. 87, [121001-22010].

[6] Euclid Langford died, testate in Hancock Co., Ga., in 1810, naming his widow, Elizabeth and children Nicholas, John, Edmund, George N., Robert, and Henry. Euclid Langford and his sons were born in Virginia, three moved to Putnam Co., in the early 1820's, and George N. (Nicholson in one report) Langford lived next door to Henry N. Langford in Muscogee Co., Ga., in 1830. This suggested a relationship between these two families. Recently, use of Y-DNA testing has shown that two of the male descendants of 1810 Euclid Langford of Hancock Co., Ga., are J2a, while two male descendants of 1860 Richard Langford of Macon Co., Ala., have been found to be R1b1. This effectively excludes any kinship between these two families. http://www.familytreedna.com/public/Langford. Accessed 10 August 2008.

personal property (three slaves) after his death to his children: Henry, Martha, John, Albert, Elizabeth, Carmila, and Rutha Ann Langford.[7] This was witnessed by George N. Langford. On 8 January 1827, Richard Langford, as the assignee of Henry N. Langford, petitioned to court to require the administrators of the estate of George Meadows to issue a deed for Lot 59, 14th District, Butts Co., formerly Monroe Co., Ga., because Henry N. Langford and George Meadows had entered into a contract 3 January 1822 for the sale, but the deed had not been executed. The Court decided in favor of Richard Langford in February 1827. On 27 May 1827 Richard Langford entered the deed for lot 59 in Butts Co., Georgia. Richard Langford of Talbot Co., Ga., sold the lot in Butts County to Robert J. Smith 6 February 1830 for $500, which was the price Henry N. Langford had originally paid George Meadows.

Richard Langford was found in Talbot Co., Ga., in the 1830 Census.[8] In the 1832 Land Lottery, Richard Langford of Talbot Co., Ga., won lot 199, district 21, Sec. 3. On 26 December 1835 Richard Langford of Harris Co., Ga., bought lot 250 in the 17th Dist. for $400 in a deed recorded in Butts Co., Ga. He bought 50 acres in lot 250 of the 17th District for $400 on 29 January 1836 in Harris Co., Ga., and the same day both tracts to Lewis Peters of Wilkes Co., Ga., for $1550. Richard Langford appeared on the records of an estate sale in Troup Co., Ga., 9 June 1836, but was probably visiting from nearby Harris County, as he was still there in 1840.[9] On 15 January 1843 Richard Langford sold lot 282 of the 17th District for $900. He appeared in Muscogee Co., Ga., court 9

---

[7] Putnam Co., Ga., Deed Book K:419.

[8] 1830 Census Talbot Co., Ga., one male under five, two 15-20, one 50-60; one female under 5, two 15-20, 1 20-30. He also had three slaves boys under 10, two slave girls under 10, and one girl 10-24.

[9] 1840 Census Harris Co., Ga., one male under five, two 5-10, one 15-20, one 60-70, one female 5-10, one 15-20, one 30-40, one slave boy under 10, three men 10-24, two girls under 10, and one 24-36.

June 1843 as agent for Elizabeth Langford, widow of a Revolutionary War soldier (probably Euclid Langford) to claim lot 151, dist. 3, Lee Co., Ga., awarded to Elizabeth Langford of Putnam Co., Ga., in the 1827 Land Lottery. Whether he lived in Muscogee Co., Ga., or was just visiting is uncertain.

He moved to Macon Co., Alabama, by May 1845, when he bought at public auction the southwest ¼ of section 32, township 19, range 25. He must have acquired additional land, for on 17 January 1848 he sold 80 acres in the northeast ¼ of section 6, township 18, range 25 for $200. On 11 January 1849 they sold the northwest ¼ of the same section for $75. He sold the 80 acres of the NE ¼ of section 6 for $200 on 16 May 1850.

Richard Lankford, 77, born Virginia, was recorded in the 1850 Census with real estate valued at $1800. Nancy was 50, Richard, 19, William 16, Robert 12, Amanda 10, and Anne E., all born in Georgia, were also present.

Nancy Langford probated the will of Richard Langford in Macon Co., Alabama, 23 May 1860. The estate was declared insolvent in 1865 and probate was closed.

Children of RICHARD LANGFORD and AMELIA SOPER:

2. i. HENRY NORMAN[2] LANGFORD, b. 13 March 1802 Montgomery Co., Maryland; d. after 12 Dec 1881 Chilton Co., Alabama; m. (1) ELIZABETH DAVIS 12 July 1827 Putnam Co., Ga., dau. of THOMAS DAVIS and ELIZABETH _____; b. about 1810 Georgia; d. about 1838 Harris Co., Ga.; m. (2) ADELINE CHEATHAM 14 December 1838 Muscogee Co., Ga.

ii. ANN TURNER[2] LANGFORD, b. 27 May 1803 Montgomery Co., Md.; d. before 1 December 1824.

Ann was not listed as one of the children of his first wife to whom Richard Langford left three slaves the day prior to his marriage to Nancy Heath. She may well have died much earlier in childhood.

iii. MARTHA[2] LANGFORD, b. about 1805 Montgomery Co., Md.; d. after 1827 Putnam Co., Ga.; m. (1) REUBEN HERNDON[10] 28 February 1825 Putnam Co., Ga.; m. (2) JAMES WILSON 29 August 1827 Putnam Co., Ga.

iv. ALBERT   G.[2]   LANGFORD,   b.   about   1806 Montgomery Co., Md.; d. after 1880 Floyd Co., Ga.; m. (1) EMELINE BRANNAN 12 November 1839 Harris Co., Ga.; m. (2) EMILY R. _____ about 1875 in Georgia.

Albert Langford, 33, and Emaline, 24, along with children Martha 8, Joshua 6, Margaret 4, and John 7/12, are living in Talbot Co., Ga., in 1850.[11] He was living in Macon Co., Ala., when his father's will was probated in May 1860, and they are recorded in the Southern District in the Census.[12] In 1880 they were living in Floyd Co., Ga., where he stated he was 73 and born in DC. Also in the household, presumably as a second family, are Emily R. 37, Albert G. 4 AL, and Lucy P. 2 AL.[13] This implies a move to Floyd Co., Ga., about 1878. It is certainly possible that Emily R. Langford is the wife of one of his sons, but she is certainly not his daughter.

Children of ALBERT LANGFORD and EMELINE:

1. MARY E.[3] LANGFORD, b. 1840 Georgia
2. MARTHA[3] LANGFORD, b. 1842 Georgia;
3. JOSHUA[3] LANGFORD, b. 1844 Georgia;
4. MARGARET[3] LANGFORD, b. 1846 Georgia;

---

[10] The name was transcribed as Reuben Herrendery in another source. http://freepages.genealogy.rootsweb.ancestry.com/~langford/marriages.htm. Accessed 8 August 2008.

[11] 1850 Census Talbot Co., Ga., p. 237, #205/205.

[12] 1860 Census Macon Co., Ala., p. 736, #265/275. Albert is 50, born in DC, Emaline is 34, b. in Ga. The children show Mary E. 18 GA, Martha 16 GA, Joshua 14 AL, Margaret 12 AL, John 10 AL, Sugar 6 AL, Emma 4 AL, and Jane 2 AL. He was an overseer.

[13] 1880 Census Floyd Co., Ga., Chiulo, p. 325, Dist. 72, #73/73.

5. JOHN[3] LANGFORD, b. March 1850 Talbot Co., Ga.;

6. SUGAR[3] LANGFORD, b. 1854 Alabama;

7. EMMA[3] LANGFORD, b. 1856 Alabama;

8. JANE[3] LANGFORD, b. 1858 Alabama;

v. JOHN T.[2] LANGFORD., b. 3 July 1807 Montgomery Co., Md.; d. 20 January 1893 Yalobusha Co., Mississippi; m. MARTHA JANE CHAMPION 12 September 1843 Muscogee Co., Ga.

Muscogee Co., Ga., records include many references to the family of George N. Langford, son of 1810 Euclid Langford of Hancock Co., Ga. The marriage of John T. Langford and Jane Champion is of record.[14] John T. Langford of Capt. Marcus' Dist., Putnam Co., Ga., was a fortunate drawer in the 1827 Land Lottery of section 1, district 32, lot 180, Lee Co., Ga.[15] John T. Langford was listed as a resident of Georgia in his father's probate record in 1860. He appears in Columbus, Ga., in the census of that year.[16] He was in Harris Co., Ga., in 1870,[17] and in 1880 he and Martha were in Yalobusha Co., Miss.[18]

Children of JOHN LANGFORD and MARTHA:

1. WILLIAM[3] LANGFORD, b. 1845 Georgia
2. EMILY[3] LANGFORD, b. 1849 Georgia
3. REBECCA[3] LANGFORD, b. 1854 Georgia

vi. ELIZABETH[2] LANGFORD, b. about 1809 Md.; d. before 1844 in Ga.; m. JOHN W. CARTER 15 December 1829 Putnam Co., Ga., son of JOHN CARTER and MARY KENDRICK.

---

[14]http://files.usgwarchives.net/ga/muscogee/vitals/marriages/musc marr.txt.

[15] http://files.usgwarchives.net/ga/deeds/1827/sur/surn-ll.txt.

[16] 1860 Census Muscogee Co., Ga., Columbus, p. 368, #528/528. He was said to be 50, and like his brother, also an overseer. Martha J. is 41, William 15, Emily 11, and Rebecca 6, all born in Georgia.

[17] 1870 Census Harris Co., Ga., p. 187B, #1989. He was a farmer. His wife and two daughters were with him.

[18] 1880 Census Yalobusha Co., Miss., ED 206, p. 142D, #159/160. Also living in the household was a granddaughter, Ida McKee, 15, born in Georgia.

Mary Kendrick died testate 1822 in Putnam Co., Ga., with Richard Wright, probably Richard W. Wright, as a witness.[19]

John Carter and the children of Elizabeth Carter were heirs of Richard Langford in 1860, but their whereabouts were unknown.[20]

vii. CARMILLA[2] LANGFORD, b. 7 September 1811 Montgomery Co., Md.; d. about 1846 Macon Co., Ala.; m. GREEN B. STEPHENS 15 September 1834 Talbot Co., Ga.; b. 25 March 1812 Georgia; d. 18 August 1890 Randolph Co., Ala.;[21] m. (2) ALAMEDA HOWARD 12 October 1847 Macon Co., Ala.; m. (3) PENNY FRANCES TILLMAN 25 July 1861 Macon Co., Ala.;[22] b. 25 December 1836 Alabama; d. 16 December 1912 Randolph Co., Ala.[23]

The children of Carmilla Stephens, ages and addresses unknown, were legatees of Richard Langford in 1860.

Green B. Stephens, 38, Ga., is head of household in Macon Co., Ala., in 1850 with Alameda, 21.[24] In 1866, he was still in Macon Co., Ga.[25] In 1880, he and Penny were in Heard Co., Ga.[26]

Children of CARMILLA and GREEN STEPHENS:

1. MARTHA J.[3] STEPHENS, b. 1835 Ga.

---

[19] 1865 Richard W. Wright of Decatur Co., Ga., son of 1832 John Wright of Clarke Co., Ga. This family was presented by me in *Southside Virginia Wright Families, 1760-1820.* (Berwyn Heights, MD: Heritage Press, 2014.)

[20] There is a John W. Carter, 59 GA, farmer, with wife Gatsey M., 46 GA, and daughter Eliza W., 10 F AL, who seems likely in the 1860 Census Walker Co., Texas, Newport, p. 104, #185/182.

[21] Paran Missionary Baptist Church Cemetery, Randolph Co., Ala. http://www.findagrave.com., #77508300.

[22] Alabama, Select Marriages, 1816-1957. Accessed 4 April 2014 at Ancestry.com.

[23] Paran Missionary Baptist Church Cemetery, Randolph Co., Ala. http://www.findagrave.com., #77508285.

[24] 1850 Census Macon Co., Ala., p. 259A, #913.

[25] 1866 Alabama State Census. Accessed 4 April 2014 at Ancestry.com.

[26] 1880 Census Heard Co., Ga., Dist. 939, ED 64, p. 68C, #144.

322

2. SARAH J. [3] STEPHENS, b. 1837 Ga.
3. EUGENIA[3] STEPHENS, b. 1840 Ga.; m. IRA B. WRIGHT 23 July 1861 Macon Co., Ala.[27]
4. ALEXANDER H.[3] STEPHENS, b. 1843 Ga.; m. S. WILHITE 16 November 1866 Macon Co., Ga.[28]
5. CHARLES[3] STEPHENS, b. 1845 Macon Co., Ala.

viii. RUTHA ANN[2] LANGFORD, d. before 1850; m. HENRY DUDNEY 15 April 1838 Harris Co., Ga.

Neither Rutha Ann, Henry Dudney, or any children of Rutha Ann were identified as heirs of Richard Langford, so she probably died *sine prole*.

Children of RICHARD LANGFORD and NANCY HEATH:

ix. SAMUEL TROUP[2] LANGFORD, b. about 1825 Putnam Co., Ga.; d. before 1870; m. ELIZA ANN PIERCE 13 March 1847 Upson Co., Ga.

They are living in the Northern Division of Macon Co., Ala., in 1860.[29] She is probably the Eliza Langford living in Upson Co., Ga., in 1870.[30] Eliza Langford is living with son John in Pike County, Ga., 1880, and with son William J. Langford in Spalding Co., Ga., in 1900[31] and 1910.[32]

Children of SAMUEL LANGFORD and ELIZA PRINCE:

1. JAMES R.[3] LANGFORD, b. 1848 Macon Co., Ala.
2. WILLIAM JACKSON[3] LANGFORD, b. 1850 Macon Co., Ala.; d. 5 September 1926 Spalding Co., Ga.;[33] m. FANNIE SEARS; b.

---

[27] Alabama, Select Marriages, 1816-1957. Accessed 4 April 2014 at Ancestry.com.

[28] Alabama, Select Marriages, 1816-1957. Accessed 4 April 2014 at Ancestry.com.

[29] 1860 Census Macon Co., Ala., Northern Div., p. p. 94, #697/708.

[30] 1870 Census Upson Co., Ga., p. 138B, #1032.

[31] 1900 Census Spalding Co., Ga., Union, ED 95, p. 16A, #300.

[32] 1910 Census Spalding Co., Ga., Griffin, ED 117, p. 3B, #19/32. They lived at 515 W. Solomon St.

[33] Oak Hill Cemetery, Griffin, Ga. http://www.findagrave.com., #36725980.

about 1854 Ga.; d. after 1930 Spalding Co., Ga.[34]

3. MARY[3] LANGFORD, b. 1852 Macon Co., Ala.

4. ELIZABETH[3] LANGFORD, b. 1854 Georgia.

5. THOMAS[3] LANGFORD, b. 1856 Macon Co., Ala.; d. 1891-1900 Hempstead Co., Ark.;[35] m. THOMIE F. about 1877 Pike Co., Ga.;[36] b. March 1861 Pike Co., Ga.

6. JOHN E.[3] LANGFORD, b. 28 August 1858 Macon Co., Ala.; d. 5 July 1921 Chambers Co., Ala.;[37] m. MARY JANE HOWELL 1880 Pike Co., Ga.,[38] dau. of WILLIAM HOWELL and MARY KNIGHT;[39] b. 6 May 1857 Pike Co., Ga.; d. 19 March 1940 Chambers Co., Ala.[40]

x. FRANCES G.[2] LANGFORD, b. about 1827 Putnam Co., Ga.; d. 7 July 1914 Coosa Co., Ala.;[41] m. ISHAM GWINN FUNDERBURK 28 January 1848 Macon Co., Ala.;[42] b. about 1817 S. C.;

They are in Macon Co., Ala., in 1850, with daughter Mary A., less than 1 year old.[43] Isham G. Funderburk patented 80 acres of land in Butler Co., Ala., 1 October 1860.[44] In 1870[45] and 1880[46]

---

[34] 1930 Census Spalding Co., Ga., Griffin, ED 3, p. 26A, #594/614. She was living with her step-mother, Nannie Sears, 86.

[35] 1900 Census Hempstead Co., Arkansas, Redland, ED 51, p. 9A. #150/151.

[36] 1880 Census Pike Co., Ga., Dist. 581, ED 107, p. 158A, #33.

[37] Penton Church of God Cemetery, Chambers Co., Ala. http://www.findagrave.com., #50931649.

[38] 1880 Census Pike Co., Ga., Zebulon, ED 107, p. 141C, #58. 1900 Census Chambers Co., Ala., Lanette, ED 9, p. 2B, #29/31.

[39] Alabama Deaths, 1908-1974. Accessed 25 April 2014 at Ancestry.com.

[40] Penton Church of God Cemetery, Chambers Co., Ala. http://www.findagrave.com., #50931697.

[41] Alabama Deaths, 1908-59, Vol. 7, #162. Accessed 26 April 2014 at Ancestry.com.

[42] Alabama, Select Marriages, 1816-1957. Accessed 4 April 2014 at Ancestry.com.

[43] 1850 Census Macon Co., Ala., Dist. 21, p. 250A, #791.

[44] U. S. General Land Office Records, 1796-1907. Accessed 26 April 2014 at Ancestry.com. The land was described as the east half of the northeast quarter, section 36, Twp. 8N, Range 13-E.

[45] 1870 Census Butler Co., Ala., Twp. 8, p. 335A, #79. He is listed as a carpenter. Also lost 10 years in age, but this is clearly an error.

they are in Butler Co., Ala. In 1910 she is living with her youngest daughter and her husband in Coosa Co., Ala.[47]

Children of FRANCES and ISHAM FUNDERBURK:

1. MARY[3] FUNDERBURK, b. 1850 Macon Co., Ala.;
2. ROBERT PERRY[3] FUNDERBURK, b. 16 December 1854 Macon Co., Ala.; d. 24 October 1930 Luverne, Crenshaw Co., Ala.;[48] m. KANSAS NEBRASKA LAWLESS, dau. of GEORGE LAWLESS and RACHEL SMITH; b. 3 August 1855 Ala.; d. 14 January 1940 Luverne, Crenshaw Co., Ala.[49]
3. WILLIAM[3] FUNDERBURK, b. about 1857 Macon Co., Ala.; d. after 1900 Oklahoma.[50]
4. JOHN[3] FUNDERBURK, b. 1859 Macon Co., Ala.
5. MALISSA[3] FUNDERBURK, b. 1864 Butler Co., Ala.
6. MINNIE[3] FUNDERBURK, b. 1868 Butler Co., Ala.; m. JOHN W. PARKER 4 July 1885 Butler Co., Ala.
7. MAGGIE[3] FUNDERBURK, b. 1871 Butler Co., Ala.; d. after 1940 Coosa Co., Ala.; m. WILLIAM PRESTON SHAW 1893,[51] son of WILLIAM C. SHAW and MARY JANE BANKS; b. about 1868 Ala.; d. 20 January 1952 Coosa Co., Ala.[52]

xi. RICHARD[2] LANGFORD, b. about 1831 Talbot Co., Ga.; d. before 1860 Macon Co., Alabama.

---

[45] 1880 Census Butler Co., Ala., Georgiana, ED 41, p. 456A, not numbered.

[47] 1910 Census Coosa Co., Ala., Goodwater, ED 58, p. 4A, #68.

[48] Alabama, Deaths and Burials Index, 1881-1974. Accessed 26 April 2014 at Ancestry.com.

[49] Alabama, Deaths and Burials Index, 1881-1974. Accessed 26 April 2014 at Ancestry.com.

[50] He was a boarder with Joseph F. Hunter and family in Twp. 8, Chickasaw Nation, Indian Territory, ED 129, p. 28B, #512/527. He was manager of a stock farm.

[51] 1900 Census Coosa Co., Ala., Goodwater, ED 21, p. 5A, #95/101. They are living with his brother and another couple in the same dwelling.

[52] Alabama, Deaths and Burials Index, 1881-1974. Accessed 26 April 2014 at Ancestry.com.

He is not named in his father's estate record, so presumably died between 1850 and 1860.

xii. WILLIAM J.[2] LANGFORD., b. about 1835 Harris Co., Ga.

W. J. Langford, 25, clerk, is in Opelika, Alabama in 1860.[53]

xiii. ROBERT WATTS[2] LANGFORD, b. 31 December 1837 Harris Co., Ga.; d. 4 December 1862 Scopes River, Rutherford Co., Indiana; m. MARGARET HILL HARRIS 28 February 1860 Macon Co., Ala.;[54] b. 3 May 1841 Jasper Co., Ga.; d. 11 July 1884 Johnson Co., Texas.[55]

Margaret Harris is living with her mother J. M. Harris, in Johnson Co., Texas, in 1880.[56] Her son, Robert H., 16, is living with them.

Child of ROBERT LANGFORD and MARGARET:

1. NANCY E.[3] LANGFORD, b. 31 December 1860 Macon Co., Ala.; d. 18 September 1873 Cleburne, Johnson Co., Tex.[57]
2. ROBERT HARRIS[3] LANGFORD, b. 26 November 1862 Macon Co., Ala.; d. 3 June 1935 Jones Co., Tex.;[58] m. (1) LELAH A. POWELL 1887 Johnson Co., Tex.;[59] b. 30 January 1868; d. 5 January 1901 Johnson Co., Tex.;[60] m. (2)

---

[53] 1860 Census Russell Co., Ala., Opelika, p. 1079, #48/46. There is a William Langford, 33 GA, living in Canton, Madison Co., Miss., in 1870 [Beat 1, ED 37, p. 29.] He is still there in 1880, but said both parents were born in Georgia, so I am not sure this is the same William Langford.

[54] Alabama, Select Marriages, 1816-1957. Accessed 4 April 2014 at Ancestry.com.

[55] Laramore Cemetery, Cleburne, Texas. http://www.findagrave.com., #15180664.

[56] 1880 Census Johnson Co., Texas, Pct. 5, ED 85, p. 359A, #347.

[57] Laramore Cemetery, Cleburne, Texas. http://www.findagrave.com., #15180651.

[58] Texas Death Certificates, #29331, [Texas Death Certificates, 1903-1982, accessed 26 April 2014 at Ancestry. com] in Jones Co., although the physician who certified the death lived in Stamford, and he was buried in Highland Cemetery, Stamford, Tex. http://www.findagrave.com., #40553256. He gave his birth year as November 1862 in the 1900 census, as the death certificate does also, although it was shown as 1861 on the tombstone.

[59] 1900 Census Johnson Co., Tex., J. P. 1, ED 55, p. 11B, #197.

[60] Sand Flat Cemetery, Johnson Co., Tex.

NANCY LULA EMMALINE HARRELL; b. 17 December 1868; d. 21 December 1946 Haskell Co., Tex.[61]

xiv. AMANDA M.[2] LANGFORD, b. about 1842 Harris Co., Ga.; m. JOHN B. WATSON 10 December 1856 Macon Co., Ala.;[62] b. about 1833 Georgia.

They are living in Russell Co., Ala., in 1860.[63]
They have two sons: E. L., 2, and D. R., 6/12.

xv. ANN E.[2] LANGFORD, b. about 1842 Harris Co., Ga.

She was in Macon Co., Alabama, in 1860.

2. HENRY NORMAN[2] LANGFORD was born 13 March 1802 in Montgomery Co., Maryland, and died after 12 December 1881 in Chilton Co., Alabama. He married (1) ELIZABETH DAVIS 12 July 1827 Putnam Co., Georgia, daughter of THOMAS DAVIS and ELIZABETH _____. She was born about 1810 in either Hancock or Putnam Co., Georgia, and died about 1838 in Harris Co., Georgia. He married (2) ADELINE CHEATHAM 14 December 1838 Muscogee Co., Georgia.

Henry N. Langford married Elizabeth Davis 12 July 1827. Her father, Thomas Davis, had died the year previously, and they received significant money and personal property from his estate.[64]

H. A. Langford is living in Muscogee Co., Ga., in 1830.[65] Henry N. Langford sold lot 158 in the 19th

---

http://www.findagrave.com., #65861519.
[61]

[62] Alabama, Select Marriages, 1816-1957. Accessed 4 April 2014 at Ancestry.com.

[63] 1860 Census Russell Co., Ala., Opelika, p. 1075, #707.

[64] Langford, Dan A. Henry Norman Langford. Tap Roots 1995;33:22-34.

[65] 1830 Census Muscogee Co., Ga., p. 284. Two males under 5, 1 20-30, one female 20-30, two slave boys under 10, and one 10-24, one female

district of then Muscogee, now Harris Co., Ga., to Thomas Kimbrough of Muscogee Co., Ga., 16 December 1836.[66] The fact that Elizabeth Langford did not sign the deed suggests she may have died before this date. Although he was described as a resident of Muscogee County in the deed, it appears he was appointed a Justice of the Peace in Militia District 696 (Harris Co.) 19 February 1836.

Henry Langford moved to Macon Co., Alabama, shortly after his marriage to Adeline Cheatham, probably in 1837 or 1838, as they are there in 1840.[67] His first recorded land purchase was made in 1842, when he purchased the NW ¼ of sec. 31, twp. 19, range 25 from John J. and Frances Harper for $550.[68] The second tract with the S ½ of the SE ¼ section 25, twp. 19, range 26.[69] The third was the SW ¼ section 32.[70] The fourth was for the south ½ and the east ½ of SW ¼ of section 25.[71] (This is clearly mostly the same tract as before, suggesting a title problem.) The final purchase in this batch was for the E ½ of section 36, all in the same township.[72]

Henry N. "Sangford", 48 year old farmer, born in Maryland, had real estate valued at $26,311 in the 1850 Census.[73] On 2 November 1854 Henry N. and Adeline M. Langford sold to Elijah Evans the east and west ½ of section 36, twp. 19, range 25 and all of the SE ¼ of section 25 south of Tuskegee Road for

---

10-24. The relationship with George N. Langford, whose family recurs in the Muscogee Co., Ga., records is discussed under Richard's entry.

[66] Muscogee Co., Ga., Deed Book C:519, 16 Dec 1836. The 202.5 acre lot was sold for $1600.

[67] 1840 Census Macon Co., Ala., p. 15. He has one son under 5, two 5-10, one 10-15, and he is 30-40. He has one daughter under 5, and his wife is 20-30. He also has one male slave 10-14, two 24-36, and one female slave 10-24, one 24-36, and one 36-55.

[68] Macon Co., Ala., Deed Book F:69, [8 August 1846].

[69] Macon Co., Ala., Deed Book F:68, [17 July 1843/8 August 1846.]

[70] Macon Co., Ala., Deed Book D:119 [5 June 1844/17 March 1845.]

[71] Macon Co., Ala., Deed Book F:67, [28 Jan 1845/8 Aug 1846.]

[72] Macon Co., Ala., Deed Book F:70, [10 Apr 1845/8 Aug 1846.]

[73] 1850 Census Macon Co., Ala., p. 215.

$1900.[74] In March 1855 they sold several lots in the town of Auburn to Jane E. Smith, formerly Patton, executor of William K. Patton.[75] On 26 December 1857 he sold a 3 ½ acre tract to the Montgomery and West Point Railroad.[76]

Dan Langford found a confusing deed made in Autauga Co., Ala., 18 December 1858, that was filed 12 April 1859 in Macon Co., Ala., that sold the NW ¼ of section 34 and the SE ¼ of section 28, and 200 acres in section 27 to C. L. and Lee Crofts for $2750.[77] Henry Langford and his family may have resided in Autauga Co., Ala., before moving to Decatur, Mississippi, to join their eldest son, Thomas Davis Langford.

> Very little is known about Henry during his stay in Newton County, Mississippi other than the 1860 census[78] and the 1863 tax rolls. The Newton Court House burned in 1876, but the 1860 census indicated that Henry owned real estate and had substantial personal property. He was a landowner and farmer for many years, so it is reasonable to assume he also owned property in Mississippi. I suspect that he and the family returned to Alabama about 1864 as a result of another war very close to home.[79]

Given that Vicksburg fell 3 July 1863 and their daughter Emma married James O. Jeffries in Autauga Co., Ala., February 1864, it is likely they left in the fall

---

[74] Macon Co., Ala., Deed Book J:10, [2 November 1854/16 November 1854.]

[75] Macon Co., Ala., Deed Book J:511 [March 1855/8 January 1856.] The lots were #13, the west ½ of lot 2, the SE corner of lot 9, known as the Eagle Hotel.

[76] Macon Co., Ala., Deed Book K:436, [26 Dec 1857/28 Dec 1857.]

[77] Macon Co., Ala., Deed Book L:104, [18 Dec 1858/12 Apr 1859.]

[78] 1860 Census Newton Co., Miss., p. 762, #470/487. John and Emma were still living with him. His real estate was valued at $1800 and his personal estate at $10,784.

[79] Langford, Dan A. Henry Norman Langford. Tap Roots 1995;33:27-28.

of 1863. Henry Langford purchased the west ½ of section 24, the NE ¼ of section 23, and 15 acres in the north end of the SE ¼ of sec 23, twp. 20, range 16, all in Autauga Co., Ala., totaling 300 acres from Martin Johnson.[80] A special census was done in 1866, which records the death of a soldier from disease during the war. This most likely was John H. Langford.

In 1870, Henry Langford and Adeline were living in Montgomery, Alabama, with no children, but with three blacks, and one black infant.[81] They apparently still owned land in the "country," as on 14 November 1876, Henry N. and Adeline M. Langford sold to Joseph Lake, et. al., for $250 the NE ¼ and the NW ¼ of section 25, twp. 20, range 16 in Autauga County, adjoining the land acquired in 1864.[82] On 25 October 1878 they sold the NE ¼ of NE ¼ section 29, less 1 acre in the extreme southeast corner of the 40 acre tract to E. L. Powers for $200.[83] (The reserved 1 acre is probably a cemetery.)

In 1880 Henry Langford and A. M. Langford were living on Bridge Street in Wetumpka, Alabama.[84] Dan Langford found two newspaper references to Henry N. Langford [16 November 1876, and 28 May 1879] that show he was a bridge keeper for a bridge over the Coosa River at Wetumpka. His occupation in the 1880 Census in Wetumpka, Alabama, is listed as

---

[80] Autauga Co., Ala., Deed Book 15:262, [1 Oct 1864/3 Oct 1864.] Dan commented that the north line of sections 23 and 24 is the boundary between Chilton and Autauga County, and the east line of section 24 is boundary between Elmore and Autauga County. Neither Chilton nor Elmore counties had been formed at this time. The land is near the headwaters of Shoal Creek, about two miles east of the town of Marbury.

[81] 1870 Census Montgomery Co., Ala., Montgomery 4th Ward, p. 503, #318/336.

[82] Autauga Co., Ala., Deed Book 23:383, [14 Nov 1876/30 Dec 1876.] Dan commented that he had not found a record for the purchase of this land.

[83] Elmore Co., Ala., Deed Book Q:1, [25 Oct 1878/10 June 1879.] This land is near Deatsville, and again, no record was found of its acquisition.

[84] 1880 Census Elmore Co., Ala., Ward 2, Beat 8, Wetumpka, ED 73, p. 1, #1/1.

bridge keeper. On 12 December 1881 Henry and Adeline Langford sold to A. T. Mitchell the W ½ of section 24 and the NE ¼ of sec. 23, and 15 acres in the N end of SE ¼ of section 23, all in twp. 20, range 16, totaling 300 acres, the land purchased in 1864.[85] Although the deed was executed in Chilton Co., Ala., there is no certainty he was actually living there. This deed is the last written record of Henry N. Langford, who was 79 years old at the time.

Henry N. Langford died in Jemison, Chilton Co., Alabama, in 1891, and is buried in Pine Hill Cemetery along with Adeline and daughter Emma and son-in-law J. O. Jeffries.

Children of HENRY N. LANGFORD and ELIZABETH DAVIS:

3. i. THOMAS DAVIS[3] LANGFORD, b. 3 June 1828 Putnam Co., Ga.; d. 22 January 1909 Meridian, Lauderdale Co., Miss.; m. LUCY FRANCES WILSON 11 September 1859 Newton Co., Miss., dau. of HENRY WILSON and ELIZA HOWE; b. about 1841 Monroe Co., Ga.; d. 27 May 1910 Meridian, Lauderdale Co., Miss.

ii. JOEL J.[3] LANGFORD, b. May 1830 Muscogee Co., Ga.; d. December 1910 Chilton, Falls Co., Texas; m. WINNIE JANE CASSIDY 20 December 1855 Henry Co., Ala.; b. 4 August 1835 in Alabama; d. 24 August 1880 Newton Co., Miss.[86]

"They raised at least eight children in Alabama and moved to Newton County, Miss., sometime after 1874 and on to Texas between 1885 and 1895. Joel was a farmer and an Alabama veteran of the Civil War."

---

[85] Autauga Co., Ala., Deed Book 28:165, [12 December 1881 Chilton Co., Ala.]

[86] Conehatta Methodist Cemetery, Newton Co., Miss. http://www.findagrave.com, #18690184. Tombstone is modern and does not include the dates, which are from another source.

In 1860 they were living in the Southern District of Macon Co., Ala., and in 1870 in Beat 10, Dale Co., Ala.[87] In 1880, they were listed in Beat 3, Newton Co., Miss., where Winnie died 24 August 1880.[88]

In 1900, he was living in Justice Precinct 4 of Limestone Co., Texas,[89] and on 4 May 1910 was living with his son in Justice Precinct 5 of Falls Co., Texas.

Children of JOEL LANGFORD and JANE CASSIDY:

1. WILLIAM[4] LANGFORD, b. 1856; d. 25 May 1923 Cooke Co., Texas;
2. MARY[4] LANGFORD, b. 1858
3. JOHN C.[4] LANGFORD, b. 1860
4. JOSEPH ALEXANDER[4] LANGFORD, b. 1862
5. SARAH[4] LANGFORD, b. 1866
6. HENRY[4] LANGFORD, b. 1868
7. CHARLES[4] LANGFORD, b. 1873
8. JOSEPHINE R.[4] LANGFORD b. 22 October 1874 Newton Co., Miss; d. 27 May 1942 San Angelo, Tom Green Co., Tex.; m. THOMAS BRITTON HARTHCOCK 30 March 1899 Chilton, Falls Co., Texas; b. 11 September 1873 Miss.; d. 4 March 1939 Kerrville, Kerr Co., Texas.[90]

iii. HENRY[3] L. LANGFORD, b. September 1832 Muscogee Co., Ga.; d. 1911 Neshoba Co., Miss.; m. CAROLINE ELIZABETH PHIPPS 5 January 1854 Macon Co., Ala.[91]

"They had eight children, three born in Alabama and the others in Mississippi. The family moved to Neshoba Co., Miss., in about 1858."

---

[87] 1870 Census Dale Co., Ala., Beat 10, p. 236B, #135/137

[88] 1880 Census Newton Co., Miss., Beat 3, ED 87, p. 602C, #103/95.

[89] 1900 Census Limestone Co., Tex., Justice Pct. 4, ED 58, p. 18B, #322. He is living a household headed by Thomas B. Harthcock, who is listed as his son-in-law. The wife, Jodie R., was born in October 1883 in Mississippi.

[90] "Harthcock Family Tree." Accessed 5 February 2014 at http://trees.ancestry.com/tree/20815747/person/993051561

[91] Alabama, Select Marriages, 1816-1957. Accessed 4 April 2014 at Ancestry.com.

In 1870 H. L. and Caroline are living in Leake Co., Miss., with six children.[92] In 1880 they are in Neshoba Co., Miss., with seven children.[93]

Children of HENRY LANGFORD and CAROLINE:

1. NORMAN L.[4] LANGFORD, b. 24 July 1854 Macon Co., Ala.; d. 17 January 1905 Leake Co., Miss.;[94] m. FRANCES ALMA BRANTLEY 1889; b. 30 November 1873 Miss.; d. 20 August 1941 Leake Co., Miss.[95]

2. MARY E.[4] LANGFORD, b. 22 February 1856 Macon Co. Ala.; d. 26 April 1929 Leake Co., Miss.;[96] m. JONES PATRICK BRANTLEY 1889 Neshoba Co., Miss.;[97] b. 10 January 1851 Marion Co., Ga.;[98] d. 24 August 1915 Leake Co., Ga.;[99] m. (1) ARABELLA MANTRY about 1871; b. 25 January 1850 Ga.; d. 2 March 1887 Neshoba Co., Miss.

3. HENRY EDWARD[4] LANGFORD, b. November 1864 Leake Co., Miss.;[100] m. (1) EUNICE THORNTON 25 April 1889 Bienville Par., La.;[101] b. July 1870 Miss.; d. before 1910 Miss.;[102] m. (2) DONNA DIXON 16 March 1910 Covington Co., Miss.;[103] b. 1892 Miss.

---

[92] 1870 Census Leake Co., Miss., p. 354A, #1770. His place of birth was listed as S. Carolina.

[93] 1880 Census Neshoba Co., Miss., Dixon, ED 59, p. 508C, #136/139.

[94] Salem Cemetery, Leake Co., Miss. http://www.findagrave.com., #11867945.

[95] Salem Cemetery, Leake Co., Miss. http://www.findagrave.com., #37333631.

[96] Salem Cemetery, Leake Co., Miss. http://www.findagrave.com., #11867715.

[97] 1900 Census Neshoba Co., Miss., Dixon and Waldo, ED 45, p. 19A, #326/334.

[98] Beech Springs Memorial Cemetery, Neshoba Co., Miss. http://www.findagrave.com., #20908246.

[99] Beech Springs Memorial Cemetery, Neshoba Co., Miss. http://www.findagrave.com., #20908255.

[100] 1900 Census Neshoba Co., Miss., Dixon and Waldo, ED 45, p. 19B, #332/340.

[101] Louisiana Marriage Records, 1851-1900. Located 7 April 2014 at Ancestry.com.

[102] 1910 Census Simpson Co., Miss., Beat 1, ED 120, p. 5B, #85/86. He was a boarder doing "odd jobs." Daughter Callie was the link with the

4. WALTER K.[4] LANGFORD, b. November 1865 Leake Co., Miss.; d. 1 December 1928 Leake Co., Miss.;[104] m. GEORGIA HAWKINS 5 January 1896 Leake Co., Miss.;[105] b. August 1873 Miss.; d. about 1920 Leake Co., Miss.[106]

5. CHARLES A.[4] LANGFORD, b. 21 June 1869 Leake Co., Miss.; d. 21 February 1937 Rusk Co., Texas;[107] m. FANNIE LITTLE 1896; b. April 1874 Miss.;[108] d. 1905 Trenton, Miss.;[109] m. (2) LILLIAN PACKMAN about 1906 Smith Co., Miss.; b. 19 February 1874 Miss.; d. 18 March 1931 Nacogdoches Co., Texas.[110]

6. ELIZABETH T.[4] LANGFORD, b. 14 January 1871 Leake Co., Miss.; d. 18 October 1940 Leake Co., Miss.;[111] m. JOHN E. Jackson 9 September 1889 Leake Co., Miss.; b. 12 September 1868 Miss.; d. 16 July 1949 Leake Co., Miss.[112]

7. LAURA A.[4] LANGFORD, b. 1875; m. C. I. JONES 17 October 1895 Leake Co., Miss.;[113] b. November 1871 Miss.[114]

1900 Census data. He was still in Simpson Co., Miss., with Donnie, 38, in 1930. [Beat 3, ED 10, p. 4A, #77.

[103] Mississippi Marriages, 1776-1935. Located 7 April 2014 at Ancestry.com.

[104] Salem Cemetery, Leake Co., Miss. http://www.findagrave.com., #37333622.

[105] Mississippi Marriages, 1776-1935. Located 7 April 2014 at Ancestry.com.

[106] Salem Cemetery, Leake Co., Miss. http://www.findagrave.com., #71532682. Grave in not marked.

[107] Tatum Cemetery, Rusk Co., Tex. http://www.findagrave.com., #72941764.

[108] 1900 Census Smith Co., Miss., Trenton, ED 106, p. 9B, #157/159.

[109] Zion Cemetery, Smith Co., Miss. http://www.findagrave.com., #11487026.

[110] Black Jack Cemetery, Nacogdoches Co., Tex. http://www.findagrave.com., #84815773.

[111] Salem Cemetery, Leake Co., Miss. http://www.findagrave.com., #377333057.

[112] Salem Cemetery, Leake Co., Miss. http://www.findagrave.com., #377333045.

[113] Mississippi Marriages, 1776-1935. Located 7 April 2014 at Ancestry.com.

iv. PHILEMON O.[3] LANGFORD, b. January 1835 Harris
Co., Ga.; d. after 1909 Montgomery, Ala.; m.
SUSAN R. MAY 12 April 1860 Lowndes Co.,
Ala.; b. December 1843 Lowndes Co., Ala.

They raised at least seven children in
Montgomery, Alabama, some of whom stayed and
raised their children there. Philemon was a man of
many talents. On succeeding census records he
was listed as a teacher, merchant, and dentist. He
had one son, Edward Davis Langford (1867-1945)
who was a dentist in Montgomery for many years
and another son, Marcus Lee Langford (1865-1946)
who was a physician who practiced in Texas from
the 1890's to the 1940's.

In 1870 Philemon Lankford is listed in
Montgomery Ward 4.[115] He was listed as a school
teacher. In 1900 he was a dentist.[116]

Children of PHILEMON LANGFORD and SUSAN:

1. MARCUS LEE[4] LANGFORD, b. 1865
Montgomery Co., Ala.; d. 11 December 1946
Mart, McLennan Co., Texas;[117] m. MINNIE
SMILIE, dau. of HENRY SMILIE and OLLIE
HUSON; b. 8 August 1874 Baileyville, Milam
Co., Texas; d. 29 April 1960 Houston, Harris
Co., Texas.[118]

2. EDGAR DAVIS[4] LANGFORD, b. January 1866
Montgomery Co., Ala.;[119] d. 13 May 1945

[114] 1900 Census Leake Co., Miss., Walnut Grove, ED 37, p. 21A,
#346/359. They are next door to Norman L. Langford and family. In 1910,
he was living in Harperville, Scott Co., Miss., with wife "Bettie" 32, b. Miss.
There was a gap of five years between the two listed in 1900, May, 13, and
Carl, 11, and Herbert, 6. This suggests Laura died about 1905. [1910
Census Scott Co., Miss., Harperville, ED 97, p5B, #58/59.

[115] 1870 Census Montgomery Co., Ala., Montgomery Ward 4, p. 501A,
#284/362.

[116] 1900 Census Montgomery Co., Ala., Montgomery Ward 5, ED 106,
p. 1A, #5. 110 N. Jackson St.

[117] Texas Death Certificate 56570. Accessed 5 April 2014 at
Ancestry.com. He has a double marker with his wife. Mart Cemetery,
McLennan Co., Texas. http://www.findagrave.com., #7041663.

[118] Texas Death Certificate 24077. Accessed 5 April 2014 at
Ancestry.com.

[119] 1900 Census Jefferson Co., Ala., Birmingham Ward 2, ED 135, p.
31B, #46/58.

Montgomery, Ala.;[120] m. BESSIE LEE ARRINGTON 1893; b. April 1874 Alabama; d. 30 January 1941 Montgomery, Ala.[121]

3. ELIZABETH[4] LANGFORD, b. August 1869; d. before 1880.

4. CHARLES H.[4] LANGFORD, b. 1871 Montgomery; d. 30 June 1892 Montgomery.[122]

5. RUTH CAROLINE[4] LANGFORD, b. 1873 Montgomery Co., Ala.; d. after 1910; m. THOMAS JOSEPH MCKENZIE 20 December 1893 Montgomery Co., Ala.;[123] b. January 1868 Georgia.[124]

6. ANNA T. [4] LANGFORD, b. May 1876 Montgomery.

7. MARVIN SIMEON[4] LANGFORD, b. 15 July 1878 Montgomery Co., Ala.;[125] d. 10 July 1919 Montgomery, Ala.[126]

8. KATE C. [4] LANGFORD, b. 4 January 1882 Montgomery; d. 28 March 1956 Lubbock, Lubbock Co., Texas;[127] m. JOHN D. HAMILTON about 1905; b. about 1886 South Carolina; d. before 1930 Dallas, Texas.[128]

Children of HENRY LANGFORD and ADELINE CHEATHAM:

---

[120] Alabama, Deaths and Burials Index, 1881-1974. Accessed 6 April 2014 at Ancestry.com.

[121] Alabama, Deaths and Burials Index, 1881-1974. Accessed 6 April 2014 at Ancestry.com.

[122] Buried at Oakwood Cemetery, Montgomery.

[123] Montgomery Co., Ala., Marriage Book 10:508. http://trees.ancestry.com/tree/56356695/person/40008810705?ssrc=

[124] They were living with P. O. Langford in 1900 and are in Jacksonville, Fla., in 1910. (Jacksonville Ward 3, ED 75, p. 10B, #291/333. 408 Lafayette St., near intersection with E. Duval.

[125] World War I Draft Registration Cards, 1917-1918. Accessed 6 April 2014 at Ancestry.com. He listed his next of kin as Edgar Davis Langford, so was likely not married.

[126] Alabama, Deaths and Burials Index, 1881-1974. Accessed 6 April 2014 at Ancestry.com.

[127] Texas Death Certificate 14984. Accessed 6 April 2014 at Ancestry.com.

[128] 1920 Census Dallas Co., Texas, Dallas Ward 31, ED 66, p. 14A, #265/335. They appear to be on a cove between North and South Bishop St. They have one son, Earl, who was with her in 1930, but John D. was not.

v. MARY[3] LANGFORD, b. May 1838 Ga.; d. before 1910 Marengo Co., Ala.; m. WILLIAM BRADY LANGFORD 1863 Macon Co., Alabama;[129] b. about 1837 Marengo Co., Ala.; d. 3 March 1910 Chilton Co., Ala.[130]

The relationship of William B. Langford to this family is not known.[131] Mary's nickname was "Scrap" according to Judge Amis. They lived in Dayton, Marengo Co., Ala., and had at least four children. He was a hotel keeper and merchant.

William Langford, 72, W. B., 35, M. J., 30, Emma and Mary, are living in Marengo Co., Ala., in 1870,[132] 1880,[133] and 1900.[134]

William B. Langford was listed as a private in Co. E, 43rd Alabama Infantry in April 1862.[135]

Children of MARY and WILLIAM LANGFORD:

1. MARY JANE[4] LANGFORD, b. 15 March 1866 Marengo Co., Ala.; d. 3 September 1940 Jacksonville, Mobile Co., Ala.[136] (unm.)
2. EMMA COTTON[4] LANGFORD, b. 1870; d. 12 February 1934 Marengo Co., Ala.;[137] m. JEFFERSON DAVIS WIMBERLY 28 September

---

[129] Daughter Mary Jane Langford's death certificate states her father was William B. Langford, b. Auburn, Ala., and that Mary was born in Dayton, Alabama.

[130] Confederate Memorial Park, Mountain Creek, Chilton Co., Alabama. http://www.findagrave.com., #14099797.

[131] William Langford was in Marengo Co., Ala., in 1830, 30-39, with another male, 20-29, his wife, 15-19, and three girls under 10. William Langford m. Nancy Moore 16 January 1823 Clarke Co., Ala. In 1850, he was widowed, and had Elizabeth, 18, Nancy, 16, and William, 14, living at home along with Hugh McAn, 23. [1850 Census Marengo Co., Ala., p. 29A, #410.

[132] 1870 Census Marengo Co., Ala., Spring Hill, p. 543B, #524/452.

[133] 1880 Census Marengo Co., Ala., Dayton, ED 88, p. 431C, #18. He was a hotel keeper.

[134] 1900 Census Marengo Co., Ala., Dayton, ED 63, p. 21B, #395/411. He was a merchant.

[135] Accessed 7 April 2014 at http://files.usgwarchives.net/al/marengo/military/civilwar/rosters/companye141nmt.txt

[136] Alabama, Deaths and Burials Index, 1881-1974. Accessed 7 April 2014 at Ancestry.com.

[108] Alabama, Deaths and Burials Index, 1881-1974. Accessed 7 April 2014 at Ancestry.com.

1888 Marengo Co., Ala.;[138] b. April 1866
Alabama;[139] d. before 1910 Marengo Co.,
Ala.[140]

  3. LILLIE B.[4] LANGFORD, b. 1871

  4. HENRY NORMAN[4] LANGFORD, b. 3 September
1875 Dayton, Marengo Co., Ala;[141] d. 7
October 1943 Tampa, Fla.;[142] m. MATTIE
WILLIAMS 18 July 1897 Marengo Co.,
Ala.;[143] b. November 1875 Ala.; d. 13 June
1939 Tampa, Fla.[144]

vi. JOHN H.[3] LANGFORD, b. about 1841 Macon Co.,
Ala.; d. 1861-1865.[145]

  John Langford, 19, is living at home with his
parents in Newton Co., Miss., in 1860.[146]

vii. EMMA J.[3] LANGFORD, b. August 1844 Macon Co.,
Ala.; m. JAMES OSCAR JEFFRIES 1864; b.
January 1842 Alabama; d. 13 June 1923
Jefferson Co., Ala.[147]

---

[138] Alabama, Select Marriages, 1816-1957. Accessed 7 April 2014 at Ancestry.com.

[139] 1900 Census Marengo Co., Ala., Dayton, ED 64, p. 21B, #396/412. She was living as a widow in Mobile, ED 57, p. 1A, in 1930.

[140] 1910 Census Marengo Co., Ala., Dayton, ED 44, p. 2B, #31. Sister Mary Langford, 41, was living with her that year. She had six children at home.

[141] WW1 Draft Registration, 12 September 1918. He was living in Tampa, Hillsboro Co., Fla., and was working for the Atlantic Coast Railroad. He listed his next of kin as Mrs. Emma Wimberly of Mobile, Ala.

[142] Woodlawn Cemetery, Tampa, Hillsborough Co., Fla. http://www.findagrave.com., #27906441.

[143] Alabama, Select Marriages, 1816-1957. Accessed 7 April 2014 at Ancestry.com.

[144] Woodlawn Cemetery, Tampa, Hillsborough Co., Fla. http://www.findagrave.com., #27906610.

[145] John Langford of Co. E, 21st Ala. Inf., died of measles 13 November 1863, but I do not know if this is the same man. The unit history says that it was organized in Mobile, Ala., Oct., 1861, and moved to Corinth, and was then involved in the battle at Shiloh. Afterward, it went back to Mobile, and most of the Regiment was lost at the fall of the town in 1864. (http://www.nps.gov/civilwar/search-regiments-detail.htm?regiment_id=CAL0021RI, accessed 7 April 2014.)

[146] 1860 Census Newton Co., Miss., p. 762, #470/487.

[147] Alabama, Deaths and Burials Index, 1881-1974. Accessed 7 April 2014 at Ancestry.com.

In 1880, they were in Autauga Co., Ala.[148] In 1900, they were living in Chilton Co., Ala., with daughter Eva, 20, and son-in-law, Charley H. Root, 21 and their son Walter, 5, along with Henry G., 17, and Oscar C., 7.[149]

Children of EMMA LANGFORD and J. O. JEFFREYS:

1. LULA[4] JEFFREYS, b. August 1865; d. 16 March 1954 Shelby Co., Ala.;[150] m. JOEL REUBEN SWINFORD 6 April 1884 Chilton Co., Ala.,[151] son of HENRY ROLAND SWINFORD and SOFIA REEDER; b. about 1861 Alabama; d. 9 July 1945 Montevallo, Shelby Co., Ala.[152]

2. WALTER H.[4] JEFFREYS, b. 1868; d. before 1900 Chilton Co., Ala.

3. LEILA CHEATHAM[4] JEFFREYS, b. 23 October 1869 Ala.; d. 13 June 1955 Chilton Co., Ala.;[153] m. GILBERT C. MCNEILL 15 December 1885 Chilton Co., Ala., son of JOHN A. MCNEILL and MARY ANN COBB; b. 15 December 1867; d. 31 October 1932 Chilton Co., Ala.[154]

4. JEWELL[4] JEFFREYS, b. 1877

5. EVA[4] JEFFREYS, b. 1879; d. 24 May 1973 Birmingham, Jefferson Co., Ala.;[155] m. CHARLES HARRIS ROOT 16 September 1898 Elmore Co., Ala.,[156] son of WILLIAM D. ROOT

---

[148] 1880 Census Autauga Co., Ala., Pine Flat, ED 6, p. 124D, #283/345.

[149] 1900 Census Chilton Co., Ala., Jemison, ED 25, p. 16A, #280.

[150] Alabama, Deaths and Burials Index, 1881-1974. Accessed 7 April 2014 at Ancestry.com.

[151] Alabama, Select Marriages, 1816-1957. Accessed 7 April 2014 at Ancestry.com.

[152] Alabama, Deaths and Burials Index, 1881-1974. Accessed 7 April 2014 at Ancestry.com.

[153] Cobb Cemetery, Chilton Co., Ala. http://www.findagrave.com., #91312654.

[154] Cobb Cemetery, Chilton Co., Ala. http://www.findagrave.com., #91312602.

[155] Alabama, Deaths and Burials Index, 1881-1974. Accessed 7 April 2014 at Ancestry.com.

[156] Alabama, Select Marriages, 1816-1957. Accessed 7 April 2014 at Ancestry.com.

and LAURA TATUM; b. abt. 1878; d. 4
February 1949 Birmingham.[157]

    6. HENRY C.[4] JEFFREYS, b. 1883 Chilton Co.,
       Ala.; d. before 1910.

    7. OSCAR C.[4] JEFFREYS, b. 1893; d. 24 March
       1914 Birmingham, Jefferson Co., Ala.[158]

3. THOMAS DAVIS[3] LANGFORD was born 3 June 1828
Putnam Co., Georgia, and died 22 January 1909
Meridian, Lauderdale Co., Mississippi. He married
LUCY FRANCES WILSON 11 September 1859 Newton Co.,
Mississippi, daughter of HENRY WILSON and ELIZA
HOWE. She was born about 1841 in Monroe Co.,
Georgia, and died 27 May 1910 Meridian, Lauderdale
Co., Miss.

*Dr. Thomas Davis Langford was born June 3,
1828. He studied medicine at Charleston, S. C.,
and graduated about 1856. Shortly afterward he
came to Newton County, Miss. and located for
the practice of his profession, making his
headquarters at the old tavern home of Henry
Wilson, on the Jackson and Livingston Stage
Road. In 1859 he married Lucy Francis Wilson,
daughter of Henry Wilson and Eliza Howe. After
their marriage they continued to reside in the
same community until 1871 when they moved to
Anderson County, Texas, where they stayed two
years, but becoming discouraged, returned and
settled on a farm about a mile east of Conehatta
in Newton County, Miss. They continued to
reside there until about 1905 when they broke
up housekeeping, sold the farm to their sons,
Willie and George, and went to live with their*

---

[157] Alabama, Deaths and Burials Index, 1881-1974. Accessed 7 April
2014 at Ancestry.com.
   [158] Alabama, Deaths and Burials Index, 1881-1974. Accessed 7 April
2014 at Ancestry.com.

340

son Howard in Meridian. He died in March 1909 and she died in May 1910. They were both buried in the Methodist Churchyard at Conehatta, Newton Co., Miss.[159]

Children of THOMAS LANGFORD and LUCY WILSON are:[160]

i. WILLIAM H.[4] LANGFORD, b. August 1861 Newton Co., Miss.; d. after 1920 Buckner Co., La.; m. ODELLA C. MITCHELL December 1891 Newton Co., Miss.; b. 8 Sept. 1872 Ala.; d. 12 November 1934 Newton Co., Miss.[161]

The family are in Newton Co., in 1900[162] and 1910.[163] In 1920 William Langford, Della, Howard, and Leon, are all in Hadley, Arkansas.[164] In 1930 Della, Leon, and Howard are all back in Newton.[165] It appears that Howard and Leon were handicapped and never married.

Children of WILLIAM LANGFORD and ODELLA:

1. HOWARD[5] LANGFORD, b. October 1893 Newton Co., Miss.; d. after 1930 Newton Co., Miss.
2. LEON[5] LANGFORD, b. October 1893 Newton Co., Miss.; d. after 1940 Lauderdale Co., Miss.[166]
3. FRANK MITCHELL[5] LANGFORD, b. 8 October 1896 Newton Co., Miss.; d. 27 March 1968 Glendale, California.[167]

---

[159] Conehatta Methodist Cemetery, Newton Co., Miss. http://www.findagrave.com, #64498936; #64489637.

[160] Additional data obtained from Kay. Our Winding Family Vine. 22 April 2008. http://wc.rootsweb.ancestry.com, (db. ourtexasfolks.)

[161] Conehatta Methodist Cemetery, Newton Co., Miss. http://www.findagrave.com, #64490571.

[162] 1900 Census Newton Co., Miss., Beat 3, ED 52, p. 2B, #36/37.

[163] 1910 Census Newton Co., Miss., Union, ED 87, p. 3B, #43.

[164] 1920 Census Lafayette Co., Ark., Hadley, ED 116, p. 12A, #97.

[165] 1930 Census Newton Co., Miss., Beat 3, ED 12, p. 20A, #394/398.

[166] He was listed as an inmate of East Mississippi State Hospital in Meridian in the 1940 Census. [Lauderdale Co., Meridian, ED 38-6, p. 5A.

[167] Forest Lawn Cemetery (Glendale), Los Angeles Co., Cal. http://www.findagrave.com., #85447409.

Frank Mitchell Langford was single 5 June 1917, when he registered for the draft while living in Buckner, Lafayette Co., Miss.[168] He was still single when listed in the 1940 Census when living at 139½ S. Main St., Los Angeles, as a lodger.[169]

    4. EVA MAY[5] LANGFORD, b. 1898 Newton Co., Miss.; d. before 1910 Newton Co., Miss.

ii. LARKIN DAVID[4] LANGFORD, b. 2 May 1862 Newton Co., Miss.; d. 15 Aug 1913 Austwell, Refugio Co., Texas;[170] m. ELLA MORGAN LOPER 2 Sep 1891 Newton Co., Miss.; b. 22 Oct 1867 Newton Co., Miss; d. 1 Apr 1952 Shreveport, Caddo Parish, La.

Larkin D. Langford was at home in the 1880 Census, and in 1910 was living in Grant Parish, La.[171] He has a step-son, Torvel M. Soper, 20, Miss., living with them. It is uncertain if the name was Soper or Loper, given the conflict between the two records.

Children of LARKIN LANGFORD and ELLA are:

    1. MARY RUTH[5] LANGFORD, b. 15 July 1892 Lake, Scott Co., Miss.; d. January 1985 Mobile, Mobile Co., Ala.;[172] m. JOHN DAVID WITZELL 20 October 1920 Shreveport, Caddo Par., La.; b. 21 November 1890 Pokemouche, New Brunswick, Canada;[173]

    2. LARKIN JOSEPH[5] LANGFORD, b. 5 April 1894 Gulfport, Miss.;[174] d. 6 July 1988 Des

---

[168] WWI Draft Registration Cards. Accessed 8 April 2014 at Ancestry.com.

[169] 1940 Census Los Angeles Co., California, Los Angeles, ED 60-1104, p. 2A, #2.

[170] Tivoli Cemetery, Refugio Co., Texas. http://www.findagrave.com., #40753096.

[171] 1910 Census Grant Parish, La., Police Jury Ward 5, ED 62, p. 39B, #530/534.

[172] SSDI. Accessed 7 April 2014 at Ancestry.com.

[173] Petition for Naturalization, 25 April 1944, Shreveport, La. Accessed 7 April 2014 at Ancestry.com.

[174] WWI Draft Registration Card, Refugio Co., Texas. Accessed 7 April 2014 at Ancestry.com

Moines, Wash.;[175] m. EVELYN SPARKS 6 April 1917 Refugio Co., Texas;[176] b. 18 April 1895 Pike Co., Ark.;[177] d. 6 September 1994 Seattle, King Co., Wash.[178]

3. CORLEE[5] LANGFORD, b. 9 May 1896 Newton Co., Miss.; d. 22 July 1989 Shreveport, Caddo Parish, La.;[179] m. EDGAR F. POWELL 15 January 1919 Caddo Par., La.; b. 12 September 1887; d. 3 May 1941 Caddo Parish, La.[180]

4. THELMA MARTHA[5] LANGFORD, b. 27 September 1898 Newton Co., Miss.; m. HOMER LEE 9 September 1923 Caddo Parish, La.

5. JAMES MCNAMARA[5] LANGFORD, b. 4 September 1900 Newton Co., Miss.; d. 28 September 1957 Texarkana, Bowie Co., Texas;[181] m. ELIZABETH MCKENZIE; b. 2 April 1911 Ark.; d. 1 April 1991 Shreveport, Caddo Par., La.

6. LEO[5] LANGFORD, b. 15 March 1901 Newton Co., Miss.; d. 12 April 1980 Fayetteville, Washington Co., Ark.[182]

7. KATHERINE ELVA[5] LANGFORD, b. 1904 Grant Parish, La.; m. GEORGE A. ZIMMERMAN 27

---

[175] Washington Death Index 1940-1996. Accessed 7 April 2014 at Ancestry.com.

[176] Moore, Orene. Davis, Folsom, Merchant, Sparks, Nelson, Vickery, Crain, and others. 4 October 2006. http://wc.rootsweb.ancestry.com., (db. orenem.) Cited hereafter as Moore. Another source says they divorced in Seattle in 1952, and that he married three more times after this.

[177] 1920 Census Victoria Co., Texas, Justice Precinct 4, ED 154, p. 13B, #228/293.

[178] Washington Death Index 1940-1996. Accessed 7 April 2014 at Ancestry.com.

[179] Jewella Cemetery, Shreveport, La. http://www.findagrave.com., #87130543.

[180] Jewella Cemetery, Shreveport, La. http://www.findagrave.com., #87130601.

[181] Forest Park East Cemetery, Shreveport, La. http://www.findagrave.com., #118502296.

[182] Fayetteville National Cemetery. U. S. Veterans' Gravesites, 1775-2006. Accessed 7 April 2014 at Ancestry.com. In the 1920 Census he was a private on active duty in Europe with Headquarters Troop, A. F. G2.

April 1924 Caddo Par., La.;[183] b. 15 December 1899; d. 19 February 1963 Shreveport, La.[184]

8. THOMAS BLACKWOOD[5] LANGFORD, b. 10 March 1906 Grant Parish, La.; d. 27 December 1956 Tyler, Smith Co., Texas.;[185] m. ESTA YOUNGER,[186] b. about 1909 Kansas.

9. PATRICK VARDAMAN[5] LANGFORD, b. 4 January 1909 Minden, Grant Parish, La.; d. 24 June 1975 Dallas, Dallas Co., Texas;[187] m. CATHERINE FULCO 2 December 1938.[188]

iii. ELIZA ROBERTA[4] LANGFORD, b. 7 July 1865 Newton Co., Miss.; d. 14 October 1939 Newton Co., Miss.;[189] m. JOSEPH ANDERSON PACE 1 Nov 1883 Newton Co., Miss.;[190] b. 18 October 1861; d. 21 Apr 1944 Newton Co., Miss.[191]

They were listed in Newton Co., Miss., in 1900,[192] 1910,[193]

Children of ELIZA LANGFORD and JOSEPH PACE:

---

[183] Kay. Roots, Branches, Twigs, and Winding Vines. 13 June 2009. http://wc.rootsweb.ancestry.com., (db. adamsfamil7328.) Cited as Kay. Another source says this was the second of her three marriages.

[184] St. Joseph Cemetery, Shreveport, La. http://www.findagrave.com., #30663373. He said he was single in the 1940 census, and she does not appear to be buried near him. This will need further invesigation.

[185] Texas Death Certificate 67583. His wife was informant, and he was buried in Forest Park Cemetery, Shreveport. He had lived in Tyler for 13 years prior to his death.

[186] Kay.

[187] Texas Death Certificate 50333. Accessed 7 April 2014 at Ancestry.com. His place of birth was listed as Minden (Webster, Par.), but the informant was a nurse. He was buried at Forest Park Cemetery, Shreveport (Caddo Parish), La. In 1930 he was in Los Angeles.

[188] Kay. Another source says this was his second marriage.

[189] Pace Cemetery, Hazel, Miss. http://www.findagrave.com., #16837246.

[190] Mississippi Marriages, 1776-1935. Accessed 8 April 2014 at Ancestry.com.

[191] Pace Cemetery, Hazel, Miss. http://www.findagrave.com., #16837261.

[192] 1900 Census Newton Co., Miss., Beat 4, ED 55, p. 13B, #237/238. They are living with his extended family.

[193] 1910 Census Newton Co., Miss., Beat 4, ED 91, p. 12A, #175/180.

1. FELIX MERTON[5] PACE, b. 14 August 1885 Newton Co., Miss.; d. 16 July 1927 Newton Co., Miss.;[194] m. NINA MAY about 1906 Newton Co., Miss.; b. 17 July 1883; d. 28 August 1967 Newton Co., Miss.[195]

2. MARY EDNA[5] PACE, b. 10 February 1887 Newton Co., Miss.; d. 19 February 1975 Columbia Co., Fla.;[196] m. WILLIAM P. MABRY about 1908 Newton Co., Miss.; b. 7 July 1885 Newton Co., Miss.; d. 19 May 1954 Newton Co., Miss.[197]

3. THOMAS MARVIN[5] PACE, b. 9 March 1889 Newton Co., Miss.; d. 22 August 1915 Newton Co., Miss.;[198] m. LILLA B. CLARK about 1914 Newton Co., Miss.; b. 31 October 1892; d. 18 September 1993 Newton Co., Miss.[199]

4. JOHNNY FORREST[5] PACE, b. 1 June 1891 Newton Co., Miss.; d. 9 October 1912 Newton Co., Miss.[200]

5. JOSEPH VERNON[5] PACE, b. 9 April 1894 Newton Co., Miss.; d. 14 May 1984 Starkville, Miss.;[201] m. RUTH COX; b. 27 September 1896; d. 14 December 1990 Starkville.[202]

---

[194] Pace Cemetery, Hazel, Miss. http://www.findagrave.com., #123695948.

[195] Pace Cemetery, Hazel, Miss. http://www.findagrave.com., #123695959.

[196] Florida Death Index, 1877-1998. Accessed 8 April 2014 at Ancestry.com. Pace Cemetery, Hazel, Miss. http://www.findagrave.com., #123011168.

[197] Pace Cemetery, Hazel, Miss. http://www.findagrave.com., #123095948.

[198] Pace Cemetery, Hazel, Miss. http://www.findagrave.com., #123011158.

[199] Pace Cemetery, Hazel, Miss. http://www.findagrave.com., #93915874. She is living with their two children with Joseph Pace and family in 1920, Newton Co., Beat 4, ED 97, p. 11B, #228/231.

[200] Pace Cemetery, Hazel, Miss. http://www.findagrave.com., #16837253.

[201] Odd Fellows Cemetery, Starkville, Oktibbeha Co., Miss. http://www.findagrave.com., #59170382.

[202] Odd Fellows Cemetery, Starkville, Oktibbeha Co., Miss. http://www.findagrave.com., #59170364.

6. TALMAGE[5] PACE, b. 13 November 1896 Newton Co., Miss.;[203] m. MAE before 1920 Newton Co., Miss.[204]

7. LUCY[5] PACE, b. 17 February 1899 Newton Co., Miss.; d. 24 January 1998 Newton Co., Miss.;[205] m. REUBEN STANLEY KELLY; b. 12 December 1891; d. 24 September 1965 Newton Co., Miss.[206]

8. NANCY L.[5] PACE, b. 1902 Newton Co., Miss.

9. ANNIE L.[5] PACE, b. 28 November 1903 Newton Co., Miss.; d. 12 January 1984 Newton Co., Miss.;[207] m. CLARENCE ELMER MCCOY about 1928 Newton Co., Miss.; b. 13 December 1899 Newton Co., Miss.; d. 3 August 1968 Newton Co., Miss.[208]

iv. MARY SALOME[4] LANGFORD, b. 1 February 1868 Newton Co., Miss.; d. 7 December 1942 Meridian, Lauderdale Co., Miss.; m. ALPHONSO BOBBITT AMIS 11 June 1892 Newton Co., Miss., son of ALBERT GALLATIN AMIS and LUVENIA BREWER; b. 7 February 1867 Newton Co., Miss.; d. 6 July 1949 Meridian, Lauderdale Co., Miss.

Her children are discussed in Chapter 4.

v. THOMAS HOWARD[4] LANGFORD, b. November 2, 1869; d. 1937 Conehatta, Newton Co., Miss.; m. INA JOE BAILEY December 1899 Newton Co., Miss.; b. September 1874; d. 1932.

---

[203] WWI Draft Registration Card. Accessed 8 April 2014 at Ancestry.com. They were in Conehatta in 1940.

[204] 1920 Census Newton Co., Miss., Beat 4, ED 97, p. 12B, #245/248.

[205] Pace Cemetery, Hazel, Miss. http://www.findagrave.com., #123696049.

[206] Pace Cemetery, Hazel, Miss. http://www.findagrave.com., #123696096.

[207] Pace Cemetery, Hazel, Miss. http://www.findagrave.com., #123695987.

[208] Pace Cemetery, Hazel, Miss. http://www.findagrave.com., #123695973.

Howard Langford, 40, and Ina, 35, along with Lucy F., 69, are living in Meridian, Miss., in 1930.[209] There are no children recorded.

vi. LUCY VIRGINIA[4] LANGFORD, b. November 5, 1871, in Texas; d. 12 March 1905 Newton Co., Miss.; m. WILLIAM W. RUSSELL 1892 Newton Co., Miss.; b. October 1868 Miss.

They were in Newton County in 1900.[210]

Child of LUCY LANGFORD and WILLIAM RUSSELL:

1. ETHEL[5] RUSSELL, b. 23 February 1893 Decatur, Newton Co., Miss.; d. 20 March 1965 Riviera, Kleberg Co., Texas;[211] m. HORACE NEWTON HARRISON about 1912 Texas; b. 9 January 1891; d. 8 April 1980 Taft, Patricio, Co., Texas.[212]

vii. ROBERT LEE[4] LANGFORD, b. 11 December 1873, Newton Co., Miss.; d. 27 Feb 1955 Meridian, Miss.; m. ETHEL BROWN after 1903; b. 1887 Louisiana.

Robert and Ethel Langford are in Meridian in 1920,[213] 1930,[214] and 1940.[215] I have not found him in 1900 and 1910. When he registered for the draft 9 September 1918, he listed Mrs. A. B. Amis as his next of kin.

In 1920, Felix Brown, 17, "son", was living with them. He may be the H. Felix Brown, Jr., living with H. Felix Brown and Ethel in Monroe,

---

[209] 1930 Census Lauderdale Co., Miss., Meridian, Ward 2, ED 41, p. 7B, #118/131. They are living at 3518 10th Street. A. B. Amis lived at 1203 38th Avenue, which would have been only a couple of blocks away.

[210] 1900 Census Newton Co., Miss., Beat 1, ED 48, p. 5B, #80.

[211] Texas Death Certificates, 1903-1982. Accessed 7 April 2014 at Ancestry.com.

[212] Riviera Cemetery, Kleberg Co., Tex. http://www.findagrave.com., #35370261. Also Texas Death Certificates, 1903-1982. Accessed 7 April 2014 at Ancestry.com.

[213] 1920 Census Lauderdale Co., Miss., Meridian, Ward 2, ED 48, p. 3B, #71/77. They had Felix Brown, 17, "son" living with them. Clearly this was Ethel's son.

[214] 1930 Census Lauderdale Co., Miss., Meridian, ED 1, p. 1A, #5/6. He was living at 1926 23rd Avenue. He was a conductor on the railroad.

[215] 1940 Census Lauderdale Co., Miss., Meridian, ED 38-11A, p. 19A, #417. They lived at 926 23rd Avenue. He was a conductor on the railroad.

La., in 1910.[216] It does not appear that they had children.

viii. LOIS PALLIE[4] LANGFORD, b. 27 July 1877 Newton Co., Miss; d. 10 Oct 1935 Alcorn Co., Miss.;[217] m. WILLIAM WYATT BASS; b. 20 June 1873 Alcorn Co., Miss.;[218] d. 1959 Tishomingo Co., Miss.;[219] m. (2) BLANCHE WYNN about 1937 Tishomingo Co., Miss.; b. 21 February 1891 Tishomingo Co., Miss.; d. September 1968 Tishomingo Co., Miss.[220]

In 1910, William Wyatt Bass, 36, and Lois Langford Bass, 32, and children are living in Okolona, Miss.[221] They were in Alcorn Co., Miss., in 1920,[222] and 1930.[223] In 1940 he and wife Blanche were living in Tishomingo Co., Miss.[224]

Children of LOIS LANGFORD and WILLIAM BASS:

1. WILL DAVIS[5] BASS, b. 27 September 1902; d. 13 February 1973 Batesville, Miss.[225]
2. HUBBARD EDWARD[5] BASS, b. 10 February 1904; d. 24 August 1974 Batesville, Miss.;[226] m. HAZEL BINGHAM about 1928 Alcorn Co., Miss.; b. 27 November 1908

---

[216] 1910 Census Ouachita Parish, La., Monroe, Ward 3, ED 102, p. 10B, #49.

[217] Conehatta Methodist Cemetery, Newton Co., Miss. http://www.findagrave.com., #64489539. Tombstone says birth was 12 Sept 1877. Date recorded was from Judge Amis.

[218] WWI Draft Registration Cards, 1917-1918. Accessed 8 April 2014 at Ancestry.com. They were living in Corinth at that time.

[219] New Prospect Cemetery, Iuka, Miss. http://www.findagrave.com., #36810690.

[220] New Prospect Cemetery, Iuka, Miss. http://www.findagrave.com., #36810687.

[221] 1910 Census Chickasaw Co., Miss., Okolona, Ward 3, ED 46, p. 25A, #123.

[222] 1920 Census Alcorn Co., Miss., Beat 4, ED 9, p. 15A, #197/209. They were living on Polk Road.

[223] 1930 Census Alcorn Co., Miss., Beat 4, ED 15, p. 5A, #91/94. They were living in West Corinth.

[224] 1940 Census Tishomingo Co., Miss., ED 71-7, p. 8A, #141. They were living in Corinth in 1935.

[225] Forrest Memorial Park, Batesville, Panola Co., Miss. http://www.findagrave.com., #15036346.

[226] Forrest Memorial Park, Batesville, Panola Co., Miss. http://www.findagrave.com., #15036346.

348

Alcorn Co., Miss.; d. 9 July 2005 Batesville, Panola Co., Miss.[227]

3. MAURICE[5] BASS, b. 1907; m. JANET about 1927.[228]

4. HOWARD[5] BASS, b. 1914; m. ADELE P.; b. 1920.[229]

ix. GEORGE MARVIN[4] LANGFORD, b. 16 May 1879 Newton Co., Miss; d. 28 July 1959 Conehatta, Newton Co., Miss.;[230] m. ALMA BLACKBURN 1904 Newton Co., Miss.; b. 30 Nov 1855 Miss.; d. 20 June 1944 Newton Co., Miss.

Children of GEORGE LANGFORD and ALMA:

1. JOHN DAVIS[5] LANGFORD, b. 15 July 1905 Newton Co., Miss.; d. September 1972 Leake Co., Miss.;[231] m. ONEITA MCMORROUGH 16 October 1935 Holmes Co., Miss.[232]

2. LESLIE[5] LANGFORD, b. 10 April 1907 Newton Co., Miss.; d. 25 February 1984 Newton Co., Miss.;[233] m. ETHA MEYRL; b. 28 September 1915; d. 2007 Newton Co., Miss.[234]

3. HENRY WILSON[5] LANGFORD, b. 3 July 1909 Newton Co., Miss.; d. 16 May 1928 Newton Co., Miss.

---

[227] Forrest Memorial Park, Batesville, Panola Co., Miss. http://www.findagrave.com., #13813524. The site has her obituary posted as well. She was survived three daughters, one son, 11 grandchildren, 24 great-grandchildren, and 19 great-great grandchildren.

[228] 1930 Census Shelby Co., Tenn., Memphis, ED 108, p. 12A, #138/166. They were living at 1598 Fleetwood.

[229] 1940 Census Alcorn Co., Miss., Corinth, Beat 1, ED 2-3, p. 8A, #128. Both were working in a hosiery mill.

[230] Conehatta Methodist Cemetery, Newton Co., Miss. http://www.findagrave.com, #64490571.

[231] http://trees.ancestry.com/tree/23504326/person/1395012929

[232] 1940 Census Jones Co., Miss., Northeast, ED 34-25A, p. 9A, #129. He was in Newton Co., in 1935, and she was in Holmes Co., so marriage was after that date.

[233] Conehatta Methodist Cemetery, Newton Co., Miss. http://www.findagrave.com, #64483158.

[234] Conehatta Methodist Cemetery, Newton Co., Miss. http://www.findagrave.com, #64479568.

4. MARVIN GEORGE[5] LANGFORD, b. 3 May 1912 Newton Co., Miss.; d. 1977 Lauderdale Co., Miss.[235]

4. FRANCIS[5] LANGFORD, b. 1914 Newton Co., Miss.

5. ROBERT[5] LANGFORD, b. 1916 Newton Co., Miss.

6. HERBERT[5] LANGFORD, b. 1923 Newton Co., Miss.;

7. JUNE NILA[5] LANGFORD, b. 1925 Newton Co., Miss.

8. IRVIN[5] LANGFORD, b. 23 March 1926 Newton Co., Miss.; d., 4 December 1994 Meridian, Lauderdale Co., Miss.[236]

9. LILLIAN[5] LANGFORD, b. 1930 Newton Co., Miss.

x. ERNEST[4] LANGFORD, b. 15 July 1881 Newton Co., Miss; d. 30 Sep 1925 Newton Co., Miss.[237]

xi. HERBERT BAILEY[4] LANGFORD, b. May 27, 1883 Newton Co., Miss.; d. 28 July 1965 Shreveport, Caddo Parish, La.; m. MARY BEATRICE CURTIS 20 Nov 1912 Shreveport, La.; b. 12 Dec 1891 Pass Christian, Miss.; d. 27 Jan 1977 Shreveport, La.

Dan Langford, the youngest child, and source of much information on the Langford family told me he felt close to the Amis family, because A. B. Amis, Sr., had sent his father, Herbert Bailey Langford, Sr., to college, which had helped all of his family to "get ahead."

Children of HERBERT LANGFORD and MARY:

1. HERBERT BAILEY[5] LANGFORD, JR., b. 4 February 1914 Shreveport, Caddo Par., La.;

---

[235] U. S., Social Security Death Index, 1935-current. Accessed 9 April 2014 at Ancestry.com.

[236] Conehatta Methodist Cemetery, Newton Co., Miss. http://www.findagrave.com, #64480822. Place of death from SSDI.

[237] Conehatta Methodist Cemetery, Newton Co., Miss. http://www.findagrave.com, #64479517.

d. 26 December 2003 Texas City, Galveston Co., Texas.[238]

2. THOMAS DAVIS[5] LANGFORD, b. 1916; m. BILLIJUNE FEW 1950; b. 1901 Natchitoches Par., La., dau. of WILLIAM BENJAMIN FEW and PEARL DUFLOT; d. 30 September 1913 Baton Rouge, La.[239]

3. JOHN CURTIS[5] LANGFORD, b.4 July 1919 Shreveport; d. 24 October 2007 Bryan, Brazos Co., Texas;[240] m. IDA TIXIER; b. 27 September 1919 Clayton, Union Co., N. M.;

---

[238] SSDI.

[239] Obituary published in *The Advocate*, Baton Rouge, La., 1-5 October 2013. Accessed 9 April 2014 at
http://www.legacy.com/obituaries/theadvocate/obituary.aspx?n=billijune -few-langford&pid=167290728

Billijune Few Langford, a native of Natchitoches Parish, died in Baton Rouge on Monday, September 30th at the age of 92 after a brief illness. She was the daughter of William Benjamin Few and Pearl Duflot Few. She is survived by her husband of 63 years, Thomas Davis (Dave) Langford. She is also survived by her two daughters, Shirley Langford Young and husband John C. (Jack) Young of Baton Rouge and Amy Langford Berry and husband Patrick G. (Pat) Berry of San Francisco, and one granddaughter, Elizabeth L. Young of New Orleans. Other surviving relatives include a sister, Frances Few Clark, and a brother-in-law, Dr. Richard B. Langford, both of Shreveport, and several nieces and nephews. Among these are Susan Marshall Rewoldt, Jane Marshall Henslee, Nancy Clark Victory, Rebecca Clark, Cindy Langford Miller, Christina Langford Kluth, and Richard B. Langford, Jr. Billijune attended Louisiana Normal College (Northwestern State) and graduated from LSU with a B.A. in sociology in 1943. Before finally settling in Baton Rouge, she and Dave lived in Shreveport, El Dorado (Arkansas), Billings (Montana), Metairie, and Covington/Mandeville and spent six years overseas in England, Japan, and Australia. Her hobby was the art of Ikebana, which she taught for many years. She was an active member of Ikebana International in New Orleans and Baton Rouge. Above all, she enjoyed doing altar flowers at Trinity Episcopal in Baton Rouge and Christ Church Episcopal in Covington. Memorial services will be held at Trinity Episcopal Church, 3552 Morning Glory, at 10:00 a.m. Saturday, October 5th, the Rev. Ralph Howe officiating. Visitation begins at 8:00 a.m. The family wishes to thank Hospice of Baton Rouge, particularly nurse Susan Boudinot, and the wonderful staff of the Health and Wellness Center at St. James Place for the excellent care Billijune received during her final illness. In lieu of flowers, the family would encourage memorial donations to either the Hospice of Baton Rouge (9063 Siegen Lane, BR LA 70810) or the St.James Place Foundation (333 Lee Drive, BR LA 70808).

[240] College Station Cemetery, College Station, Texas. http://www.findagrave.com., #80804398. Obituary is posted on the site.

d. 13 August 2000 College Station, Brazos Co., Texas.[241]

4. RICHARD[5] B. LANGFORD, b. 1921; m. HELEN.[242]

5. STEVEN E.[5] LANGFORD, b. 6 December 1922 Shreveport; d. 21 November 2006 Shreveport;[243] m. CATHERINE.

6. MARY B.[5] LANGFORD, b. 1931; d. before 2006.

7. DAN A.[5] LANGFORD, b. 25 October 1932 Shreveport, Caddo Par., La.; d. 1 April 2010 Spring, Harris Co., Texas;[244] m. LARUE.

xii. ALBERT LEON[4] LANGFORD, b. 22 June 1888 Newton Co., Miss.; d. 13 Oct 1891 Newton Co., Miss.[245]

---

[241] The Bryan-College Station Eagle. Accessed 9 April 2014 at http://www.edensfamily.com/geneology/raw/research/ida-tixier-langford-new-mexico.htm

[242] Living in Shreveport, La., in 2006.

[243] Forest Park East Cemetery, Shreveport, Caddo Parish, La. http://www.findagrave.com., #16784470. The newspaper obituary was attached to the posting.

[244] Obituary Houston Chronicle, 8 April 2010. Accessed 9 April 2014 http://www.legacy.com/obituaries/houstonchronicle/obituary.aspx?n=dan-a-langford&pid=141597635.

DAN A. LANGFORD passed away unexpectedly in his home in Spring, Tx at the age of 77. He was the youngest of 7 children born to H.B. and Mary Curtis Langford in Shreveport, LA on October 25, 1932. He is preceded in death by his parents, his wife of 49 years, LaRue, sister Manie, brothers Herb, Curt, and Steve and sisters-in-law, Betty, Ida, Irma, Kay, and Helen. Dan is survived by his children, Daniel Langford, Jr, Christina Kluth and husband John Kluth, brothers Dick, Dave and sister in law Billijune. He is also survived by his grandchildren Jessica, Cameron and Kirby Kluth, numerous nieces and nephews and friend, Alice Agafon. Born in Louisiana, he came to Texas as soon as he could as a Texas Longhorn, graduating in 1954 with a degree in Petroleum Engineering. His career took the family to New Mexico, Oklahoma, Arkansas and Louisiana but he always came back to Houston, living here 3 different times. Moving to Spring in 1973 was the last stop. Dan was very active and a fixture at St Dunstan's Episcopal Church and on the tennis court. A memorial service will be held at 3:00 p.m. on Monday, April 12, 2010 at St Dunstan's Episcopal Church, 14301 Stuebner Airline Road, Houston, TX 77069. A reception will follow in the church Parish Hall. In lieu of flowers, memorial contributions may be sent to St Dunstan's.

[245] Conehatta Methodist Cemetery, Newton Co., Miss. http://www.findagrave.com, #64481810.

Chapter 9: Descendants of 1706 Robert Davis of Accomack County, Virginia

Thomas Davis Langford was named after his maternal grandfather. Fortunately, court records in Georgia link his father, 1803 James Davis of Hancock Co., Georgia, to 1706 Robert Davis of Accomack County, Virginia.[1]

Genealogical Summary

1. ROBERT[1] DAVIS was born in England and died May 1706 in Accomack Co., Va. He married ELIZABETH _____.

Robert Davis was claimed as a headright by Richard Hill, Sr., who patented a 1,000 acre tract of land on Hunting Creek, Accomack Co., Va., on 23 February 1663.[2] On 26 March 1672 Robert Davis patented 350 acres in Northampton Co., Va., at the head of the branches of Muddy (Guilford's) Creek, adjacent to John Parker of Mattapony, Thomas Nixon, Miles Gray, and Griffen Savage.[3]

Robert Davis' will was written 2 May 1706 and probated 4 June 1706 Accomack Co., Va.[4] His will bequeathed to son Samuel, land on the south side of Muddy or Guilford Creek, to son Thomas, land on the north side of the same creek, and to son James a tract of 100 acres apparently below the creek. His wife Elizabeth was mentioned by name. Additional bequests of one shilling were made to sons William and Robert and to daughters Elizabeth Parks, Mary

---

[1] Hendershot, Stan. Stan Hendershot's Family Tree. 3 January 2007. Located on http://worldconnect.rootsweb.com, (db. standhendershot). The original research on this family was done by Robert M. Davis of Salisbury, Maryland.

[2] Nugent, Nell M. Cavaliers and Pioneers,1:482; 2:105, 119, 127.

[3] Worcester Co., Maryland DB H:245-246.

[4] Nottingham and Stratton. Wills and Administrations of Accomack County, Virginia, 1663-1800. (Cottonport, LA: Polyanthus, 1973,) pp. 27, 28. Accomack Co., Virginia Wills (1692-1715):197-198.

Reed, and Sarah Davis. Also mentioned were daughters Jean, Comfort, and Easter Davis, who were to share in the division of the remainder of the estate with their mother. The will was witnessed by John Morris, Obedience Pitman, and Thomas Bell.

Children of ROBERT DAVIS and ELIZABETH are:

    i. SAMUEL[2] DAVIS, d. 1761 Accomack Co., Va.; m. SEBELLA WALKER.
    ii. THOMAS[2] DAVIS.
    iii. JAMES[2] DAVIS.
    iv. WILLIAM[2] DAVIS, d. about 1754 Worcester Co., Md.; m. ELIZABETH TRUITT, daughter of GEORGE TRUITT and ELEANOR _____.
2. v. ROBERT[2] DAVIS was b. about 1674 Accomack Co., Va.; d. 1769 Worcester Co., Maryland; m. ELIZABETH LAWSON.
    vi. ELIZABETH[2] DAVIS, d. 20 February 1753 Somerset Co., Md.; m JOHN READ.
    vii. MARY[2] DAVIS.
    viii. SARAH[2] DAVIS.
    ix. JEAN[2] DAVIS.
    x. COMFORT[2] DAVIS.
    xi. EASTER[2] DAVIS.

2. ROBERT[2] *(ROBERT[1])* DAVIS was born about 1674 in Accomack Co., Virginia, and died 1769 in Worcester Co., Maryland. He married ELIZABETH LAWSON.

    1769 Robert Davis of Worcester Co., Maryland, outlived many of his children, and was the subject of a study by William D. Patrick.[5] He wrote his will 8 February 1767, but it was annulled by court decree 10 January 1771. In the will he named five sons, seven grandsons, and one great-grandson. Mr.

---

[5] Patrick, William D. Robert Davis, Sr.: A Man Who Broke New England's Monopoly on Grandparents. Maryland Historical Magazine 81:345-348, 1986.

Patrick notes that at the time of his will he twenty-five grandchildren and six great-grandchildren had been born by the time he made his will. Robert may also have had several daughters, but their names have not been found and we know nothing of their descendants. In addition to the five named sons, he had two other sons listed by his administrator, William Davis, in the final accounting in November 1772.

Robert Davis, "weaver," and William Davis, "carpenter," purchased a six hundred acre tract in Somerset County, Maryland, known as *Adventure* on 15 September 1708. Robert appears to have prospered as a planter and continued to live on his half of *Adventure* for the rest of his life. He made only one small addition to his land-holdings, an adjoining fifty-acre tract called Pig Penn Ridge, which he patented in 1750. These tracts were disposed of in the contested will.

The will was contested by sons Robert and Matthias Davis on a technicality that the two surviving witnesses had not heard Robert Davis say that the will was his—the implication being that William Davis, the executor, had benefited by a fraudulent will. As noted by Mr. Patrick:

> It is difficult to see what Robert and Matthias Davis hoped to gain by having their father's will set aside. In the absence of a valid will all of Robert's land went to their eldest brother, William, as Robert's heir at law. Apparently in recognition of his father's wishes regarding the bequest to Henry Davis son of Thomas, William in his own will, probated 4 June 1773, made a bequest of fifty acres of land to his "cousin" (nephew) Henry Davis, leaving the rest of his plantation to his sons Robert and Nixon Davis.[6]

---

[6] Will of William Davis, Sr., prob. 1773, Worcester Co., Md., JW No. 4 Wills (Worcester) 161. (cited by Patrick.)

Children of ROBERT DAVIS and ELIZABETH LAWSON:

    i. WILLIAM³ DAVIS, b. about 1707, d. about 1773 Worcester Co., Md.; m. ANN PORTER.

    ii. THOMAS³ DAVIS, b. about 1708 Somerset Co., Md., d. 1777 Worcester Co., Md.

3. iii. ISHMAEL³ DAVIS, b. about 1712 Somerset Co., Md., d. 1760 Worcester Co., Md.; m. PATIENCE _____.

    iv. BENJAMIN³ DAVIS, b. about 1716 Worcester Co., Md.; d. 1760 Worcester Co., Md.; m. MARY BADDARD.

    v. ROBERT³ DAVIS, b. about 1720 Worcester Co., Md.; d. April 1794 Kent Co., Del.; m. SUSANNAH HART.

    vi. JOHN³ DAVIS, b. about 1723 Worcester Co., Md., d. 1783 Worcester Co., Md.; m. MARTHA GIVEN.

        1. JOHN⁴ DAVIS.

        2. MARY⁴ DAVIS.

    vii. MATHIAS³ DAVIS.

    viii. boy

3. ISHMAEL³ *(ROBERT²⁻¹)* DAVIS was born about 1712 Worcester Co., Md., and died before 21 February 1761 Worcester Co., Md. He married PATIENCE _____.

    The tract in Worcester Co., Md., known as "Hoggs Den" was patented 20 May 1696 by George Truitt, at which time it was described as "300 acres in Mattapony."[7] Samuel Truitt sold 200 acres of this tract to Donnock Dennis on 20 February 1735, at which time it became known as "Dennis his purchase." Donnock Dennis, Jr., sold the tract to

   [7] Dryden, Ruth T. Land Records of Worcester County, Maryland, 1666-1810. (n. p. d., 1987) p. 300. Copy located at Pratt Library, Baltimore, Md., March 2007.

Ishmael Davis 11 December 1749, and which time it was repatented with additional land for a total of 549 acres. On 8 March 1758 Samuel Truitt of Sussex Co., Md., sold the remaining 100 acres of the original tract to Ishmael Davis or Worcester Co., Md.

Hogg's Den was transferred from Ishmael Davis to his son, Benjamin, in 1760 by will. On 29 March 1776 Benjamin Davis sold 12 acres to John Givens, and on 13 July 1790 he sold 143 acres to William Round. On 13 July 1791 he sold 10 acres to James Davis. On 5 March 1787, James Davis had sold six acres of the tract to William Brittingham, and on 20 Feb 1793 James Davis and William Brittingham sold to John Jarman tracts of six acres and two acres 15 perches. On 29 March 1793, James Davis, Sr., son of Ishmael Davis, sold 10 acres to William Round, Sr. Then, on 28 Oct 1794 James Davis and William Brittingham sold eight acres to John Jarman, and on the same date, James Davis sold 211 ½ acres to William Bassett, Jr. The remaining part of the land was transferred by William Round to his son, Joshua, by will in 1815.

The last will and testament of Ishmael Davis has been published online.[8]

In the Name of God, Amen, 10th day of February in the year of our Lord seventeen hundred sixty, I, Ishmael Davis of Worcester County in Maryland being in perfect sense and memory of mind thanks be to God for the same and calling to mind the mortality of my body and knowing that it is appointed for all men to die, do make and ordain this my last will and testament.

Item: I leave to my beloved wife, Patience Davis, my plantation and all the land I now possess, til my son Benjamin comes to years of eighteen and the part that I shall give to him for her to have no right

[8] Kay. Our Winding Family Vine. 24 Sep 2005. http://worldconnect.rootsweb.com, (db texasfolks).

to after he comes to that age and the remainder part to be hers during life or widowhood.

Item: I give and bequeath to my daughter Martha Davis a cow that goes by the name of her cow and all the increase, the bed she lies in and furniture and two head of sheep—one feather bed, two chairs, cow and calf and 2 head of sheep to Rachell.

Item: I give to my daughter Mary Davis one cow and calf two sheep and feather bed and my smallest pot.

Item: I give to my son Benjamin Davis part of my tract of land call Hoggs Den to divide from a marked white gum marked with eight notches standing at the going over to the Bid Place then, with a line drawn east to the original line, then my cart road to divide to the westward. I give to him one cow and calf and one yoke of oxen.

Item: I give to my son James Davis the remainder part of my tract of land whereon I now live and two cows and calves and my gun.

Item: I give to my son Shadrack one negro fellow called Peter and one cow and calf and two sheep.

Item: I give to Patience my beloved wife all the remainder part of my estate to her during her widowhood and likewise I do appoint her executrix of this my sole will and testament.

Item: I give to my three daughters eight pounds cash and each after the death of my wife.

Item: I give all the rest of my estate to be equally divided among all my surviving children.

I do hereby acknowledge this to be my last will and testament in testimony whereof I have hereunto set my hand and seal the day and year above written—sealed and delivered in the presence of

Joseph Jones Senr
Savory Wing
Robert Wilson   Ishmael Davis (seal)

February 23, 1761 came Joseph Jones, Savory Wing, and Robert Wilson the subscribing witnesses to the foregoing will and made oath on the Holy Evangelis of Almighty God that they saw Ishmael Davis the testator sign, seal, and hear him publish, pronounce, and declare the same to be his last will and testament and that at the time of his so doing he was to the best of their apprehension of a sound disposing mind and memory and that they subscribed their names as witnesses to the said will in the presence of the testator and at his request.
Examined Benton Harris, court clerk

February 28, 1761 came Patience Davis widow and relict of the above deceased and quitted claim to the devise made to her in the foregoing will and elected in lieu thereof to have a third of said estate real and personal as by law allotted.
Benton Harris

Children of ISHMAEL DAVIS and PATIENCE are:

  i. MARTHA[4] DAVIS.
  ii. MARY[4] DAVIS.
  iii. RACHEL[4] DAVIS.
  iv. BENJAMIN[4] DAVIS.
4. v. JAMES[4] DAVIS, b. about 1750 Worcester Co., Md.; d. after 27 April 1803 Hancock Co., Ga.; m. ELIZA VICTOR, daughter of THOMAS VICTOR and ELIZABETH BEVANS; b. about 1762 Worcester Co., Md.; d. before 4 September 1826 Hancock Co., Ga.
  vi. SHADRACK[4] DAVIS.

4. JAMES[4] (ISHMAEL[3], ROBERT[2-1]) DAVIS was born about 1750 in Worcester Co., Maryland and died after 27 April 1803 Hancock Co., Ga. He married ELIZA VICTOR, daughter of THOMAS VICTOR and ELIZABETH BEVANS. She was born about 1762 Worcester Co., Maryland, and died before 4 September 1826 Hancock Co., Ga.

Dan Langford did extensive research on James Davis and his son Thomas Davis and provided me a copy of his research notes in 2001. He compiled his data in 1995. Many of his sources were personal communications, and he did not provide full references for all of his public sources.[9]

4 Feb 1795 Archibald Smith, Sen., to James Davis, both of Hancock Co. for $154 a tract of land on west side of road leading from Archibald Sr. to Archibald Jr., being part of a tract purchased of John Hannock, originally granted to Sanders Walker on 14 July 1787. Wit: Zackary Williamson, Alex'd Reed, JP.[10]

1795 Hancock Co., Ga. James Davis paid tax on 140.5 ac. on Shoulder Bone Creek, adj. Smith, land originally granted to Walker.

19 Nov 1801 Eliza Davis appointed Samuel Turner her attorney to act in her place on matters in Worcester Co., MD.[11]

1802 Hancock Co., Ga; Capt. F. Lewis' District: James Davis paid tax for Ishmael Davis on 130 ac. on Shoulder Bone Cr., adj. to Jackson, originally granted to Simmons; also paid tax on the land as in 1795.

27 Apr 1803 James Davis prepared his will in Hancock Co., Ga. Three sons, Ishmael, James, and Thomas left 1 shilling plus property already given. The balance of the estate lent to Eliza to raise the younger children all named. He signed in presence of Daniel Melson, Elizabeth Greene, Nancy Hunt, and M. Greene.[12]

1805 Georgia Land Lottery James Davis Draw 510 (one lucky draw, married) resident Hancock Co.

---

[9] Where I have found the references, I have added that here.

[10] Hancock Co., Ga., Deed Book C:227-228, [24 Feb 1795/15 Feb 1799]. Cited in Marsh, Helen, and Marsh, Tim. Land Deed Genealogy of Hancock County, Georgia. (Greenville, SC: Southern Historical Press, 1997,) p. 156. Cited hereafter as Marsh.

[11] Hancock Co., Ga., Deed Book E:332, [19 May 1801.] Marsh.

[12] Hancock Co., Ga., Will Book F:165-166.

10 February 1810 Inventory and appraisal of estate made. Value $606.8125. Appraisers Myles Greene, Jethro Jackson, William Wallace.[13]

1813 Hancock Co., Ga., Capt. Harper's District. Eliza Davis as executor of J. Davis paid tax on two slaves and 143 ac. on Shoulder Bone Creek adjacent Ellis.

James Davis wrote his will 27 April 1803, and the inventory of his estate was made 10 February 1810, so he probably died late in 1809 or early in 1810. His will is of record.[14]

In the name of God Amen, I James Davis of the County of Hancock and State of Georgia, being in a good state of health and of perfect mind, memory & understanding and calling to mind the uncertainty of this life, do make and ordain this my last Will and Testament, in manner & form following, (to wit), first I recommend my Soul to God who gave it and my body to the earth to be buried in a Christian like manner at the discretion of my Executors. And as touching such worldly goods wherewith it has pleased God to bless me in this life I give devise and bequeath in the following manner.
Item. I give and bequeath unto my son Ishmael Davis one shilling Sterling besides the property which I have heretofore given and no more, to him and his heirs forever.
Item. I give and bequeath to my son James Davis, on shilling Sterling besides the property I have heretofore given him & no more, to him & his heirs forever.
Item. I give and bequeath to my son Thomas Davis, the sum of one shilling Sterling besides the property

---

[13] Hancock Co., Ga., Will Book F:166-168. The annual return for 1809 was filed by Eliza Davis, executrix at WB F:169-170, which implies that James Davis died early enough in 1810 that he had not completed his taxes for the previous year.

[14] Hancock Co., Ga., Will Book F:165. The inventory follows on page 166.

I have heretofore given him & no more, to him & his heirs forever.

Item. I lend unto my beloved wife Eliza Davis all the rest and remaining part of my estate real and personal during her natural life or widowhood for the purpose of raising and educating my younger children, Saul Davis, Mary Davis, Eliza Davis, Jehu Davis, Archibald Davis and Henrietta Davis and at the death of or marriage of my said wife Eliza Davis, it is my will and meaning that all the property lent to my wife as above shall be equally divided between my younger children above mentioned, Saul, Mary, Eliza, Jehu, Archibald and Henrietta. And I ordain and constitute my wife Eliza Davis sole executrix to this my last will and Testament. In witness whereof I have hereunto set my hand and seal this 27th day of April 1803.

James Davis

Signed, sealed, and acknowledged
As the last will of the Testator
In the presence of us
Daniel Melson
Elizabeth Greene
Nancy (x) Hart
M. Greene

Eliza Davis, age greater than 45, is head of household in the 1820 Census and has one male 26-45 living with her.[15] The estate records of James Davis establish that Eliza (Victor) Davis died before 4 September 1826 when Archibald Davis was granted letters of administration *de bonis non* for the estate of James Davis, with Joshua Ellis as his security.[16] Archibald Davis was granted permission to sell the remaining property of the estate on 5 November 1827. The appraisers were Edmund Abercrombie, George L.

---

[15] 1820 Census Hancock Co., Ga., Clayton's Dist., p. 94 [000010-00001].

[16] Hancock Co., Ga., Will Book M:175-178.

362

Scott, Wilkins Smith, William Hurt, and Job Harton. On 4 December 1827 130 acres were sold to William Hurt on 12 months credit for $300. On 2 January 1828 an inventory was recorded that showed debts found among the papers of Elizabeth Davis, deceased, widow and executrix of James Davis' estate totaling $178.12. The personal property was sold for cash to Henry N. Langford and Archibald Davis on 3 January 1828. Finally, on 13 December 1828 Joshua Ellis paid $92.38 for his property as part of the estate, except for land in Wayne Co., and on 26 December 1828 John Davis did the same.

There are several hints that the James Davis family (including son Thomas) was originally from Maryland. At least three of Thomas' brothers died after the 1850 census when the birth states and ages of individuals were recorded. Both brother James, (born about 1780) found in Putnam Co., Ga., in 1850, and Saul, (born about 1785) found in Dallas Co., Ala. in 1850 indicated their birth place as Maryland. (Ishmael died in Montgomery Co., Ala., in 1848). Archibald, born about 1796 in Georgia is found in Monroe Co., Ga., in 1850.

In 1801 Hancock Co., Ga., Eliza Davis (Thomas' mother) appointed Samuel Turner attorney to handle legal matters in Worcester Co., Md. Mrs. Davis obviously had a matter requiring someone to represent her back in Maryland. Perhaps disposal of property or settlement of a dispute over inheritance was the reason.

Worcester Co. is on the Eastern Shore, east of Chesapeake Bay The occurrence of unusual given names might also be a clue. In the early and middle 1700's land and probate records of Worcester Co., Md., are full of transactions by Ishmael, Saul, and

Solomon Davis as well as the more common given names.[17]

The 1790 Census for Worcester Co., Maryland shows James Davis with one male over 16, four males under 16, two females, and no slaves.[18] This matches the known information about the children of 1810 James Davis of Hancock Co., Ga. While there are many men named Davis in this county, the nearest to this entry for James Davis are Philip Davis (#124 2-0-3-0-0), Samuel Davis, (#133, 3-0-2-1-0), Joshua Davis, (#136, 2-2-3-0-0) and Thomas Davis, (#138, 2-2-2-0-0).[19]

On 10 January 1795 Thomas Victor made his will in Worcester Co., Maryland in which he named as one of his heirs a daughter, Jemina Davis.[20] Since the

---

[17] Quoted from Dan Langford's report, with minor corrections of grammatical errors.

[18] 1790 Census Worcester Co., Md., p. 127, #132. (1-4-2-0-0).

[19] Thomas Victor, Sr., Thomas, Jr., and James Victor are on p. 126, #64, 65, and 66. Thomas Beavins, Jr., Roland Beavins, Sr., and William Beavins are on p. 126, #88, 94, and 95. Thomas Beavins, Sr., is on p. 127, #114. Benjamin Davis (2-2-4-0-0) and Shadrack Davis (1-1-1-0-0) are on p. 125, #267 and 268. Unfortunately, there is another cluster of Davis men known to be related to 1760 Ishmael Davis of Worcester Co., MD on p. 124: Shadrack, #222 (1-2-5-0-0), Edmond, #223 (2-2-2-0-0); Benjamin #224 (3-1-3-0-0); Thomas, son of Benjamin, #225 (2-1-2-0-0); Charles, #227 (1-3-2-0-0); Nehemiah, #228, (1-4-2-0-0); and John (Mill), #229 (1-1-1-0-1).

[20] The LWT of Thomas Victor was written 10 Jan 1792 and proved 17 Mar 1797 Worcester Co., Md., Will Book JW:290. He left his son James a 150 ac. tract known as "Partnership" and a 7 ac. tract known as "Victor's industry." He left his son Thomas the remainder of the land. His son, John Victor, received 1 shilling. He left two negroes for the support of his daughter Peggy. He left his personal estate to his daughters Peggy, Sarah, and Ann; to daughter Jemima Davis he left 1 shilling. He left his plantation to his wife Elizabeth for life or widowhood. Cited in Kay. Our Winding Family Vine. 24 Sep 2005. http://worldconnect.rootsweb.com, (db texasfolks.) She also reports the following deeds. Worcester Co., MD DB C:34 [6 June 1753] James Bratten to Thomas Victor, £20, a 50 ac. tract "James' Choice," n side of Pocomoke River. DB M:526 [8 May 1789] John Victor to William Dryden (son Samuel), a 210 ac. tract acquired from Thomas Victor known as "Broad Neck." tract now called "Black Soil" 259 acres, sold for £350 with dower release by James' wife, Hannah. Dryden's Land Records shows Victor's Industry patented 15 October 1750 by Thomas Victor, 70 ac. in Coulborn Dist, #6, map 34. In 1795 willed 5 ac.

Georgia records show 1810 James Davis' wife as Eliza, it is not as clear as one would like that this refers to the same woman, but the naming patterns of the children supports a connection. The date of emigration to Georgia can therefore be narrowed from between August 1791 and fall 1794 when James Davis appears on the Hancock Co., Ga., tax list.

The connection between James Davis and Ishmael Davis is made on the basis of his will, plus the land transactions involving "Hogg's Den" in Worcester Co., Md., discussed previously. James Davis sold the remaining part of his tract in 1794, which matches the data outlined above.

Children of JAMES DAVIS and ELIZA VICTOR are:

i. ISHMAEL[5] DAVIS b. about 1778 Worcester Co., Md.[21], d. after 21 February 1843 Montgomery Co., Ala.; m. REBECCA SIMMONS about 1800 Hancock Co., Ga., daughter of JOHN SIMMONS and REDECCA ____; b. 1794 Hancock Co., Ga., and d. before 1860 Montgomery Co., Ala.

Ishmael Davis and Myles Green witnessed the sale of a 10 acre tract on the waters of Fort Creek on Long Dam Creek adjacent Myles Greene from Archibald Smith to Danielson Melson on 4 Feb 1799.[22]

The following data were accumulated by Dan Langford.

30 Dec 1801 Thomas Simmons of "Linkom" Co., to Ishmael Davis of Hancock 143 ¾ acres for $718.25, a tract on Oconee River at the mouth of Shoulder Bone Creek, being half of a tract granted to John Simmons 12 Oct

---

to James, rest to Thomas; Victor's Addition, 121 ac. same district, patented 1759.

[21] Eliza Mothershed, daughter, reported her father was b. in MD in the 1880 Census. [DAL]

[22] Hancock Co., Ga., Deed Book C:332-333, [6 May 1800.] Marsh, p. 169.

1785. Wit: James Davis, Jos. Cooper, JP.

26 Feb 1803 Ishmael Davis to William Wallace, both of Hancock Co., $1500, a tract of 130 acres on Oconee River and the mouth of Shoulder Bone Creek, being half of tract granted to John Simmons in 1785. Wit: Myles Green, Jethro Jackson.

1805 Georgia Land Lottery: Ishmael Davis Draw 509, BB (2 draws, married, no luck) Resident Hancock Co.

17 Feb 1808 John Nixon of Clarke Co. to Ishmael Davis of Baldwin Co. for $500, 202 ½ acre, lot 102, 14th Dist., orig. Baldwin, now Putnam Co., granted to John Nixon. Wit: Thomas Hill, Peter Randolph, JJC.

18 Apr 1808 Ishmael Davis to Robert B. Knight, both of Putnam, for $800, lot 102, 14th Dist. originally Baldwin, now Putnam Co.

29 Aug 1808 Ishmael Davis, original grantee, to Reuben Westmoreland, both of Putnam, $275, 109.9 ac. lot 62, 3rd Dist., orig. Baldwin, now Putnam Co., Wit: Hannah Taylor, Shephard Mize.

30 Oct 1824 Ishmael Davis received patent from US Land Office, Cahaba, Ala., 80 ac. E½ , SE¼ sec. 28, twp. 12N, range 18 E, St. Stephens, now Montgomery Co., Ala.

1830 Census, Montgomery Co., Alabama. Ishmael Davis, 50-60; one woman 50/60, one woman 15-20, and 4 slaves.

1840 Census, Montgomery Co., Alabama, p. 189, Ishmael Davis, 60-70, one woman 50-60, and one male 15-20, and 11 slaves.

LWT Ishmael Davis of Montgomery Co., Ala., written 21 Feb 1845, probated 19 June 1848, gives all lands, live stock, etc., except for 1 ac. incl. Meeting house and grave yard to wife Rebecca, and at her death to be divided among children: John V. Davis, Mary Jackson, Eliza Mothershed, Rebecca Moore, and Cornelia Hurt. Slaves were granted to children and their heirs. John V. Davis was named executor. Wit: Benjamin Mitchell, A. Dubberly, Bartlett Williams.

The Oakes source cited above reports that John Simmons made a deed of gift to his children, including Rebecca, at Old Wilkes County, formerly Washington Co., now Hancock Co., Ga.

Montgomery County, Alabama, May 24th, 1848. Died at his residence, in this county, on the 14th instant, Ishmael Davis, who had lived to see the full number of years allotted to man in this world. He died as he professed to live—a Christian. He belonged to the Christian Church and had spent all of the prime of his life in the service of God. He was highly devoted to the Reformation, and taught in public during a great number of years. Suffice to say, that we are confident that we hazard nothing in saying that society, in this vicinity, is bereaved of its best pattern. We furthermore say to the friends of the deceased, that they should, in signal manner, show their gratitude to God for permitting such an example of piety to dwell so long among them, and their love for the deceased by practicing the virtues for which they esteemed him.[23]

---

[23] The Millennial Harbinger, Vol. 5, p. 419. Cited by Tom Childers. http://www.findagrave.com, #48783243.

Rebecca Davis, 66, b. GA, is living next to her son, John V. Davis, in the 1850 Census, and has a two year old boy, Gustavus Adolphus Davis, b. Alabama living with her. In the 1860 census he is living with John V. Davis' family, and Rebecca no longer appears in the census.

Children of ISHMAEL DAVIS and REBECCA:

1. JOHN V.[6] DAVIS, b. 26 September 1801 Hancock Co., Ga., d. 10 May 1871 Montgomery Co., Ala.;[24] m. JULIA PARKER KNIGHT 10 July 1823 Montgomery Co., Ala.,[25] dau. of ALLEN KNIGHT and MARY ELIZABETH FOREMAN, b. 3 May 1805 in South Carolina; d. 17 Dec 1876 Montgomery Co., Ala.[26]
      He appears in the 1850 Census for Montgomery Co., Ala. aged 48, b. Georgia. Julia P., is 45, b. SC, and the children are listed.[27]

Children of JOHN DAVIS and JULIA KNIGHT:

a. MARY ANN REBECCA[7] DAVIS, b. 13 April 1827 Montgomery Co., Ala.; d. 30 January 1891 Montgomery Co., Ala.;[28] m. ANSOM HIRAM COURTNEY, son of JOHN HIRAM COURTNEY and MARY HELLUMS; b. 4 March 1819; d. 6 August 1894 Montgomery Co., Ala.[29]

a. SIMEON DEROLLO[7] DAVIS, b. 24 August 1825 Montgomery Co., Ala.; d. before 1870 Henderson Co., Texas;[30] m. SARAH M. (OWEN) BROWN.

---

[24] Fair Prospect Cemetery, Naftel Montgomery Co., Ala. http://www.findagrave.com, #23887357.

[25] Alabama Select Marriages, 1816-1957. Accessed 9 February 2014 at Ancestry.com.

[26] Fair Prospect Cemetery, Naftel, Montgomery Co., Ala. http://www.findagrave.com, #23887376.

[27] 1850 Census Montgomery Co., Ala., Dist. 2, p. 157B, #99.

[28] Ebenezer Church Cemetery, Ramer, Montgomery Co. ,Ala. http://www.findagrave.com, #23688462.

[29] Ebenezer Church Cemetery, Ramer, Montgomery Co. ,Ala. http://www.findagrave.com, #17330295.

[30] D. M. LeForce, http://www.findagrave.com, #98766729. He died in Henderson Co., Texas, and married Sarah Emmanitus Owen, b. 15 September 1833 Pike Co., Ala.; d. 20 April 1891 Okla., (#98766996.) She

They are present in 1860 in Henderson Co., Texas with Joella, 2, Aaron, 10/12, and William W. Brown, 9, and also William G. Middleton.[31]

b.   WILLIAM DEWITT CLINTON[7] DAVIS, b. 5 January 1827, Montgomery Co., Ala., d. 4 February 1894 Henderson Co., Texas.[32]

c.   ELIZABETH ELMINE[7] DAVIS, b. 19 June 1828 Montgomery Co., Ala.; d. 17 July 1862 Montgomery Co., Ala.;[33] m. JAMES S. TUCKER 4 May 1852 Montgomery Co., Ala.;[34] d. about 1857 Montgomery Co., Ala.[35]

d.   THOMAS JEFFERSON[7] DAVIS, b. 14 April 1830 Montgomery Co., Ala.; d. 7 June 1893 Pike Co., Ala.[36]; m. SARAH F. WOOD 3 January 1861 Pike Co., Ala.,[37] dau. of

---

had married (1) John W. Brown; m. (2) Simeon Davis and had Joella, Aaron, Beauregard Arlington Lee, Sarah Addiline, and Simeon de Kalb Washington Lafayette. She m. (3) James W. Hannah, and m. (4) S. T. Brinson. Simeon was b. 28 January 1864 Rusk Co., Texas; d. 8 December 1925 Tulsa, Tulsa Co., Okla. (Rose Hill Memorial Park, Tulsa, #45857096.)

[31] 1860 Census Henderson Co., Texas, Beat 4, p. 60, #605/586. He was listed as a wagoner. The census notes that "Mr. Middleton was not given in at his boarding house."

[32] Owen Cemetery, Henderson Co., Texas. http://www.findagrave.com, #44224668. Tombstone states his date of birth was 6 February 1827 in Alabama. He was single and listed as a lawyer in the 1880 Census Henderson Co., Texas, Athens, ED 31, p. 103A, #1.

[33] The date is from online sources. There is a modern tombstone without dates for Elizabeth Tucker in Ebenezer Church Cemetery, Ramer, Montgomery Co., Ala. http://www.findagrave.com, #23886940.

[34] Elizabeth E. Davis married James B. Collin(s) 3 August 1846 Montgomery Co., Ala. However, Elizabeth E. Davis was still living with her father in the 1850 Census. [Montgomery Co., Ala., Dist. 2, p. 157B, #99.] Elizabeth E. Davis m. James S. Tucker 4 May 1852 in Montgomery Co., Ala. [Alabama Select Marriages, 1816-1957. Accessed 11 February 2014 at Ancestry.com.]

[35] "E." Tucker, b. about 1829 Georgia, is head of household in Dist. 2, Montgomery Co., Ala., in 1860 [p. 8, #60] with children Helen, 7; Julia, 5; and Joann, 3. In 1870, Lou H. Tucker, 16; Julia, 15; and Jane A., 13, are living with John W. Davis, 36, Louisa J. Boyd, 30; James P. Boyd, 10; and Caroline S. Boyd, 6. [Montgomery Co., Ala., Twp. 12, p. 9A, #448.] Hence James S. Tucker appears to have died around the time of the birth of his last daughter, and before 1860.

[36] Elam-Davidson Memorial Cemetery, Goshen, Pike Co., Ala. http://www.findagrave.com, #23595670.

[37] Alabama Select Marriages, 1816-1957. Accessed 9 February 2014 at Ancestry.com.

JONATHAN WOOD and CYNTHIA;[38] b. 1846 Pike Co., Ala.; d. after 1920 Pike Co., Ala.

He was a physician. They are in Pike County in 1870,[39] and 1880.[40] She was still there in 1920,[41] but I have not found her in the 1930 Census.

e.   JAMES ANDERSON MONROE[7] DAVIS, b. 9 October 1832 Montgomery Co., Ala.; m. MALISIA JANE CASTELLAW 22 April 1858 Lowndes Co., Ala.,[42] dau. of BENJAMIN F. CASTELLAW and MARY LOUISA JORDAN; b. 3 February 1842 Ala.; d. 22 December 1935 Scurry Co., Texas.[43]

He is enumerated in the 1870 and 1880 Census for Henderson Co., Texas. His brother William D. C. Davis, attorney, was listed in the household in 1880.

Malissa, age 67, was widowed and living with her son, John V. Davis, in Scurry Co., Texas, in 1910.[44]

f.   JOHN WHITAKER[7] DAVIS, b. 28 November 1834 Montgomery Co., Ala.; d. 27 February 1880 Montgomery Co., Ala.[45]

g.   ELIZA VICTOR[7] DAVIS, b. 4 February 1837, d. 29 August 1838, Montgomery Co., Ala.

h.   NUBAL ANDREW JACKSON[7] DAVIS, b. 13 December 1838 Montgomery Co., Ala.,; d. during the Civil War.

i.   LOUISA JEFFELONA[7] DAVIS, b. 19 December 1840 Montgomery Co., Ala.; d. before 1880

---

[38] 1860 Census Pike Co., Ala., Western Division, p. 26, #174.

[39] 1870 Census Pike Co., Ala., Beat 10, p. 405A, #6/6. Listed are children: Julia E., 8, Martha C., 7, Thomas J., 5, Celia O., 3, and Cullen G., 8/12 (male).

[40] 1880 Census Pike Co., Ala., Mitchells, ED 150, p. 220B, #26/65.

[41] 1920 Census Pike Co., Ala., Goshen Hill, ED 154, p. 3A, #61. She was living on South Street.

[42] Alabama Select Marriages, 1816-1957. Accessed 11 February 2014 at Ancestry.com.

[43] Ira Cemetery, Scurry Co., Texas. http://www.findagrave.com, #76589112.

[44] 1910 Census Scurry Co., Texas, Justice Pct. 3, ED 233, p. 5B, #91/93. They were described as at the intersection of Bluff Creek and Red Bluff Road.

[45] Ebenezer Church Cemetery, Ramer, Montgomery Co. ,Ala. http://www.findagrave.com, #17330299.

370

Montgomery Co., Ala.;[46] m. JAMES P. BOYD 28 September 1859 Montgomery Co., Ala.;[47] b. about 1838 Montgomery Co., Ala.; d. before 1870.[48]

j. SAUL CICERO[7] DAVIS, b. 10 June 1842 Montgomery Co., Ala.; d. 15 Nov. 1902 Henderson Co., Texas;[49] m. NANCY CUMI; b. 13 June 1845; d. 7 April 1930 Henderson Co., Texas.[50]

k. JULIA MISSOURI[7] DAVIS, b. 11 February 1844 Montgomery Co., Ala., d. 26 April 1866.

l. WILLIAM ZACHARY TAYLOR[7] DAVIS, b. 18 March 1848 Montgomery Co., Ala., d. 15 July 1918 Henderson Co., Texas;[51] m. CELINA ELIZA SMITH, Athens, Texas; b. 22 September 1851 Arkansas; d. 27 June 1939 Henderson Co., Tex.[52]

Mrs. W. T. Davis, 87, one of the oldest residents of the county, died at 8:10 Tuesday night at the residence of Mrs. M. J. Millender on Madole Street, where she had been making her home. Mrs. Davis suffered a stroke of paralysis early Monday morning and little hope had been held out for her. All her children except one reached her bedside before the end came...Burial will be by the side of her husband, who died in 1918. Six of her children are also buried there. The

---

[46] James P. Boyd is living with his uncle, G. A. Davis, in Mitchells, Pike Co., Ala., ED 150, p. 220B. He was b. 18 January 1862 Montgomery Co., Ala.; d. 14 September 1927 Hopkins Co., Texas. http://www.findagrave.com, #27209392. I have not located his mother in the 1880 Census, nor have I located a grave record.

[47] Alabama Select Marriages, 1816-1957. Accessed 12 February 2014 at Ancestry.com.

[48] 1860 Census Montgomery Co., Ala., Dist. 2, p. 87, #676/631. They are living next to his parents, Alfred and Caroline Boyd. [cf. 1850 Census Montgomery Co., Ala., Dist. 2, p. 170A, #270.]

[49] Davis Cemetery, Athens, Henderson Co., Texas. http://www.findagrave.com, #25604233.

[50] Davis Cemetery, Athens, Henderson Co., Texas. http://www.findagrave.com, #25604257.

[51] Davis Cemetery, Athens, Henderson Co., Texas. http://www.findagrave.com, #25587526.

[52] Davis Cemetery, Athens, Henderson Co., Texas. http://www.findagrave.com, #25587572.

death of Mrs. Davis marked the passing of the last of her immediate family...Mrs. Davis is survived by six children.[53]

  m. GUSTAVUS ADOLPHUS[7] DAVIS, b. 19 April 1848 Montgomery Co., Ala.; d. 14 August 1932 Hunt Co., Texas;[54] m. (1) MARTHA V. WOOD 16 January 1868 Pike Co., Ala., dau. of JONATHAN WOOD and CYNTHIA; b. 8 August 1848 Pike Co., Ala.; d. 17 January 1889 Henderson Co., Texas;[55] m. (2) EUGENIA DAWSON about 1895 Henderson Co., Texas; b. 1859; d. 1926.[56]

2. MARY[6] DAVIS, b. 1805 Georgia; m. HARMAN JACKSON; b. about 1805 S. C.

  In 1850 Harman Jackson, 45, SC, and Mary, 45, are in Montgomery Co., Ala.[57]

3. ELIZA[6] DAVIS m. JAMES MOTHERSHED 25 January 1826 Montgomery Co., Ala.[58]

  The 1860 Census shows James Mothershed, 59, b. SC, and Eliza, 50, b. Ga., along with their children.[59]

4. REBECCA[6] S. DAVIS b. about 1811 Putnam Co., Ga., d. after 1860 Montgomery Co., Ala.; m. NUBAL A. MOORE 5 February 1829 Montgomery Co., Ala.;[60] b. about 1810 Georgia; d. after 1870 Coffee Co., Ala.

  N. A. Moore is listed in the 1850 Census Montgomery Co., Ala. (#384) and again in 1860

---

[53] Ibid.

[54] Simmons Cemetery, Cash, Hunt Co., Texas. http://www.findagrave.com, #25590109. The obituary gives his birth date as 19 September 1848. He does not appear in the 1850 Census, but is listed in 1860. [Montgomery Co., Ala., Dist. 2, p. 15, #108/99.]

[55] Simmons Cemetery, Cash, Hunt Co., Texas. http://www.findagrave.com, #66341296. The grave is unmarked, but several of her children are buried there.

[56] Hart Cemetery, Cash, Henderson Co., Texas. http://www.findagrave.com, #20867096.

[57] 1850 Census Montgomery Co., Ala., Dist. 2, p. 170A, #269.

[58] Alabama Select Marriages, 1816-1957. Accessed 9 February 2014 at Ancestry.com.

[59] 1860 Census Lowndes Co., Ala., p. 556, #645/556. There is also a book by Mattie Logsdon, My Mothershed Family, (Ada, OK.: 1975), which details some of this information. Dan Langford listed this in his reference list, but did not cite it in his notes on Eliza Mothershed.

[60] Alabama Select Marriages, 1816-1957. Accessed 9 February 2014 at Ancestry.com. She is shown as Carolina P. in this database.

(#821/775.) The names of the children are from these lists. Reuben Wilson, 35, farmer, is living in the household in 1850. In 1860 Robert C. Hill, 22, and Mary P., 12 AL, John, 9, AL, and Wm. G., 6, AL., are also living in the household. These are probably kin on the Moore side of the family. They are living in Coffee Co., Ala., in 1870.[61]

5. CORNELIA[6] DAVIS b. 1814; d. after 1880 Coffee Co., Ala.; m. KINDRED HURT 13 March 1831 Montgomery Co., Ala.; b. about 1810 S. C.; d. after 1880 Coffee Co., Ala.

Cornelia Hurt and Kindred are living in Pike Co., Ala., in 1850[62] and 1860,[63] and in Coffee Co., Ala., in 1870[64] and 1880.[65]

ii. JAMES[5] DAVIS was b. 16 April 1781 Md., d. 30 Dec 1851 Eatonton, Putnam, Co., Ga.; m. MARY DARNELL 14 May 1812 Prince George Co., Md.; b. 15 November 1785 Virginia.[66]

Diane Killian references a Davis family Bible for her dates. She indicates that James, Jr., was in Putnam Co., Ga., by 1815, and that five children married in Putnam Co., with records extant. She reports that the research was done by her father, Patillo Edwin Langford. Dan Langford cited personal communications from Rhoda A. Bowen sent to him by Aline Chesnutt Anderson for the data.

Dan Langford reported that James Davis was in Putnam Co., Ga., on the 1815 Tax List.

24 Feb 1819 James P. Knowles to James Davis, both of Putnam Co., for $500 a tract of 50 ¼ acres part of lot 59, 3rd Dist., Putnam Co. Wit: Edw. Varnes, H. B. Rees, JP.

---

[61] 1870 Census Coffee Co., Ala., Twp. 6, Range 19, p. 421A, #90. Robert and Rachel Hurt are at #91, and J. J. Davis is #93.

[62] 1850 Census Pike Co., Ala., p. 203A, #727

[63] 1860 Census Pike Co., Ala., Western Div., p. 122, #822.

[64] 1870 Census Coffee Co., Ala., Twp. 3, Range 20, p. 431B, #12.

[65] 1880 Census Coffee Co., Ala., Grants, ED 44, p. 304D, #302.

[66] Killian, Dianne L. James Davis, Jr., Putnam, Ga. father of William Arnold Davis, Lowndes, AL. 15 July 2004. http://genforum.genealogy.com/davis/messages/32776.html. Dan Langford listed his date of death as 29 September 1856 Putnam Co., Ga.

James Davis is 26-45 in the 1820 census as is his wife.[67] Archibald Davis is on the next line.

James Davis of Buckner's District, Putnam Co., Ga., was a fortunate drawer in the 1821 Georgia Land Lottery, drawing lot 66, sec.16, Houston Co., and lot 145, sec. 8, Henry Co.

9 Feb 1821 Archibald Davis to James Davis, both of Putnam Co., $1200, 149 ac. part of lot 59, 3rd Dist. Putnam Co.

1824 and 1826 Tax Lists show James Davis with 3 polls, (two slave), and 200 acres of second quality land; 200 acres third quality land in Putnam Co., on Little River, adjacent Lynch & others; 2 wheeled carriages, and 202 ½ acres in Houston Co., 16th Dist., lot 66.

In 1827 James Davis had five polls and only the 400 acres in Putnam Co. In 1828 he had seven polls with 253 acres of 2nd quality land, and 200 acres of 3rd quality land in Putnam Co.

James Davis, age 70, b. Maryland is living in Putnam Co., Ga., on the 1850 Census along with Mary, 57, b. Virginia, Lucinda Rainey, 25, John Callaway, 14, James Callaway, 12, Mary A. Copeland 3, and Butten Reid, 12, all born in Georgia.

James Davis wrote his last will and testament 11 August 1852 in Putnam Co., Ga. He mentions that his son-in-law Larkin Barnet of Floyd Co., Ga., is not to participate in the division of the estate. He gave $500 in trust to Richard Copeland for granddaughter Mary Ann Augusta Copeland. He then divided the remainder of the estate into four shares and gave one each to his sons John V.

---

[67] 1820 Census Putnam Co., Ga., p. 101 (Capt. Buckner's District.) 10010-20010 plus six slaves.

Davis, and William A. Davis, and to his daughters Eliza J. Stubbs, wife of James Stubbs, and Martha J. Stubbs, wife of William B. Stubbs. He named his sons John V. and William A. Davis as executors. Wit: A. O. Moseley, Evan Harvey, and B. O. Adams.

Children of JAMES DAVIS and MARY DARNELL:

1. OLIVE[6] DAVIS d. after 1844 in Georgia; m. LARKIN BARNETT 21 August 1828 Putnam Co., Ga.; b. about 1802 Tennessee; he m. (2) EMELINE ____ about 1848 Floyd Co., Ga.
2. ELIZA J.[6] DAVIS b. 17 April 1815 Putnam Co., Ga., d. 6 February 1872 Putnam Co., Ga.; m. JOHN J. STUBBS 21 August 1834 Putnam Co., Ga.

    In the 1850 Census for Putnam Co., John J. Stubbs, 35 and Eliza J. Stubbs, 34, have the children listed living with them. John J. Stubbs died before the 1860 Census[68] and probably after 1854, when his last son was born.
3. JOHN V.[6] DAVIS was b. about 1817 Putnam Co., Ga. and d. after 1870 Monroe Co., Ga.; m. MARY R. WALKER 16 October 1845 Monroe Co., Ga.

    John V. Davis is listed in the 1850 Census for Putnam Co., Ga. age 33, b. GA, along with Mary T., 22, Emeline T., 4, and Mary S., 2. He is listed in Forsyth Dist., Monroe Co., in 1860, along with children E. T., (f) 13, Mary S., 12, Mattie G., 5, and L. E. A. (f), 1.[69]

    J. V. Davis was a member of the Rising Star Lodge No. 4, of Eatonton, Putnam Co., Ga., in 1854.[70]

    J. V. Davis served in Co. D., 8th Monroe Infantry State Guard during the civil war. He is in the 1870 Census for Monroe Co., Forsyth, #252/269, along with Mattie G., 14, and Lou A., 11.

---

[68] 1860 Census Putnam Co., Ga., p. 402, Eatonton, #262/262.
[69] 1850 Census Putnam Co., Ga., Dist. 70, p. 286.
[70]
http://ftp.rootsweb.com/pub/usgenweb/ga/putnam/history/risstar4.txt.

Children of JOHN DAVIS and MARY WALKER:

a. EMELINE T.[7] DAVIS, b. 1846 Putnam Co., Ga.
b. MARY S.[7] DAVIS, b. 1848 Putnam Co., Ga.
c. MATTIE G.[7] DAVIS, b. 1855 Monroe Co., Ga.
d. LOU E. A.[7] DAVIS, b. 1859 Monroe Co., Ga.

4. MARTHA JANE[6] DAVIS b. about 1821 Putnam Co., Ga.; d. aft. 1850 Putnam Co., Ga.; m. WILLIAM B. STUBBS 1 February 1841 Putnam Co., Ga.; b. about 1817 Georgia.

5. WILLIAM ARNOLD[6] DAVIS b. about 1825 Putnam Co., Ga., d. aft. 1870 Lowndes Co., Ala.; m. MARTHA JEFFERSON WARD 25 January 1849 Putnam Co., Ga.

William A. Davis migrated, perhaps with his brother John V. Davis, to Lowndes Co., Ala. This immigration occurred prior to the death of James Davis in 1851, as the probate records show that William Davis did not return to Putnam Co., Ga., to serve as an executor of his father's will. (Dianne Killian)

They are in the 1860 Census in Cahaba P. O., Dallas Co., Ala.[71] In 1870 they are in Lowndes Co., Ala.[72] Children are from the Census.

Children of WILLIAM DAVIS and MARTHA WARD:

a. CAROLINE[7] DAVIS, b. 1851 Putnam Co., Ga.
b. JAMES ARCHIBALD[7] DAVIS, b. 1856 Putnam Co., Ga.
c. WILLIAM[7] DAVIS, b. 1861 Dallas Co., Ala.
d. BEULAH[7] DAVIS, b. 1864 Dallas Co., Ala.
e. EMMA[7] DAVIS, b. 1869 Alabama

6. MARY ANN[6] DAVIS d. before 1850 Putnam Co., Ga.; m. WILLIAM COPELAND 15 January 1846 Putnam Co., Ga.

5. iii. THOMAS[5] DAVIS was b. about 1788 and d. August 1826 Putnam Co., Ga.

---

[71] 1860 Census Dallas Co., Ala., p. 789, #195/189.
[72] 1870 Census Lowndes Co., Ala., p. 388, #76/77. Braggs Store.

iv. SAUL[5] DAVIS was b. 1788 Maryland, d. 20 August 1859 Dallas Co., Ala.;[73] m. NANCY HOLLINGSWORTH.

"Sal" Davis, 65, Maryland, and George Davis, 21, Alabama, are in Dallas Co., Ala., in 1850.[74]

Children of SAUL DAVIS and NANCY:

1. GEORGE T.[6] DAVIS, b. 1829 Ala.; d. after 1880 Dallas Co., Ala.; m. TENNESSEE R. KENNEDY 22 April 1852 Dallas Co., Ala.;[75] d. before 1880 Dallas Co., Ala.
   George T. Davis is in Dallas Co., Ala., in 1860,[76] 1870,[77] and 1880.[78]
2. ARCHIBALD[6] DAVIS, b. 1837; d. April 1860 Dallas Co., Ala.
3. WILLIAM L.[6] DAVIS, b. about 1832 Ala.; m. MARY.
   William L. Davis, 28, and Mary, 21, La., are living next door to George T. Davis in 1860.[79] They are there in 1870.[80]
4. ADALINE[6] DAVIS.

v. MARY[5] DAVIS.

vi. ELIZA[5] DAVIS.

vii. JEHU[5] DAVIS.

Jehu Davis served as a corporal in 3rd Regt. Ga. Militia under Col. Ignatius A. Few in the War of 1812. He is likely the male 26-45 living with Eliza Davis in the 1820 Census for Hancock Co.,

---

[73] Adams Grove Cemetery, Central Mills, Dallas Co., Ala. http://www.findagrave.com, #25198729.

[74] 1850 Census Dallas Co., Ala., River, p. 250A, #245.

[75] Alabama Select Marriages, 1816-1957. Accessed 11 February 2014 at Ancestry.com.

[76] 1860 Census Dallas Co., Ala., River, p. 790, #203/196. Children are Saul A., 6; George A., 2; and William, 7/12.

[77] 1870 Census Dallas Co., Ala., River, p. 620A, #285/331. Children are Saul, 16; James, 10; Adaline, 8; William, 5; Robert, 4; Harrell, 2; and Julia, 4/12.

[78] 1880 Census Dallas Co., Ala., Liberty Hill, ED 60, p. 332D, #559/457. He was a widower. Children living with him were Saul A., 26; William B., 15, and Robert C., 16.

[79] 1860 Census Dallas Co., Ala., River, p. 790, #204/197. No children.

[80] 1870 Census Dallas Co., Ala., River, p. 620A, #291/337. Children are Elizabeth, 8; Archibald, 6; Roberta, 5; and James, 2.

Ga. In 1821, Jehu Davis of Capt. Clayton's District, Hancock Co., Ga., drew lot 119, 12th Dist. Monroe Co. in the 1821 Georgia Land Lottery. In 1824 "John" Davis of Putnam Co., Ga., deeded 2.5 acres in lot 119, 12th Dist. Monroe Co., to the Methodist Episcopal Church for $15. In 1825 Jehu Davis of Monroe Co. made a deed to Archibald Davis of Putnam Co. for lot 119, 12th District of Monroe Co. The deed was made in Putnam Co., Ga., and recorded in Monroe Co. in 1882. Jehu Davis is on p. 185 of the 1840 Census for Monroe Co., Ga., age 40-50, with one boy and one girl under five and his wife 20-30.

viii. ARCHIBALD[5] DAVIS, b. about 1796 Hancock Co., Ga., d. 1867 Monroe Co., Ga.;[81] m. NANCY ———.

Archibald Davis is living in Monroe Co., Ga., in the 1850 census.[82]

Children of ARCHIBALD DAVIS and NANCY are:

1. ELIZABETH REEVES[6] DAVIS, b. 27 September 1820 Putnam Co., Ga.; d. 25 February 1886 Monroe Co., Ga.;[83] m. LEONIDAS B. ALEXANDER 26 February 1837 Monroe Co., Ga., son of PETER W. ALEXANDER and ELIZABETH A. BANKS; b. 29 October 1819 Elbert Co., Ga.; d. 1 March 1864 Monroe Co., Ga.[84]

   "Died at her home on Thursday, in the 65th year of her age, Mrs. Elizabeth, widow of the late L. B. Alexander, after an illness of several months. The deceased was born in Monroe, spent her life here and was buried at the old family homestead. She was daughter of the late

---

[81] Maddox-Davis Cemetery, Forsyth, Monroe Co., Ga. http://www.findagrave.com, #85248958. The stone, which is later, says he was a veteran of the War of 1812 and served in Capt. Simmons' Co., Butts Co., Ga.

[82] 1850 Census Monroe Co., Ga., Div. 60, p. 3B, #36. Amanda H. Davis is 26 and living at home.

[83] Maddox-Davis Cemetery, Forsyth, Monroe Co., Ga. http://www.findagrave.com, #66076619.

[84] Maddox-Davis Cemetery, Forsyth, Monroe Co., Ga. http://www.findagrave.com, #66076590.

Archibald Davis; has long been a member of the Methodist Episcopal Church...leaves six children..."[85]

2. MARTHA J.[6] DAVIS, b. 1822 Putnam Co., Ga., d. after 1882 Monroe Co., Ga.; m. WILLIAM B. DAVIS 21 February 1836 Monroe Co., Ga.;[86] b. about 1819 Georgia; d. after 1870 Monroe Co., Ga.

3. AMANDA H.[6] DAVIS, b. 1824 Georgia.[87]

ix. HENRIETTA[5] DAVIS.

5. THOMAS[5] DAVIS was born about 1788 and died 9 August 1826 Putnam Co., Ga. He m. ELIZABETH (LITTLE?) She was born about 1791 and died November 1846 Harris Co., Ga.

Thomas Davis is in Capt. Jerneghan's district of Putnam Co., Ga., in the 1820 census.[88] He is 26-45 and has five children, including three girls 16-26 years of age. A published obituary for Thomas Davis indicates he died in Putnam Co., Ga., at the age of 38.[89] The date of his marriage was estimated from the

---

[85] Ibid.

[86] Georgia Marriages, 1699-1944. Accessed 11 February 2014 at Ancestry.com.

[87] Georgia Marriages, 1699-1944. Accessed 11 February 2014 at Ancestry.com. There is also a marriage for an Amanda Davis to James H. Mays. James H. Mays appears to have died in Ruston, La., in 1911. His wife, Amanda, died there in 1875, but was born about 1830, which is off too much even for census errors. Joseph R. Banks m. Amanda M. Davis 25 June 1850 in Monroe Co., Ga. The census was done 4 August 1850, and still showed Amanda H. Davis living with her father. This Joseph Ralph Banks married Caroline Smith Stevens 30 December 1852 in Monroe Co., Ga., and died in Monroe Co., Ga., 3 July 1910. Forsyth City Cemetery, Monroe Co., Ga., http://www.findagrave.com, #48809114. Neither of these women seem to be the daughter of Archibald.

[88] 1820 Census Putnam Co., Ga., Jerneghan's Dist., p. 82 [20010-00310-3]. There is a Thos. Davis in Hancock Co., Ga., as well, p. 98 [10010-00010-2]. In fact, there is evidence of another unrelated Davis family in Hancock Co., Ga., at the same time as the family of 1810 James Davis.

[89] Marriages & Deaths 1820-1830, Warren (Newspapers) "Davis, Thomas, 38 years, died 8/9/1826 in Putnam Co. An affectionate husband and father, half of his lifetime was humbly devoted to the service of God."

marriage of his oldest daughter, Bethia, who married in 1824. He died intestate 9 August 1826.[90] His estate was billed by Dr. Cochran for daily visits from 1 to 10 July 1826, and again from 28 July 28 to 10 Aug 1826. The estate was also billed for two coffins by Thomas Reeves, one for Thomas Davis, and one for his son, Warren Davis. Included in his estate were books, bought by Henry N. Langford. He also owned land and slaves as evidenced by census, probate and land records.

Georgia) Know all men by these Putnam County) presents that I, Elizabeth Davis reposing special trust and confidence in Kinchen Little do hereby ____ in my name and for my individual risk to make application to the honorable Inferior Court of Putnam County when sitting for ordinary purposes for a child's portion of the estate of Thomas Davis, dec'd, in as full and ample a manner as if I was formally present. Whereunto I set my hand and seal

Her

Elizabeth X Davis

Mark

Teste: Stephen Meadow, J. P.

Kinchen Little, attorney-in-fact for Elizabeth Davis, widow of Thomas Davis, did come into court and made choice of a child's portion of the estate of Thomas Davis as the first claim of the said Elizabeth Davis, widow of said dec'd.[91]

Elizabeth Davis is head of household in the 1830 census for Putnam Co., Ga. On 29 October

(Georgia Reporter and Christian Gazette, Sparta, GA.) Cited by Kay. Our Winding Family Vine. 28 Dec 2006. http://worldconnect.rootsweb.com, (db. texasfolk).

[90] Kinchen Little was appointed administrator of the estate and guardian for Eliza Davis on November 20, 1826. (Putnam Co., Ga., Court of Ordinary Minutes B (1819-1826): (page # illegible.) Division of the estate was made 11 December 1826.

[91] Putnam Co., Ga., Court of Ordinary Minutes B (1819-1826): (page # illegible.) 8 July 1827.

1832, Elizabeth Davis, (widow) replaced Kinchen Little as guardian for William T. Davis.[92] She also sold 120 acres of land in Putnam Co., Ga., on 11 December 1832, to Kinchen Little. She filed annual returns for 1833 and 1834 in Harris Co. On 4 May 1835, Elizabeth Davis and Thomas Clower were jointly held responsible by the Harris Co. Inferior Court after posting a $6000 bond to guarantee Elizabeth's performance as guardian. In 1837, Thomas Clower was the guardian and James Cox was jointly responsible for a $5000 bond. Mr. Clower filed returns for William Davis through 1843, presumably the year William turned 21.

Elizabeth Davis bought 101 acres in the southeast corner of Harris Co., near the present-day community of Ellersley. She bought additional land in 1841, 1842, and 1843, all of which were sold by William T. Davis in 1848 after his mother's death. Elizabeth Davis died in Harris Co., Ga., shortly after her will was prepared 7 October 1846. Her daughter, Malinda, died about the same time. Both wills were submitted to probate in Harris Co., Ga., 27 November 1846.

Children of THOMAS DAVIS and ELIZABETH LITTLE?:

    i. BETHIA[6] DAVIS, b. about 1808 Putnam Co., Ga.; d. 1827 Putnam Co., Ga.; m. LITTLETON WYNN 7 December 1824 Putnam Co., Ga.;[93] b. 9 May 1799 Georgia; d. 26 May 1852 Auburn,

---

[92] The fact that Kinchen Little was both attorney in fact and guardian to Matthew T. Davis suggests to me that Elizabeth's maiden name was Little. Kinchen Little was documented in a DAR application. He was born 1780 Edgecombe Co., N. C., son of Frederick Little, and died 1865 Putnam Co., Ga. The files do not list the other children of Frederick Little, but do suggest a line of inquiry. Frederick appears to have died in Georgia about 1807. Kinchen Little, 61 NC, with wife "C" and children Wm. F, 32, James 32, Alex, 18, Milton 12, Stincheon 10, and Algernon 8, all b. Ga, are shown on the 1850 Census Putnam Co., Ga., 70th Dist., p. 300, #397. Jesse Batchelor is #395 and Blakey is #396.

[93] Marriages and Obituaries from Early Georgia Newspapers. Cited by Kay. Our Winding Family Vine. 28 Dec 2006.
http://worldconnect.rootsweb.com, (db. texasfolk).

Lee Co., Ala.;[94] m. (2) AMANDA FRANCES
HARPER about 1827 Georgia; b. 1815 Pike Co.,
Ga.; d. 1866 Pike Co., Ga.[95]

Littleton Wynn is listed in the 1850 Census
with his wife, Amandia F., 35, and Thomas L.
Wynn, 24. He is almost certainly a son of Bethia
Davis

Child of BETHIA DAVIS and LITTLETON WYNN:

    1. THOMAS LITTLETON[7] WYNN, b. 20 December
       1825 Putnam Co., Ga.; d. 8 April 1878
       Chattahoochee Co., Ga.[96]

ii. ELIZABETH[6] DAVIS, b. about 1810 Putnam Co.,
    Ga.; d. 1838 Harris Co., Ga.; m. HENRY
    NORMAN LANGFORD 12 July 1827 Putnam Co.,
    Ga., son of RICHARD LANGFORD and AMELIA
    SOPER; b. 13 March 1802 Montgomery Co.,
    Maryland; d. 1881 Chilton Co., Ala.[97]

iii. MALINDA[6] DAVIS, b. about 1813 Putnam Co.,
    Ga.; d. before 27 November 1846 Harris Co.,
    Ga.

iv. WARREN[6] DAVIS, b. about 1815 Putnam Co.,
    Ga.; d. 1826 Putnam Co., Ga.

v. WILLIAM T.[6] DAVIS, b. 1822 Putnam Co., Ga.

---

[94] Pine Hill Cemetery, Auburn, Ala. http://www.findagrave.com,
#8678383.

[95] Littleton Wynn Family Tree. Accessed 9 February 2014 at
http://trees.ancestry.com/tree/51066533/

[96] Cusetta City Cemetery, Chattahoochee Co., Ga.
http://www.findagrave.com, #33493629. There is also a Dr. David Wynn,
b. 30 November 1827, d. 6 August 1903, who may be another son.
(#33493599.)

[97] See Chapter 8.

Chapter 10: Descendants of Larkin Wilson

1. LARKIN[1] WILSON was born in England and died about 1788 in Botetourt Co., Virginia.

Neither the date of his birth, nor the date of his emigration is known, although it seems certain that he came from England. The last name of his wife is likewise uncertain. The family legend has it that Larkin died of a broken neck sustained in a fall while helping a neighbor raise a barn.[1]

The names of his children were from Dan Langford, and to date, I have not found where this list came from, nor have I been able to confirm the presence of any of these people in Botetourt County, Virginia. The 1784 Personal Property Tax lists 16 men with the surname Wilson in the first district, and nine men in the second district.[2] Unfortunately, none of them is identifiable as Larkin Wilson.[3]

Reportedly, Larkin Wilson was the son of Roger Wilson, born about 1722 in England, and his wife Elizabeth. Larkin had a brother, Richard, who also came to America, and died in Georgia. This file shows Larkin Wilson marrying Mary Jane Hansen, but lists her as the daughter of William Swanson and Mary McGuire. The original source for most of this information seems to be a letter written in Thomas

---

[1] Dan Langford shared the results of his research with me for this report. He was not able to confirm many details about Larkin Wilson, Sr., as much of his information came from Ms. Millie Stewart, who had also researched the Wilson family. I have subsequently found Mrs. Stewart's report in Abbott, Frank M. History of the People of Jones County, Georgia, Vol. 6, p. 58, at the Washington Library, Macon, Georgia. She lived in Macon.

[2] 1784 Personal Property Tax List, Botetourt Co.,, Virginia. http://newrivernotes.com. Accessed 2 Nov 2006.

[3] I have found one family listing that shows his name as Larkin William James Roger Wilson. She does not indicate where this came from. Gubbins, Beth. Beth's Family History. 29 Oct 2006. Located at http://worldconnect.rootsweb.com, (db. :3087208.)

Wilson of Milner, Ga., to Mrs. A. G. White of Lueders, Texas, 11 June 1940.[4]

Answering your inquires, about your father's people. 1st, I am a first cousin of his. My father was Z. W. Wilson, who was 12 years younger than E. G. N. Wilson. His father, Jasper Wilson, was another brother, two years older than E. G. N. Wilson. My father was born in 1824, Jasper Wilson in 1812, and E. G. N. Wilson I think in 1813. Our grandfather and grandmother were the very first settlers in Monroe County, Georgia, settling in 1817. Monroe County was founded in 1821. Our grandfather and his wife came to Georgia from Bedford County, Virginia. Grandmother was a Cabanis, and a first cousin to William Henry Harrison, who was President about 1840. Grandfather was born in 1770; his father came to America from Scotland, they were Scotch-English people. Grandmother was born in 1785. Her and grandfather were married in 1800. They raised 14 children to be grown and married, except one who was a cripple from birth.

There were seven boys and seven girls. The oldest was a girl named Pallie Harrison Wilson, born in 1801. Next, Henry Wilson, a son, born in 1803, then a girl named Sonnell born in 1805, then another son named George Jefferson, born in 1808. This kinsman settled in Tyler, Texas, between 1845 and 1850. He never had any sons. His youngest daughter died there about three years ago. Next to him was Uncle Jasper, then your grandfather, then aunt Mary was born in 1816. She married a Speer. Then Aunt Lucy in 1819, who married a LeSeuer. The twins, aunt Permeliar and uncle

[4] http://trees.ancestry.com/tree/40227163/person/19466006458/ Accessed 7 March 2014.

Larkin in 1822. Then my father and aunt Lizzie who were twins; aunt Lizzie married John W. Cauthen. Then Uncle Columbus C. Wilson in 1826, then aunt Sue in 1828 who married an Atkinson. Grandfather died in 1845. He had at the time of his death 150 Negroes, 2000 acres of land, all in Monroe County. He brought with him from Virginia his wife, younger brother, and sister. His wife's brother became the first Ordinary of Monroe County which he held for forty years. He was also a Judge of the Superior Court of the Flynt Circuit from 1855 to 1861, then his son, Thos. B. Cabanis, was elected to Congress from 1892 to 1894. Then Judge of the City Court of Forsyth for a number of years. Your father's first cousin, Thos. J. Speer, was the first man elected to Congress from Georgia after the great Civil War.

When your grandfather died, he had seven hundred and 80 acres of land. His farm is owned or controlled by the W. G. Weldone estate. I never did know just your father got out of E. G. N. Wilson's estate. But I have understood from others that Jeff, who was the only child living anywhere in this section, got the lion's share of the estate which amounted to a good sum. Your father's mother was a Morris, the daughter of old Capt. Morris of Monroe County. She died before my birth. Well if you can read this and want more of the family's history I will write you more fully.

s./ Thomas S. Wilson

Children of LARKIN WILSON and MARY HANSON:

2.   i. LARKIN[2] WILSON, b. 7 May 7 1770 Botetourt Co., Va.; d. July 1845 Monroe Co., Ga.
     ii. NELSON[2] WILSON, b. 1771 Botetourt Co., Va.; d. 1859 Georgia; m. (1) SUSANNAH WOODRUFF 6

March 1797 Oglethorpe Co., Ga.,[5] daughter of CLIFFORD WOODRUFF; d. before 1820 Georgia;[6] m. (2) ELLA GEE.

Nelson Wilson is in Capt. Collier's District in the 1800 Census for Oglethorpe Co., Ga.[7] Clifford Woodruff wrote his will in Oglethorpe Co., Ga., on 17 May 1831 and left $10 to be divided between his daughters "Molly Colquitt and Susan Wilson, along with bequests to his other children.[8]

iii. ARKELLIS[2] WILSON, b 1774 Botetourt Co., Va.; d. before 1850 Jasper Co., Ga.; m. (1) SARAH MASON; m. (2) NANCY SWANSON; d. 1870 Jasper Co., Ga.

Arkillis Wilson is listed in Jasper Co., Ga., in the 1830 Census.[9] The 1850 Census shows Arkellis Wilson, 23, b. Ala., along with wife Nancy, as newlyweds,[10] which suggests Arkellis Wilson moved to Alabama shortly after the 1830 census. Nancy Wilson, 70, born in Georgia, is listed nearby in the household of A. J. Wilson, 31, b. in Georgia.[11] In 1860 "Mary" Wilson, widow, 78, born in Georgia, is living in the house with A. J. Wilson,

---

[5] Georgia Marriages to 1850. Accessed 6 March 2014 at Ancestry.com.

[6] 1820 Census Jasper Co., Ga., Monticello, p. 254. He is over 45 with two boys, 10-16 and no women in the household.

[7] Accessed 5 Nov 2006 at http://ftp.rootsweb.com/pub/usgenweb/ga/oglethorpe/census/1800/coll iers.txt. Also listed is Jos. Wilson, whose connection is unknown to me. James Wilson is listed in Capt. Hardeman's district along with Bennett Wilson. (http://ftp.rootsweb.com/pub/usgenweb/ga/oglethorpe/census/1800/ha rdmans.txt) Joseph Wilson is Capt. Lee's District. (http://ftp.rootsweb.com/pub/usgenweb/ga/oglethorpe/census/1800/lee s.txt).

[8] Oglethorpe Co., Ga., Will Book D:75-76. [9 September 1840] Copy accessed 5 November 2006 at http://ftp.rootsweb.com/pub/usgenweb/ga/oglethorpe/wills/woodruff.txt

[9] 1830 Census, Jasper Co., Ga., p. 372 [He is age 60-70, and is listed three males and three females, one of whom is probably his wife, and 11 slaves. http://ftp.rootsweb.com/pub/usgenweb/ga/jasper/census/1830/1830pt 3ja.txt

[10] 1850 Census, Jasper Co., Ga., p. 13, #88. http://ftp.rootsweb.com/pub/usgenweb/ga/jasper/census/1850/1850.tx t

[11] 1850 Census, Jasper Co., Ga., p. 13, #81.

and others of her family, but she is listed as the head of household.[12]

The marriage records of Jasper Co., Ga., show Arkellis Wilson married Judah Finley on 18 July 1833.[13]

iv. LEONARD[2] WILSON.

Leonard Wilson is listed in Jasper Co., Ga., in 1830, aged 50-60.[14]

v. WILLIAM[2] WILSON.

On 10 May 1810 John Gresham of Oglethorpe Co., Ga., deeded two lots in Lexington to Joel Bridge, of Chatham Co., Ga., executor of William Wilson, to clear a debt owed by Gresham to William Wilson for $2902.16.[15] Presently, I have no information as to the likelihood this is the same man. Another possibility is William Wilson who died in Jasper Co., Ga., before 26 Sep 1816. This deed was written by John Wilson, clerk.[16]

vi. JOHN[2] WILSON, d. 1842 Jones Co., Ga.; m. ESTHER ____.

vii. MARTHA (PATSY)[2] WILSON, d. 1815 Oglethorpe Co., Ga.; m. SAMUEL EDMONDSON 24 Dec 1800 Oglethorpe Co., Ga.

viii. MARY[2] WILSON, b. 1773 Botetourt Co., Va.; d. 1824 Oglethorpe Co., Ga.; m. JOHN MASON.

ix. SUSANNA[2] NANCY WILSON, d. 1812 Monroe Co., Ga.

---

[12] 1860 Census, Jasper Co., Ga., p. 308, #557/563.

[13] Jasper Co., Ga., Marriage Book B:150.
http://ftp.rootsweb.com/pub/usgenweb/ga/jasper/vitals/marriages/marr2.txt Also shown is the marriage for John Wilson to Nancy Phillips 1 April 1832, (p. 148);

[14] 1830 Census, Jasper Co., Ga., p. 380. He is listed with one female slave, and no other persons in his household.

[15] Oglethorpe Co., Ga., Deed Book F:151.
http://ftp.rootsweb.com/pub/usgenweb/ga/oglethorpe/deeds/b6320001.txt

[16] Jasper Co., Ga., Deed Book B:36-37. John Ward sold to Sally Wilson, executor of William Wilson, a tract of land of 100 acres, the southeast half of Lot 95 17th Dist.
http://files.usgwarchives.net/ga/jasper/deeds/dd149surnames.txt

2. LARKIN[2] WILSON was born 7 May 1770 in Botetourt Co., Virginia and died July 1845 Monroe Co., Georgia.[17] He married MARY ANN CABINESS 28 December 1803 in Greene Co., Ga., daughter of GEORGE CABINESS and PALATEA HARRISON. She was born 4 January 1785 in North Carolina and died December 1862 in Monroe Co., Ga.

Larkin Wilson's marriage to Mary Ann Cabiness is recorded in the marriage records of Greene Co., Ga.[18] They had moved to Jones Co., Ga., with her father before October 1809, when he was listed as a juror.[19] He paid a poll tax in Jones Co., Ga., in 1811, on land located next to that owned by his wife's family, and paid taxes there regularly through 1823.[20] He also won lot 65, 4th District, Houston Co., Ga., in the 1821 Georgia Land Lottery. Sometime prior to 1830, he moved to Monroe Co., Ga., where he appears in the 1830[21] and 1840 Census.[22]

Larkin Wilson wrote his will in Monroe Co., Ga., 20 April 1845 and it was proved by the three subscribing witnesses 7 July 1845.[23]

Georgia   )
Monroe County)

---

[17] Both are buried in Stewart Cemetery, Jones Co., Ga., near their eldest daughter. http://www.findagrave.com., #73988875 and #73988713.

[18] Accessed 4 November 2006 at http://ftp.rootsweb.com/pub/usgenweb/ga/greene/vitals/marriages/grm/180050.txt.

[19] Abbott, Frank M. History of the People of Jones County, Georgia, Vol. 2, p. 3. Copy located at the Washington Library, Macon, Georgia.

[20] 1811 Jones Co., Ga. Tax Record, p. 59, Larkin Wilson, 1 poll, 3 slaves, 101.25 #2, acq. Golsby, adj. Cabeniss [sic] on Shoal Cr. Dan Langford also found him in 1813, no page cited; 1814, p. 96; 1819, p. 118; 1820, 1823, no page cited.

[21] 1830 Census Monroe Co., Ga., p. 215, [12120001-21210101+18 slaves]

[22] 1840 Census Monroe Co., Ga., Mil. Dist. 632, p. 153. He is listed as 60-69, she is listed as 50-59 and they have five sons and three daughters living at home.

[23] Monroe Co., Ga., Will Book A:234-236. Copy located 8 March 2014 at http://trees.ancestry.com/tree/43194817/person/12634039158

388

In the name of God, Amen. I, Larkin Wilson of the County and State aforesaid do make this my last will and testament utterly discarding all others by me made—

And first of all, I will that my body be buried in a decent and Christian manner in the burial ground at my plantation.

2nd I will that all my just debts be paid out of my property.

3rd I will and bequeath unto my wife Mary Wilson all my property both real and personal during her natural lifetime with the exception of four hundred dollars and a good home which I will to each of my children as they may become of age or may be paid out of my estate, and at the time of the death of my wife I will that my Negroes be lotted off and drawn for and equally divided among my children and the balance of my estate to be sold by my executors and be equally divided among my children. And my will further is that what I have given my children during my lifetime may be all rendered in at the time of the division of my estate and be all added to the amount of my estate and be equally divided between all my children. I further will that my son Larkin Franklin Wilson be paid one thousand dollars out of my estate over and above a child's part on account of his afflictions.

4th I will that the part or share of my estate which may be coming to my daughters be left to them during their natural lifetime, and at their death to go to the heirs of their body.

5th I nominate and appoint George J. Wilson, Wm. J. Wilson, and Simeon F. Speer as my Executors to carry this my last will and testament into full force and effect 20th April in the year of our Lord 1845.

Larkin (W) Wilson

Signed & Sealed in the presence of
Thomas Stewart
David Proctor
B. F. Wilson

His wife stayed on in Monroe Co., Ga., after his death in 1845, as she appears as the head of household in the 1850 Census.[24] At that time her holdings were valued at $5000. In the 1849 tax record she was shown as holding 13 slaves and three parcels of land, as well as a four wheel carriage.[25]

Additional information about the children were obtained from Mrs. Stewart's report.[26] The marriage books for Monroe Co., Ga., confirmed dates of marriage for many of the children.[27] Larkin Wilson's Bible Record was transcribed and filed in the Monroe Co., Historical Society, and is the original source for the birth dates.[28]

Children of LARKIN WILSON and MARY CABANISS:

i. PALATIA HARRISON[3] WILSON, b. 22 April 1805 Greene Co., Ga.; d. 11 July 1866 Jones Co., Ga.;[29] m. THOMAS WARE STEWART 22 June 1821 Jones Co., Ga., son of WILLIAM STEWART and JANE SMITH; b. 15 Feb 1787 Mecklenburg Co., N. C.; d. 19 Nov 1846 Jones Co., Ga.[30]

"Pallie" Harrison Wilson Stewart and her husband, as well as a son, Washington Jackson

---

[24] "May" Wilson, 66, b. Ga., has Columbus Wilson, 22, and Zachariah W. Wilson, 28; Eliza Wilson, 20, and Larkin Wilson, 4/12 living with her. 1850 Census Monroe Co., Ga., Div. 60, p. 49B, #732.

[25] 1849 Monroe Co., Ga., Tax Record; Morris District, p. 111.

[26] History of the People of Jones County, Georgia, Vol. 6, p. 58.

[27] Accessed 2 November 2006 at http://ftp.rootsweb.com/pub/usgenweb/ga/monroe/vitals/marriage/1850.txt.

[28] Copy found 7 March 2014 at http://trees.ancestry.com/tree/40227163/person/19466006458

[29] Stewart Cemetery, Jones Co., Ga. http://www.findagrave.com., #77623080.

[30] Stewart Cemetery, Jones Co., Ga. http://www.findagrave.com., #30243899.

Stewart (10 Nov 1830—13 Feb 1858) are buried in the Stewart Cemetery, Jones Co., Ga.[31]

"Palacia Harrison Wilson Stewart, known as Dr. Poly Stewart was one of the first woman doctors in Georgia.[32] She was a descendant of the Harrisons of Jamestown, Virginia, and her mother was Mary Cabaniss the daughter of George and Palacia Harrison Cabiness. Her father was Larkin Wilson from Virginia, born in 1770.

Palacia H. W. Stewart was born April 2, 1805 in Jones County, Georgia, on a large plantation two miles east of Bradley. Her home still stands, and has recently been restored by a descendant, Mrs. Doris Hungerford Fraley. In front of this home at the time when Polly was growing up were the drill grounds for the Militia. Later she lived not far away at the home built by Thomas Ware Stewart, now known as the Joseph Glawson Place, built in 1842.

Polly Harrison Wilson grew up on the plantation and was an attractive brunette. Her eyes werc largc and gray with heavy lashes, she had black hair, an exquisite complexion, regular features with full lower lip (which the artists called an Egyptian nether lip). She was strong, healthy and very active. At sixteen, she married a man twice her age. On June 22, Thomas Ware Stewart took his girl-bride to his small plantation near Fortville. There Thomas and Polly brought their strength and knowledge to bear, and soon they had two thousand acres and many slaves and were successful planters. Polly had thirteen children. When the thirteenth child was six weeks old her husband, Thomas Ware Stewart suddenly died. Polly faced life with thirteen children, a large plantation and almost one hundred slaves.

---

[31] Colvin, Earl and Colvin, Beth. Fields of Stone: Cemeteries of Jones County, Georgia. (2004), p. 503. His parents are also buried there, with William Stewart's date of death 10 April 1827 and Jane Smith Stewart's date of death, 20 April 1836.

[32] History of the People of Jones County, Georgia, cited by Medders, Richard. Medders Family Tree. 30 Sep 2006. Located at http://worldconnect.rootsweb.com, (db medders_family).

Polly had studied and managed to get a fair medical education, and on May 13, 1848 she had passed examinations and was given a diploma in Medicine by "The Botanico-Medical Society," of Hartford, Connecticut. This diploma is now in the possession of Miss May Stewart, (granddaughter) at Gray, Georgia, and is signed by H. A. Archer, M.D., Pres., J. J. Jacques, M.D., Vice-Pres., T. S. Sperry, M.D., Sec.

Her services to the counties of Baldwin, Jasper and Jones during the Civil War was a heroic effort. She was constantly called to the bedside of the sick, and gave of her time, means and efforts. She was practical and when the occasion demanded, could use her temper. She was reared an Episcopalian, later joined the Presbyterians and after marriage was a Baptist. She attended church as much as her time would allow, but when she was absent she was distributing alms or caring for the sick. No man in Jones County did more for the Confederacy than Dr. Polly Stewart.

Her six sons were in the Confederate Army and all returned after the war except Polk who was killed and buried in Savannah. It was during the terrible war days that her executive abilities counted most for her country and community. Other women whose impulses were equally generous and patriotic did little or nothing because they were without means, but Polly Harrison W. Stewart provided the means for her purposes. She had her farms producing at a maximum during the war, with all of the drawbacks and difficulties of that period."

Children of PALLIE WILSON and WILLIAM STEWART:

1. THOMAS JEFFERSON[4] STEWART, b. 6 April 1822 Jones Co., Ga.; d. 6 January 1902 Jones Co., Ga.;[33] m. (1) MARTHA J. FINNEY, dau. of BENJAMIN FINNEY and SARAH CARSON; b. 9 September 1823; d. 28

---

[33] Stewart Cemetery, Jones Co., Ga. http://www.findagrave.com., #77622958.

October 1847 Jones Co., Ga.;[34] m. (2) MARGARET SMITH 16 January 1849 Jones Co., Ga.; m. (3) SARAH T. FINNEY 6 April 1851 Jones Co., Ga.;[35] (4) MARTHA (GODARD) PITTS 21 November 1858 Jones Co., Ga., relict of DAUPHIN LEWIS PITTS, dau. of JAMES DANIEL GODARD, SR., and ARDECIA CALLAWAY; b. 8 September 1834; d. 26 July 1896 Jones Co., Ga.[36]

2. WILLIAM NEWTON[4] STEWART, b. 22 May 1825 Jones Co., Ga.; d. 14 November 1861 Russell Co., Ala.;[37] m. CAMELIA S. LESTER 2 October 1849 Jones Co., Ga.;[38] b. 1828 Georgia; d. after 1870 Russell Co., Ala.

2. LARKIN WILSON[4] STEWART, b. about 1827 Jones Co., Ga.; d. about 1875 Houston Co., Ga.; m. (1) MARTHA A. MCCANTS 23 December 1851 Bibb Co., Ga.[39]; m. (2) CATHERINE C. BRYAN 10 November 1865 Jones Co., Ga.;[40] m. (3) about 1876 ELLIOTT V. STEADMAN.[41]

4. SAMUEL SMITH[4] STEWART, b. 28 May 1828 Jones Co., Ga.; d. 1839 Jones Co., Ga.[42]

5. WASHINGTON JACKSON[4] STEWART, b. 10 November 1830 Jones Co., Ga.; d. 13 February 1858 Jones Co., Ga.[43]

---

[34] Finney Family Cemetery, Jones Co., Ga. http://www.findagrave.com., #92087375.

[35] Georgia Marriages, 1699-1944. Accessed 9 March 2014 at Ancestry.com.

[36] Clinton UMC Cemetery, Jones Co., Ga. http://www.findagrave.com., #21787148.

[37] Stewart Burying Ground, Glenville, Ala. http://www.findagrave.com., #110854718.

[38] Georgia Marriages to 1850. Accessed 9 March 2014 at Ancestry.com.

[39] 1860 Census Twiggs Co., Ga., Mil. Dist. 372, p. 353, #47. He was a railroad contractor.

[40] Georgia Marriages, 1699-1944. Accessed 9 March 2014 at Ancestry.com. 1870 Census Houston Co., Ga., p. 20B, #1477/1592. Eula, the child from the 1860 Census is still there, but there is a gap. There is also a Mary Park, 11, who is probably her daughter from a previous marriage.

[41] 1880 Census Houston Co., Ga., Fort Valley, ED 29, p. 280D, #397. The Wilson children are listed as "step," and their "son" was born 1878.

[42] http://trees.ancestry.com/tree/5765079/person/1096100714

6. HENRY JASPER[4] STEWART, b. 27 December 1832 Jones Co., Ga.; d. 29 March 1909 Jones Co., Ga.;[44] m. ANNE FINNEY 19 December 1865;[45] b. 4 July 1838; d. 5 December 1915.[46]

7. MARION F.[4] STEWART, m. MARY A. OTIS about 1870 Autauga Co., Ala.[47]

8. PALATIA MARY JANE[4] STEWART, b. 7 September 1836 Jones Co., Ga.; d. 10 December 1923 Jones Co., Ga.; m. JAMES PARK 27 February 1857 Bibb Co., Ga.;[48] d. before 1880 Jones Co., Ga.[49]

9. MARTHA P. T.[4] STEWART, b. 15 January 1839 Jones Co., Ga.; d. 15 September 1908 Jones Co., Ga.;[50] m. HENRY SHORTER GREAVES 1857 Jones Co., Ga.;[51] b. 17 April 1830 Ga.; d. 18 January 1908 Jones Co., Ga.[52]

10. COLUMBUS M.[4] STEWART, b. 1840 Jones Co., Ga.; m. LAURA AVERETTE BRYAN 9 December 1867 Jones Co., Ga.[53]

11. SARAH LOUISE[4] STEWART, b. 17 October 1842 Jones Co., Ga.; d. 14 May 1906 St.

---

[43] Stewart Cemetery, Jones Co., Ga. http://www.findagrave.com., #77623253.

[44] http://www.findagrave.com., #77622817. He served as a private in Slaten's Battery, Macon Light Artillery.

[45] Georgia Marriages, 1699-1944. Accessed 9 March 2014 at Ancestry.com.

[46] SAR Application of Henry Stewart Wootten, 29 April 1930. Accessed 9 March 2014 at Ancestry.com.

[47] 1870 Census Autauga Co., Ala., Beat 5, p. 14A, #278. 1880 Census Russell Co., Ala., Girard, ED 151, p. 414B, #285/326. Some files suggest he died young and this is a different man.

[48] Georgia Marriages, 1699-1944. Accessed 9 March 2014 at Ancestry.com. Georgia Death Index, 1914-1927. Accessed 9 March 2014 at Ancestry.com. Also Clinton UMC Cemetery, Jones Co., Ga. http://www.findagrave.com., #21770064.

[49] 1880 Census, Jones Co., Ga., Clinton, ED 77, p. 390C, #22. She is listed as a "school marm." In 1900 Census Jones Co., Ga., Pope, ED 57, p. 1A, #1, she is living with her son-in-law, James T. Finney.

[50] Clinton UMC Cemetery, Jones Co., Ga. http://www.findagrave.com., #21769988.

[51] 1900 Census Jones Co., Ga., Clinton, ED 63, p. 5A, #72/73.

[52] Clinton UMC Cemetery, Jones Co., Ga. http://www.findagrave.com., #21769975.

[53] http://trees.ancestry.com/tree/5765079/person/1096100709

Johns Co., Fla.;[54] m. SAMUEL M. CALHOUN
2 April 1861 Jones Co., Ga.;[55] d. before
1900. [56]

    12. METHVIN C. POLK[4] STEWART, b. 1845 Jones
        Co., Ga.; d. after 1860.

    13. JOSEPH DAY[4] STEWART, b. 17 September
        1846 Jones Co., Ga.; d. 5 March 1930
        Miami, Dade Co., Fla.;[57] m. EMMA M. HAND;
        b. 18 April 1848; d. 22 February 1942
        Miami, Dade Co., Fla.[58]

3. ii. HENRY BAILEY[3] WILSON, b. 24 March 1807 Jones
        Co., Ga.; d. 4 July 1880 Newton Co., Miss.; m.
        ELIZA HOWE about 1833 Monroe Co., Ga.,
        daughter of DAVID HOWE and ELIZABETH _____;
        b. 12 Aug 1812 Putnam Co., Ga.; d. 8 Nov
        1888 Newton Co., Miss.

  iii. SANDAL ORGAN[3] WILSON, b. 15 April 1809 Jones
        Co., Ga.; m. ROBERT WATSON about 1830[59]
        Monroe Co., Ga.; b. 27 December 1803
        Georgia; d. 2 January 1845 Monroe Co., Ga.[60]

Children of SANDAL and ROBERT WATSON:[61]

---

[54] San Lorenzo Cemetery, Saint Augustine, Fla.
http://www.findagrave.com., #43888289.

[55] Georgia Marriages, 1699-1944. Accessed 9 March 2014 at
Ancestry.com.

[56] In 1880 they were living in Columbus, Muscogee Co., Ga., ED 50, p.
574B, #272/268. They were living on Oglethorpe St. 1900 Census St.
Johns Co., Fla., New Augustine, ED 139, p. 7B, #166/169.

[57] Lived in Americus, Ga., and is buried in Oak Grove Cemetery,
Americus, Sumter Co., Ga. http://www.findagrave.com., #71240521.

[58] She was living in Miami in 1940, but is buried in Oak Grove
Cemetery, Americus, Sumter Co., Ga. http://www.findagrave.com.,
#71240834. She is identified on the stone as the wife of Joseph Stewart
and is buried next to him.

[59] 1840 Census Monroe Co., Ga., Mil. Dist. 467, p. 155. Robert
Watson, 30-39, and wife of similar age along with two boys under five and
two girls under five are living in Monroe Co., Ga., in 1840.

[60] Watson Plantation Cemetery, Cabaniss, Monroe Co., Ga.
http://www.findagrave.com, #41622325.

[61] 1850 Census Monroe Co., Ga., Div. 60, p. 76B, #1126. Sandel
Watson, 41, is head of household with children Benjamin F., 19, Larkin,
16, Mary, 14, Martha, 11, and Robert, 6. 1860 Census Butts Co., Ga., Iron
Spring, p. 49, #318/326, she is living in a household headed by Benjamin
F., 28, and wife, Georgia Ann, 21. 1870 Census Jasper Co., Ga.,
Monticello, p. 487A, #294/282, she is probably "Saunders O." Watson,

1. BENJAMIN F.[4] WATSON, b. January 1832 Georgia; d. 1920 Gadsden Co., Fla.;[62] m. GEORGIA ANN _____ 1856; b. December 1836 Georgia; [63] d. before 1910 Butts Co., Ga.

2. LARKIN DOUGLAS[4] WATSON, b. 15 March 1837 Monroe Co., Ga.; d. 11 October 1910 Butts Co., Ga.;[64] m. MARY BUTTRILL 15 November 1866 Butts Co., Ga., dau. of ASA BUTTRILL and LUCIE JANE MANLY; b. 25 October 1842 Ga.; d. 25 March 1942 Butts Co., Ga.[65]

3. MARY[4] WATSON, b. about 1836 Ga.

4. MARTHA F.[4] WATSON, b. 8 September 1839 Monroe Co., Ga.; d. 29 October 1919 Butts Co., Ga.;[66] m. NUDIGATE O. ALEXANDER about 1859 Jasper Co., Ga.; b. 22 August 1836 Ga.; d. 24 May 1885 Butts Co., Ga.[67]

5. ROBERT[4] WATSON., b. 1844 Monroe Co., Ga.[68]

iv. GEORGE JEFFERSON[3] WILSON, b. 9 July 1813 Jones Co., Ga.; d. April 1873 Rusk Co., Texas;[69] m. MARY JANE FORTSON 20 September 1848 Russell Co., Ala.;[70] d. February 1872 Rusk Co., Texas.[71]

---

living with Martha Alexander, 29, and husband "Nudigut" in Jasper Co., Ga.

[62] 1920 Census Gadsden Co., Fla., Quincy, ED 63, p. 9B, 194/195. He is living with his son, Benjamin F. Watson and family, and his daughter, Mary Blackmore. His death is recorded as 1920 in Florida Death Index, 1877-1998. Accessed 6 March 2014 at Ancestry.com.

[63] 1900 Census Butts Co., Ga., Indian Springs, ED 39, p. 14A, #257/274. Daughter Mary E. Blackamore, 55, is living with them.

[64] Jackson City Cemetery, Jackson, Ga. http://www.findagrave.com, #17617835.

[65] Jackson City Cemetery, Jackson, Ga. http://www.findagrave.com, #17617878.

[66] Indian Springs Cemetery, Butts Co., Ga. http://www.findagrave.com, #46580744.

[67] Indian Springs Cemetery, Butts Co., Ga. http://www.findagrave.com, #46580728.

[68] I have not found him after 1850, suggesting he died young.

[69] Fortson Cemetery, Rusk Co., Texas. http://www.findagrave.com, #5739825.

[70] Alabama Marriages, 1809-1920. Accessed 8 March 2014 at Ancestry.com.

[71] Henderson, Betty A. 11 Aug 2001. Located at

Children of GEORGE WILSON and MARY FORTSON:

1. MARY P. E.[4] WILSON, b. 21 June 1849 Monroe Co., Ga.; d. 27 June 1934 Rusk Co., Texas;[72] m. HENRY C. MINOR 22 November 1873 Rusk Co., Texas;[73] b. 9 November 1847 Miss.; d. 28 February 1915 Rusk Co., Texas.[74]

2. SARAH LOU[4] WILSON, b. 18 March 1851 Monroe Co., Ga.; d. 17 March 1935 Rusk Co., Texas; [75] m. HARVEY S. MINOR 25 August 1877 Rust Co., Texas;[76] b. 3 March 1849; d. 2 December 1879 Rusk Co., Texas.[77]

3. SUSAN ANSOPHIA[4] WILSON, b. 22 March 1853 Monroe Co., Ga.; d. 18 December 1938 Bossier Par., La.;[78] m. JAMES ALLEN EASON 29 February 1872 Rusk Co., Texas;[79] b. 12

---

http://genforum.genealogy.com/wilson/messages/15928.html. She posted a more expansive message on findagrave.com under his name. "George Jefferson Wilson and Mary Jane Fortson moved from Russell Co., Ala., to Rusk Co., Texas, in 1854, where her father, and brother Richard Fortson owned land. She died there in 1872 and he died in April 1873. Both are buried in Fortson Cemetery, but the markers are largely gone." 1850 Census Monroe Co., Ga., Div. 60, p. 42A, #623. 1860 Census Rusk Co., Texas, Beat 11, p. 300, #672/690.

[72] Overton Cemetery, Rusk Co., Texas. http://www.findagrave.com., #99884267. The posting gives the year as 1847, but I believe it should be 1849 based on marriage and census records.

[73] Texas, Marriage Collection, 1814-1909 and 1966-2011. Accessed 8 March 2014 at Ancestry.com.

[74] Overton Cemetery, Rusk Co., Texas. http://www.findagrave.com., #99883790.

[75] Texas, Death Certificates, 1903-1982. Accessed 8 March 2014 at Ancestry.com.

[76] Texas, Marriage Collection, 1814-1909 and 1966-2011. Accessed 8 March 2014 at Ancestry.com.

[77] Fortson Cemetery, Rusk Co., Texas. http://www.findagrave.com., #90420601.

[78] Overton Cemetery, Rusk Co., Texas. http://www.findagrave.com., #5738571. Ms. Henderson says she died in Shreveport, but the Louisiana Statewide Death Index, 1900-1949, (Ancestry.com), lists her parish as Bossier. She was living in Rusk Co., in 1930, so was either in the hospital or at the home of one of her children. I have not attempted to resolve this.

[79] Texas, Marriage Collection, 1814-1909 and 1966-2011. Accessed 8 March 2014 at Ancestry.com.

August 1849 Lonoke Co., Ark.; d. 19 January 1908 Rusk Co., Texas.[80]

4. ADDIE J.[4] WILSON, b. 1856; m. JOHN W. MORRIS 25 November 1876 Rusk Co., Texas;[81] b. about 1853 Miss.

5. JEFFIE[4] WILSON, b. 1860 Rusk Co., Texas; d. before 1896 Rusk Co., Texas; m. ARTHUR H. RAYFORD 20 May 1878 Rusk Co., Texas;[82] b. 21 July 1857 Mobile, Ala.; d. 14 October 1942 Rusk Co., Texas; [83] m. (2) SARAH L. (PARKER) ESTES, widow of JOHN WESLEY ESTES 1896[84] Rusk Co., Texas; b. 16 September 1850 Georgia; d. 2 May 1937 Rusk Co., Texas.[85]

6. CORA WYN[4] WILSON, b. 2 March 1862 Rusk Co., Texas; d. 23 April 1957 Henderson, Rusk Co., Texas;[86] m. CHARLES GORDON RAYFORD; b. 7 November 1860 Mobile Co., Ala.; d. 27 November 1946 Rusk Co., Texas.[87]

7. FANNIE[4] WILSON, b. 1867 Rusk Co., Texas.

v. WILLIAM JASPER[3] WILSON, b. 9 July 1813 Jones Co., Ga.; m. ELIZA H. HANSFORD 7 March 1839 Monroe Co., Ga.[88]

William J. Wilson and family are in Monroe Co., Ga., in 1850,[89] 1860,[90] and 1870.[91] In that

---

[80] Fortson Cemetery, Rusk Co., Texas. http://www.findagrave.com., #5738558.

[81] Texas, Marriage Collection, 1814-1909 and 1966-2011. Accessed 8 March 2014 at Ancestry.com. 1880 Census Rusk Co., Texas, Overton, ED 74, p. 55D, #94/95. Cora Wilson is living with them.

[82] Texas, Marriage Collection, 1814-1909 and 1966-2011. Accessed 8 March 2014 at Ancestry.com.

[83] Pleasant Hill Cemetery, New London, Texas. http://www.findagrave.com., #29563554.

[84] 1900 Census Rusk Co., Texas, Justice Precinct 2, ED 82, p. 7A, #118/119.

[85] Pleasant Hill Cemetery, New London, Texas. http://www.findagrave.com., #29563359.

[86] Lakewood Memorial Park, Henderson, Texas. http://www.findagrave.com, #65473056. Also Texas Death Certificate 22141. Accessed 8 March 2014 at Ancestry.com.

[87] Lakewood Memorial Park, Henderson, Texas. http://www.findagrave.com., #65472762.

[88] Monroe Co., Ga., Marriage Book A:155. Also Georgia, Marriages 1808-1967, accessed 7 March 2014 at familysearch.org.

year, Mary Wilson, 78, is living with them, but in her own household with two black servants. They were still there in 1880.[92]

Children of W. J. WILSON and ELIZA HANSFORD:

1. MARY E.[4] WILSON, b. 1841 Monroe Co, Ga.; d. after 1880 Monroe Co., Ga.
2. GEORGE LARKIN[4] WILSON, b. 1843 Monroe Co., Ga.; d. 1861-1865.
3. BENJAMIN F.[4] WILSON, b. 1845 Monroe Co., Ga.
4. GEORGIANNA JOSEPHINE[4] WILSON, b. 27 June 1846 Monroe Co., Ga.; d. 29 April 1938 Johnston Co., Okla.;[93] m. WILLIAMSON CAMPBELL HOOD; b. 16 November 1832; d. 24 January 1912 Johnston Co., Okla.[94]
5. JAMES KNOX POLK[4] WILSON, b. 16 November 1849 Monroe Co., Ga.; d. 13 April 1935 Smith Co., Texas;[95] m. EMMA BEALL TOWNSEND 1877 Pike Co., Georgia;[96] b. 20 June 1843, Alabama; d. 30 September 1926 Smith Co., Texas.[97]
6. SUSAN ANNA[4] WILSON b. 1850 Monroe Co., Ga.; d. 10 November 1938 Augusta, Ga.;[98] m. DAVID G. W. HOOD 26 December 1868 Monroe Co., Ga.; b. 21 October 1837; d. 12 May 1910 Augusta, Richmond Co., Ga.[99]

---

[89] 1850 Census Monroe Co., Ga., Div. 60, p. 50A, #742.

[90] 1860 Census Monroe Co., Ga., Unionville, p. 850, #1054/1023.

[91] 1870 Census Monroe Co., Ga., p. 133A, #718.

[92] 1880 Census Monroe Co., Ga., Monroeville, ED 88, p. 24C, #257/261.

[93] Oak Grove Cemetery, Nida, Johnston Co., Okla. http://www.findagrave.com., #59148783.

[94] Oak Grove Cemetery, Nida, Johnston Co., Okla. http://www.findagrave.com., #59148744.

[95] Elkins Cemetery, Smith Co., Texas. http://www.findagrave.com, #107565855.

[96] 1880 Census Pike Co., Ga., Dist. 540, ED 105, p. 95A, #353/375. 1900 Census Smith Co., Texas, Justice Precinct 2, ED 99, p. 3A, #38.

[97] Elkins Cemetery, Smith Co., Texas. http://www.findagrave.com, #107565903.

[98] Georgia Deaths, 1919-1998. Accessed 9 March 2014 at Ancestry.com. Original statements from Gubbins.

[99] U. S. Veterans Gravesites, ca. 1775-2006. Accessed 9 March 2014 at Ancestry.com. Buried at Westover Memorial Park, Augusta, Ga.

7. LUCY R.[4] WILSON, b. 1854 Monroe Co., Ga.

8. ROBERT E.[4] WILSON, b. 1856 Monroe Co., Ga.

9. FRANCIS BARTOW[4] WILSON, b. 1859 Monroe Co., Ga.; d. 29 January 1940 Monroe Co., Ga.[100]

vi. ELBRIDGE GERRY[3] NEWTON WILSON, b. 4 Feb 1815 Jones Co., Ga.; d. before 15 October 1907 Pike Co., Ga.;[101] m. (1) MARY L. MORRIS 30 December 1841 Monroe Co., Ga.; [102] d. about 1860 Pike Co., Ga.; m. (2) MARY J. CAUTHEN about 23 July 1861 Pike Co., Ga.;[103] m. (3) AMANDA (CAUTHEN) MCLEOD 1866 Pike Co., Ga.; b. October 1837 Ga.[104]

E. G. N. Wilson, 33 and Mary L., 21, have Jenn L. Wilson, 7, and Sarah E. Wilson, 1, in 1850 Monroe Co., Ga.,[105] and they are living in Pike Co., Ga., in 1860, along with John L. Wilson, 17, Mary C. Wilson, 8, Elbridge G. Wilson 6, Augustine B. Wilson, 2, Martha W. Wilson, 10/12, and Frances A. Smith, 19, domestic.[106] In 1870 he has Amanda L. Wilson, 32, Augustus B, 12, Lucy Ann, 6, William N., 5, and Thomas J., 2, along with Caroline McCloud, 12, and four staff.[107]

T. M. Cauthen, Sr., wrote his will in Pike Co., Ga., 8 December 1885, and it was proved 4 January 1886. He named his daughter, Amanda L. Wilson, and her husband, E. G. Wilson in that document.[108] The executors, E. G. N. Wilson, and

---

http://www.findagrave.com., #58586315.

[100] Ga. Death Certificate #1854; Georgia Death, 1919-98. Accessed 9 March 2014 at Ancestry.com

[101] Letters of Administration were granted that date to T. J. Wilson, executor. Accessed 8 March 2014 at http://trees.ancestry.com/tree/43194817/person/12634033371

[102] Monroe Co., Ga., Marriage Book A:199.

[103] Marriage License located 8 March 2014 at http://trees.ancestry.com/tree/43194817/person/12634033371

[104] 1900 Census Pike Co., Ga., Mil. Dist. 592, ED 105, p. 4A, #

[105] 1850 Census Monroe Co., Ga., Div. 60, p. 70B, #1045.

[106] 1860 Census, Pike Co., Ga., p. 82, #587/559. Near neighbors are Seaborn Jones and Joseph H. Bragg.

[107] 1870 Census Pike Co., Ga., p. 124A, #153.

[108] http://files.usgwarchives.net/ga/pike/wills/cauthen1.txt. Accessed 7 March 2014.

Z. Gardiner, had to defend the will, since the children of a third daughter were ignored. In the end, the court decided the will was invalid and set it aside.[109]

Child of E. WILSON and MARY MORRIS:[110]

1. AUGUSTUS BAILEY[4] WILSON, b. 11 November 1857 Pike Co., Ga.; d. 2 July 1947 Dennison, Grayson Co., Texas;[111] m. MARY FRANCES MANLEY 13 October 1874 Fayette Co., Ga.; b. 1858 Georgia; d. 5 May 1935 Grayson Co., Texas.[112]

Children of E. WILSON and MARY CAUTHEN:

2. LUCY ANN[4] WILSON, b. 1862; d. 18 January 1944 Fulton Co., Ga.;[113] m. JOSEPH M. WILLIAMS about 1880 Monroe Co., Ga.
3. WILLIAM NEWTON[4] WILSON, b. 17 November 1864 Pike Co., Ga.; d. after 1900 Harrison Co., Miss.;[114] m. LEE BARBER DOOLITTLE 13 December 1889 Newton Co., Miss.;[115] b. about 1876 Newton Co., Miss.; d. after 1910 Harrison Co., Miss.
4. PAMELIA JOSIE TRENT[4] WILSON, b. 1863 Pike Co., Ga.; d. 1964 Atlanta, Fulton Co., Ga.;[116] m. _____ MORGAN.

Children of E. WILSON and AMANDA CAUTHEN:

5. THOMAS J.[4] WILSON, b. 6 March 1868 Pike Co., Ga.; d. 16 December 1942 Miami, Dade

---

[109] The Pike County Journal, Tuesday, 16 September 1890. Accessed 7 March 2014 at http://files.usgwarchives.net/ga/pike/wills/tcauthen.txt

[110] The others listed appear to have died young.

[111] Texas Death Certificate #29601. Accessed 8 March 2014 at Ancestry.com.

[112] Newspaper clipping about him at age 82, (1957), accessed 8 march 2014 at http://trees.ancestry.com/tree/43194817/person/12686687218

[113] Oakland Cemetery, Atlanta, Ga. http://www.findagrave.com., #52112501.

[114] 1900 Census Harrison Co., Miss., Mississippi City, ED 32, p. 10B, #197/199.

[115] Mississippi Marriages, 1776-1935. Accessed 8 March 2014 at Ancestry.com.

[116] http://trees.ancestry.com/tree/43194817/person/12782370155

Co., Fla.; m. BERTHA MIRANDA MCCOWELL 29 January 1899 Pike Co., Ga.

    6. ELBRIDGE DRURY[4] WILSON, b. 20 October 1873 Pike Co., Ga.; d. 7 December 1886 Pike Co., Ga.

vii. MARY ANN[3] WILSON, b. 30 Jan 1818 Jones Co., Ga.; d. before 1860 Pike Co., Ga.;[117] m. SIMEON FRANKLIN SPEER 1 December 1836 Monroe Co., Ga.; [118] b. about 1811 Georgia; d. before 1860.

Children of MARY WILSON and SIMEON SPEER:

    1. THOMAS J.[4] SPEER, b. 21 August 1837 Monroe Co., Ga.; d. 18 August 1872 Pike Co., Ga.[119]

    2. GEORGE W.[4] SPEER, b. 1839 Ga.; d. 11 March 1870 Fulton Co., Ga.;[120] m. AMANDA MELVINE BLOODWOOD[121] 29 May 1859 Carroll Co., Ga., b. 4 September 1842 Pike Co., Ga.; d. 14 September 1928 Houston, Harris Co., Texas.[122]

    3. LARKIN WILSON[4] SPEER, b. 1843 Ga.; d. before 1870.

    4. JOHN H. P.[4] SPEER, b. 1844 Ga.; d. before 1870

---

[117] 1860 Census Pike Co., Ga., p. 106, #756/726. All of boys are living with Thomas S. M. Bloodworth and family in 1860. 1850 Census Pike Co., Ga., Dist. 68, p. 196B, #1041.

[118] Monroe Co., Ga., Marriage Book A:110.

[119] Greenwood Cemetery, Barnesville, Lamar Co., Ga. http://www.findagrave.com., #7987452. He was a Ga. State Senator 1868-1870 and was elected to Congress where he served from 1870 to his death.

[120] Amanda J. Speer made application for a pension in his name in Harris Co., Texas, 6 September 1921. She stated he served as secretary to General Henry S. Wayne, and in 1864 was appointed by Gov. Joseph E. Brown as Chief Quartermaster, Ga. Militia, attaining the rank of Major. Application #37647, Confederate Pension Applications, 1899-1975. Accessed 9 March 2014 at Ancestry.com.

[121] The death certificate said James Bloodwood, but I suspect her maiden name may have been Bloodworth, since the George, Amanda, and his brothers were living in the household of Thomas and Frances Bloodworth in 1860.

[122] Texas Death Certificate 53416. Accessed 9 March 2014 at Ancestry.com.

5. MARY L.[4] SPEER, b. 1849 Pike Co., Ga.; d. before 1860 Pike Co., Ga.

viii. LUCY ANN REBECCA[3] WILSON, b. 12 May 1820 Jones Co., Ga.; d. about 1854 Pike Co., Ga.; m. STEPHEN LESUEUR 10 August 1837 Monroe Co., Ga.;[123] b. about 1812 Elbert Co., Ga.; d. 1886 Pike Co., Ga.;[124] m. (2) REBECCA MARY MANN 2 November 1854 Spalding Co., Ga.; b. 31 March 1833 Monroe Co., Ga.; d. 1887 Pike Co., Ga.[125]

Children of LUCY WILSON and STEPHEN LESUEUR:

1. JORDAN ELDRIDGE MEADE[4] LESUEUR, b. 15 August 1838 Pike Co., Ga.; d. 10 May 1916, Chula, Tift Co., Ga.;[126] m. NANCY SUE DUKES about 15 August 1861 Spalding Co., Ga.; b. 6 September 1845 Pike Co., Ga.; d. 4 March 1910 Tift Co., Ga.[127]

2. MARY S. V.[4] LESUEUR, b. 1841 Pike Co., Ga.; d. 1880 Pike Co., Ga.;[128] m. JOHN WESLEY CRAWLEY, SR. 9 December 1853 Pike Co., Ga.; b. 1836 Pike Co., Ga.; d. 1876 Pike Co., Ga.[129]

3. SARAH S. E.[4] LESUEUR, b. 1842 Pike Co., Ga.[130]

4. MCPHERSON C.[4] LESUEUR, b. 1844 Pike Co., Ga.; d. 19 August 1863 Murfreesboro, Rutherford Co., Tenn.;[131] m. GEORGIA WILLIAMS.

---

[123] Jasper Co., Ga., Marriage Book A:113.

[124] Midway Baptist Church Cemetery, Lamar Co., Ga. http://www.findagrave.com., #31585641.

[125] Midway Baptist Church Cemetery, Lamar Co., Ga. http://www.findagrave.com., #32620407.

[126] Hickory Springs Cemetery, Tifton, Tift Co., Ga. http://www.findagrave.com., #12817354.

[127] Hickory Springs Cemetery, Tifton, Tift Co., Ga. http://www.findagrave.com., #12817379.

[128] Crawley Cemetery, Lamar Co., Ga. http://www.findagrave.com., #49886049.

[129] Crawley Cemetery, Lamar Co., Ga. http://www.findagrave.com., #49886041.

[130] 1850 Census Pike Co., Ga., Dist. 68, p. 196A, #1038.

[131] Stones River National Cemetery, Murfreesboro, Tenn.

5. JOHN BERRION[4] LESUEUR, b. 19 April 1846 Pike Co., Ga.; d. 2 September 1879 Barnesville, Pike Co., Ga.;[132] m. MARION ELLA PORCH 10 January 1878 Monroe Co., Ga.; d. 8 January 1914 Forsyth, Monroe Co., Ga.;[133] m. (1) HENRY COGGINS; m. (3) WALTER STEEL CHILDS 13 February 1881 Monroe Co., Ga.

6. ZACHARY TAYLOR[4] LESUEUR, b. 20 August 1848 Pike Co., Ga.; d. 22 November 1933 Johnson Co., Texas;[134] m. EULA G. DARDEN 9 October 1873 Macon, Bibb Co., Ga.; b. 27 August 1854 Monroe Co., Ga.; d. 7 September 1926 Johnson Co., Texas.[135]

ix. BENJAMIN LARKIN[3] WILSON, b. 12 February 1822 Jones Co., Ga..; d. 1839 Monroe Co., Ga.

x. PERMELIA A.[3] WILSON, b. 19 February 1822 Jones Co., Ga.; d. 1 May 1892; m. MATTHEW TRENT FARLEY 15 Nov 1843 Monroe Co., Ga.;[136] b. about 1819 Georgia; d. before 1880.[137]

Children of PERMELIA WILSON and M. T. FARLEY:

1. SUSAN C.[4] FARLEY, b. about 1843 Monroe Co., Ga.; d. after 1920 Dalton, Whitfield Co., Ga.;[138] m. DANIEL G. MAYS 11 December 1859 Monroe Co., Ga.; d. 22 October 1904 Murray Co., Ga.[139]

---

http://www.findagrave.com., #62048343.

[132] Reeves-Askin Cemetery, Lamar Co., Ga. http://www.findagrave.com., #32108873.

[133] Forsyth City Cemetery, Forsyth, Ga. http://www.findagrave.com., #49118007

[134] Cleburne Memorial Cemetery, Cleburne, Texas. http://www.findagrave.com., #75863980.

[135] Cleburne Memorial Cemetery, Cleburne, Texas. http://www.findagrave.com., #75864405.

[136] Monroe Co., Ga., Marriage Book A:237.

[137] 1850 Census Monroe Co., Ga., Div. 60, p. 56B, #836. 1860 Census Monroe Co., Ga., Unionville, p. 849, #1049/1018. 1880 Census Monroe, Co., Ga., Unionville, ED 88, p. 23A, #239/242.

[138] 1920 Census Whitfield Co., Ga., Dalton, ED 195, p. 9B, #179/195.

[139] Susan C. Mays applied for a widow's pension in Whitfield Co., Ga., 16 June 1906. Georgia Confederate Pension-480. Accessed 9 March 2014 at Ancestry.com.

2. JAMES ALEXANDER[4] FARLEY, b. 8 August 1846 Monroe Co., Ga.; d. 19 August 1927 Monroe Co., Ga.;[140] m. MARY J. PHINAZEE 1877 Monroe Co., Ga.,[141] dau. of JAMES GLENN PHINAZEE and ELIZABETH STEWART; b. 5 January 1856; d. 19 March 1924 Monroe Co., Ga.[142]

3. LARKIN F.[4] FARLEY, b. September 1848 Monroe Co., Ga.; d. 27 January 1927 Upson Co., Ga.;[143] m. MARY LUCY FAMBROUGH 1872 Monroe Co., Ga.,[144] dau. of THOMAS FAMBROUGH and LUCY DARDEN;[145] b. 1864 Monroe Co., Ga.; d. 17 February 1926 Monroe Co., Ga.[146]

4. BENJAMIN[4] FARLEY, b. 1850; d. young.

5. JOHN M.[4] FARLEY, b. 25 August 1850 Monroe Co., Ga.; d. 16 September 1914 Forsyth, Monroe Co., Ga.;[147] m. MINNIE 1893;[148] b. 11 January 1869; d. 2 June 1887 Pike Co., Ga.[149]

6. WILLIAM ARTHUR[4] FARLEY, b. 20 February 1858 Monroe Co., Ga.; d. 22 October 1931 Lamar Co., Ga.;[150] m. ELIZABETH SUTTON 1885 Monroe Co., Ga.; b. 1 June 1862; d. 1 February 1943 Forsyth, Monroe Co., Ga.[151]

---

[140] Providence Congregational Methodist Church Cemetery, Jackson, Ga. http://www.findagrave.com., #25672895.

[141] 1900 Census Monroe Co., Ga., Unionville, ED 71, p. 9A, #152.

[142] Providence Congregational Methodist Church Cemetery, Jackson, Ga. http://www.findagrave.com., #25672907.

[143] Glenwood Cemetery, Thomaston, Ga. http://www.findagrave.com., #87250735. Georgia, Deaths Index, 1914-1927. Accessed 9 March 2014 at Ancestry.com.

[144] 1900 Census Pike Co., Ga., Milner, ED 82, p. 12A, #

[145] Georgia, Deaths Index 1914-1927. Accessed 9 March 2014 at Ancestry.com.

[146] Glenwood Cemetery, Thomaston, Ga. http://www.findagrave.com., #87250681.

[147] Forsyth City Cemetery. http://www.findagrave.com., #49118429.

[148] 1900 Census Pike Co., Ga., Milner, ED 82, p. 18B, #227/221.

[149] Milner Baptist Church Cemetery. http://www.findagrave.com., #35214826.

[150] Forsyth City Cemetery. http://www.findagrave.com., #49118431.

[151] Forsyth City Cemetery. http://www.findagrave.com., #49118428.

7. JEFFIE[4] FARLEY, b. July 1862 Monroe Co., Ga.; m. JOHN H. WILSON 1884 Pike Co., Ga.;[152] b. February 1860 Ga.

8. FRANCES TRENT[4] FARLEY, b. 24 October 1865 Monroe Co., Ga.; d. 8 July 1904 Spalding Co., Ga.;[153] m. ARTHUR MIDDLETON SPEER 1887 Ga., son of ALEXANDER MIDDLETON SPEER and MARY BATTLE; b. 22 October 1862 Ga.; d. 23 June 1931 Spalding Co., Ga.[154]

xi. ELIZABETH EDNA[3] WILSON, b. 5 April 1824 Jones Co., Ga.; d. 1902 Griffin, Ga.;[155] m. JOHN WADE CAUTHEN 15 June 1845 Monroe Co., Ga.;[156] b. 1817 S. C.; d. 1892 Griffin, Spalding Co., Ga.[157]

"John Cauthen, son of Thomas H. Cauthen and his wife, Rebecca Williamson, was born in Lancaster Dist., S. C., about 1817, and was a teenager when his father moved to Pike Co., Ga. He married 16 January 1845 (Monroe Co., Ga., Marriage Records) Elizabeth Wilson, daughter of Larkin Wilson, and his wife, Mary Ann Cabiness.

John Cauthen was a well to do farmer in the Milner area, raised his large family in the trying days after the Civil War, and died in 1892 at the age of seventy-five."[158]

Children of ELIZABETH and JOHN CAUTHEN:

1. JANE[4] CAUTHEN, b. 10 March 1846 Monroe Co., Ga.; d. 10 May 1932 Lampasas,

[152] 1900 Census Pike Co., Ga., Milner, ED 82, p. 2A, #29.

[153] Oak Hill Cemetery, Griffin, Spalding Co., Ga. http://www.findagrave.com., #16201208.

[154] Oak Hill Cemetery, Griffin, Spalding Co., Ga. http://www.findagrave.com., #16201196.

[155] Oak Hill Cemetery, Griffin, Ga. http://www.findagrave.com., #15077496.

[156] Monroe Co., Ga., Marriage Book A:238.

[157] Oak Hill Cemetery, Griffin, Ga. http://www.findagrave.com., #24080960.

[158] Westenhaver, Maryline Cauthen. The Cauthen Family History. (Opelika, Ala., 1981), p. 260. Accessed at familysearch.org., 22 April 2014. She has an extended discussion on the children. Cited hereafter as Westenhaver.

Texas;[159] m. PASCHAL HARRISON TAYLOR 5 December 1866 Pike Co., Ga.;[160] b. 20 June 1832 Jasper Co., Ga.; d. 17 January 1905 Lampasas Co., Texas.[161]

2. JOHN WILLIAM[4] CAUTHEN, b. 17 March 1848 Pike Co., Ga.; d. 26 April 1904 Milner, Pike Co., Ga.;[162] m. KATE MARTIN 16 January 1890 Pike Co., Ga.; b. 12 January 1871 Georgia; d. 12 July 1962 Lamar Co., Ga.[163]

3. LUCY REBECCA[4] CAUTHEN, b. 20 September 1850 Pike Co., Ga.; d. 9 June 1924 Baldwin Co., Ga.;[164] m. (1) THOMAS J. SPEER;[165] m. (2) JAMES FRANCES WEST; b. 22 January 1849 Pike Co., Ga.; d. 13 March 1883 Spalding Co., Ga.[166]

4. THOMAS L.[4] CAUTHEN, b. 20 January 1853 Pike Co., Ga.; d. 10 April 1903 Lampasas Co., Texas;[167] m. EMMA JANE REID 1875 Pike Co., Ga.;[168] b. 19 March 1857 Ga.; d. 23 August 1945 Lampasas, Texas.[169]

5. JAMES SIMEON[4] CAUTHEN, b. 6 September 1855 Pike Co., Ga.; d. 4 June 1872 Pike Co., Ga.[170]

---

[159] Oak Hill Cemetery, Lampasas, Lampasas Co., Texas. http://www.findagrave.com., #46322971.

[160] Texas Confederate Pension Applications #29230 22 September 1914 Lampasas, Texas. Accessed 10 March 2014 at Ancestry.com.

[161] Oak Hill Cemetery, Lampasas, Lampasas Co., Texas. http://www.findagrave.com., #46322866.

[162] Milner Baptist Church Cemetery, Lamar Co., Ga. http://www.findagrave.com., #35214734.

[163] Westenhaver, p. 260.

[164] Oak Hill Cemetery, Griffin, Ga. http://www.findagrave.com., #15077457.

[165] Westenhaver, p. 261.

[166] Oak Hill Cemetery, Griffin, Ga. http://www.findagrave.com., #15077459.

[167] Oak Hill Cemetery, Lampasas, Lampasas Co., Texas. http://www.findagrave.com., #46304873.

[168] 1900 Census Lampasas Co., Texas, Lampasas, ED 103, p. 8B, #166/182.

[169] Oak Hill Cemetery, Lampasas, Lampasas Co., Texas. http://www.findagrave.com., #46304934.

[170] Greenwood Cemetery, Barnesville, Lamar Co., Ga. http://www.findagrave.com., #34399891.

6. MARTHA FRANCES[4] CAUTHEN, b. 19 November 1858 Pike Co., Ga.; d. 17 August 1939 Lampasas, Texas;[171] m. (1) JEFFERSON EVANS BLOODWORTH; d. 1884 Pike Co., Ga.; m. (2) WILLIAM H. BREWER 1884 Pike Co., Ga.;[172] d. after 1900 Spalding Co., Ga.

7. JEFFERSON[4] HAMILTON CAUTHEN, b. 25 December 1862 Pike Co., Ga.; d. 17 October 1938 Lampasas, Tex.;[173] m. CORA ETTA EDWARDS; b. 21 August 1864 Brazos Co., Tex.; d. 29 November 1916 Lampasas Co., Tex.[174]

8. LODIE[4] CAUTHEN, b. 1865 Pike Co., Ga.; d. 1903 Griffin, Spalding Co., Ga.;[175] m. WILLIAM MATTHEW THOMAS 1884 Pike Co., Ga.;[176] b. 1851; d. 1906 Spalding Co., Ga.[177]

9. WADE HAMPTON[4] CAUTHEN, b. 1865 Pike Co., Ga.; d. 1903 Atlanta, Fulton Co., Ga., unm.[178]

10. JORDAN DENNIS[4] CAUTHEN, b. 21 March 1868 Pike Co., Ga.; d. 25 January 1944 Glendale, Los Angeles Co., Calif.;[179] m. LOUISE REED 1900 Lampasas, Texas;[180] b. 27 September 1875 La.; d. 12 July 1949 Glendale, Calif.[181]

---

[171] Oak Hill Cemetery, Lampasas, Lampasas Co., Texas. http://www.findagrave.com., #35208082.

[172] 1900 Census Spalding Co., Ga.; Town, ED 90, p. 29A, #

[173] Oak Hill Cemetery, Lampasas, Lampasas Co., Texas. http://www.findagrave.com., #51718785.

[174] Oak Hill Cemetery, Lampasas, Lampasas Co., Texas. http://www.findagrave.com., #35208082

[175] Oak Hill Cemetery, Griffin, Ga. http://www.findagrave.com., #17026022.

[176] 1900 Census Spalding Co., Ga., Griffin, ED 90, p. 7B, #110/120.

[177] Oak Hill Cemetery, Griffin, Ga. http://www.findagrave.com., #17026027.

[178] Oak Hill Cemetery, Griffin, Ga. http://www.findagrave.com., #15077479. Westenhaver, p. 261.

[179] Forest Lawn Memorial Park, Glendale, Calif. http://www.findagrave.com., #85363669.

[180] 1900 Census Lampasas Co., Texas, Lampasas, ED 103, p. 5B, #102/109.

[181] [181] Forest Lawn Memorial Park, Glendale, Calif. http://www.findagrave.com., #85363670.

xii. ZACHARIAH WESLEY[3] WILSON, b. 5 April 1824 Jones Co., Ga.; d. 27 April 1904 Monroe Co., Ga.; m. JANE E. ROBERTS 5 May 1847 Monroe Co., Ga.;[182] b. 1838 Ga.; d. before 1880 Pike Co., Ga.[183]

Children of ZACH. WILSON and JANE ROBERTS:

1. CORNELIUS FRANKLIN[4] WILSON, b. 23 August 1848 Monroe Co., Ga.; d. 29 June 1919 Henderson Co., Texas;[184] m. FANNIE RAY 1885 Pinto Co., Texas;[185] b. 27 December 1861 Mississippi; d. 13 October 1907 Navarro Co., Texas.[186]

2. LARKIN J.[4] WILSON, b. 16 August 1850 Monroe Co., Georgia; d. 7 April 1923 Navarro Co., Texas;[187] m. GEORGIA ELIZABETH CANNIFAX 26 November 1873 Pike Co., Ga.,[188] dau. of WILLIAM OSBORN CANNIFAX and FRANCES ELIZABETH BOYD; b. 12 December 1850 Ga.; d. 4 January 1910 Navarro Co., Texas.[189]

3. ALICE M.[4] WILSON, b. 1854.

4. WILLIAM W.[4] WILSON, b. 25 January 1854 Pike Co., Ga.; d. 25 June 1900 Navarro Co., Texas;[190] m. CHARLOTTE MCDANIEL 24

---

[182] Monroe Co., Ga., Marriage Book B:22. Georgia, County Marriages, 1785-1950. Accessed 7 March 2014 at familysearch.org.

[183] 1860 Census Pike Co., Ga., p. 101, #723/695. 1870 Census Pike Co., Ga., p. 114A, #2. He was a widower in 1880 and Alice, Newton, "Zolikoffer, 20, Homer, 14, and Jeff, 12, were still at home.

[184] La Rue Cemetery, Henderson Co., Texas. http://www.findagrave.com, #65846338.

[185] She is living with her parents, Thomas C. and Mary A. Ray, in Palo, Precinct 3, Pinto Co., Texas, ED 157, p. 164D, #131. They gave their marriage year as 1885 in the 1900 Census Jack Co., Tex., Justice Prect. 3, ED 39, p. 21B, #324.

[186] Dresden Cemetery, Navarro Co., Tex. http://wwwfindagrave.com, #70953731.

[187] Dawson Cemetery, Navarro Co., Tex. http://www.findagrave.com, #48950237.

[188] Georgia, County Marriages, 1785-1950. Accessed 7 March 2014 at familysearch.org.

[189] Dawson Cemetery, Navarro Co., Tex. http://www.findagrave.com, #48950254.

[190] Hamilton Beeman Cemetery, Navarro Co., Texas. http://www.findagrave.com, #4649401.

October 1876 Pike Co., Ga., dau. of GEORGE MCDANIEL and JANE SLADE;[191] b. 30 October 1857; d. 30 January 1931 Navarro Co., Texas.[192]

5. NEWTON HENRY[4] WILSON, b. 7 March 1857 Pike Co., Ga.; d. 23 June 1910 Pike Co., Ga.;[193] m. MARY BETHEMIE REEVES 21 December 1880 Pike Co., Ga.;[194] b. 14 December 1858; d. 9 October 1908 Pike Co., Ga.[195]

6. CLARA J.[4] WILSON, b. 1860, Pike Co., Ga.

7. BRAXTON ZOLLICOFER[4] WILSON, b. 16 December 1861 Pike Co., Ga.; d. 19 April 1926 Barnesville, Lamar Co., Ga.;[196] m. DEANA REEVES 1889 Pike Co., Ga.;[197] b. 14 February 1867; d. 21 June 1962 Lamar Co., Ga.[198]

8. THOMAS J.[4] WILSON, b. 1866 Pike Co., Ga.

9. GEORGIA L.[4] WILSON., b. 1868 Pike Co., Ga.

xiii. SUSAN A.[3] WILSON, b. 12 May 1826 Jones Co., Ga.; d. after 1880 Newton Co., Miss.; m. MATTHEW LEWIS ATKINSON 4 May 1848 Monroe Co., Ga.;[199] b. about 1826 Georgia; d. after 1880 Newton Co., Miss.

---

[191] Accessed 7 March 2014 at http://files.usgwarchives.net/ga/pike/vitals/marriages/mr1909mcdaniel.txt

[192] Hamilton Beeman Cemetery, Navarro Co., Texas. http://www.findagrave.com., #41687345.

[193] Kendrick Cemetery, Zebulon, Ga. http://www.findagrave.com, #25689116.

[194] Georgia, County Marriages, 1785-1950. Accessed 7 March 2014 at familysearch.org.

[195] Kendrick Cemetery, Zebulon, Ga. http://www.findagrave.com, #25689160.

[196] Greenwood Cemetery, Barnesville, Lamar Co., Ga. http://www.findagrave.com, #34403208. Parents are listed in entry Georgia, Deaths Index, 1914-1927. Accessed 6 March 2014 at Ancestry.com.

[197] 1900 Census Pike Co., Ga., Zebulon, ED 85, p. 11A, #201/214.

[198] Greenwood Cemetery, Barnesville, Lamar Co., Ga. http://www.findagrave.com, #34403210.

[199] Jasper Co., Ga., Marriage Book B:34.

In 1850 they are living in Butts Co., Ga.,[200] and are in Newton Co., Miss., in 1870,[201] and 1880.[202]

Children of SUSAN WILSON and LEWIS ATKINSON:

1. FRANCES L.[4] ATKINSON, b. about 1849 Butts Co., Ga.; unm. 1900.[203]
2. MARY O. [4] ATKINSON, b. about 1853 Butts Co., Ga.
3. WILLIAM H.[4] ATKINSON, b. November 1854 Butts Co., Ga.;[204] d. 1945 Lamar Co., Miss.;[205] m. NANCY C. WALL 14 November 1877 Newton Co., Miss.;[206] b. February 1859 Miss.; d. 1927 Lamar Co., Miss.[207]
4. THOMAS JEFFERSON[4] ATKINSON, b. 13 December 1862 Butts Co., Ga.; d. 10 November 1927 Newton Co., Miss.;[208] m. KATHRYN L. LEWIS 9 January 1897 Rankin Co., Miss.;[209] b. 1872; d. 1959 Newton Co., Miss.[210]
5. LEWIS[4] ATKINSON, b. July 1864 Newton Co., Ga.[211] (unm.)

---

[200] 1850 Census Butts Co., Ga., Dist. 8, p. 364A, #460.

[201] 1870 Census Newton Co., Miss., Twp. 7, Range 11, p. 469A, #1. From the births of the children, they moved to Newton Co. after 1857 and before 1863.

[202] 1880 Census Newton Co., Miss., Beat 1, ED 85, p.570A, #179/195. The township is the same, so they probably did not move.

[203] 1900 Census Newton Co., Miss., Beat 1, ED 47, p. 9B, #152. She is living with her brother, Thomas Jefferson, 38, and his wife.

[204] 1900 Census Newton Co., Miss., Beat 1, ED 47, p. 9B, #151.

[205] Dan Sumrall Cemetery, Lamar Co., Miss. http://www.findagrave.com., #55158396.

[206] Mississippi Marriages, 1776-1935. Accessed 23 April 2014 at Ancestry.com.

[207] Dan Sumrall Cemetery, Lamar Co., Miss. http://www.findagrave.com., #55158395.

[208] Midway Missionary Baptist Church Cemetery, Little Rock, Miss. http://www.findagrave.com., #98542682.

[209] Mississippi Marriages, 1776-1935. Accessed 23 April 2014 at Ancestry.com.

[210] Midway Missionary Baptist Church Cemetery, Little Rock, Miss. http://www.findagrave.com., #98542711.

[211] In 1900 he is boarding with George and Mary A. Doolittle in Newton Co., Miss., Beat 1, ED 47, p. 10B, #167. By 1920 he had moved to Tunnel Hill in Lauderdale County, and in 1940 was in Jones County.

6. SARAH[4] ATKINSON, b. 11 August 1866 Newton Co., Miss.; d. 19 February 1941 Newton Co., Miss.;[212] m. NEWTON DOOLITTLE 18 March 1889 Newton Co., Miss.;[213] b. April 1857 Newton Co., Miss.;[214] d. after 1920 Newton Co., Miss.

xiv. CHRISTOPHER COLUMBUS[3] WILSON, b. 10 May 1828 Jones Co., Ga.; m. MARY F. HARVEY 25 January 1852 Monroe Co., Ga.; [215] b. 1836 Georgia.[216]

3. HENRY BAILEY[3] (*LARKIN[2-1]*) WILSON was born 24 March 1807 in Greene Co., Ga. and died 4 July 1880 in Newton Co., Mississippi. He married ELIZA HOWE about 1833 Monroe Co., Ga., daughter of DAVID HOWE and ELIZABETH _____. She was born 12 August 1812 in Putnam Co., Ga., and died 8 November 1888 in Newton Co., Mississippi.

In 1832, as a resident of Jones Co., Ga., he bought land in Monroe Co., Ga. In 1835, he bought 100 acres of land from Elizabeth Howe, Eliza's mother, in Monroe Co. Both of these tracts of land were subject to a Sheriff's sale in 1842. Henry and his family, along with four slaves, appear in Monroe Co. for the 1840 Census, so his move to Mississippi

---

[212] Masonic Cemetery, Newton, Miss. http://www.findagrave.com., #28336120.

[213] Mississippi Marriages, 1776-1935. Accessed 23 April 2014 at Ancestry.com.

[214] 1900 Census Newton Co., Miss., Beat 1, ED 47, p. 10B, #168.

[215] Georgia, County Marriages, 1785-1950. Accessed 7 March 2014 at familysearch.org.

[216] Columbus C. Wilson, 30, and Mary, 24, are living with Sallie, 8, Lucy, 5, Albert J., 3, and William, 1, along with Rufus James, W. S. Nolan, and Robert Y. Harvey in Monroe Co., Ga., in 1860.1860 Census Monroe Co., Ga., Forsyth, p. 713, #73. He is listed as a grocer. Rufus James was a clerk, and W. L. Nolan was Clerk of Court. C. C. Wilson, 42, M. F. Wilson, 31, along with S. E.,17, M. L., 15, and N. J., 13 are living in Atlanta in 1870. 1870 Census Fulton Co., Ga., Atlanta, Ward 1, p. 116A, #335. He is listed as a "RR Fgt Cndctr" which I think should be read as a railroad freight conductor.

412

occurred between 1841 and 1846. With the Sheriff's sale of his land in 1842, this seems the most likely year for removal. Lucy, age 9, born in Ga., and her family are listed in Neshoba County, Miss., for the 1850 Census. Lucy was the youngest child born in Georgia, again supporting 1842 as the likely year for removal

In the 1850 Census Henry B. Wilson listed his occupation as "farmer,"[217] but according to Judge Amis, he operated a stage coach inn as well, as described in the Amis history for Albert. G. Amis. The 1850 Slave Schedule for Neshoba Co., Miss.[218] shows he had one adult female and four young children. In the 1860 Census he had an estimated value of $5400 and the slave schedule showed that he had four adult women, two adult men, two teenage males, and six younger children.[219] His stage stop was burned by Sherman during the Civil War, and in the 1870 Census, his personal value was estimated at $200.[220]

Henry B. Wilson and Eliza (Howe) Wilson are buried in the Wilson Cemetery, Newton Co., Miss.[221] It appears that all of their children except Lucy Frances Wilson are buried there. (She is buried with her husband in the Methodist Church Cemetery, Conehatta, Miss.)

Children of HENRY WILSON and ELIZA HOWE are:

i. MARY E.[4] WILSON, b. 4 April 1834 Monroe Co., Ga.; d. 5 Nov 1906 Newton Co., Miss; m. ENOCH M. HATTAWAY about 1860 Newton Co., Miss.

Mary E. Hattaway is living with Henry B. Wilson in the 1870 Census, age 37, along with a

---

[217] 1850 Census, Neshoba Co., Miss., p. 149.
[218] 1850 Slave Schedule, Neshoba Co., Miss., p. 736.
[219] 1860 Census, Newton Co., Miss., p. 758.
[220] 1870 Census, Newton Co., Miss., Newton P. O., p. 497, #142/142.
[221] Garrett, Cathy. Wilson Family Cemetery, Newton Co., MS. 1 June 2000. Located at
http://genforum.genealogy.com/wilson/messages/9498.html.

daughter, Eliza, age 9. This suggests she married about 1860.[222]

The 1860 Census for Mississippi shows only three men named Hattaway, all in Newton Co. Enoch, 24, b. Ala., is married to Mary, 24, b. GA, and they have no children. James, 33, b. Ga., and his wife Eliza, 26, b. Ala., have two children, while William, 26, is working as a farm laborer for James A. Haroldson, whose household is in between the brothers.[223] Mary is living with her daughter Eliza and her sister, Pallie Wilson with William L. Pace in 1900.[224]

Child of MARY WILSON and HATTAWAY:

1. ELIZA J.[5] HATTAWAY, b. September 1860 Newton Co., Miss.; m. WILLIAM L. PACE 1888 Newton Co., Miss.; b. October 1862 Newton Co., Miss.; d. 1939 Newton Co., Miss.[225]

ii. LARKIN DAVID[4] WILSON, b. 17 February 1836 Monroe Co., Ga.; d. 6 January 1873 Newton Co., Miss.; m. NANCY ELIZABETH (ANDERSON?); b. 29 December 1842; d. 24 Dec 1935 Newton Co., Miss.

In the 1870 Census Larkin D. Wilson and Nancy E. Wilson are living in their own household with Thomas, 4, George 2, and Anna 1.[226]

Children of LARKIN WILSON and NANCY are:

1. THOMAS M.[5] WILSON, b. 18 December 1865 Newton Co., Miss.; d. 13 July 1933 Newton Co., Miss.; m. ORA LATTISHA _____; b. 10

---

[222] 1870 Census Newton Co., Miss., Twp. 8, Range 10, p. 497B, #142.

[223] 1860 Census, Newton Co., Miss., p. 761, #549/476; #463/480; and #464/481. (Enoch, William, and James in that order.) By the process of elimination, Mary Wilson married Enoch Hattaaway.

[224] 1900 Census Newton Co., Miss., Beat 3, ED 52, p. 15B, #258/264.

[225] Wilson Cemetery, Newton Co., Miss.

[226] 1870 Census, Newton Co., Miss., Newton P. O., p. 493, #90/90.

April 1874; d. 18 October 1894 Newton Co., Miss.[227]

    In the 1900 census, Thomas M. Wilson is widowed, with son Tommy, 5, and living with him are his mother Nancy E., 55, and his sister, Larkin, b. November 1872.[228]

2. GEORGIA[5] WILSON, b. 24 September 1867 Newton Co., Miss.; d. 9 October 1870.

3. ANNIE K.[5] WILSON, b. 31 December 1869 Newton Co., Miss.; d. 16 March 1945 Smith Co., Miss.;[229] m. ANDREW J. HEMBREE 10 January 1886 Newton Co., Miss.;[230] b. 25 January 1859 Neshoba Co., Miss.;[231] d. 10 April 1938 Smith Co., Miss.[232]

4. JOHN H.[5] WILSON, b. 1871 Newton Co., Miss.;[233] m. LAURA PACE 10 February 1899 Newton Co., Miss.[234]

5. MARY LARKIN[5] WILSON, b. 28 December 1872 Newton Co., Miss.; d. 7 February 1957 Newton Co., Miss.

iii. GEORGIA S.[4] WILSON, b. 18 April 1839 Monroe Co., Ga.; d. 10 May 1861 Newton Co., Ga.; m. JOSEPH SPEAR.

    The tombstone for Georgia S. Spear matches the birth date recorded for Georgia S. Wilson. Also recorded is a tombstone for Georgia Spier Finlayson, b. 1861, d. 1929. This suggests to me that Georgia (Wilson) Spear/Spier died in

---

[227] Erin Presbyterian Church Cemetery, Newton Co., Miss. Accessed at http://files.usgwarchives.net/ms/newton/cemeteries/erin.txt 11 March 2014

[228] 1900 Census Newton Co., Miss., Beat 3, ED 52, p. 15A, #258, 262.

[229] Union Cemetery, Raleigh, Miss. http://www.findagrave.com., #24085119.

[230] Mississippi Marriages, 1776-1935. Accessed 11 March 2014 at Ancestry.com.

[231] 1850 Census Neshoba Co., Miss., Twp. 12, Range 10, p. 688, #1034/1071. Parents are D. W. and Lenora A.

[232] Union Cemetery, Raleigh, Miss. http://www.findagrave.com., #24085096.

[233] They are in Newton Co., Miss., Beat 3, ED 95, p. 6B in 1920; and in Yazoo Co,. Miss., in 1930, Beat 4, ED 17, p. 8B, and 1940, Yazoo Co., Miss., Eden, ED 82-82, p. 2A, #24.

[234] Mississippi Marriages, 1776-1935. Accessed 11 March 2014 at Ancestry.com.

childbirth and that her daughter later married Mr. Finlayson, whose tombstone is not recorded.

Georgia Spear, 21, b. GA, is living with Joseph Spear, 27, Ala., schoolteacher, in Scott Co., Mississippi in the 1860 Census. She has no children listed.[235] He is probably the son of Hardy Spear, who is 64, NC, and Ada, 65, NC, who are also living in Scott Co., Miss.[236]

iv. LUCY FRANCES[4] WILSON, b. 6 September 1841 Monroe Co., Ga.; d. 27 May 1910 Meridian, Lauderdale Co., Miss.; m. THOMAS DAVIS LANGFORD 11 September 1859 Newton Co., Miss., son of HENRY NORMAN LANGFORD[237] and ELIZABETH DAVIS;[238] b. 3 June 1828 Putnam Co., Ga.; d. 22 Jan 1909 Meridian, Lauderdale Co., Miss.

v. ANDREW J.[4] WILSON, b. 16 August 1845 Neshoba Co., Miss.; d. 10 August 1861 Newton Co., Miss.

vi. PALLIE SANDAL[4] WILSON, b. 27 April 1849 Neshoba Co., Miss.; d. 25 September 1948 Newton Co., Miss. (unm.)

vii. JEFFIE[4] WILSON, b. 9 April 1853 Neshoba Co., Miss.; d. 18 August 1878 Newton Co., Miss. (unm.)

---

[235] 1860 Census, Scott Co., Miss, p.16, #96/96.
[236] 1860 Census, Scott Co., Miss., p. 15, #93/93.
[237] See Chapter 8.
[238] See Chapter 9.

Chapter 11: Descendants of 1820 David Howe of Jones County, Georgia

David Howe was born in Scotland according to the 1880 Census entry for his daughter, Eliza (Howe) Wilson.[1] The earliest certain appearance of David How(e) in the record is 11 June 1810 when David How bought half of lot 99, 14th District of Putnam Co., Ga., from Samuel Berry for $500.[2] He sold this land to James Brooks on 3 August 1811 for $632.[3] He purchased another tract in Putnam County on 2 June 1813 from David Thrash for $800, being half of lot 117 in the Third District, containing 101¼ acres.[4] This tract was sold to Christopher B. Strong for $600 on 8 November 1817, at which time David How was living in Jones Co., Ga.[5] Betsey Howe released her dower right to this tract on the same date.

Dan Langford found in the estate file of Robert Iverson a note which showed:

> 1811, Nov. 18 to 2 schollars 1 quarter—$6.00;
> 1812, Sept. to 2 schollars 6 months—$21.00.
> Approved 1815 by David Howe, late Rector of Union Academy.[6]

This certainly suggests that David Howe was a teacher. Dan Langford has investigated the deeds of Putnam Co., Ga., and found a group of trustees for the Union Academy on a mortgage from 1808, and in

---

[1] I received the name of Eliza Howe's parents from Dan Langford, who supplied most of the information contained here on the Langford, Davis, and Wilson families. However, when I had contacted him, he had not done much work on the Howe family. As I began to research the question in 2004, I found an internet correspondent, who forwarded me a copy of his work on the Howe family, some of which I had already found. However, the majority of the work is his.

[2] Putnam Co., Ga., Deed Book B:112. [9 April 1811.]

[3] Putnam Co., Ga., Deed Book C:212.

[4] Putnam Co., Ga., Deed Book C:232.

[5] Putnam Co., Ga., Deed Book H:187. [24 April 1818.]

[6] Estate case file for Robert Iverson.

1810 they sold a town lot in Eatonton.[7] In 1814 the trustees bought two lots from the Sheriff in Putnam Co. One of the trustees listed in 1816 was Christopher B. Strong, who purchased the land listed above. There is indirect evidence that this was a Presbyterian school, which is certainly consistent with the idea that David Howe was an immigrant from Scotland.

On 9 May 1810 David Howe was appointed administrator for Benjamin Edgar Atkinson, minor son of Joseph Atkinson, deceased. He was released from his surety on 4 March 1816. On the same dates, he was also appointed guardian for Ernest L. Young, child of Alexander Young, deceased.

David Howe applied for letters of administration with the will attached on the estate of Alexander Young, deceased, in Jones Co., Ga., 20 May 1817.[8]

David Howe was on the tax rolls of Putnam Co., Ga., in 1815, but had moved to Jones Co., Ga., by 1816 when he appeared on the tax rolls there.[9] In 1817, David Howe gifted slaves to his wife and two children.[10]

Georgia
Jones County
Know all men by these presents that I David Howe for and in consideration of the love and affection which I have and in regards my daughter Eliza Ann Howe and my son Wm. Joshua Howe and for their use and occupation; my property

---

[7] Trustees were Brice Gaither, Robert Iverson, Barney Holloway, Edmund Lane, and Simeon Holt. In 1814 the trustees were Bruce Gaither, Simeon Holt, Henry Branham, Stephen W. Harris, and John H. Posey.

[8] Georgia Journal, Tuesday 3 June 1817. Cited in Evans, Tad. Georgia Newspaper Clippings Jones County Extracts, Vol. 1. (1810-1831). (Savannah:2001,) p. 61. An attempt to find this in the Ordinary Court Minutes was not successful. There are two separate books covering the time of interest, and they appear somewhat out of order. At any rate, the will was not copied.

[9] Taylor, Robert J. An Index to Georgia Tax Digests, Vol. V. (1814-1817). (Spartanburg, SC: The Reprint Co., 1986.)

[10] Jones Co., GA, Deed Book L:250-251.

disenthralled and unencumbered by debts, I do hereby freely give, grant, and convey to my said daughter Eliza Ann a negro girl named Hannah now about five years old and to my son William Joshua a negro girl named Lucy, now about two years and six months old and their increase the negro girl Hannah to belong to Eliza Ann while she lives and at the time of her death to go and be vested in her issue if any, if none then to go and be vested in my son William Joshua if then is alive and it is especially conditioned that my said daughter has not the power to sell or convey away the said negro girl Hannah nor is she or her increase to be subject to the payment of any debts that may be contracted by herself or any companion, she may hereafter think proper to marry, and in case either of said children dies without issue the negroes then with all their increase to go to the survivor and the issue thereof and in case both should die without issue then both the negroes and their increase to go to and be vested in my two step sons Benjamin E. Atkinson and Ernest L. Young share and share alike , which said two negroes I do hereby consider as given by my heirs, Executors and administrators and from all and every other person or parties whatsoever will defend forever. In witness whereby I have hereunto set my hand and seal in common form on this ninth day of April in the Year of Our Lord Eighteen Hundred and Seventeen.

David Howe (LS)

This deed of Gift signed sealed and acknowledged by the said David Howe and the negro girl Hannah delivered to Eliza Ann Howe and Lucy to William Joshua Howe by the father placing the hand of each negro girl in the hand of each of them as given. In presence of
Benjamin Stripling
William Clopton
John C. Armstrong
N. B. The words {"after the time of my death and") were destroyed before signing.

Georgia
Jones Co.[11]

Know all men by these presents that I David
Howe for and in consideration of the love good will
and duty I give to my present wife Elizabeth Howe
and for her better support and maintenance I give,
settle and confirm to her a negro man named Peter
about twenty four years old and woman Hannah
about twenty years old, to belong and be vested in
her until she marries or dies, in either event, the
said negroes with their increase to go to and be
vested in my daughter Eliza Ann Howe and my son
William Joshua Howe and their issue share and
share alike, and in case either of my said children
should die without issue said property to go to and
be vested in the survivor and issue, if both my said
children should die without issue then to go to and
be vested in my two step sons Benjamin E. Atkinson
and Ernest L. Young share and share alike which
said negroes in the manner given, I hereby warrant
from me and my heirs Executors administrators and
assigns and from all and every party and persons
whatsoever will forever defend. In witness whereof I
the said David Howe have hereto set my hand and
seal on the ninth day of April in the Year of our Lord
Eighteen Hundred and Seventeen.

David Howe (LS)

Signed sealed and acknowledged &
the negroes delivered in presence of
Benjamin Stripling
John C. Armstrong

David Howe purchased one half of Lot 3 in the
Sixth District of "Baldwin County when surveyed, now
Jones County, and known by the name of Caney Fork
Spring," from Arrington Hooten. The deed was
witnessed by Edmund C. Beard and Benjamin A.

Young.[12] This land was sold by the sheriff 4 July 1820 at public outcry to settle a suit in *fiere facias* filed against David Howe by John P. Speir and Company. The land was characterized by both the legal description and also as the tract "whereon the said David Howe now lives."[13] The indenture was endorsed by James Hayes, the purchaser, on July 15, 1820 to

David Howe his heirs & assigns forever against myself my heirs forever given under my hand this 15th July 1820. Signed Sealed in the presence of Benj.A.Young, Robert Thompson. S/ James Hayes.[14]

This land was sold again by "Elizabeth Howe, administratrix of David Howe, deceased," to Joseph Stiles for $391 on 7 March 1822. The land was described as Lot 3, 6th District of Baldwin, now Jones Co., "it being the south half lying on the waters of Dry Creek containing eighty seven acres more or less..."[15] This deed was proved by the oath of Nicholas Summers on 28 September 1834 and recorded 2 November 1835.

The indenture between these two deeds was made 15 November 1821 between Benjamin Stripling, Senior, and Joseph Stiles, in which the latter bought 187 acres of land consisting of 101¼ acres, being the southwest half of lot 2, 6th district of Baldwin when surveyed, also 50¾ acres being the northeast fourth of lot 3, 6th district, and also 35 acres of which 25 are on the west side of Lot 2, and the other 10 are Lot 2 in the 7th District of Baldwin Co. when surveyed.[16] This deed was recorded 3 November 1835.

[12] Jones Co., Ga., Deed Book J:51. [7 February 1817.] These pages had been removed from the deed book before filming in the microfilm copy at the Georgia State Archives and at the Washington Library, Macon, Ga., (2006.)

[13] Jones Co., Ga., Deed Book P:351. [15 July 1820.]

[14] Jones Co., Ga., Deed Book P:352. [31 October 1831]

[15] Jones Co., Ga., Deed Book P:352-353.

[16] Jones Co., Ga., Deed Book P:352.

David Howe was taxed in 1820 for one poll, six slaves, 86 acres of third quality land in Jones County adjacent Mangrum on Big Sandy Creek, and 202½ acres in Telfair County, 9th Dist., lot 237.

Elizabeth Humphries and Elizabeth Howe initially applied for letters of administration on the estate of David Howe on 18 November 1820.[17] They must have been unable to obtain security, as John Humphries and Elizabeth Howe then applied for letters of administration on the estate of David Howe 8 December 1820.[18] Administration was finally granted on 5 January 1821. Bond was posted for $3000 with Moses Stripling, Willis Wilder, Benjamin Stripling, Isaac Burnett and John Stallings as appraisers and security.[19] Taken together, these three documents imply that David Howe was in poor health, had become unable to meet his debts, and had his farm saved by James Hayes, who basically gave him $75 to meet the debt.

The inventory of David Howe was presented on 5 January 1821 when his wife was granted letters of administration. His estate was valued at $1,547 of which the land was valued at $400, and two slaves, a woman and a girl, were valued at $400. A silver watch was also noted among the possessions. The appraisal was signed by Willis Wilder, John Vinson, Moses Stripling, Senior, and Benjamin Stripling.[20] The property sale was held 16 April 1821 with Elizabeth Howe and Benjamin A. Young as the major purchasers, with small purchases by Daniel Hughes, Isaac Barnett, Robert Proctor, John B. Jones, Matthew Beard, John Vinson, Thomas S. Humphries, John S.

---

[17] *Georgia Journal*, Tuesday 5 Dec 1820. Cited in Evans, Tad. Georgia Newspaper Clippings Jones County Extracts, Vol. 1. (1810-1831). (Savannah: 2001,) p. 120. Cited as Evans hereafter.

[18] *Georgia Journal*, Tuesday 19 Dec 1820. Evans, p. 120.

[19] Jones Co., Ga., Court of Ordinary Minute Book 2:37.

[20] Jones Co., Ga., Annual Returns, Inventories & Appraisements, Sales, Divisions of Estates Book C:86-87.

Porter, John Winslett, and John Hughes, Jr. The total of the sale was $344.68.[21]

In May 1821 John Stallings said that Elizabeth Howe was mismanaging the estate. The court ordered her to find other security or be discharged as administratrix.[22] In September 1821 John Stallings was released from his obligation and replaced by Benjamin Stripling and Benjamin A. Young. [23]

Search for the Ancestry of David Howe

William Howe died in Greene Co., Ga., in 1795. His will was dated 12 October 1794 and was proved 31 December 1795. He named his wife Genet, and his daughters, Mary Long and "Moty Leget" and ordered his real estate in South Carolina to be sold and the proceeds divided among the rest of his children. He named as executors Andrew Armor, John Armor, and Jane Howe. The will was witnessed by William Green, John Shaw, and E. Park.[24]

George Deane, Burkit Deane, and Charles Deane sold lot #15 in the town of Greensboro, "being the lot where William How now lives" in January 1795 to Andrew Armor.[25] Andrew Armor, in turn, sold lot #15 to Jane How 31 December 1799.[26]

Jannet Howe, widow of William Howe, died before 27 November 1812 in Greene Co., Ga., when

---

[21] Jones Co., Ga., Annual Returns, Inventories & Appraisements, Sales, Divisions of Estates Book D:18.

[22] Jones Co., Ga., Court of Ordinary Minute Book 2:44.

[23] Jones Co., Ga., Court of Ordinary Minute Book 2:47.

[24] Lucas, Silas Emmet, Jr. Some Georgia County Records, Vol. 2. (Easley, SC: Southern Historical Press, 1986,) p. 317. Cited by Varner, Cheryl. Glick/Foster Ancestry. 29 December 2003. http://worldconnect.rootsweb.com (db :2753682).

[25] Ibid., p. 266.

[26] Ibid., p. 280. Gerry Hill, of Albany, Ga., says that Andrew Armor married Jennett Howe, daughter of William and Jennet Howe of Greene Co., Ga. She also says that Susannah Gray was the daughter of James Gray and Mary Riley, and that she left a family Bible. (HOWE-L, 21 Dec 1997. Located on http://rootsweb.com.

her executor, Robert Howe, filed an inventory.[27] There is a record of the marriage of Catherine Howe to George Ponsonbry on July 6, 1803 Greene Co., Ga.[28] Robert Howe and Janet Howe are the only two persons named Howe found on the Greene Co., Ga., tax list for 1809.[29] As noted, Janet was probably dead, but her estate had not been settled. Robert Howe is present in Putnam Co., Ga., in the 1815 tax list, [30] and in the 1820 Census. He appears in Crawford Co., (p. 414) in 1830 and 1840, (p. 378.) On 7 September 1807 the Trustees of the University of Georgia sold to Robert Howe a lot in the commons of Greensboro containing 25 ½ acres of land, "distinguished in the plat as No. 19."[31] Robert Howe and Susan, his wife, are shown in the Grantor Index as selling land on 9 October 1816, but I was not able to locate the deed itself.[32]

On 11 December 1807 Robert How of Greene Co., Ga., sold to Hamner Fitzpatrick of Baldwin Co., for $200 a tract of 202 ½ acres in the 4th District of Baldwin Co., Ga., lot 92. The indenture was signed Robert Howe, and witnessed by Allen Greene, Edward Rowell, John Armer, J. P., and recorded in Morgan Co., Ga., on 31 December 1810.[33] An Internet source says that Robert Howe was born 22 Jan 1782 in York Co., S. C., and died 10 February 1858 in Crawford Co., Ga. Susannah Gray was born 13 September 1786

---

[27] Greene Co., Ga., Ordinary Office Appraisements and Returns of Estates. G:160.

[28] Dodd, Jordan R. Georgia Marriages 1801-1825. (Orem, Utah: Liahona Research, 1993.)

[29] Captain Carleton's District. However, the 1811 tax list shows William Howe and Robert Howe in Capt. Thomas Dawson's District.

[30] Taylor, Robert J. An Index to Georgia Tax Digests, Vol. IV (1809-1811). (Spartanburg, S. C.: The Reprint Co., 1986.)

[31] Greene Co., Ga., Deed Book 4:704.

[32] Greene Co., Ga., Deed Book HH:217. There is also a purchase recorded 29 Jan 1814, Deed Book EE:410 that I did not locate.

[33] Morgan Co., Ga., Deed Book B:383. Cited in Farmer, Michael M. Morgan County, Georgia Deed Books A-G (1808-1820). (Dallas: npd, 2002,) p. 93.

in Pike Co., Ga., and died 1 Oct 1846 in Taylor Co., Ga.[34]

The Howe Family Bible[35] shows James Gray, born 1 May 1758, died 20 November 1832. He married Mary (   ) Gray, born 25 May 1762, died 16 July 1834. Their children included Archibald, who married Cynthia Armour and Susannah Gray, born 13 September 1786, died 1 October 1846. She married Robert Howe 17 December 1807. Gerry Hill has added that Susannah Gray was born in Orange Co., N. C., and died in Taylor Co., Ga. She is buried in the Harris-Gray Cemetery. She also identifies Robert Howe as the son of William Howe and Jennet Armour.

The will of James Gray was written May 20, 1831 and proved December 6, 1833 in Pike Co., Ga.[36] He specifically mentions his daughter, Susannah Howe.

A slightly different Gray ancestry was reported by Ferdinand Carson.[37]

John Thomas Carson, eldest child of Joseph Jefferson Carson and Martha Goodwin Raines, was born November 11, 1825. He married Susan Saphronia Howe of Crawford County, Georgia, the daughter of Robert Howe, Jr., and Susanna Gray, on February 2, 1847. Susan Saphronia Howe was born May 17, 1826, and died in Columbus, Georgia, on September 15, 1898. Her father, Robert Howe, Jr., was the son of Robert Howe, who served as a

---

[34] Conroy, Lonna Jean. Hudson Working File. 18 Feb 2004. http://worldconnect.rootsweb.com (db huds). She also lists birthdates for Joseph Howe, b. 11 Sep 1784, York Co., SC; d. 21 Sep 1802, Greene Co., Ga.; William Howe, b. 8 Nov 1786 York Co., SC; Katherine Howe b. 24 Sept 1788 in York Co., SC; Andrew Armour Howe, b. 25 Apr. 1790 York Co., SC; d. Greene Co., Ga.; and James A. Howe, b. 15 June 1794 Greene Co., Ga., d. 22 Aug 1859. I do not know the source of her information.

[35] Howe Family Bible. http://files.usgwarchives.org/ga/pike.howegray.txt.

[36] Pike Co., Ga., Will Book B. http://files.usgwarchives.org/ga/gafiles/wl340gray.txt.

[37] Carson, Ferdinand. http://files.usgwarchives.org/ga/macon/carson.txt.

lieutenant in the Revolutionary War. His wife, Susanna Gray, was the daughter of Archibald Gray and Cynthia Armour. Cynthia Armour was the daughter of John Armour and Nancy Caldwell of Greene County, Georgia. Robert Howe, Jr., and Susanna Gray were married on December 17, 1807.

William Howe appears on the 1811 Greene Co., Ga., Tax List along with Robert Howe. On 12 September 1818 William A. Howe of Putnam Co., Ga., sold to Jonas Fancher of Greensboro, Greene Co., Ga., for $2500 a 100 acre tract of land in Greene Co., Ga., "being one of the Academy Lots near the town of Greensborough known in the plan of said Academy lots by No. 39."

Thomas T. Howe married Nancy Rivers 27 June 1816 Putnam Co., Ga. Thomas Howe is listed in the 1840 Census in Randolph Co., Ga., p. 251.

I have found no data showing a relationship among David Howe, Robert Howe, William A. Howe, and Thomas T. Howe, or to 1795 William Howe of Greene Co., Ga. The latter was from York Co., S. C., where the 1790 Census lists David, Joseph, and Robert Howe.[38] From the will of 1799 Joseph Howe of York Co., S. C., it seems likely that William and Thomas Howe are brothers, and probably first cousins to Robert Howe.

Elizabeth (_____) Howe

Benjamin A. Young was the agent for Elizabeth Howe, administratrix of David Howe, deceased on the 1821 Tax List, Flowers District. She was taxed for two slaves, 86 acres of land in Jones County, adjacent Stripling, on Watts Creek, 202½ acres by patent in Telfair Co., 9th District, lot 237, 250 acres by patent in

---

[38] 1790 Census, York Co., S. C., p. 31, col. 3, line 10 (David); p. 31, col. 2, line 10 (Joseph); and p. 28, col. 1, line 94, (Robert.) There is on record the LWT of Joseph Howe of York Co., S. C., written 7 July 1799, inventory presented 17 Sep 1799, [York Co., S. C., Will Book A:155] that lists sons William Howe, John Howe, Joseph Howe, and Thomas Howe, and daughters Isabella Howe and Mary Dunlap Howe.

Early County, 2nd District, lot 315; and 250 acres by patent in Early County, 4th District, lot 40. The records of the 1820 land lottery show that David How of Waller's District of Jones County was awarded land in Early County 4th Dist., lot 40 and 2nd Dist., lot 315. In the 1821 land lottery the orphans of David How of Flowers District, Jones county were awarded Houston Co. 12th Dist., lot 40, and Elizabeth How, widow, of Flowers District, Jones Co., was awarded lot 128, 2nd Dist., Monroe County.

Elizabeth Howe moved to Monroe Co., Ga., by 13 October 1828 when Earnest L. Young of Jasper Co., Ga., sold to Elizabeth Howe of Monroe Co., Ga., for $600 par of lot 161, 6th District of Monroe Co., containing 101¼ acres. This deed was witnessed by Benjamin A. Young and John Stuart.[39] This appears to be the same Earnest Young who was the ward of David Howe in Putnam County from 1810 to 1816.[40]

Elizabeth Howe is in the 1830 Monroe Co., Census, p. 212 with one son between five and 10, one daughter between 10 and 15 years old, and herself between 40 and 50 years of age.

David Howe's orphans of Collier's district, Monroe County, were again fortunate drawers in the 1832 Cherokee Lottery, being awarded Floyd Co., 22nd District, 3rd section, lot no. 267.

On 17 December 1832 Henry B. Wilson of Jones Co., Ga., bought parts of lot 192 and 161 in the 6th District of Monroe County totaling 100 acres, from William S. Chappel, also of Monroe Co., for $375.[41] This deed was witnessed by his father, Larkin Wilson and Stephen Proctor, J. P. This deed appears on the same page as the purchase of land by Elizabeth Howe in 1828—both deeds were recorded in February 1836.

[39] Monroe Co., Ga., Deed Book I:188.

[40] E. L. Young is shown in the 1830 Census for Jasper Co., Ga., (p. 371) with one male 20-30, one female 15-20, and one boy under five, along with one male and two female slaves. This is consistent with the notion that he was born about 1800, and was a ward until about the age of 16.

[41] Monroe Co., Ga., Deed Book I:188.

On 17 December 1835 Elizabeth Howe sold to Henry B. Wilson for $900 a 100 acre tract, lot 161 in the 6th District of Monroe County, "whereon said Elizabeth now lives." The witnesses were William J. Howe and William E. Aiken, J. P.[42]

The 1834 Tax List for Monroe County shows Elizabeth Howe with five polls, and 500 acres of third quality land in Early County, 4th Dist., lot 40 and 2nd Dist., lot 115.

Elizabeth Howe has not been found in the 1840 census, and she is not on the tax lists for 1841 and 1843 for Monroe County, Ga.[43] William J. Howe appears on the 1847 Tax Roll, p. 47, as agent for Elizabeth Howe, when she was taxed on 250 acres in Lot 40, District 4, Early County. In 1849 she was taxed on the same land. She has not been located in the 1850 census.

Elizabeth Howe was buried in a family cemetery in Monroe Co., Ga. along with members of the Robinson and Fambrough families. When the cemetery was disturbed by the farmer owning the land, her marker was moved to Providence Congregational Methodist Church, Monroe Co., Ga. Her marker listed her date of birth as 14 September 1779 and her date of death as 31 October 1857.[44]

If Elizabeth and David Howe married about 1810, then she would have been about thirty years old, and possibly married previously. The deeds cited suggest Elizabeth Howe was the widow of Alexander Young or Joseph Atkinson, or possibly both.

Young Family Connections

---

[42] Monroe Co., Ga., Deed Book I:207.

[43] Dan Langford notes that Henry B. Wilson and William J. Howe were also not on these tax lists, although they were on the census in 1840. Neither has an older woman in the household, so she may have been living with another family member.

[44] Bobby Ellis. 1 December 2004. Personal communication.

428

Elizabeth Howe was associated with Benjamin A. Young in Jones Co., Ga., in settlement of David Howe's affairs. The 1816 Tax List for Jones Co., Ga., (Capt. Waller's Dist.) shows David Howe, Benjamin A. Young, and John Young. John Young is also present in the 1811 Tax List. The marriage records of Jones Co., Ga., show that John Young married Betsey Barfield 1 December 1812, that Benjamin Young married Mariah Holstead 4 July 1819, Nelly Young married James Kelly 26 Jan 1818, and Ellinder Young married Stephen Mills 28 Sept 1826.[45]

The land record showing the purchase of land in Jones Co., Ga., by John Young is helpful in defining his origins, as it was originally written in Jackson Co., Ga.[46]

Georgia   )
Jackson County)
This indenture hath been made the twenty fifth of March in the year of our Lord Eighteen hundred and nine and in the thirty third and fourth year of American independence between Edward Williams of the county and state aforesaid of the one part, and John Young of the other part, know all men by these presents that I, Edward Williams, of the State and County aforesaid within the consideration of two hundred dollars to me paid by John Young, doth hereby bargain and deed and lease and release a certain tract of land unto the said Young of two hundred two and one half acres situated in Baldwin County in the Sixth District and in the Twenty second number, survey on the ninth day of December Eighteen hundred and six by Abner Davis, surveyor, with the beginning on a pine post corner running N45 E45, to a pine post corner, then N45 W45, along the said line to a hickory station, and thence to a dogwood corner post, and thence

[45] Jones Co., Ga., Marriage Book A. Accessed 30 October 2006 at ftp.rootsweb.com/pub/usgenweb/ga/jones/vitals/marriages/1811.txt.
[46] Jones Co., Ga., Deed Book D:177, [24 Sep 1812.]

along the said line to Barretts Ford, and thence along said line to a pine corner, and thence along said line to the beginning corner pine post, together with all and singular the abovementioned premises I doth hereby bargain and sell, lease and release, all that lot of land unto John Young unto him, his heirs and assigns (executors?) and administrators I doth warrant and defend forever from any person or persons, who hath or may claim the same against myself and my heirs and assigns and Executors and administrators or assigns I doth hereby warrant and defend forever all and singular the premises thereunto belong to the said John Young to him and his heirs and assigns and free common usage Witness I the said Edward Williams hath hereunto set my hand and seal .

Edward (X his mark) Williams
Signed, sealed & delivered in the presence of us
Daniel Young
J. Montgomery

Georgia   )
Jackson County)
    Personally came before me James Montgomery and on oath saith that he saw Edward Williams Senr., make and acknowledge the above deed. Sworn to before me this 17th day of May 1809.   M. Montgomery J. P.   J. M. Gomsey

Georgia   )
Jones County)
    Recorded the 14th day of September 1812.
                      Jno. B. Gregory, Clk.

    Robert Isaiah Young, eight day old son of Alexander Young, storekeeper, died at his father's in Smith's building on Market Place in Savannah, Ga., 15 May 1807.[47] Alexander Young acknowledged receipt of $7000 from Frederick Colham for the

[47] Genealogical Committee of Georgia Historical Society. Register of Deaths in Savannah, Georgia, Vol. 2. (1807-July 1811,) p. 7.

account of John James, merchant in Philadelphia; the assignment having been made by Colham at his store in Savannah, and he had taken possession at his store on the Oconee River in Greene County, Ga., 14 July 1810.[48] Presently, I have no information to say whether this Alexander Young is related to the Young family of Jones Co., Ga., or not.[49]

Genealogical Summary

1. DAVID[1] HOWE was born in Scotland and died before 18 November 1820 in Jones Co., Ga. He married ELIZABETH _____. She was born September 14, 1779 in Georgia and died 31 October 1857 in Monroe Co., Ga.

Children of DAVID HOWE and ELIZABETH are:

   i. ELIZA ANN[2] HOWE, b. 12 August 1812 Putnam Co., Ga.; d. 8 Nov 1888 Newton Co., Miss.; m. HENRY BAILEY WILSON about 1833 Monroe Co., Ga., son of LARKIN WILSON and MARY ANN CABINESS, b. 24 Mar 1807 Greene Co., Ga.; d. 4 July 1880 Newton Co., Miss.
     This family is described in Chapter 10.
  ii. WILLIAM JOSHUA[2] HOWE, b. about 1814 Putnam Co., Ga.; d. October 1873 Pike Co., Ga.; m. LUCINDA R. FAMBROUGH 2 November 1837 Monroe Co., Ga., daughter of ALLEN R. FAMBROUGH and MARY.;[50] b. 1821 Georgia; d. before 3 November 1873 Pike Co., Ga.

---

[48] Greene Co., Ga., Deed Book DD:39, [24 Dec 1810]. Cited in Turner, Freda R. Greene Co., Georgia, Land Records, Vol. 2. Deeds 1810-1815. (Milledgeville, Ga.: Boyd Publ. Co., 2005,) pp. 8-9.

[49] Another intriguing possibility is Alexander Young of Camden Co., Ga. He was described as a captured British soldier from Lt. Col. Ferguson's regiment. (Camden Co., Ga., DB B:350-352). He was a captain of Militia in Camden Co., Ga., in 1787, and seems to be unrecorded after 1803. Unfortunately, many early Camden Co. records were not available at the Washington Library or at the Ga. Archives.

[50] Monroe Co., Ga., marriage records also show the marriage of Eliza Fambrough to Thomas D. Jones on 15 January 1835, Nancy H. Fambrough to William M. White on 27 May 1841.

William How appears on the Monroe Co., Ga., census for 1840 (p. 199) with one son under five, himself 20-30 and his wife, 15-20. The index I consulted listed the marriage of William J. Howe and Lucinda R. Fambrough as 2 November 1837.

The estate of Allen R. Fambrough was sold on 15 November 1843 in Monroe Co., Ga. His widow Mary, and son Allen A. Fambrough divided the slave property between them.[51] In 1844 a note was made that the four notes due from William J. Howe, listed on the initial appraisement, had been returned as insolvent.[52]

William J. Howe and his family are listed in the 1850 census for Monroe Co., Ga.[53] He is shown as 35 years old, born in Georgia, farmer, with real estate valued at $2000. Lucinda R. Howe is shown as 39, born in Georgia. In 1860, they are listed in Pike County[54] He is shown as 43 years old, farmer, with real estate valued at $8250 and personal estate valued at $15,075. Lucinda R. Howe is still shown as 39. Also listed in the household were Virgil H. Terryman, 28, overseer, and William H. S. Potts, 17, farm laborer. In 1870 they still in Pike Co., Ga.,[55] with real estate valued at $10,500 and a personal estate of $1500. All of the children except Mary, Matthew, and Benjamin are still living at home, as is Mary Fambrough, 79. Also in the family are Elijah Bradshaw, 62, Postmaster, and four "mulatto" domestic servants: Rebecca Fambrough 40, Nancy 12, Robert 8, Emmett, 3.

The will of William J. Howe was written 11 August 1873 and proved in Pike Co., Ga., 3 November 1873.[56]

State of Georgia
Pike County

---

[51] Monroe Co., Ga., Returns of Estates E:551.

[52] Monroe Co., Ga., Returns of Estates E:552.

[53] 1850 Census Monroe Co., Ga., p. 70, #1043.

[54] 1860 Census Pike Co., Ga., p. 103, #734.

[55] 1870 Census Pike Co., Ga., p. 219, #1529/1543

[56] Pike Co., Ga., Will Book C:478-479. Accessed 10 April 2014 at http://files.usgwarchives.net/ga/pike/wills/howe671wl.txt.

In the name of God Amen I William J. Howe of said State and County being in feeble health but of sound and disposing mind and memory deem it right and proper that I should make a disposition of the property with which a kind Providence has blessed me I do therefore make this my last Will and Testament hereby revoking all others heretofore made by me.

Item 1st I desire and direct that my body be buried in a decent and Christian like manner suitable to my circumstances and condition in life.

Item 2nd I desire and direct that all my just debts be paid by my executors hereinafter named, as soon as they are due or as soon thereafter as proper arrangements can be made to settle them.

Item 3rd I desire and direct that my beloved wife Lucinda R. Howe shall take charge of all my Estate both real and personal and that the same shall by her kept together and managed as by her should be deemed best for the same, for the maintenance [and education marked out] of herself and for the maintenance and education of my minor children until they shall arrive at the age of maturity or majority.

Item 4th I desire and direct that upon the marriage of my beloved wife Lucinda R. Howe after my death that all my Estate both real and personal shall be by my Executors hereinafter named equally among my heirs at law share and share alike: my personal Estate to be sold for division , and my real estate to be either sold and the proceeds of the sale distributed among my heirs or the same to be divided in kind as shall be deemed best for my executors.

Item 5th I desire and direct that all my estate upon the death of my beloved wife Lucinda R. Howe if not distributed before that time as hereinbefore provided shall be by my executors distributed by my according to the fourth Item of this Will

Item 6th I desire and direct that if it shall become necessary for any of my property to be sold for the purpose of paying any of my outstanding debts that the two store houses and lots in the town of Milner now occupied by Manny and Brawner and J. P. Hunt be sold for that purpose unless my wife Lucinda R. Howe shall deem it better to sell some other property in which event I hereby empower her to exercise her discretion in the matter.

Item 6th [7th] I hereby nominate my son William R. Howe and my son in law, Marion [?] Green executors of this my last will and Testament this August 11th 1873

s/W. J. Howe

Signed sealed declared and published by William J. Howe   as his last will and testament in the presence of us the subscribers who subscribed our names hereto in the presence of each other and in the presence of the testator at his special instance and request this August 11th 1873

J. A. Hunt

Geo. A. Gardner

Jno. P. Hunt

Pike Court of Ordinary November Term 1873

Came into open court John P. Hunt and George A. Gardner two of the subscribing witnesses being duly sworn depose and say that William J. Howe signed and sealed the foregoing instrument in their presence and that they heard him declare the same to contain his Will and Testament that he signed the same freely and voluntarily and that he was of sound and disposing mind and memory at the time that they signed the same at his request as witnesses in his presence and in the presence of each other on the day it purports to be

434

Jno. P. Hunt
Geo. A. Gardner
Sworn to and subscribed [before marked out]
in open court this November 3rd 1873
T. J. Blasingame   Ordinary
Georgia
Pike County
We William R. Howe and M. B. Green do
solemnly swear that this writing contains the
true last Will and Testament of William J.
Howe deceased so far as we know or believe
and that you will well and truly execute the
same by paying first the debts and then the
legacies contained in the said will as far as his
goods and chattels will thereunto extend and
the law charges you and that you will make a
true and perfect inventory of all such goods
and chattels so help you God
W. R. Howe
W. B. Green
Sworn to in open Court November 3rd 1873
T. J. Blasingame   Ordinary
Recorded November 10th 1873
T. J. Blasingame

The will of Mary R. Fambrough was written 23
March 1871 and proved 4 November 1873. She
directed her body to be buried "handsomely," and
left Elvira White $100 and $25 for each of her
children: William P. White, Thomas White, Julius
White, and Lucy White. She left to the four
children of Eliza Jones $25: Mary A. Flynt,
William Jones, Henry Jones, and Wiley Jones. She
left to Emmit and Monty Fambrough $50 each.
She left $50 each to W. R. Howe, Ernest Howe,
Mary Arnold, Lizer Howe, and Mattie Greene. To
William J. Howe she left $600, to Lucinda Howe,
$300 and the balance of her estate to be divided
equally among the minor children of William J.
and Lucinda Howe. William R. Howe applied for
letters of administration on 4 November 1873.[57]

---

[57] Pike Co., Ga., Will Book C:480.

The inventory of Mary Farmbrough's estate shows the above disbursements with the genealogically significant notes that H. T. Arnold was paid for his wife Mary E. L. Howe, and M. B. Green for his wife Mattie.

William Howe of Pike County was a representative to the Republican Georgia Constitutional Convention of 1868 for the 22nd District including Pike County.[58] William J. Howe and J. M. Howe were privates in the Barnesville Rifles, later Co. D., 3rd Georgia Battalion, who enlisted 29 June 1861.[59]

Children of WILLIAM HOWE and LUCINDA FAMBROUGH:

1. WILLIAM J.[3] HOWE, b. 9 October 1839 Monroe Co., Ga.;[60] d. after 10 January 1902 Pike Co., Ga.; m. M. VIRIGINIA HUNT 5 October 1871 Pike Co., Ga.

2. DAVID ERNEST L.[3] HOWE, b. 1842 Monroe Co., Ga.; m. ANNIE GENTRY 28 December 1873 Pike Co., Ga.[61]

3. MARY E.[3] HOWE, b. 1843 Monroe Co., Ga.; m. (1) A. J. PUGSLEY 1863 Pike Co., Ga.;[62] m. (2) WILLIAM T. ARNOLD 26 December 1869 Jefferson Co., Ga.; b. 1850 Georgia.[63]

4. ELIZA E.[3] HOWE, b. 1848 Monroe Co., Ga.; m. M. B. GREEN.

5. ROBERT T.[3] HOWE, b. 1851 Ga.

---

[58] Mitchell, Lizzie R. History of Pike County, Georgia, 1822-1932. (Spartanburg, SC: The Reprint Co., 1980), p. 64. Cited hereafter as Mitchell.

[59] Mitchell, p. 132.

[60] He filed a pension application 1 July 1896 reporting that he had sold his house and lot in Milner, Ga., in 1890 for debt, and had six minor children, that he was too disabled to make a living, and attributed it to nervous prostration following his capture 16 December 1864 and subsequent imprisonment at Camp Chase, Ohio. He took the oath in June 1865 and was released from prison. He had enlisted in May 1861. Georgia, Confederate Pension Applications, 1879-1960. Accessed 10 April 2014 at Ancestry.com.

[61] http://files.usgwarchives.net/ga/pike/vitals/marriages/1873-1883groom.txt, 10 April 2014

[62] Accessed 10 April 2014 at http://files.usgwarchives.net/ga/pike/vitals/marriages/marchro2.txt

[63] 1870 Census Jefferson Co., Ga., Dist. 81, p. 57B, #137.

6. MATTHEW F. [3] HOWE, b. 1853
7. MILLARD F. [3] HOWE, b. 1857
8. LUCINDA J. [3] HOWE, b. 1858
9. BENJAMIN A. HOWE, b. 1860; d. young.

Chapter 10: Ancestry of Martha Wadkins

Judge Amis reported that his grandmother, Martha Wadkins Amis, lived "around Macon, Ga., and that she came to Mississippi with Seth Corley some time prior to her marriage to J. W. Amis, in 1824." He reported that she had a sister named Temperance and identified Seth Corley as her uncle. The 1850 Census for Scott Co., Mississippi, shows a number of people named Corley living in close proximity to the Amis family, so I considered the possibility that her mother was actually a "Corley."[1] A search for Corley turned up records in Jones Co., Georgia, which is, indeed, near Macon, Bibb Co., Georgia.

It is ordered that letters of administration on the estate of Edmund Corley be granted to Nancy Corley, Kinchen Curl, & James Stubbs.[2]

On application of the administrators of Edmund Corley deceased. It is ordered that James Lucas, William Butler, Evans Myrick, Thomas Hill, & Peter Clowers be & they are hereby appointed commissioners to divide fifteen Negroes that belong to said estate giving to Nancy Corley and her nine children viz: Seth Corley, Isham, Sally, Silas, John, Evelina, James, Edmund, and Kinchen Corley, or their legal representatives an equal share each and on said distributors giving their bond and security according to laws to refund their proportional part of any debt & cost that may be established against said estate, and said commissioners acting on what will

---

[1] 1850 Census Scott Co., Miss., p. 257, Silas Corley, age 49, b. Ga., #56, Isham Corley, 52, b. Ga., #55, Kinchen Corley, 34, b. Ga., #55, living next to the Grahams, then the Amis family, the Brewer family, and then the Petty family.

[2] Jones Co., GA Ordinary Court Minutes 1808-1818, p. 111, 6 May 1816

make return of their actings and doings therein to next term of this court.[3]

On application of Nancy Corley, administratrix of the estate of Edmund Corley, deceased, stating that the intestate had in his lifetime made a settlement in the Mississippi Territory & carried part of his property there, & she and her children being desirous to prosecute his intended removal. It is ordered that she have leave to remove the children & their property after a legal division takes place & it recorded with the distributees that may remain in this State.[4]

Sally Corley & Silas Corley children of Edmund Corley deceased being about 14 years of age came into court & made choice of their mother Nancy Corley to be their Guardian & there being also other children under that age viz: John Corley, Evelina Corley, Edmund Corley, and Kinchen Curly [sic]. It is therefore ordered that she be their guardian also upon her giving bond and security of $11,200.00. And Isham Corley another child of said Edmund Corley dec'd. above 14 years makes choice of Kinchen Curl to be his Guardian. Ordered that he be guardian on giving bond & security in $1600.00.[5]

Ordered that Nancy Corley, Kinchen Curl, & James Stubbs administrators of Edmund Corley deceased have leave to sell three hundred three and three fourth acres of land in the waters of Walnut Creek whereon Edmund Corley lived to be sold on a credit until the first day of January 1818 they giving the legal notice."[6]

November Term 1818: "Ordered on application of James Stubbs that Nancy Corley, ~~Kinchen~~ [as written in the text] be cited to appear at this next term of this court & show cause why she should not

---

[3] Jones Co., GA Ordinary Court Minutes 1808-1818, p. 122, 2 September 1816

[4] Jones Co., GA Ordinary Court Minutes 1808-1818, p. 124.

[5] Jones Co., GA Ordinary Court Minutes 1808-1818, pp. 133-134.

[6] Transcript of Jones Co, GA Ordinary Court Minutes 1808-1818, p. 138, May 1817.

be discharged from the guardianship of the children of Edmund Corley dec'd. & a new guardian appointed.[7]

John Corley orphan of Edmund Corley dec. being over 14 years of age came into court and made choice of Chilmon[?] Johnson as his guardian who is ordered to be appointed of _____ accordingly bond & security in $2000.00.[8]

Ordered that Nancy Corley be appointed guardian of Silas Corley orphan of E. Corley dec. having made that choice in open court.   Bond $2000.00"[9]

Ordered that Nancy Corley be & she is hereby appointed guardian of her infant children Arvelina, James H., Edmund, & Kinchen Corley orphans of Edmund Corley dec'd. in $8000.00.[10]

Ordered that Kinchen Curl administrator of Edmund Curley deceased be & he is hereby discharged from the administration of said estate having published the ____pany made in the Georgian [?] Journal & satisfied the court that he has fully administered the same and the Clerk is hereby authorized to issue the _____ letters of _____ to him accordingly.[11]

John F. Corley orphan of Edmund Corley dec'd. came into court and made choice of Nancy Corley to be his guardian bond $2000.00."[12]

These records make it clear that Seth Corley must have been Martha Wadkins' brother-in-law, and that they moved to Mississippi sometime after 2 September 1816, when his mother received permission to move to the land Edmund Corley had

---

[7] Jones Co, GA Ordinary Court Minutes 1818-1826, p. 10, December 1818.

[8] Jones Co, GA Ordinary Court Minutes 1818-1826, p. 12, January 1819.

[9] Jones Co, GA Ordinary Court Minutes 1818-1826, p. 13.

[10] Jones Co, GA Ordinary Court Minutes 1818-1826, p. 14, July 1819.

[11] Jones Co, GA Ordinary Court Minutes 1818-1826, p. 19, July 1819.

[12] Jones Co, GA Ordinary Court Minutes 1818-1826, p. 19.

already purchased in Mississippi. The records also establish that Jones Co., Georgia, was the area "near Macon" where Martha Wadkins came from.

> Ordered that Lucretia Watkins be & she is hereby appointed guardian over her persons & property of her two children to wit Temperance Watkins & Patsey Watkins, orphans of James Watkins deceased.
> Amount of bond $1200
> Securities: Lucretia Watkins, Kinchen Curl, Drury Spane. Approved.[13]
>
> Patsy Watkins being a minor under the age of fourteen the Court have appointed Kinchen Curl as her Guardian being the Orphan of James Watkins late of Tennessee dec'd and the said Kinchen Curl come forward & bound himself with Thomas Lockett his security their heirs executors etc. in the sum of six hundred dollars for his faithful performance of duty as Guardian of said orphan."
> (signed) Kinchen Curl LS
> (signed) Thomas Lockett LS[14]
>
> Ordered that Temperance Watkins an Orphan do come forward and choose a Guardian on the first Monday in September next and that she Temperance Watkins be forthwith served with a copy of the same.[15]
>
> Ordered that the clerk issue a citation to Temperance Watkins to appear July Term next to choose a Guardian.[16]

---

[13] Jones Co., GA Ordinary Court Minutes 1808-1818, p. 42, September 1811.

[14] Jones Co., GA Ordinary Court Minutes 1808-1818, p. 62, April 1814.

[15] Jones Co., GA Ordinary Court Minutes 1808-1818, p. 78, August 1814.

[16] Jones Co., GA Ordinary Court Minutes 1808-1818, p. 89, May 1815.

An internet source reported that Seth Corley, son of Edmund and Nancy Corley married Temperance Watkins on 16 July 1815.[17] Temperance was able to choose her guardian, but chose to get married instead. Martha (Patsy) was born in 1805, and so was appointed a ward of Kinchen Curl.

These records established that Martha Wadkins Amis was the daughter of James Watkins and Lucretia Watkins, and the probability that she was the niece of Kinchen Curl. She said she was born in Tennessee in the 1850 Census, and her sister Temperance was born in North Carolina, so James Watkins and Lucretia Watkins must have moved from North Carolina to Tennessee in the interim, and then moved to Jones County, Georgia, where James died before September 1811.

Wilson Curl died testate in Montgomery Co., Tennessee, between 25 November 1802 and the January term of court 1803, naming his eldest daughter, Lucretia, and his youngest son, Kinchen.[18] The 1800 tax list for Montgomery Co., Tenn., lists James Watkins with one poll and no property. [19] However, detailed analysis of the available records of Montgomery Co., Tenn., are somewhat confusing, and it is likely there is more than one James Watkins living in the area.

Wilson Curl moved to Montgomery Co., Tenn., from Nash Co., North Carolina, and James Watkins can be shown to be in Nash Co., N. C., at the time of the 1790 Census, consistent with the idea that

---

[17] Corley, Jennifer. Corleys of Jones/Hancock Co., Ga. 25 Mar 2001. Located on http://genforum.genealogy.com/corley/messages/844.html.

[18] Montgomery Co., Tenn., WB 1. A transcription, which I have confirmed was posted at
http://genforum.genealogy.com/curl/messages/662.html.

[19] Published in Montgomery Co. (TN) Genealogical Journal 4:25-26,1974. (Copy located in Tennessee Room, Jackson-Madison Co. Library.)

Temperance Watkins Corley was born in Nash Co., North Carolina, 21 November 1798.

Nash Co., North Carolina was formed in 1779 from Edgecombe County, and it appears that the Watkins, Curl, and Horn families all had property on or near the Tar River as it crossed the county line in what was then western Edgecombe County. The Watkins men do not appear in the land deeds of Edgecombe with the frequency of the Curl and Horn men, so some of the extant records are subject to interpretation. However, what follows is what I think is a fair representation of the genealogy of the family in North Carolina. I have not been able to find any clues that suggest where the Watkins family came from, and the commonness of the name makes any associations even more problematic.

The Watkins Families of Edgecombe and Nash Counties, North Carolina

Probate records of Edgecombe County, North Carolina, show John Watkins died intestate before the end of October 1764, when his widow, Agnes, was granted administration of his estate.[20] The fact that she did the administration suggests, but does not prove, that John had no sons over the age of 21. An "additional" inventory of the estate was presented in court in July 1766,[21] and Agnes Dunbar, wife of Robert Dunbar, petitioned as administrator of the estate of John Watkins for its distribution.[22] Settlement of the account was ordered in May 1769.[23]

---

[20] Dorman, Marvin K. Edgecombe County North Carolina Abstracts of Court Minutes: 1744-46, 1757-94. (Winston-Salem: Hutchison-Allgood Printing, 1968,) p. 24.

[21] Ibid., p. 27.

[22] Ibid., p. 31.

[23] Ibid., p. 33.

A second John Watkins died before 26 May 1772 when administration of his estate was granted to his widow, Jane.[24] The inventory was presented on August 26, 1772,[25] and division of the estate was ordered 24 February 1773.[26]

Henry Watkins left a will dated 23 March 1804, which was probated at the May Court, in Nash County, North Carolina.[27]

> Henry (x) Watkins 23 Mar 1804; May Ct. 1804
> Wife: Mary Watkins
> Son: Thomas Watkins-50 acres on north side of Kirby's Creek
> 5 shillings each to: son, Stephen Watkins, dau. Anna Ammons, dau. Susanna Robbins, dau. Sarah Clibon, dau. Elizabeth Weaver, son Henry Watkins, son James Watkins, son Joseph Watkins, dau. Jinney Watkins, dau. Cobb, dau. Rhodo Sanders, dau. Mary Revell, dau. Beveton Watkins, dau. Mourning Winstead, dau. Rachel Watkins.
> Exec. Friends Jacob Horn, Jno. Atkinson
> Wit: Jno. Atkinson, Elizabeth Patrick

The same source also shows a will for John Watkins, who left a will dated 2 May 1808, in Nash Co., North Carolina.[28] Note that his land, which was much more extensive than that of Henry Watkins, was also located on Kirby's Creek. Furthermore, both wills named Jacob Horn as executor.

> John Watkins 2 May 1808; May Ct. 1808
> Wife Nancy, 400 acres on north side of Kirby's Creek for life or widowhood

---

[24] Ibid., p. 39.
[25] Ibid., p. 40.
[26] Ibid., p. 41.
[27] Bradley, Stephen E. The Wills of Nash County, North Carolina, Vol. 1, 1777-1848, p. 88.
[28] Ibid.

Dau: Charlotte Watkins, dau. Sally Ricks, son Isaac Watkins, my land on south side of Kirby's Creek, including the Falls of Tar River.
4 youngest children: Betsy, Nancy, Delilah, John Watkins (John gets land on n. side of Kirby's creek, excluding reserve for wife, which is split between John and Isaac after Nancy's death.)
Exec. Friend Jacob Horn, son Isaac Watkins
Wit; Sam. Smith, Marmaduke Mason

Since we are primarily interested in the Watkins family connected with the Curl family, it was helpful to find an analysis of Curl family deeds. .[29] Mr. Curl compiled a list of near neighbors from those people who witnessed deeds involving Wilson, Joseph, Lewis, or Willis Curl, and developed a geographic list based upon common recurrence of some of these names. From this analysis he concludes that Wilson Curl probably lived between Joseph and Lewis Curl and they shared neighbors. Of significance, Wilson and Joseph shared Henry Watkins, while Joseph Curl was also associated with John and Isaac Watkins.[30] These deeds make it clear that there is a close relationship among John, Henry, and Isaac Watkins. Since Wilson Curl named his eldest daughter Lucretia in his will, cited previously, and since the will of Henry Watkins lists a son named James, and they appear to

[29] Curl, Clarence L. Curl, May, et al.: A Compilation of Family Records. (El Paso, TX: High Desert Publishing Co., 1995,) pp. 258-261.
[30] This work shows other interesting relationships. For instance, Henry Horn, Isaac Horn, and Lewis Hines appear only on the deeds of Wilson Curl, and are in a group with several others. In the group with Henry Watkins, he has placed John Davenport, Andrew Ross, Nicholas Skinner, and Josiah Horn. This group is associated with deeds for both Joseph and Wilson Curl. Associated with Joseph alone is a group including William Horn, Joseph Exum, Micajah Revel, John Watkins, and Isaac Watkins. This latter pairing makes it clear that this John Watkins is the same as John Watkins, 1808, who left 400 acres to his son, Isaac. At the other end, in a group associated only with Lewis Curl, are James Watkins and others, whose names do not appear here.

have been near neighbors, I think it likely that James Watkins was the son of Henry.

Edgecombe and Nash County deed records appear largely intact. The following deeds bear upon this family of men named Watkins. On 30 August 1779 Henry Watkins of Nash County sold to Lewis Hines for £500 current money a 100 acre plantation on Compass Creek adjoining Henry Horn, Lewis, Hines, and Wilson Curl, being part of a tract granted to Jacob Whitehead by Earl Granville on 16 March 1761 containing 650 acres. The tract was conveyed by Whitehead to Francis Jinkins on 11 February 1762, by Jinkins to Henry Horn on 4 August 1768, and by Henry Horn to said Henry Watkins. The deed was witnessed by Wilson Curl and Lewis Moore.[31] The same day John Moore of Nash County sold to Henry Watkins of Nash County for £500 a 200 acre tract on both sides of Kirby's Creek adjoining Moore, Wilson Curl, Micajah Revel, and Emmanuel Skinner, being part of a 700 acre tract granted to John Moore by Earl Granville on 1 June 1762. The deed was witnessed by Wilson Curl and Lewis Hines.[32] These deeds leave little doubt that 1804 Henry Watkins of Nash Co., N. C., is the same as the man of these 1779 deeds. Trading land apparently did not help, though, as Henry Watkins, with one poll, was listed as one of the insolvents in Capt. Horn's District for 1786 at the Nash County Quarterly Court for Monday 23 July 1787.[33]

There are three other deeds in Nash County of interest. First, on 7 February 1779, Stephen Watkins of Edgecombe County sold to Moses Harrell of Nash

---

[31] Nash Co., N. C., Deed Book 1:112, 30 August 1779.

[32] Nash Co., N. C., Deed Book 1:112, 30 August 1779.

[33] Dorman, Marvin K. Edgecombe County North Carolina Abstracts of Court Minutes:
1744-46, 1757-94. (Winston-Salem: Hutchison-Allgood Printing, 1968,) p. 72. This might be Henry Watkins, Jr., of course.

County for £50 proclamation a 150 acre tract on both sides of Kirby's Creek adjoining the Folsom Road and Thomas' Road, it being part of a tract granted to Thomas Williams 2 March 1781. This deed was witnessed by Nicholas Skinner and William Barnes.[34] Second, on 30 October 1778 Joel Horn of Edgecombe Co., sold to Hardy Harris, Wilson Curl, and John Watkins, son of John Watkins of Edgecombe County for £110 proclamation a 540 acre tract adjoining William Bridges, Philip Thomas, James Ricks, Horn's Creek, and Redman Bunn.[35] Lastly, John Watkins of Edgecombe County sold to Gray Jordan for £19, 1 a tract of 127 acres on Horn's Creek adjoining William Bridges and Thomas.[36]

James Watkins appeared as a witness to the sale of a 150 acre tract on Maple Creek from Joseph Sealy to Lewis Curl 10 January 1788.[37]

The 1790 Census for Nash Co., N. C., shows James Wadkins (10100), Henry Watkins (21500), and another James Watkins (11200). It is tempting to speculate that 1807 James Watkins of Jones Co., Ga., is the first man in this list. The 1790 Census for Edgecombe Co., N. C., shows John Watkins (20302) living next to William Horn, Sr., Henry Watkins, (10000), Stephen Watkins (14500), living near Michael and Ann Horn, Daniel Watkins (12200) living near Josiah Watkins (12200).

John Watkins witnessed the sale of a tract of land from John Sikes of Hanover Co., N. C., to William

---

[34] Nash Co., N. C., Deed Book 1:94, 7 February 1779.

[35] Edgecombe Co., N. C. Deed Book 5:303; 30 October 1778, February Court 1790; quoted in Bradley, Stephen E. Edgecombe County, North Carolina Deeds, Vol. 4: 1786-1794. (Lawrenceville, VA: 1996,) p. 43.

[36] Edgecombe Co., N. C., Deed Book 6:136; 28 December 1790, August Ct., 1791; quoted in Bradley, Stephen E. Edgecombe County, North Carolina Deeds, Vol. 4: 1786-1794. (Lawrenceville, VA: 1996,) p. 65.

[37] Nash Co., N. C. Deed Book 1:406. Located 28 March 2012 at http://files.usgwarchives.net/nc/nash/deeds/cain002.txt

Bell of Edgecombe Co., N. C., on 30 November 1761.[38] John Watkins witnessed by mark the sale of a tract from Jacob Pope to Pilgrim Pope, for love and affection, a 150 acre tract on the south side of Swift Creek on 3 November 1763.[39] These appear to be the earliest references to anyone named Watkins in the records. I have found no indication as to where they came from before this date. I also cannot tell which, if either of the two John Watkins who died in 1764 and 1772 this might be.

Thomas Watkins was described as living adjacent White Oak Swamp and James Spears in 1765.[40] Thomas Watkins sold to Caleb Coker for £20 a tract on the north side of Indian Cabin Branch, adjacent James Speir, being part of a tract for 115 acres granted by Lord Granville to Speir on 8 December 1760.[41] Stephen Watkins land is described as adjacent Tyancoke Swamp, Holland's Branch, Willis Dade and William Cohoon in a grant from the State of North Carolina to Aaron Proctor.[42] It appears that his land was inherited by Jarrett Watkins, who died and had the land divided by lot amongst his three heirs at law.[43]

---

[38] Edgecombe co., N. C., Deed Book 1:37, 30 November 1761/December Ct., 1761. Accessed 30 March 2012 at http://files.usgwarchives.net/nc/edgecombe/deeds/ebk1.txt.

[39] Edgecombe Co., N. C., Deed Book C:133, 3 November 1763/January Ct., 1764. Accessed 30 March 2012 at http://files.usgwarchives.net/nc/edgecombe/deeds/ebkc.txt.

[40] Edgecombe Co., N. C., Deed Book C:375, 26 October 1765/January Ct., 1766. Accessed 30 March 2012 at http://files.usgwarchives.net/nc/edgecombe/deeds/ebkc.txt

[41] Edgecombe Co., N. C., Deed Book C:546, 9 March 1768/May Ct., 1768. Accessed 30 March 2012 at http://files.usgwarchives.net/nc/edgecombe/deeds/ebkc2.txt. The same land appears by reference in Deed Book D:61, 27 September 1768/February Ct., 1769.

[42] Edgecombe Co., N. C., Deed Book E:291, 28 October 1782/May Ct., 1783. Accessed 30 March 2012 at http://files.usgwarchives.net/nc/edgecombe/deeds/ebke.txt.

[43] Edgecombe Co., N. C., Deed Book 20:401, January 1833/February Ct. 1833. Accessed 30 March 2012 at

Descendants of after 1700 Pasco Curl of Elizabeth City County, Virginia

The English ancestry of the Curle family of Elizabeth City County, Virginia, has been determined.[44]

Nicholas Curle was apparently a lifelong resident of St. Michael's Parish, Lewes, Sussex County, England. He was likely born there although no birth record has been found yet. He was a haberdasher by occupation...

The Lewes Town Book records show Nicholas served as High Constable in 1647 and again in 1659. He was a Society of Twelve member in 1647, 1649, 1657, 1661, and 1663...

Judith Havoll of Lewes married Nicholas Curle on 2 February 1626/7. There were twelve children born of this marriage: four daughters and eight sons. They were Susan, Nicholas, Allen, Mary, Allen, Susannah, Elizabeth, Joshua, Thomas, Pasco, John, and Samuel...Present research has located the will records for both Nicholas and his wife Judith, along with the birth and baptism records for the children. In addition, some marriage and burial records have been found. All these records give proof positive there was a Nicholas Curle of Lewes and he was the father of Thomas, Pasco, and Samuel, who did emigrate to Virginia.

Thomas Curle served as a justice of Elizabeth City County, Virginia, and his tombstone records his birth as 24 November 1640 and his death 30 May 1700. He died without issue, and left his property to

---

http://files.usgwarchives.net/nc/edgecombe/deeds/ebk20.txt.
[44] Curl, Clarence. Curl Family Genealogy. Located at http://clarencecurl.com/. Accessed 7 March 2009. Cited hereafter as Curl.

his nephews, Pasco and Joshua, sons of his brother Pasco Curle.[45]

1. PASCO[1] CURLE was born in Lewes, Sussex, and died after 1700 in Elizabeth City Co., Virginia. He married SARAH _____. She died after 19 March 1712/13 in Elizabeth City Co., Virginia.

The earliest extant record of Pasco Curle is 18 May 1688, when he participated in settlement of the estate of William Myles.[46] He was a justice of the peace in 1688.[47] He was one of the first three "feofees" of Hampton Town in 1691.[48] There seems to be no extant record of his death. Sarah Curle's will was written 19 March 1713 and proved before 15 September 1715 in Elizabeth City Co., Virginia.[49] She made bequests to her daughter Mary Jenkins, daughter Sarah, wife of Joshua Curle, daughter Judith "Bayley", son Joshua, son John, and son Nicholas. Witnesses were Elizabeth Jennings, Mary Ballard, and Euphan Roscow. Nicholas Curle, son, was executor of the will.

Children of PASCO CURL and SARAH ____ are:[50]

.   i.   SARAH[2] CURLE, m. JOSHUA CURLE 1702 Elizabeth City Co., Virginia, son of SAMUEL CURLE and MARY ____. He died before 18 May 1737 Elizabeth City Co., Virginia.

---

[45] Merrill, Kathy, transcriber. Old Kecoughtan, Elizabeth City County, Va.—Old Records. From Wm & Mary Q 9(i. ser.):125. Accessed 7 March 2009. Cited hereafter as "Merrill." Located at http://files.usgwarchives.net/va/elizabethcity/court/kecoughtan.txt.

[46] Curl,.

[47] Merrill.

[48] Kennedy, Mary Selden. Seldens of Virginia and Allied Families. (1911),pp. 265-275. Located at http://books.google.com/books?id=X6xRAAAAMAAJ. Cited hereafter as Kennedy.

[49] Chapman, Blanche A. Wills and Administrations of Elizabeth City County, Virginia, 1688-1800. (Baltimore: Genealogical Publ. Co., repr. 1980,) p. 29. Cited hereafter as Chapman

[50] Kennedy.

Sarah and Joshua were first cousins. His mother is sometimes identified as Mary Armistead, but I have not seen the basis for this conclusion.

Joshua Curle's estate was appraised by William Tucker, Samuel Hawkins, and George Wray 18 May 1737.[51]

Joshua and Sarah Curle had a son named Nicholas, who was named in the will of Nicholas Curle 14 August 1714.[52]

Another possible son is John Curle, who died before 21 February 1732, with administration granted to John King.[53]

Another possible son is Samuel Curle, who died in Elizabeth City Co., Va., before 26 June 1767.[54] He directed his son Samuel to bring up his three youngest children, Sarah, John, and Mary Baker Curle. He mentioned his son, Darby Tools Curle, and gave his son John Curle land on Harris Creek adjoining John Shepherd, William Lattimore, and Hannah Avent; daughter Mary Baker Curle a Negro bought of my brother Joshua Curle, and names his wife Mary Curle as executor along with friends Daniel Barraud and Col. Cary Selden. The will was dated 25 October 1766 and proved 26 June 1767. Witnesses were Charel King, Robert Kipplin Brown, and Robert Bowrey. Mary Curl qualified as executrix with Thomas Dixon, Curle Tucker, and William Wager as security. Appraisal of the estate was done by Samuel Watts, James Naylor, and William Lattimore 26 November 1767.

Samuel Curle had a sister, Sarah Curle, who wrote her will 25 February 1764 and it was proved 5 August 1766 in Elizabeth City Co., Va.[55] She

---

[51] Chapman, p. 28.

[52] Chapman, p. 28.

[53] Chapman, p. 28. This may or may not be the John King who was a bondsman for the executors of Nicholas Curle.

[54] Chapman, p. 29.

[55] Chapman, p. 29.

mentions niece Sarah Curle Barraud, nephew Thomas Pierce, niece Frances Prevost Barraud, brother in law Daniel Barruad, sister Catherine Barraud, niece Martha Pierce, niece Sarah Curle, daughter of Samuel Curle, nephew Darby Curle, niece Jane Summerell, sister Judith Pierce, niece Mary Bridger. Executors were brother-in-law Daniel Barraud, Mr. James Westwood, and Col. Joseph Bridger. Witnesses were Augustine Moore, Ann Moore, and James Westwood.

From this will, we can deduce there were sisters Catherine Curle, who married Daniel Barraud, and Judith Curle, who married Mr. Pierce. There may be sisters who married Joseph Bridger, and one who married Mr. Summerell.

ii. MARY[2] CURLE; d. before 1737 Elizabeth City Co., Va.; m. (1) HENRY JENKINS before 1713 Elizabeth City Co., Va.; m. (2) before 1728 ANTHONY TUCKER son of CHARLES TUCKER and PHEBE CHANDLER; d. before 2 January 1759 Elizabeth City Co., Va.

Mary Jenkins, wife of Westwood Armistead was the daughter of Henry Jenkins and Mary Curle.[56] Mary Jenkins was granted bond for administration of the estate of John Curle with Thomas Wythe and Joshua Curle as bondsmen, with Henry Jenkins later added as a bondsman, with the bond dated 19 February 1718.[57] The appraisal of the estate took place at the house of Mrs. Mary Jenkins by Hind Armistead, John Moore, Henry Irwin, 17 November 1719. This almost surely refers to her brother, John Curle, although it is not clear to me why Joshua was not the administrator. Perhaps he was living with his sister at the time of his death. He was certainly of age, as he was an executor of his father's will.

iii. JUDITH[2] CURLE, m. JOHN BAILEY.

---

[56] Garber, Virginia A. The Armistead Family, 1635-1910. (1910,) p. 117.

[57] Chapman, p. 28.

2. iv. NICHOLAS[2] CURLE, b. abt. 1679; d. 15 August 1714 Elizabeth City Co., Va.; m. (1) ELIZABETH GUTHERICK 14 June 1700 Elizabeth City Co., Va., dau. of QUINTILIAN GUTHERICK; d. 1757 Elizabeth City Co., Va.; m. (2) JANE WILSON; she m. (2) JAMES RICKETTS; m. (3) MERRITT SWEENEY.

   v. PASCO[2] CURLE, b. after 1681; d. 1701 Elizabeth City Co., Va.

  vi. JOSHUA[2] CURLE, d. before 21 February 1732;[58] m. ROSEA _____ about 1714 Elizabeth City Co., Va.; d. before 6 January 1767 Elizabeth City Co., Va.;[59] she m. (2) ANTHONY TUCKER son of CHARLES TUCKER and PHEBE CHANDLER; d. before 2 January 1759 Elizabeth City Co., Va.

     Rosea Curle was granted administration of the estate of Joshua Curle, Jr., 21 February 1732. Appraisers appointed were Anthony Tucker, (brother-in-law), Servant Ballard, John Moore, and Richard Hawkins.[60]

     "William[2] (Michael[1]) King married Mary, daughter of Joshua Curle and Rosea, his wife, afterward Rosea Tucker. Mary survived her husband, who died about 1747, and her will (October 1778-December 24, 1778) mentions daughters Mary Hudson, Rosea Latimer, son William King, and grandson Thomas King. She named Miles King and Henry Jenkins her executors."[61]

 vii. JOHN[2] CURLE, d. before 19 February 1718 Elizabeth City Co., Va.

     See note under Mary Curle.

---

[58] Everingham, Kimball G. Kimball G. Everingham's Genealogical Database. 1 March 2009. Located at http://wc.rootsweb.ancestry.com, (db. kgeveringham.)

[59] Everingham. He identifies her as Rosea Tyler, daughter of Nicholas Tyler, but the basis for this identification is not clear to me from his posting.

[60] Chapman, p. 28.

[61] King Family of Virginia. Wm & Mary Q 16(ser. i.):105-107, 1907.

2. NICHOLAS[2] CURLE was born about 1679 and died 15 August 1714 Elizabeth City Co., Virginia. He married (1) ELIZABETH GUTHERICK 14 June 1700 Elizabeth City Co., Va. He married (2) JANE WILSON about 1707 Elizabeth City Co., Va., daughter of WILLIAM WILSON. She died about 1757 in Elizabeth City Co., Va. She married (2) JAMES RICKETTS. She married (3) MERRITT SWENEY.

"Jane Wilson...also married three times, first Nicholas Curle, who died August 15, 1714."[62] Nicholas Curle was a Justice for Elizabeth City Co., Va., in 1700, and both Clerk and Sheriff in 1702. He represented Elizabeth City County as a burgess in the session of 10 October 1710. He died 15 August 1714 "at the age of 35 years."[63]

The original will for Nicholas Curle was found in the papers of Northampton Co., Virginia, dated 14 August 1714.[64] This document names his wife Jane as executrix, with executors George Walker, John Curle and Henry Jenkins. Legatees include son Pasco, son Wilson, and provision for an unborn child. The document also mentions his brother, John Curle, Nicholas Curle, son of Joshua Curle, to Nicholas Bailey, son of John Bailey, and to kinswoman Lydia Curle, to each of his natural brothers and sisters. Henry Jenkins, John Curle, Jane and James Ricketts qualified as executors to the will with bondsmen being Anthony Armistead, John King, Thomas Wythe, and John Bailey.

Settlement of the estate was delayed, for an estate account for James Ricketts "due to Mr. Curle's children" and to Mrs. Ricketts, was paid from the account with Major Merritt Sweney on 17 July 1745. This estate account is the basis for naming the second

---

[62] Kennedy.

[63] Curl, Clarence. Curl Family Genealogy. Located 7 March 2009 at http://clarencecurl.com/

[64] Chapman, p. 28.

and third husbands of Jane (Wilson) Curle. Merritt Sweney's first wife was apparently the sister of James Ricketts if internet files are to be accepted, although I have not pursued documentation for this.

Children of NICHOLAS CURLE and JANE WILSON are:

3. i. WILSON[3] CURLE, b. 18 December 1709 Elizabeth City Co., Va.; d. 7 June 1748 Elizabeth City Co., Va.; m. PRISCILLA MEADE dau. of ANDREW MEADE and MARY LATHAM.

   ii. PASCO[3] CURLE, d. before 21 August 1745 Elizabeth City Co., Va.

      The court records for Elizabeth City Co., Virginia, show a land dispute involving Pasco Curl, described as an "infant," meaning under the age of 21 on 16 May 1717.[65] Co-defendants in the suit were James Ricketts and wife Jane, widow of Nicholas Curle. It appears the plaintiff, Thomas Poole, had claimed a tract of land inherited from his father, John Poole, and had rented the land to Robert Westlock. However, Pasco Curl claimed ownership of the land as devised to him by the will of his father, Nicholas Curl, whose will was attached. It appears the land in question had escheated from Jane (Poole) Avery to the crown in an inquisition held 26 November 1702, but had been re-granted to Thomas Poole 16 April 1704. The court held in favor of the plaintiff, but damages were limited to one shilling. More than likely, Nicholas Curle thought he had obtained title to the land in 1703 following the escheatment.

      Pasco Curle was dead before 21 August 1745, when sundry debts for his estate and his

---

[65] Elizabeth City Co., Va., Deeds Wills & Court Orders 1715-1721, transcribed by Rosemary C. Neal. Cited by William and Sarah Avery. The Avera/Avery Families of VA, NC, AL, & Putnam Co., GA. Descendants of Henry Avera, Sr. Updated 27 June 2008. Accessed 7 March 2009 at http:// familytreemaker.genealogy.com/users/a/v/e/William-J-Avery-OK/GENE10-0001.html

schooling in England were paid, and receipt of a legacy from Mr. Dandridge and his part of his father's estate. The receipt was signed by Merritt Sweeny.[66]

iii. JANE[3] CURLE, m. GEORGE WALKER,[67] son of GEORGE WALKER and ANN KEITH.[68]

"The will abstract of George Walker (md Jane Curle) that I've read names a son George, executor, and daughter Jane Crooker. I know nothing about her (except I believe she more likely was a Jane Booker. There were several Booker families associated with this family in Hampton, but I have never come across a "Crooker" name.) The son George sold Nansemond Co. property to Daniel Meade in Feb 1768 (from Hening's Statues, vol 8.). And was married by 1764 to Susan, with whom they buy property from Mary Bell (from Elizabeth City Co, OB). He evidently died by 1787; in that year Susan Walker is listed with 5 slaves and a minor levy, George Walker, in the Mecklenburg Co property list."[69]

iv. MARY[3] CURLE, m. (1) ALEXANDER HAMILTON; m. (2) JOHN NASH.[70]

3. WILSON[3] CURLE was born 18 December 1709 (?) in Elizabeth City Co., Virginia, and died 7 June 1748 in Elizabeth City Co., Virginia. He married PRISCILLA MEADE about 1731, daughter of ANDREW MEADE and MARY LATHAM. She died before 22 December 1785 in Elizabeth City Co., Virginia.

---

[66] Chapman, p. 28.
[67] Kubinski, Elaine K. Extended. 3 July 2008.
http://wc.rootsweb.ancestry.com, (db. ekubinski.)
[68] Bateman, Sondra. Bateman and Related Branches. 30 May 2008.
http://wc.rootsweb.ancestry.com, (db. sbb0004).
[69] Cosgriff, John. Re: Jane Curle married George Walker. 16 May 2007. http://genforum.genealogy.com/curl/messages/817.html.
[70] Kubinski.

Wilson [Curl] was born 18 Dec 1709.[71] (A land dispute in 1742 gives his birth date, mentions his parents and grandfather—see Hampton County, Virginia, Deeds, Wills, and Orders, film #31122, page 45.) He married Priscilla Meade (the daughter of Andrew Meade) and died in Elizabeth City in 1748. Their children were: Wilson; David, who died 1767; Hamilton, who died 1760; Nicholas, who died 1768; Andrew, who died 1762; Jane, Mary, William Roscoe, who married Euphan Wallace.[72]

The earliest mention of the name Curle which the records, now extant, furnish, occurs in 1693, when Pascho Curle gives bond as High Sheriff of Elizabeth City County, with his brothers Samuel and Thomas as surety...His eldest, if not only, son, Wilson, was born December 18, 1799 (sic.)[73] married Priscilla, daughter of Andrew and sister of David Meade...and died in June 1748 leaving six sons and two daughters: Wilson Roscoe, born 1732; David Wilson, d. s. p. 1770; Nicholas Wilson, Lt. R. N., d. s. p. after 1771; Andrew Hamilton; and William Roscow Wilson Curle, a member of the Virginia Convention of 1776; Judge of the Admiralty and First Court of Appeals of Virginia....[74]

The will of Wilson Curle was dated 15 December 1746, and was proved in Elizabeth City Co., Virginia, 7 June 1748.[75] He mentioned his wife, Priscilla, his son Wilson, who was not of age, and his

---

[71] Sherwood, JoAnn. Pasco Curle of Elizabeth City, Virginia, Emigrant Ancestor. 6 June 2002.
http://genforum.genealogy.com/curl/messages/629.html.
[72] Sherwood.
[73] There is a dispute about his date of birth. The 1699 date comes from a deposition which I have seen cited, but not published.
[74] Spotswood, Alexander. The Official Letters of Alexander Spotswood, Lieutenant-Governor of the Colony of Virginia, 1710-1722. (Richmond: Va. Hist. Soc., 1882,) p. 32. Located at http://books.google.com/books?id _k4SAAAAYAAJ. Accessed 8 March 2009.
[75] Chapman, pp. 29-30.

son David, who was to be left to the management of David Meade until he was of age. David received lots contiguous to George Waffe, with reversion to son Hamilton if there were no heirs. His son, Nicholas, received a tract called Scones Dam plantation, son Andrew received land at Foxhill and Harris' Creek, son William Roscow received the land called Ridgeland, son Hamilton a lot adjoining Henry Irwin and George Waffe, and son Wilson the land on Back River bought of "Merett Sweny," he paying to his sister Jane money when she is 18, and mentioned daughter Mary Curle. Executors of the will were Miles Cary, Cary Selden, and David Meade. Witnesses were Alexander Rhonnald, Wilson Curle, Catherine Batts, and Mary Hamilton. Priscilla Curle renounced the will, and David Meade qualified as executor, with the inventory returned by David Meade 2 June 1749.

The will seems to name all of the children of Wilson Curle and Priscilla Meade. However, there was an estate settlement for Joshua Curle 6 February 1760, where there was a division of slaves. Mr. David Wilson Curle came into court and made choice of Lot #2 for his brother Nicholas Curle, he to pay Mr. George Walker, Sr., as guardian to Mary and Jane Curle, orphans, he also made choice of lot #5 for his brother Andrew Curle and William Roscow Curle made choice of lot #3 and is to pay the difference to Andrew Curle and George Walker, Sr., guardian to Mary and Jane Curle, orphans. Division of the estate made by Rt. Brough, John Jones, and W. Wager.[76] The heirs are clearly the children of Wilson Curle, so the best explanation is that this is the division of an inheritance of Wilson Curle from Joshua Curle. Was Joshua Curle the "unborn child" named in the will of Nicholas Curle?

---

[76] Chapman, pp. 28-29.

This estate division also establishes that Mary and Jane Curle were "orphans" and their guardians were uncles, George Walker, wife of Wilson Curle's sister, Jane, and Andrew Curle, brother of Wilson Curle. They were presumably still minors in 1760, and so were born after 1744, but before 1748.

The will also poses some problems about birth order for the children. Wilson Curle was described as a minor, but also served as a witness. I have not seen the original, but I think it more likely that it was William R. W. Curle who served as a witness. On the other hand, the will does not specify his guardian, which suggests he was at least 14 years old, which would yield a birth year of 1732 or so. David is clearly the youngest son, but was able to deed land in his own right in 3 April 1762, so was born before 3 April 1741. If they used traditional naming patterns, Andrew would be the oldest son, followed by Nicholas and William, followed by Hamilton, Wilson, and David. It appears that all except Wilson, David, and the two daughters had reached majority by December 1746, but there is documentation that Wilson Curle was born in 1709, so would not have reached age 21 until 1730. Since the youngest son would have to be born in 1725, he would have had to start having children by 1720, which is not biologically plausible, if he were only 11 years old. I suspect the document giving his birth year as 1709 is incorrect, and that he was likely at least 10 years older.

Priscilla Campbell of Elizabeth City Co., Va., made her will 6 October 1784 leaving her estate to Mary Armistead, wife of son-in-law William Armistead. The will was witnessed by Wilson Curle and proved 22 December 1785.[77] It is not certain if this was her son, Wilson Curle, or her grandson, Wilson Curle, son of

---

[77] Tylers Q. Hist. & Gen. Mag. 9:139,1927.

William Roscoe Curle, although the later seems more likely.

Children of WILSON CURLE and PRISCILLA MEADE are:

    i. ANDREW[4] CURLE, d. after 27 March 1762 in Liverpool, Lancaster; m. ANN ____.

        Andrew Curle, mariner, listed his wife Ann as his legatee and executrix in his will, dated 27 March 1762. He listed himself as of Liverpool, Lancaster. Witnesses were John Wilson, Michael Robinson, and Samuel Selden.[78]

    ii. NICHOLAS WILSON[4] CURLE, d. before 27 June 1771, probably in England.

        Nicholas Wilson Curle wrote his will 31 May 1768 as he was about to leave the country. He instructed his brother Will. Roscow Wilson Curle to hold his estate during the life of his mother, with reversion of the estate to his brother upon her death. The will was witnessed by James Armistead, Francis Mallory, and William Face. William R. W. Curle proved the will 27 June 1771, and qualified as executor with Richard Cary as bondsman.[79]

    iii. WILLIAM ROSCOE WILSON[4] CURLE, d. before 30 March 1782 Warwick Co., Va.; m. (1) EUPHAN WALLACE about 1762, dau. of JAMES WALLACE and MARTHA ____; d. 1773; m. (2) SARAH (____) LYON August 1776, widow of WALTER LYON; m. (3) MARY KELLO abt. 1781.

        William Roscow Curle married Mary Wilson, sister to Jane Wilson, which may explain why the name was preserved in the family.[80] William Curl served as a Colonel of militia in the Revolutionary War, was captured by the British, a delegate to

---

78 Chapman, p. 27.
79 Chapman, p. 28.
80 Kennedy.

the Virginia Convention of 1776, and a judge of the Admiralty Court.[81]

William Curl and Euphan Wallace had one son, Wilson Curl, who married Lockey Langhorne. "Wilson Curle of the Parish and County of Warwick, formerly of Elizabeth City County, Virginia, was dead by September 23, 1793, when his widow Lockey Curle made a signed deed to Philemon Morris, for 200 pounds money, 640 acres on both sides of Great Creek in Halifax County, North Carolina, taken up on June 30, 1760 by David Curle and going at his death to William Roscow Curle and at his death to said Wilson Curle whose will directed that William Langhorne, Maurice Langhorne, Richard Cary be his executors and administer the estate of his wife Lockey Curle (Halifax Co., N. C. Deed Book 17, p. 575.)"[82]

This Wilson Curle wrote his will 25 May 1792 and it was proved 26 July 1792. He directed that his lands in North Carolina be sold to pay his debts and left his "beloved wife" all the slaves I acquired by her. He made a bequest to his daughter, Elizabeth, with reversion of that bequest to the children of Moss Armistead if she did not survive with heirs, and mentioned his sister, Elizabeth Curle, along with William and Moss Armistead, and relation Wilson Wallace. Executors were William Langhorne the Elder, Richard Cary, and Maurice Langhorne.[83]

William Curl was listed as an adjoining landowner in two deeds from Northampton Co., N. C., in 1758, indicating he was born before 1737.[84]

---

[81] Kennedy.

[82] Johnston, Hugh Buckner. Some Notes on the Curle Family. (mss. located in North Carolina State Library, Raleigh.) Accessed September 2001.

[83] Chapman, p. 30.

[84] Northampton Co., N. C., Deed Book 2:474, 12 April 1758; Northampton Co., N. C., Deed Book 2:516, 3 July 1758. Cited by Hofmann, Margaret M. Abstract of Deeds Northampton County, North

iv. HAMILTON[4] CURLE, d. before 6 May 1760 Elizabeth City Co., Va.

Priscilla Curle, mother of Hamilton Curle, relinquished administration and William Roscow Curle qualified with David Wilson Curle as security for the estate on 6 May 1760.[85]

4. v. WILSON[4] CURLE, b. say 1732 Elizabeth City Co., Va.; d. December 1802 Montgomery Co., Tenn.; m. MOURNING HORN 17 March 1769 Nash Co., N. C., dau. of HENRY HORN and ANN PURCELL; b. 10 March 1748/49 Edgecombe Co., N. C.; d. 15 Feb 1829 Tuscaloosa Co. Ala.

vi. DAVID WILSON[4] CURLE, b. before 3 April 1741 Elizabeth City Co., Va.; d. before June 1767; m. MARY ____. She married (2) JOSEPH SELDEN; d. before 28 March 1776 Elizabeth City Co., Va.[86]

David Wilson Curle[87] "of the Town of Hampton in the Colony of Virginia" on April 3, 1762 for 20 pounds proclamation money, deeded to Edward Mumford 30 slaves, cattle, horses, hogs, sheep on said Curle's plantation in Halifax County, N. C., (DB 8:167) signed. On April 3, 1762, he made a second signed deed to Edward Mumford, for 2,400 pounds current Virginia money, 640 acres south of Roanoke River in Halifax County, North Carolina, and also two other tracts left to said Curle in the will of the late Andrew Meade of Nansemond County, Virginia (Deed Book 8, p. 184). On November 21, 1763, David Wilson Curle of Elizabeth City County, Virginia, made a signed deed to William Roscoe Curle of Bertie County,

Carolina, Public Registry, Deed Book One and Deed Book Two. 1741-1759. (Weldon NC: Roanoke Press, 1965,) pp. 142 and 146.

[85] Chapman, p. 27.

[86] Tyler's Q. Hist. Gen. Mag. 10:52-58,1928. The last will and testament of Joseph Selden was written 23 August 1774 and proved 28 March 1776 on the oaths of W. R. Wilson Curle and John Selden.

[87] Johnston, Hugh Buckner. Some Notes on the Curle Family. (mss. located in North Carolina State Library, Raleigh.)

North Carolina, for 10 pounds money, 640 acres on both side of Great Creek, Edgecombe Parish, Halifax County, North Carolina (Deed Book 8, p. 363.) This land was also mentioned in the last will and testament of Montfort Selbeck, who bequeathed to his daughter Elizabeth Shine "land on Pretty Creek formerly belonging to David Curle and Edward Montfort."[88]

This land passed to his nephew, Wilson Curle, son of William Roscow Curle following his death in 1767. (See note below.)

The appraisal of the estate of David Wilson Curle was ordered in June 1767 Elizabeth City Co., Va., which was performed by Rt. Brough, John Riddlehurst, and Benjamin Crooker, and signed by William Roscow Wilson Curle. William Roscow Wilson Curle signed the account of sales 22 February 1770. Included within the inventory, were two Negroes, "being dower Negroes, which David W. Curle bought of Mrs. Stretch and sold at public auction to William Selden." The Negroes were sold during the life of Mrs. Stretch.

vii. JANE[4] CURLE, m. MOSS WALLACE ARMISTEAD.

viii. MARY[4] CURLE, m. (1) ROBERT WALLACE; m. (2) WILLIAM ARMISTEAD.

She was named as the sole legatee of her mother's will, (see above), suggesting Jane (Curle) Armistead was already dead.

4. WILSON[4] CURLE was born say 1732 in Elizabeth City Co., Virginia, and died December 1802 in Montgomery Co., Tenn. He married MOURNING HORN 17 March 1769 in Edgecombe Co., North Carolina, daughter of HENRY HORN and ANN PURCELL. She was

---

[88] Hofmann, Margaret M. Genealogical Abstracts of Wills 1758 through 1824 Halifax County, North Carolina. (Weldon NC: Roanoke News Co., 1970,) p. 81.

born 10 March 1748/49 in Wayne Co., N. C., and died 15 February 1829 in Tuscaloosa Co., Ala.

Wilson Curl appeared in Edgecombe Co., N. C. when he married Mourning Horn on 17 March 1769. If the birth estimate discussed in the previous section is reasonable, he was about 37 years old.[89] To date, I have seen no documents to directly link Wilson Curl of Edgecombe Co., N. C. to the Wilson Curle son of Wilson Curle and Priscilla Meade. It is a reasonable guess that this is the same man, but some of the uncertainty is due to his relationship to Lewis, Willis, and Joseph Curl. I will return to this question after presenting the information found about Wilson Curl in Edgecombe and Nash County, North Carolina.

Henry Horn of Edgecombe Co., N. C., first purchased 250 acres of land on the north side of the Tar River in 1741. He and his wife, Susannah, sold this land in 1742. He was certainly in the area of Edgecombe County on the Tar River and Kirby's Creek by 10 March 1743/44, when he bought 299 acres of land from Isaac Kirby.[90]

The first recorded purchase for Wilson Curl occurred 7 March 1770, when he bought a 124 acre plantation on the south bank of Compass Creek adjoining Thomas Exum for £25 proclamation money. This indenture was witnessed by Isaac Horn and Nicholas Skinner, Jr.[91] Compass Creek enters the Tar

---

[89] Some have suggested a first wife, named Mourning Armistead. However, I can find no indication there was ever a person named Mourning Armistead. Cf Garber, Virginia Armistead. The Armistead Family, 1635-1910. (Richmond, Va.:Whittet and Shepperson, 1910.) Copy located on Heritage Quest, 21 March 2009.

[90] Horn, Robert G. William Horn of Nansemond. (n.p.d, 2006,) p. 47. Cited hereafter as Horn.

[91] Edgecombe Co., N. C., Deed Book D:232, 7 March 1770; recorded May Ct., 1770. Cited in Watson, Joseph W. Abstracts of Early Deeds of Edgecombe Co., North Carolina, 1759-1772. (New Bern, NC: Owen G. Dunn Co., 1966), p. 293. Cited hereafter as Watson. The same information has been re-abstracted and reported online: Colbert, C. T.

River at the northeast edge of Rocky Mount, N. C., on today's maps, and runs to the west-northwest. The area of interest in these deeds is proximate to the boundary of Nash Co., N. C., which was cut off from the western portion of Edgecombe Co., N. C., in 1777. Thus, Wilson Curl's name appears in deeds in both counties.

Wilson Curl, Isaac Horn, and Joseph Exum witnessed the sale of a 200 acre tract of land on both sides of Compass Creek at the mouth of Stony Branch from Thomas Spight to Solomon Edwards of Southampton Co., Va., 4 Jan 1775.[92]

On 27 September 1780, Wilson Curl, Joel Horn and Lewis Hines witnessed the sale of a 100 acre tract of land "lying in Nash Co." on the north bank of Compass Creek adjoining both parties, from Isaac Horn to Jacob Horn, both of Edgecombe Co., "it being part of a grant to Isaac Horn 1 June 1762.[93]

John Barnes of Edgecombe Co., sold a 543 acre tract of land to Joel Horn, Wilson Curl, and Hardy Harris "of Edgecombe and Nash" counties, for £80. The land was described as "a few miles from the Tar River on the south side and Horn's Creek, adjoining William Bridges, formerly Lewis Curl, Philip Thomas, James Ricks, and Redmun Bunn. Redmun Bunn and Josiah Bunn were the subscribing witnesses.[94] This same tract of land was sold to John Watkins, son of John, of Edgecombe Co., N. C., by Joel Horn, Wilson Curl, and Hardy Harris on 30 October 1788.[95]

The final entry for Wilson Curl I have found in the land records of Edgecombe Co., N. C., occurred 2

http://files.usgwarchives.net/nc/edgecombe/deeds/ebk24d.txt. Accessed 12 March 2009 at Cited hereafter as Colbert.

[92] Edgecombe Co., N. C., Deed Book 3:32. Watson, p. 78.

[93] Edgecombe Co., N. C., Deed Book E:160. Watson, p. 191.

[94] Edgecombe Co., N. C., Deed Book 4:300. Watson, p. 305.

[95] Edgecombe Co., N. C., Deed Book 5:303. C. T. Colbert. http://files.usgwarchives.net/nc/edgecombe/deeds/ebk5.txt. Accessed 12 March 2009.

January 1787, when he and Redmun Bunn witnessed the sale of a 200 acre tract on both sides of the "Little Swamp" to Willis Curl by Sam Hammock.[96]

Wilson Curl added to his original 124 acre tract of Compass Creek when he purchased from William Hamlin, son and heir of Stephen Hamlin, deceased, of Sussex Co., Va., a 440 acre tract for £40 Virginia money, adjoining Henry Horn and the Compass Creek on 11 February 1779.[97]

He made another major purchase on 26 August 1779, when he purchased 300 acres of land on both sides of Kirby Creek for £2000 current money, from John Moore, who had obtained the land by grant from Earl Granville 1 July 1762.[98] He also received a tract of 150 acres of land on the south side of Compass Creek adjoining Stephen Hamlin, Isaac Horn, Henry Watkins, John Exum, and his own line from the State of North Carolina 10 November 1779.[99] To this point, he acquired in less than 10 years a total of 574 acres on the waters of Compass Creek and 300 acres on the waters of Kirby's Creek., all in the easternmost part of Nash County.

He sold 300 acres of the land on Compass Creek to Lewis Hines 27 September 1780 for £10,000 proc. money.[100] He then went and purchased a 200 acre tract from Nicholas Skinner 24 November 1783 for £100 described as on the north side of the Tar River adjoining David Bunn.[101] The deed was witnessed by H. Horn, Thomas Hunter, Howell Ellen,

---

[96] Edgecombe Co., N. C., Deed Book 5:336. Recorded May Ct., 1790. Colbert, http://files.usgwarchives.net/nc/edgecombe/deeds/ebk5.txt. Accessed 12 March 2009.

[97] Nash Co., N. C., Deed Book 1:63. Watson, Joseph W. Abstracts of Early Deeds of Nash County North Carolina, Books 1-6. (Fort Worth: Arrow Printing Co.,) p. 19. Cited hereafter as Watson.

[98] Nash Co., N. C., Deed Book 1:83. Watson, p. 21.

[99] Nash Co., N. C., Deed Book 3:246. Watson, p. 108.

[100] Nash Co., N. C., Deed Book 1:130. Watson, p. 26.

[101] Nash Co., N. C., Deed Book 1:261. Watson, p. 40.

and Michael Atkinson. The same day he purchased a 250 acre tract on both sides of Stony Creek from Nicholas Skinner for £110 Virginia money. This deed was witnessed by the same men.[102] Examination of the map for this area suggests Wilson Curl was simply adding to his holdings in a southerly direction.

On 26 March 1784 Wilson Curl and wife, Mourning, of Nash Co., sold the 200 acre tract on the north side of the Tar River adjoining David Bunn for £75 to John Watkins of Edgecombe Co., N. C. On the face of it, he seems to have lost £25 on the transaction, which suggests the possibility that John Watkins had married another of his daughters.[103] In a second deed executed the same day, Wilson and Mourning Curl sold John Watkins of Edgecombe Co., N. C., for £65, a tract of 102 acres on the south side of Stony Creek adjoining Benjamin Bunn and Michajah Revel.[104] The deed was witnessed by Joseph Exum and H. Horn. These sales reduced his holdings on Compass Creek to about 173 acres, and reduced his holdings on Stony Creek to about 148 acres.

On 10 August 1786, Wilson Curl bought from William Horn a 225 acre tract on the river, adjoining Andrew Ross, the meeting house, and Stony Creek for £185 Virginia money. On 14 September 1786, Wilson Curl sold the 300 acre tract on Kirby's Creek that he had purchased 26 August 1779, to Edward Wilson for £150[105] On 17 January 1787, Wilson Curl sold a 150 acre plantation on the north side of Stony Creek to Joseph Curl adjoining Andrew Ross and Thomas Hunter for £110 Virginia money.[106] The State of North Carolina granted Wilson Curl title to 17 acres on the east side of Stony Creek adjoining his own land and

---

[102] Nash Co., N. C., Deed Book 1:262. Watson, p. 40.
[103] Nash Co., N. C., Deed Book 1:275. Watson, p. 41.
[104] Nash Co., N. C., Deed Book 1:276. Watson, p. 41.
[105] Nash Co., N. C., Deed Book 1:321. Watson, p. 46.
[106] Nash Co., N. C., Deed Book 1:337. Watson, pp. 47-48.

that of Ross 20 December 1791.[107] This series of transactions left him with about 240 acres of land on the River near the entrance of Stony Creek, and left him cleared of his holdings along the waters of Stony Creek.

He also appears to have about 173 acres remaining on the waters of Compass Creek, but in fact he must have acquired more, as on 11 January 1793, he sold a tract of 340 acres on Compass Creek adjoining Lewis Hines to Randolph Harris of Southampton Co., Virginia.[108] On 18 February 1793, Lewis Curl sold to John Sedgley for £100 Virginia money, a 150 acre tract on the north side of the Tar River adjoining the road and Stony Creek.[109] This deed was witnessed by Wilson Vick and "Lewrancy" Curl. This is the only instance I have found of Luraney Curl appearing in the record.

This last transaction would appear to have left him with about 90 acres on the river, but, again, there appear to be unrecorded deeds, for on 15 May 1794 Wilson Curl sold to John Holley of Bertie Co., N. C., for $125 a tract of 250 acres adjoining Lewis Curl, Wade Moore, William Joyner, Lamon, Lamon's Road, and the Polecat Branch. The deed was witnessed by Wilson Vick and Benjamin Whitfield.[110]

This is the last recorded deed for Wilson Curl, and suggests he was getting ready to move to Tennessee. This supposition is strengthened by the fact that Edward Moore, a known son-in-law of Wilson Curl, sold a 100 acre tract for £100 specie to John Bone, the tract being described as adjacent said Bone, said Moore, and John Brantley.

Exactly when he left for Montgomery Co., Tennessee is uncertain. He is not listed in the 1798

---

[107] Nash Co., N. C., Deed Book 2:108. Watson, p. 69.
[108] Nash Co., N. C., Deed Book 4:227. Watson, p. 162.
[109] Nash Co., N. C., Deed Book 4:212. Watson, p. 161.
[110] Nash Co., N. C., Deed Book 6:4. Watson, p. 237.

tax list, (there is no extant 1800 census,) but I did find the following item: [111]

Indenture made this 10th day of April 1801, between Vinson Cooper of Montgomery County, and Wilson Curl of the same county, for and in consideration of the sum of two hundred and eighty dollars to him in hand paid, for a tract of land lying on the west side of Blooming Grove Creek on Payne's Branch, and containing one hundred and forty-four acres.
Attest: William Curl
      Vinson Cooper

Wilson Curl did not move to Montgomery Co., Tenn., by himself, and was probably in the area at least a year before he purchased land. On 16 January 1800, Edward Prince of Montgomery Co., Tenn., sold to Josiah Horn a 230 acre tract on Blooming Grove Creek, and the same day sold to Edward Moore, Wilson Curl's son-in-law, a 150 acre tract on Blooming Grove Creek.[112] James Watkins also moved to Montgomery Co., Tenn.,[113] but as yet I have not located any land purchases for him.

---

[111] Montgomery Co., Tenn., Deed Book B:419; abstracted in Willis, Laura. Montgomery County, Tenn. Deeds, Vol. Two, 1797-1804. (Melber, KY: Simmons Historical Publications, 1996), p. 32

[112] Horn, p. 90. Josiah Horn's lineage is in some dispute, but he is certainly a cousin of Mourning Horn, and was living near Wilson Curl in Nash Co., N. C., too.

[113] He signed a petition for formation of a new county (Stewart) from the western portion of Montgomery Co., Tenn., on 20 January 1803. William Curl also signed the petition. [Accessed 21 March 2009. Located at http://www.tngenweb.org/montgomery/pet1803.html.]

The Last Will and Testament of Wilson Curl, Montgomery Co., Tenn. [114]

In the name of God Amen. I Wilson Curl of the County of Montgomery and State of Tennessee, calling to mind the mortality of my body and knowing it is one appointed for all mankind to die, being weak of body but of sound mind and memory, hath made and ordained this to be my last will and testament in manner as follows, viz:

1st I commit my soul to god who gave it and my body to the earth to be decently buried at the discretion of my executors.

2nd I give and bequeath to my dear and beloved wife Mourning Curle my negro man Jiff together with all my stock of every kind, farming utensils and household furniture to be at her disposal.

3rd I give and bequeath to my eldest son William Curl the house & land whereon I now live to belong to him & his heirs forever.

4th I give and bequeath to my eldest daughter Lucrecy one dollar. I will and bequeath to my 2nd daughter Sarah the sum of one dollar, I will and bequeath to my 3rd daughter Lurany the sum of one dollar, I will and bequeath to my 4th daughter Ester the sum of one dollar, I will and bequeath to my 5th daughter Elizabeth the sum of one dollar, I will and bequeath to my 6th daughter Millicent the sum of one dollar, I will and bequeath to my youngest son Kinchen Curl the sum of one dollar. I here lastly appoint my wife Mourning Curl and my eldest son William Curl to be the executors of this my last will and testament, N.B. the seven last legacies to be paid by my wife Mourning Curl out of her part.

---

[114] Sherwood, JoAnn. 27 March 2003.
http://genforum.genealogy.com/curl/messages/662.html. She replied to my email by sending the transcript of the will made by Clarence Curl. I have subsequently viewed the microfilm copy of the will at the Tennessee State Archives, and agree with this transcription.

In testimony whereof I have set my hand and affixed my seal this 25th day of November in the year of our Lord 1802.

Wilson Curl
Witness:
Prefant
Wm Weathersbee
Proven in open Court January Term 1803

The land Wilson Curl purchased in 1801 was sold by his eldest son, William, in 1804, by which time William was in Stewart County, formed in 1804.[115]

Indenture made this 21st day of December 1804, between William Curl of Stewart County, and William Potts of Montgomery County, for an in consideration of the sum of four hundred and thirty two dollars to him in hand paid, for a tract of land lying on the west side of Blooming Grove on Pain's Branch, running north on William Weathersby's line, and containing one hundred and forty-four acres.
Attest: Thomas Randle
William Curl

The following bill of sale recorded in Stewart County, Tennessee.[116]

I, Mourning Curl of Montgomery County, have in consideration of the sum of six hundred dollars to me in hand paid by my son William Curl, sold to him a negro man known by the name of Jeffery,

---

[115] Montgomery Co., Tenn., DB D:12;abstracted in Willis, Laura. Montgomery County, Tenn. Deeds, Vol. Three, 1802-1807. (Melber, KY: Simmons Historical Publications, 1996), p. 63.
[116] Stewart Co., Tenn., DB 1:195; in Willis, Laura. Stewart County, Tenn. Deeds, Vol. 1, (1791-1806) (Melber, KY: Simmons Historical Publications, 1995,) p. 28.

about twenty-six years old. Dated this 15th day of June 1807.

Attest:David Hogan
Caleb Williams
    Mourning Curl

Mourning Curl apparently moved to Maury Co., Tenn., along with her daughter Sarah and her husband, Edward Moore, as demonstrated by a deed there dated 8 December 1814, in which she identified herself as one of the children of Henry Horn, deceased, of Wayne Co., N. C. She asserted her rights to her portion of his slaves, which were left in charge of Thomas Horn of Wayne Co., N. C., and she deeded her interest in these slaves to her grandsons, Bennett W. Moore and William I. Moore, both of Maury Co., Tenn.[117]

Children of WILSON CURL and MOURNING HORN are:

i. WILLIAM[5] CURL, b. 24 August 1779 Nash Co., N. C.; d. 20 October 1854 Cherokee Co., Texas.

William Curl was elected sheriff of Stewart Co., Tenn., at the first meeting of the County Court 12 March 1804.[118] William Curl sold 923 acres of land in Stewart Co., Tenn., to William Allen on 24 January 1806.[119] In a deed dated 17 March 1808, William Curl, former Sheriff, sold a 640 acre tract of land on Crosses Trace Creek, in range 21, section 7, and had been sold as part of a judgment.[120] He appears in numerous other deeds from 1808 in his role as sheriff. He was still active in affairs through 1818.

---

[117] Maury Co., Tenn. Deed Book B:39, May 1815. Quoted in Horn.

[118] Stewart Co., Tenn., County Court Minutes (1804-1807):1. http://www.tngenweb.org/stewart/minutes1804.htm. Accessed 8 March 2009.

[119] Stewart Co., Tenn., Deed Book 2:10. Accessed 8 March 2009 at http://www.tngenweb.org/stewart/deed/deed2.htm.

[120] Stewart Co., Tenn., Deed Book 2:168. Accessed 8 March 2009 at http://www.tngenweb.org/stewart/deed/deed2.htm.

William Curl was head of household in Stewart Co., Tenn., in 1820.[121] He was born after 1775 and before 1794 based on this report.

In March 1829, Elizabeth Curl sued William Curl for divorce. In her trial in September 1829, she showed that William Curl had married another woman in Alabama in 1823.[122] Elizabeth Curl is head of household in the 1830 Census for Stewart Co., Tenn.[123]

In an Act of the Alabama Legislature passed 20 December 1828, "Nancy Steel, natural child of Wm. Curl be hereafter known and called by the name Nancy Curl, and that said child be legitimated, and that she be entitled to all the rights and privileges of the legitimate children of William Curl."[124]

William Curl appears in the census for St. Clair Co., Ala., with himself, age 50-60, one woman 20-30, and one female child, 5-10.[125] Jeri Steele has identified him as William Curl, b. 2 August 1779 in North Carolina and died 20 October 1854 in Shelby Co., Texas.[126] Her data do not cite a source for his birth and death dates. He

---

[121] 1820 Census Stewart Co., Tenn., p. 5. [110010-0101] This indicates William Curl was 26-45 years old, which gives a birth year 1775-1794, which is not accurate.

[122] Stewart Co., Tenn., Circuit Court Minutes 1A. Accessed 8 March 2009 at
http://www.tngenweb.org/stewart/circminutes.htm.

[123] 1830 Census Stewart Co., Tenn., p. 233, [010201-200001, plus 4 slaves.] It is not clear who the man in the household might be.

[124] Acts Passed at the Tenth Annual Session of the General Assembly of the State of Alabama: Begun and held in the Town of Tuscaloosa, on the Third Monday in November, One Thousand Eight Hundred and Twenty Eight. (Tuscaloosa: McGuire, Henry, and McGuire, 1829,) p. 83. Located at http://books.google.com/books?id=jao3AAAAIAAJ. Accessed 11 March 2009.

[125] 1830 Census St. Clair Co., Ala., p. 232.

[126] Steele, Jeri. Jeri Steele's Research in Progress (includes non-ancestors.) 17 August 2003. Located at http://wc.rootsweb.ancestry.com., (db. txpioneers.)

married Nancy Steel 31 March 1831 in St. Clair Co., Alabama.[127]

William Curl entered Texas in November 1837, and was awarded a 320 acre tract of land in Nacogdoches County, Texas, on 4 July 1839.[128] He was paid $15 for service as a private in Capt. H. B. Stephens' Company of Mounted Rangers in East Texas.[129]

Nancy Curl married John Bishop Renfro 9 Jan 1838 in Benton (now Calhoun) Co., Ala., son of William Renfro and Mary Pelt. He was born 20 May 1817 in Knox Co., Tenn., and died 5 December 1880 in Dangerfield, Morris Co., Texas. She died in 1882 in Larissa, Cherokee Co., Texas.

William Curl is listed in the 1850 Census living with his daughter and her family in Rusk, Rusk Co., Texas. He was 73, born in North Carolina, Nancy Curl was 50 and born in Tennessee.[130] Nancy Curl appears in the 1860 Census for Cherokee Co., Texas, age 51 (amazingly she aged only one year, and now was born in SC), living next door to her daughter with one grandson in the house.[131]

ii. LUCRETIA[5] CURL, b. about 1770 Nash Co., N. C.; d. 1814 Jones Co., Ga.; m. JAMES WATKINS, son of HENRY WATKINS before 1799 Nash Co., N. C.; d. before 1811 Jones Co., Ga.
See Genealogical Summary below.

---

[127] Steele. She cites Gandrud, but I was not able to find the relevant volume.

[128] White, Gifford. 1840 Citizens of Texas, Vol. 1, Land Grants. (Austin, 1983,) p. 60. Kinchen Curl arrived 25 May 1838 and was awarded 320 acres in San Augustine Co., Texas, 23 April 1839.

[129] Steele, Jeri. She cites Davis, Kathryn H. East Texas Militiamen 1838-1839, Vol. 2. (Nacogdoches, TX: Ericson Books, 1992,) p. 55.

[130] 1850 Census Rusk Co., Texas, p. 302, #940/940. John B. Renfro was head of household, 33, b. TN, and his wife, Nancy was 26, b. Alabama. This information is consistent with the data reported by Steele. John B. Renfro was listed as a Baptist clergyman.

[131] 1860 Census Cherokee Co., Texas, Rusk P. O., p. 471, #798/798. John B. Renfro, 43, and Nancy (Curl) Renfro, 36, b. Alabama, are living next door at #797/797.

iii. SARAH[5] CURL, b. 11 October 1771 Nash Co., N. C.; d. 12 February 1829 Tuscaloosa Co., Ala.; m. EDWARD MOORE 1791 Nash Co., N. C.; b. 8 March 1772 Nash Co., N. C.; d. 17 February 1823 Tuscaloosa Co., Ala.

Sarah Curl and Edward Moore moved from Nash Co., N. C. to Montgomery Co., Tenn., along with Wilson Curl and Josiah Horn.[132] They moved to Maury Co., Tenn., before 1814, when Mourning Curl gave her grandsons Bennett Moore and William Moore a gift of two Negroes.[133]

"Mourning Curl, one of the daughters of Henry Horn, dec'd, of Wayne Co., N. C., entitled to equal part with the rest of heirs of slaves of which he did possess, which were left in charge of Thomas Horn of same place, for love and affection to two grandsons, Bennett W. Moore and William I. Moore, both of Maury Co., Tenn., of interest in aforementioned slaves, dated 8 December 1814; registered May 1815. Witnessed A. H. Goforth, William Goforth, signed Mourning Curl."

Edward Moore, his wife, mother-in-law and children moved to Tuscaloosa Co., Ala., and settled on the Sipsey River north of Northport, Ala., an area now known as Moore's Bridge. Unfortunately, the land was marshy and typhoid was epidemic.

Edward Moore died 17 February 1823, and his family were supported by the county. Three children died in epidemics in 1826: James Edward, Polly Jane, and William Curl Moore. Sarah (Curl) Moore died of typhoid 12 February 1829, and Mourning (Horn) Curl died 15 February 1829, also of typhoid. The cemetery has been restored, and many of the graves identified.[134]

---

[132] Edgeworth-Smith, Annette. 3 May 2005. Accessed 11 March 2009. Located at http://boards.ancestry.com/surnames.curl/218.1.1.1/mb.ashx.

[133] Maury Co., Tenn., Deed Book B:39. Cited in Horn.

[134] Smith, Annette. 24 May 2005. Accessed 11 March 2009. Located at

Another source reports his will was written 9 January 1821 and is recorded in Tuscaloosa Co., Ala., Will Book 1:11.[135] This same source was used for information on their children.

Children of EDWARD MOORE and SARAH CURL:[136]

1. BENNETT WRIGHT[6] MOORE, b. 4 August 1792 Nash Co., N. C.; d. 17 March 1863 Webster Co., Miss.; m. MARY RANKIN 31 March 1816 Maury Co., Tenn.; b. 26 July 1797 Kentucky; d. 2 September 1865 Webster Co., Miss.[137]

2. WILLIAM L.[6] MOORE, b. 11 May 1795 Nash Co., N. C.; d. 28 Jan 1815 Maury Co., Tenn.?[138]

3. SARAH[6] MOORE, b. 26 February 1800; m. ELIJAH BREEN 15 November 1827 Tuscaloosa Co., Ala.[139]

4. LUCRETIA[6] MOORE, b. 6 January 1802 Montgomery Co., Tenn.; d. 3 February 1882 Choctaw Co., Miss. m. SAMUEL BOON FRANKS 18 November 1817 Maury Co., Tenn.

5. ELIZABETH[6] MOORE, b. 26 June 1804 Montgomery Co., Tenn.; d. 9 February 1873 Choctaw Co., Miss.; m. HENRY PICKARD 2 September 1819 Maury Co., Tenn.[140]

6. SUSANNAH[6] MOORE, b. 6 September 1806 Montgomery Co., Tenn.; d. 1856 Tuscaloosa Co., Ala.; m. (1) ARCHIBALD MOORE 15

---

http://newsarch.rootsweb.com/th/read/WINDHAM/2005-05/1116981033.

[135] Horn.

[136] This list is incomplete, based upon the findings in the Windham Cemetery, which shows the three children unaccounted for. They may have been grandchildren, of course.

[137] Additional information from Barnes, John. John Barnes Ancestory. 7 Jan 2008. Located at http://wc.rootsweb.ancestry.com, (db. :2819274.)

[138] There is the possibility he is the William Moore in the 1850 Census for Neshoba Co., Miss.

[139] Barnes.

[140] Barnes.

November 1827 Tuscaloosa Co., Ala.; m. (2) WILLIS RICHARDS about 1847.

7. MARTHA[6] MOORE, b. 1 July 1809 Montgomery Co., Tenn.; m. ELIJAH EMBRY 13 July 1830 Tuscaloosa Co., Ala.

8. TABITHA CURL[6] MOORE, b. 16 May 1814 Maury Co., Tenn.; m. ALFRED POE 6 February 1831 Tuscaloosa Co., Ala.

iv. LURANY[5] CURL, b. before 18 February 1771 Nash Co., N. C.?

On 18 February 1793, Lewis Curl sold to John Sedgley for £100 Virginia money, a 150 acre tract on the north side of the Tar River adjoining the road and Stony Creek.[141] This deed was witnessed by Wilson Vick and "Lewrancy" Curl.a deed in Nash Co., N. C., 1793, implying she was born before 18 February 1771 and was not married on that date.[142] However, Wilson Curle did indicate he was listing his daughters in birth order, so she was more likely born about 1772 or 1773, since Sarah Curl was born 11 October 1771.

v. ESTHER[5] CURL.

vi. ELIZABETH[5] CURL.

vii. MILLICENT[5] CURL.

viii. KINCHEN[5] CURL.

Kinchen Curl was in Jones Co., Ga., by 1811, when he was a bondsman for Lucretia Curl's guardian bond. (see below.) He served as a justice of the peace in Jones Co., Ga., in 1813, 1814. He was present in Jones Co., Ga., in the 1820 Census, aged 26-45, with two boys aged 16-26 and one 10-16, plus two women, one 26-45 and one 16-26.[143]

Kinchen Curl was a grand juror of the Inferior Court for Houston Co., Ga., at the time of its formation in 1821.[144] He was sued (and lost) for

[141] Nash Co., N. C., Deed Book 4:212. Watson, p. 161.
[142] Nash Co., N. C., Deed Book 4:212. Watson, p. 161.
[143] 1820 Census Jones Co., Ga., p. 124.
[144] Mills, William A. Accessed 15 March 2009. Located at

debt by Nicholas Loyd in Bibb Co., Ga., Superior Court in 1823.[145] Kinchen Curl was in Bibb Co., Ga., and a fortunate drawer of a lot in the 11th District, 3rd Section of Cherokee Co., Ga., in the 1832 Land Lottery, which he qualified for as a "soldier."[146]

Kinchen Curl entered Texas 25 May 1838, and was granted 320 acres of land in San Augustine Co., Texas, 23 April 1839.[147] I have not found Kinchen Curl in the 1850 Census, but there is a Henry H. Curl, 39, born in Tennessee living in San Augustine County, with his family. From the birthplaces of his children, it appears that he moved to Alabama about 1832, to Arkansas about 1838, to Missouri about 1840, and to Texas before 1847.[148] He certainly is the age to be a child of either Kinchen or William Curl.[149]

Genealogical Summary

1.   HENRY[1] WATKINS died before May 1804 Nash County, N. C. He married MARY _____.

---

http://archiver.rootsweb.ancestry.com/th/read/gahouston/2004-04/0955167672.

[145] Elliott-Kashima, Trish. Bibb County Superior Court Records, 1823. http://archiver.rootsweb.ancestry.com/th/read/gabibb/2005-07/1121301138. Accessed 15 March 2009.

[146] Smith, James F. The Cherokee Land Lottery. (repr.) (Baltimore: Genealogical Publ., Co., 1969,), p. 184. I have found Norflet Curl listed as a resident of Bibb Co., Ga., and a fortunate drawer in the 1827 Land Lottery. I have not been able to find either one in the 1830 Census yet.

[147] White, Gifford. 1840 Citizens of Texas, Vol. 1, Land Grants. (Austin, 1983,) p. 60.

[148] 1850 Census San Augustine Co., Texas, San Augustine Dist., pp. 335-36. His wife, Nancy, is probably his second wife, as she was 29, and the oldest child was 19. Further, were three children William Cartwright, Julia Cartwright, and John Cartwright, all born in Tennessee living in the household, ages 6-12. The only sons listed were Henry 3, and James 1, who are likely children of Nancy.

[149] Edgeworth-Smith, Annette.   3 May 2005.   Accessed 11 March 2009. Located at http://boards.ancestry.com/surnames.curl/218.1.1.1/mb.ashx. She lists him as a son of William Curl. She also says he was the father of Thomas J. Curl.

Children of HENRY WATKINS and MARY are:

    i. STEPHEN² WATKINS.

    ii. ANNA² WATKINS, m. _____ AMMONS.

    iii. SUSANNA² WATKINS, m. _____ ROBBINS.

    iv. SARAH² WATKINS, m. _____ CLIBON.

    v. ELIZABETH² WATKINS, m. _____ WEAVER.

    vi. HENRY² WATKINS.

2. vii. JAMES² WATKINS, died about 1811 Jones County, Georgia; m. LUCRETIA CURL about 1770 Edgecombe Co., N. C., daughter of WILSON CURL and MOURNING HORN; d. about before 1816 Jones County, Georgia.

    viii. JOSEPH² WATKINS.

    ix. JENNY² WATKINS.

    x. _____ m. _____ COBB.

    xi. RHODA² WATKINS, m. _____ SAUNDERS.

    xii. MARY² WATKINS, m. _____ REVELL.

    xiii. BEVETON² WATKINS.

    xiv. MOURNING² WATKINS, d. after 1827 Hawkins Co., Tenn.; m. EZEKIEL WINSTEAD, b. 26 November 1775 Northumberland Co., Va.; d. 23 November 1832 Hawkins Co., Tennessee.[150]

    xv. RACHEL² WATKINS.

2. JAMES² WATKINS was born in Edgecombe County, North Carolina about 1765 and died about 1811 in Jones County, Georgia. He married LUCRETIA CURL before 1790 in North Carolina, daughter of WILSON CURL and MOURNING HORN. She died before 1816 in Jones County, Georgia.

---

[150] Kimberly. Slagle-Downs. 5 Jan 2009. Located at http://wc.rootsweb.ancestry.com, (db. kslagle.) She cites Smith, Michael K. The Winstead Family in America, and Families of Hawkins County, Tennessee.

Children of JAMES WATKINS and LUCRETIA CURL are:

i. TEMPERANCE[3] WATKINS, TEMPERANCE b. 21 November 1798 Nash Co., N. C.; d. 1 December 1876 Copiah Co., Mississippi;[151] m. SETH CORLEY 16 July 1815 Jones Co., Georgia, son of EDMOND CORLEY; b. 3 November 1796 Georgia; d. 30 October 1872 Copiah Co., Mississippi.[152]

Seth Corley served as a fifer in the 4th Regt. Ga. Militia (Jones Co.,) in the War of 1812.[153]

Seth Corley was in Marion Co., Miss., in 1820, with one son and one daughter under 10, one woman 10-15 (Martha Watkins), and his wife, 16-25.[154] Seth Corley appears in the Copiah County in censuses of 1830[155] and 1840.[156] Family structure suggests three, or perhaps four sons and two daughters born before 1840.

In 1850 Seth and Temperance have Margaret F., 15, and Mary Jane, 6, living with them.[157]

In 1870 Seth and Temperance have Edmond W. Corley, 51, Thomas Tillman, 16, Margaret Corley, 9, plus three others who do not appear to be family.

Children of TEMPERANCE and SETH CORLEY:

1. LUCRETIA ANN[4] CORLEY, b. 5 February 1817 Marion Co., Miss.; d. 28 July 1891 Copiah Co., Miss.;[158] m. JAMES DOUGLAS CAMMACK

---

[151] Damascus Cemetery, Hazelhurst, Copiah Co., Miss. http://www.findagrave.com, #27590493.

[152] Damascus Cemetery, Hazelhurst, Copiah Co., Miss. http://www.findagrave.com, #27590487.

[153] U. S. War of 1812 Service Records, 1812-1815, Roll Box 46. Located at Ancestry.com, 13 February 2014.

[154] 1820 Census Marion Co., Miss., p. 77.

[155] 1830 Census Copiah Co., Miss., p. 104. [112002-1100101] The older woman is probably his mother. The other adult male is probably his brother.

[156] 1840 Census Copiah Co., Miss., p. 112. [0011101-0101001]

[157] 1850 Census Copiah Co., Miss., p. 228A. #274.

[158] Poplar Springs Cemetery, Crystal Springs, Copiah Co., Miss. http://www.findagrave.com, #26202118.

16 April 1833 Copiah Co., Miss.;[159] b. 1812 Sumner Co., Tenn.; d. 1901 Copiah Co., Miss.[160]

2. EDMUND W.[4] CORLEY, b. 18 April 1819 Marion Co., Miss.; d. 1 October 1892 Shelby Co., Texas;[161] m. M. ADALINE MCLEMORE 20 November 1871 Copiah Co, Miss.;[162] b. July 1854 Miss.[163]

3. JAMES[4] CORLEY, b. 17 May 1821 Marion Co., Miss.; d. 29 July 1894 Copiah Co., Miss.;[164] m. ELEANOR SCOTT 15 December 1842 Copiah Co., Miss.;[165] m. (2) ELIZABETH STRAHAN 25 February 1847 Copiah Co., Miss.; b. 18 January 1825; d. 19 July 1904 Copiah Co., Miss.[166]

4. JOHN FRANKLIN[4] CORLEY, b. April 1828 Copiah Co., Miss.; d. 4 November 1852 Copiah Co., Miss.;[167] m. ELIZA HARRIS 12 November 1850 Copiah Co., Miss.[168]

---

[159] Jeremy Clay Dunn Family Tree. Accessed 13 February 2014 at http://trees.ancestry.com/tree/40295321/

[160] Poplar Springs Cemetery, Crystal Springs, Copiah Co., Miss. http://www.findagrave.com, #15970512.

[161] Bradley Springs Cemetery, Tenaha, Shelby Co., Texas. http://www.findagrave.com, #62501680.

[162] Mississippi Marriages 1776-1935. Accessed 12 February 2014 at Ancestry.com.

[163] 1880 Census Copiah Co., Miss., Brown's Store, ED 27, p. 275D, #31. Their children are Edmond W., 7, and Mary T., 5. 1900 Census Shelby Co., Texas, Timpson, ED 92, p. 8A, #125/138. She said she was the mother of two children, both living, and is living with her son, E. W. Corley. Mary has presumably married before then.

[164] Gallman Cemetery, Copiah Co., Miss. http://www.findagrave.com, #26228508.

[165] Mississippi Marriages 1776-1935. Accessed 12 February 2014 at Ancestry.com.

[166] Gallman Cemetery, Copiah Co., Miss. http://www.findagrave.com, #26228485.

[167] Damascus Cemetery, Hazelhurst, Copiah Co., Miss. http://www.findagrave.com, #27590478.

[168] Mississippi Marriages 1776-1935. Accessed 12 February 2014 at Ancestry.com.

5. MARTHA[4] CORLEY, b. 1825 Copiah Co., Miss.;[169] d. before 1860 Copiah Co., Miss.;[170] m. ANDREW JACKSON TILLMAN 3 February 1842 Copiah Co., Miss.; b. 2 December 1814 Bedford Co., Tenn.; d. 11 March 1883 Copiah Co., Miss.[171]

6. MARGARET F.[4] CORLEY, b. 16 March 1835 Copiah Co., Miss.; d. 5 September 1865 Copiah Co., Miss.;[172] m. ELISHA SUMRALL 24 October 1850 Copiah Co., Miss.;[173] b. 28 January 1828 Copiah Co., Miss.; d. 29 November 1875 Copiah Co., Miss.;[174] m. (2) MARY ELIZABETH COOPER; b. 10 December 1841 Hinds Co., Miss.; d. 23 February 1923 Copiah Co., Miss.[175]

7. MARY JANE[4] CORLEY, b. 1844 Copiah Co., Miss.; d. before 1903 Little Rock, Pulaski Co., Ark.;[176] m. THOMAS BENTON TILLMAN 17 February 1865 Copiah Co., Miss., son of THOMAS TILLMAN and ELIZABETH;[177] b. 10 October 1842 Copiah Co., Miss.; d. 10 April

---

[169] 1850 Census Copiah Co., Miss., Gallatin, p. 277B, #1031. She has children Senith, 6; Alice, 4; and Virginia, 2.

[170] 1860 Census Copiah Co., Miss., p. 959, #1293/1304. A. J. is head of household with children Arsenith, 15; Alice, 13; Emma, 11; Benjamin 10; Andrew, 8; and Thomas 6. Also C. J. Perser is a farmhand living with them. She died between 1856 and 1860.

[171] Damascus Cemetery, Hazelhurst, Copiah Co., Miss. http://www.findagrave.com, #12231052.

[172] Gorman, Shannon A. Mostly Mississippi Database Compiled by Shannon Gorman. 31 January 2014. http://wc.rootsweb.ancestry.com, (db. shannon50.)

[173] Mississippi Marriages 1776-1935. Accessed 12 February 2014 at Ancestry.com.

[174] New Zion Cemetery, Crystal Springs, Copiah Co., Mississippi. http://www.findagrave.com, #11443789.

[175] New Zion Cemetery, Crystal Springs, Copiah Co., Mississippi. http://www.findagrave.com, #11443833.

[176] 1900 Census Pulaski Co., Ark., Little Rock Ward 4, ED 81, p. 11A, 1324 13th Street, #224/239. They are living with son Walter E. Tillman, 35.

[177] 1850 Census Copiah Co., Miss., Gallatin, p. 232A, #339. He was 8, so born about 1842.

1911 Monroe Co., Ark.;[178] m. (2) JULIA _____ about 1903 Arkansas.[179]

ii. MARTHA[3] WATKINS, b. 28 June 1805 Montgomery Co., Tenn.; d. 10 September 1887 Scott Co., Mississippi; m. JOHN WOODSON AMIS 10 February 1824 Copiah Co., Mississippi, son of WILLIAM AMIS and JUDITH KNIGHT; b. 22 September 1795 Granville Co., N. C.; d. 4 February 1849 Scott Co., Miss.

Her children are shown in Chapter 3.

---

[178] Roe Cemetery, Monroe Co., Ark. http://www.findagrave.com, #47296981.

[179] 1910 Census Monroe Co., Ark., Roc Roe, ED 102, p. 1A, #8.

INDEX

Atkinson, Benjamin Edgar, 418, 419
Atkinson, Frances L., 411
Atkinson, Joseph, 418, 428
Atkinson, John, 445
Atkinson, Lewis, 412
Atkinson, Michael, 468
Atkinson, Mary O., 411
Atkinson, Matthew Lewis, 411
Atkinson, Sarah, 412
Atkinson, Thomas Jefferson, 411
Atkinson, William H., 411
Avent, Hannah, 452
Aycock, Richard M., 47

-B-

Baddard, Mary, 356
Bagley, George, 32
Bailey, Finis, 196
Bailey, Ina Joe, 346
Bailey, John, 453, 455
Bailey, Nicholas, 455
Bailey, Worth, 196
Raine, Mary E., 244
Baker, Andrew, 281
Baldridge, Michael, 173
Ballard, Mary, 451
Ballard, Servant, 454
Banks, Elizabeth A., 378
Banks, Mary Jane, 325
Banks, William Cameron, 167
Barber, Claude, 124
Barfield, Betsey, 429
Barker, Thomas, 267
Barksdale, Peter, 276
Barnes, John, 466
Barnes, William, 448
Barnett, Isaac, 422
Barnett, Joseph N., 52
Barnett, Larkin, 374, 375
Barraud, Catherine, 453
Barraud, Daniel, 452, 453
Barraud, Frances Prevost, 453
Barraud, Sarah Curle, 453
Barruad, Daniel, 453
Barrow, John G., 216
Bass, Howard, 349
Bass, Hubbard Edward, 348
Bass, Maurice, 349
Bass, Will Davis, 348
Bass, William Wyatt, 348
Bassett, William, 357
Bates, Ann, 229, 242

Bates, Anna Clarke, 235
Bates, Fleming, 236, 242
Bates, John F, 227
Batson, James C., 149
Battle, Mary, 406
Batts, Catherine, 459
Bayless, Abigail, 291
Bayley, Judith,, 451
Beard, Edmund C., 420
Beard, Matthew, 422
Beasley, Elizabeth S. M, 206
Beasley, Ellis B., 38
Beasley, Jonathan, 38
Beasley, William H., 207, 223
Bell, George W., 255
Bell, Mary, 457
Bell, William, 449
Bellefant, Joseph, 173
Berry, Samuel, 417
Berryman, Benjamin, 9
Bethune, Mary, 261
Bevans, Elizabeth A., 378
Bevill, William V., 207
Bingham, Hazel, 348
Bishop, Bennett, 198
Bishop, Lita, 198
Blackburn, Abigail, 14
Blackburn, Alma, 349
Blackburn, Christopher, 14
Blackburn, Elias, 14
Blackburn, Mary, 14
Blalock, Ascension Amis, 101
Blalock, Harriet Parisade, 109
Blalock, John Millanton, 102, 107, 109, 280
Blalock, Louisa Lavinia, 110
Blalock, Richard, 280
Blalock, Samuel, 107
Blalock, William, 280
Bledsoe, Albert Percy, 304
Bledsoe, Alonzo Bailey, 304
Bledsoe, Anna Celestia, 298
Bledsoe, Arthur Franklin, 303
Bledsoe, Bailey, 302
Bledsoe, Benjamin Franklin, 302
Bledsoe, C. D., 303
Bledsoe, Carl Davis, 304
Bledsoe, Clarence Warner, 305
Bledsoe, Daisy Mae, 305
Bledsoe, Fannie, 304
Bledsoe, Frances Delia, 299
Bledsoe, Gussie, 304
Bledsoe, Hiram Floyd, 299
Bledsoe, Hollis D., 303

Brewer, Thomas G., 242
Brewer. Thomas I., 237
Brewer, Thomas J., 228, 240
Brewer, Thomas P., 206
Brewer, Thomas Pinckney, 215
Brewer, William, 190, 200, 201, 202, 205, 210, 217, 227, 228, 229, 231, 239, 242, 258
Brewer, William A., 227
Brewer, William F., 244
Brewer, William George, 228, 246
Brewer, William P., 202, 206, 226
Brewer, Willie Edith, 227
Brewer, Willis, 201, 228, 245
Brewer, Wyche, 189, 190, 191, 192, 203, 258, 261, 263, 294, 297, 313
Bridge, Joel, 387
Bridger, Joseph, 453
Bridger, Mary, 453
Bridges, William, 448, 466
Briggs, Eli N., 216
Briggs, Eli Nelson, 220
Briggs, Elkanah, 220, 224
Briggs, Henry, 206, 222
Briggs, Jacob, 216, 225
Briggs, Leroy Marshall, 222
Briggs, Mary, 206, 223
Briggs, Michael, 225
Briggs, Nancy, 206
Briggs, Simeon, 225
Briggs, Syrena, 221
Briggs, Thomas H., 225
Briggs, William E, 206, 222
Brittingham, William, 357
Brogdon, Mary, 262
Brookings, William, 15
Brooks, James, 417
Brooks, Thomas Price, 46
Broooks, Patti Maud, 148
Brunson, Alex T., 125
Brown, Ethel, 347
Brown, Flora, 254
Brown, John F., 200
Brown, Joseph, 173
Brown, Mary, 210
Brown, Mary V., 200
Brown, Nancy, 254
Brown, Robert, 231
Brown, Robert Kipplin, 452
Brown, Sarah M. (Owen), 368
Brown, William. P., 210

Bryan, Catherine C., 393
Bryan, Cynthia, 291
Bryan, Laura Averette, 395
Bryant, Albert, 81
Bryant, Alexander, 74
Bryant, Andrew, 99
Bryant, Andrew Daniel Daily, 75
Bryant, Ann Robertson, 89
Bryant, Archibald S., 88
Bryant, Cornelia, 100
Bryant, Edward T., 79
Bryant, Elizabeth, 82
Bryant, Ellen G., 82
Bryant, Frances Daily, 88
Bryant, Harriett D.[6], 81
Bryant, Henrietta, 75
Bryant, Ida, 100
Bryant, Isaiah Burney, 89, 100
Bryant, James Alonzo, 90
Bryant, James D., 82
Bryant, James E., 97
Bryant, James Jackson, 73
Bryant, John Amis, 77
Bryant, John Farrington, 72, 90
Bryant, Judith W., 92
Bryant, Junius A., 93
Bryant, Lavinia Lemon, 90
Bryant, Lewis Amis, 81
Bryant, Louisiana Bee, 89
Bryant, Lucius Rhodes82
Bryant, Lucy H., 81
Bryant, Martha, 82
Bryant, Martha Elizabeth, 89
Bryant, Mary Judith88
Bryant, Minerva Emaline, 89
Bryant, Missniah Eugenia, 90
Bryant, Patrick Henry, 76
Bryant, Robert D., 88
Bryant, Robertson, 74
Bryant, Robertson, 85
Bryant, Rowland Edward, 90
Bryant, Rowland Farrington, 78
Bryant, Theophilus Compton, 90
Bryant, Thomas H., 83
Bryant, Wiley T., 91
Bryant, William D., 91
Bryant, William H., 89
Bryant, William Rowland, 80
Bryant, William Thrower, 75
Bunn, David, 467
Bunn, Josiah, 466
Bunn, Redman, 448
Bunn, Redmun, 466
Burke, Elias, 176

Burleson, Margaret, 116
Burnett, Isaac, 422
Burns, Eliza Jane, 222
Burton, Robert, 141
Burt, Pearl, 312
Bush, Abraham, 265, 267
Bush, Richard, 11
Butler, Mary Ann, 296
Butler, William, 439
Buttrill, Asa, 396
Buttrill, Mary, 396
Buyck, Sarah J., 300

-C-

Cabaniss, George, 388, 391
Cabaniss, Mary Ann, 388, 391,
    431
Caffee, Cleaveland, 281
Caldwell, Nancy, 426
Calhoun, Samuel M., 395
Callaway, Ardecia, 393
Callaway, James, 374
Callaway, John, 374
Cameron, Dennis, 264
Cameron, Dennis, 266
Cameron, Jane, 266
Cameron, Jane, 264
Cammack, James Douglas, 481
Campbell, Ann, 254
Campbell, Catharine, 254
Campbell, Daniel, 253
Campbell, Daniel, 255
Campbell, Gracey Downey, 254
Campbell, John M., 254
Campbell, John P, 254
Campbell, John P., 254
Campbell, Malcolm Hugh, 253
Campbell, Priscilla, 460
Campbell, William, 254
Cannifax, Georgia Elizabeth, 409
Cannifax, William Osborn, 409
Carlton, David, 290
Carr, Elizabeth, 220
Carson, John Thomas, 425
Carson, Joseph Jefferson, 425
Carson, Sarah, 393
Carter, John, 321
Carter, John W., 321
Carver, James Richard, 297
Cary, Miles, 459
Cary, Richard, 462
Cassidy, Winnie Jane, 331
Cast, Elisha, 283

Castellaw, Benjamin F., 370
Castellaw, Malisia Jane, 370
Cater, Eliza, 262
Cauthen, James Simeon, 408
Cauthen, Jane, 407
Cauthen, Jefferson, 408
Cauthen, John Wade, 406
Cauthen, John William, 407
Cauthen, Jordan Dennis, 408
Cauthen, Lucy Rebecca, 407
Cauthen, Martha Frances, 408
Cauthen, Mary J., 400
Cauthen, Thomas L., 407
Cauthen, Wade Hampton, 408
Champion, Martha Jane, 321
Chandler, Annie H., 66
Chandler, James Lee, 65
Chandler, James P., 65
Chandler, Julia Amis, 65
Chandler, Lillian, 66
Chandler, Mary Elizabeth, 65
Chandler, Phebe, 453, 454
Chandler, Robie Thomas, 65
Chandler, Rufus Edward, 65
Chandler, Sallie Ann, 65
Chapman, Samuel, 287
Chapman, Penelope, 93
Chappel, William S., 427
Caskey, Robert, 90
Caskey, William Spark, 90
Cheatham, Adeline, 319, 327
Cheatham, Amanda, 97
Cheatham, Cynthia Elizabeth,
    99
Cheatham, David T., 99
Cheatham, Fletcher H., 96
Cheatham, James, 97, 99
Cheatham, John, 183
Cheatham, Judith C., 97
Cheatham, Lewis Robertson, 96
Cheatham, Martha H., 97
Cheatham, Mary E., 96
Cheatham, Nancy P., 97
Cheatham, Sarah A., 97
Cheatham, William, 97
Childs, Walter Steele, 404
Claiborne, Sarah, 445
Clark, Lilla B., 345
Clement, Frank L., 227
Clement, John, 16
Cleaveland, John, 281
Cleveland, Amanda, 198
Cleveland, J. M., 301
Cleveland, Junie, 301

490

Cleveland, Mimms I., 301
Cleveland, Thomas Grover, 301
Clopton, David, 231
Clopton, William, 419
Cloud, Dick, 193
Cloud, Lafayette, 313
Clower, Thomas, 381
Clowers, Peter, 439
Cobb, Mary Ann, 339
Coffman, DeWitt, 224
Coffman, Erasmus, 224
Coffman, Mary, 224
Coffman, Samuel, 224
Coffman, Samuel H., 224
Coffman, Susan B, 224
Coffman, Virginia Elizabeth, 224
Coggin, Henry, 404
Cohoon, William, 449
Coker, Caleb, 449
Colquitt, Molly, 386
Cooper, Jos., 366
Cooper, Mary Elizabeth, 483
Cooper, Vinson, 470
Copeland, Mary A., 374
Copeland, Mary Ann Augusta, 374
Copeland, Richard, 374
Copeland, William, 376
Corley, Edmund, 439, 440, 481
Corley, Edmund W., 482
Corley, Evelina, 439
Corley, Isham, 439
Corley, James, 439, 482
Corley, John, 439
Corley, John Franklin, 482
Corley, Kinchen, 439
Corley, Lucretia Ann, 481
Corley, Margaret F, 483
Corley, Martha, 483
Corley, Mary Jane, 483
Corley, Nancy, 439, 440
Corley, Sally, 439
Corley, Sarah, 270
Corley, Seth, 102, 439, 481
Corley, Silas, 439
Corry, Nicholas, 274
Cottrell, Anna F., 244
Courtney, Ansom Hiram, 368
Courtney, John Hiram, 368
Cox, James, 381
Cox, Ruth, 345
Cox, William, 198
Cramphin, Thomas, 317

Craig, Christian,, 11
Craig, William, 11
Crawley, John Wesley, 403
Crews, Rebecca, 99
Crews, Joseph, 279, 280
Crews, William, 279,
Crofts, C. L., 329
Crofts, Lee, 329
Crook, James, 33
Crooker, Benjamin, 464
Cumi, Nancy, 371
Cummins, Karin, 172
Curl, Elizabeth, 474, 478
Curl, Esther, 478
Curl, Henry H., 479
Curl, Joseph, 446, 468
Curl, Kinchen, 439, 440, 442, 478
Curl, Lewis, 446, 448, 469
Curl, Lucretia, 101, 475, 480
Curl, Luraney, 469, 478
Curl, Millicent, 478
Curl, Mourning, 473
Curl, Nancy, 474
Curl, Sarah, 476
Curl, William, 473
Curl, Willis, 446
Curl, Wilson, 443, 446, 447, 448, 466, 480
Curle, Andrew, 459, 461
Curle, Darby, 453
Curle, Darby Tools, 452
Curle, David, 459
Curle, David Wilson, 463
Curle, Hamilton, 459, 463
Curle, Jane, 457
Curle, John, 451-455
Curle, Joshua, 451, 453, 454, 455, 459
Curle, Judith, 453
Curle, Lydia, 455
Curle, Mary, 453, 457
Curle, Mary Baker, 452
Curle, Nicholas, 450-452, 454, 455, 459
Curle, Nicholas Wilson, 461
Curle, Pasco, 451, 454, 456
Curle, Rosea, 454
Curle, Samuel, 451, 452
Curle, Sarah, 451, 452, 453
Curle, Thomas, 450
Curle, William Roscow Wilson, 459, 461

492

Hamilton, Mary, 459
Hamlin, Stephen, 467
Hamlin, William, 467
Hammock, Sam, 467
Hammond, John W., 223
Hammond, William, 281
Hampton, Elizabeth, 240
Hand, Emma M., 395
Hannock, John, 360
Hansford, Eliza H., 399
Harbin, Mary Lou Driver, 287
Hardin, Pauline, 167
Harding, Elizabeth, 134
Hargrove, Francis, 285
Harkness, John W, 93
Harkness, Sarah J., 93
Harper, Amanda Frances, 382
Harper, Frances, 328
Harper, John J, 328
Harper, T. B., 139
Harrell, Nancy Lula Emmaline, 327
Harrell, Moses, 447
Harrington, Jeptha, 274
Harris, Anna, 192, 193, 290, 292
Harris, Benton, 359
Harris, Eliza, 482
Harris, Hardy, 448, 466
Harris, Margaret Hill, 326
Harris, Mary, 22, 23
Harris, Randolph, 469
Harris, Sarah, 293
Harrison, Diane Martin, 290
Harrison, George A., 94
Harrison, Horace Newton, 347
Harrison, Palatea, 388, 391
Hart, Nancy, 362
Hart, Susannah, 356
Harthcock, Thomas Britton, 332
Harton, Job, 363
Harvey, Mary F., 412
Havoll,Judith, 450
Hawkins, Coleman, 275
Hawkins, Georgia, 334
Hawkins, Milly, 275
Hawkins, Richard, 454
Hawkins, Samuel, 452
Hawkins, Susannah, 271
Hayes, James, 421, 422
Heath, Nancy, 315, 317
Hellums, Mary, 368
Hembree, Andrew J., 415
Henderson, Elizabeth Polk, 178

Herman, Charles, 212
Herndon, Reuben, 320
Herring, Elizabeth, 32
Hickerson, Charles, 289
Hickerson, David, 288
Hickerson, John, 288
Hickerson, John W, 288
Hickerson, Little, 288
Hickerson, William P., 289
High, Ruth, 40
Hill, Eliza, 71
Hill, Isaac, 75
Hill, Jane, 90
Hill, Mary Elizabeth, 75
Hill, Richard Sr., 353
Hill, Sarah Williams, 75
Hill, Thomas, 366, 439
Hines, Lewis, 447, 466, 467, 469
Hitt, David, 205
Hodges, Alice Amis, 8. 263
Hodges, Vernon Seymour, 166
Hogan, David, 473
Hogan, Elizabeth, 47
Holladay, Frances, 169
Holley, Amanda Caroline, 218
Holley, John, 469
Holley, Pinckney, 231
Holley, William F, 217
Hollingsworth, Carrie E., 136
Hollingsworth, Nancy, 377
Holloway, Jeremiah, 217
Holman, Elizabeth, 235, 239
Holman, Samuel, 239
Holstead, Mariah, 429
Holt A.M., 289
Hood, David G. W., 400
Hood, Williamson Campbell, 399
Hooten, Arrington, 420
Horn, Ann, 448
Horn, Henry, 447, 463, 464, 467
Horn, Isaac, 465, 467
Horn, Jacob, 445, 446
Horn, Joel, 448, 466
Horn, Josiah, 470, 476
Horn, Michael, 448
Horn, Mourning, 463, 464, 480
Horn, Thomas, 473, 476
Horn, William, 468
Horn, William Sr, 448
Horton, Eula Mae, 306
Houston, Matthew C, 205
Houston, Robert H., 207
Howard, Alameda, 322
Howard, William, 295

495

497

501

Reed, Alexander, 360
Reeves, Deana, 410
Reeves, John, 38
Reeves, Mary Bethemie, 410
Reid, Butten, 374
Renfro, Frances Cordelia
    (Garrett), 82
Renfro, James H., 83
Renfro, John Bishop, 475
Renfro, William, 475
Renn, Joseph J., 100
Revell, Micajah, 468, 447
Revell, Mary, 445
Rhonnald, Alexander, 459
Richards, James, 38
Richards, Willis, 478
Richardson, Miriam Brewer, 202
Ricketts, James, 454-456,
Ricketts, Jane, 455
Ricks, James, 448, 466
Ricks, Sally, 446
Riddlehurst, John, 464
Roane, Alexander, 15
Robbins, Susanna, 445
Robinson, Michael, 461
Roberts, Caroline A., 303
Roberts, Louisa Whyte, 291, 295
Robertson, Mary, 178
Roffe, Sarah (Knight), 67
Roffe, William, 39
Root, Charles Harris, 339
Root, William D., 339
Roscow, Euphan, 451
Ross, Andrew, 468
Ross, Benjamin A., 298
Ross, Stephen N., 298
Rowell, Edward, 424
Round, William, 357
Russ, Bernice, 145
Russell, Buckner, 283
Russell, Ethel, 347
Russell, Mittie Eloise, 124
Russell, Simon J., 92
Russell, William W., 347
Ryan, Solomon, 269

-S-

Sanders, Kiziah Jane, 283
Sanders, Mary, 283
Sanders, Rhoda, 445
Satterfield, Annis, 49
Satterfield, William, 49
Saunders, George B., 210

Saunders, William. B., 210
Savage, Griffen, 353
Scarborough, James, 230
Schreefer, Ina L., 305
Scott, Bettie R., 55
Scott, David C., 184
Scott, Eleanor, 482
Scott, George L., 363
Scott, Hannah M., 91
Scott, Ibby, 176
Scott, Mary Nash, 54
Sealy, Joseph, 448
Sears, Fannie, 323
Sedgley, John, 469
Selbeck, Montfort, 464
Selden, Cary, 452, 459
Selden, Joseph, 463
Selden, Samuel, 461
Selden, William, 464
Self, Carolyn, 194
Sellers, Lemuel M., 305
Shackelford, Rebecca, 290
Shampine, Beulah, 147
Shaw, John, 423
Shaw, William C, 325
Shaw, William Preston, 325
Shepherd, John, 452
Shermer, W. Waldo, 209
Shine, Elizabeth, 464
Short, Thomas, 14
Simmons, Anne, 213
Simmons, John, 365. 366
Simmons, Rebecca, 365
Simmons, Thomas, 365
Sims, Rebecca, 270
Sims, Thomas, 267
Sims, William, 269
Skinner, Emmanuel, 447
Skinner, Mittie Theo, 310
Skinner, Nicholas, 448, 465, 468
Slade, Jane, 410
Smilie, Henry, 335
Smilie, Minnie, 335
Smith, Alexander, 43
Smith, Anderson B., 191
Smith, Archibald, 360
Smith, Buckner, 180
Smith, C. D., 35
Smith, Celina Elizabeth, 371
Smith, Charlotte, 38
Smith, Daniel, 39
Smith, Francina Almeta, 90
Smith, Hardaway, 48
Smith, H. C., 312

Smith, Isaac, 217
Smith, James M., 196
Smith, Jane, 20, 329, 391
Smith, John, 20
Smith, Lucy, 48
Smith, Margaret, 393
Smith, Mary, 11, 20, 31
Smith, Myrtice (Batson), 149
Smith, Nettie, 90
Smith, Rachel, 325
Smith, Robert J., 318
Smith, Samuel, 11, 17, 19, 20.
    446
Smith, Stephen W., 173
Smith, Susannah, 20
Smith, Thomas, 97
Smith, Wilkins, 363
Smith, William E., 48
Snodgrass, Florence, 80
Soper, Amelia, 315, 382
Soper, Torvel M., 342
Soper, Zadok, 315
Soutston, James H., 207
Spain, Drury, 442
Sparks, Evelyn, 343
Spears, James, 449
Speer, Alexander Middleton, 406
Speer, Arthur Middleton, 406
Speer, John H. P., 403
Speer, Larkin Wilson, 403
Speer, Mary L., 403
Speer, Simeon Franklin, 389,
    402
Speer, Thomas J., 402
Spight, Thomas, 466
Spratt, Robert, 228
Stallings, John, 422, 423
Stanley, Charles A., 217
Stanley, Julia, 124
Starling, Luther, 200
Steadman, Elliott V., 393
Steel, Nancy, 474
Steele, Margaret, 75
Steele, Nathaniel, 173
Stephen, Sarah Elizabeth, 290
Stephens, Alexander H., 323
Stephens, Charles, 323
Stephens, Eugenia, 323
Stephens, Green B., 322
Stephens, Martha J., 322
Stephens, Sarah J., 323
Stevens, Richard, 284
Stewart, Columbus M., 395
Stewart, Elizabeth, 405

Stewart, Henry Jasper, 394
Stewart, Joseph Day, 395
Stewart, Larkin Wilson, 393
Stewart, Marion F., 394
Stewart, Martha P. T., 394
Stewart, May, 392
Stewart, Methvin C. Polk, 395
Stewart, Palatia Mary Jane, 394
Stewart, Samuel Smith, 394
Stewart, Sarah Louise, 395
Stewart, Thomas, 390
Stewart, Thomas Jefferson, 392
Stewart, Thomas Ware, 390
Stewart, Washington Jackson,
    394
Stewart, William, 390
Stewart, William Newton, 393
Stiles, Joseph, 421
Stone, John, 281
Stone, Susan Ann, 292
Strahan, Elizabeth, 482
Stripling, Benjamin, 419-423
Stripling, Moses, 422
Strong, Christopher B., 417
Strother, Margaret, 19
Stuart, John, 427
Stubbs, James, 439, 440
Stubbs, John, 15
Stubbs, John J., 376
Stubbs, Wiliam B., 376
Summerell, Jane, 453
Summerhill, Horace, 181
Summerhill, Rebecca E., 181
Summerlin, Calvin L, 226
Summerlin, Cornelia A., 226
Summerlin, Fesenton, 206
Summerlin, Henry, 222
Summerlin, Lavinia A., 226
Summerlin, Margaret A., 226
Summerlin, Pheasonton K., 221
Summerlin, Sarah, 206
Summerlin, Serena, 206
Summerlin, William D., 206,
    210, 225
Summerlin, Wylie, 222
Summers, Nicholas, 421
Sumrall, Elisha, 483
Sutton, Elizabeth, 406
Swanson, Nancy, 386
Sweeny, Merritt, 454, 455, 459
Swepson, Thomas, 15
Swinney, B. O., 111

-T-

505

Wood, Jonathan, 370, 372
Wood, Martha V., 372
Wood, Sarah F., 369
Wood, William, 271
Woodruff, Clifford, 386
Woodruff, Susanna, 386
Woodson, Charles, 40
Woodson, Elizabeth, 27
Woodson, Joseph, 31, 35, 40
Woodson, Judith, 22, 23, 31,
    35, 40, 41, 67, 173
Woodson, Miller, 31
Woodson, Mirnia, 7
Woodson, Robert, 27
Woodson, Sarah, 40
Wooster, Ruth, 145
Wooten, Keziah, 39
Wooten, William, 39
Wray, George, 452
Wright, George Denny, 171
Wright, Ira B., 323
Wright, John, 282, 284
Wright, Judith, 171
Wright, Lucius F., 170, 171
Wright, Lucretia, 282, 284
Wyche, Abigail, 236
Wynn, Littleton, 381
Wynn, Thomas Littleton, 382
Wynne, Sarah, 45
Wythe, Thomas, 453, 455

-Y-

Yarbrough, Lillian, 301
Yelverton, Adele, 147
Young, Alexander, 418, 428, 430
Young, Benjamin A., 421, 423,
    426, 429
Young, Daniel, 430
Young, Earnest L., 427
Young, Ellinder, 429
Young, Ernest L., 418, 419
Young, John, 429
Young, Nelly, 429
Young, Robert Isaiah,, 430
Younger, Esta, 344

-Z-

Zimmerman, George A., 343

www.ingramcontent.com/pod-product-compliance
Lightning Source LLC
Chambersburg PA
CBHW060948280326

41935CB00009B/657